Taking Sides: Clashing View in United States History, Volume 2, 18/e

Kevin R. Magill

Tony L. Talbert

create.mheducation.com

ISBN-13: 9781260184860

ISBN-10: 1260184862

Contents

Detailed Table of Contents

Unit 2: Reform, War, and Depression

Ronald J. Pestritto and William J. Atto provide significant evidence from the Progressive Party Platform of 1912 and Woodrow Wilson's 1913 campaign addresses demonstrating the impact of progressivism's influence of policy and practice throughout the 20th century and into the 21st century. Professor of history Richard Abrams maintains that progressivism was a failure because it tried to impose a uniform set of values upon a culturally diverse people and never seriously confronted the inequalities that still exist in American society.

Thomas A. Bailey argues that a physically infirm Woodrow Wilson was unable to make the necessary compromises with the U.S. Senate to join the League of Nations and convince America that the United States should play a major role in world affairs. The late William G. Carleton believed that Woodrow Wilson understood better than any of his contemporaries the role that the United States would play in world affairs.

Edward Bernays believes that the media propaganda plays a vital role in developing the opinions, habits, tastes, and ideas within a democratic society. He suggests that this conscious and intelligent manipulation is vital because it helps to establish a basic framework by which citizens can understand the world, thereby avoiding chaos. Noam Chomsky rejects the idea that this type of propaganda is helpful, instead suggesting that it and other media mechanisms limit the exchange of democratic ideas by furthering the interests of those in power and business elites.

Gabriel Kolko asserts that instead of implementing a successful progressive New Deal agenda President Franklin Delano Roosevelt and his administrative cabinet of advisors closely aligned with conservative "big business" interests that took advantage of the economic crises during America's twentieth century Great Depression to protect their financial and social power bases at the expense of the common person. To counter Gabriel Kolko's critical analysis of the FDR's New Deal motives, a primary document representing one of President Roosevelt's many "fire side chats" is offered as evidence that FDR's New Deal policies called upon all segments of the U.S. population to enter into a common commitment of sacrifice and service to address the economic and social crises of the day.

Unit 3: The Cold War and Beyond

Issue: Did President John F. Kennedy Cause the Cuban Missile Crisis?
YES: **Thomas G. Paterson**, from "When Fear Ruled: Rethinking the Cuban Missile Crisis," *New England Journal of History* (1995)
NO: **Robert Weisbrot**, from "Maximum Danger: Kennedy, the Missiles, and the Crisis of American Confidence," Ivan R. Dee, Publisher (2001)

Professor Thomas G. Paterson believes that President Kennedy, even though he moderated the American response and compromised in the end, helped precipitate the Cuban missile crisis by his support for both the failed Bay of Pigs invasion in April 1961 and the continued attempts by the CIA to assassinate Fidel Castro. Historian Robert Weisbrot argues that the new sources uncovered in the past 20 years portray Kennedy as a president who had not only absorbed the values of his time as an anti-Communist cold warrior but who nevertheless acted as a rational leader and was conciliatory toward the Soviet Union in resolving the Cuban missile crisis.

Issue: Did Southern White Christians Actively Support Efforts to Maintain Racial Segregation?
YES: **Carolyn Renée Dupont**, from "A Strange and Serious Christian Heresy: Massive Resistance and the Religious Defense of Segregation," New York University Press (2013)
NO: **David L. Chappell**, from "Broken Churches, Broken Race: White Southern Religious Leadership and the Decline of White Supremacy," University of North Carolina Press (2004)

Carolyn Renée Dupont argues that in the post-*Brown* years of the 1950s and 1960s, most white Mississippians, including Christian ministers and laypersons, zealously drew upon biblical texts, religious tracts, and sermons to craft a folk theology supporting massive resistance to racial segregation. David L. Chappell concludes that white southern religious leaders from the mainline Protestant denominations, preferring peace and social order, failed to provide sufficient support to enable segregationist politicians to mount a united front in defending the doctrine of white supremacy.

Issue: Did the Nixon–Kissinger "Peace with Honor" Strategy Fulfill the Conservative Commitment to Containment of Communism?
YES: **Richard Nixon**, from "Peace with Honor" and "14 Addresses to the Nation on Vietnam," Richard Nixon (1973)
NO: **Jeffrey Kimball**, from "Debunking Nixon's Myths of Vietnam," *The New England Journal of History* (2000)

Richard Nixon believed his policy of Vietnamization and the Paris Peace Accords of 1973 would bring lasting peace in Vietnam, ultimately fulfilling his promise of containment and satisfying his "Peace with Honor" strategy. Jeffrey Kimball suggests the Nixon–Kissinger "Peace with Honor" promise remained unfulfilled at the conclusion of the Vietnam war due to misrepresentations of the truth used to salvage the reputations of the president and his conservative staff.

Issue: Has the Women's Movement of the 1970s Failed to Liberate American Women?
YES: **F. Carolyn Graglia**, from "Domestic Tranquility: A Brief against Feminism," Spence Publishing (1998)
NO: **Jo Freeman**, from "The Revolution for Women in Law and Public Policy," McGraw-Hill Education (1995)

Writer and lecturer F. Carolyn Graglia argues that women should stay at home and practice the values of "true motherhood" because contemporary feminists have discredited marriage, devalued traditional homemaking, and encouraged sexual promiscuity. Jo Freeman claims that the feminist movement produced a revolution in law and public policy in the 1960s and 1970s that completed a drive to remove discriminatory laws regarding opportunities for women in the United States.

Milton Friedman argues that liberalism, in its quest to combat authoritarian elements, has naturally aligned with markets, individualism, and freedom. He further claims that the so-called economic freedom (meaning privatization) is a way of maintaining the personal liberties of people against the government and tries to give historical examples attempting to illustrate this point. Daniel Stedman Jones critiques and tracks how privatization has come to be understood as neoliberalism, the economic ideology that has come to permeate all American political life. Jones argues that in understanding the history of neoliberal thought can help us better make sense of the complexity of the present economic situation.

Andrew Bacevich argues that the American Century is over. He believes we need to see ourselves as we are now by casting aside the problematic mythology of the American Century. Joseph S. Nye Jr. believes the American Century will continue; however, he suggests that if the United States would like to maintain its leadership role, it must recognize that the role will look very different from what it was in the 20th century.

Preface

The authors' academic and professional theory and practice have been significantly influenced by the belief that the study of history, and all humanities and social sciences, is most powerful and transformative when it is meaningful, active, challenging, integrative and value-based (NCSS, 2016). For these reasons, we have designed and organized this eighteenth edition of *Taking Sides: Clashing Views in United States History* in a way that will engage both the teacher and learner in a participatory process of academic and civic discourse. Each of the primary and secondary documents found in the three units of this text have been carefully selected to provide all readers the opportunity to develop a depth and breadth of insights through *critical historical inquiry* (Blevins, Salinas, and Talbert, 2015) and active learning (Bonwell and Eison, 1991).

Inherent in the act of *critical historical inquiry* and *active learning* are the powerful and transformative teaching and learning behaviors of asking probing questions, thinking critically and reflectively, making reasoned inferences based upon data, and developing reasoned explanations and interpretations of events and issues in the past and present" (Singleton & Giese, 1999, p. 148). Because this project is guided by the authors' belief that the reader is an equal partner in the interpretation of the meaning and impact of the issues and ideas presented in this text, each of the 16 issues are designed to engage the reader in the process of *dialogical problem posing* which compels the reader to actively participate in their own learning. It involves placing students in situations that compel them to take responsibility for gathering, organizing, and interpreting information (Bonwell & Eison, 1991).

As you immerse yourself in this text, we encourage you the teacher and learner to not simply read the exemplary primary and secondary documents offered to you but to also incorporate the learning outcomes, the critical thinking and reflection questions, and the common ground summaries into your lesson and study plans. Taken as a whole, this eighteenth edition of *Taking Sides* will provide the teacher and learner the opportunity to critique historical and contemporary texts not only as academic historians, but also as critical minded citizens committed to the Jeffersonian ideal that democracy is intrinsically dependent on a citizenry that is educated, informed, and active with concern of civic, might we also add, critical issues. Inside the pages you will discover a diversity of narratives that at time will collide with traditional interpretations of historical events and texts. It is our hope that your history classrooms will become "the places where the contending voices in the debate over what history means, or should mean, in a democracy come together" (Stearns, Seixas, & Wineburg, 2000; Blevins, Salinas, and Talbert, 2015).

Book Organization

This eighteenth edition of *Taking Sides: Clashing Views in United States History* continues the organizational format of presenting critical historical issues and their accompanying pairs of primary and secondary documents and essays in a chronological thematic structure that facilitates the inclusion of the whole text into any United States history, social studies, and even American Studies survey courses. The 16 critical historical issues presented in this 18th edition offer an Introduction, which provides a summary of the content and context that follows in the contrasting views represented in the carefully selected primary and secondary documents and essays. This edition, like the one before it, continues the expanded focus on *alternative perspectives* and *diverse voices* that are applicable to the issues, problems, and questions posed in the text. It is our intent to offer you the reader the opportunity to engage in critical historical inquiry and active learning as a means of encountering the complexity and nuances of the historical issues that cannot be addressed in a simple Yes/No response. The teacher and student-focused *Learning Outcomes* have been designed to both guide and engage all readers in a well-focused scope and sequence of content knowledge that will inform both the learning and teaching process. To better contextualize the origins of the contrasting primary and secondary documents and essays, we have provided a brief biographical sketch of each of the authors.

Following the contrasting primary/secondary documents and essay selections, there are several features that are designed to generate further understanding through critical historical inquiry of the topical issues. First, the feature entitled *Critical Thinking and Reflection* is comprised of several probing questions that are designed to stimulate challenging and integrative dialogue related to the learning outcomes and the dueling perspectives found in the documents and essays. The second feature, *Is There Common Ground?*, encourages the teacher and the student to think more deeply about the issue by highlighting areas of consensus that the contributors share on the topic being debated as well as alternative perspectives within the debate as offered by we the editors. Third, *Additional Resources* is a feature that offers a brief list of important books and/or journal articles relating to the issue. In addition to text-based resources, we have provided updated Internet sites (URLs) to aid in further exploration of the historical topics being debated and to extend the diversity of voices that better facilitate critical historical inquiry.

Acknowledgments

Live life like you're playing jazz. Improvised, off beat, behind the note and feel the syncopation that comes from living in the moment.
—Tony L. Talbert

Just as jazz is an eclectic fusion of individual musicians strategically and serendipitously giving one another space to create a uniquely unified sound so is this partnership in brainstorming, writing, and editing this book where individuals graciously share their gifts and talents for the benefit of the whole. Indeed, the synergy of many contributors has led to the successful completion of this eighteenth edition of *Taking Sides: Clashing Views in United States History*. The cornerstone of the *Taking Sides: Clashing Views in United States History* is Jill Meloy, senior product developer for McGraw-Hill Create®/CLS, and the entire staff of McGraw-Hill Education. Jill entrusted in us to continue the tradition of excellence that this seminal series has established over the last three plus decades. We are sincerely grateful for Jill's professional guidance, patient encouragement, and persistent humor. Special thanks to our colleagues Lauren Bagwell, Victoria A. Davis, Justin Kruger, Ashleigh Maldonado, and Nathan G. Scholten whose contributions to this edition provided a diversity of voices that enriched the analysis of the 20 historical topics presented. Finally, we are endearingly grateful to our wives Dr. Sandra A. Talbert and Ms. Elizabeth Harrelson-Magill for their constructive feedback as they listened to us compose multiple drafts, their constant encouragement as deadlines approached, and their caring and creative spirits shared unconditionally. Dr. Magill would like to thank Dr. Talbert for his diligence, brilliance, mentorship, and most of all his friendship. He is forever grateful for his brother. In turn, Dr. Talbert shares his abiding admiration for Dr. Magill who as a scholar embodies the mind of Thoreau seeking truth amidst confusion and the heart of Emerson never failing to look for the best in others or give the best

of himself. And now we turn the page to write the next chapter.

Editors of This Volume

Kevin R. Magill is an assistant professor of Secondary and Social Studies Education at Baylor University. Dr. Magill received PhD in Social Studies Education from The University of Texas at Austin, and holds Masters Degrees in Education and Public Administration from The University of California, Davis, and California State University, Stanislaus, respectively. He also earned a BA in Communication Studies while attending California State University, Stanislaus. Dr. Magill's research explores two areas, first, how social studies teachers understand the relationship between teaching and civics and how their own ontologies and ideologies inform their pedagogical practices. Second, he considers how and when teachers help social studies students utilize cultural knowledge and critical inquiry to do the authentic work of civics. Dr. Magill's most recent scholarly works include "The primacy of relation: Social studies teachers and the praxis of critical pedagogy" with Professor Cinthia Salinas and "Critically civic teacher perception, posture and pedagogy: Negating civic archetypes" published in *Theory and Research in Social Education* and *The Journal of Social Studies Research*, respectively. He also recently published a co-edited book with Professor Arturo Rodriguez called, *Imagining Education: Beyond the Logic of Global Neoliberal Capitalism*. Prior to his work in the academy, Dr. Magill was a middle and high school teacher in public and private schools in Seaside, Vacaville, and Sacramento, California where he taught Social Studies, English Language Arts, and Opportunity/Intervention.

Tony L. Talbert is a Professor of Social/Cultural Studies Education and Qualitative Research in the School of Education at Baylor University. He received a BA in History and Political Science from Stephen F. Austin State University in 1986, an MA in American Studies from Baylor University in 1991, and an EdD in Social/Cultural Studies and Qualitative Research from the University of Houston in 1998. Dr. Talbert refers to his field of research and teaching as Education As Democracy which integrates social and cultural studies education into a focused discipline of qualitative inquiry examining school and community stakeholder empowerment through activist engagement in political, economic, and social issues. Dr. Talbert's 33 years of experience as an educator has allowed him to serve as a public high school teacher, education specialist and consultant for the Texas Education Agency, professor, associate dean, department chair, and graduate program director at such institutions as Sam Houston State University, Mississippi State University, The University of Houston, and Baylor University. Over his career in academia, Dr. Talbert has published over 45 peer-reviewed journal articles and book chapters, presented more than 85 peer-reviewed and invited research presentations, collaboratively obtained in excess of $2.8 million in funded research, served as the chair and methodologist for dozens of masters and doctoral theses and dissertations, co-editor of two academic journals, chair of several special interest groups for national professional organizations and a popular invited speaker and consultant for education organizations and conferences, private corporations, and government entities where he has showcased his creative teaching, research, and public activism seminars. In 2013, Dr. Talbert decided that it had been far too long since he had been fully immersed in the real world of teaching. After a twenty-year absence from the public-school classroom, he returned to a local high school where he taught world history to 166 10th-grade students. His experiences have been captured in both academic journal and popular press articles and will be the subject of a book in the future. Dr. Talbert was named as the recipient of the 2014 McGraw-Hill Distinguished Scholar Award for his contributions to qualitative research in the field of education.

References

Blevins, B., Salinas, C., and Talbert, T. L. (2015). Critical Historical Thinking: Enacting the Voice of the Other in the Social Studies Curriculum and Classroom. In C.S. White, Editor (Eds.), *Critical Qualitative Research for Social Education*. Charlotte, NC: IAP Information Age Publishing.

Bonwell, C. C., & Eison, J. A. (1991). Active Learning: Creating Excitement in the Classroom. ASHE-ERIC Higher Education Report, Washington, DC: School of Education and Human Development, George Washington University.

Epstein, T. (2009). *Interpreting national history: Race, identity, and pedagogy in classrooms and communities*. New York: Routledge.

National Council for the Social Studies—NCSS. (2016). *A vision of powerful teaching and learning in the social studies*. Retrieved from https://www.socialstudies.org/publications/socialeducation/may-june2016/vision-of-powerful-teaching-and-learning-in-social-studies.

Singleton, L., & Giese, J. (1999). Using online primary sources with students. *The Social Studies*, 90(4), 148–151.

Stearns, P. N., Seixas, P. C., & Wineburg, S. (Eds.). (2000). *Knowing, teaching, and learning history: National and international perspectives*. NYU Press.

Academic Advisory Board Members

Members of the Academic Advisory Board are instrumental in the final selection of articles for Taking Sides books. Their review of articles for content, level, and appropriateness provides critical direction to the editors and staff. We think that you will find their careful consideration reflected in this volume.

Introduction

Democracy must be built through open societies that share information. When there is information, there is enlightenment. When there is debate, there are solutions. When there is no sharing of power, no rule of law, no accountability, there is abuse, corruption, subjugation and indignation.

—Atifete Jahjaga, Former President of Kosovo

Informed dialogue and dialectic are the bulwarks of civic discourse in a thriving democracy. Diversity of opinion is unavoidable within a pluralist community where unlimited access to global digital media requires us to ask ourselves, *What is fact, what is fiction, and how do I discern what might be a confluence of the two?* Inherently embedded within the complex process of discerning the trustworthiness of information is the belief of the authors of this text that all citizens must have experience in researching, analyzing, organizing and/or engaging in professional and civic issues and discourse if we are to achieve what President Jahjaga deems as *enlightenment.* Through active researching, analyzing, organizing, and engaging in civic discourse, the *enlightened citizen* is better able to develop a broader knowledge and experience base that ultimately leads to a depth of intellectual skills and attitudes necessary to confront, discuss, and consider actions on the most pernicious issues of past, present, and future.

Substantive knowledge and understanding of the multiple perspectives of any issue is an essential ingredient of the learning and teaching process. After all, it is useless, if not impossible, to engage in effective inquiry unless there is a base of understanding on what is being questioned and analyzed. In turn, a deep abiding understanding of the issues through active pursuit and participation in information gathering and dissemination serves to better prepare the student, the teacher, the citizen in encountering transformative instructional, learning, and decision-making opportunities. For these reasons, the epistemological foundations of this text are like the Gordian Knot inextricably entangled with a methodological structure that will engage the reader in reflective inquiry intended to generate enduring questions, critical analysis, evidence-based assertions, and hopefully a better understanding of differences in beliefs, philosophies, and principles as revealed through the human narratives represented throughout this text.

The success of democracy is intrinsically dependent on a citizenry that is educated, informed, and active with concern to civic issues. This idea best championed by Thomas Jefferson as he asserts,

If a nation expects to be ignorant and free, in a state of civilization, it expects what never was and never will be. The functionaries of every government have propensities to command at will the liberty and property of their constituents. There is no safe deposit for these but with the people themselves; nor can they be safe with them without information. Where the press is free and every man able to read, all is safe[i]. (Ford, P.L. (1899). *The writings of Thomas Jefferson: Volume 10 1816–1826.* New York City: G.P. Putnam's Sons Publishing)

Thomas Jefferson, among others, emphasized that the vitality of a democracy depends upon the education and participation of its citizens. While such active civic participation includes becoming informed about issues and voting in elections, we must also engage in other forms of intellectual exploration that expose us to a diverse array of lenses that guide our analysis, synthesis, and ultimately our discerning evaluation of the fidelity of information that guide the actions of others and ourselves. For this reason, we offer the following guiding framework that provides a diverse array of lenses for the reader to apply throughout the text.

Conceptual Framework: Political–Economic–Religious–Social–Intellectual–Area (PERSIA)

In the previous volume 1 edition 18 of the *Taking Sides: Clashing Views in United States History, The Colonial Period to Reconstruction,* we introduced to you our readers the acronym PERSIA which serves as the conceptual and organizational structure in which this text has been developed. The unifying thread that binds these six thematic areas of PERSIA is the assertion that to fully understand human history, one must acquire the skills of historical inquiry, analysis, and synthesis to recognize the ever-present impact of time, continuity, and change as evidenced through the values, beliefs, cultures, and institutions that comprise the storied legacies of women and men past and present.

As a reminder to you our readers of this volume 2 edition 18 of *Taking Sides: Clashing Views in United States History, Reconstruction to the Present*, PERSIA is once again applied as a graphic organizer that structures the general knowledge of the academic disciplines that comprise Social Studies Education into six thematic areas. For example,

- **P**olitical influences and concerns (e.g., issues of power, authority, governance, civic ideals, and practices as manifest in the rise of dominant individual leaders and governing institutions);
- **E**conomic influences and concerns (e.g., issues of production, distribution, and consumption as evidenced by the development of agrarian, industrial, and technological systems of exchange and investment);
- **R**eligious influences and concerns (e.g., issues of individual and group beliefs and practices as they influence cultural and institutional norms and deviations);
- **S**ocial influences and concerns (e.g., issues of individuals, groups, institutions and how they influence and are influenced by the multiple variables of identity development and the subsequent cultural formations that evolve from these individual, group, and institutional identities);
- **I**ntellectual influences and concerns (e.g., issues of science, technology, arts, philosophy, and the interdependent nature of human intellectual evolution emanating from local innovations to global phenomenon); and
- **A**rea/geographical influences and concerns (e.g., issues of people, places, and environments as framed within the spatial concepts of geography and interpreted through the cultural lenses that guide the interpretive exploration of between human beings, the environment, and the global interdependence of people and their limited resources).

As scholars within Social Studies Education, we believe that the complexity of the issues presented in this text requires an overarching framework that integrates academic disciplines that originate from both the liberal arts and social sciences. Social Studies Education, both in theory and practice, provides opportunities to explore issues and ideas, problems and solutions through interconnected and often overlapping fields of study. From history to sociology, political science to economics, the encompassing study of geography, and perhaps a half-dozen supporting disciplines (i.e., anthropology, archeology, law, philosophy, psychology, and theology), the comprehensive and indeed complex field of Social Studies Education provides the ideal academic landscape with which to explore the fascinating issues offered in this edition of the highly successful *Taking Sides: Clashing Views in United States History* series.

Thematic Content and Contours

History is certainly about the past, but it is also about the present, and the future. It is within this present and future tense that we find ourselves posing questions and seeking answers to pernicious unresolved issues that linger in our human experiences. Throughout the text, the reader will experience the explicit representation of historical knowledge (i.e., *Progressive*, *Neo-Conservative/ Consensus*, and *New Left* schools) and skills (i.e., historical inquiry, analysis, and synthesis) while also encountering the implicit presence of PERSIA's six thematic areas as represented in the 16 carefully selected and articulated issues of political, economic, religious, social, intellectual, and area-related historical importance. We consider how and why history has been interpreted in particular ways and attempt to reveal implications for acting as stewards of our democracy.

Metaphorically speaking, understanding the essential nature of the Gordian Knot begins with its examination. Through study, we might think beyond the structures that regulate one's thinking about it. Solving its mythological puzzle requires unique analysis, thinking past what has been given, and acting to transform the ways it has existed. We suggest the intellectually curious can similarly unlock the secrets of US history through shared inquiry. New analysis can lead us to new interpretation for social analysis and transformation. However, this task requires our active Historical learning, critical historical inquiry, and authentic acting. We therefore ask the reader to consider what we have presented and then to conduct their own deep dive into these issues so you will further reveal the social, intellectual, political, economical, spiritual, cultural, and intersectional aspects of historical relation. We hope you proceed by seeking new information that will nuance author interpretations and support your agency as a historical informed social actor.

Upon first appearance the organization of this text appears to adhere to a linear chronological structure that presents the opportunity for the reader to develop a cause and effect understanding of historical events. Yet, with closer examination, one begins to recognize that the six thematic areas of PERSIA provide a breadth of interdependence among the topics presented, while the sources chosen to represent these contrasting views on the topics offer a depth of historiographical interpretation that challenge the linear view of history with an entwined narrative. Indeed, the cause and effect phenomenon within history is always in play. Or as is oft misquoted and wrongly attributed to Mark Twain, "History doesn't repeat itself, but it often rhymes." Following Twain's insights, the following "rhyming" organizational structure of this text has been developed to present to you the reader 16 historical topics as presented through the lens of significant historians, theorists, authors, and even a handful of pundits, patriots, philosophers, politicians, and pamphleteers. The clashing views articulated through both primary and secondary documents offer an intriguing analysis and interpretation of historical events that continue to resonate as significant issues to be considered and debated by each of us in our contemporary lives.

A Summary of the Units

Unit 1: The Gilded Age

Mark Twain's coining of the term *The Gilded Age* most assuredly captures the essence of an era where economic expansion, technological innovations, and seemingly endless horizons of opportunities for human flourishing shined brightly in the American experience. Yet this thin decorative veneer could not hide the economic corruption, environmental degradation, and human inequities that became further ensconced in this period after Reconstruction and prior to United States involvement in World War I. Robber Barons or Entrepreneurs? Immigrants or Invaders? United Workers or Untethered Radicals? These and other labels became the nomenclature for the age as the social, economic, political, and indeed cultural institutions from east to west and north to south across the United States landscape experienced transformative upheaval and opportunities.

Throughout this unit, three issues are examined that capture the voices and visions of the characters that helped to write the script for this episode of American history at the close of the 19th century. Jeffrey Pugh and William Appleman Williams examine the question *Has U.S. Style Western Liberal Democracy Led to a New Historical Stage of Human Freedom?* Though Pugh does not emphatically settle\ this question on democratic peace theory he does suggest that the theory is a viable way to examine democratic relations internationally and ultimately reveals a consistent body of evidence as a primary framework

forunderstanding a new historical rise in human freedom. Williams challenges this notion as obfuscating the what he deems as the realities of *Western Liberal Democracy's* means of imposing a gentler form of empire that has served to contain class and race tensions at home and allowed for imperial expansion abroad.

Continuing this close examination of the conflicting interpretations of *The Gilded Age* are Ronald D. Eller, James Tice Moore, Michael Hudson and primary documents capturing the voices of James Monroe, Car Schurz, and John Hobson each confront the impact of aggressive entrepreneurialism and expansive industrialization on the traditional rural economies and societies throughout the Southern and Mid/Western regions of the United States. In asking *Did a New South Emerge Following Reconstruction?* and *Should We Understand U.S. Imperial Power as Primarily Emerging from its Financial Diplomacy Following the World Wars?*, Eller, Moore, Hudson, Monroe, Schurz, and Hobson require the reader to confront the complexities inherent within issues of race, ethnicity, nationalism, class privilege and power that are integrated within the topics examined.

Unit 2: Reform, War, and Depression

The arch of the pendulum's swing is predictable in its extremes. Just as *The Gilded Age* revealed the unbridled potential of human invention and excess, the Progressive Era ushered in a new age of social, economic, and cultural reforms that served as a preface to pending global wars and depressions. Where *laissez faire* sentiments dominated the political landscape of the preceding era, activism and re-activism became the *cause célèbre* for this era between the close and advent of the 20th century into the midst of a second global war. Socialists, Suffragists, Reformers, Racists, Internationalists, and Isolationists all gave voice to this intriguing era in American history.

The beginning and ending of the First World War exposed the nation's young citizenry to the horrors of human conflict enabled by technologies of war intended to inflict mass deconstruction and chaos with indiscriminate force. Amidst the devastations of war, the young citizen soldiers would also be equally influenced by the alluring cultures of Europe that challenged traditional values and provincial worldviews. Returning home from the trenches of war were men and women with more progressive ideas of their place and purpose in the social, economic, and political constructs of the United States. Equally restless on in migration (both domestic and foreign) were U.S.

citizens of colour and women at-large who were forming a solidarity of purpose to challenge the value-propositions on which American institutions were founded.

Five issues explore this era of reform, war, and depression through provocative questions that are intended to reflect the synergy as well as the maelstrom of the competing movements of the period. Sorting out winners and losers, though certainly not as simple a proposition, are Ronald J. Pestritto, William J. Atto, and Richard M. Abrams who offer distinctive responses to the inquiry *Did the Progressives Succeed?* A similar focus on success and failure is the issue inquiry *Was Woodrow Wilson Responsible for the Failure of the United States to Join the League of Nations?* Thomas A. Bailey and William G. Carlton address this matter with a nuanced interpretation that offers the reader a complex insight into the conjoined realities of foreign policy and human philosophy.

The questions of the catalysts of the American Great Depression and entry into World War II are examined through the lenses of political manoeuvring and propaganda. The two issues that raise the prospects of *Is Propaganda in Media Helpful to United States Democracy?* and *Were the First 100 Days of the New Deal Essentially Political Manoeuvring?* confront important insights regarding media literacy that draw from past insights to inform present and perhaps future deliberations. Edward Bernays and Noam Chomsky skilfully engage in an analysis of the symbiotic relationship of propaganda and democracy. A fireside chat offered by President Franklin D. Roosevelt is paired with the counterarguments of Gabriel Kolko to examine the extent to which the New Deal was grounded in progressive values or simply a sophisticated example of political manoeuvring that secured power among the corporate elites.

Reform and resistance are certainly highlighted throughout this unit but perhaps no more poignantly than with a critical examination of the individuals and organizations that comprised the mid-twentieth century African American civil rights movement as James A. Nuechterlein and Harvard Sitkoff debate the question *Was the World War II Era a Watershed for the Civil Rights Movement?*

Unit 3: The Cold War and Beyond

Let every nation know, whether it wishes us well or ill, that we shall pay any price, bear any burden, meet any hardship, support any friend, oppose any foe to assure the survival and the success of liberty.

—President John F. Kennedy,
inaugural address, January 20, 1961.

If ever there were a misnomer, it would have to be the notion that there was anything *cold* about the so-called Cold War era and beyond. The fire that burned white hot in the town squares, city halls, and collective consciousnesses of citizens both domestic and international was an all-consuming flame of political, economic, religious, social, intellectual, and area (geographic) upheaval. Whether it was the fear of a communist or a capitalist around every corner or the threat of nuclear bomb or a new rock-n-roll song that would destroy a culture the era following the Second World War revealed a dizzying array events that would lead to the toppling of institutions and the triumph of ideas (and ideals). President John F. Kennedy's inaugural address laid waste to the fears the skeptical political establishment in the United States and beyond that the young, yet to be tested, leader of the Western world would turn his back on the Nation's founding value of liberty as the historic bookmark in the American narrative.

World War II reemphasized liberty as driving force to commit a nation to war. Equally so, the rise of race, ethnic, gender, sex, and sexuality civil rights movements, music, literature, and art cultural movements, and an eclectic amalgam of political, economic, and social movements marched across the United States and the globe echoing Kennedy's clarion call for liberty at all costs in the face of all opposition. Imbued with a confidence born out of surviving an economic depression and another world war, the American citizenry embraced a victorious sense of exceptionalism that would serve as the fuel for the fire that was to be the era of the Cold War and beyond.

Throughout this unit, the reader will examine Walter LeFeber's and John Lewis Gaddis' point and counterpoint inquiring *Was President Truman responsible for the Cold War?* Complementing this issue of the role of a U.S. President's cause and effect relationship with catalysts to international crises is Thomas G. Paterson and Robert Weisbrot who debate the John F. Kennedy's role in causing the Cuban Missile Crisis. The Vietnam War continues to serve as litmus test for all U.S. Presidents and policy makers when assessing the costs of venturing into foreign entanglements as a nation. Thus, we examine Nixon's comments in "Peace with Honor" and "14 Addresses to the Nation on Vietnam," as compared to Kimbal's critiques of the Presidents discourse and presentation of Vietnam to the American people.

Milton Freidman and Daniel Stedman Jones broaden the scope of inquiry by including world leaders and economic theorist in equation by asking, *Do Economic Policies*

Associated with Reagan, Thatcher, and Friedman Promote Freedom in a Liberal Democracy?

No examination of the post-World War II and Cold War era(s) would be complete without venturing into popular uprisings and culture as a venue for social reform. The story of rock and roll, women's liberation organizations, and even Southern Christian traditions tells the tale of issues of race, ethnic, sex, and gender inequity of attribution and inclusion in American. Jody Pennington and Bruce Harrah-Conforth debate the role of rock and roll in dismantling so-called traditional family values, while Carolyn Renée Dupont, David L. Chappell, F. Carolyn Graglia, and Jo Freeman seek to bring clarity and context to entrenched racial segregation as a part of religious doctrine and the lingering resistance to passage of the Equal Rights Amendment as championed by the American feminist movement of the 1970s to present. Unit 3 ends with a provocative challenge to America's place in the world at the dawn of a new 20th century. Andrew Bacevich and Joseph S. Nye bring the text to an end by revisiting the question, *Is the American Century over?*

"Without history, we cannot undertake any sensible inquiry into the political, social, or moral issues in society. And without historical knowledge and inquiry, we cannot achieve the informed, discriminating citizenship essential to effective participation in the democratic processes of governance and the fulfillment for all our citizens of the nation's democratic ideals" (Crabtree & Nash, 1995). It is with this call for a commitment to reasoned discernment that we the authors of *Taking Sides: Clashing Views in United States History, Reconstruction to the Present, Volume 2, Edition 18* invite you to join us.

Humanizing Historical Inquiry

Paulo Freire insists that, *Humanization is the process of becoming more fully human as social, historical, thinking, communicating, transformative, creative persons who participate in and with the world* (Freire, 1972).

The teaching of American history is crucial not only to student achievement, but also to the future of our democratic nation. According to the National Standards for United States History: Exploring the American Experience, "history opens to students the great record of human experience, revealing the vast range of accommodations individuals and societies have made to the problems confronting them, and disclosing the consequences that have followed the various choices that have been made. By studying the choices and decisions of the past, students can confront today's problems and choices with a deeper awareness of the alternatives before them and the likely consequences of each" (Crabtree & Nash, 1994).

Michael Hartoonian, past President of the National Council for the Social Studies asserts that

> *The ultimate work of education is to learn to be a human being. As human beings, we are always active with two kinds of tasks—reconstructing civilization and reconstructing ourselves. We are always in the process of trying to be better, to live better, and to construct better places. And, we do this through conversations with each other and with the cultural heritage of the human family. Unless we engage in this conversation, we cannot become fully human* (Hartoonian, 1996).

If we are to be enlightened (Jahjaga) and fully human (Freire and Hartoonian), it appears that we must deliberately engage in the quest for a broader understanding of the diversity of the human condition as told in the narratives that capture our individual stories informed by our past and present experiences in order to write tale of our collective future. It is this belief in the capacity of humans to engage in critically reflective dialogue and dialectic that inspire we the authors and editors of *Taking Sides: Clashing Views in United States* History, *Volume 2, Edition 18* to offer the reader opportunities to consider a diverse array of theories, conjectures, and even emboldened opinions found in primary and secondary documents that we hope will *inform, enlighten,* and *humanize* the study of history in your days ahead.

Dr. Kevin R. Magill
Dr. Tony L. Talbert
Baylor University

References

Crabtree, C., & Nash, G. B. (1994). *National Standards for United States History: Exploring the American Experience. Grades 5-12. Expanded Edition. Including Examples of Student Achievement.* National Center for History in the Schools, University of California, Los Angeles, 10880 Wilshire Blvd., Suite 761, Los Angeles, CA 90024-4108.

Ford, P. L. (1899). *The writings of Thomas Jefferson: Volume 10 1816–1826.* New York City: G.P. Putnam's Sons Publishing.

Crabtree, C., & Nash, G. (1995). Chapter 1: Developing Standards in United States and World History for Students in Grades 5-12: Significance of History for the Educated Citizen. *The History Teacher, 28*(3), 301–314. doi:10.2307/494679. Retrieved from http://www.jstor.org/stable/49467

Freire, P. (1972). *Pedagogy of the oppressed.* New York: Herder and Herder.

Hartoonian, M. H. 1996. "The Price of Civilization: Competence and Constant Vigil." *Social Education* 60 (1): 6–8.

Soley, M. 1996. "If It's Controversial, Why Teach It?" *Social Education,* 60 (1): 9–14.

Talbert, T. L., & Rodgers, M. J. B. (2011). Social Education Teacher as Activist. In C.S. White's *Journeys in Social Education* (pp. 227–239). Sense Publishers.

Torney-Purta, J., & Lopez, S. V. (2006). Developing Citizenship Competencies from Kindergarten Through Grade 12: A Background Paper for Policymakers and Educators. *Education Commission of the States (NJ3).*

The Gilded Age

The Gilded Age

*T*he nation that emerged from the Civil War had choices to make about the future of the nation. How would she reconcile the material realities of a fundamentally divided and inequitable country supposedly founded on enlightenment ideals that now extended to one of its traditionally marginalized groups? Economic expansion and the seemingly unlimited resources available in the postbellum United States offered great opportunities and created new political, social, and economic challenges. After an initial burst of freedom, African Americans were disfranchised and segregated from mainstream America and limited in their opportunities for full citizenship.

As the United States became more heavily industrialized in the years following the Civil War, the need for cheap labor to run the machinery of the Industrial Revolution created an atmosphere for potential exploitation, which was intensified by the concentration of wealth in the hands of a few capitalists. Even the defeated South experienced the impact of industrialization, but questions remain as to how much the South remained tied to the political, economic, and social institutions of the Old South. In regions where industry thrived, the labor movement took root, with some elements calling for an overthrow of capitalism, whereas others sought to establish political power within the existing system. The formation of labor unions demanding rights for workers produced industrial warfare as management sought the support of the federal government to counter the efforts of strikers. The contentious struggles moved labor movements toward reforms rather than revolution, a condition that would have profound affects on the nation. So called "Robber Barons" manipulated markets to their ends monopolizing industry, exploited unregulated markets, and led to a new stage of investment capitalism. These efforts resulted in both positive and negative outcomes economically, socially, and politically that exists in the 21st century. The novel "The Gilded Age: A Tale of Today" by Mark Twain's and Charles Dudley Warner's described an era of significant social problems superficially covered by a thin gold layer and lent its name to this era of US history.

Concurrently, relative political freedom and economic opportunity provided incentives for immigration to the United States, but strains began to develop between immigrants and native-born workers. At the same time, thousands of Americans sought their opportunities in the trans-Mississippi West where they sought to earn their livelihoods in farming, herding, and mining. The era saw the United States begin its imperialist efforts cementing her place on the world stage under the banner of freedom and democracy, without really troubling its social organizing or problematic past.

Selected, Edited, and with Issue Framing Material by:
Kevin R. Magill and Tony L. Talbert, *Baylor University*

ISSUE

Has the Democratic Peace Theory Helped Lead U.S. Style and Other Western Democracies to a New Historical Stage of Human Freedom?

YES: Jeffrey Pugh, from "Democratic Peace Theory: A Review and Evaluation," *CEMPROC Working Paper Series* (2005)

NO: William Appleman Williams, from "Conclusion: History as a Way of Breaking the Chains of the Past," Verso (2011)

Learning Outcomes
After reading this issue, you will be able to:
• Discuss the history of the democratic peace theory in Western political thought.
• Contextualize some of the ways ideologies of the 20th century have been framed and discussed by historians.
• Understand the ways the Democratic Peace Theory fits within the historical and current geopolitical climate.
• Notice the similarities and differences in democratic thinking related to international relations within different historical eras.

ISSUE SUMMARY

YES: Jeff Pugh suggests that the *Democratic Peace Theory* remains a viable way to examine democratic relations internationally. He also notes legitimate critiques of the theory: that a democratic nation's desire to maintain power is a means of ensuring self-preservation (not necessarily democracy), that data presented by democratic peace theorists is limited and causal, and that it is also important for us to trouble the ways we perceive, define, and apply the theory.

NO: William Appleman Williams argues that Liberal Democracy has been a means of imposing a gentler form of empire that has served to contain class and race tensions at home and allowed for imperial expansion abroad.

T he Democratic Peace Theory has been used to describe aspects of western thought and philosophy for many years. It has more recently been applied to history and political science in the late 1960s to describe Cold War and other more recent Western coalitions. The theory argues that democracies are hesitant to engage in armed conflict with other identified powerful democracies. Enlightenment thinkers like Thomas Paine and Immanuel Kant introduced the theory to western philosophy after making their own observations about democratic social organization. Alexis de Tocqueville and others continued to use the theory, taking it up in complementary ways. In "Common Sense" written in 1776, Paine argued that the democratic and economic realities he observed in Europe at the time were swayed by the emotional nature of a sovereign leader's whims and could therefore draw these nations into war. Further, Paine believed that the benefits of trading among like nations would keep republics from going to war because each nation benefits from a favorable trading partnership. Like Paine, Kant suggested that the European republics would have many representative voices that could limit war-like impulses, particularly against other republics. Based on these ideas, Kant suggested, in 1795, that most people would naturally avoid war unless it was for personal interest or for self-defense. He contended that the nature of a Republic would naturally dissuade a government from summarily going to war because people would need to democratically agree to such a conflict. Kant suggested that governments would be able to better understand the perspectives of similarly governed nations. Kant therefore surmised that if all nations became republics, then war would necessarily end without aggressors of differing governing ideologies coming into conflict. Between 1835 and 1840 de Tocqueville studied Democracy in America and, similarly, observed that democratic nations were unlikely to go to war because of the shared values needed for the foundations of a democratic society.

While the democratic peace theory was not widely discussed or used to describe political relations in Kant's time, it found resurgence in Western thought in the 1960s as a way to describe the international relations during the Cold War. A number of studies were done between 1976 and 1989 that suggested a statistically significant correlation between democratic societies and peace. However, many objected to these findings, including scholars called political realists. According to Haslam (2010) realists believe that the international political system is anarchic, as there is no supranational authority to enforce rules; states act in their rational self-interest within the international system; and states desire power to ensure self-preservation. Realists come from the Machiavellian perspective and argue that every nation comes from a perspective of power, survival, and glory and will therefore go to war in whichever ways they must in order to achieve their aims. Other historical challengers to the idea have come from historians that have noted the Spanish American War and the Kargil War (among others) as examples which disprove the theory.

Despite challenges to the theory, Francis Fukuyama famously took up the idea in 1989 during the fall of the Berlin Wall claiming that Western-style liberal democracy had won out over all other systems and would be the last form of human government. Writing in the deregulation era in the 1980s, he believed that the United States had entered new stage of human freedom, arguing that the collapse of the Soviet Union led to humanity reaching, "not just . . . the passing of a particular period of post-war history, but the end of history as such: that is, the end point of mankind's ideological evolution and the universalization of Western Liberal democracy as the final form of human government." Fukuyama ironically drew on aspects Hegel and Marx for his more conservative analysis to claim that this new epoch was a new stage of historical materialism (Marxist historiographers often suggest that history is the result of material conditions, production, mode of production, and relations of production will fundamentally determine social organization and development.). Despite Fukuyama's claims, many have argued that his idea of a "new era" through democratic peace represents one of the major problems with the democratic peace theory. Critics like Jacques Derrida suggest that Fukuyama's use of Hegel and Marx are superficial and his social analysis therefore exist within a Western centric bubble that assumes US beneficence. In Derrida's words, "never have violence, inequality, exclusion, famine, and thus economic oppression affected as many human beings in the history of the earth and of humanity . . . no degree of progress allows one to ignore that never before, in absolute figures, have so many men, women and children been subjugated, starved or exterminated on the earth." Derrida believed that, if in fact we were in a new stage of peace, it is not one in which Liberal democracy exists as part of the Enlightenment tradition.

Similarly, some have suggested that we need only look to the social relations in the United States to reveal that the United States and many other Western "democracies" are undemocratic. Consider that institutional racism, sexism, classism, the rewriting of history, changing artifacts in the name of heritage, the relationship between democracy and capitalism, money in political elections, and a myriad of other antagonisms all restrict proper democratic function and disenfranchise much of the population. Historically, we need only look to African Americans, Asian Americans, Indigenous Persons, Women and even (albeit to a much lesser degree) Irish Americans, Italian American, German Americans, and so on to see the ways this functions in society, limiting their access to political decision-making. Therefore, even the term liberal democracy includes insidious forms of racism (classism, sexism, etc.) that make it undemocratic. Kwame Ture and Martin Luther King considered this form of democracy White Liberalism—a condition in which individuals know and understand racism is bad, but they still limited their acting to end it. Much like King and Ture, many nations realize that the international democracy functions in similar ways. They are held to democratic standards while the United States is not. These arguments suggest that certain social and political realities exist, which are undemocratic, and therefore these nations are not democratic, but use the term as a form of propaganda.

Author William Appleman Williams wrote in what is now called the civil rights era and critiques the idea of the United States as a Liberal Democratic paragon. He argues that one cannot read the idea of a Western-style liberal democracy without considering the relationships between it, the oppression of capitalism, the incompatibility of its structures to democracy, and the reality of U.S. Empire. Appleman Williams traces this history of these relationships in the United States back to the British Empire and argues that Liberal Democracy has been used, not as a means to achieve freedom or democratic peace but as a means of imposing a gentler form of empire. He argues Liberal U.S. Democracy has also been a mechanism to contain class and race tensions at home while supporting imperial expansion abroad. Appleman Williams believed the relationship between capitalism, empire, and "Western Liberal democracy" has not led to a new stage of human freedom or to democratic peace, but as a mechanism of international and civic control. He argues the social control has fragmented people and limited their democratic access. He suggests Western Liberal democracy has tied citizens at individual and systematic level to "the rat-race" of a capitalist system designed to encourage accumulation of private property and support business interest over people. The result, propaganda has convinced people that empire can be democratic. Jeff Pugh offers us a balanced view of the democratic peace theory as it has been framed. He provides a measured analysis of the strengths and weaknesses of the theory accepting the definitions and premises those arguing for it have outlined. He begins by providing the foundations of the theory and offering data that seem to imply democratic peace has indeed led to a more peaceful Western world. However, Pugh also acknowledges the shortcomings of the theory and the validity of political realism's critiques. Ultimately, Pugh suggests that the theory can be helpful to consider as a political approach, but that we need to trouble taken for granted perceptions, definitions, and applications of the theory.

YES ↩

Jeffrey Pugh

Democratic Peace Theory: A Review and Evaluation

According to Jack Levy, the democratic peace thesis is "the closest thing we have to an empirical law in the study of international relations."[1] This theory refers to the idea that democracies by nature do not go to war with one another, a fact which historically has guaranteed peace between democratic states, arguably without exception. The democratic peace thesis offers a strong empirical attack in the liberal arsenal against the traditional intellectual hegemony of realism in American IR theory. Perhaps for this reason, there has been a spirited debate between proponents of democratic peace theory and critics who level a number of counterattacks. Among others, these include charges that the theory is a statistical artifact, that the terms of its definition ('democratic' or 'liberal', 'war', etc.) are defined in a tautological and self-serving manner, and that insufficient historical evidence is available to make accurate, generalizable conclusions since both war between states and the existence of democracy is historically relatively rare.

Democratic peace is rooted theoretically in the writings of Immanuel Kant, and in particular his work "Perpetual Peace". Kant claims that peace is a reasonable outcome of the interaction of states with a republican form of government. He believes that the republican constitution "gives a favorable prospect for the desired consequence, i.e., perpetual peace. The reason is this: if the consent of the citizens is required in order to decide that war should be declared (and in this constitution it cannot but be the case), nothing is more natural than that they should be very cautious in commencing such a poor game, decreeing for themselves all the calamities of war." Contrasting republicanism with other forms of governments, Kant argues, "On the other hand, in a constitution which is not republican, and under which the subjects are not citizens, a declaration of war is the easiest thing in the world to decide upon, because war does not require of the ruler, who is the proprietor and not a member of the state, the least sacrifice of the pleasure of his table, the chase, his country houses, his court functions, and the like."[2]

Because peace under Kant's paradigm is a function of the form of government of the two potential parties to a conflict, the logical implication is that liberal republicanism must be diffused and made universal in order to achieve perpetual peace among states. Until states share a common liberal perspective, war will be necessary to prevent autocratic and despotic governments from oppressing their own people and from threatening the freedom of citizens in the liberal states themselves. This semi-evangelical view of liberalism may also contribute to strengthening the democratic peace theory. Authoritarian regimes may view liberal states as particularly threatening because of this ideology that values the diffusion of liberalism to other states, which would of course threaten the authoritarian leader's own power. Liberal states, on the other hand, would not feel threatened by the universalistic outlook of other liberal republics since they already share a similar form of government.

It is important to recognize that the term 'democratic peace' is somewhat ambiguous, even misleading, as it tends to conflate democracy (which can be ambiguously defined itself) with other terms. Some scholars prefer to talk about the 'liberal peace theory' instead of democratic peace, saying that this formulation is more relevant and easier to define in empirical analyses.[3] Kant himself notes that democracy (a form of sovereignty) is often confused with republicanism (a form of government). The presence of a republican constitution is one of his primary criteria for attaining perpetual peace. He claims that "The mode of government is incomparably more important to the people than the form of sovereignty."[4]

Liberal states in Kant's paradigm are characterized by certain criteria that distinguish them from authoritarian and other autocratic, nondemocratic forms of government. These include a republican form of government based on the rule of law that is governed in a representative manner

Pugh, Jeffrey. 2005. "Democratic Peace Theory: A Review and Evaluation." CEMPROC Working Paper Series: In peace, conflict, and development (April): 1–19.

through a separation of powers; respect for human rights; and interdependent social and economic relations. Taken together, these criteria are necessary and sufficient to create stable peace between two states with the expectation that this peace will endure, according to Kant.[5]

An important part of democratic peace is that liberal, democratic states[6] share a common normative dedication to liberal ideals, and they frequently employ liberal justifications for going to war. Michael Doyle argues that quite often, the violent interventions that liberal states engage in "are publicly justified in the first instance as attempts to preserve a 'way of life': to defend freedom and private enterprise."[7] When the potential adversary shares a commitment to the protection of basic freedoms and human rights, and its government truly represents the wishes of the population (as evidenced by free and fair, competitive elections), it is much more difficult for democratic governments to justify war to their own citizens.

Perception is an important component of liberal peace. Put crudely, liberal states are peaceful toward one another because they trust other liberal states to behave rationally and sensibly, whereas they are suspicious that non-liberal states may not behave in this manner. John Owen explains that "liberals view foreign states with prejudice. Prima facie, they believe that, irrespective of physical capability, liberal states are safe and illiberal states potentially dangerous. The ground of this belief is the premise that states whose governments respect their citizens' autonomy will behave rationally and responsibly, while coercive governments may not."[8]

By extension, it does not matter whether illiberal states are actually inherently prone to irresponsible or aggressive behavior; if liberal states believe that this is possible, they will act accordingly, basing their foreign policy decisions on the perception that liberal states are to be trusted while autocratic and despotic regimes must be regarded with some suspicion. This can become a self-fulfilling prophesy, in which the liberal state instigates a conflict with the illiberal state (or vice versa) in an example of what Owen calls 'liberal war'.

In addition to the enhanced accountability inherent in states with republican constitutions and the perceptions of the citizens and elites of these states which view illiberal states with suspicion, there are several other possible reasons for the peace which prevails between liberal states (and by extension, the fact that this peace does not apply reliably between liberal states and autocratic counterparts). The checks and balances and separation of powers that characterize liberal republics place restraints on the executive in making a decision to go to war. The delays and debate that are natural parts of such republics

introduce a period of deliberation in which conflicts are fully examined from a variety of vantage points. Two liberal republics facing a joint conflict, because of their deliberative structures maintained by separation of power, are likely to find any number of opportunities to address the issue before it escalates to the point of war.[9]

In order to create a better 'big picture' of liberal peace, Maoz and Russett condense several of the preceding factors into two explanatory models of liberal peace, which they then test with empirical cases. They describe the normative model and the structural model: "The normative model suggests that democracies do not fight each other because norms of compromise and cooperation prevent their conflicts of interest from escalating into violent clashes. The structural model asserts that complex political mobilization processes impose institutional constraints on the leaders of two democracies confronting each other to make violent conflict unfeasible."[10] Based on their empirical analysis, Maoz and Russett conclude that both models are supported by the data, but that the normative model is stronger, more robust, and more consistent across the data set than is the structural model.

Liberal republics facing conflicts with other liberal states are likely to benefit from the increased credibility of their claims. Stephen Van Evera has argued that war is made much more likely by states' frequent misperception of international conditions, their own capabilities, and the intentions of other states.[11] James Fearon, however, points out that liberal states are much more credible and effective in signaling their intentions to potential rivals, because leaders are held accountable by the electorate for their threats and statements, and bluffs that are called are likely to lead to the leader's recall as an example of 'domestic audience costs'.[12]

The secrecy of an authoritarian regime, on the other hand, would likely mean that the leader could bluff with impunity, and that other states might easily misperceive his true motives and determination to carry through, unlike a liberal republic, which would be transparent enough in its decision-making process that another democracy would be able to recognize its intention if it were willing to go to war. The result of all this is that war is less likely to occur as a result of a liberal state's misperception that another liberal state is making empty threats or is bluffing.

Much of the strength of liberal peace theory lies in the empirical record that supports the proposition. Michael Doyle has surveyed historical wars from 1790 to 1983, and concluded that "The near absence of war between Liberal states, whether adjacent or not, for almost two hundred years thus may have significance."[13] One of the key elements in the debate over liberal peace is the way liberal republics or democracies are defined (and indeed the actual term used varies among a number of similar concepts, including liberal state, constitutional republic, libertarian state, democracy, polyarchy, and others). Doyle acknowledges the approximate nature of the liberal state concept, but he nonetheless attempts to provide careful and clear criteria for the selection of the states that he lists as liberal, drawing on the theoretical base established by Kant to do so. He explains,

> I have drawn up this *approximate* list of Liberal regimes (including regimes that were Liberal democratic as of 1990) according to the four "Kantian" institutions described as essential: market and private property economies; polities that are externally sovereign; citizens who possess juridical rights; and 'republican' (whether republican or parliamentary monarchy), representative government. This last includes the requirement that the legislative branch have an effective role in public policy and be formally and competitively (either inter- or intraparty) elected. Furthermore, I have taken into account whether male suffrage is wide (that is, 30 percent) or, as Kant would have had it, open to 'achievement' by inhabitants (for example, to poll tax payers or householders) of the national or metropolitan territory. (This list of Liberal regimes is thus more inclusive than a list of democratic regimes, or polyarchies.) Female suffrage is granted within a generation of its being demanded by an extensive female suffrage movement, and representative government is internally sovereign (for example, including and especially over military and foreign affairs) as well as stable (in existence for at least three years."[14]

Other studies have refined the definitions employed in analysis of wars or have focused on particular intervening variables that may affect the liberalism-peace relationship. Singer & Small, for example, set a definition for war corresponding with that of the Correlates of War (COW) project at the University of Michigan that included only those conflicts with more than one thousand battlefield deaths; this measure has been used frequently by other scholars.[15] Subsequent scholars, however, have also tested the liberal peace thesis using data from the Militarized Interstate Dispute (MID) data set of the COW, which measure interstate conflict at lower levels short of fulls-cale war. This allows for a more robust test of the proposition that pairs of democracies go to war against each other much less frequently (perhaps not at all) than other state dyads, since there are multiple levels of conflict that are included in the data set. Henry Farber and Joanne Gowa

found using MID data that there is a significantly lower chance of lower-level conflict between pairs of democracies than between other sets of states, a finding that is consistent with the conventional conclusion in studies of higher-level conflict (war) and liberal peace.[16]

Farber & Gowa developed the research program further by segmenting the historical time periods in which wars were analyzed, studying separately the conflicts prior to World War I; the First World War years; the period between world wars; World War II, and the Cold War period. This examination produced the potentially interesting result that, although war did not occur between liberal states during these periods[17], this finding was statistically significant only during World War I, which the authors dismiss as too unique to be relevant or generalizable, and during the post-WWII period of the Cold War.[18] It is important to add the caveat that the empirical evidence does not seem to indicate that liberal states are any less prone to engage in war than other types of regimes; they simply do not go to war against other liberal states.

Most early democratic peace theorists relied on some form of categorical division between liberal and illiberal regimes. This provided ammunition for critics, who alleged that this arbitrary dichotomy made the definition of a liberal state particularly arbitrary and open to manipulation. Maoz and Russett, however, attempted to capture sophisticated empirical data by using a continuum to describe a state's level of democracy (vs. autocracy), as well as using the traditional dichotomous measures. The continuum, based on the work of Ted Gurr, Harry Eckstein, and other scholars working on the Polity II data set, measured the degree of democracy on a number of factors, as well as the degree of autocracy, which was expressed as a negative number, then combined the two measures into an aggregate score.

The analysis of Maoz and Russett, which drew on two major data sets which differed somewhat in case selection, definitions, and other details that could serve as a test of the robustness of the authors' models, produced mixed results. The results from one of the data sets showed a strong relationship between democracy and peace for both the dichotomous and continuous measures of democracy, whereas the other data set indicated a significant correlation only for the dichotomous category (in which states were labeled either democratic or not, rather than being assigned a score between democracy and autocracy).[19]

Oneal & Ray attempt to reconcile some of the inconclusive and mixed results of Maoz & Russett and other scholars who utilize continuum scales of democracy rather than dichotomous categories. They claim that these measures fail to capture adequately the important but distinct elements of total level of democracy shared in a particular state dyad and the political distance between the two regimes. Oneal & Ray conclude,

> Our pooled analyses of the politically relevant pairs of states, 1950–85, indicate that democracies are more peaceful dyadically and individually, and democracies and autocracies are especially prone to conflict. The prospects for peace are influenced by the level of democracy in a dyad; but they are also significantly affected by the political distance separating the regimes along the democracy-autocracy continuum. Democratic pairs are less conflict-prone than average, all else being equal; but a high level of democracy in one state does not compensate for the dangers associated with autocracy in a strategic partner. Making the less democratic state in a dyad more democratic is unambiguously good; it increases the average democracy score for the pair and reduces the political distance separating the states, lowering the likelihood of conflict. Increasing the level of democracy in the more democratic state, holding the regime score of the other state constant, raises the danger of a dispute, however. The average level of democracy within the dyad increases, but so does political distance . . . A dichotomous measure of joint democracy yields strong support for the democratic peace because it identifies dyads for which the combined democracy scores are a maximum and political distance is a minimum. Continuous measures produce weaker evidence because the strong influence of political distance is not fully taken into account.[20]

Some liberal peace proponents have advanced the claim that liberal states are inherently less violent, both in their relations with other states and with respect to internal violence. R.J. Rummel, one of the early pioneers of the study of democratic peace, advanced four propositions—that interstate violence will occur only if at least one state is not 'libertarian'; that the more libertarian two states are, the less likely they will engage in mutual violence; that libertarian states tend to engage less in interstate violence in general; and that the more libertarian a state is, the less internal violence it will have. Based on empirical tests, Rummel found positive support for all of these propositions, but only the proposition that interstate war will occur only if at least one state is not libertarian could be supported at a level of significance that he called 'robust'. As the subsequent literature has reflected, it is probably not true that liberal states are less likely to engage in war in general or to have lower levels of internal conflict.

Criticisms and Weaknesses of Liberal Peace Theory

By no means is the liberal peace thesis accepted universally within the field of international relations. It represents a robust and active research program, but like most such groups of theory, it has attracted energetic criticism from several sides. One weakness of liberal peace theory is that there is a fairly small sample from which to draw conclusions. Democracies were quite rare until relatively recently, and combined with the fact that war is actually fairly rare (when considered from the perspective that of all interactions between sets of two countries, or dyads, across time and space, only a few develop into war), the data set is quite limited. Some scholars have alleged that this creates uncertainty about whether the lack of war between democratic states is any more significant than would be a statistical analysis that revealed a lack of war between states whose names begin with a particular letter.

In addition to this criticism, Farber & Gowa concluded from their segmented analysis of historical war periods that most new democracies emerged during the Cold War, and that liberal peace was only significantly different during this period (as opposed to earlier periods, when the difference in the occurrence of war between democracies and that between other types of states was not significant).[21] This suggests the possibility that liberal peace during this period could have been explained by the need to balance against a hostile and threatening Communist bloc. For this reason, liberal states would have avoided going to war against each other for fear of presenting weakness before the greater perceived threat which was the Soviet bloc. In other words, the statistical evidence for liberal peace could actually be an artifact reflecting alliance factors during the Cold War.

James Lee Ray refutes this attack, saying that it is inconsistent to apply the expectation that opposition to a common enemy leads to peace only to democracies without applying it also to the nondemocratic allies against communism and to the Communist bloc itself, which faced a formidable set of common enemies in the West. He claims,

> One might reasonably infer that if the opposition of the communists was sufficient to create common interests guaranteeing peace among the democratic (or anticommunist) states of the world, then the opposition of the 'Free World' (even more formidable, by most measures) should have been sufficient to guarantee peace among the communist states. Yet during the Cold War the Soviet Union invaded Hungary and Czechoslovakia, as

well as Afghanistan, and experienced serious border clashes with communist China. Meanwhile, Vietnam attacked and occupied most of Cambodia, provoking a retaliatory attack by communist China. The 'opposition leads to common interests leads to peace' idea would also be hard-pressed to account for the fact that peace did not prevail uniformly on the anticommunist side of the Cold War divide. For example, El Salvador fought a war with Honduras in 1969, Turkey and Greece became embroiled in a war over the fate of Cyprus in 1974, and Great Britain clashed with Argentina over the Falkland/Malvinas islands in 1982. These cases are not anomalies for advocates of the democratic peace proposition; each of those wars involved at least one undemocratic state.[22]

Raymond Cohen argues that democracy is not adequate as an explanation for the phenomenon of 'liberal peace' that has been noted so extensively by scholars. He argues that,

> Contrary to received truth, the existence of a general law of behaviour that *democracies as a class do not fight each other* has not been demonstrated. Rather, the soundest conclusion to draw from the evidence is that democratic states in the North Atlantic/Western European area, sharing a particular set of historical circumstances and a common cultural heritage, have avoided going to war. This is in line with Karl Deutsch's 1955 observation that a 'security community', a community of nations resolved to settle their disputes peacefully, had come into being in the North Atlantic area. The finding has not been proved to hold throughout history, outside the North Atlantic area, or for non-Western cultures.[23]

Similarly to those mentioned earlier who claim the liberal peace to be an artifact or coincidence attributable to other factors such as time period, Cohen concludes that "No causal mechanism has been shown to exist providing a necessary link between democracies and mutually peaceful behaviour. On the contrary, there is reason to suspect that pacific unions are liable to occur in particular historical circumstances irrespective of regime type."[24] If Cohen is correct, then democracies are just as likely to go to war with one another as with any other type of regime, given similar circumstances and controlling for extraneous variables. The problem with this criticism, of course, is that democracies have not gone to war against one another, and a number of significant empirical studies that have attempted to control for any variable that seems remotely relevant to international war have found that controlling for the extraneous variables does not negatively affect the statistical significance and importance of the absence of war between democracies.[25]

One further weakness exhibited by liberal peace theory is similar to the scientifically questionable action in an experiment of peeking at data before formulating one's hypotheses. It is possible that some of the power of the empirical support for the liberal peace proposition comes from the careful crafting of the criteria used to define concepts like 'democracies' and 'war'. The Correlates of War project, which has produced much of the empirical data used by scholars on all sides of the liberal peace debate, defines interstate war as being conflict between two independent states resulting in at least 1,000 battlefield casualties. The definition of a 'liberal' or democratic state includes several criteria, such as external sovereignty, private property and market economies, juridical rights of citizens and representative government.[26] Both of these definitions are potentially controversial, and they have been subject to charges that they were shaped to fit existing data. The research on liberal peace may be driven to some extent by scholars' assumptions, which reflect the widespread belief that mutual democratic institutions result in peaceful relations, and that the central research agenda, beyond confirming empirical support for the correlation between peace and liberalism, is to figure out why this phenomenon occurs.

Cohen expands on this criticism, saying that "the only way to eliminate counter-examples of war between democracies is by defining democracy in such a way that it applies only to a handful of states, but a narrow definition of democracy limits the validity of the generalization to the North Atlantic/West European area after 1945. Before 1945 there were few opportunities for democracies to fight. After 1945 many states classified as democratic by early researchers such as Doyle turn out, on closer examination, to possess dubious credentials."[27]

In addition, Cohen points out that as the international system evolved during the twentieth century, the concept of war also has changed. It is now difficult to define war as being significant only when it is conflict between two independent states resulting in at least 1,000 battlefield deaths. In the wake of World War II, overt war between Great Powers has become essentially nonexistent (possibly due to immense increases in violence interdependence), while Great Powers and other democracies continue to engage in conflict through proxy wars posing as civil conflicts as well as through less bloody conflicts that are still extremely significant from a political standpoint. The significance of new types of conflict that do not fall neatly into either the realist or liberal peace paradigms are borne out by a number of scholars, especially those writing on areas of the world outside of Western Europe and the United States.[28]

Liberal peace, despite the doubts of its critics, is still a very active and robust set of theories and research programs. It offers perhaps the most comprehensive and persuasive attack on the theoretical hegemony of realism within the field of international relations. Furthermore, the empirical evidence is difficult to deny—liberal states generally do not go to war against each other. The criticism of the theory has mostly focused on questioning the validity of interpreting causal relationships from limited empirical data, not on the actual lack or presence of war between democracies (although there are a couple of exceptions in the literature). This is an important proviso to remember for advocates and critics alike—both democracies and wars are still rather rare, so it may still be somewhat premature to proclaim based on empirical evidence that democratic peace should be considered to have the strength of a law. The combined evidence, however, of the Cold War period when democracies proliferated enormously, plus the past fifteen years after the fall of the Soviet Union, when presumably any intervening variable having to do with alliance effects against the USSR would have collapsed, serve as persuasive support for the theory. Every year that passes in which democracies behave peacefully toward one another simply reinforces the validity of democratic peace theory.

Notes

1. Jack S. Levy, "Domestic Politics in War," in Robert I. Rotberg and Theodore K. Rabb, eds., *The Origin and Prevention of Major Wars* (New York: Cambridge University Press, 1989), p. 88.

2. Immanuel Kant, "Perpetual Peace." *On History*, trans L.W. Beck, R.E. Anchor, & E. Fackenheim (New York: The Liberal Arts Press, 1957), p. 94–95.

3. See John M. Owen, *Liberal Peace, Liberal War* (Ithaca: Cornell University Press, 1997); Michael Doyle, *Ways of War and Peace: Realism, Liberalism, and Socialism* (New York: W.W. Norton & Company, 1997).

4. Immanuel Kant, "Perpetual Peace", p. 97.

5. Michael Doyle, *Ways of War and Peace: Realism, Liberalism, and Socialism*, p. 286–287.

6. The definitions offered for democracy are varied and contentious, and are very important for the empirical examination of the theory's claim. Bruce Russet gives a typical if slightly broad (by excluding liberal protections of rights from the criteria) definition, which considers democratic states to be those with governments that are popularly selected through periodic contested elections in which a substantial portion of citizens are eligible to vote, and that the possibility exists for the leaders to be defeated and replaced through election and a peaceful transfer of power. Finally, he indicates that democracy must exist and exhibit some minimum level of stability or institutionalization: "some period must have elapsed during which democratic processes and institutions could become established, so that both the citizens of the 'democratic' state and its adversary could regard it as one governed by democratic principles." (p. 16) Bruce Russett, *Grasping the Democratic Peace* (Princeton: Princeton University Press, 1993).

7. Michael Doyle, "Kant, Liberal Legacies, and Foreign Affairs", p. 335.

8. John M. Owen, *Liberal Peace, Liberal War*, p. 38.

9. Michael Doyle, *Ways of War and Peace*, p. 281.

10. Maoz and Russett, 'Normative and Structural Causes of Democratic Peace, 1946–1986', *American Political Science Review*, 87 (1993), pp. 624–37.

11. Stephen Van Evera, *Causes of War: Power and the Roots of Conflict* (Ithaca: Cornell University Press, 1999).

12. James Fearon, "Domestic Political Audiences and the Escalation of International Disputes," *American Political Science Review*, 88 (1994), pp. 577–582.

13. Michael Doyle, *Ways of War and Peace*; See also Michael Doyle, "Kant, Liberal Legacies, and Foreign Affairs," Part I, *Philosophy and Public Affairs*, vol. 12, no. 3 (Summer, 1983).

14. Michael Doyle, *Ways of War and Peace*, p. 264.

15. David Singer & Melvin Small, *Resort to Arms* (Beverly Hills: Sage, 1982).

16. Henry Farber & Joanne Gowa, "Polities and Peace," *International Security* vol. 20, no. 2 (Fall, 1995), pp. 108–132.

17. Farber & Gowa note that the United States and Spain engaged in war during the Spanish-American War, and that Finland was on opposite sides during World War II from a number of democracies that were Allied Powers, both of which could be considered examples of democracies engaging in war against one another. A number of scholars, however, have questioned whether Spain could be accurately defined as a democracy in 1898 and have challenged the Finnish example because Finland was fighting against the Soviet Union, and only indirectly against the liberal allies of the USSR, which calls into question the legitimacy of calling this a war between democracies.

18. Farber & Gowa, "Polities and Peace".

19. See Maoz and Russett, 'Normative and Structural Causes of Democratic Peace, 1946–1986'.

20. John R. Oneal & James Lee Ray, "New Tests of the Democratic Peace: Controlling for Economic Interdependence, 1950–85," *Political Research Quarterly*, vol. 50, no. 4 (December 1997), p. 770.

21. Farber & Gowa, "Polities and Peace".

22. James Lee Ray, "Does Democracy Cause Peace?" *Annual Review of Political Science* (1998), p. 38.

23. Raymond Cohen, "Pacific Unions: A Reappraisal of the Theory That 'Democracies Do Not Go to War with Each Other'," *Review of International Studies*, vol. 20 no. 3 (July 1994), p. 208.

24. Ibid.

25. See Maoz and Russett, 'Normative and Structural Causes of Democratic Peace, 1946–1986'.

26. Michael Doyle, "Kant, Liberal Legacies, and Foreign Affairs".

27. Raymond Cohen, "Pacific Unions," p. 222.

28. See Steven David, "Explaining Third World Alignment," *World Politics*, vol. 43 (January 1991), pp. 233–56; K.J. Holsti, "International Relations Theory and Domestic War in the Third World: The Limits of Relevance" in Stephanie G. Neuman, ed., *International Relations Theory and the Third World* (New York: St. Martin's Press, 1998); Arlene Tickner, "Seeing IR Differently: Notes from the Third World," *Millennium: Journal of International Studies*, vol. 32, no. 2 (2003), pp. 295–324; Steven David, "Why the Third World Still Matters," *International Security*, vol. 17 no. 3 (Winter 1992–1993), pp. 127–59.

JEFFREY PUGH is an assistant professor of Conflict Resolution at the University of Massachusetts, Boston. His research focuses on political conflict and peacebuilding in Latin America, especially the role of non-state actors as conflict resolution actors.

William Appleman Williams

 **NO**

Conclusion: History as a Way of Breaking the Chains of the Past

I see what you are not making, oh, what you are so vividly not . . .

—Henry James, The American Scene, 1907

Imperceptibly, the junction of nostalgia reduces the ability to function.

—Wright Morris, The Territory Ahead, 1958

We cannot begin until we have said farewell to the assumption that Utopia is in the old American frontier.

—Walter Lippmann, 1935

I'm not concerned with the New Jerusalem. I'm concerned with the New Atlanta, the New Birmingham, the New Montgomery, the New South.

—Reverend Martin Luther King, Jr., 1960

HISTORY as a way of learning has one additional value beyond establishing the nature of reality and posing the questions that arise from its complexities and contradictions. It can offer examples of how other men faced up to the difficulties and opportunities of their eras. Even if the circumstances are noticeably different, it is illuminating, and productive of humility as well, to watch other men make their decisions, and to consider the consequences of their values and methods. If the issues are similar, then the experience is more directly valuable. But in either case the procedure can transform history as a way of learning into a way of breaking the chains of the past.

For by watching other men confront the disparity between existing patterns of thought and a reality to which they are no longer relevant, the outsider may be encouraged to muster his own moral and intellectual courage and discipline and undertake a similar re-examination and re-evaluation of his own outlook. Whether the student of

history follows the responses of earlier men remains a matter of his own choice, and even if he accepts their views he is obtaining his answers from men, not History. History offers no answers per se, it only offers a way of encouraging men to use their minds to make their own history.

This essay in the review and interpretation of American history has suggested that several elements have emerged as the major features of American society, and that those have in turn defined the central issues faced by contemporary Americans. One is the functional and syndicalist fragmentation of American society (and hence its individual citizens) along technological and economic lines. The personal and public lives of Americans are defined by, and generally limited to, their specific functional role. To an amazing extent, they share very little on a daily basis beyond a common duty as consumers and a commitment to anti-communism. The persistent cliche of being "caught in the rat-race" dramatizes that alienation, as does the attempt to "play it cool" in order to maintain some semblance of identity and integration.

The second theme is the persistence of a frontier-expansionist outlook a conception of the world and past American history which holds that expansion (or "growth," as Walter Lippmann put it in 1960) offers the best way to resolve problems and to create, or take advantage of, opportunities. A third is a commitment to private property as the means of insuring personal identity, and of thereby guaranteeing democratic politics, and of creating material well-being. And finally, Americans have displayed a loyalty to an ideal of humanity which defines man as more than a creature of property; which defines him as a man by reason of his individual fidelity to one of several humane standards of conduct and by his association with other men in a community honoring those codes.

None of those themes is unique, or even of recent origin, in American history. One example will suffice to establish that. Bernard Baruch raised in 1944 the specter of a dangerous fragmentation of American society into functional groups bent on pursuing the short-run satis-faction of their interests to the detriment of the general welfare, and his report was followed by many related or separate comments on the same problem. But Herbert Hoover had discussed the same issue at great length in the 1920s; the founders of the National Civic Federation had been motivated in large part by a similar concern at the turn of the 20th century; Abraham Lincoln had come to stress the same issue after he became President in 1861; James Madison and other Founding Fathers had grappled with the identical problem in the late 18th and early 19th centuries; and Shaftesbury had struggled to provide a resolution of the same dilemma during the Restoration Era in England. Hence it was not the issues that were new in 1944. The crisis was of a different nature, being instead defined by the progressive failure of the approach that Americans had evolved to solve the problems. That approach no longer provided a satisfactory resolution.

From Shaftesbury's time forward, the solution developed by Americans had been compounded of two conflicting themes or answers. One was the interpretation of Christianity advanced by the Levellers during the English Revolution, and later reasserted wholly within that tradition by Karl Marx in the form of a secular socialism. It held that the problems raised by faction, interest, fragmentation, and alienation could only be resolved and man restored to a true wholeness and identity by de-emphasizing private property in favor of social property and through the co-operative building of a community rather than the mere construction of an organized collective system. Save for the first two decades of the 20th century, that outlook never played a large and direct role in American history. Indirectly, however, it did exert a sustained influence.

The other approach accepted private property as necessary and desirable. For guidance in defining and honoring the ideal of a commonwealth, its followers looked to different religious and secular traditions. One of these was Calvin's conception of a corporate Christian commonwealth in which the trustee accepted and discharged the responsibility for the general welfare; at the same time, all men were charged to honor the axiom that their choice between callings should be made in favor of the one that contributed most to the common good. Another tradition involved the ideal and practice of feudal noblesse oblige. That view had of course arisen within the Christian world, but by the 17th century had developed a secular life of its own. Finally, such men also relied upon a secular argument which held that expansion offered the only feasible way of underwriting private property while at the same time improving the general or collective welfare.

Put simply, the mercantilists such as Shaftesbury sought to integrate those three themes into a coherent and consistent Weltanschauung. That outlook on the world was, and remained, the essence of all class consciousness among upper-class groups in England and the United States from the Age of Elizabeth I. Thus Shaftesbury accepted the responsibility of those who enjoyed the possession of consolidated property for maintaining the general welfare and viewed the state as the natural and appropriate instrument for implementing that obligation. At the same time, he tried to organize political affairs on the basis of parties which included men of all functional interests (or factions) who accepted a broad conception of the general welfare and the means to achieve it. By thus coming together as men who shared an ideal of community a Utopia they would be able to override the tendency of functional activity to fragment and divide them both internally (or personally) from their fellow men.

Shaftesbury extended that outlook into foreign affairs. He accepted the necessity of expansion and acted vigorously to co-ordinate the various aspects of commerce and colonization. But he also sought to build such an empire as a mutually beneficial and responsible commonwealth. He had few qualms about waging war against outsiders to protect or extend the empire, and certainly intended to control its members; but he did have a strong sense of partnership that guided his actions toward the colonies. Shaftesbury and other mercantilists made many false starts, and they failed to control all factions (or to subordinate their own particular interests) at all times. It is nevertheless true that they did to a rather remarkable degree develop and act upon such a class-conscious outlook that combined a defense of private property with a belief in the necessity of expansion, and with an ideal of community and commonwealth.

That outlook was carried to America by the Puritans, by other emigrants, and by the empire directives prepared by Shaftesbury and his successors. It was thereby established, in various versions, in every colony. In many respects, moreover, it continued to mature and develop beyond its English origins and precedents. Indeed, Jonathan Edwards integrated its various themes perhaps more successfully and infused them with a more noble vision of Christian community than any English or American philosopher either before or after his time. His corporate Christian commonwealth was one of the few American visions worthy of the name Utopia.

But in any of its versions, that outlook was a demanding Weltanschauung. As Frederick Jackson Turner pointed out three centuries after the colonies had become firmly established (and in doing so offered a revealing insight into his own generation), the urge to escape the responsibilities of that ideal of a corporate Christian commonwealth was powerful, persistent, and without regard for the direct and indirect costs of such flight. In England, for example, expansion offered a progressively more appealing substitute for the self-discipline and fidelity to ideals that was essential in maintaining the general interest against the factional. And in America the presence of a continent defended only by weaker souls made that solution even more convenient. Americans proceeded in the space of two generations to substitute the Manifest Destiny of empire for the Christian Commonwealth of Jonathan Edwards. Thomas Jefferson was the great epic poet of that urge to escape, to run away and spend one's life doing what one wanted or in starting over time after time. Jackson, Benton, and Polk were but the type-cast protagonists of that dream, and through his early years even Lincoln was a man who charted his career by that same western star.

James Madison was the theorist of the outlook, and in offering expansion as the way of controlling faction, he articulated the guiding line of American history from the end of the 18th century through the 1950s. Yet unlike most who followed his theory, Madison recognized the grave implications of the solution; along with such men as Calhoun, Monroe, Clay, and especially John Quincy Adams, he sought to prevent the complete devaluation of the self-restraint and other ideals that Shaftesbury and Edwards had stressed. The continent was too much for them. By making escape so easy, it produced an unrestrained and anti-intellectual individualist democracy that almost destroyed any semblance of community and commonwealth. Even before the continent was filled up, the frontier had become a national Utopia and Madison's theory the New Gospel. Men largely ceased to think about problems, and merely reacted to them by reciting the frontier catechism and pushing the Indians off another slice of the continent. Following the general lines of Seward's reformulation of Madison's argument to fit the conditions of an industrial society, Hay's Open Door Notes merely restated the principle in terms appropriate to the 20th century.

Less than 60 years later, however, the open door of escape was no more than ajar. Two forces had combined to all but close it: Russian and Chinese industrial and nuclear power and potential; and the growing refusal by societies that had formerly served as the frontier to continue in the role any longer. As a result, the frontier Utopia had ceased to offer a practical substitute for the more demanding

Weltanschauung of class-conscious leadership and responsibility. Expansion as escape meant nuclear war. Yet the cold war was essential to those who still, consciously or unconsciously, saw expansion as the means of adjusting and controlling factions and at the same time providing some measure of welfare. In typical frontier fashion, such people saw defeat or war as the only other solutions.

Expansion of a vastly different character and drastically more limited nature was still possible, but even that could be sustained only by strengthening the self-discipline necessary to honor the commonwealth ideal that Shaftesbury, Edwards, and Adams had tried to sustain. Expansion of any sort was only possible without war, and that is to say, only possible if the frontier were abandoned as a Utopia. Expansion of that kind would of necessity be channeled through the United Nations, without political or economic strings, in an effort to help other societies solve their own problems within their own traditions. Hence the possibility of any full maturation of the class-conscious industrial gentry that had slowly been created by the corporation between the 1890s and the 1950s turned on one very simple test. Did that gentry have, or would it manage to muster, the nerve to abandon the frontier as Utopia, to turn its back on expansion as the open door of escape?

It is of course fair to ask whether any precedents exist for encouraging such a display of intelligence and courage. For while it is helpful to find examples in the past, it is too much to ask that contemporary corporation executives and political leaders model themselves on Shaftesbury or John Quincy Adams. Very few, if any of them, are men of sufficient empathy. Nor would it be wise for them to follow such a course even if they could. Not only are the circumstances different, but it is the attitude and the ideals that are important, not the personal styles or the specific policies. But there is no need to return to the past in that sense, for some of the very Americans who restated the expansionist outlook in the 20th century also realized that there was another choice.

Brooks Adams, for example, admitted that America did not have to embark upon a program to control China and Siberia. It was merely the easier way out of the dilemma, and one which in his opinion offered more glory and riches. And as late as 1944, Dean Acheson acknowledged that he and his colleagues in government could invest an indefinite amount of energy and time in discussing alternatives to expansion as a way of building "a successfully functioning political and economic system." Acheson dismissed such approaches, however, on the grounds that they would weaken the rights of private property, require modifications of the Constitution, and limit the frontier-style liberties to which Americans had become accustomed.

Herbert Hoover and Charles Beard had more intellectual courage and imagination than either Adams or Acheson. They argued that it was possible to build a community a commonwealth based on private property without relying on imperial expansion. Whatever his other failings, Hoover did at least refuse to go to war for the Open Door in Asia, and did try very hard to change the character of America's overseas economic expansion. In some ways, at least, Beard advocated an even more rigorous effort to restore the ideal of a commonwealth as the American Utopia. But in its commitment to the frontier as a Utopia of escape, the American public refused to give that approach a serious or a fair trial.

Finally, the mid-century industrial gentry might draw even more encouragement from the example provided by the southern Negro. During approximately a century after the Civil War, the Negro modeled his aspirations and ideals on the white society in which he existed. Briefly at the end of the Civil War, again in the 1890s, and then with a rush during World War I, the Negro adapted the frontier-expansionist outlook to his own position. He defined northern urban centers as his frontier of escape from the conditions of survival in the south. For a generation or more, Negroes streamed into that supposed Utopia only in the end to discover that it was largely a mirage. Then, under the leadership of deeply religious and courageous men like the Reverend Martin Luther King, Jr., they broke with that traditional view of the frontier as escape and defined the south, the cities and the states where they lived, as the only meaningful frontier that existed.

Having made that magnificently courageous and deeply intelligent decision, they stood their ground and faced the issue in the present, reasserting as their solution the ideal and the practice of a Christian community or commonwealth. In a way that dramatized their abandonment of the frontier outlook, they organized themselves in such groups as "The Montgomery Improvement Association." No longer did they rally under the old slogan of the frontier, "Kansas or Bust," merely changing Kansas to read New York or Chicago or Detroit or Cleveland or Pittsburgh. They made no mention of the frontier: they simply talked about the here and the now, and set about to improve it guided by the Utopia of a Christian commonwealth. And to do so they chose the appropriate weapon—nonviolent resistance. Within one year they had effected more fundamental progress than in a century of following the white man's theory of escape through the frontier. Not merely did they begin to obtain food in formerly closed cafes: that was really a minor point. What they really won

was respect for themselves as men who no longer ran away. The frontier never had and never could give a man that kind of self-respect.

But while Reverend King and the Montgomery Improvement Association offered the class-conscious industrial gentry inspiring proof that wealth and welfare were obtainable without running off to some new frontier, they also posed some crucial questions. Even if the gentry could regenerate such a Christian vision of a corporate commonwealth, would corporation capitalism be able to function if operated according to its precepts? Perhaps it would not. Perhaps the corporation economy could not function without the indirect but vital help of the citizen in the form of taxes paid to the government and then handed on to the corporation in the form of subsidies. If that were the case, then how and by what secular ideal and hierarchy of values by what Utopia would the class-conscious industrial gentry transform such double jeopardy into a system of true equity in which every citizen, along with the corporations, received a fair share of wealth and welfare? It might be rather difficult to convince the citizen that his sacrifices were worthwhile on the grounds that the gentry would then take an honest interest in him. For even under the best of circumstances, is having an interest taken in one a sufficient substitute for active participation in the present and future affairs of one's own society?

Those are fundamental and very difficult questions. Even to ask them is to understand why the frontier as a Utopia of escape has been so attractive in the past, and why it still exerts such influence in the middle of the 20th century. But to ask these questions is also to raise the issue as to whether Americans have any other traditions that are appropriate to the present. Is it really a choice between, on the one hand, a continuance of government by a syndicalist oligarchy relying on expansion or, on the other, a government by a class-conscious industrial gentry? To be sure, the choice does offer some measure of meaningful difference; for a class-conscious industrial gentry with the nerve to abandon the Utopia of frontier expansion would clearly provide at least the chance of a more equitable, humane, creative, and peaceful future. But if that is all Americans can offer themselves, then they are apt to become unique in the sense of becoming isolated from the mainstream of 20th-century development.

For the rest of the world, be it presently industrial or merely beginning to industrialize, is very clearly moving toward some version of a society modeled on the ideal and the Utopia of a true human community based far more on social property than upon private property. That is what the editors of The Wall Street Journal meant in 1958 when they candidly admitted that the United States was on "the wrong side of a social revolution." That socialist reassertion of the essence of the ancient ideal of a Christian commonwealth is a viable Utopia. It was so when the Levellers asserted it in the middle of the 17th century, and it remains so in the middle of the 20th century. It holds very simply and clearly that the only meaningful frontier lies within individual men and in their relationships with each other. It agrees with Frederick Jackson Turner that the American frontier has been "a gate of escape" from those central responsibilities and opportunities. The socialist merely says that it is time to stop running away from life.

And in Eugene Debs, America produced a man who understood that expansion was a running away, the kind of escape that was destructive of the dignity of men. He also believed and committed his life to the proposition that Americans would one day prove mature and courageous enough to give it up as a child's game; that they would one day "put away childish things" and undertake the creation of a socialist commonwealth. Americans therefore do have a third choice to consider alongside that of an oligarchy and that of a class-conscious industrial gentry. They have the chance to create the first truly democratic socialism in the world.

That opportunity is the only real frontier available to Americans in the second half of the 20th century. If they revealed and acted upon the kind of intelligence and morality and courage that it would take to explore and develop that frontier, then they would have finally broken the chains of their own past. Otherwise, they would ultimately fell victims of a nostalgia for their childhood.

WILLIAM APPLEMAN WILLIAMS, a former president of the Organization of American Historians, taught for many years at the University of Wisconsin and Oregon State University. His books include *The Contours of American History, The Tragedy of American Diplomacy,* and *Empire as a Way of Life*. Modern Library ultimately chose *Contours* as one of the best 100 nonfiction books of the 20th Century.

EXPLORING THE ISSUE

Has the Democratic Peace Theory Helped Lead U.S. Style and Other Western Democracies to a New Historical Stage of Human Freedom?

Critical Thinking and Reflection

1. What criteria would you put forth to test the Democratic Peace Theory?
2. How does Appleman Williams argue that history is a means of breaking the chains of the past and how does this relate to the democratic peace theory?
3. Can the United States have capitalism, democracy, and empire?
4. When, if ever, has the history of the nation been authentically democratic and when, if ever, has democracy been used as propaganda?
5. How does the democratic peace theory, or rejecting it, frame the ways you understand US history?

Is There Common Ground?

There is indeed common ground between the authors on this issue. First, however, let us consider the question framing the major differences between authors. What do the authors believe about the nature of US democracy? Appleman Williams believes that US democracy is a means of imposing social controls on her citizens. Internationally, his argument suggests that US democracy is used as a tool of imperialism. Therefore, he asks us to question is US democracy, democratic in practice. Pugh differs from Appleman Williams analysis in that he accepts the foundational points of the democratic peace theory. However, Pugh does critique the theory lacks consistent data. Further, he acknowledges the Rationalist arguments that suggest democratic nations will manipulate relations to serve their own ends. Despite these critiques, Pugh still feels the theory is helpful making better sense of international relations, while Appleman Williams would likely attack the theory as being developed from faulty assumptions. Appleman Williams would also likely argue that accepting the democratic peace theory requires disregarding US activity that has overthrown and opposed democracies in many places around the world. For Appleman Williams, we need only look at international relations, surveillance policies, assassinations, disinformation, and organization busting within US history to understand democratic peace as something different than what has been presented to us in the theory. Pugh would likely disagree.

A point of commonality between Pugh and Appleman Williams might be that both authors acknowledge Realist critiques to the Democratic Peace Theory, though Appleman Williams would take the argument further. He suggests that the coalition of Western nations provides an international peace that is undemocratic version of "democratic." Appleman Williams would also likely agree with Pugh that liberal democracies are good. The values of a liberal democracy include freedom, self-rule, and human exchange. Both authors would also likely concede, as Pugh and Fukuyama both argued, that "mature" democracies have not gone to war with each other. Both would also likely argue that we are called to deeply consider the definitions of "mature democracy" and "war" as participants in democracies. Each author would likely conclude that liberal democracies have generally led to a higher standard of living for people when those countries have important elements such as free speech and remained free from major conflicts with other (perhaps so called) Western democratic powers.

Additional Resources

Huntington, S. (2011). *The clash of civilizations and the remaking of world order*. New York: Simon & Schuster.

Williams, W. (2007). *Empire as a way of life: an essay on the causes and character of America's present predicament along with a few thoughts about an alternative*. Brooklyn, NY: Ig Publishing.

Korab-Karpowicz, W. J. (2010). Political realism in international relations. From: https://plato.stanford.edu/entries/realism-intl-relations/

Wiebrecht, F. (2013). *Democratic Peace Theory*. Munich: GRIN Verlag GmbH.

Fukuyama, F. (2006). *The end of history and the last man*. New York: Free Press.

Internet References . . .

At the "End of History" Still Stands Democracy: Twenty-five years after Tiananmen Square and the Berlin Wall's fall, liberal democracy still has no real competitors

https://www.wsj.com/articles/at-the-end-of-history-still-stands-democracy-1402080661

Iraq and the Democratic Peace: WHO SAYS DEMOCRACIES DON'T FIGHT? By John M. Owen IV

https://www.foreignaffairs.com/reviews/review-essay/2005-11-01/iraq-and-democratic-peace

Oxford Bibliographies: "Democratic Peace Theory" by Dan Reiter

https://www.oxfordbibliographies.com/view/document/obo-9780199756223/obo-9780199756223-0014.xml

Selected, Edited, and with Issue Framing Material by:
Kevin R. Magill and Tony L. Talbert, *Baylor University*

ISSUE

Did a "New South" Emerge Following Reconstruction?

YES: Ronald D. Eller, from "A Magnificent Field for Capitalists," University of Tennessee Press (1982)

NO: James Tice Moore, from "Redeemers Reconsidered: Change and Continuity in the Democratic South, 1870–1900," *Journal of Southern History* (1978)

Learning Outcomes

After reading this issue, you will be able to:

- Define what scholars mean when they talk about a "New South" following the era of Reconstruction.
- Evaluate the extent to which the "New South" differed from the "Old South."
- Discuss the degree to which industrial processes were introduced into the southern economy after Reconstruction.
- Compare and contrast the characteristics of southern political leadership from the antebellum period to the late nineteenth century.
- Understand the concepts of "continuity" and "change" as they apply to historical processes in general and the realities of the post-Reconstruction South in particular.

ISSUE SUMMARY

YES: Ronald D. Eller describes the post-Reconstruction entrepreneurial spirit that altered the traditional rural economy of the Mountain South through the introduction of the railroad and the development of coal, iron, and lumber industries in Appalachia.

NO: James Tice Moore challenges the view that the white, Democratic political elite that ruled the post-Reconstruction South abandoned antebellum rural traditions in favor of business and commerce and concludes that these agriculturally oriented "Redeemers" actually represented a continuity of leadership from the Old South to the New South.

One of the critical questions confronting those empowered to restore the former Confederate states to the Union following the Civil War was "What would the New South be like?" This rather large question can be broken down into several more specific parts: (1) "Who would take the reins of leadership in the South now that the war was over?"; (2) "How would the southern economy differ, if at all, in light of the fact that the plantation system had been dealt a blow by the end of chattel slavery?"; and (3) "What would be the nature of race relations in the South in the wake of emancipation?" Over the course of the Reconstruction period, the Republican politicians who seized control of the southern state governments in the late 1860s sought to impose their image of America upon the vanquished South, but they confronted intense resistance from most white southerners, who railed against "Yankee oppression" and the imposition of "Negro rule." Most of the "radical Republican" governments fell quickly, and within a decade, conservative white Democrats had regained control of the South and were in a position to determine the economic and social meanings of the New South.

Prior to the Civil War, the southern economy had been based overwhelmingly on agricultural production dominated by the plantation-slave system. The South was not without its manufacturing operations, but as the sectional conflict began, the region lacked a sufficient industrial base to sustain a people at war. By the late 1870s, some influential white southerners realized that the economic future of the South, and their ultimate reconciliation with the North, depended upon their willingness to participate actively in the industrial expansion that was sweeping much of the nation north of the Mason-Dixon line. What would such a program entail? It would require the exploitation of the South's abundant natural resources of timber, coal, and iron; the establishment of local industries funded by local capital; the expansion of the southern railway system; the creation of new banks to extend credit; and the building of new towns as mercantile and industrial centers.

The proponents of the New South looked forward to the prospect that one day their region would support a business culture associated with cities, factories, and trade. Their supporting statements found robust voice in language that would have been unimaginable only a few years before, among a handful of southern newspaper editors who propagandized the goals of a diversified southern economy. Francis Dawson, editor of the *Charleston News and Courier,* wrote: "As for Charleston, the importation of about five hundred Yankees of the right stripe would put a new face on affairs, and make the whole place throb with life and vivid force." Henry Waterson of Louisville, Kentucky's *Courier-Journal,* proclaimed that the "ambition of the South is to out-Yankee the Yankee." The most outspoken proponent of a New South, however, was Henry Grady, editor of the *Atlanta Constitution.* Grady traveled widely to promote his vision of the New South, and in a speech to the New England Society of New York in 1886, he offered a message of regional reconciliation when he told his audience, "There was a South of slavery and secession—that South is dead. There is now a South of union and freedom—that South, thank God, is living, breathing, and growing every hour."

There was more than a rhetorical flourish to the idea of the New South; cotton textiles, iron and steel manufacturing, sulfur and phosphate production, and tobacco products made significant headway in diversifying the southern economy. For example, from 1880 to 1900, the number of spindles of cotton thread produced in the textile states of North and South Carolina, Georgia, and Alabama increased from 423,000 to 3,792,000. The capital invested in the textile industry alone increased from $17.4 million to $124.6 million, an increase of over 600 percent. Iron and steel manufacturing became major industries in the middle and lower South. This activity led Richard Edmonds, editor of the *Manufacturer's Record* to report that "the easy-going days of the South have passed away, never to return." On another occasion, he proclaimed that throughout the South one could hear "a continuous and unbroken strain of what has been termed 'the music of progress'—the whir of the spindle, the buzz of the saw, the roar of the furnace and the throb of the locomotive." By 1914, the New South had become industrialized in ways that few Americans could have imagined at the end of the Civil War. More importantly, this was permanent change, despite the fact that the great majority of southerners (and other Americans for that matter) continued to earn their livelihoods from the soil. This industrial growth marked the beginning of the South's integration into the nation.

The first generation of professionally trained historians, many of them native-born southerners, were, along with propagandists like Henry Grady, largely responsible for the pronouncement that a New South had emerged from the Civil War. For these scholars, the New South had reconciled with the North and become more urbanized and industrialized. Businessmen and manufacturers enjoyed a prominent place in southern society, but members of the antebellum planter aristocracy—the Bourbons—were most responsible for overthrowing the Reconstruction regimes and continued to wield significant economic and political power. This view of the post-Reconstruction Gilded Age remained largely intact until C. Vann Woodward published his monumental *The Origins of the New South, 1877–1913* (Louisiana State University Press, 1951). Woodward argued vigorously for a New South that had broken the back of the antebellum planter class. The architects of the elimination of Republican rule in the 1870s were "Redeemers"—white, conservative, business-oriented Democrats who, in Woodward's view, tried but failed to close the gap between the North and the South in terms of industrial production. At the same time, Woodward's Redeemers oversaw corrupt governments that failed to respond to the real needs of the southern population, especially African Americans, and pursued economic policies that ultimately left the South as little more than a colony of northeastern corporate interests. In the years since 1951, virtually every book and essay written about the South in the period from 1877 to 1913 has been crafted as a response to the "Woodward thesis." This is certainly the case in the two selections that follow.

Ronald D. Eller recognizes Woodward's claim that southern industrialization did not match the exaggerated claims of many New South proponents, but he is convinced that the southern economy made impressive strides in numerous enterprises, such as railroads and extractive industries, that rose to national prominence with the aid of local and outside capitalization. Perhaps more importantly, this industrial activity touched the lives of thousands of Appalachian residents, providing opportunities for them that might not otherwise have existed.

James Tice Moore focuses his attack on Woodward's depiction of the Redeemers. Where Woodward finds discontinuity in leadership from the antebellum period, Moore insists that the South's post-Reconstruction political elite were neither subservient to business interests nor willing to abandon the region's antebellum rural traditions. Southern politicians, he concludes, depended upon rural constituencies, held the same types of occupations as antebellum leaders, and are best characterized as members of agriculturally oriented elite.

YES

Ronald D. Eller

A Magnificent Field for Capitalists

In the summer of 1888, Charles Dudley Warner, a New York journalist and coauthor with Mark Twain of *The Gilded Age,* made a journey along the Wilderness Road from Pineville to Cumberland Gap in eastern Kentucky. As was the fashion with northern journalists who ventured into the southern backcountry in the late nineteenth century, Warner published an account of his travels the following spring in *Harper's New Monthly Magazine.* This was not Warner's first trip to the mountains, nor was this his first effort to describe the region which Will Wallace Harvey had labeled "A Strange Land and Peculiar People." Four years earlier, after riding through the Blue Ridge country of southwest Virginia, east Tennessee, and western North Carolina, Warner had written a major travelogue entitled "On Horseback." The latter had established its author as one of the leading figures in the new literary "discovery" of Appalachia. His journey into eastern Kentucky in 1888 promised to provide more of the same local-color material that had interested his urban middle-class readers.

Leaving the railroad near Pineville, Warner and his party traveled the thirteen miles to Cumberland Gap by wagon and then, crossing into Virginia, rode horseback up the Powell River Valley to Big Stone Gap. The scenery along the way was much the same as that which Warner had found in the Blue Ridge. "The road had every variety of badness conceivable—loose stones, ledges of rock, boulders, sloughs, holes, mud, sand, deep fords." Settlements were few—only "occasional poor shanties" and "rugged little farms"—but the landscape was spectacular with "the great trees . . . frequent sparkling strearns, and lovely mountain views." The ineffable beauty of this virgin land, however, hid a "primitive and to a considerable extent illiterate" population that had long been isolated from the moving world. Amid the splendors of the great forests and swift streams were depressing scenes of poverty, ignorance, and lawlessness. . . .

Yet, in contrast to his adventure in the Blue Ridge, Warner found much in eastern Kentucky to inspire hope for the region's future. The picturesque hills, which had so long secluded the natural beauty of the region and had isolated the mountaineers from the currents of modern life, had also guarded the treasures of the mountains—the rich stores of coal, timber, and iron ore. The Civil War had removed major obstacles to the exploitation of this vast supply of natural wealth, and recent "scientific investigation [had] made the mountain district . . . the object of the eager competition of both domestic and foreign capital." The entire country from the Breaks of the Big Sandy River to Big Creek Gap in the Cumberland Mountain was "on the eve of an astonishing development—one that will revolutionize eastern Kentucky, and powerfully affect the iron and coal markets of the country." This region of "clear, rapid streams, stuffed with coals, streaked with iron, abounding in limestone, and covered with superb forests . . . [appealed] as well to the imagination of the traveller as to the capitalist." As Warner observed; "I saw enough to comprehend why eager purchasers are buying the forests and the mining rights, why great companies, American and English, are planting themselves there and laying the foundations of cities, and why the gigantic railway corporations are straining every nerve to penetrate the mineral and forest heart of the region. . . It is a race for the prize."

And what of the mountaineers? The arrival of the "commercial spirit," Warner believed, would transform this benighted society. Other writers had found the mountain people to be a "worthless, good-for-nothing, irreclaimable" lot, but Warner was not so despondent about their future. "Railroads, trade, the sight of enterprise and industry, will do much with this material." Business and enterprise would bring law and order, sobriety, education, health care, and the other fruits of the modern age. Now that an industrializing America had need for the abundance of fuel that had been so long stored in the mountains, a new day was dawning for the mountaineers. Because of the vast developments about to occur in the Cumberlands, this land had become "one of the most important and interesting regions in the Union."

Warner was not alone in his optimism about the potential industrialization of the Appalachians. As early as the 1870s, politicians, businessmen, and journalists had begun to promote the wealth of the mountains in newspapers and boardrooms throughout the United States and Europe. The untapped treasures of the hill country, these individuals believed, offered innumerable possibilities for the accumulation of personal wealth. Nowhere in the eastern United States could one find the vital industrial elements of coal, iron ore, timber, and water in such vast quantities and so close to one another. Among many promoters in the South, the natural resources of the Appalachians offered not only the opportunity for the accumulation of great personal wealth but for the revitalization of southern society as well. Lying in the very heartland of the South, the mountains harbored the materials necessary for building a "new civilization"—a New South constructed from the ashes of the old, but patterned in a more modern industrial mold. In the years from 1870 to 1900, therefore, for both personal and social reasons, advertising the mountains became an important component of the New South creed.

Yet the promotion of industrial development of the Appalachians reflected more than just opportunism or the romantic visions of a defeated South. The coming of what Warner called "the commercial spirit" to the mountains was part of a larger drama taking place in the nation as a whole. Throughout most of the nineteenth century, the forces of modernization had largely bypassed the mountains while fundamentally restructuring the fabric of American life. In the years following the Civil War, those forces were rapidly moving the nation down the road toward urban-industrial maturity, and the abundant resources of Appalachia provided vital fuel for that final industrial drive. As technological developments increased the productive capacities of urban centers in the Northeast, South, and Midwest, capitalists began to turn to surrounding rural areas for the human and natural resources to undergird expansion. The exploitation of peripheral rural areas for the benefit of industrializing urban centers became a requisite of industrial growth, resulting in unequal economic development and prolonged social tension between urban and rural communities. Appalachia, being one of the most rural areas of eastern America and rich in natural resources, provided a stage upon which much of this great social drama was played out. In a rapidly industrializing society, the wealth of the Appalachians became a passkey to affluence and power. Indeed, "it was a race for the prize." . . .

The emergence of economic and intellectual interest in the Appalachians in the late nineteenth century marked the beginning of the decline of the stable, traditional society that had evolved in the mountains. Although major aspects of modernization were not to be felt in the region until after the turn of the century (and even later-in some remote areas), the years from 1880 to 1900 were among the most critical decades in the region's history. The penetration of the region during these years by outside speculators, land developers, and industrialists launched a revolution in land use and ownership that drastically altered the mountaineer's relationship to the land. As ownership and control of the land were transferred from the mountaineers to the spokesmen of the new industrial order, the fate of the region became irretrievably tied to that of the larger society. The selling of the mountains and the subsequent arrival of the railroads were, as Warner noted, the first stage in the remaking of mountain life.

The Selling of the Mountains

By the year in which Charles Dudley Warner made his journey into eastern Kentucky, the mineral and timber wealth of the Appalachians was already well known to American capitalists, . . . but it was not until the post-Civil War years that interest in the potential of these resources quickened. Throughout most of the antebellum period, the difficulties of transportation, the absence of any real market, and the deep agrarian biases of southern leaders had prevented the large-scale development of the mountain reserves. In the years immediately following the war, however, a sudden rush of activity in commerce, investment, and new technology focused increasing attention on the mountains as a source of materials to fuel the industrial revolution. Among a new generation of southern leaders, moreover, the road to wealth seemed no longer to lead to the plantation but rather to the coal and iron fields of the Appalachians.

The rise of the industrial spirit in the South after Reconstruction did not substantially alter the basic structure of southern society. The South remained primarily an agricultural region until well into the twentieth century. Yet, changes in the character and outlook of southern leadership did take place in these years, opening large areas of the South, especially the Appalachians, to exploitation by absentee investors. Whether or not southern leaders themselves benefited economically from the new commercial enterprises (and many did), their receptive attitude toward industrial development eased the way for the penetration of southern regions by northern capital. To that outspoken band of southerners who believed that the future of their region lay in commercial and industrial growth, the abundant resources of the Appalachians provided a major incentive for capital investment. Beginning in the 1870s and growing in intensity in the 1880s and 1890s, advocates of the New South creed ardently promoted the industrialization of the South and the development of the timber and mineral reserves of the southern mountains. If the South was to fulfil its destiny as a leading center of industry, they argued, it must exploit the "exhaustless treasures" of its mountains.

The New South creed was part of a national booster spirit that emerged in the late nineteenth century, and, like its larger counterpart, was predominantly an urban phenomenon. Its loudest proponents were members of the new middle class that had begun to rise in major southern cities. Proselytes of the creed could be found in most towns and many villages throughout the postwar South, but the industrial faith burned brightest in three cities of the Southeast: Atlanta, Louisville, and Richmond. Each had evolved as an important railroad center, had developed a large manufacturing base, and supported a powerful business community. Moreover, each was home to a leading newspaper whose pages became fliers for the dissemination of the faith.

The Richmond *Whig,* under the control of conservative politician and railroad president William Mahone, was without equal in its promotion of railroads, mining, timber, and iron manufacturing in the Virginias. General Mahone had acquired extensive railroad interests in southwest Virginia, and his newspaper became a major advocate of "new ways for the Old Dominion." Across the mountains in Louisville, the *Courier-Journal* and its fiery editor Henry Watterson—sometimes spokesman for the Louisville and Nashville Railroad—called for the industrial development of Kentucky and the attraction of "Eastern Capital" to that state's coal fields. But the most outspoken apostle of the new order was Henry Grady of the Atlanta *Constitution.* In his years with the *Constitution,* Grady developed a national reputation as the leading disciple of the New South creed. As orator and editor, he advertised the opportunities for investment in the South and encouraged southern businessmen to exploit the industrial potential of their region.

These three metropolitan newspapers combined to spread the gospel of industrialism throughout the South and much of the nation. A line drawn through the urban headquarters of each of these presses would form a triangle completely enclosing the heartland of the Appalachian South. It was only natural, therefore, that as these centers of modernization sought to expand their industrial bases, they turned to their own "internal periphery" and to the natural resources of the mountains. In the years after 1870, these and other New South papers brought increasing pressure to bear upon politicians and state officials to publicize this backcountry wealth.

Convincing southern state leaders of the need for publicity was relatively easy during the initial postwar years. In this era of social and economic depression, politicians from all parties were interested in improving business conditions. During the 1870s and 1880s, campaigns were launched in every southern Appalachian state aimed at attracting foreign immigration and commercial investment. State authorities established immigration bureaus and dispatched agents to New York and Europe to spread the word of southern opportunities. Exhibitions of state resources were creatively displayed at commercial conventions throughout America and Europe, and by the turn of the century geological surveys were being commissioned to detail the extent of the states' mineral wealth for the benefit of potential buyers. . . .

Notwithstanding the efforts of organized groups, the promotional activity that was most influential in the development of the mountains was that carried on by private speculators. Riding into the mountains in the years following the Civil War, these men surveyed iron and coal deposits, purchased land or mineral rights from local residents, and attempted to entice railroads and industrialists to the area. Many of these "mineral men"—or "mineral hunters," as mountain people called them—were ex-military officers who had served in the region during the Civil War and had become familiar with the untapped wealth of the land. Others were the paid agents of northern capitalists who sought to invest in the lucrative resource potential of the South. Together with a zealous band of local promoters, they prepared the way for the invasion of the larger corporations.

Among the earliest and most ardent promoters of coal and iron development in the southern mountains were two former Confederate officers, General John Daniel Imboden and Major Jedidiah Hotchkiss. As early as 1872, General Imboden was urging legislators and prominent citizens of Virginia to exploit the forgotten coal and iron fields of the Appalachians. "Within this imperial domain of Virginia," he told a Richmond gathering, "lie almost unknown to the outer world, and not fully appreciated by their owners," greater mineral deposits than could be found in all of England and which, if tapped, would "attract hither millions of money, and enterprising thousands of people to aid in the restoration of the 'Old Dominion' to a foremost rank amongst the States of the Union." Such developments, he argued, would make Richmond the southern rival of Pittsburgh and Philadelphia. . . .

The work of General Imboden, however, was surpassed by that of his friend, Major Jedidiah Hotchkiss, who might fairly be called the father of coal development in parts of southwest Virginia and southern West Virginia.

Long before the coming of the railroad, Hotchkiss was promoting the mineral wealth of the Flat Top Mountain region along the headwaters of the Bluestone, Elkhorn, Big Sandy, and Guyandotte rivers. He was primarily responsible for attracting the Philadelphia capital that constructed the Norfolk and Western Railroad (N & W) and transformed the Flat Top area into one of the most productive coal fields in the world. . . .

In 1873, the owners of the Wilson Cary Nicholas grant, a Revolutionary war grant of 500,000 acres around Flat Top Mountain, hired Hotchkiss to make a survey and evaluation of their holdings. Hotchkiss in turn hired Captain Isaiah Welch, a fellow Confederate officer and noted geologist, to make a detailed examination of the property and report on timber and mineral deposits. Welch entered the tract along Laurel Creek in Tazewell County, Virginia, and quickly discovered a seam of coal thirteen feet thick, which was then being used to fuel a local blacksmith shop. Since this seam was "about twice the height of the highest seams then known," he continued to follow the outcroppings north into Mercer, McDowell, and Wyoming counties in West Virginia before returning home. Welch's report thoroughly confirmed the presence of valuable coal deposits in the Flat Top district and generated a flurry of interest in developing the area. Major Hotchkiss subsequently persuaded a group of Philadelphia capitalists headed by Thomas Graham to purchase "some of the best land in the territory" and to begin construction of a narrow-gauge railroad, but the business depression of the 1870s prevented the realization of these plans. . . .

A similar rush of interest in land speculation swept the mountains of Tennessee and North Carolina in these years, although the prize was primarily the virgin timber and purported iron deposits of the territory. Expectations for the development of iron in the mountains failed to mature, partly because of the low quality of the ore, but speculators in the late nineteenth century were convinced of the region's potential for iron production. Great iron centers had evolved to the north of the mountains in Pittsburgh and on the region's southern fringe in Birmingham. It seemed logical that East Tennessee, with its proximity to the new coal fields and its purported deposits of iron ore, would become one of the leading industrial centers of the South. As one developer maintained in 1889,

What we need to make East Tennessee the most prosperous and desirable section of the South is capital. That would be a panacea for our financial ills and would disarm poverty of its terrors.

It would put us on the high road to wealth. . . . We need hundreds of blazing furnaces distributed over this region, along the foothills of our mountains, lighting up their gorges and developing and utilizing the iron embedded in their bowels. . . . What a magnificent field for capitalists!

Spurred by the rise of the industrial spirit, two cities in East Tennessee, Knoxville and Chattanooga, became centers for speculative activity in the surrounding mountains. After the revival of the economy in 1880, northern financiers sent an army of agents into these urban centers to survey the possibilities for investment. One of the leading examples of this northern invasion was H.B. Wetzell, a native of Pennsylvania and former Michigan businessman who came to live in Knoxville in the early 1880s to investigate "the natural resources of the southern Appalachian region from West Virginia to Alabama." Finding that the region was "A Country of Infinite Wealth-Creating Possibilities," Wetzell stayed on for over a decade, traveling on foot and horseback throughout the mountains and buying timber and mineral properties for northern investors.

In eastern Kentucky, the pioneer coal prospector of these years was Richard M. Broas of New York City. An engineer and former captain in the Union Army, Broas had spent the postwar years searching for oil in Pennsylvania and for gold and silver in the Sierras. In 1881, he came to the Big Sandy Valley between West Virginia and Kentucky to examine coal lands for the "Walbridge interests" of Toledo, Ohio. Failing to discover coal at the mouth of the Tug and Levisa forks of Big Sandy, Broas was hired by Nathanial Stone Simkins of Massachusetts to push on up the river and examine lands in the Miller's Creek section of Pike County. There, and later in the valley of the Elkhorn, he found seams of coal with immense possibilities and began a ten-year effort to promote the development of the mineral lands of the Elkhorn district. Like Hotchkiss in southwest Virginia, Broas met with repeated rebuffs, but this did not prevent his acquiring options on large tracts of land and mineral rights in the area. Between 1887 and 1891, Broas purchased or leased thousands of acres of mineral property in Pike and Letcher counties. At the height of his buying venture, he employed about twenty surveyors and a number of title attorneys. Most of his mineral leases were purchased at one dollar per acre in tracts of from 100 to 400 acres, generally from poor, often illiterate farmers. . . .

Some buyers, moreover, like Richard M. Broas, offered to purchase only the minerals under the land, leaving the surface to the ownership and use (and tax liability) of the farmer. The land would be disturbed at some future date, but it was difficult for the mountaineer to envision the scale and impact of industrial change. These "broad form deeds," as they were known in eastern Kentucky, effectively transferred to the land agents all of the mineral wealth and the right to remove it by whatever means necessary, while leaving the farmer and his descendants with the semblance of land ownership. It was not until the railroads penetrated the district that those who had concluded such deals realized their mistake. Not only had they lost all rights to the minerals below the land, but they had also relinquished such other rights to the surface of the land as to limit its use for residential or agricultural purposes.

In this way, millions of acres of land and even greater quantities of timber and mineral rights passed out of the hands of mountain residents and into the control of absentee owners. Most mountain families sold their land voluntarily, but the negotiations were hardly between equals. The mountaineer had little knowledge of the value his natural resources had to distant industrial centers, nor was he able to comprehend the changes that would come to the mountains as a result of efforts to tap those resources. Despite its importance to mountain life and culture, land was often taken for granted by the mountaineers, for it had always been plentiful and ownership had never been a deterrent to common use. The prices paid by land agents during these early years varied greatly from state to state and according to the potential wealth of the property, but amounts generally ranged from twenty-five cents to three dollars per acre. Some mountaineers were reported to have sold entire mountains rich in coal and timber for a mule, a saddle horse, or a hog rifle. . . .

Despite the crucial role played by outside agents in the selling of the mountains, that played by local speculators was almost equally important. Especially after many residents began to question the integrity of outside interests, native middle-class entrepreneurs served as effective brokers for absentee investors and as energetic missionaries of the new industrial faith. Particularly in the larger villages and towns, the relatively small mountain middle class and landed elite actively promoted the development of Appalachian natural resources as a panacea for their own as well as the region's financial ills. Local merchants and lawyers speculated widely in timber and mineral lands and advertised the potential of mountain property in the leading business journals and newspapers. Often serving as agents of northern capitalists, such individuals quietly bought up land from their neighbors at nominal prices.

By 1900, the emergence of new urban centers within the region had brought about the concentration of many resident speculators and promoters in towns such as Charleston, Bluefield, Ashland, Paintsville, Bristol, and Asheville. These development centers (called "growth centers" by modern planners) served as convenient extensions of the eastern industrial core into the Appalachian heartland. In many ways, they functioned in the same exploitative relationship to their surrounding rural counties as did the larger metropolises of the South and Northeast to the region as a whole. Promoters of industrialization increasingly used these centers as bases of operation from which to launch their invasions of the outlying rural districts.

The mountains had always contained a small ruling class whose economic power and political influence were derived from longstanding ownership of large tracts of land. Having evolved over the years into a planter-lawyer-merchant class, these mountain elites had much in common with the wealthier planters of the lowland South. Many had remained loyal to the Confederacy and the Democratic party. After Reconstruction, they joined with other "Redeemer" or "Bourbon" Democrats in writing new state constitutions and enacting a new series of land laws. While these laws further confused the system of land registry in the mountains, they benefited many of the same lawyer-politicians, who specialized in litigation of disputed land titles. When outside capitalists sought to acquire land in the mountains in the 1870s and 1880s, resident lawyers grew rich on corporation retainers and through ownership of valuable real estate. During the next three decades, the new laws passed by "conservative" politicians not only contributed to the wealth of the mountain elite but facilitated, with the help of that elite, "the eventual transfer of titles and mineral rights from small proprietors to mining and lumber corporations.". . .

Early Industrial Developments, 1870–1900

To urban middle-class Americans of the late nineteenth century, nothing symbolized the progress of American civilization quite as much as the railroad. Not only had the great surge in railroad construction after the Civil War helped to create a modern market economy, but the iron horse itself seemed to embody the energy, force, and technology of the new order. In fact, the fanning out of railroads from urban centers was an integral part of the modernizing process, tying the natural and human resources of rural areas to the industrializing core. If the mountains were to fuel the advance of industrial capitalism, they too would have to be breeched by the iron horse. "Capitalists and speculators," wrote a western North Carolinian in 1889, "have but very little wish to visit and examine counties without a railroad." Those resident mountain speculators who were most successful in their efforts, therefore, were those who were able to attract the interest of railroad men.

The coming of railroads to the Appalachian South was almost as dramatic as the selling of the land itself. In 1870, only one railroad line penetrated the region, and it ran down the valleys of southwest Virginia and eastern Tennessee, connecting Norfolk with Knoxville. This valley line had little impact on the surrounding mountain communities. By 1900, however, four major railroads had extended branch lines into the heart of the region: the Chesapeake and Ohio (C&O) into southern West Virginia, the Norfolk and Western (N&W) into southwest Virginia, the Louisville and Nashville (L&N) into eastern Kentucky and eastern Tennessee, and the Southern into western North Carolina. . . .

The last major extension of the N&W during these feverish days of the railroad's growth was an extension into the Clinch Valley of southwest Virginia, where rich coal deposits had been discovered in Wise County along the Kentucky border. Construction of the Clinch Valley Branch began in 1887 on a line running from Bluefield, on the New River Division, to Norton, near the Kentucky state line, a distance of 103 miles. The tracks of the N&W reached Norton in 1891, along with those of the L&N Railroad, which had constructed a branch up the Powell River Valley from Cumberland Gap. About this time another line, the Virginia and Southwestern—originally backed by Massachusetts interests—was completed from Bristol to Appalachia, Virginia, just below Norton. The completion of these three lines opened up markets for Wise County coal in the Southeast, the West, and the eastern seaboard, and the rapid economic development that followed quickly turned Wise County into the leading coal-producing county in the state. In 1902, the coal production for Wise County totaled more than 2.4 million tons, three times that of any other county in Virginia.

The two largest developers of the Wise County fields were the Virginia Coal and Iron Company, a Pennsylvania firm, and the Virginia Iron, Coal and Coke Company, financed by New York capital. Together, these two companies controlled a majority of the coal and coke produced in the county. The older of the two firms was the Virginia Coal and Iron Company, founded in 1882 by Edward K. Hyndman, Judge John Leisenring, and others of the Connellsville, Pennsylvania, coal region. These men had been attracted to Wise County by General J.D. Imboden, who had convinced them of the potential wealth of Virginia coal. With Imboden serving as their attorney and land agent, the Connellsville syndicate had purchased about 67,000 acres of coal lands on the headwaters of the Powell River, paying as little as 35 cents an acre for some tracts. In the late 1880s, other companies began to acquire land in the area, and a new town sprang up at Big Stone Gap, near the Virginia Coal and Iron Company properties. Shortly thereafter, the company hired Rufus A. Ayers to manage its development, and in 1890 the first coal openings were made and the first coke was produced at Stonega, near Big Stone Gap. Progress was slow until railroads reached the area, but by 1896 the company was producing over 7,000 tons of coal a month and operating more than five hundred coking ovens. . . .

Riding from Pineville to Middlesborough and Big Stone Gap in 1889, Charles Dudley Warner had stumbled upon the revolution that was transforming the mountains. Everywhere about him industrialists, speculators, railroad men, and coal barons were busy remaking the civilization and structure of mountain life. "It is my belief," he wrote, "that this central and hitherto neglected portion of the United States will soon become the theatre of vast and controlling industries." The "remarkable progress" that was taking place in the mountains, he added, would inevitably provide for this region a "prosperous" and "great future."

Unfortunately for Appalachia, only "Warner's first prediction was correct. By the turn of the century, the Appalachian South had become the economic colony of the urban Northeast, and Warner's "vast and controlling industries" had begun to sap the region of its mineral and timber wealth. As the resources of the mountains flowed wantonly out of the region, so did any hope for the independence and prosperity of the mountain people. The selling of the mountains, therefore, was only the first stage in the eventual modernization of Appalachia, but it marked the beginning of the process that would make miners and millhands out of the southern mountaineers.

RONALD D. ELLER earned his PhD degree from the University of North Carolina-Chapel Hill and is currently Distinguished Professor of History at the University of Kentucky. A specialist on the Appalachian region, he served 15 years as the director of the Appalachian Center at Kentucky. His most recent book is the award-winning *Uneven Ground: Appalacia Since 1945* (University Press of Kentucky, 2008).

James Tice Moore

 **NO**

Redeemers Reconsidered: Change and Continuity in the Democratic South, 1870–1900

The political leaders of the post-Reconstruction South have experienced a curious fate at the hands of historians. Variously known as "Bourbons," "Redeemers," or "New Departure Democrats" (*Redeemers* is used in this essay), these men were lionized by scholars well into the twentieth century—only to suffer a sharp decline in their reputations from the 1920s to the 1950s. The sources of their initial popularity are readily apparent, for they had expelled the hated carpetbag governments from the South, reestablished white supremacy on the wreckage of a defunct Radicalism, and put an end to the humiliating military occupation of the region. Reflecting this favorable climate, historians in the first four or five decades after Reconstruction rarely questioned the motives or personal integrity of the Democratic leaders. Instead, scholars generally contented themselves with eulogies on the Redeemers' Confederate war records, their heroism and sagacity in the struggles against "Negro rule," and their ties in blood and sentiment to the chivalric aristocracy of antebellum days.

Occasional criticisms crept into these early analyses, to be sure; students of the period sometimes suggested that the region's Gilded Age Democrats had been too parsimonious in their spending policies and too conservative in their political outlook, too resistant to new men and new ideas. Even so, historians excused these short-comings because of the politicians' service on the battlefields and in the legislative halls. Repeatedly hailed as the heirs and equals of the patriots of 1776, the Redeemers' place in history seemed assured. They were—in the eyes of scholars and public alike—the patrician saviors of their homeland, the natural leaders of the South.

This exalted image has not survived. Attacks on the post-Reconstruction leadership began to appear in the 1920s and became increasingly vitriolic for a generation. Inspired by Charles Austin Beard and other reformist historians of the Progressive Era, scholars . . . emphasized the negative aspects of the Redeemer establishment, and an image of the Democratic elite took shape that was far different from the heroic vision of previous years.

Where an earlier generation had perceived courage, self-sacrifice, and a sincere devotion to good government, the revisionist historians of the 1930s and 1940s by and large saw only intolerance, avarice, and a shocking indifference to popular needs. Many historians examined long-forgotten Democratic financial scandals and conflicts of interest, and they attacked the Redeemers' inadequate funding for schools, asylums, and prisons. Most important of all, students of the period questioned the social and economic origins of the post-Reconstruction leadership. Rejecting the previous emphasis on the Redeemers' "good blood" and patrician heritage, hostile scholars described the Democratic politicians of the 1870s and 1880s as an essentially new class of money-hungry townsmen, as upstart capitalists who had muscled their way to prominence in the turbulent post-Civil War era. This revisionist trend culminated in the 1951 publication of C. Vann Woodward's *Origins of the New South,* a work which brilliantly synthesized the findings of the preceding decades.

According to Woodward, the collapse of the carpetbaggers neither restored the South's prewar leaders to office nor revitalized the region's traditional values and beliefs. The secessionist firebrands of the planter class never regained their old preeminence, and the powers of government gravitated inexorably into the hands of urban-oriented parvenus, men who had enjoyed little influence in the antebellum years. Railroad executives, corporation lawyers, and speculators of various kinds set the political tone in Professor Woodward's New South. Revisionist historians also emphasized the importance of erstwhile Whigs in the Democratic hierarchy, and Woodward exploited this theme with particular effectiveness.

He insisted that probusiness Whigs monopolized public offices in the Redeemer period, displacing the old-line adherents of Jefferson and Jackson. He described a Democratic elite that allegedly ignored the farmers' demands, lavished favors on the corporate interests, and aligned itself with northeastern capital on the great economic issues of the Gilded Age. In Woodward's opinion, therefore, the Redeemer hegemony represented fundamental, irreversible change. Parvenus presumably gained power over traditionalists, Whigs over Jacksonians, capitalists over agrarians. New men with new ideas clearly held sway in the revisionist South. . . .

In spite of its wide acceptance by historians, the revisionist appraisal, dominant for at least three decades, is now itself in need of revision. This claim is supported by the marked increase in historical research and writing on the Redeemer years since the publication of *Origins of the New South*. . . . This abundant new information should make possible a reassessment of the revisionist argument. Were the Democratic leaders in fact townsmen instead of farmers? Did parvenus take the place of aristocrats? Were old-line Jacksonians overshadowed by erstwhile Whigs? Did the Redeemers actually abandon antebellum traditions and favor industry and commerce at the expense of agriculture? The extent of change in the South's Gilded Age ruling class is obviously at issue, and this essay will attempt to gauge the strength of the contending forces of continuity and discontinuity, tradition and innovation.

As noted previously, revisionist scholars have concluded that the Redeemers were much more urban in occupation and attitude than were the prewar elite. Analysis of this claim suggests, however, that the evidence supporting it is too narrowly based to be conclusive. In 1922 Alex Mathews Arnett demonstrated that townsmen controlled the Georgia legislature and held almost all of the state's congressional seats in the 1870s and 1880s, but subsequent investigations have offered only the most tenuous proof of similar developments elsewhere. Revisionist arguments on this point have by and large been founded more on untested assumptions and sweeping generalizations than on substantive research.

C. Vann Woodward attempted to bolster the case for Redeemer urbanism, but his evidence was insufficient. Although Woodward cited examples of urban Democratic spokesmen throughout the region, including a number of governors and senators, he offered no systematic proof that these men were representative of the Redeemer leadership. On the contrary, much of the pertinent statistical data supports the concept of a continuing and potent agricultural influence. Publishing his findings in 1926, Francis Butler Simkins noted that farmers occupied most of the seats in South Carolina's legislature in the mid-1880s (several years before the upsurge of Tillmanite "agrarianism"), and Willie D. Halsell's 1945 analysis of Mississippi's "Bourbon" regime documented the predominance of rural lawmakers in that state as well. William Best Hesseltine in his 1950 survey of the post-Civil War careers of 656 former Confederate leaders—men whose activities shaped the economic and political life of the Gilded Age South—acknowledged that many of these prestigious individuals pursued new opportunities in the business world, but he also showed that the percentage of agriculturalists among them increased from 20 percent in the antebellum era to almost 30 percent after the war. The number of lawyers in the group, by contrast, actually declined, further indicating that the urban ascendancy over the countryside may have been less pronounced than historians have assumed. The argument that rural interests were eclipsed should be modified.

Approaching Redeemer urbanism from another direction, it is inaccurate to argue (as revisionists typically do) that the presence of a sizable group of lawyers or businessmen in a postwar southern legislature or congressional delegation constitutes *prima facie* evidence of a sharp break with antebellum or agrarian ideals, attitudes, or even personnel. Definitive statistical evidence on this point is lacking, but some of the "urban-oriented" Redeemer leaders may have emerged from the old plantation elite and borne its impress on their personal values and intellectual heritage. A planter or his son could move to the city and begin a new career with relative ease, but abandoning the ideological trappings of a lifetime was undoubtedly more difficult. Perhaps an even larger number of the postwar Democratic leaders lived in crossroads hamlets or courthouse towns. Although they were no longer planters, these Redeemer "urbanites" depended on rural constituencies for their livelihood and political preferment and were only little more independent of agricultural interests than the antebellum leadership had been. Such circumstances offer as great, if not greater, support for notions of continuity as for change in Gilded Age political patterns. To complicate the issue still further, Ralph Ancil Wooster has demonstrated that nonfarm occupational groups, especially lawyers, were already assuming dominant governmental roles in the upper South before the Civil War and held a smaller (though sizable) number of positions in the antebellum cotton states also. Developments in the 1870s and 1880s consequently represented, to some extent at least, a continuation of long-established trends. In other words, evidence concerning Redeemers' occupations does not appear adequate in and of itself to sustain the concept of a sharp break with the prewar regime. . . .

The revisionists' stress on the emergence of new men in the Redeemer leadership appears at first glance to contradict another, more vital tenet of their interpretation—their emphasis on the continuing importance of Old Whigs in the southern Democratic regimes of the 1870s and 1880s. The Whigs had been a vigorous political force in the antebellum South, battling the Democrats on relatively even terms for a generation before the Civil War. The presence of many erstwhile Whigs in the Gilded-Age Democratic ranks (their own party having collapsed in the 1850s) would seem, therefore, to provide yet another link between antebellum and postbellum days, another evidence of continuity with the past. Accentuating change, however, Woodward and like-minded scholars have contended that former Whigs not only survived into the New South era but actually achieved a dominant role in the politics of the period—successfully imposing their nationalistic, capitalistic views on their old-line Democratic rivals. This dramatic upsurge of Whigs and Whiggery, according to the Woodward appraisal, thus further differentiated the New South from the Old. . . .

Professor Woodward's revisionist interpretation of Redeemer origins is itself in need of revision. City dwellers, parvenus, and persistent Whigs undoubtedly participated in Democratic politics in the 1870s and 1880s, but there is little evidence that they were numerically dominant in the party councils. Indeed, historical scholarship for the past three decades strongly supports the opposite conclusion. Recent state studies for the most part suggest that traditionalist, agriculturally oriented elites grasped the New South as firmly as they had the Old. William James Cooper provided the most forceful statement of this viewpoint in his analysis of Wade Hampton's South Carolina, but support for it can be found in other works as well. Allen Johnston Going and William Warren Rogers stressed the influence of black-belt planters in Redeemer Alabama, and Roger L. Hart wrote about the return to power of a similar group in Tennessee at the start of the 1880s. C. Alwyn Barr, Jr., emphasized the preeminence of cotton farmers, cattlemen, and other rural interests in post-Reconstruction Texas. William Ivy Hair and Edward Charles Williamson noted the continuing power of old-line "Bourbons" in Louisiana and Florida respectively, and Willie D. Halsell documented the influence of agricultural representatives in Mississippi's Redeemer government, especially in the state legislature. Jack P. Maddex, Jr., broke with the prevailing trend by accentuating the capitalistic, entrepreneurial character of Virginia's ruling elite in the 1870s. But Allen Wesley Moger argued instead that antebellum attitudes and values permeated the Old Dominion's Conservative regime.

These developments were paralleled in the other states. Indeed, only in the case of Georgia has the revisionist interpretation been fully sustained. In that state, according to Judson Clements Ward, Jr., the corporate interests set the political tone and controlled the operations of the Democratic machine. Elsewhere in the Redeemer South, by contrast, Whiggish innovators apparently continued to function as subordinate elements or junior partners—just as they had before the Civil War. Such findings necessarily point to the need for a reassessment of other aspects of the revisionist interpretation. If traditionalist groups dominated most of the post-Reconstruction Democratic regimes, it seems unlikely that those governments actually adopted the one-sidedly prourban and pro-industrial approach to the region's problems that Woodward describes. A new appraisal of Redeemer economic policies is, therefore, essential to a more accurate reinterpretation of the period.

Revisionist historians have devoted considerable attention to Redeemer economic programs, and, as noted previously, their findings have done little to enhance the image of the South's Democratic regimes. Exposés of pro-business bias fill their pages, and the evidence they advance to support their accusations is impressive. Seeking to attract capital investments, five of the post-Reconstruction state governments granted tax exemptions to new manufacturing enterprises. Legislatures and state constitutional conventions granted monopolies to such companies as the infamous Louisiana State Lottery, and the convict-lease system provided cheap labor for ambitious entrepreneurs, especially for owners of railroads, mines, and lumber camps. Railroads, in particular, became prime beneficiaries of Redeemer largesse. Democratic regimes in North Carolina and Virginia sold state-owned railroad properties to private interests at bargain prices, and the governments of Texas and Florida encouraged the construction of new lines with massive grants of government land. Further exploiting this Redeemer generosity, speculators purchased millions of additional acres of timber and mineral lands from state and federal governments at extremely low prices. Such developments, according to the revisionists, constituted nothing less than a southern-style "great barbecue," a wholesale plundering of the region's resources by avaricious capitalists.

This indictment of Redeemer economic policies is damning in tone and, for the most part, convincing in its main thrust. The Democratic regimes undoubtedly made numerous errors in their quest for economic growth. They squandered resources with little or no thought for the future and frequently confused private greed with public good. Even so, the revisionist argument is misleading in several significant respects. For one thing, the Woodward school employs this evidence of probusiness activity to support the concept of a radical break between New South and antebellum attitudes toward economic growth—a highly questionable assumption. Working essentially within the interpretive framework established by Charles A. Beard, the revisionists view the Redeemer program as marking the ascendancy of industry over agriculture in the region, the collapse of pre–Civil War agrarianism before the onslaughts of triumphant capitalism. . . .

In addition to exaggerating the innovative character of the Redeemer program, the dominant Woodward interpretation of New South economic policies suffers from another significant defect: the revisionists' stress on Democratic favoritism toward business led them for the most part to neglect Redeemer attempts to exact concessions from the corporate interests, to tap their financial resources for the public benefit. The post-Reconstruction politicians' efforts along these lines are evident in their revenue policies. Railroad magnates and other businessmen made handsome profits from the convict-lease system, as noted previously, but they also had to pay hundreds of thousands of dollars into southern state treasuries each year in return for the privilege. Louisiana derived forty thousand dollars annually from lottery interests in compensation for gambling rights, and South Carolina reaped even greater profits from its abundant phosphate beds. Allowing private contractors to mine the rich deposits, the state siphoned off mineral royalties which amounted to over $250,000 a year by 1890. Public-land sales, even at bargain prices, provided another source of funds for the Democratic regimes. Florida's Redeemer administration obtained a million dollars from one such sale during the 1880s, while Texas officials employed half the state's land receipts to support the public school system.

Revenues from these sources, however trifling by modern standards, constituted major windfalls at a time when a typical southern state's budget ranged from one to two million dollars a year. Carrying this approach still further, the Democratic leaders also demonstrated a willingness to exact license fees, sales taxes, and property taxes from the business community. Although liberal in their treatment of new factories and the railroads (many of which continued to enjoy tax exemptions under their original antebellum charters), the Redeemers showed much less consideration for the mercantile and professional classes. Southern legislatures imposed a bewildering variety of levies on storekeepers, insurance agents, traveling salesmen, liquor dealers, expressmen, money lenders, and other urban occupational groups. The enactment of such measures suggests a significant conclusion:

the Redeemers were less subservient to business than has generally been assumed. They granted important concessions, but they expected those interests to pay part of the cost of providing public services.

The Democrats' pragmatic attitude toward businessmen was also expressed in their penchant for retracting privileges they had previously bestowed. The opportunism of South Carolina politicians in this respect is particularly notable. After witnessing the rapid expansion of the state's textile industry at the start of the 1880s, the Redeemers in 1885 repealed the tax exemption for new factories. Tax incentives in South Carolina rapidly gave way to tax levies. Southern Democrats also retreated from favoritism toward the railroads, especially after many of the lines fell under the control of Wall Street financiers during the depression of the 1870s. This northern takeover reignited old sectional antagonisms, and anti-railroad sentiment surged through the former Confederacy. Responding to this unrest, Redeemer legislatures passed laws requiring the rail corporations to maintain adequate depots, to fence their rights-of-way, and to compensate farmers for livestock killed by trains. Democratic regimes in Arkansas and Florida manifested the new hostility by defeating the rail lines in the courtroom, enabling them to raise the tax assessments on railroad property early in the 1880s—in the Florida case abolishing tax exemptions granted in 1855. Most important of all, the Redeemers joined with western politicians in pioneering the practice of governmental railroad regulation. Between 1877 and 1891 all the states of the former Confederacy except Arkansas and Louisiana established regulatory commissions of one sort or another. Significant rate cuts ensued, even though the commissions were frequently hampered by corporate intransigence and judicial conservatism. Not satisfied with these efforts, the region's Democrats played prominent roles in the struggle for federal railroad regulation as well. Texas Senator John H. Reagan led the fight to establish the Interstate Commerce Commission, and Alabama Redeemer Walter Lawrence Bragg, another champion of the regulatory cause, served as one of the original members of the new agency.

Paralleling these developments, moreover, Democratic attitudes toward the public lands underwent a similar transformation. Eager for economic growth, southerners had generally favored liberal land policies at the start of the Redeemer era. Northern lumber interests had bought timber tracts in the South in order to forestall potential competition, and other capitalists had purchased large acreages for purely speculative purposes, making no immediate effort to promote the region's prosperity. Misgivings arose about the land boom, and in 1888 southern congressmen led a successful movement to suspend cash sales of federal land, a maneuver which paved the way for reorganization of the entire public-land system along conservationist lines. Two Redeemers in Grover Cleveland's cabinet also worked to improve the management of natural resources. Secretary of the Interior Lucius Q. C. Lamar of Mississippi and Attorney General Augustus Hill Garland of Arkansas took action against illegal encroachments on the federal domain, and together they expelled speculators, ranchers, and railroads from an estimated 45,000,000 acres in the South and West. In land policies as well as railroad regulations, therefore, southern Democrats manifested an increasingly sophisticated attitude toward Gilded Age capitalism. Skepticism gradually supplanted gullibility; restrictions accompanied and sometimes overshadowed concessions.

Abounding in such ambiguities, the Redeemer economic program offered uncertain and tenuous encouragement for the entrepreneurial classes. Indeed, a case can be made that the Democratic elite provided more consistent and reliable support for farmers than for businessmen. Gathering most of their electoral strength from the countryside, Redeemer politicians generally reflected agrarian biases on such issues as debt scaling and railroad regulation, and their tax policies followed a similar pattern. As noted previously, they veered from one direction to another in their revenue demands on business. But they pursued a much more uniform and straightforward course with reference to property taxes—the exactions which fell most heavily on rural areas. Appalled by the high property levies of the Reconstruction years, Democratic leaders moved in the 1870s and 1880s to prevent the recurrence of such abuses. They wrote strict limits on property taxes into their state constitutions, severely curtailing the revenue-gathering authority of local as well as state governments. Southern legislatures accelerated this trend with numerous tax cuts, and the results were impressive. Mississippi set the pace for the entire region by slashing its state property levy from 14 mills in 1874 to 2.5 mills in 1882, a reduction of more than 80 percent. Alabama's less drastic adjustment from 7.5 mills in 1874 to 4 mills in 1889 was more typical, but substantial reductions occurred in state after state. These cuts, together with the South's traditionally low assessments of property values, offered massive tax savings for the agricultural population. The impact of these reforms was readily apparent, for millions of acres which had been forfeited for delinquent taxes during Reconstruction were reclaimed by farmers in the Redeemer era.

Applying political pressure through the Grange and Alliance, the rural interests derived many additional benefits from the Democratic regimes. Agricultural and mechanical colleges received increased funding, and the Redeemers established new land-grant schools in the Carolinas, Mississippi, and Virginia. Government-supported agricultural experiment stations proliferated as well. North Carolina pioneered the development of experimental farms in the 1870s, setting a pattern which the rest of the South followed during the next decade. Democratic legislatures provided another recognition of the farmers' importance by creating state departments of agriculture. Although hampered by inadequate budgets, these new agencies became increasingly innovative and efficient. By the 1880s state agriculture departments were inspecting commercial fertilizers, analyzing soil samples, conducting geological surveys, encouraging immigration, providing veterinary services, dispatching speakers to farm meetings, and collecting statistics on crop yields. In Alabama the Department of Agriculture eventually became the second most powerful agency in the state, enjoying an influence exceeded only by that of the governor.

Southern Democrats also demonstrated their support for farmers by sponsoring agricultural societies. Legislatures appropriated thousands of dollars each year to subsidize these groups (primarily to enable them to hold state fairs). Further belying the notion of the Redeemers' indifference to rural needs, the region's legislators passed hundreds of laws regarding the crop-lien system, the maintenance of fences and roads, and the conservation of fish and wildlife—all issues of concern to farm areas. These activities reflected an essential fact: the agriculturalists still constituted the most important interest group in the South, and they received due consideration from the Democratic elite.

The Redeemers' favoritism toward farmers also influenced developments at the national level, undermining another facet of the revisionist interpretation. According to Professor Woodward, investment-hungry southern congressmen generally subordinated the needs of their section and its people to the demands of the capitalistic, conservative Northeast. If this in fact was the case, the Democratic leaders manifested their subservience in an extremely curious way—by opposing the northern business interests on almost all the great economic issues of the Gilded Age. Southern crusades for federal railroad regulation and the conservation of the public domain have been noted previously, but the Redeemers assumed anticorporate stands in other national controversies as well. The great majority of the region's political leaders denounced protective tariffs and for decades battled to reinstitute the low duties of the antebellum years. Gaining particular prominence in these struggles, newspaper editor Henry Watterson of

Kentucky, together with Senator Lamar of Mississippi, formulated the famous "tariff for revenue only" pledge in the 1880 Democratic platform, and House Ways and Means Chairman Roger Quarles Mills of Texas led the unsuccessful congressional fight for tariff reform in 1888. . . .

The Redeemers' commitment to an increased money supply also led them to criticize the restrictive policies of the national banking system. They opposed the rechartering of many of the national banks in the 1880s, and they urged the repeal of the federal government's prohibitive tax on state bank notes. Far from endorsing the Hamiltonian financial structure which had emerged during the Civil War, as revisionist historians have maintained, the southern Democrats were instead among the more persistent critics of that structure. Only with reference to federal aid to internal improvements did they find themselves in harmony with the prevailing system. Having witnessed the destruction of their ports, railroads, and levees by federal power during the war years, southerners requested federal money for rebuilding them. Even on this issue, surprisingly enough, the Redeemers' stand placed them in opposition to northern sentiment. Northeastern congressmen—Democrats and Republicans alike—had turned against government-financed internal improvements after the scandals of the Grant era, and the southerners were only able to vote the funds for their projects with the help of the West. On issue after issue, therefore, the Redeemers took sides against, not with, the masters of capital.

These national developments, together with similar trends at the state level, clearly point up inadequacies in the revisionist interpretation of Redeemer origins and views. Parvenus, urbanites, and persistent Whigs made their way into the Democratic leadership during the post–Civil War years, as Woodward and others have argued, but these potentially innovative groups proved either unable or unwilling to alter the entrenched patterns of southern government. Traditionalist forces enjoyed too much strength in both the electorate and the party hierarchy to permit any wholesale departure from established practices and policies. As a result the southern Democrats neither abandoned the farmers nor embraced Whiggery in the aftermath of Reconstruction. Indeed, their economic programs were more congruent with the ideals of Jefferson, Jackson, or even Calhoun than with those of Clay or Webster. Although they promoted limited industrial growth, the Redeemers continued to acknowledge and reward the primacy of agriculture in their region's life. Although they accepted the defeat of secession and the collapse of the slave system, most of them also continued to regard the capitalistic North with a deep-seated antagonism. . . . In the decisive economic clashes of the Gilded Age, . . . the Redeemer South consistently joined forces with the other great agricultural section of the United States, the West. Such facts lend further support to the notion of continuity between the Old and New Souths. All things had not changed with Appomattox, much less with the Compromise of 1877.

James Tice Moore (1946–2009) was a professor of history and former department chair at Virginia Commonwealth University where he taught for 31 years. His scholarly works focused on the American South, especially Virginia and include *Two Paths to the New South: Virginia Debt Controversy, 1870–83* (University Press of Kentucky, 1974) and (with Edward Younger) *The Governors of Virginia* (University of Virginia Press, 1982).

EXPLORING THE ISSUE

Did a "New South" Emerge Following Reconstruction?

Critical Thinking and Reflection

1. Based on the YES and NO selections, what is meant by the term "New South"?
2. How did the political leadership of the post-Reconstruction South differ from that of the antebellum period?
3. What impact did industrial production have on the South in the last quarter of the nineteenth century?
4. Based on your understanding of the YES and NO selections, to what extent did the economic and political character of the post-Reconstruction South represent continuity with the antebellum period?

Is There Common Ground?

Although the Civil War and Reconstruction clearly produced changes in the South, scholarly debates continue as to the extent of this change. For example, despite the introduction of impressive industrial processes, the vast majority of southerners continued to depend upon farming for their livelihoods. Moreover, Woodward recognizes that the South's postwar industries were tied to raw materials and natural resources extracted from southern lands. Even Woodward's argument in support of the discontinuity between the antebellum South and the postwar South suggests that the distinctions were not always complete. Whether or not the post-Reconstruction political leaders of the New South were "Bourbons" or "Redeemers," they still were white, conservative Democrats. In addition, the attitudes of post-Reconstruction politicians toward urban-industrial growth differed from state to state, making generalizations about change more difficult.

Another important aspect of this question, one that is not addressed in the YES and NO selections, is the social change in the post-Civil War South. Specifically, how different were patterns of race relations once the war had ended and slavery had been abolished? On the one hand, efforts by some Radical Republicans to promote a truly egalitarian society resulted in a framework to extend citizenship rights to African Americans through the Civil Rights Acts of 1866 and 1875 and the Fourteenth and Fifteenth Amendments. These actions held out the promise of a dramatic departure from the antebellum slave statutes or the quasi-freedom of the Black Codes in the immediate postwar South. On the other hand, the demise of the Reconstruction governments resulted in a general withdrawal of any commitment to advancing the status of black southerners and paved the way by the end of the century to firmly entrenched policies of peonage, political disfranchisement, and racial segregation. From the perspective of most black southerners, then, the prospect of fully participating in the benefits of American democracy seemed just as remote in 1900 as it had been in 1860.

Additional Resources

Edward L. Ayers, *The Promise of the New South: Life After Reconstruction* (Oxford University Press, 1992).

James C. Cobb, *Industrialization and Southern Society, 1877–1984* (University Press of Kentucky, 1984).

Pete Daniel, *Breaking the Land: The Transformation of Cotton, Tobacco, and Rice Cultures Since 1880* (University of Illinois Press, 1985).

Paul Gaston, *The New South Creed: A Study in Southern Mythmaking* (Alfred A. Knopf, 1970).

Gavin Wright, *Old South, New South: Revolutions in the Southern Economy Since the Civil War* (Basic Books, 1986).

Internet References . . .

History of the United States:
Industrialization and Reform (1870–1916)

www.theusaonline.com/history/industrialization.htm

The New South

http://www.apstudynotes.org/us-history/topics/
the-new-south/

The South After the Civil War

www.cs.unm.edu/~sergiy/amhistory/ch21.html

Selected, Edited, and with Issue Framing Material by:
Kevin R. Magill and Tony L. Talbert, *Baylor University*

ISSUE

Should We Understand Modern U.S. Imperial Power as Primarily Emerging from Its Financial Diplomacy Following the World Wars?

YES: **Michael Hudson,** from "Introduction to Super Imperialism," Pluto Press (2003)

NO: **James Monroe,** from "Transcript of Monroe Doctrine (1823)," OurDocuments.gov (1823); **Carl Schurz,** from "Platform of the American Anti-Imperialist League," The Policy of Imperialism (1899); **John Hobson,** from "The Economic Bases of Imperialism," Imperialism: A Study (1902)

Learning Outcomes

After reading this issue, you will be able to:

- Discuss the evolution of the United States as an imperial power.
- Understand how and why the U.S. sphere of imperial influence developed from annexing imperial power to occupying imperial force to economic imperial sovereign.
- Understand how economic mechanisms, such as the IMF and World Bank have served to support U.S. imperial economic domination.
- Understand on aspect of imperial hegemony.

ISSUE SUMMARY

YES: Michael Hudson suggests that the imperial watershed moment is when United States used their position as world creditor to establish the economic conditions that would evolve lead to future economic mechanisms, such as the IMF and World Bank, which would plunge certain countries into a debt crisis to maintain US economic and imperial dominance worldwide.

NO: James Monroe writes that the United States would oppose European colonialism in the Americas beginning in 1823. Carl Schurz argues that the United States was becoming an imperial nation, committing criminal aggression by annexing the Philippines. John Hobson provides us with the reasons for and state of imperialism around the world. He discusses the economic basis for imperial expansion suggesting it is driven by the search for new markets and investment opportunities overseas. He names how the United States was entering this imperial quest in relations to other world powers at the turn of the century. The authors provide examples of historical shifts in imperial policy prior to the World Wars.

Imperialism is generally characterized by extending a country's political, economic, and/or cultural control beyond its immediate borders. It has certainly been a major driving force for geopolitical activities of the last 600 years. Often efforts to subjugate have been paired with misinformation and nationalism to win the support of the population. Consider too the psychology of imperial efforts which have ranged from the use of named implying othering (terms like savages); political cartoons that marginalize subjugated people while supporting the "civilizing mission" of Western culture; and pseudo-science as justification for genocide or marginalization. Imperialism has also included more straightforward subjugation such as the stripping of legal rights from particular groups. Indigenous and African American populations have certainly experienced all of these injustices, while more European populations tended to be subjected to those that were less dehumanizing.

Looking at US imperialism, scholars like Richard H. Immerman (2010) have suggested that the quest for empire has been a part of the fabric of US thought from the nation's history. Historians like W. L. Williams (1980) have argued that we need to only look to colonial wars with Indigenous Americans to see how and why US imperialism evolved to become imperial activity we saw in the Philippines and beyond, and why imperialism remained part of the U.S. ethos. The narrative of the Revolutionary War shares a story of British oppression and a colony wanting to be free. While true, many wealthy landowning colonists also wished to extend their sphere of influence into the Ohio River Valley, which had been forbidden by Great Britain as part of their agreement to the Treaty of Paris after the French and Indian War. Naturally, the United States broke this Treaty when they severed colonial ties with Britain in order to secure this land (among other reasons). Later, Manifest Destiny served as an imperial force that pushed the United States further across the continent. The nation has since continued imperial expansion in different ways including economic and physical forms of imperialism.

Often historians point to examples of U.S. imperialism prior to World War II. Examples they have considered included but are not limited to: The Louisiana Purchase, Mexican American War, The Annexation of the Dominican Republic, The Spanish American War, The Roosevelt Corollary, Panama Canal, Occupation of Haiti, and the Good Neighbor Policy. The long history of U.S. imperialism has included extensions of these geopolitical efforts to secure a sphere of influence and new forms of empire. As the United States became a greater international power, new types of imperialism developed to become part of their globalized empire. These efforts included everything from privatization of public goods in nations across the globe to forceful regime change. Imperialist planning has included the developing global policy such as The Truman Doctrine, The Reagan/Thatcher Doctrine and The Cold War Foreign Policy, and international interventions and institutions such as NATO, the overthrow of governments (democratic and otherwise), Oil Protectionism, and the War on Terror. Insidiously, these U.S policies have economically and politically penetrated (and in some cases destroyed) nations

and their ability to exist as sovereign state. Many have called these efforts neocolonialism, an idea that suggests an imperial power uses economic system that they have created and manipulated to achieve their imperial aims. The United States has used these and other measures to control much of the globe. The nation has and continues to occupy nations all across the world, using air force bases as staging grounds for military intervention while tying nation's economic interests to US interests. Other more warlike imperial activity has included military conquests such as Vietnam and Korea that have served as warnings to states that might reject US policy goals.

In many ways, the United States is like every imperial power in human history. Forced treaties and military aid have ensured these states support the United States, while she maintains a favorable balance of power. Like most empires, the United States has enforced certain treaties and rules while working outside them. As the preeminent imperial power, the United States has violated international law, required that countries accept aid for access, and ensured particular leaders and styles of government last that support her aims. While these efforts are not unique, the United States has been the most forceful and successful behaving in this way over the last century. An example of this type of incursion (and occupation rather than annexation) was the U.S.'s extensive dealings in Iraq and Iran. The United States first placed Saddam Hussein in power in 1979 in an effort to help control the Middle East and establish a government favorable to the United States. Placing Hussein in power was also an effort to offer a check to Iranian influence because Revolution had begun which had a distinctly anti-imperialist and anti-American sentiment. The United States provided Hussein with weapons to fight Iran and to maintain control of his own people. The Iraq–Iran War happened in 1980 and lasted to 1988 resulting in a stalemate of sorts. Estimates include over one million dead. Iran was supported by Syria and Libya who they themselves have suffered bombings, regime change, and covert actions from the United States for their defiance of imperialist aims. Iraq lost support from the West and Hussein became concerned about Iran smoothing relations with the West in order to attack Iraq. In 1990, the United States invaded Iraq when Hussein interfered with Kuwaiti pipelines that were sending oil to the West. The 9/11 terror attacks later provided the cover needed to invade Iraq for a second time to punish Hussein for rejecting Western imperial power.

The occupation of Iraq or Vietnam is simply one way the United States occupies other nations and is one piece of the occupational imperial puzzle. We can also look to the drug war in South America as an example of another type of occupation that has become a part of US policy over the last century. Many South American countries were forced or bribed to allow the United States into their countries with the idea that drugs were entering the United States illegally and needed to be stopped. Imagine if another country required them to allow their law enforcement and intelligence agencies into the United States. Being in South America was an ideal way for the United States to occupy without annexing to destabilize or coerce nations and governments for US economic benefit.

Like other historical imperial powers the United States has also amassed a remarkable military arsenal. In recent years, much has been made of China's rise as a world power. The Pentagon recently complained to the government and media that China increased their military arsenal to 400 offensive missiles hoping to secure additional military funding. What the Pentagon did not mention and what the media did not report was that the United States has close to 10,000 missiles (Chomsky, 2008). When others do take these actions, the United States calls it terrorism or a threat to world peace, when the United States does it the United States calls it the defense of democracy.

How then should we understand the origins of US imperialism in our modern world? Williams (1980) suggests we should understand it emerging from US clashes with indigenous populations. Others believe it began as we know it in the late 19th century or with World War I. Adam Burns argues that the US imperial intervention and occupation emerges from what we saw in the Caribbean between 1916 and 1925. Occupation, rather than annexation, came to characterize US interventional imperialism and exists in many forms today. Our "YES" author Michael Hudson suggests that the imperial watershed moment for the United States was the use of their position as world creditor to establish the economic conditions that would evolve into the IMF and World Bank. These organizations would plunge certain countries into debt with the United States and maintain US economic and imperial dominance worldwide. He argues American foreign politics after World War II were designed to restrain the economic development of Third World countries to prevent competition. Concurrently, the United States imposed free trade policies on developing countries while not adhering to free trade themselves. As Noam Chomsky (1999) has noted, globalization and neoliberalism has made it easier to "for corporations and the wealthy to dominate the economies of nations around the world without having obligations to the peoples of those nations." To Hudson, the relationship between the private and public sectors is how we should understand modern U.S. imperial activity.

Our "NO" authors speak to several different times in US history where imperialism was a topic of debate and national policy. President Monroe's Doctrine attempted to assert a US sphere of influence in the Americas. The declaration was generally disregarded by European powers, other than Britain, because the United States did not have a strong Navy or Army at the time. The British approved as they would likely benefit from the mercantilism within the emerging markets former emerging markets that had been Spanish and Portuguese colonies. The Monroe Doctrine was generally praised in the Americas, but also met with prophetic critiques. For example, Chilean Diego Portales wrote, "we have to be very careful: for the Americans of the north [believe], the only Americans are themselves." Regardless, the statement signaled a US path toward imperial activity. In 1899, the anti-imperialist league platform argues that the US imperialist behavior in the Philippines was antithetical to founder intentions. The league invoked the declaration of independence, Lincoln, Washington, and the constitution to critique certain imperialist tendencies. Similarly, in 1902, English economist John Hobson discussed the drive for economic oligarchy and hegemony, rather than nationalism, which served as the basis for imperial activity. He notes the ways the United States and other situated themselves well within this International imperial activity prior to its ascendency to a global hegemon. In some ways, his analysis might provide context for better understanding imperial forms and allowing us to see imperial/colonial relationships between annexation, occupation, and economic manipulation.

Without question U.S. Empire has developed a complex structure with many nuances. When looking at its history, should we understand U.S. imperialism as demonstrated primarily through the economic practices and organizations established following World War II or in previous more physical efforts to assert itself as an International power?

Chomsky, N. (2008). We Own The World. Retrieved from https://chomsky.info/20080101/

Chomsky, N. (1999). *Profit over people: Neoliberalism and global order*. Seven Stories Press.

Immerman, R. H. (2010). *The CIA in Guatemala: The foreign policy of intervention*. University of Texas Press.

Williams, W. L. (1980). United States Indian policy and the debate over Philippine Annexation: implications for the origins of American imperialism. *The Journal of American History*, 66(4), 810–831.

YES ⬅   Michael Hudson

Introduction to Super Imperialism

It would be simplistic to view the United States' rise to world dominance as following the European model characterized by the drives of private finance capital. . . . The United States has achieved its global position through novel policies that were not anticipated by economists writing prior to World War I, or indeed prior to the 1970s.

One lesson of U.S. experience is that the national diplomacy, embodied in what now is called the Washington Consensus, is not simply an extension of business drives. It has been shaped by overriding concerns for world power (euphemized as national security) and economic advantage as perceived by American strategists quite apart from the profit motives of private investors. Although the roots of imperialism and its diplomatic rivalries always have been economic in character, these roots—and especially their tactics—are not the same for all nations in all periods.

The United States' ascent to world creditor status after World War I resulted from the unprecedented terms on which its government extended armaments and reconstruction loans to its wartime allies. In administering these Inter-Ally debts, U.S. Government aims and objectives were different from those of the private sector investment capital. The United States had a unique perception of its place and role in the world, and hence of its self-interest.

. . . The American School of political economy believed that their nation's rise to world power would be achieved by protecting their economy from that of Britain and other European nations. The objective was to create nothing less than a new civilization, one based on high wages as a precondition for achieving even higher productivity. The result would be a society of abundance rather than one whose cultural and political principles were based on the phenomenon of scarcity.

. . .

America as a new civilization, whose dynamics were those of increasing returns in agriculture as well as industry, and the perception that rising living standards would bring about a new social morality. Juxtaposing American civilization to European society wracked by class conflict, pauper labor and a struggle for foreign markets based on reducing wage levels. Teaching at the University of Pennsylvania from the 1890s through the 1910s, Patten's students included such future luminaries as Franklin Roosevelt's brainstruster Rex Tugwell and the socialist Scott Nearing.

Europe's imperial rivalries were viewed as stemming from its competing princely ambitions and an idle landed aristocracy, and from the fact that its home markets were too impoverished to purchase industrial manufactures of the type that were finding a ready market in the United States. To nationalists, the United States did not need colonies. Its tariff revenues would better be spent on internal improvements than on vainglorious foreign conquests.

This attitude helps explain America's belated commitment to World War I. The nation declared war in 1917 only when it became apparent that to stay out would entail at least an interim economic collapse as American bankers and exporters found themselves stuck with uncollectible loans to Britain and its allies. Reflecting the ideological and moral elements in America's entry, President Wilson viewed the nation's political and cultural heritage as stemming largely from England. He was a Democrat, and a southerner to boot, whereas most of the leading Republican intellectuals felt a closer kinship to Germany. That nation was after all in much the same position as the United States in seeking to shape its social evolution by state policy to build a high-income, technologically innovative economy, marked by government leadership in social spending and the financing of heavy industry.

This social philosophy helps explain America's particular form of isolationism preceding and after World War I, and especially the government's demand to be repaid for its wartime loans to its allies. U.S. officials insisted that the nation was merely an associate in the war, not a full ally. Its $12 billion in armaments and reconstruction loans to Europe were more of a business character than a contribution to a common effort. America saw itself as economically and politically distinct.

The Dilemma of U.S. Economic Diplomacy in the Interwar Years

The United States emerged from the war not only as the world's major creditor, but a creditor to foreign governments with which it felt little brotherhood. It did not see its dominant economic position as obliging it to take responsibility for stabilizing world finance and trade. If Europe wished to channel its labor and capital to produce armaments instead of paying its debts, and if it persisted in its historical antagonisms—as evidenced by the onerous Treaty of Versailles imposed on Germany—the United States need feel no obligation to accommodate it.

The government did not seek to create a system capable of extending new loans to foreign countries to finance their payments to the United States, as it was to do after World War II. Nor did it lower its tariffs so as to open U.S. markets to foreign producers as a means of enabling them to pay their war debts to the U.S. Treasury. The United States rather wished to see Europe's empires dissolved, and did not mind seeing imperial governments stripped of their wealth, which tended to be used for military purposes with which few Americans sympathized . . .

Economically, the U.S. attitude was to urge European governments to reduce their military spending and/or living standards, to permit their money to flow out and their prices to fall. In this way, it was hoped, world payments equilibrium might be re-established even in the face of rising American protectionism and full payment of the Inter-Ally debts that were the legacy of the Great War.

This was not a clearly thought-out position but many leading Europeans shared these attitudes. In trying to cope with the international financial breakdown of the 1920s, their governments were advised by anti-German writers who insisted that Germany could repay its assessed reparations if only it would submit to sufficient austerity.

Chicago School attitudes towards today's debtor economies view of international payments adjustment was as self-defeating in the 1920s as are the IMF's austerity programs today. By insisting on repayment of its allies' war debts in full, and by simultaneously enacting increasingly protectionist tariffs at home, the U.S. Government made repayment of these debts impossible.

Private investors traditionally had been obliged to take losses when debtors defaulted, but it became apparent that the U.S. Government was not about to relinquish its creditor hold on the Allies. This intransigence obliged them to keep tightening the screws on Germany.

To review the 1920s is to examine how nations were not acting in their enlightened self-interest but in an unquestioning reaction against obsolete economic attitudes. The orthodox ideology carried over from the prewar era was anachronistic in failing to recognize that the world economy emerged from World War I shackled with debts far beyond its ability to pay. . . . U.S. bankers and investors lent money to German municipalities, which turned the dollars over to the central bank to pay reparations to the Allies, which in turn used the dollars to pay their war debts to the U.S. Treasury. The world financial system thus was kept afloat simply by intergovernmental debts being wound down by a proportional build-up in private sector and municipal debts.

The ensuing débâcle introduced a behavioral difference from theorists of prewar world diplomacy. . . . After World War I, the U.S. Government pursued. An enlightened imperialism would have sought to turn other countries into economic satellites of the United States. But the United States did not want European exports, nor were its investors particularly interested in Europe after its own stock market outperformed those of Europe.

The United States could have named the terms on which it would have supplied the world with dollars to enable foreign countries to repay their war debts. It could have specified what imports it wanted or was willing to take. But it did not permit, debtor countries to pay their debts in the form of exports to the United States. . . . On both the trade and financial fronts, the U.S. Government pursued policies that impelled European countries to withdraw from the world economy and turn within.

Even the United States' attempt to ameliorate matters backfired. To make it easier for the Bank of England to pay its war debts, the Federal Reserve held down interest rates so as not to draw money away from Britain. But low interest rates spurred a stock market boom, discouraging U.S. capital outflows to European financial markets.

America's failure to recycle the proceeds of its intergovernmental debt receipts into the purchase of European exports and assets was a failure to perceive the implicit strategy dictated by its unique position as world creditor. The U.S. Government's economic isolationism precluded it from collecting its intergovernmental debts. Its status as world creditor proved ultimately worthless as the world economy broke into nationalist units, each striving to become independent of foreign trade and payments, and from the U.S. economy in particular. In this respect, America forced its own inward-looking attitude on other nations.

The upshot was the breakdown of world payments, competitive devaluations, tariff wars and international autarchy that characterized the 1930s. Less an explicit attempt at imperialism than an inept result of narrowly legalistic and bureaucratic intransigence regarding the war debts, coupled with a parochial domestic tariff policy. It was just the opposite of a policy designed to establish the United States as the world's economic center based on a reciprocity of payments between creditor and periphery, a complementarity of imports and exports, production and payments. A viable U.S.-centered world economic system would have required some means of enabling Europe to repay its war debts. What occurred instead was isolationism at home, prompting drives for national self-sufficiency abroad.

. . . Although it certainly was logical in the 1920s for private U.S. investors to extend their power throughout the world, the financial policies pursued by the U.S. Government made this impossible. The Government narrowly construed America's national self-interest in terms of the Treasury's balance sheet, putting this above the cosmopolitan tendencies of private financial capital. This forced country after country to withdraw from the internationalism of the gold exchange standard and to abandon policies of currency stability and free trade.

. . . Depression spread as the world financial crisis was internalized in one country after another. As world trade and payments broke down utterly, the national socialist governments of Italy and Germany became increasingly aggressive. Governments throughout the world responded to falling incomes and employment by vastly extending their role in economic affairs, prompting Keynes to proclaim the end of laissez-faire.

The Great Depression extinguished private capital throughout the world, just as intergovernmental capital had been extinguished by the shortsightedness of governments seeking to derive maximum economic benefit from their financial claims on other governments. This poses the question of why such debts were allowed to become so problematic in the first place.

Britain's agreement to begin paying its war debts to the United States no doubt was inspired largely by its world creditor ideology of maintaining the "sanctity of debt." Yet this policy no longer was appropriate in a situation where Britain, along with continental Europe, had become an international debtor rather than a creditor. There was little idea of adjusting the traditional ideology concerning the sanctity of debts to their realistic means of payment.

The Great Depression and World War II taught governments the folly of this attitude, although they were to lose it again with regard to Third World and Eastern Bloc debts within a few decades of the close of World War II.

American Plans for a Postwar "Free Trade Imperialism"

Since 1945, U.S. foreign policy has sought to reverse foreign state control over economic policies generally, and attempts at economic self-reliance and independence from the United States in particular.

As U.S. diplomats and economists theorized during 1941–45 over the nation's imminent role as dominant power in the postwar world, they recognized that it would emerge from the war by far the strongest national economy, but would have to be a major exporter in order to maintain full employment during the transition back to peacetime life. This transition was expected to require about five years, 1946–50. Foreign markets would have to replace the War Department as a source of demand for the products of American industry and agriculture. This in turn required that foreign countries be able to earn or borrow dollars to pay the United States for these exports.

It was clear that the United States could not impose war debts on its Allies similar to those that had followed World War I. The Allies had been stripped of their marketable international assets. If they were obliged to pay war debts to the United States, they would have no remaining funds to buy American exports. The U.S. Government would have to provide the world with dollars, by government loans, private investment or a combination of both. In exchange, it would be entitled to name the terms on which it would provide these dollars. The question was, what terms would U.S. economic diplomats stipulate?

In January 1944, the American Economic Association was dominated by proposals for postwar U.S. economic policy. "For the first time in many decades," wrote J. B. Condliffe attention is now being paid by soldiers and political scientists, but little as yet by economists, to the power position of the United States in the modern world ". . . this war has shown the folly of complacent and self-centered isolationist theorist and attitudes." Examination should not be thought of as Machiavellian or evil but as a necessity if U.S. ideals were to carry real force behind them.

A central theme of the meeting was the relative roles that government and business would play in shaping the postwar world. Former presidents of the American Economic Association on "What Should be the Relative Spheres of Private Business and Government in our Postwar American Economy?" most respondents held that the distinction between private business and government policy was becoming fuzzy, and that some degree of planning was needed to keep the economy working at relatively full employment.

This did not necessarily imply a nationalist economic policy, although that seemed to be an implicit long-term tendency. Speaking on "The Present Position of Economics," Arthur Salz observed "government and economics have drawn close together and live in a real and, to a large extent, in a personal union. The economist made his reputation by constructive[ly] criticizing governments, he is now hand and glove with them . . ."

The problem of government/private sector relations was put in most rigorous form by Jacob Viner, the laissez-faire theoretician from the University of Chicago. . . . Viner concluded hopefully: "The pattern of international economic relations will be much less influenced by the operation of national power and national prestige considerations in a world of free-enterprise economies than in a world of state-operated national economies."

This was just the opposite of socialist theory, which assumed that national governments were inherently peaceful, except when goaded by powerful business cartels. . . .

The war debts and reparations after World War I had brought into question the tendency for conflict among nations—and hence the chances of war—would be greater rather than smaller in a world of state-controlled economies. Looking back on the experience of the 1930s in particular, he found that "The substitution of state control for private enterprise in the field of international economic relations would, with a certain degree of inevitability, have a series of undesirable consequences, to wit: the injection of a political element into all major international economic transactions; the conversion of international trade from a predominantly competitive to a predominantly monopolistic basis; a marked increase in the potentiality of business disputes to generate international friction." From this perspective national rivalries as conceived and carried out by governments were inherently more belligerent than commercial rivalries among private exporters, bankers and investors.

. . . Government planning was the problem as an autonomous force based on the inherently nationalistic ambitions of political leaders. No room was acknowledged for planning even of the kind that had led American industry to achieve world leadership from the end of the U.S. Civil War in 1865 to the end of World War I under a program of industrial protectionism and active internal improvements.

. . .

It seemed to many observers that U.S. officials were structuring the IMF and World Bank to enable countries to pursue laissez-faire policies by insuring adequate resources to finance the international payments imbalances that were anticipated to result from countries opening their markets to U.S. exporters after the return to peace. Special reconstruction lending would be made to war-torn Europe, followed by development loans to the colonies being freed, and balance-of-payments loans to countries in special straits so that they would not need to resort to currency depreciation and tariff barriers. It was believed that free trade and investment would settle into a state of balanced international trade and payments under the postwar conditions being created under U.S. leadership. Bilateral foreign aid would serve as a direct inducement to governments to acquiesce in the United States' postwar plans, while ensuring the balance-of-payments equilibrium that was a precondition for free trade and an Open Door to international investment.

When President Truman insisted that "World trade must be restored—and it must be restored to private enterprise," this was a way of saying that its regulation must be taken away from foreign governments that might be tempted to try to recover their prewar power at the expense of U.S. exporters and investors. America's laissez-faire stance promoted the United States as the center of a world system vastly more extensive and centralized, yet also more flexible, less costly and less bureaucratic than Europe's imperial systems had been.

Given the fact that only the United States possessed the foreign exchange necessary to undertake substantial overseas investment, and only the U.S. economy enjoyed the export potential to displace Britain and other European rivals, the ideal of laissez-faire was synonymous with the worldwide extension of U.S. national power. American commercial strength would achieve the government's underlying objective of turning foreign economies into satellites of the United States. The objectives of U.S. exporters and international investors thus were synonymous with those of the government in seeking to maximize U.S. world power, and this was best achieved by discouraging government planning and economic statism abroad.

The laissez-faire ideology that American industrialists had denounced in the nineteenth century, and that the U.S. Government would repudiate in practice in the 1970s and 1980s, served American ends after World War II. Europe's industrial nations would open their doors and permit U.S. investors to buy in to the extractive industries of their former colonies, especially into Near Eastern oil. These less developed regions would provide the United States with raw materials rather than working them up into their own manufactures to compete with U.S. industry. They would purchase a rising stream of American foodstuffs and manufactures, especially those produced by the industries whose productive capacity had expanded greatly during the war. The resulting U.S. trade surplus would provide the foreign exchange to enable American investors to buy up the most productive resources of the world's industry, mining and agriculture.

To the extent that America's export surplus exceeded its private sector investment outflows, the balance would have to be financed by growth in dollar lending via the World Bank, the Export-Import Bank and related intergovernmental aid-lending institutions. Under the aegis of the U.S. Government, American investors and creditors would accumulate a growing volume of claims on foreign economies, ultimately securing control over the non-Communist world's political as well as economic processes.

This idealized model never materialized for more than a brief period. The United States proved unwilling to lower its tariffs on commodities that foreigners could produce less expensively than American farmers and manufacturers, but only on those commodities that did not threaten vested U.S. interests. The International Trade Organization, which in principle was supposed to subject the U.S. economy to the same free trade principles that it demanded from foreign governments, was scuttled. Private U.S. investment abroad did not materialize to the degree needed to finance foreign purchases of U.S. exports, nor were IMF and World Bank loans anywhere near sufficient to buoy up the payments-deficit economies.

Much of Europe's remaining gold was stripped by the United States, as was that of Latin America in the early postwar years. By 1949 foreign countries were all but faced with the need to revert to the protectionism of the 1930s to prevent an unconscionable loss of their economic independence. The U.S. Treasury accumulated three-fourths of the world's gold, denuding foreign markets of their ability to continue buying U.S. exports at their early postwar rates. . . . America's payments surplus position thus was threatening its prospective export potential.

. . . Beyond a point, a creditor and payments surplus status can be decidedly uncomfortable.

It was in America's enlightened self-interest to extend foreign aid program, perhaps under the emerging Cold War's military umbrella.

. . .

The other major obstacle to U.S. Government plans for the postwar world did not derive from foreign countries, but from Congress. Despite the overwhelming domestic benefits gained by foreign aid, Congress was unwilling to extend funds to impoverished countries as outright gifts, or even as loans beyond a point. The problem was not that it failed to perceive the benefits that would accrue from extending further aid, after the pattern of the British Loan and the subsequent Marshall Plan. It was just that Congress gave priority to domestic spending programs. What was at issue was not an abstract cost-benefit analysis for humanity at large, or even one of overall U.S. long-term interests, but one of parochial interests putting their local objectives ahead of foreign policy.

America Embarks on a Cold War That Pushes Its Balance of Payments into Deficit

As matters turned out, the line of least resistance to circumvent this domestic obstacle was to provide Congress with an anti-Communist national security hook on which to drape postwar foreign spending programs. Dollars were provided not simply to bribe foreign governments into enacting Open Door policies, but to help them fight Communism which might threaten the United States if not nipped in the bud. This red specter carried Marshall Aid through Congress, along with most subsequent aid lending down through the present day. Congress would not appropriate funds to finance a quasi-idealistic worldwide transition to laissez-faire, but it would provide money to contain Communist expansion, conveniently defined as being virtually synonymous with spreading poverty nurturing seedbeds of anti-Americanism.

The U.S. Government hoped to keep its fellow capitalist countries solvent. U.S. diplomats remembered the 1930s well enough to recognize that economies threatened with balance-of-payments insolvency would move to insulate themselves, foreclosing U.S. trade and investment opportunities accordingly.

. . .

Former U.S. Ambassador to Britain Joseph Kennedy was among the first to urge U.S. credits for that nation, "largely to combat communism." He even urged an outright gift, on the ground that Britain was for all practical purposes broke.

. . .

It was to become the political lever to extract U.S. foreign aid for the next two decades. International policies henceforth were dressed in anti-Communist garb in order to facilitate their acceptance by non-liberal congressmen whose sympathies hardly lay with the laissez-faire that had afforded the earlier window dressing for the government's postwar economic planning.

The problem from the government's point of view was that the U.S. balance of payments had reached a surplus level unattained by any other nation in history. It had an embarrassment of riches, and now required a payments deficit to promote foreign export markets and world currency stability. Foreigners could not buy American exports without a means of payment, and private creditors were not eager to extend further loans to countries that were not creditworthy.

The Korean War seemed to resolve this set of problems by shifting the U.S. balance of payments into deficit. Confrontation with Communism became a catalyst for U.S. military and aid programs abroad. Congress was much more willing to provide countries with dollars via anti-Communist or national defense programs and after the Korean War U.S. military spending in the NATO and SEATO countries seemed to be a relatively bloodless form of international monetary support. In country after country, military spending and aid programs provided a reflux of some of the foreign gold that the United States had absorbed during the late 1940s.

What at first seemed to be a stabilizing economic dynamic became destabilizing. The United States, the only nation capable of financing a worldwide military program, began to sink into the mire that had bankrupted every European power that experimented with colonialism. America's Cold War strategists failed to perceive that whereas private investment tends to be flexible in cutting its losses, being committed to relatively autonomous projects on the basis of securing a satisfactory rate of return year after year. . . . Such programs are by no means as readily reversible as those of private industry, for military spending abroad, once initiated, tends to take on a momentum of its own. The government cannot simply say that national security programs have become economically disadvantageous and therefore must be curtailed. That would imply they were pursued in the first place only because they were economically remunerative—something involving the sacrifice of human lives for the narrow motives of economic gain, even if national gain. What began as pretense became a new reality.

The New Characteristics of American Financial Imperialism

If the United States had continued to run payments surpluses, if it had absorbed more foreign gold and dollar balances, the world's monetary reserves would have been reduced. This would have constrained world trade, and especially imports from the United States. A US payments surplus was incompatible with continued growth in world liquidity and trade. The United States was obliged to buy more foreign goods, services and capital assets than it supplied to foreigners, unless they could augment monetary reserves with non-U.S. currencies.

What was not grasped was the corollary implication. Under the key-currency dollar standard the only way that the world financial system could become more liquid was for the United States to pump more dollars into it by running a payments deficit. The foreign dollar balances being built up as a result of foreign military and foreign aid spending in the 1950s and 1960s were, simultaneously, debts of the United States.

At first, foreign countries welcomed their surplus of dollar receipts. At the time there was no doubt that the United States was fully capable of redeeming these dollars with its enormous gold stock. But in autumn 1960 a run on the dollar temporarily pushed up the price of gold to $40 an ounce. . . . It became clear that just as the U.S. payments surplus had been destabilizing in the late 1940s, so in the early 1960s a U.S. payments deficit beyond a point likewise would be incompatible with world financial stability.

The run on gold had followed John Kennedy's victory in the 1960 presidential election, waged largely over a rather demagogic debate over military preparedness. It seemed unlikely that the incoming Democratic administration would do much to change the Cold War policies responsible for the U.S. payments deficit.

Growing attention began to be paid to the difference between domestic and international money. Domestic currency attempts by governments to repay their debts beyond a point would extinguish their monetary base. Back in the 1890s high U.S. tariffs produced a federal budget surplus that obliged the Treasury to redeem its bonds, causing a painful monetary deflation. But in the sphere of international money and credit, most investors expect debts to be paid on schedule.

. . . The problem is that international money (viewed as an asset) is simultaneously a debt of the key-currency nation. Growth in key-currency reserves accumulated by payments-surplus economies implies that the nation issuing the key currency acts in effect, and even in reality, as an international borrower. To provide other countries with key-currency assets involves running into debt, and to repay such debt is to extinguish an international monetary asset.

. . . By the early 1960s it became clear that the United States was approaching the point at which its debts to foreign central banks soon would exceed the value of the Treasury's gold stock. This point was reached and passed in 1964, by which time the U.S. payments deficit stemmed entirely from foreign military spending, mainly for the Vietnam War.

It would have required a change in national consciousness to reverse the military programs that had come to involve the United States in massive commitments abroad. America seemed to be succumbing to a

European-style imperial syndrome weighed down by the cost of maintaining its worldwide empire. As World Wars I and II had bankrupted Europe, so the Vietnam War threatened to bankrupt the United States.

If the United States had followed the creditor-oriented rules to which European governments had adhered after World Wars I and II, it would have sacrificed its world position. Its gold would have flowed out and Americans would have been obliged to sell off their international investments to pay for military activities abroad. This was what U.S. officials had demanded of their allies in World Wars I and II, but the United States was unwilling to abide by such rules itself. Unlike earlier nations in a similar position, it continued to spend abroad, and at home as well, without regard for the balance-of-payments consequences.

One result was a run on gold, whose momentum rose in keeping with sagging military fortunes in Vietnam. Foreign central banks cashed in their surplus dollars for U.S. gold reserves almost on a monthly basis.

Official reserves were sold to meet private demand so as to hold down the price of gold. . . . Two prices for gold emerged, a rising open-market price and the lower "official" price of $35 an ounce at which the world's central banks continued to value their monetary reserves.

In August 1971, President Nixon made the gold embargo official. The key-currency standard based on the dollar's convertibility into gold was dead. The U.S. Treasury bill standard—that is, the dollar-debt standard based on dollar inconvertibility—was inaugurated. Instead of being able to use their dollars to buy American gold, foreign governments found themselves able to purchase only U.S. Treasury obligations (and, to a much lesser extent, U.S. corporate stocks and bonds).

As foreign central banks received dollars from their exporters and commercial banks that preferred domestic currency, they had little choice but to lend these dollars to the U.S. Government. . . . The world's richest nation was enabled to borrow automatically from foreign central banks simply by running a payments deficit. The larger the U.S. payments deficit grew, the more dollars ended up in foreign central banks, which then lent them to the U.S. Government by investing them in Treasury obligations of varying degrees of liquidity and marketability.

The U.S. federal budget moved deeper into deficit inflating a domestic spending stream that spilled over to be spent on more imports and foreign investment and yet more foreign military spending to maintain the hegemonic system. But instead of U.S. citizens and companies being taxed or U.S. capital markets being obliged to finance the rising federal deficit, foreign economies were obliged to buy the new Treasury bonds being issued. America's Cold War spending thus became a tax on foreigners. It was

their central banks who financed the costs of the war in Southeast Asia.

There was no real check to how far this circular flow could go . . .

This shift from asset money (gold) to debt money (U.S. Government bonds) inverted the traditional relationships between the balance of payments and domestic monetary adjustment. Conventional wisdom prior to 1968 held that countries that ran deficits were obliged to part with their gold until they stemmed their payments outflows by increasing interest rates so as to borrow more abroad, cutting back government spending and restricting domestic income growth. . . .

The United States flouted this adjustment mechanism. It announced that it would not let its domestic policies be "dictated by foreigners." This go-it-alone policy had led it to refrain from joining the League of Nations after World War I, or to play the international economic game according to the rules that bound other nations. It had joined the World Bank and IMF only on the condition that it was granted unique veto power, which it also enjoyed as a member of the United Nations Security Council. No economic rules could be imposed that U.S. diplomats judged did not serve American interests.

These rules meant that the United States was able to pursue its Cold War spending in Asia and elsewhere in the world without constraint, as well as social welfare spending at home. This was just the reverse of Britain's stop–go policies or the austerity programs that the IMF imposed on Third World debtors when their balance of payments fell into deficit.

Thanks to the $50 billion cumulative U.S. payments deficit between April 1968 and March 1973, foreign central banks found themselves obliged to buy all of the $50 billion increase in U.S. federal debt during this period. In effect, the United States was financing its domestic budget deficit by running an international payments deficit. . . . Failure to absorb these dollars would have led the dollar's value to fall vis-à-vis foreign currencies, as the supply of dollars greatly exceeded the demand. A depreciating dollar would have provided U.S. exporters with a competitive devaluation, and also would have reduced the domestic currency value of foreign dollar holdings.

Foreign governments had little desire to place their own exporters at a competitive disadvantage, so they kept on buying dollars to support the exchange rate—and hence, the export prices—of Dollar Area economies. . . . Thanks to the extraordinary demand by central banks for government dollar-debt instruments, yields on U.S. Government bonds fell relative to those of corporate securities, which central banks did not buy.

This inverted the classical balance-of-payments adjustment mechanism, which for centuries had obliged nations to raise interest rates to attract foreign capital to finance their deficits. In America's case it was the balance-of-payments deficit that supplied the "foreign" capital, as foreign central banks recycled the dollar outflows—that is, their own dollar inflows—into Treasury securities. U.S. interest rates fell precisely because of the balance-of-payments deficit. The larger the balance-of-payments deficit, the more dollars foreign governments were obliged to invest in U.S. Treasury securities, financing simultaneously the balance-of-payments deficit and the domestic federal budget deficit.

The stock and bond markets boomed as American banks and other investors moved out of government bonds into higher-yielding corporate bonds and mortgage loans, leaving the lower-yielding Treasury bonds for foreign governments to buy. U.S. companies began to buy up lucrative foreign businesses. The dollars they spent were turned over to foreign governments, which had little option but to reinvest them in U.S. Treasury obligations at abnormally low interest rates. Foreign demand for these Treasury securities drove up their price, reducing their yields accordingly. This held down U.S. interest rates, spurring yet further capital outflows to Europe.

The U.S. Government had little motivation to stop this dollar-debt spiral. It recognized that foreign central banks hardly could refuse to accept further dollars, lest the world monetary system break down. Not even Germany or the Allies had thought of making this threat in the 1920s or after World War II, and they were not prepared to do it in the 1960s and 1970s. It was generally felt that such a breakdown would hurt foreign countries more than the United States. U.S. strategists recognized this, and insisted that the U.S. payments deficit was a foreign problem, not one for American citizens to worry about.

In the absence of the payments deficit, Americans themselves would have had to finance the growth in their federal debt. This would have had a deflationary effect. But under circumstances where growth in the national debt was financed by foreign central banks, a balance-of-payments deficit was in the U.S. national interest, for it became a means for the economy to tap the resources of other countries.

All the government had to do was to spend the money to push its domestic budget into deficit. Spending flowed abroad, both directly as military spending and indirectly via the overheated domestic economy's demand for foreign products, as well as for foreign assets. The excess dollars were recycled to their point of origin, the United States, spurring a worldwide inflation along the way. A large number of Americans felt they were getting rich from this inflation as incomes and property values rose.

. . .

This unique ability of the U.S. Government to borrow from foreign central banks rather than from its own citizens is one of the economic miracles of modern times. Without it the war-induced American prosperity of the 1960s and early 1970s would have ended quickly, as was threatened in 1973 when foreign central banks decided to cut their currencies loose from the dollar, letting them float upward rather than accepting a further flood of U.S. Treasury IOUs.

. . .

Implications for the Theory of Imperialism

It is not to the corporate sector that one must look to find the roots of modern international economic relations as much as to U.S. Government pressure on central banks and on multilateral organizations such as the IMF, World Bank and World Trade Organization. Already in the aftermath of World War I, but especially since the end of World War II, intergovernmental lending and debt relationships among the world's central banks have overshadowed the drives of private sector capital.

At the root of this new form of imperialism is the exploitation of governments by a single government, that of the United States, via the central banks and multilateral control institutions of intergovernmental capital rather than via the activities of private corporations seeking profits. What has turned the older forms of imperialism into a super imperialism is that whereas prior to the 1960s the U.S. Government dominated international organizations by virtue of its preeminent creditor status, since that time it has done so by virtue of its debtor position.

Confronted with this transformation of postwar economic relations, the non-Communist world seemed to have little choice but to move toward a defensive regulation of foreign trade, investment and payments. This objective became the crux of Third World demands for a New International Economic Order in the mid-1970s. But the United States defeated these attempts, in large part by a strengthening of its military power.

. . .

U.S. diplomats pressed foreign governments to regulate their nations' trade and investment to serve U.S. national objectives. Foreign economies were to serve as residual markets for U.S. output over and above domestic U.S. needs, but not to impose upon these needs by buying U.S. commodities in times of scarcity. When world food and timber prices exceeded U.S. domestic prices in the early 1970s, American farmers were ordered to sell their output at home rather than export it.

The United States thus imposed export controls to keep down domestic prices while world prices rose. In order that prices retain the semblance of stability in the United States, foreign governments were asked to suffer shortages and inflate their own economies. The result was a divergence between U.S. domestic prices and wages on the one hand, and worldwide prices and incomes on the other. The greatest divergence emerged between the drives of the U.S. Government in its worldwide diplomacy and the objectives of other governments seeking to protect their own economic autonomy. Protectionist pressures abroad were quickly and deftly defeated by U.S. diplomacy as the double standard implicit in the Washington Consensus was put firmly in place.

When the prices of U.S. capital goods and other materials exceeded world prices, for instance, the World Bank was asked (unsuccessfully) to apportion its purchases of capital goods and materials in the United States so as to reflect the 25 per cent subscription share of its stock. Japan was asked to impose "voluntary controls" on its imports of U.S. timber, scrap metal and vegetable oils, while restricting its exports of textiles, iron and steel to the United States. U.S. Government agencies, states and municipalities also followed "buy American" rules.

All this was moving in just the opposite direction from early idealistic postwar planners had anticipated. In retrospect they look like "useful fools" who failed to perceive who actually benefits from ostensibly cosmopolitan liberalism. In this regard today's laissez-faire and monetarist orthodoxy may be said to play the academic role of useful foolishness as far as U.S. diplomacy has been concerned. Reviewing the 1945 rhetoric about how postwar society would be structured, one finds idealistic claims emanating from the United States with regard to how open world trade would promote economic development. But this has not materialized. Rather than increasing the ability of aid borrowers to earn the revenue to pay off the debts they have incurred, the Washington Consensus has made aid borrowers more dependent on their creditors, worsened their terms of trade by promoting raw materials exports and grain dependency, and forestalled needed social modernization such as land reform and progressive income and property taxation.

Even as U.S. diplomats were insisting that other nations open their doors to U.S. exports and investment after World War II, the government was extending its regulation of the nation's own markets. . . .

World commerce has been directed by an unprecedented intrusion of government planning, coordinated by the World Bank, IMF and what has come to be called the Washington Consensus. Its objective is to supply the United States with enough oil, copper and other raw materials to produce a chronic over-supply sufficient to hold down their world price. The exception to this rule is for grain and other agricultural products exported by the United States, in which case relatively high world prices are desired. If foreign countries still are able to run payments surpluses under these conditions, as have the oil-exporting countries, their governments are to use the proceeds to buy U.S. arms or invest in long-term illiquid, preferably non-marketable U.S. Treasury obligations. All economic initiative is to remain with Washington Consensus planners.

U.S. officials created a Dollar Area more tightly controlled by their government than any prewar economy save for the fascist countries. By the mid-1960s the financing of overseas expansion of U.S. companies was directed to be undertaken with foreign rather than U.S. funds, and their dividend remission policies likewise were controlled by U.S. Government regulations overriding the principles of foreign national sovereignty. Overseas affiliates were told to follow U.S. Government regulation of their head offices, not that of governments in the countries in which these affiliates were located and of which they were legal citizens.

The international trade of these affiliates likewise was regulated without regard either for the drives of the world marketplace or the policies of local governments. U.S. subsidiaries were prohibited from trading with Cuba or other countries whose economic philosophy did not follow the Washington Consensus. Protests by the governments of Canada and other countries were overridden by U.S. Government pressure on the head offices of U.S. multinational firms.

Matters were much the same in the financial sphere. Although foreign interest rates often exceeded those in the United States, foreign governments were obliged to invest their surplus dollars in U.S. Treasury securities. The effect was to hold down U.S. interest rates below those of foreign countries, enabling American capital investments to be financed at significantly lower cost (and at higher price/earnings ratios for their stocks) than could be matched by foreign companies.

The U.S. economy thus achieved a comparative advantage in capital-intensive products not through market competition but by government intrusion into the global marketplace, both directly and via the Bretton Woods institutions it controlled. This intrusion often aimed at promoting the interests of U.S. corporations, but the underlying motive was the perception that the regulated activities of these companies promoted U.S. national interests, above all the geopolitical interests of Cold War diplomacy with regard to the balance of payments.

. . .

A century ago national states were permitted to exploit only their own citizens by creating money and credit. The unique feature of this new system is that governments in Europe and Asia, the Third World and the former Soviet sphere may now tap the wealth of their citizens, only to be tapped in turn by the imperial American center, which defies the world's creditor central banks to burst the international financial bubble and let the most open economies fall into bankruptcy. The U.S. economy remains the most self-reliant and hence readily able to insulate itself from any European and Asian breakdown, but the financial sector remains most highly leveraged, as it was in the 1920s. . . . The United States played both sides of the creditor/debtor street.

The way to break such financial dependency is to do what America itself did as the world's major debtor: default. This is what Europe did in 1931. But rather than taking this path, Third World countries (following the lead of General Pinochet's Chile and Mrs. Thatcher's Britain) have agreed to sell off their public utilities, fuel and mineral rights and other parts of their public domain. They are playing by the classical creditor rules, while America itself plays by new debtor rules against Europe and Asia. The euro for its part has not been created as a political reserve currency, but only as a unit of account to function as a satellite currency to the dollar. Russia's rouble likewise has been dollarized.

The upshot has been to create a system in which the dollar is artificially supported by central bank capital flows offsetting those of the private sector. Capital movements in turn have become the byproduct of increasingly unstable, top-heavy stock and bond markets. It is these capital movements—mainly debt service for many countries—that determine currency values in today's world, not relative commodity prices for exports and imports. The classical adjustment mechanism of interest rate and price changes thus have been unplugged by the Washington Consensus.

The World's Need for Financial Autonomy from Dollarization

. . .

The early system was supposed to grow stronger and stronger until it culminated in armed conflict, but economically developing the periphery in the process. But the tendency of today's Washington Consensus is to retard world development by loading down the economies of

almost every country with dollar-denominated debt, and to require America's own dollar debts as the medium to settle payments imbalances in every region. The upshot is to exhaust the system until local economies assert their own sovereignty and let the chips fall where they may.

In today's world the form of breakdown is likely to be financial, not military. Vietnam showed that neither the United States nor any other democratic nation ever again can afford the foreign exchange costs of conventional warfare, although the periphery still is kept in line by American military initiatives, most recently in Yugoslavia and Afghanistan. The lesson is that peace will be maintained by governments refusing the finance the military and other excesses of the increasingly indebted imperial power.

Yet Europe, Japan and some Third World countries have made only feeble attempts to regain control of their economic destinies since 1972, and since 1991 even Russia has relinquished its fuels and minerals, public utilities and the rest of the public domain to private holders. Its overhead in acquiescing to the Washington Consensus has been to sustain a capital flight of about $25 billion annually for the past decade. Asian and Third World countries have permitted their domestic debts to be denominated in dollars, despite the fact that domestic revenues accrue in local currencies. This creates a permanent balance-of-payments outflow as a result of the privatization sell-offs that provided governments with enough hard currency to keep current on their otherwise bad dollarized debts, but demand future interest and dividend remittances, while the state must tax labor, not these enterprises.

This is a system that cannot last. But what is to take its place?

If foreign economies are to achieve financial independence, they must create their own regulatory mechanisms. Whether they will do so depends on how thoroughly America has succeeded in making irreversible the super imperialism implicit in the Washington Consensus and its ideology.

Financial independence presupposes a political and even cultural autonomy.

. . .

The key to understanding today's dollar standard is to see that it has become a debt standard based on U.S. Treasury IOUs, not one of assets in the form of gold bullion. While applying creditor-oriented rules against Third World countries and other debtors, the IMF pursues a double standard with regard to the United States. It has established rules to monetize the deficits the United States runs up as the world's leading debtor, above all by the U.S. Government to foreign governments and their central banks.

The World Bank pursues its own double standard by demanding privatization of foreign public sectors, while financing dependency rather than self-sufficiency, above all in the sphere of food production. While the U.S. Government runs up debts to the central banks of Europe and East Asia, U.S. investors buy up the privatized public enterprises of debtor economies. Yet while imposing financial austerity on these hapless countries, the Washington Consensus promotes domestic U.S. credit expansion—indeed, a real estate and stock market bubble—untrammeled by America's own deepening trade deficit.

The early twenty-first century is witnessing the emergence of a new kind of centralized global planning. It is not by governments generally, as anticipated in the aftermath of World War II, but is mainly by the U.S. Government. Its focus and control mechanisms are financial, not industrial. Unlike the International Trade Organization envisioned in the closing days of World War II, today's WTO is promoting the interests of financial investors in ways that transfer foreign gains from trade to the United States, not uplift world labor.

MICHAEL HUDSON is a distinguished research professor of Economics at the University of Missouri, Kansas City (UMKC), and a professor of Economics at Peking University in China. Before moving into research and consulting, Prof. Hudson spent several years applying flow-of-funds and balance-of-payments statistics to forecast interest rates, capital, and real estate markets for Chase Manhattan Bank and The Hudson Institute. His academic focus has been on financial history and, since 1980, on writing a history of debt, land tenure, and related economic institutions from the Sumerian period, antiquity, and feudal Europe to the present.

James Monroe   **NO**

Transcript of Monroe Doctrine (1823)

At the proposal of the Russian Imperial Government, made through the minister of the Emperor residing here, a full power and instructions have been transmitted to the minister of the United States at St. Petersburg to arrange by amicable negotiation the respective rights and interests of the two nations on the northwest coast of this continent. A similar proposal has been made by His Imperial Majesty to the Government of Great Britain, which has likewise been acceded to. The Government of the United States has been desirous by this friendly proceeding of manifesting the great value which they have invariably attached to the friendship of the Emperor and their solicitude to cultivate the best understanding with his Government. In the discussions to which this interest has given rise and in the arrangements by which they may terminate the occasion has been judged proper for asserting, as a principle in which the rights and interests of the United States are involved, that the American continents, by the free and independent condition which they have assumed and maintain, are henceforth not to be considered as subjects for future colonization by any European powers . . .

It was stated at the commencement of the last session that a great effort was then making in Spain and Portugal to improve the condition of the people of those countries, and that it appeared to be conducted with extraordinary moderation. It need scarcely be remarked that the results have been so far very different from what was then anticipated. Of events in that quarter of the globe, with which we have so much intercourse and from which we derive our origin, we have always been anxious and interested spectators. The citizens of the United States cherish sentiments the most friendly in favor of the liberty and happiness of their fellow-men on that side of the Atlantic. In the wars of the European powers in matters relating to themselves we have never taken any part, nor does it comport with our policy to do so. It is only when our rights are invaded or seriously menaced that we resent injuries or make preparation for our defense.

With the movements in this hemisphere we are of necessity more immediately connected, and by causes which must be obvious to all enlightened and impartial observers. The political system of the allied powers is essentially different in this respect from that of America. This difference proceeds from that which exists in their respective Governments; and to the defense of our own, which has been achieved by the loss of so much blood and treasure, and matured by the wisdom of their most enlightened citizens, and under which we have enjoyed unexampled felicity, this whole nation is devoted. We owe it, therefore, to candor and to the amicable relations existing between the United States and those powers to declare that we should consider any attempt on their part to extend their system to any portion of this hemisphere as dangerous to our peace and safety. With the existing colonies or dependencies of any European power we have not interfered and shall not interfere. But with the Governments who have declared their independence and maintain it, and whose independence we have, on great consideration and on just principles, acknowledged, we could not view any interposition for the purpose of oppressing them, or controlling in any other manner their destiny, by any European power in any other light than as the manifestation of an unfriendly disposition toward the United States. In the war between those new Governments and Spain we declared our neutrality at the time of their recognition, and to this we have adhered, and shall continue to adhere, provided no change shall occur which, in the judgment of the competent authorities of this Government, shall make a corresponding change on the part of the United States indispensable to their security.

The late events in Spain and Portugal shew that Europe is still unsettled. Of this important fact no stronger proof can be adduced than that the allied powers should have thought it proper, on any principle satisfactory to themselves, to have interposed by force in the internal concerns of Spain. To what extent such interposition may be carried, on the same principle, is a question in which all independent powers whose governments differ from

Message of President James Monroe at the commencement of the first session of the 18th Congress (The Monroe Doctrine), 12/02/1823; Presidential Messages of the 18th Congress, ca. 12/02/1823-ca. 03/03/1825; Record Group 46; Records of the United States Senate, 1789–1990; National Archives.

theirs are interested, even those most remote, and surely none of them more so than the United States. Our policy in regard to Europe, which was adopted at an early stage of the wars which have so long agitated that quarter of the globe, nevertheless remains the same, which is, not to interfere in the internal concerns of any of its powers; to consider the government de facto as the legitimate government for us; to cultivate friendly relations with it, and to preserve those relations by a frank, firm, and manly policy, meeting in all instances the just claims of every power, submitting to injuries from none. But in regard to those continents circumstances are eminently and conspicuously different.

It is impossible that the allied powers should extend their political system to any portion of either continent without endangering our peace and happiness; nor can anyone believe that our southern brethren, if left to themselves, would adopt it of their own accord. It is equally impossible, therefore, that we should behold such interposition in any form with indifference. If we look to the comparative strength and resources of Spain and those new Governments, and their distance from each other, it must be obvious that she can never subdue them. It is still the true policy of the United States to leave the parties to themselves, in hope that other powers will pursue the same course . . .

JAMES MONROE was the fifth President of the United States, serving two terms from 1816 to 1825. His presidency is probably most well-known for the Monroe Doctrine, which made it official U.S. policy to treat colonization of land in North or South America by European powers as an act of aggression against the United States.

Carl Schurz October 18, 1899

Platform of the American Anti-Imperialist League

We hold that the policy known as imperialism is hostile to liberty and tends toward militarism, an evil from which it has been our glory to be free. We regret that it has become necessary in the land of Washington and Lincoln to reaffirm that all men, of whatever race or color, are entitled to life, liberty, and the pursuit of happiness. We maintain that governments derive their just powers from the consent of the governed. We insist that the subjugation of any people is "criminal aggression" and open disloyalty to the distinctive principles of our government.

We earnestly condemn the policy of the present national administration in the Philippines. It seeks to extinguish the spirit of 1776 in those islands. We deplore the sacrifice of our soldiers and sailors, whose bravery deserves admiration even in an unjust war. We denounce the slaughter of the Filipinos as a needless horror. We protest against the extension of American sovereignty by Spanish methods.

We demand the immediate cessation of the war against liberty, begun by Spain and continued by us. We urge that Congress be promptly convened to announce to the Filipinos our purpose to concede to them the independence for which they have so long fought and which of right is theirs.

The United States have always protested against the doctrine of international law which permits the subjugation of the weak by the strong. A self-governing state cannot accept sovereignty over an unwilling people. The United States cannot act upon the ancient heresy that might makes right.

Imperialists assume that with the destruction of self-government in the Philippines by American hands, all opposition here will cease. This is a grievous error. Much as we abhor the war of "criminal aggression" in the Philippines, greatly as we regret that the blood of the Filipinos is on American hands, we more deeply resent the betrayal of American institutions at home. The real firing line is not in the suburbs of Manila. The foe is of our own household.

The attempt of 1861 was to divide the country. That of 1899 is to destroy its fundamental principles and noblest ideals.

Whether the ruthless slaughter of the Filipinos shall end next month or next year is but an incident in a contest that must go on until the declaration of independence and the constitution of the United States are rescued from the hands of their betrayers. Those who dispute about standards of value while the foundation of the republic is undermined will be listened to as little as those who would wrangle about the small economies of the household while the house is on fire. The training of a great people for a century, the aspiration for liberty of a vast immigration are forces that will hurl aside those who in the delirium of conquest seek to destroy the character of our institutions.

We deny that the obligation of all citizens to support their government in times of grave national peril applies to the present situation. If an administration may with impunity ignore the issues upon which it was chosen, deliberately create a condition of war anywhere on the face of the globe, debauch the civil service for spoils to promote the adventure, organize a truth-suppressing censorship, and demand of all citizens a suspension of judgement and their unanimous support while it chooses to continue the fighting, representative government itself is imperiled.

We propose to contribute to the defeat of any person or party that stands for the forcible subjugation of any people. We shall oppose for re-election all who in the white house or in congress betray American liberty in pursuit of un-American ends. We still hope that both of our great political parties will support and defend the declaration of independence in the closing campaign of the century.

We hold with Abraham Lincoln, that "no man is good enough to govern another man without that other's consent. When the white man governs himself, that is self-government, but when he governs himself and also governs another man, that is more than self-government—that

Schurz, Carl. "The policy of imperialism" Address at The Anti-Imperialist Conference in Chicago, October 17, 1899.

is despotism." "Our reliance is in the love of liberty which God has planted in us. Our defense is in the spirit which prizes liberty as the heritage of all men in all lands. Those who deny freedom to others deserve it not for themselves, and under a just God cannot long retain it."

We cordially invite the co-operation of all men and women who remain loyal to the declaration of independence and the constitution of the United States.

CARL SCHURZ was a German revolutionary and an American statesman, journalist, and reformer. He emigrated to the United States after the German revolutions of 1848–1849 and became a prominent member of the new Republican Party.

John Hobson 1902

The Economic Bases of Imperialism

John A. Hobson, an English economist, wrote one the most famous critiques of the economic bases of imperialism in 1902.

Amid the welter of vague political abstractions to lay one's finger accurately upon any "ism" so as to pin it down and mark it out by definition seems impossible. Where meanings shift so quickly and so subtly, not only following changes of thought, but often manipulated artificially by political practitioners so as to obscure, expand, or distort, it is idle to demand the same rigour as is expected in the exact sciences. A certain broad consistency in its relations to other kindred terms is the nearest approach to definition which such a term as Imperialism admits. Nationalism, internationalism, colonialism, its three closest congeners, are equally elusive, equally shifty, and the changeful overlapping of all four demands the closest vigilance of students of modern politics.

During the nineteenth century the struggle towards nationalism, or establishment of political union on a basis of nationality, was a dominant factor alike in dynastic movements and as an inner motive in the life of masses of population. That struggle, in external politics, sometimes took a disruptive form, as in the case of Greece, Servia, Roumania, and Bulgaria breaking from Ottoman rule, and the detachment of North Italy from her unnatural alliance with the Austrian Empire. In other cases it was a unifying or a centralising force, enlarging the area of nationality, as in the case of Italy and the PanSlavist movement in Russia. Sometimes nationality was taken as a basis of federation of States, as in United Germany and in North America.

It is true that the forces making for political union sometimes went further, making for federal union of diverse nationalities, as in the cases of Austria, Hungary, Norway and Sweden, and the Swiss Federation. But the general tendency was towards welding into large strong national unities the loosely related States and provinces with shifting attachments and alliances which covered large areas of Europe since the breakup of the Empire. This was the most definite achievement of the nineteenth century. The force of nationality, operating in this work, is quite as visible in the failures to achieve political freedom as in the successes; and the struggles of Irish, Poles, Finns, Hungarians, and Czechs to resist the forcible subjection to or alliance with stronger neighbours brought out in its full vigour the powerful sentiment of nationality.

The middle of the century was especially distinguished by a series of definitely "nationalist" revivals, some of which found important interpretation in dynastic changes, while others were crushed or collapsed. Holland, Poland, Belgium, Norway, the Balkans, formed a vast arena for these struggles of national forces.

The close of the third quarter of the century saw Europe fairly settled into large national States or federations of States, though in the nature of the case there can be no finality, and Italy continued to look to Trieste, as Germany still looks to Austria, for the fulfillment of her manifest destiny.

This passion and the dynastic forms it helped to mould and animate are largely attributable to the fierce prolonged resistance which peoples, both great and small, were called on to maintain against the imperial designs of Napoleon. The national spirit of England was roused by the tenseness of the struggle to a self-consciousness it had never experienced since "the spacious days of great Elizabeth." Jena made Prussia into a great nation; the Moscow campaign brought Russia into the field of European nationalities as a factor in politics, opening her for the first time to the full tide of Western ideas and influences.

Turning from this territorial and dynastic nationalism to the spirit of racial, linguistic, and economic solidarity which has been the underlying motive, we find a still more remarkable movement. Local particularism on the one hand, vague cosmopolitanism upon the other,

Hobson, John Atkinson. Imperialism: A Study. United States: J. Pott, 1902.

yielded to a ferment of nationalist sentiment, manifesting itself among the weaker peoples not merely in a sturdy and heroic resistance against political absorption or territorial nationalism, but in a passionate revival of decaying customs, language, literature and art; while it bred in more dominant peoples strange ambitions of national "destiny" and an attendant spirit of Chauvinism.

No mere array of facts and figures adduced to illustrate the economic nature of the new Imperialism will suffice to dispel the popular delusion that the use of national force to secure new markets by annexing fresh tracts of territory is a sound and a necessary policy for an advanced industrial country like Great Britain . . .

But these arguments are not conclusive. It is open to Imperialists to argue thus: "We must have markets for our growing manufactures, we must have new outlets for the investment of our surplus capital and for the energies of the adventurous surplus of our population: such expansion is a necessity of life to a nation with our great and growing powers of production. An ever larger share of our population is devoted to the manufactures and commerce of towns, and is thus dependent for life and work upon food and raw materials from foreign lands. In order to buy and pay for these things we must sell our goods abroad. During the first three quarters of the nineteenth century we could do so without difficulty by a natural expansion of commerce with continental nations and our colonies, all of which were far behind us in the main arts of manufacture and the carrying trades. So long as England held a virtual monopoly of the world markets for certain important classes of manufactured goods, Imperialism was unnecessary."

After 1870 this manufacturing and trading supremacy was greatly impaired: other nations, especially Germany, the United States, and Belgium, advanced with great rapidity, and while they have not crushed or even stayed the increase of our external trade, their competition made it more and more difficult to dispose of the full surplus of our manufactures at a profit. The encroachments made by these nations upon our old markets, even in our own possessions, made it most urgent that we should take energetic means to secure new markets. These new markets had to lie in hitherto undeveloped countries, chiefly in the tropics, where vast populations lived capable of growing economic needs which our manufacturers and merchants could supply. Our rivals were seizing and annexing territories for similar purposes, and when they had annexed them closed them to our trade. The diplomacy and the arms of Great Britain had to be used in order to compel the owners of the new markets to deal with us: and experience showed that the safest means of securing and developing such markets is by establishing 'protectorates' or by annexation . . .

It was this sudden demand for foreign markets for manufactures and for investments which was avowedly responsible for the adoption of Imperialism as a political policy . . . . They needed Imperialism because they desired to use the public resources of their country to find profitable employment for their capital which otherwise would be superfluous . . .

Every improvement of methods of production, every concentration of ownership and control, seems to accentuate the tendency. As one nation after another enters the machine economy and adopts advanced industrial methods, it becomes more difficult for its manufacturers, merchants, and financiers to dispose profitably of their economic resources, and they are tempted more and more to use their Governments in order to secure for their particular use some distant undeveloped country by annexation and protection.

The process, we may be told, is inevitable, and so it seems upon a superficial inspection. Everywhere appear excessive powers of production, excessive capital in search of investment. It is admitted by all business men that the growth of the powers of production in their country exceeds the growth in consumption, that more goods can be produced than can be sold at a profit, and that more capital exists than can find remunerative investment.

It is this economic condition of affairs that forms the taproot of Imperialism. If the consuming public in this country raised its standard of consumption to keep pace with every rise of productive powers, there could be no excess of goods or capital clamorous to use Imperialism in order to find markets: foreign trade would indeed exist . . .

Everywhere the issue of quantitative versus qualitative growth comes up. This is the entire issue of empire. A people limited in number and energy and in the land they occupy have the choice of improving to the utmost the political and economic management of their own land, confining themselves to such accessions of territory as are justified by the most economical disposition of a growing population; or they may proceed, like the slovenly farmer, to spread their power and energy over the whole earth, tempted by the speculative value or the quick profits of some new market, or else by mere greed of territorial acquisition, and ignoring the political and economic wastes and risks involved by this imperial career. It must be clearly understood that this is essentially a choice of alternatives; a full simultaneous application of intensive and extensive cultivation is impossible. A nation may either, following the example of Denmark or Switzerland, put brains into agriculture, develop a finely varied system of public education, general and technical, apply the ripest science to its special manufacturing industries, and so support in progressive comfort and character a considerable population upon a strictly limited area; or it may, like Great Britain, neglect its agriculture, allowing its lands to go out of cultivation and its population to grow up in towns, fall behind other nations in its methods of education and in the capacity of adapting to its uses the latest scientific knowledge, in order that it may squander its pecuniary and military resources in forcing bad markets and finding speculative fields of investment in distant corners of the earth, adding millions of square miles and of unassimilable population to the area of the Empire.

The driving forces of class interest which stimulate and support this false economy we have explained. No remedy will serve which permits the future operation of these forces. It is idle to attack Imperialism or Militarism as political expedients or policies unless the axe is laid at the economic root of the tree, and the classes for whose interest Imperialism works are shorn of the surplus revenues which seek this outlet.

JOHN HOBSON was an English economist and social scientist. Hobson is best known for his writing on imperialism, which influenced Vladimir Lenin and informed his theory of under consumption.

EXPLORING THE ISSUE

Should We Understand Modern U.S. Imperial Power as Primarily Emerging from Its Financial Diplomacy following the World Wars?

Critical Thinking and Reflection

1. How has US imperialism evolved from the foundation of the country through today?
2. How was the United States able to create and modify economic system that allowed her to maintain imperial power without traditional conquest?
3. Should U.S. imperialism be seen as a global force for good? Why or why not?
4. Why do you think the United States shifted its imperial strategy at different points in her history?
5. What role do you believe the Monroe Doctrine and anti-imperialist league had in affecting US policy?

Is There Common Ground?

Without question, U.S. Empire has developed a complex structure with many nuances and has been present, to some degree, through the entirety of its history. To understand the nature of U.S. Empire requires inter-disciplinarily across the work of traditional historians, labor historians, political scientists, economists, and sociologists. It also calls us to seek out primary source documents that speak to the political identity and different types of imperial strategies used. These authors do just this, and together provide us a more complete picture of the evolution of the United States as a world power.

Michael Hudson's study provides many details about economic imperialism and its organization. However, he would likely argue that occupation, policy, and its economic basis have been a major part of the U.S. imperial project. The "NO" authors provide writings that suggest the US imperial spirit reached back to the founding of the nation. Though his assertion that the new economic imperialism represent how we ought to look at imperialism today, Hudson would likely agree that the historical authors provide us with a sense of how the conditions

for his theory developed. Given that these authors were writing before WW2, it is difficult to say how they would have understood the US imperial project. However, taking these writing together provides us a nuanced view of US imperialism.

Additional Resources

Burns, A. (2017). *American imperialism: the territorial expansion of the United States, 1783–2013*. Edinburgh University Press.

Suwandi, I. (2019) *Value chains: the new economic imperialism*. Monthly Review Press.

Immerwahr, D. (2019). *How to hide an empire: a history of the greater United States*. New York: Farrar, Straus and Giroux.

Perkins, J. (2016). *The new confessions of an economic hit man*. Oakland, CA: Berrett-Koehler Publishers.

Bender, D. & Lipman, J. (2015). *Making the empire work: labor and United States imperialism*. New York London: New York University Press.

Internet References . . .

Imperialism: Fordham University

https://sourcebooks.fordham.edu/mod/modsbook34.
asp#American%20Imperialism

Newspapers.com: Age of American Imperialism

https://www.newspapers.com/topics/american-imperialism/

Southern Connecticut State University: United States History - Primary Resources: American Imperialism

https://libguides.southernct.edu/c.
php?g=200161&p=1316579

White, H., & Langer, E. (2015, June 29). American Imperialism: This Is When It All Began.

Retrieved from https://www.thenation.com/article/american-imperialism-when-it-all-began/

Reform, War, and Depression

UNIT

Reform, War, and Depression

*T*he maturing of the industrial system, a major economic depression, agrarian unrest, and labor violence all came to a head in 1898 with the Spanish–American War. The progressives brought about major domestic reforms to ameliorate the worst abuses of rapid industrial growth and urbanization.

The United States entered World War I to assert its position as an imperialist player on the world stage. Progressive Era presidents advanced a proactive foreign policy, but the nation's role as a mediator of global conflicts was pushed to the limit when Woodrow Wilson tried and failed to get the United States to join the League of Nations at the end of World War I.

The end of the war brought on the "new era" of the 1920s, marked by political conservatism in the political arena, economic prosperity and the rise of a consumer culture, and what some have termed a "revolution of morals and manners." Within this rapidly changing environment, a new Ku Klux Klan appeared. There is controversy over whether the Klan created a climate of lawlessness in the 1920s or was primarily a mainstream organization committed to traditional white, middle-class, Protestant values. Common people and workers negotiate difference within this racist, sexist, and classist society that potentially led to an inability to develop more universal solidarity. Progressive Era reforms were powerful but perhaps resulted in versions of social movements that were contained by political power.

The rise of a more activist federal government accelerated with the Great Depression. In the midst of widespread unemployment, Franklin D. Roosevelt was elected on a promise to give Americans a "New Deal." Every sector of the economy was affected by the proliferation of the alphabet soup New Deal agencies, and historians continue to debate whether the New Deal measures ameliorated or prolonged the Great Depression or whether they were more beneficial to common people or Big Business.

The emergence of a conservative Congress and the impending world war killed the New Deal by 1939. With the fall of France to the Germans in 1940, FDR tried to abandon the traditional foreign policy of isolationism by aiding allies in Europe and Asia without involvement in the war. The effort failed, and on December 7, 1941, the Japanese attacked Pearl Harbor. At home, African Americans connected the struggle for democracy abroad to their own efforts to secure full citizenship rights in their own country. Again looking to increase its imperial sphere, World War II made the United States the dominant world power rivalled to a degree by the Soviet Union, as the United States became the "free" world's creditor. In return, she required access, influence, and the freedom to manipulate economic and political systems, while aligning other's interests to their own. The war also framed a debate over racial ideology in the United States, whereas the end of the war, through the introduction of weapons of mass destruction, not only introduced the world to the Atomic Age, but also produced a controversy involving the moral efficacy of deploying such weapons.

New forms of psychological propaganda were developed and deployed in mass media to ensure democratic ideals align with ruling class visions—a reality that continues to exist today as new forms of media arise. The propaganda and nationalism began to galvanize as the country entered and helped win the World War II.

Selected, Edited, and with Issue Framing Material by:
Kevin R. Magill and Tony L. Talbert, *Baylor University*

ISSUE

Did the Progressives Succeed?

YES: Ronald J. Pestritto and William J. Atto, from "Progressive Party Platform of 1912," Progressive Party National Convention (1912); **Woodrow Wilson**, from "The New Freedom," *Doubleday* (1913)

NO: Richard M. Abrams, from "The Failure of Progressivism," Little, Brown and Company (1971)

Learning Outcomes

After reading this issue, you will be able to:

- Define progressivism.
- List the supporters and opponents of progressivism.
- Distinguish between a progressive reformer and a progressive socialist.
- Critically evaluate progressivism's impact on today's society.

ISSUE SUMMARY

YES: Ronald J. Pestritto and William J. Atto provide significant evidence from the Progressive Party Platform of 1912 and Woodrow Wilson's 1913 campaign addresses demonstrating the impact of progressivism's influence of policy and practice throughout the 20th century and into the 21st century.

NO: Professor of history Richard Abrams maintains that progressivism was a failure because it tried to impose a uniform set of values upon a culturally diverse people and never seriously confronted the inequalities that still exist in American society.

Progressivism is a word used by historians to define the reform currents in the years between the end of the Spanish-American War and America's entrance into the Great War in Europe in 1917. The so-called progressive movement had been in operation for several decades before the label was first used in the 1912 electoral campaigns. Former President Theodore Roosevelt ran as a third-party candidate in the 1912 election on the Progressive party ticket, but in truth the party had no real organization outside of the imposing figure of Theodore Roosevelt. Therefore, as a label, "progressivism" was rarely used as a term of self-identification for its supporters. Even after 1912, it was more frequently used by journalists and historians to distinguish the reformers of the period from socialists and old-fashioned conservatives.

The 1890s was a crucial decade for many Americans. From 1893 until almost the turn of the century, the nation went through a terrible economic depression. With the forces of industrialization, urbanization, and immigration wreaking havoc upon the traditional political, social, and economic structures of American life, changes were demanded. The reformers responded in a variety of ways. The proponents of good government believed that democracy was threatened because the cities were ruled by corrupt political machines while the state legislatures were dominated by corporate interests. The cure was to purify democracy and place government directly in the hands of the people through such devices as the initiative, referendum, recall, and the direct election of local school board officials, judges, and U.S. senators. Social justice proponents saw the problem from a different perspective. Settlement workers moved into cities and tried to change the urban environment. They pushed for sanitation improvements, tenement house reforms, factory inspection laws, regulation of the hours and wages of women, and the abolition of child labor. Another group of reformers considered the major problem to be the trusts. They argued for controls over the power of big business and for the preservation of the free enterprise system. Progressives disagreed on whether the issue was size or conduct and on whether the remedy was trust-busting or the regulation of big business. But none could deny the basic question: How was the relationship between big business and the U.S. government to be defined?

How successful was the progressive movement? What triggered the reform impulse? Who were its leaders? How much support did it attract? More important, did the laws that resulted from the various movements fulfill the intentions of its leaders and supporters? Historians have generally been sympathetic to the aims and achievements of the progressive historians. Many, like Charles Beard and Frederick Jackson Turner, came from the Midwest and lived in model progressive states like Wisconsin. Their view of history was based on a conflict between groups competing for power, so it was easy for them to portray progressivism as a struggle between the people and entrenched interests.

It was not until after World War II that a more complex view of progressivism emerged. Richard Hofstadter's *Age of Reform* (Alfred A. Knopf, 1955) was exceptionally critical of the reformist view of history as well as of the reformers in general. Born of a mixed marriage with a Jewish immigrant mother and raised in Buffalo and New York City, the Columbia University professor argued that progressivism was a moral crusade undertaken by white Anglo-Saxon Protestant (WASP) families in an effort to restore older Protestant and individualistic values and to regain political power and status. Both Hofstadter's "status revolution" theory of progressivism and his profile of the typical progressive have been heavily criticized by historians. Nevertheless, he changed the dimensions of the debate and made progressivism appear to be a much more complex issue than had previously been thought.

Most of the writing on progressivism for the past 20 years has centered on the "organizational" model. Writers of this school have stressed the role of the "expert" and the ideals of scientific management as basic to an understanding of the progressive era. This fascination with how the city manager plan worked in Dayton or railroad regulation in Wisconsin or the public schools laws in New York City makes sense to a generation surrounded by bureaucracies on all sides. Two books that deserve careful reading are Robert Wiebe's *The Search for Order, 1877–1920* (Hill & Wang, 1967) and the wonderful collection of essays by Samuel P. Hays, *American Political History as Social Analysis* (University of Tennessee Press, 1980), which brings

together two decades' worth of articles from diverse journals that were seminal in exploring ethnocultural approaches to politics within the organizational model.

In a highly influential article written for the *American Quarterly* in spring 1970, Professor Peter G. Filene proclaimed "An Obituary for the 'Progressive Movement.'" After an extensive review of the literature, Filene concluded that since historians cannot agree on its programs, values, geographical location, members, and supporters, there was no such thing as a progressive movement. Few historians were bold enough to write progressivism out of the pantheon of American reform movements. But Filene put the proponents of the early 20th-century reform movement on the defensive. Students who want to see how professional historians directly confronted Filene in their refusal to attend the funeral of the progressive movement should read the essays by John D. Buenker, John C. Burnham, and Robert M. Crunden in *Progressivism*.

Three works provide an indispensable review of the literature of progressivism in the 1980s. Link and McCormick's *Progressivism* (Harland Davidson, 1983) deserves to be read in its entirety for its comprehensive yet concise coverage. More scholarly but still readable are the essays on the new political history in McCormick's *The Party Period and Public Policy: American Politics from the Age of Jackson to the Progressive Era* (Oxford University Press, 1986). The more advanced student should consult Daniel T. Rodgers, "In Search of Progressivism," *Reviews in American History* (December 1982). While admitting that progressives shared no common creed or values, Rodgers nevertheless feels that they were able "to articulate their discontents and their social visions" around three distinct clusters of ideas: "the first was the rhetoric of anti-monopolism, the second was an emphasis on social bonds and the social nature of human beings, and the third was the language of social efficiency."

In the first selection, Ronald J. Pestritto and William J. Atto provide significant evidence from the Progressive Party's platform of 1912 and Woodrow Wilson's 1913 campaign addresses demonstrating the impact of American progressivism's influence on policy and practice throughout the 20th century and into the 21st century. Pestritto's and Atto's representation of the actual reform minded scope of the 1912 Progressive Party platform demonstrates commitment of these middle-class reformers to bringing change to the American social, economic, and political landscape of the early 20th century. In addition to the bold agenda of the Progressive Party, the warnings and perhaps even the predictions offered by President

Woodrow Wilson (1913) in his *New Freedom* addresses speaks to a curious blending of aggressive social, economic, and political mandates while cobbling together shifting, even opposing, coalitions to bring about reforms.

As one reads the depth and breadth of reforms called for by the Progressive Party platform of 1912 and Wilson's on call for a *change to the old order* there is a sense of both urgency and commitment to preserving democracy through such social reforms as the elimination of child labor, the regulation of hours and working conditions, and the establishment of a minimum wage. Although as Neil A. Wynn (1986) asserts that some marginally reform-minded leaders in Wilson's sphere of influence were at time ambivalent in their attitude toward big business monopolies, the rank and file Progressive Party members demanded significant reforms as they called for the elimination, and at the very least the regulation, of business monopolies as the cure to America's ills. It is in this tension between radical reformers and business interests who benefitted from the inequities of economic power structures in early 20th-century American that Wilson would commit to a long-term vision of reform and restructuring of the American social, economic, and political landscape that is evident in 21st-century expansion of government influence in all segments of American society. It is in the presidential party platforms and candidates' addresses of the election of 1912 where we see the full spectrum of Woodrow Wilson's and Theodore Roosevelt's strategic positioning in framing the debate on the issues of size or conduct as the defining value proposition on whether large business monopolies should be broken up.

It is within both the nuanced and explicit arguments that Ronald J. Pestritto and William J. Atto offer support for their position on the success of the progressive movement as opposed to Richard Abrams who contends the inevitable failure of the progressive movement. Evidence of Progressivism's bold reforms in labor, safety, health, education, and social welfare programs are certainly prominent in the 21st-century American reality. Yet, lingering are the same issues of monopolies and so-called *too big to fail* business interests that dominant 21st-century banking, technology, energy, and perhaps more prominent than in the early 20th-century corruption of government via big business lobbyist interests. Ensconced in the contemporary contexts are Richard M. Abrams contention that the progressive movement has had little sustaining impact and thus must be considered a failure in meeting both the goals of the party's platform, circa 1912, and perhaps more important the movements philosophical vision.

Abrams' distinguishes the progressives from other reformers of the era such as the Populists, the Socialists, the mainstream labor unions, and the corporate reorganization movement. He argues that the progressive movement failed because it tried to impose a uniform set of middle-class traditional Protestant moral values upon a nation that was growing more culturally diverse, and that the reformers supported movements that brought about no actual changes or only superficial ones at best. The real inequities in American society, says Abrams, were never really addressed.

By 1910, says Abrams, xenophobic racism and nativism had blended with reform movements in the Far West and South. Restrictions limiting "coolie labor" and laws preventing African Americans from voting pushed the reformers to become more interested in controlling the behavior patterns of the working classes. Anti-Catholicism was also spreading, probably because of the large number of immigrants coming in from Southern and Eastern Europe. The more diverse the population, the harder it was to achieve a consensus of old-fashioned moral values. The Americanization and prohibition movements were speeded up by the United States' entrance into World War I. Since the German-Americans were the major beer brewers, the supporters of the Anti-Saloon League were able to push through Congress the Eighteenth Amendment prohibiting "the manufacture, sale or transportation of intoxicating liquors within, the importation . . . into or the exportation . . . from the United States." Many states forbade teaching the German language in the schools while grocery stores sold liberty burgers instead of hamburgers.

Abrams is particularly harsh in his criticism of the political and economic reforms of the period. Direct election of senators and legislators didn't prevent the wealthy from dominating the legislatives. The initiative and the referendum are devices used primarily by special interest groups to promote their agendas. Laws controlling the practices of the railroads didn't change the general rate structure until the 1940s. Farmers could mortgage their homes but they were still dependent upon bankers, middlemen, and the international market to make money. The Federal Reserve Act of 1913 didn't prevent the Depression of 1929 and the modification and strengthening of the Sherman Antitrust Act and the Federal Trade Commission have not seriously stopped the mergers of billion-dollar corporations.

So, the question remains, did the progressive movement succeed or fail? Perhaps the answer to this binary question cannot be fully answered when narrowly positing a "yes" or "no" response. Like most controversial issues that frame historical debates the depth and breadth of evidence must be contextualized. Pestritto's and Atto's representation of the Progressive Party platform of 1912 and Woodrow Wilson's 1913 *The New Freedom* addressed certainly offer compelling support for the lingering zeitgeist of progressivism in contemporary American society. Yet, Abrams' arguments against ultimate success of the progressive movement resonates true, given the same pernicious economic and social inequities and ubiquitous presence of big business interests in all sectors of government. History may indeed not repeat itself but the rhyme and reason certainly is familiar.

YES ⬅

Ronald J. Pestritto and William J. Atto

Progressive Party Platform of 1912

The conscience of the people, in a time of grave national problems, has called into being a new party, born of the nation's sense of justice. We of the Progressive party here dedicate ourselves to the fulfillment of the duty laid upon us by our fathers to maintain the government of the people, by the people and for the people whose foundations they laid.

We hold with Thomas Jefferson and Abraham Lincoln that the people are the masters of their Constitution, to fulfill its purposes and to safeguard it from those who, by perversion of its intent, would convert it into an instrument of injustice. In accordance with the needs of each generation the people must use their sovereign powers to establish and maintain equal opportunity and industrial justice, to secure which this Government was founded and without which no republic can endure.

This country belongs to the people who inhabit it. Its resources, its business, its institutions and its laws should be utilized, maintained or altered in whatever manner will best promote the general interest.

It is time to set the public welfare in the first place.

The Old Parties

Political parties exist to secure responsible government and to execute the will of the people.

From these great tasks both of the old parties have turned aside. Instead of instruments to promote the general welfare, they have become the tools of corrupt interests which use them impartially to serve their selfish purposes. Behind the ostensible government sits enthroned an invisible government owing no allegiance and acknowledging no responsibility to the people.

To destroy this invisible government, to dissolve the unholy alliance between corrupt business and corrupt politics is the first task of the statesmanship of the day.

The deliberate betrayal of its trust by the Republican party and the fatal incapacity of the Democratic party to deal with the new issues of the new time have compelled the people to forge a new instrument of government through which to give effect to their will in laws and institutions.

Unhampered by tradition, uncorrupted by power, undismayed by the magnitude of the task, the new party offers itself as the instrument of the people to sweep away old abuses, to build a new and nobler commonwealth.

A Covenant with the People

This declaration is our covenant with the people, and we hereby bind the party and its candidates in State and Nation to the pledges made herein.

The Rule of the People

The National Progressive party, committed to the principles of government by a self-controlled democracy expressing its will through representatives of the people, pledges itself to secure such alterations in the fundamental law of the several States and of the United States as shall insure the representative character of the government.

In particular, the party declares for direct primaries for the nomination of State and National officers, for nation-wide preferential primaries for candidates for the presidency; for the direct election of United States Senators by the people; and we urge on the States the policy of the short ballot, with responsibility to the people secured by the initiative, referendum and recall.

Nation and State

Up to the limit of the Constitution, and later by amendment of the Constitution, if found necessary, we advocate bringing under effective national jurisdiction those problems which have expanded beyond reach of the individual States.

It is as grotesque as it is intolerable that the several States should by unequal laws in matter of common concern become competing commercial agencies, barter the lives of their children, the health of their women and the safety and well-being of their working people for the benefit of their financial interests. . .

Progressive Party (Founded 1912). National Convention (1st : 1912 : Chicago)

Equal Suffrage

The Progressive party, believing that no people can justly claim to be a true democracy which denies political rights on account of sex, pledges itself to the task of securing equal suffrage to men and women alike.

Corrupt Practices

We pledge our party to legislation that will compel strict limitation of all campaign contributions and expenditures, and detailed publicity of both before as well as after primaries and elections.

Publicity and Public Service

We pledge our party to legislation compelling the registration of lobbyists; publicity of committee hearings except on foreign affairs, and recording of all votes in committee; and forbidding federal appointees from holding office in State or National political organizations, or taking part as officers or delegates in political conventions for the nomination of elective State or National officials.

The Courts

The Progressive party demands such restriction of the power of the courts as shall leave to the people the ultimate authority to determine fundamental questions of social welfare and public policy.

Administration of Justice

The Progressive party, in order to secure to the people a better administration of justice and by that means to bring about a more general respect for the law and the courts, pledges itself to work unceasingly for the reform of legal procedure and judicial methods . . .

Social and Industrial Justice

The supreme duty of the Nation is the conservation of human resources through an enlightened measure of social and industrial justice. We pledge ourselves to work unceasingly in State and Nation for:

Effective legislation looking to the prevention of industrial accidents, occupational diseases, overwork, involuntary unemployment, and other injurious effects incident to modern industry;

The fixing of minimum safety and health standards for the various occupations, and the exercise of the public authority of State and Nation, including the Federal Control over interstate commerce, and the taxing power, to maintain such standards;

The prohibition of child labor;

Minimum wage standards for working women, to provide a "living wage" in all industrial occupations;

The general prohibition of night work for women and the establishment of an eight hour day for women and young persons;

One day's rest in seven for all wage workers;

The eight hour day in continuous twenty-four hour industries;

The abolition of the convict contract labor system; substituting a system of prison production for governmental consumption only; and the application of prisoners' earnings to the support of their dependent families;

Publicity as to wages, hours and conditions of labor; full reports upon industrial accidents and diseases, and the opening to public inspection of all tallies, weights, measures and check systems on labor products;

Standards of compensation for death by industrial accident and injury and trade disease which will transfer the burden of lost earnings from the families of working people to the industry, and thus to the community;

The protection of home life against the hazards of sickness, irregular employment and old age through the adoption of a system of social insurance adapted to American use;

The development of the creative labor power of America by lifting the last load of illiteracy from American youth and establishing continuation schools for industrial education under public control and encouraging agricultural education and demonstration in rural schools;

The establishment of industrial research laboratories to put the methods and discoveries of science at the service of American producers;

We favor the organization of the workers, men and women, as a means of protecting their interests and of promoting their progress.

Country Life

The development and prosperity of country life are as important to the people who live in the cities as they are to the farmers. Increase of prosperity on the farm will favorably affect the cost of living, and promote the interests of all who dwell in the country, and all who depend upon its products for clothing, shelter and food.

We pledge our party to foster the development of agricultural credit and co-operation, the teaching of agriculture in schools, agricultural college extension, the use of mechanical power on the farm, and to re-establish the Country Life Commission, thus directly promoting the welfare of the farmers, and bringing the benefits of better farming, better business and better living within their reach.

High Cost of Living

The high cost of living is due partly to worldwide and partly to local causes; partly to natural and partly to artificial causes. The measures proposed in this platform on various subjects such as the tariff, the trusts and conservation, will of themselves remove the artificial causes.

There will remain other elements such as the tendency to leave the country for the city, waste, extravagance, bad system of taxation, poor methods of raising crops and bad business methods in marketing crops.

To remedy these conditions requires the fullest information and based on this information, effective government supervision and control to remove all the artificial causes. We pledge ourselves to such full and immediate inquiry and to immediate action to deal with every need such inquiry discloses.

Health

We favor the union of all the existing agencies of the Federal Government dealing with the public health into a single national health service without discrimination against or for any one set of therapeutic methods, school of medicine, or school of healing with such additional powers as may be necessary to enable it to perform efficiently such duties in the protection of the public from preventable diseases as may be properly undertaken by the Federal authorities, including the executing of existing laws regarding pure food, quarantine and cognate subjects, the promotion of vital statistics and the extension of the registration area of such statistics, and cooperation with the health activities of the various States and cities of the Nation.

Business

We believe that true popular government, justice and prosperity go hand in hand, and, so believing, it is our purpose to secure that large measure of general prosperity which is the fruit of legitimate and honest business, fostered by equal justice and by sound progressive laws.

We demand that the test of true prosperity shall be the benefits conferred thereby on all the citizens, not confined to individuals or classes, and that the test of corporate efficiency shall be the ability better to serve the public; that those who profit by control of business affairs shall justify that profit and that control by sharing with the public the fruits thereof.

We therefore demand a strong National regulation of inter-State corporations. The corporation is an essential part of modern business. The concentration of modern business, in some degree, is both inevitable and necessary for national and international business efficiency. But the existing concentration of vast wealth under a corporate system, unguarded and uncontrolled by the Nation, has placed in the hands of a few men enormous, secret, irresponsible power over the daily life of the citizen—a power insufferable in a free Government and certain of abuse.

This power has been abused, in monopoly of National resources, in stock watering, in unfair competition and unfair privileges, and finally in sinister influences on the public agencies of State and Nation. We do not fear commercial power, but we insist that it shall be exercised openly, under publicity, supervision and regulation of the most efficient sort, which will preserve its good while eradicating and preventing its ill.

To that end we urge the establishment of a strong Federal administrative commission of high standing, which shall maintain permanent active supervision over industrial corporations engaged in inter-State commerce, or such of them as are of public importance, doing for them what the Government now does for the National banks, and what is now done for the railroads by the Inter-State Commerce Commission.

Thus the business man will have certain knowledge of the law, and will be able to conduct his business easily in conformity therewith; the investor will find security for his capital; dividends will be rendered more certain, and the savings of the people will be drawn naturally and safely into the channels of trade.

We favor strengthening the Sherman Law by prohibiting agreement to divide territory or limit output; refusing to sell to customers who buy from business rivals; to sell below cost in certain areas while maintaining higher prices in other places; using the power of transportation to aid or injure special business concerns; and other unfair trade practices.

Currency

We believe there exists imperative need for prompt legislation for the improvement of our National currency system. We believe the present method of issuing notes through private agencies is harmful and unscientific.

The issue of currency is fundamentally a Government function and the system should have as basic principles soundness and elasticity. The control should be lodged with the Government and should be protected from domination or manipulation by Wall Street or any special interests.

We are opposed to the so-called Aldrich currency bill, because its provisions would place our currency and credit system in private hands, not subject to effective public control.

Commercial Development

The time has come when the Federal Government should co-operate with manufacturers and producers in extending our foreign commerce. To this end we demand adequate appropriations by Congress, and the appointment of diplomatic and consular officers solely with a view to their special fitness and worth, and not in consideration of political expediency.

It is imperative to the welfare of our people that we enlarge and extend our foreign commerce.

In every way possible our Federal Government should co-operate in this important matter. Germany's policy of co-operation between government and business has, in comparatively few years, made that nation a leading competitor for the commerce of the world.

Conservation

The natural resources of the Nation must be promptly developed and generously used to supply the people's needs, but we cannot safely allow them to be wasted, exploited, monopolized or controlled against the general good. We heartily favor the policy of conservation, and we pledge our party to protect the National forests without hindering their legitimate use for the benefit of all the people.

Agricultural lands in the National forests are, and should remain, open to the genuine settler. Conservation will not retard legitimate development. The honest settler must receive his patent promptly, without hindrance, rules or delays.

We believe that the remaining forests, coal and oil lands, water powers and other natural resources still in State or National control (except agricultural lands) are more likely to be wisely conserved and utilized for the general welfare if held in the public hands.

In order that consumers and producers, managers and workmen, now and hereafter, need not pay toll to private monopolies of power and raw material, we demand that such resources shall be retained by the State or Nation, and opened to immediate use under laws which will encourage development and make to the people a moderate return for benefits conferred.

In particular we pledge our party to require reasonable compensation to the public for water power rights hereafter granted by the public.

We pledge legislation to lease the public grazing lands under equitable provisions now pending which will increase the production of food for the people and thoroughly safeguard the rights of the actual homemaker. Natural resources, whose conservation is necessary for the National welfare, should be owned or controlled by the Nation.

Waterways

The rivers of the United States are the natural arteries of this continent. We demand that they shall be opened to traffic as indispensable parts of a great Nation-wide system of transportation, in which the Panama Canal will be the central link, thus enabling the whole interior of the United States to share with the Atlantic and Pacific seaboards in the benefit derived from the canal.

It is a National obligation to develop our rivers, and especially the Mississippi and its tributaries, without delay, under a comprehensive general plan covering each river system from its source to its mouth, designed to secure its highest usefulness for navigation, irrigation, domestic supply, water power and the prevention of floods.

We pledge our party to the immediate preparation of such a plan, which should be made and carried out in close and friendly co-operation between the Nation, the States and the cities affected.

Under such a plan, the destructive floods of the Mississippi and other streams, which represent a vast and needless loss to the Nation, would be controlled by forest conservation and water storage at the headwaters, and by levees below; land sufficient to support millions of people would be reclaimed from the deserts and the swamps, water power enough to transform the industrial standings of whole States would be developed, adequate water terminals would be provided, transportation by river would revive, and the railroads would be compelled to co-operate as freely with the boat lines as with each other.

The equipment, organization and experience acquired in constructing the Panama Canal soon will be available for the Lakes-to-the-Gulf deep waterway and other portions of this great work, and should be utilized by the Nation in co-operation with the various States, at the lowest net cost to the people.

Panama Canal

The Panama Canal, built and paid for by the American people, must be used primarily for their benefit.

We demand that the canal shall be so operated as to break the transportation monopoly now held and misused by the transcontinental railroads by maintaining sea competition with them; that ships directly or indirectly owned or controlled by American railroad corporations shall not be permitted to use the canal, and that American ships engaged in coastwise trade shall pay no tolls.

The Progressive party will favor legislation having for its aim the development of friendship and commerce between the United States and Latin-American nations.

Tariff

We believe in a protective tariff which shall equalize conditions of competition between the United States and foreign countries, both for the farmer and the manufacturer, and which shall maintain for labor an adequate standard of living.

Primarily the benefit of any tariff should be disclosed in the pay envelope of the laborer. We declare that no industry deserves protection which is unfair to labor or which is operating in violation of Federal law. We believe that the presumption is always in favor of the consuming public.

We demand tariff revision because the present tariff is unjust to the people of the United States. Fair dealing toward the people requires an immediate downward revision of those schedules wherein duties are shown to be unjust or excessive.

We pledge ourselves to the establishment of a non-partisan scientific tariff commission, reporting both to the President and to either branch of Congress, which shall report, first, as to the costs of production, efficiency of labor, capitalization, industrial organization and efficiency and the general competitive position in this country and abroad of industries seeking protection from Congress; second, as to the revenue producing power of the tariff and its relation to the resources of Government; and, third, as to the effect of the tariff on prices, operations of middlemen, and on the purchasing power of the consumer.

We believe that this commission should have plenary power to elicit information, and for this purpose to prescribe a uniform system of accounting for the great protected industries. The work of the commission should not prevent the immediate adoption of acts reducing these schedules generally recognized as excessive.

Inheritance and Income Tax

We believe in a graduated inheritance tax as a National means of equalizing the obligations of holders of property to Government, and we hereby pledge our party to enact such a Federal law as will tax large inheritances, returning to the States an equitable percentage of all amounts collected.

We favor the ratification of the pending amendment to the Constitution giving the Government power to levy an income tax.

Peace and National Defense

The Progressive party deplores the survival in our civilization of the barbaric system of warfare among nations with its enormous waste of resources even in time of peace, and the consequent impoverishment of the life of the toiling masses. We pledge the party to use its best endeavors to substitute judicial and other peaceful means of settling international differences.

We favor an international agreement for the limitation of naval forces. Pending such an agreement, and as the best means of preserving peace, we pledge ourselves to maintain for the present the policy of building two battleships a year.

Treaty Rights

We pledge our party to protect the rights of American citizenship at home and abroad. No treaty should receive the sanction of our Government which discriminates between American citizens because of birthplace, race, or religion, or that does not recognize the absolute right of expatriation.

The Immigrant

Through the establishment of industrial standards we propose to secure to the able-bodied immigrant and to his native fellow workers a larger share of American opportunity.

We denounce the fatal policy of indifference and neglect which has left our enormous immigrant population to become the prey of chance and cupidity.

We favor Governmental action to encourage the distribution of immigrants away from the congested cities, to rigidly supervise all private agencies dealing with them and to promote their assimilation, education and advancement.

Pensions

We pledge ourselves to a wise and just policy of pensioning American soldiers and sailors and their widows and children by the Federal Government. And we approve the policy of the southern States in granting pensions to the ex-Confederate soldiers and sailors and their widows and children.

Parcel Post

We pledge our party to the immediate creation of a parcel post, with rates proportionate to distance and service.

Civil Service

We condemn the violations of the Civil Service Law under the present administration, including the coercion and assessment of subordinate employees, and the President's refusal to punish such violation after a finding of guilty by his own commission; his distribution of patronage among subservient congressmen, while withholding it from those who refuse support of administration measures; his withdrawal of nominations from the Senate until political support for himself was secured, and his open use of the offices to reward those who voted for his renomination.

To eradicate these abuses, we demand not only the enforcement of the civil service act in letter and spirit, but also legislation which will bring under the competitive system postmasters, collectors, marshals, and all other non-political officers, as well as the enactment of an equitable

retirement law, and we also insist upon continuous service during good behavior and efficiency.

Government Supervision over Investments

The people of the United States are swindled out of many millions of dollars every year, through worthless investments. The plain people, the wage earner and the men and women with small savings, have no way of knowing the merit of concerns sending out highly colored prospectuses offering stock for sale, prospectuses that make big returns seem certain and fortunes easily within grasp.

We hold it to be the duty of the Government to protect its people from this kind of piracy. We, therefore, demand wise, carefully thought out legislation that will give us such Governmental supervision over this matter as will furnish to the people of the United States this much-needed protection, and we pledge ourselves thereto.

Conclusion

On these principles and on the recognized desirability of uniting the Progressive forces of the Nation into an organization which shall unequivocally represent the Progressive spirit and policy we appeal for the support of all American citizens, without regard to previous political affiliations.

RONALD J. PESTRITTO is the dean of the Graduate School of Statesmanship at Hillsdale College, and he holds the Charles and Lucia Shipley Chair in the American Constitution.

WILLIAM J. ATTO is an associate professor of History at the University of Dallas. Drs. Pestritto and Atto are the editors of the highly acclaimed book *American Progressivism: A Reader*.

Woodrow Wilson 1913

The New Freedom

Chapter 1. The Old Order Changeth

. . . nothing is done in this country as it was done twenty years ago. We are in the presence of a new organization of society. Our life has broken away from the past. The life of America is not the life that it was twenty years ago; it is not the life that it was ten years ago. We have changed our economic conditions, absolutely, from top to bottom; and, with our economic society, the organization of our life. The old political formulas do not fit the present problems; they read now like documents taken out of a forgotten age. The older cries sound as if they belonged to a past age which men have almost forgotten. Things which used to be put into the party platforms of ten years ago would sound antiquated if put into a platform now. We are facing the necessity of fitting a new social organization, as we did once fit the old organization, to the happiness and prosperity of the great body of citizens; for we are conscious that the new order of society has not been made to fit and provide the convenience or prosperity of the average man. The life of the nation has grown infinitely varied. It does not centre now upon questions of governmental structure or of the distribution of governmental powers. It centres upon questions of the very structure and operation of society itself, of which government is only the instrument. Our development has run so fast and so far along the lines sketched in the earlier day of constitutional definition, has so crossed and interlaced those lines, has piled upon them such novel structures of trust and combination, has elaborated within them a life so manifold, so full of forces which transcend the boundaries of the country itself and fill the eyes of the world, that a new nation seems to have been created which the old formulas do not fit or afford a vital interpretation of. We have come upon a very different age from any that preceded us. We have come upon an age when we do not do business in the way in which we used to do business—when we do not carry on any of the operations of manufacture, sale, transportation, or communication as men used to carry them on. There is a sense in which in our day the individual has been submerged. In most parts of our country men work, not for themselves, not as partners in the old way in which they used to work, but generally as employees—in a higher or lower grade—of great corporations. There was a time when corporations played a very minor part in our business affairs, but now they play the chief part, and most men are the servants of corporations.

You know what happens when you are the servant of a corporation. You have in no instance access to the men who are really determining the policy of the corporation. If the corporation is doing the things that it ought not to do, you really have no voice in the matter and must obey the orders, and you have oftentimes with deep mortification to co-operate in the doing of things which you know are against the public interest. Your individuality is swallowed up in the individuality and purpose of a great organization.

It is true that, while most men are thus submerged in the corporation, a few, a very few, are exalted to a power which as individuals they could never have wielded. Through the great organizations of which they are the heads, a few are enabled to play a part unprecedented by anything in history in the control of the business operations of the country and in the determination of the happiness of great numbers of people.

Yesterday, and ever since history began, men were related to one another as individuals. To be sure there were the family, the Church, and the State, institutions which associated men in certain wide circles of relationship. But in the ordinary concerns of life, in the ordinary work, in the daily round, men dealt freely and directly with one another. Today, the everyday relationships of men are largely with great impersonal concerns, with organizations, not with other individual men.

Now this is nothing short of a new social age, a new era of human relationships, a new stage-setting for the drama of life.

In this new age we find, for instance, that our laws with regard to the relations of employer and employee are in many respects wholly antiquated and impossible. They were framed for another age, which nobody now living remembers, which is, indeed, so remote from our life that

Hale, William Bayard, Wilson, Woodrow. The New Freedom: A Call for the Emancipation of the Generous Energies of a People. Germany: Doubleday, Page, 1913.

it would be difficult for many of us to understand it if it were described to us. The employer is now generally a corporation or a huge company of some kind; the employee is one of hundreds or of thousands brought together, not by individual masters whom they know and with whom they have personal relations, but by agents of one sort or another. Workingmen are marshaled in great numbers for the performance of a multitude of particular tasks under a common discipline. They generally use dangerous and powerful machinery, over whose repair and renewal they have no control. New rules must be devised with regard to their obligations and their rights, their obligations to their employers and their responsibilities to one another. Rules must be devised for their protection, for their compensation when injured, for their support when disabled.

There is something very new and very big and very complex about these new relations of capital and labor. A new economic society has sprung up, and we must effect a new set of adjustments. We must not pit power against weakness. The employer is generally, in our day, as I have said, not an individual, but a powerful group; and yet the workingman when dealing with his employer is still, under our existing law, an individual.

. . . Most of our laws were formed in the age when employer and employees knew each other, knew each other's characters, were associates with each other, dealt with each other as man with man . . . . Our modern corporations employ thousands, and in some instances hundreds of thousands, of men. The only persons whom you see or deal with are local superintendents or local representatives of a vast organization, which is not like anything that the workingmen of the time in which our laws were framed knew anything about. A little group of workingmen, seeing their employer every day, dealing with him in a personal way, is one thing, and the modern body of labor engaged as employees of the huge enterprises that spread all over the country, dealing with men of whom they can form no personal conception, is another thing.

. . . I want to record my protest against any discussion of this matter which would seem to indicate that there are bodies of our fellow-citizens who are trying to grind us down and do us injustice. There are some men of that sort. I don't know how they sleep o' nights, but there are men of that kind. Thank God, they are not numerous. The truth is, we are all caught in a great economic system which is heartless. The modern corporation is not engaged in business as an individual. When we deal with it, we deal with an impersonal element, an immaterial piece of society. A modern corporation is a means of co-operation in the conduct of an enterprise which is so big that no

one man can conduct it, and which the resources of no one man are sufficient to finance. A company is formed; that company puts out a prospectus; the promoters expect to raise a certain fund as capital stock. Well, how are they going to raise it? They are going to raise it from the public in general, some of whom will buy their stock . . . . Does the public deal with that president and that board of directors? It does not. Can anybody bring them to account? It is next to impossible to do so . . . . Do they even attempt to distinguish between a man's act as a corporation director and as an individual? They do not. Our laws still deal with us on the basis of the old system. The law is still living in the dead past which we have left behind. This is evident, for instance, with regard to the matter of employers' liability for workingmen's injuries. Suppose that a super[i]ntendent wants a workman to use a certain piece of machinery which it is not safe for him to use, and that the workman is injured by that piece of machinery. Some of our courts have held that the superintendent is a fellow-servant, or, as the law states it, a fellow-employee, and that, therefore, the man cannot recover damages for his injury. The superintendent who probably engaged the man is not his employer. Who is his employer? And whose negligence could conceivably come in there? The board of directors did not tell the employee to use that piece of machinery; and the president of the corporation did not tell him to use that piece of machinery . . . . Don't you see by that theory that a man never can get redress for negligence on the part of the employer? When I hear judges reason upon the analogy of the relationships that used to exist between workmen and their employers a generation ago, I wonder if they have not opened their eyes to the modern world. You know, we have a right to expect that judges will have their eyes open, even though the law which they administer hasn't awakened. Yet that is but a single small detail illustrative of the difficulties we are in because we have not adjusted the law to the facts of the new order.

Since I entered politics, I have chiefly had men's views confided to me privately. Some of the biggest men in the United States . . . are afraid of somebody, are afraid of something. They know that there is a power somewhere so organized, so subtle, so watchful, so interlocked, so complete, so pervasive, that they had better not speak above their breath when they speak in condemnation of it.

They know that America is not a place of which it can be said, as it used to be, that a man may choose his own calling and pursue it just as far as his abilities enable him to pursue it; because today, if he enters certain fields, there are organizations which will use means against him that will prevent his building up a business which they do not want to have built up; organizations that will see to it that the ground is cut from under him and the markets shut against him. For if he begins to sell to certain retail dealers, to any retail dealers, the monopoly will refuse to sell to those dealers, and those dealers, afraid, will not buy the new man's wares . . . no man is supposed to be under any limitation except the limitations of his character and of his mind; where there is supposed to be no distinction of class, no distinction of blood, no distinction of social status, but where men win or lose on their merits.

American industry is not free, as once it was free; American enterprise is not free; the man with only a little capital is finding it harder to get into the field, more and more impossible to compete with the big fellow. Why? Because the laws of this country do not prevent the strong from crushing the weak. That is the reason, and because the strong have crushed the weak the strong dominate the industry and the economic life of this country . . . any process of manufacture which has been taken under the control of large combinations of capital will presently find himself either squeezed out or obliged to sell and allow himself to be absorbed . . . it was meant to shut out beginners, to prevent new entries in the race, to prevent the building up of competitive enterprises that would interfere with the monopolies which the great trusts have built up.

The originative part of America, the part of America that makes new enterprises, the part into which the ambitious and gifted workingman makes his way up, the class that saves, that plans, that organizes, that presently spreads its enterprises until they have a national scope and character—that middle class is being more and more squeezed out by the processes which we have been taught to call processes of prosperity. Its members are sharing prosperity, no doubt; but what alarms me is that they are not *originating* prosperity. No country can afford to have its prosperity originated by a small controlling class. The treasury of America does not lie in the brains of the small body of men now in control of the great enterprises that have been concentrated under the direction of a very small number of persons. The treasury of America lies in those ambitions, those energies, that cannot be restricted to a special favored class. It depends upon the inventions of unknown men, upon the originations of unknown men, upon the ambitions of unknown men. Every country is renewed out of the ranks of the unknown, not out of the ranks of those already famous and powerful and in control.

There has come over the land that un-American set of conditions which enables a small number of men who control the government to get favors from the government . . .. Is that freedom? That is dependence, not freedom.

A corporation is very like a large tenement house; it isn't the premises of a single commercial family; it is just as much a public affair as a tenement house is a network of public highways. When you offer the securities of a great corporation to anybody who wishes to purchase them, you must open that corporation to the inspection of everybody who wants to purchase. There must, to follow out the figure of the tenement house, be lights along the corridors, there must be police patrolling the openings, there must be inspection wherever it is known that men may be deceived with regard to the contents of the premises. If we believe that fraud lies in wait for us, we must have the means of determining whether our suspicions are well founded or not.

One of the most alarming phenomena of the time—or rather it would be alarming if the nation had not awakened to it and shown its determination to control it—one of the most significant signs of the new social era is the degree to which government has become associated with business. I speak, for the moment, of the control over the government exercised by Big Business. Behind the whole subject, of course, is the truth that, in the new order, government and business must be associated closely. But that association is at present of a nature absolutely intolerable; the precedence is wrong, the association is upside down. Our government has been for the past few years under the control of heads of great allied corporations with special interests. It has not controlled these interests and assigned them a proper place in the whole system of business; it has submitted itself to their control. As a result, there have g[r]own up vicious systems and schemes of governmental favoritism (the most obvious being the extravagant tariff), far-reaching in effect upon the whole fabric of life, touching to his injury every inhabitant of the land, laying unfair and impossible handicaps upon competitors, imposing taxes in every direction, stifling everywhere the free spirit of American enterprise.

Now this has come about naturally; as we go on we shall see how very naturally. It is no use denouncing anybody, or anything, except human nature. Nevertheless, it is an intolerable thing that the government of the republic should have got so far out of the hands of the people; should have been captured by interests which are special and not general. In the train of this capture follow the troops of scandals, wrongs, indecencies, with which our politics swarm.

There are cities everywhere, in every part of the land, in which we feel that, not the interests of the public, but the interests of special privileges, of selfish men, are served; where contracts take precedence over public interest.

All over the Union people are coming to feel that they have no control over the course of affairs. I live in one of the greatest States in the union, which was at one time in slavery. Until two years ago we had witnessed with increasing concern the growth in New Jersey of a spirit of almost cynical despair. Men said: "We vote; we are offered the platform we want; we elect the men who stand on that platform, and we get absolutely nothing." So they began to ask: "What is the use of voting? We know that the machines of both parties are subsidized by the same persons, and therefore it is useless to turn in either direction."

This is not confined to some of the state governments and those of some of the towns and cities. We know that something intervenes between the people of the United States and the control of their own affairs at Washington. It is not the people who have been ruling there of late.

Why are we in the presence, why are we at the threshold, of a revolution? Because we are profoundly disturbed by the influences which we see reigning in the determination of our public life and our public policy. There was a time when America was blithe with self-confidence. She boasted that she, and she alone, knew the processes of popular government; but now she sees her sky overcast; she sees that there are at work forces which she did not dream of in her hopeful youth.

The old order changeth—changeth under our very eyes, not quietly and equably, but swiftly and with the noise and heat and tumult of reconstruction . . .

. . . We are in a temper to reconstruct economic society, as we were once in a temper to reconstruct political society, and political society may itself undergo a radical modification in the process. I doubt if any age was ever more conscious of its task or more unanimously desirous of radical and extended changes in its economic and political practice.

We stand in the presence of a revolution, not a bloody revolution; America is not given to the spilling of blood, but a silent revolution, whereby America will insist upon recovering in practice those ideals which she has always professed, upon securing a government devoted to the general interest and not to special interests.

We are upon the eve of a great reconstruction. It calls for creative statesmanship as no age has done since that great age in which we set up the government under which we live, that government which was the admiration of the world until it suffered wrongs to grow up under it which have made many of our own compatriots question the freedom of our institutions and preach revolution against them.

The whole stupendous program must be publicly planned and canvassed. Good temper, the wisdom that comes of sober counsel, the energy of thoughtful and unselfish men, the habit of co-operation and of compromise which has been bred in us by long years of free government, in which reason rather than passion has been made to prevail by the sheer virtue of candid and universal debate, will enable us to win through to still another great age without violence.

Chapter 2. What Is Progress?

The laws of this country have not kept up with the change of economic circumstances in this country; they have not kept up with the change of political circumstances; and therefore we are not even where we were when we started. We shall have to run, not until we are out of breath, but until we have caught up with our own conditions, before we shall be where we were when we started; when we started this great experiment which has been the hope and the beacon of the world. And we should have to run twice as fast as any rational program I have seen in order to get anywhere else.

I am, therefore, forced to be a progressive, if for no other reason, because we have not kept up with our changes of conditions, either in the economic field or in the political field. We have not kept up as well as other nations have. We have not kept our practices adjusted to the facts of the case, and until we do, and unless we do, the facts of the case will always have the better of the argument; because if you do not adjust your laws to the facts, so much the worse for the laws, not for the facts, because law trails along after the facts. Only that law is unsafe which runs ahead of the facts and beckons to it and makes it follow the will-o'-the-wisps of imaginative projects.

Business is in a situation in America which it was never in before; it is in a situation to which we have not adjusted our laws. Our laws are still meant for business done by individuals; they have not been satisfactorily adjusted to business done by great combinations, and we have got to adjust them. I do not say we may or may not; I say we must; there is no choice. If your laws do not fit your facts, the facts are not injured, the law is damaged; because the law, unless I have studied it amiss, is the expression of the facts in legal relationships. Laws have never altered the facts; laws have always necessarily expressed the facts; adjusted interests as they have arisen and have changed toward one another.

. . . The government, which was designed for the people, has got into the hands of bosses and their employers, the special interests. An invisible empire has been set up above the forms of democracy.

There are serious things to do. Does any man doubt the great discontent in this country? Does any man doubt that there are grounds and justifications for discontent? Do we dare stand still? Within the past few months we have witnessed (along with other strange political phenomena, eloquently significant of popular uneasiness) on one side a doubling of the Socialist vote and on the other the posting on dead walls and hoardings all over the country of certain very attractive and diverting bills warning citizens that it was "better to be safe than sorry" and advising them to "let well enough alone." Apparently a good many citizens doubted whether the situation they were advised to let alone was really well enough, and concluded that they would take a chance of being sorry. To me, these counsels of do-nothingism, these counsels of sitting still for fear something would happen, these counsels addressed to the hopeful, energetic people of the United States, telling them that they are not wise enough to touch their own affairs without marring them, constitute the most extraordinary argument of fatuous ignorance I ever heard. Americans are not yet cowards. True, their self-reliance has been sapped by years of submission to the doctrine that prosperity is something that benevolent magnates provide for them with the aid of the government; their self-reliance has been weakened, but not so utterly destroyed that you can twit them about it. The American people are not naturally stand-patters. Progress is the word that charms their ears and stirs their hearts.

There are, of course, Americans who have not yet heard that anything is going on. The circus might come to town, have the big parade and go, without their catching a sight of the camels or a note of the calliope. There are people, even Americans, who never move themselves or know that anything else is moving.

Now, movement has no virtue in itself. Change is not worthwhile for its own sake. I am not one of those who love variety for its own sake. If a thing is good today, I should like to have it stay that way tomorrow. Most of our calculations in life are dependent upon things staying the way they are . . . [many powerful men] have achieved their great success by means of the existing order of things and therefore they have been put under bonds to see that that existing order of things is not changed; they are bribed to maintain the *status quo* . . .

Progress! Did you ever reflect that that word is almost a new one? No word comes more often or more naturally to the lips of modern man, as if the thing it stands for were almost synonymous with life itself, and yet men through many thousand years never talked or thought of progress. They thought in the other direction. Their stories of heroisms and glory were tales of the past. The ancestor wore the heavier armor and carried the larger spear. "There were giants in those days." Now all that has altered. We think of the future, not the past, as the more glorious time in comparison with which the present is nothing. Progress, development, those are modern words. The modern idea is to leave the past and press onward to something new . . .

Are those thoughtful men who fear that we are now about to disturb the ancient foundations of our institutions justified in their fear? If they are, we ought to go very slowly about the processes of change. If it is indeed true that we have grown tired of the institutions which we have so carefully and sedulously built up, then we ought to go very slowly and very carefully about the very dangerous task of altering them. We ought, therefore, to ask ourselves, first of all, whether thought in this country is tending to do anything by which we shall retrace our steps, or by which we shall change the whole direction of our development?

I believe, for one, that you cannot tear up ancient rootages and safely plant the tree of liberty in soil which is not native to it. I believe that the ancient traditions of a people are its ballast; you cannot make a *tabula rasa* upon which to write a political program. You cannot take a new sheet of paper and determine what your life shall be tomorrow. You must knit the new into the old. You cannot put a new patch on an old garment without ruining it; it must be not a patch, but something woven into the old fabric, of practically the same pattern, of the same texture and intention. If I did not believe that to be progressive was to preserve the essentials of our institutions, I for one could not be a progressive . . .

The trouble with the theory is that government is not a machine, but a living thing. It falls, not under the theory of the universe, but under the theory of organic life . . .. Government is not a body of blind forces; it is a body of men, with highly differentiated functions, no doubt, in our modern day, of specialization, with a common task and purpose. Their co-operation is indispensable, their warfare fatal. There can be no successful government without the intimate, instinctive co-ordination of the organs of life and action. This is not theory, but fact and displays its force as fact, whatever theories may be thrown across its track. Living political constitutions must be Darwinian in structure and in practice. Society is a living organism and must obey the laws of life, not of mechanics; it must develop.

All that progressives ask or desire is permission—in an era when "development," "evolution," is the scientific word—to interpret the Constitution according to the Darwinian principle; all they ask is recognition of the fact that a nation is a living thing and not a machine . . .

The Declaration of Independence did not mention the questions of our day. It is of no consequence to us unless we can translate its general terms into examples of the present day and substitute them in some vital way for the examples it itself gives, so concrete, so intimately involved in the circumstanc[e]s of the day in which it was conceived and written. It is an eminently practical document, meant for the use of practical men; not a thesis for philosophers, but a whip for tyrants; not a theory of government, but a program of action. Unless we can translate it into the questions of our own day, we are not worthy of it, we are not the sons of the sires who acted in response to its challenge.

What form does the contest between tyranny and freedom take today? What is the special form of tyranny we now fight? How does it endanger the rights of the people, and what do we mean to do in order to make our contest against it effectual? What are to be the items of our new declaration of independence?

By tyranny, as we now fight it, we mean control of the law, of legislation and adjudication, by organizations which do not represent the people, by means which are private and selfish. We mean, specifically, the conduct of our affairs and the shaping of our legislation in the interest of special bodies of capital and those who organize their use. We mean the alliance, for this purpose, of political machines with selfish business. We mean the exploitation of the people by legal and political means. We have seen many of our governments under these influences cease to be representative governments, cease to be governments representative of the people, and become governments representative of special interests, controlled by machines, which in their turn are not controlled by the people . . .

Well, we are architects in our time, and our architects are also engineers. We don't have to stop using a railroad terminal because a new station is being built. We don't have to stop any of the processes of our lives because we are rearranging the structures in which we conduct those processes. What we have to undertake is to systematize the foundations of the house, then to thread all the old parts of the structure with the steel which will be laced together in modern fashion, accommodated to all the modern knowledge of structural strength and elasticity, and then slowly change the partitions, relay the walls, let in the light through new apertures, improve the ventilation; until finally, a generation or two from now, the scaffolding will be taken away, and there will be the family in a great building whose noble architecture will at last be disclosed, where men can live as a single community, co-operative as in a perfected, co-ordinated beehive, not afraid of any storm of nature, not afraid of any artificial storm, any imitation of thunder and lightning, knowing that the foundations go down to the bedrock of principle, and knowing that whenever they please they can change that plan again and accommodate it as they please to the altering necessities of their lives . . .

We said to all the world, "America was created to break every kind of monopoly, and to set men free, upon a footing of equality, upon a footing of opportunity, to match their brains and their energies" and now we have proved that we meant it.

WOODROW WILSON was an American academic and the 28th President of the United States of America (1913–1921). Wilson's academic and political writings advocating for popular democracy and progressive ideals has positioned him as a significant historical voice in the 20th and 21st centuries.

Richard M. Abrams → **NO**

The Failure of Progressivism

Our first task is definitional, because clearly it would be possible to beg the whole question of "failure" by means of semantical niceties. I have no intention of being caught in that kind of critics' trap. I hope to establish that there was a distinctive major reform movement that took place during most of the first two decades of this century, that it had a mostly coherent set of characteristics and long-term objectives, and that, measured by its own criteria—not criteria I should wish, through hindsight and preference, to impose on it—it fell drastically short of its chief goals.

One can, of course, define a reform movement so broadly that merely to acknowledge that we are where we are and that we enjoy some advantages over where we were would be to prove the "success" of the movement. In many respects, Arthur Link does this sort of thing, both in his and William B. Catton's popular textbook, *American Epoch,* and in his article, "What Happened to the Progressive Movement in the 1920s?" In the latter, Link defines "progressivism" as a movement that "began convulsively in the 1890s and waxed and waned afterward to our own time, to insure the survival of democracy in the United States by the enlargement of governmental power to control and offset the power of private economic groups over the nation's institutions and life." Such a definition may be useful to classify data gathered to show the liberal sources of the enlargement of governmental power since the 1890s; but such data would not be finely classified enough to tell us much about the *non*-liberal sources of governmental power (which were numerous and important), about the distinctive styles of different generations of reformers concerned with a liberal society, or even about vital distinctions among divergent reform groups in the era that contemporaries and the conventional historical wisdom have designated as progressive . . . .

Now, without going any further into the problem of historians' definitions which are too broad or too narrow—there is no space here for such an effort—I shall attempt a definition of my own, beginning with the problem that contemporaries set themselves to solve and that gave the era its cognomen, "progressive." That problem was *progress*—or more specifically, how American society was to continue to enjoy the fruits of material progress without the accompanying assault upon human dignity and the erosion of the conventional values and moral assumptions on which the social order appeared to rest . . ..

To put it briefly and yet more specifically, a very large body of men and women entered into reform activities at the end of the nineteenth century to translate "the national credo" (as Henry May calls it) into a general program for social action. Their actions, according to Richard Hofstadter, were "founded upon the indigenous Yankee-Protestant political tradition [that] assumed and demanded the constant disinterested activity of the citizen in public affairs, argued that political life ought to be run, to a greater degree than it was, in accordance with general principles and abstract laws apart from and superior to personal needs, and expressed a common feeling that government should be in good part an effort to moralize the lives of individuals while economic life should be intimately related to the stimulation and development of individual character."

The most consistently important reform impulse, among many reform impulses, during the progressive era grew directly from these considerations. It is this reform thrust that we should properly call "the progressive movement." We should distinguish it carefully from reform movements in the era committed primarily to other considerations.

The progressive movement drew its strength from the old mugwump reform impulse, civil service reform, female emancipationists, prohibitionists, the social gospel, the settlement-house movement, some national expansionists, some world peace advocates, conservation advocates, technical efficiency experts, and a wide variety of intellectuals who helped cut through the stifling, obstructionist smokescreen of systematized ignorance. It gained powerful allies from many disadvantaged business interests that appealed to politics to redress unfavorable trade positions; from some ascendant business interests seeking institutional protection; from publishers who discovered the promotional value of exposes; and from politicians-on-the-make who sought issues with which to dislodge long-lived incumbents from their place. Objectively it focused on or expressed (1) a concern for responsive, honest, and efficient government, on the local and state levels especially; (2) recognition of the obligations of society—particularly of an affluent society—to its underprivileged; (3) a desire for more rational use of the nation's resources and economic energies; (4) a rejection, on at least intellectual grounds, of certain social principles that had long obstructed social remedies for what had traditionally been regarded as irremediable evils, such as poverty; and, above all, (5) a concern for the maintenance or restoration of a consensus on what conventionally had been regarded as *fixed moral* principles. "The first and central faith in the national credo," writes Professor May, "was, as it always had been, the reality, certainty, and eternity of moral values . . . .. A few thought and said that ultimate values and goals were unnecessary, but in most cases this meant that they believed so deeply in a consensus on these matters that they could not imagine a serious challenge." Progressives shared this faith with most of the rest of the country, but they also conceived of themselves, with a grand sense of stewardship, as its heralds, and its agents.

The progressive movement was (and is) distinguishable from other contemporary reform movements not only by its devotion to social conditions regarded, by those within it as well as by much of the generality, as *normative,* but also by its definition of what forces threatened that order. More specifically, progressivism directed its shafts at five principal enemies, each in its own way representing reform:

1. The *socialist reform movement*—because, despite socialism's usually praiseworthy concern for human dignity, it represented the subordination of the rights of private property and of individualistic options to objectives that often explicitly threatened common religious beliefs and conventional standards of justice and excellence.

2. The corporate reorganization of American business, which I should call the *corporate reform movement* (its consequence has, after all, been called "the corporate revolution")—because it challenged the traditional relationship of ownership and control of private property, because it represented a shift from production

to profits in the entrepreneurial definition of efficiency, because it threatened the proprietary small-business character of the American social structure, because it had already demonstrated a capacity for highly concentrated and socially irresponsible power, and because it sanctioned practices that strained the limits of conventionality and even legality.

3. *The labor union movement*—because despite the virtues of unionized labor as a source of countervailing force against the corporations and as a basis for a more orderly labor force, unionism (like corporate capitalism and socialism) suggested a reduction of individualistic options (at least for wage-earners and especially for small employers), and a demand for a partnership with business management in the decision-making process by a class that convention excluded from such a role.

4. *Agrarian radicalism,* and populism in particular—because it, too, represented (at least in appearance) the insurgency of a class conventionally believed to be properly excluded from a policy-making role in the society, a class graphically represented by the "Pitchfork" Bens and "Sockless" Jerrys, the "Cyclone" Davises and "Alfalfa" Bills, the wool hat brigade and the rednecks.

5. *The ethnic movement*—the demand for specific political and social recognition of ethnic or ex-national affiliations—because accession to the demand meant acknowledgment of the fragmentation of American society as well as a retreat from official standards of integrity, honesty, and efficiency in government in favor of standards based on personal loyalty, partisanship, and sectarian provincialism.

Probably no two progressives opposed all of these forces with equal animus, and most had a noteworthy sympathy for one or more of them . . . ..

So much for what progressivism was not. Let me sum it up by noting that what it rejected and sought to oppose necessarily says much about what it was—perhaps even more than can be ascertained by the more direct approach.

My thesis is that progressivism failed. It failed in what it—or what those who shaped it—conceived to be its principal objective. And that was, over and above everything else, to restore or maintain the conventional consensus on a particular view of the universe, a particular set of values, and a particular constellation of behavioral modes in the country's commerce, its industry, its social relations, and its politics. Such a view, such values, such modes were challenged by the influx of diverse religious and ethnic elements into the nation's social and intellectual stream, by the overwhelming economic success and power of the corporate form of business organization, by the subordination of the work-ethic bound up within the old proprietary and craft enterprise system, and by the increasing centrality of a growing proportion of low-income, unskilled, wage-earning classes in the nation's economy and social structure. Ironically, the *coup de grâce* would be struck by the emergence of a philosophical and scientific rationale for the existence of cultural diversity within a single social system, a rationale that largely grew out of the very intellectual ferment to which progressivism so substantially contributed.

Progressivism sought to save the old view, and the old values and modes, by educating the immigrants and the poor so as to facilitate their acceptance of and absorption into the Anglo-American mode of life, or by excluding the "unassimilable" altogether; by instituting antitrust legislation or, at the least, by imposing regulations upon corporate practices in order to preserve a minimal base for small proprietary business enterprise; by making legislative accommodations to the newly important wage-earning classes—accommodations that might provide some measure of wealth and income redistribution, on-the-job safety, occupational security, and the like—so as to forestall a forcible transfer of policy-making power away from the groups that had conventionally exercised that power; and by broadening the political selection process, through direct elections, direct nominations, and direct legislation, in order to reduce tensions caused unnecessarily by excessively narrow and provincial cliques of policy-makers. When the economic and political reforms failed to restore the consensus by giving the previously unprivileged an ostensible stake in it, progressive energies turned increasingly toward using the force of the state to proscribe or restrict specifically opprobrious modes of social behavior, such as gaming habits, drinking habits, sexual habits, and Sabbatarian habits. In the ultimate resort, with the proliferation of sedition and criminal syndicalist laws, it sought to constrict political discourse itself. And (except perhaps for the disintegration of the socialist movement) *that* failed, too.

One measure of progressivism's failure lies in the xenophobic racism that reappeared on a large scale even by 1910. In many parts of the country, for example, in the far west and the south, racism and nativism had been fully blended with reform movements even at the height of progressive activities there. The alleged threats of "coolie labor" to American living standards, and of "venal" immigrant and Negro voting to republican institutions

generally, underlay the alliance of racism and reform in this period. By and large, however, for the early progressive era the alliance was conspicuous only in the south and on the west coast. By 1910, signs of heightening ethnic animosities, most notably anti-Catholicism, began appearing in other areas of the country as well. As John Higham has written, "It is hard to explain the rebirth of anti-Catholic ferment [at this time] except as an outlet for expectations which progressivism raised and then failed to fulfill." The failure here was in part the inability of reform to deliver a meaningful share of the social surplus to the groups left out of the general national progress, and in part the inability of reform to achieve its objective of assimilation and consensus.

The growing ethnic animus, moreover, operated to compound the difficulty of achieving assimilation. By the second decade of the century, the objects of the antagonism were beginning to adopt a frankly assertive posture. The World War, and the ethnic cleavages it accentuated and aggravated, represented only the final blow to the assimilationist idea; "hyphenate" tendencies had already been growing during the years before 1914. It had only been in 1905 that the Louisville-born and secular-minded Louis Brandeis had branded as "disloyal" all who "keep alive" their differences of origin or religion. By 1912, by now a victim of anti-Semitism and aware of a rising hostility toward Jews in the country, Brandeis had become an active Zionist; before a Jewish audience in 1913, he remarked how "practical experience" had convinced him that "to be good Americans, we must be better Jews, and to be better Jews, we must become Zionists."

Similarly, American Negroes also began to adopt a more aggressive public stance after having been subdued for more than a decade by antiblack violence and the accommodationist tactics suggested in 1895 by Booker T. Washington. As early as 1905, many black leaders had broken with Washington in founding the Niagara Movement for a more vigorous assertion of Negro demands for equality. But most historians seem to agree that it was probably the Springfield race riot of 1908 that ended illusions that black people could gain an equitable share in the rewards of American culture by accommodationist or assimilationist methods. The organization of the NAACP in 1909 gave substantive force for the first time to the three-year-old Niagara Movement. The year 1915 symbolically concluded the demise of accommodationism. That year, the Negro-baiting movie, "The Birth of a Nation," played to massive, enthusiastic audiences that included notably the president of the United States and the chief justice of the Supreme Court; the KKK was revived; and Booker T. Washington died. The next year, black nationalist Marcus Garvey arrived in New York from Jamaica.

Meanwhile, scientific knowledge about race and culture was undergoing a crucial revision. At least in small part stimulated by a keen self-consciousness of his own "outsider" status in American culture, the German-Jewish immigrant Franz Boas was pioneering in the new anthropological concept of "cultures," based on the idea that human behavioral traits are conditioned by historical traditions. The new view of culture was in time to undermine completely the prevailing evolutionary view that ethnic differences must mean racial inequality. The significance of Boas's work after 1910, and that of his students A. L. Kroeber and Clyde Kluckhohn in particular, rests on the fact that the racist thought of the progressive era had founded its intellectual rationale on the monistic, evolutionary view of culture; and indeed much of the progressives' anxiety over the threatened demise of "the American culture" had been founded on that view.

Other intellectual developments as well had for a long time been whittling away at the notion that American society had to stand or fall on the unimpaired coherence of its cultural consensus. Yet the new work in anthropology, law, philosophy, physics, psychology, and literature only unwittingly undermined that assumption. Rather, it was only as the ethnic hostilities grew, and especially as the power of the state came increasingly to be invoked against dissenting groups whose ethnic "peculiarities" provided an excuse for repression, that the new intelligence came to be developed. "The world has thought that it must have its culture and its political unity coincide," wrote Randolph Bourne in 1916 while chauvinism, nativism, and antiradicalism were mounting; now it was seeing that cultural diversity might yet be the salvation of the liberal society—that it might even serve to provide the necessary countervailing force to the power of the state that private property had once served (in the schema of Locke, Harrington, and Smith) before the interests of private property became so highly concentrated and so well blended with the state itself.

The telltale sign of progressivism's failure was the violent crusade against dissent that took place in the closing years of the Wilson administration. It is too easy to ascribe the literal hysteria of the postwar years to the dislocations of the War alone. Incidents of violent repression of labor and radical activities had been growing remarkably, often in step with xenophobic outbreaks, for several years before America's intervention in the War. To quote Professor Higham once more. "The seemingly

unpropitious circumstances under which antiradicalism and anti-Catholicism came to life [after 1910] make their renewal a subject of moment." It seems clear that they both arose out of the sources of the reform ferment itself. When reform failed to enlarge the consensus, or to make it more relevant to the needs of the still disadvantaged and disaffected, and when in fact reform seemed to be encouraging more radical challenges to the social order, the old anxieties of the 1890s returned.

The postwar hysteria represented a reaction to a confluence of anxiety-laden developments, including the high cost of living, the physical and social dislocations of war mobilization and the recruitment of women and Negroes into war production jobs in the big northern cities, the Bolshevik Revolution, a series of labor strikes, and a flood of radical literature that exaggerated the capabilities of radical action. "One Hundred Per Cent Americanism" seemed the only effective way of meeting all these challenges at once. As Stanley Coben has written, making use of recent psychological studies and anthropological work on cultural "revitalization movements"; "Citizens who joined the crusade for one hundred per cent Americanism sought, primarily, a unifying forte which would halt the apparent disintegration of their culture . . .. The slight evidence of danger from radical organizations aroused such wild fear only because Americans had already encountered other threats to cultural stability."

Now, certainly during the progressive era a lot of reform legislation was passed, much that contributed genuinely to a more liberal society, though more that contributed to the more absolutistic moral objectives of progressivism. Progressivism indeed had real, lasting effects for the blunting of the sharper edges of self-interest in American life, and for the reduction of the harsher cruelties suffered by the society's underprivileged. These achievements deserve emphasis, not least because they derived directly from the progressive habit of looking to standards of conventional morality and human decency for the solution of diverse social conflicts. But the deeper nature of the problem confronting American society required more than the invocation of conventional standards; the conventions themselves were at stake, especially as they bore upon the allocation of privileges and rewards. Because most of the progressives never confronted that problem, in a way their efforts were doomed to failure.

In sum, the overall effect of the period's legislation is not so impressive. For example, all the popular government measures put together have not conspicuously raised the quality of American political life. Direct nominations and elections have tended to make political campaigns so expensive as to reduce the number of eligible candidates for public office to (1) the independently wealthy; (2) the ideologues, especially on the right, who can raise the needed campaign money from independently wealthy ideologues like themselves, or from the organizations set up to promote a particular ideology; and (3) party hacks who pay off their debt to the party treasury by whistle-stopping and chicken dinner speeches. Direct legislation through the Initiative and Referendum device has made cities and states prey to the best-financed and organized special-interest group pressures, as have so-called nonpartisan elections. Which is not to say that things are worse than before, but only that they are not conspicuously better. The popular government measures did have the effect of shaking up the established political organizations of the day, and that may well have been their only real purpose.

But as Arthur Link has said, in his text, *The American Epoch*, the popular government measures "were merely instruments to facilitate the capture of political machinery. . . . They must be judged for what they accomplished or failed to accomplish on the higher level of substantive reform." Without disparaging the long list of reform measures that passed during the progressive era, the question remains whether all the "substantive reforms" together accomplished what the progressives wanted them to accomplish.

Certain social and economic advantages were indeed shuffled about, but this must be regarded as a short-term achievement for special groups at best. Certain commercial interests, for example, achieved greater political leverage in railroad policy-making than they had had in 1900 through measures such as the Hepburn and Mann-Elkins Acts—though it was not until the 1940s that any real change occurred in the general rate structure, as some broad regional interests had been demanding at the beginning of the century. Warehouse, farm credits, and land-bank acts gave the diminishing numbers of farm owners enhanced opportunities to mortgage their property, and some business groups had persuaded the federal government to use national revenues to educate farmers on how to increase their productivity (Smith-Lever Act, 1914); but most farmers remained as dependent as ever upon forces beyond their control—the bankers, the middlemen, the international market. The FTC, and the Tariff Commission established in 1916, extended the principle of using government agencies to adjudicate intra-industrial conflicts ostensibly in the national interest, but these agencies would develop a lamentable tendency of deferring to and even confirming rather than moderating the power of each industry's dominant interests.

The Federal Reserve Act made the currency more flexible, and that certainly made more sense than the old system, as even the bankers agreed. But depositers would be as prey to defaulting banks as they had been in the days of the Pharaoh—bank deposit insurance somehow was "socialism" to even the best of men in this generation. And despite Woodrow Wilson's brave promise to end the banker's stifling hold on innovative small business, one searches in vain for some provision in the FRA designed specifically to encourage small or new businesses. In fact, the only constraints on the bankers' power that emerged from the era came primarily from the ability of the larger corporations to finance their own expansion out of capital surpluses they had accumulated from extortionate profits during the War.

A major change almost occurred during the war years when organized labor and the principle of collective bargaining received official recognition and a handful of labor leaders was taken, temporarily, into policy-making councils (e.g., in the War Labor Board). But actually, as already indicated, such a development, if it had been made permanent, would have represented a defeat, not a triumph, for progressivism. The progressives may have fought for improved labor conditions, but they jealously fought against the enlargement of union power. It was no aberration that once the need for wartime productive efficiency evaporated, leading progressives such as A. Mitchell Palmer, Miles Poindexter, and Woodrow Wilson himself helped civic and employer organizations to bludgeon the labor movement into disunity and docility. (It is possible, I suppose, to argue that such progressives were simply inconsistent, but if we understand progressivism in the terms I have outlined above I think the consistency is more evident.) Nevertheless, a double irony is worth noting with respect to progressivism's objectives and the wartime labor developments. On the one hand, the progressives' hostility to labor unions defeated their own objectives of (1) counterbalancing the power of collectivized capital (i.e., corporations), and (2) enhancing workers' share of the nation's wealth. On the other hand, under wartime duress, the progressives did grant concessions to organized labor (e.g., the Adamson Eight-Hour Railway Labor Act, as well as the WLB) that would later serve as precedents for the very "collectivization" of the economic situation that they were dedicated to oppose.

Meanwhile, the distribution of advantages in the society did not change much at all. In some cases, from the progressive reformers' viewpoint at least, it may even have changed for the worse. According to the figures of the National Industrial Conference Board, even income was as badly distributed at the end of the era as before. In 1921, the highest 10 percent of income recipients received 38 percent of total personal income, and that figure was only 34 percent in 1910. (Since the share of the top 5 percent of income recipients probably declined in the 1910–20 period, the figures for the top 10 percent group suggest a certain improvement in income distribution at the top. But the fact that the share of the lowest 60 percent also declined in that period, from 35 percent to 30 percent, confirms the view that no meaningful improvement can be shown.) Maldistribution was to grow worse until after 1929.

American farmers on the whole and in particular seemed to suffer increasing disadvantages. Farm life was one of the institutional bulwarks of the mode of life the progressives ostensibly cherished. "The farmer who owns his land" averred Gifford Pinchot, "is still the backbone of the Nation; and one of the things we want most is more of him, . . . [for] he is the first of home-makers." If only in the sense that there were relatively fewer farmers in the total population at the end of the progressive era, one would have to say farm life in the United States had suffered. But, moreover, fewer owned their own farms. The number of farm tenants increased by 21 percent from 1900 to 1920; 38.1 percent of all farm operators in 1921 were tenants; and the figures look even worse when one notices that tenancy *declined* in the most *impoverished* areas during this period, suggesting that the family farm was surviving mostly in the more marginal agricultural areas. Finally, although agriculture had enjoyed some of its most prosperous years in history in the 1910–20 period, the 21 percent of the nation's gainfully employed who were in agriculture in 1919 (a peak year) earned only 16 percent of the national income.

While progressivism failed to restore vitality to American farming, it failed also to stop the vigorous ascendancy of corporate capitalism, the most conspicuous challenge to conventional values and modes that the society faced at the beginning of the era. The corporation had drastically undermined the very basis of the traditional rationale that had supported the nation's freewheeling system of resource allocation and had underwritten the permissiveness of the laws governing economic activities in the nineteenth century. The new capitalism bypassed the privately owned proprietary firm, it featured a separation of ownership and control, it subordinated the profit motive to varied and variable other objectives such as empire-building, and, in many of the techniques developed by financial brokers and investment bankers, it appeared to create a great gulf between the making of money and the producing of useful goods and services. Through a remarkable series of judicial sophistries, this nonconventional form of business enterprise had become, in law, a person, and had won privileges and liberties once entrusted only to men, who were presumed to be conditioned and restrained by the moral qualities that inhere in human nature. Although gaining legal dispensations from an obliging Supreme Court, the corporation could claim no theoretical legitimacy beyond the fact of its power and its apparent inextricable entanglement in the business order that had produced America's seemingly unbounded material success.

Although much has been written about the supposed continuing vitality of small proprietary business enterprise in the United States, there is no gainsaying the continued ascendancy of the big corporation nor the fact that it still lacks legitimation. The fact that in the last sixty years the number of small proprietary businesses has grown at a rate that slightly exceeds the rate of population growth says little about the character of small business enterprise today as compared with that of the era of the American industrial revolution; it does nothing to disparage the apprehensions expressed in the antitrust campaigns of the progressives. To focus on the vast numbers of automobile dealers and gasoline service station owners, for example, is to miss completely their truly humble dependence upon the very few giant automobile and oil companies, a foretold dependence that was the very point of progressives' anticorporation, antitrust sentiments. The progressive movement must indeed be credited with placing real restraints upon monopolistic tendencies in the United States, for most statistics indicate that at least until the 1950s business concentration showed no substantial increase from the turn of the century (though it may be pertinent to note that concentration ratios did increase significantly in the decade immediately following the progressive era). But the statistics of concentration remain impressive—just as they were when John Moody wrote *The Truth About the Trusts* in 1904 and Louis Brandeis followed it with *Other People's Money* in 1914. That two hundred corporations (many of them interrelated) held almost one-quarter of all business assets, and more than 40 percent of all corporate assets in the country in 1948; that the fifty largest manufacturing corporations held 35 percent of all industrial assets in 1948, and 38 percent by 1962; and that a mere twenty-eight corporations or one one-thousandth of a percentage of all nonfinancial firms in 1956 employed 10 percent of all those employed in the nonfinancial industries, should be sufficient statistical support for the apprehensions of the progressive era—*just as it is testimony to the failure of the progressive movement to achieve anything substantial to alter the situation.*

Perhaps the crowning failure of progressivism was the American role in World War I. It is true that many progressives opposed America's intervention, but it is also true that a great many more supported it. The failure in progressivism lies not in the decision to intervene but in the futility of intervention measured by progressive expectations. It is . . . clear from the biographical masterwork on Wilson that Arthur Link [completed] that nothing was quite so important in shaping the Wilson policies toward Germany as Wilson's commitment to the Anglo-American system of values by which he defined "civilization." Wilson's decision to intervene ultimately rested . . . not only on his unwillingness to see England defeated but on his desire to make certain that America would have a major decision-making role at the peace table—where it could help shape the world according to the same principles of stewardship that guided the Wilsonian program at home . . . .

The inability of progressive reform to solve the problems of a society driven by industrial alienation, by the community-dissolving experience of the industrial process, by the convention-defying influence of massive immigration, by the faith-shattering impact of modern science, and the by consensus-destroying effect of rival nationalisms at war, helps us to understand the estrangement from all causes and social purpose that seems to have characterized the generation of Americans that came out of the War era . . . .

For younger men, such as F. Scott Fitzgerald, who were just emerging from college, it seemed that they had come on the scene "with all gods dead, with all wars fought, with all faiths shaken." For progressives, the god that was dead was the one that had made them "stewards" of the people; the faith that was shaken was what had given them the criteria upon which they could confidently assert their definition of the "general interest"; and the war (to end all wars) that had been fought—to make the world safe for democracy—had been a mockery, an exercise in futility, a grand illusion, especially because even the object no longer had the hallowed shimmer they thought they had perceived.

RICHARD M. ABRAMS is a professor of history emeritus and associate director of international and area studies at the University of California, Berkeley, where he has been teaching for 47 years. He has been a Fulbright professor in both London and Moscow and has taught and lectured in many countries throughout the world, including China, Austria, Norway, Italy, Japan, Germany, and Australia. He has published numerous articles in history, business, and law journals, and he is the editor of *The Shaping of Twentieth Century America: Interpretive Essays,* 2nd ed. (Little, Brown, 1971) and the author of *The Burdens of Progress* (Scott, Foresman, 1978). His most recent book is *America Transformed: Sixty Years of Revolutionary Change, 1941–2001* (Cambridge University Press, 2006).

EXPLORING THE ISSUE

Did the Progressives Succeed?

Critical Thinking and Reflection

1. State in one or two sentences Abrams' definition of progressivism. Discuss who joined the movement, what the reformers' philosophical principles were, and who the movement's five principal enemies were.
2. Critically examine those areas where Abrams says progressivism blunted "the sharper edges of self-interest in American life, and the harsher cruelties suffered by the society's underprivileged."
3. Critically analyze the reasons why the progressives failed to achieve their goals, according to both Wynn and Abrams. In your answer consider:
    a. The progressives relied on natural science and social science reforms.
    b. The progressives had deep ambivalence about industrialism and its consequences.
    c. The progressives never came to grips with the real conflicts of American society.
4. In the introductory essay to the issue, Pestritto and Atto offer a detailed list of Progressive Platform categories of reform. Discuss which of these issues continue to challenge America's social, economic, and political system and why these issues persevere in the 21st century?
5. Compare and contrast the successes of progressivism (Pestritto and Atto) with its failures (Abrams). Point out areas where the authors are in agreement and areas where they totally disagree.

Is There Common Ground?

In spite of their differences, Ronald J. Pestritto, William J. Atto, and Richard Abrams' interpretations find a degree of confluence in the manifestation of progressive philosophy in the 21st-century American reality. A review of Pestritto's and Atto's representation of the Progressive Party's 1912 platform and Woodrow Wilson's *The New Freedoms* 1913 campaign agenda reveal examples of how the intended reforms did not necessarily produce the desired results. Moreover, all authors would certainly agree that in the midst of reform movements insensitivities to the cultural values of marginalized populations are ever more apparent against the backdrop of so-called economic and social justice reforms. Nevertheless, the historic record as articulated by the primary document offered by Pestritto and Atto reveals a strong case for asserting that the progressive reforms did ameliorate the worst abuses of the new urban industrial society. Although the progressives failed to solve all the major problems of their times, they did set the agenda that still challenges the reformers of today.

Abrams also makes a concession to his critics when he admits that "progressivism had real lasting effects for the blunting of the sharper edges of self-interest in American life, and for the reduction of the harsher cruelties suffered by the society's underprivileged." Yet the thrust of his argument is that the progressive reformers accomplished little of value. While Abrams may very well concede to Pestritto and Atto that the progressives were the first group to confront the problems of modern America, he considers their intended reforms inadequate by their very nature. Perhaps inherent in the affirmative and negative arguments offered by our authors is the reality that American progressives were unable to fully achieve the foundations of the welfare state accomplished by Great Britain or Germany because of the entrenched power of the conservative elites, the entangled big business influence through all sectors of government (local, state, national), the racial and ethnic divisions of the population, a largely conservative labor movement, and the persistent seemingly unwavering American value proposition of elevating individualism and independence over all other values.

Additional Resources

Steven J. Diner, *A Very Different Age: Americans of the Progressive Era* (Hill and Wang, 1998)

Glenda Elizabeth Gilmore, ed., *Who Were the Progressives?* (Bedford/St. Martin's, 2002)

Lewis L. Gould, *America in the Progressive Era* (Routledge, 2001)

Michael McGeer, *A Fierce Discontent: The Rise and Fall of the Progressive Movement in America* (Oxford University Press, 2003)

Robert H. Wiebe, *The Search for Order: 1877–1920* (Hill and Wang, 1967)

Internet References . . .

Teaching American History – Progressive Era Archives

> https://teachingamericanhistory.org/library/progressive/

The Eleanor Roosevelt Project

> https://erpapers.columbian.gwu.edu/

The Progressive Era

> https://www2.gwu.edu/~erpapers/teachinger/glossary/progressive-era.cfm

Theodore Roosevelt

> https://www2.gwu.edu/~erpapers/teachinger/glossary/roosevelt-theodore.cfm

Woodrow Wilson

> https://www2.gwu.edu/~erpapers/teachinger/glossary/wilson-woodrow.cfm

Theodore Roosevelt Association

> https://theodoreroosevelt.org/content.aspx?sl=1496616134

Woodrow Wilson Presidential Library

> https://www.woodrowwilson.org/

Selected, Edited, and with Issue Framing Material by:
Kevin R. Magill and Tony L. Talbert, *Baylor University*

ISSUE

Was Woodrow Wilson Responsible for the Failure of the United States to Join the League of Nations?

YES: **Thomas A. Bailey**, from "Woodrow Wilson Wouldn't Yield," Appleton-Century-Crofts (1969)

NO: **William G. Carleton**, from "A New Look at Woodrow Wilson," *The Virginia Quarterly Review* (1962)

Learning Outcomes

After reading this issue, you will be able to:

- Discuss how Woodrow Wilson performed in various presidential roles.
- Distinguish between the realist approach and the idealist approach to foreign policy and evaluate whether Wilson was a realist or idealist.
- Determine whether Wilson was either psychologically or physically impaired during the treaty fight in the Senate.
- Conclude whether Wilson or Senator Henry Cabot Lodge killed the Treaty of Versailles.
- Determine whether Wilson was ahead of his times and American public opinion during the treaty fight.

ISSUE SUMMARY

YES: Thomas A. Bailey argues that a physically infirm Woodrow Wilson was unable to make the necessary compromises with the U. S. Senate to join the League of Nations and convince America that the United States should play a major role in world affairs.

NO: The late William G. Carleton believed that Woodrow Wilson understood better than any of his contemporaries the role that the United States would play in world affairs.

The presidential polls of Arthur Schlesinger in 1948 and 1962 as well as the 1983 Murray-Blessing poll have ranked Woodrow Wilson among the top 10 presidents. William Carleton considers him the greatest twentieth-century president, only two notches below Jefferson and Lincoln. Yet, among his biographers, Wilson has been treated ungenerously. They carp at him for being naïve, overly idealistic, and too inflexible. It appears that Wilson's biographers respect the man but do not like the person.

Wilson's own introspective personality may be partly to blame. He was, along with Jefferson and to some extent

Theodore Roosevelt, America's most intellectual president. He spent nearly 20 years as a history and political science teacher and scholar at Bryn Mawr, Wesleyan, and at his alma mater Princeton University. While his multivolume *History of the United States* appears dated as it gathers dust on musty library shelves, his PhD dissertation on Congressional Government, written as a graduate student at Johns Hopkins, remains a classic statement of the weakness of leadership in the American constitutional system.

There is one other reason why Wilson has been so critically analyzed by his biographers. Certainly, no president before or since has had less formal political experience than Wilson. Apparently, academic work does not constitute the proper training for the presidency. Yet, in addition to working many years as a college professor and a short stint as a lawyer, Wilson served eight distinguished years as the president of Princeton University. He turned it into one of the outstanding universities in the country. He introduced the preceptorial system, widely copied today, which supplemented course lectures with discussion conferences led by young instructors. He took the lead in reorganizing the university's curriculum. He lost two key battles. The alumni became upset when he tried to replace the class-ridden eating clubs with his "Quadrangle Plan," which would have established smaller colleges within the university system. What historians most remember about his Princeton career, however, was his losing fight with the Board of Trustees and Dean Andrew West concerning the location and eventual control over the new graduate school. Wilson resigned when it was decided to build a separate campus for the graduate school.

Shortly after Wilson left Princeton in 1910, he ran for governor of New Jersey and won his only political office before he became the president. As a governor, he gained control over the state Democratic Party and pushed through the legislature a litany of progressive measures—a primary elections law, a corrupt practices act, workmen's compensation, utilities regulation, school reforms, and an enabling act that allowed certain cities to adopt the commission form of government. When he was nominated on the 46th ballot at the Democratic convention in 1912, Wilson had enlarged the power of the governor's office in New Jersey and foreshadowed the way in which he would manage the presidency.

If one uses the standard categories of the late Professor Clinton Rossiter, Wilson ranks very high as a textbook president. No one, with the exception of Franklin Roosevelt and perhaps Ronald Reagan, performed the ceremonial role of the presidency as well as Wilson. His speeches rang with oratorical brilliance and substance. No wonder he abandoned the practice of Jefferson and his successors by delivering the president's annual State of the Union address to Congress in person rather than in writing.

During his first four years, he also fashioned a legislative program rivaled only by FDR's later "New Deal." The "New Freedom" pulled together conservative and progressive, rural and urban, as well as southern and northern Democrats in passing such measures as the Underwood-Simmons Tariff, the first bill to significantly lower tariff rates since the Civil War, and the Owens-Keating Child Labor Act. It was through Wilson's adroit maneuvering that the Federal Reserve System was established. This banking measure, the most significant in American history,

established the major agency that regulates money supply in the country today. Finally, President Wilson revealed his flexibility when he abandoned his initial policy of rigid and indiscriminate trust busting for one of regulating big business through the creation of the Federal Trade Commission.

More controversial were Wilson's presidential roles as commander-in-chief of the armed forces and chief diplomat. Some have argued that Wilson did not pay enough attention to strategic issues in the war, whereas other writers said he merged the proper dose of force and diplomacy. Thomas A. Bailey's *Woodrow Wilson and the Lost Peace* (Macmillan, 1944) and *Woodrow Wilson and the Great Betrayal* (Macmillan, 1945) were written as guidance for President Franklin Roosevelt to avoid the mistakes that Wilson made at home and abroad in his failure to gain ratification of the Treaty of Versailles. Specifically, Bailey blamed Wilson for failing to compromise with Republican senator Henry Cabot Lodge. Similarly, Wilson was the target of diplomat George F. Kennan whose chapter in *American Diplomacy, 1900–1950* (Mentor Books, 1951) protested vehemently about the "legalistic-moralistic" streak that he believed permeated Wilson's foreign policy. Scholars have criticized the realist approach to Wilson for a number of reasons. Some say that it is "unrealistic" to expect an American president to ask for a declaration of war to defend abstract principles such as the balance of power or the American national interest. Presidents and other elected officials must have a moral reason if they expect the American public to support a foreign war in which American servicemen might be killed. More recently, former Secretary of State Henry Kissinger, in his scholarly history *Diplomacy* (Simon & Schuster, 1994), insisted that Wilson was excessively moralistic and naïve in telling the American people that they were entering the war to "bring peace and safety to all nations and make the world itself at last free." Other realistic critics included influential journalist Walter Lippman and political scientists Robert Endicott Osgood and Hans Morgenthau. Osgood's study *Ideals and Self-Interest in American Foreign Relations* (University of Chicago Press, 1953) established the realist/idealist dichotomy later utilized by former Secretary of State Henry Kissinger in his scholarly history of *Diplomacy* (Simon & Schuster, 1994).

Many recent historians agree with David F. Trask that Wilson developed realistic and clearly articulated goals and coordinated his larger diplomatic aims with the use of force better than any other wartime U.S. president. See his essay "Woodrow Wilson and the Reconciliation of Force and Diplomacy, 1917–1918," *Naval War College Review* (January/February 1975). John Milton Cooper, Jr., in *The Warrior and the Priest: Woodrow Wilson and Theodore Roosevelt* (Harvard University Press, 1984), presents Wilson as the realist and Theodore Roosevelt as the idealist. Arthur S. Link, coeditor of the *Papers of Woodrow Wilson,* 60 vols. (Princeton, 1966–1993), gives a blow-by-blow response to Kennan in revised lectures given at Johns Hopkins University in *Woodrow Wilson: Revolution, War and Peace* (Harlan Davidson, 1979), nicely summarized in "The Higher Realism of Woodrow Wilson," in a book of essays with the same title (Vanderbilt University Press, 1971). Kennan himself acknowledged that his earlier criticism of Wilson had to be viewed within the context of the Cold War. "I now view Wilson," he wrote in 1991, "as a man who, like so many other people of broad vision and acute sensitivities, was ahead of his time, and did not live long enough to know what great and commanding relevance his ideas would acquire before this century was out." See "Comments on the Paper, Entitled 'Kennan Versus Wilson'" by Thomas J. Knock in John Milton Cooper et al., eds., *The Wilson Era: Essays in Honor of Arthur S. Link* (Harlan Davidson, 1991).

Wilson's health has received serious scrutiny from scholars. In the early 1930s, Sigmund Freud and William C. Bullitt, a former diplomat, wrote a scathing and highly inaccurate biography of Thomas Woodrow Wilson (Houghton Mifflin, 1967) published posthumously in 1967. The book was poorly received and scathingly reviewed by Arthur S. Link, "The Case for Woodrow Wilson," in *The Higher Realism of Woodrow Wilson and Other Essays.* The major controversy seems to be those who stress psychological difficulties—see Alexander and Juliette George, *Woodrow Wilson and Colonial House: A Personality Study* (Dover Press, 1956, 1964)—versus medical illnesses—see Edwin A. Weinstein, *Woodrow Wilson: A Medical and Psychological Biography* (Princeton University, 1981). For the best summaries of the controversy, see Thomas T. Lewis, "Alternative Psychological Interpretations of Woodrow Wilson," *Mid-America* (vol. 45, 1983), and Lloyd E. Ambrosius, "Woodrow Wilson's Health and the Treaty Fight, 1919–1920," *The International History Review* (February 1987). Phyllis Lee Levin, *Edith and Woodrow: The White House Years* (Scribners, 2001), and Robert J. Maddox, "Mrs. Wilson and the Presidency," *American History* (February 1973), makes the case that we have already had America's first woman president.

The four best bibliographies of Wilson are as follows: the introduction to Lloyd E. Ambrosius's *Wilsonianism: Woodrow Wilson and His Legacy in American Foreign Relations* (Palgrave Macmillan, 2002), which is a collection of his articles from the leading realist Wilsonian scholar. John A. Thompson, a British scholar, has an up-to-date analysis of the Wilson scholarship in *Woodrow Wilson* (Pearson Macmillan, 2002), a short, scholarly sympathetic

study in the "Profiles in Power" series designed for student use. Advanced undergraduates should consult David Steigarwald, "The Reclamation of Woodrow Wilson," *Diplomatic History* (Winter 1999). Political Science majors should consult Francis J. Gavin, "The Wilsonian Legacy in the Twentieth Century," *Orbis* (Fall 1997).

Thomas Bailey claims that Wilson made mistakes at home that affected his foreign policies. For example, by attempting to politicize the war issue by asking voters to elect a Democratic Congress in the off-year elections in 1918, voters responded by restoring the Republicans to power in the Senate. Wilson also failed to name any prominent Republicans to the peace delegation he took to Paris. This was the first time a president was going outside the United States to conduct foreign affairs. Had he brought any prominent Senate Republicans with him, including Henry Cabot Lodge, he might have successfully negotiated a treaty acceptable to Senate ratification. During the negotiations at Paris, Wilson was forced to compromise on issues of self-determination for settling territorial disputes, parceling out "mandates" to the winners over former German clinical possessions, and saddling Germany with a high reparations bill. Bailey mentions but does not dwell on the attempts by Senator Lodge to privately negotiate a compromise treaty with the Democrats. Might the real villain have been the irreconcilable isolationist Senator William Borah who threatened to remove Lodge as Senate majority leader? Was Lodge afraid that an open fight with Borah could have split the Republican Party as had occurred in 1912 when ex-President Theodore Roosevelt walked out of the convention and ran as a third-party candidate? Wilson, who hated the sound of Lodge's name, had also privately worked out his own set of reservations with Democratic Senate minority leader Gilbert M. Hitchcock. Bailey maintains the compromise reservations differed only slightly in degree from those of Senator Lodge. If this was the case, would Wilson have been better off staying at home and negotiating a compromise with the Senate instead of delivering emotional appeals to the American public on the ill-fated tour where he suffered a paralyzing stroke to the left side of his body?

The late William G. Carleton presents an impassioned defense of both Wilson's policies at Versailles as well as their implications for the future of American foreign policy. Carleton responds to the two main charges historians continue to level against Wilson: his inability to compromise and his naïve idealism. In contrast to Bailey, Carleton excoriates Lodge, as the chairman of the Senate Foreign Relations Committee, for adding "nationally self-centered" reservations that he knew would emasculate the League of Nations and most likely cause other nations to add reservations to the Treaty of Versailles. Wilson, says Carleton, was a true realist when he rejected the Lodge reservations. In his article, Carleton advanced many of the arguments that historians Trask, Link, and Kennan later used in defending Wilson's "higher realism." Rejecting the view of Wilson as a naïve idealist, Carleton maintains: "He recognized the emergence of the anti-imperialist revolutions . . . the importance of social politics in the international relations of the future . . . the implications for future world politics of the technological revolutions in war, of total war, and of the disintegration of the old balance of power."

YES ⤴   Thomas A. Bailey

Woodrow Wilson Wouldn't Yield

"As a friend of the President . . . I solemnly declare to him this morning: If you want to kill your own child [League of Nations] because the Senate straightens out its crooked limbs, you must take the responsibility and accept the verdict of history."

—Senator Henry F. Ashurst, in Senate, 1920

I

The story of America's rejection of the League of Nations revolves largely around the personality and character of Thomas Woodrow Wilson.

Born in Virginia and reared in Yankee-gutted Georgia and the Carolinas, Wilson early developed a burning hatred of war and a passionate attachment to the Confederate-embraced principle of self-determination for minority peoples. From the writings of Thomas Jefferson he derived much of his democratic idealism and his invincible faith in the judgment of the masses, if properly informed. From his stiff-backed Scotch-Presbyterian forebears, he inherited a high degree of inflexibility; from his father, a dedicated Presbyterian minister, he learned a stern moral code that would tolerate no compromise with wrong—as defined by Woodrow Wilson.

As a leading academician who had first failed at law, he betrayed a contempt for "money-grubbing" lawyers, many of whom sat in the Senate, and an arrogance toward lesser intellects, including those of the "pygmy-minded" senators. As a devout Christian keenly aware of the wickedness of this world, he emerged as a fighting reformer, whether as president of Princeton, governor of New Jersey, or President of the United States.

As a war leader, Wilson was superb. Holding aloft the torch of idealism in one hand and the flaming sword of righteousness in the other, he aroused the masses to a holy crusade. We would fight a war to end wars; we would make the world safe for democracy. The phrase was not a mockery then. The American people, with an amazing display of self-sacrifice, supported the war effort unswervingly.

The noblest expression of Wilson's idealism was his Fourteen Points address to Congress in January, 1918. It compressed his war aims into punchy, placard-like paragraphs, expressly designed for propaganda purposes. It appealed tremendously to oppressed peoples everywhere by promising such goals as the end of secret treaties, freedom of the seas, the removal of economic barriers, a reduction of arms burdens, a fair adjustment of colonial claims, and self-determination for oppressed minorities. In Poland, university men would meet on the streets of Warsaw, clasp hands, and soulfully utter one word, "Wilson." In remote regions of Italy peasants burned candles before poster portraits of the mighty new prophet arisen in the West.

The fourteenth and capstone point was a league of nations, designed to avert future wars. The basic idea was not original with Wilson; numerous thinkers, including Frenchmen and Britons, had been working on the concept long before he embraced it. Even Henry Cabot Lodge, the Republican senator from Massachusetts, had already spoken publicly in favor of a league of nations. But the more he heard about the Wilsonian League of Nations, the more critical of it he became.

A knowledge of the Wilson–Lodge feud is basic to an understanding of the tragedy that unfolded. Tall, slender, aristocratically bewhiskered, Dr. Henry Cabot Lodge (Ph.D., Harvard), had published a number of books and had been known as "the scholar in politics" before the appearance of Dr. Woodrow Wilson (Ph.D., Johns Hopkins). The Presbyterian professor had gone further in both scholarship and politics than the Boston Brahmin, whose mind was once described as resembling the soil of his native New England: "naturally barren but highly cultivated." Wilson and Lodge, two stubborn men, developed a mutual antipathy which soon turned into freezing hatred.

II

The German armies, reeling under the blows of the Allies, were ready to surrender November, 1918. The formal armistice terms stipulated that Germany was to be guaranteed a peace based on the Fourteen Points, with two reservations concerning freedom of the seas and reparations.

Meanwhile the American people had keyed themselves up for the long-awaited march on Berlin; eager voices clamored to hang the Kaiser. Thus the sudden end of the shooting left inflamed patriots with a sense of frustration and letdown that boded ill for Wilson's policies. The red-faced Theodore Roosevelt, Lodge's intimate of long standing, cried that peace should be dictated by the chatter of machine guns and not "the clicking of typewriters."

Wilson now towered at the dizzy pinnacle of his popularity and power. He had emerged as the moral arbiter of the world and the hope of all peoples for a better tomorrow. But regrettably his wartime sureness of touch began to desert him, and he made a series of costly fumbles. He was so preoccupied with reordering the world, someone has said, that he reminded one of the baseball player who knocks the ball into the bleachers and then forgets to touch home plate.

First came his tactlessly direct appeal for a Democratic Congress in October, 1918. The voters trooped to the polls the next month and, by a narrow margin, returned a Republican Congress. Wilson had not only goaded his partisan foes to fresh outbursts of fury, but he had unnecessarily staked his prestige on the outcome—and lost. When the Allied leaders met at the Paris peace table, he was the only one not entitled to be there—on the European basis of a parliamentary majority.

Wilson next announced that he was sailing for France, presumably to use his still enormous prestige to fashion an enduring peace. At that time no President had ever gone abroad, and Republicans condemned the decision as evidence of a dangerous Messiah complex—of a desire, as former President Taft put it, "to hog the whole show."

The naming of the remaining four men to the peace delegation caused partisans further anguish. Only one, Henry White, was a Republican, and he was a minor figure at that. The Republicans, now the majority party, complained that they had been good enough to die on the battlefield; they ought to have at least an equal voice at the peace table. Nor were any United States senators included, even though they would have a final whack at the treaty. Wilson did not have much respect for the "bungalow-minded" senators, and if he took one, the logical choice would be Henry Cabot Lodge. There were already enough feuds brewing at Paris without taking one along.

Doubtless some of the Big Business Republicans were out to "get" the President who had been responsible for the hated reformist legislation of 1913–14. If he managed to put over the League of Nations, his prestige would soar to new heights. He might even arrange—unspeakable thought!—to be elected again and again and again. Much of the partisan smog that finally suffocated the League would have been cleared away if Wilson had publicly declared, as he was urged to do, that in no circumstances would he run again. But he spurned such counsel, partly because he was actually receptive to the idea of a third term.

III

The American President, hysterically hailed by European crowds as "Voovro Veelson," came to the Paris peace table in January, 1919, to meet with Lloyd George of Britain, Clemenceau of France, and Orlando of Italy. To his dismay, he soon discovered that they were far more interested in imperialism than in idealism. When they sought to carve up the territorial booty without regard for the colonials, contrary to the Fourteen Points, the stern-jawed Presbyterian moralist interposed a ringing veto. The end result was the mandate system—a compromise between idealism and imperialism that turned out to be more imperialistic than idealistic.

Wilson's overriding concern was the League of Nations. He feared that if he did not get it completed and embedded in the treaty, the imperialistic powers might sidetrack it. Working at an incredible pace after hours, Wilson headed the commission that drafted the League Covenant in ten meetings and some thirty hours. He then persuaded the conference not only to approve the hastily constructed Covenant but to incorporate it bodily in the peace treaty. In support of his adopted brain child he spoke so movingly on one occasion that even the hard-boiled reporters forgot to take notes.

Wilson now had to return hurriedly to the United States to sign bills and take care of other pressing business. Shortly after his arrival the mounting Republican opposition in the Senate flared up angrily. On March 4, 1919, 39 senators or senators-elect—more than enough to defeat the treaty—published a round robin to the effect that they would not approve the League in its existing form. This meant that Wilson had to return to Paris, hat in hand, and there weaken his position by having to seek modifications.

Stung to the quick, he struck back at his senatorial foes in an indiscreet speech in New York just before his departure. He boasted that when he brought the treaty back from Paris, the League Covenant would not only be tied in but so thoroughly tied in that it could not be cut out without killing the entire pact. The Senate, he assumed, would not dare to kill the treaty of peace outright.

IV

At Paris the battle was now joined in deadly earnest. Clemenceau, the French realist, had little use for Wilson, the American idealist. "God gave us the ten commandments and we broke them," he reportedly sneered. "Wilson gave us the Fourteen Points—we shall see." Clemenceau's most disruptive demand was for the German Rhineland; but Wilson, the champion of self-determination, would never consent to handing several million Germans over to the tender mercies of the French. After a furious struggle, during which Wilson was stricken with influenza, Clemenceau was finally persuaded to yield the Rhineland and other demands in return for a security treaty. Under it, Britain and America agreed to come to the aid of France in the event of another unprovoked aggression. The United States Senate shortsightedly pigeonholed the pact, and France was left with neither the Rhineland nor security.

Two other deadlocks almost broke up the conference. Italy claimed the Adriatic port of Fiume, an area inhabited chiefly by Yugoslavs. In his battle for self-determination, Wilson dramatically appealed over the head of the Italian delegation to the Italian people, whereupon the delegates went home in a huff to receive popular endorsement. The final adjustment was a hollow victory for self-determination.

The politely bowing Japanese now stepped forward to press their economic claims to China's Shantung, which they had captured from the Germans early in the war. But to submit 30,000,000 Chinese to the influence of the Japanese would be another glaring violation of self-determination. The Japanese threatened to bolt the conference, as the Italians had already done, with consequent jeopardy to the League. In the end, Wilson reluctantly consented to a compromise that left the Japanese temporarily in possession of Shantung.

The Treaty of Versailles, as finally signed in June, 1919, included only about four of the Fourteen Points essentially intact. The Germans, with considerable justification, gave vent to loud cries of betrayal. But the iron hand of circumstance had forced Wilson to compromise away many of his points in order to salvage his fourteenth point, the League of Nations, which he hoped would iron out the injustices that had crept into the treaty. He was like the mother who throws her younger children to the pursuing wolves in order to save her sturdy first born son.

V

Bitter opposition to the completed treaty had already begun to form in America. Tens of thousands of homesick and disillusioned soldiers were pouring home, determined to let Europe "stew in its own juice." The wartime idealism, inevitably doomed to slump, was now plunging to alarming depths. The beloved Allies had apparently turned out to be greedy imperialists. The war to make the world safe for democracy had obviously fallen dismally short of the goal. And at the end of the war to end wars there were about twenty conflicts of varying intensity being waged all over the globe.

The critics increased their clamor. Various foreign groups, including the Irish-Americans and the Italian-Americans, were complaining that the interests of the "old country" had been neglected. Professional liberals, notably the editors of the *New Republic,* were denouncing the treaty as too harsh. The illiberals, far more numerous, were denouncing it as not harsh enough. The Britain-haters, like the buzz-saw Senator James Reed of Missouri and the acid-penned William R. Hearst, were proclaiming that the British had emerged with undue influence. Such ultra-nationalists as the isolationist Senator William E. Borah of Idaho were insisting that the flag of no superstate should be hoisted above the glorious Stars and Stripes.

When the treaty came back from Paris, with the League firmly riveted in, Senator Lodge despaired of stopping it. "What are you going to do? It's hopeless," he complained to Borah. "All the newspapers in my state are for it." The best that he could hope for was to add a few reservations. The Republicans had been given little opportunity to help write the treaty in Paris; they now felt that they were entitled to do a little rewriting in Washington.

Lodge deliberately adopted the technique of delay. As chairman of the powerful Senate Committee on Foreign Relations, he consumed two weeks by reading aloud the entire pact of 264 pages, even though it had already been printed. He then held time-consuming public hearings, during which persons with unpronounceable foreign names aired their grievances against the pact.

Lodge finally adopted the strategy of tacking reservations onto the treaty, and he was able to achieve his goal because of the peculiar composition of the Senate. There were 49 Republicans and 47 Democrats. The Republicans consisted of about twenty "strong reservationists" like Lodge, about twelve "mild reservationists" like future Secretary of State Kellogg, and about a dozen "irreconcilables." This last group was headed by Senator Borah and the no less isolationist Senator Hiram Johnson of California, a fiery spellbinder.

The Lodge reservations finally broke the back of the treaty. They were all added by a simple majority vote, even though the entire pact would have to be approved by a two-thirds vote. The dozen or so Republican mild reservationists were not happy over the strong Lodge reservations, and if Wilson had deferred sufficiently to these men, he might have persuaded them to vote with the Democrats. Had they done so, the Lodge reservations could have all been voted down, and a milder version, perhaps acceptable to Wilson, could have been substituted.

VI

As the hot summer of 1919 wore on, Wilson became increasingly impatient with the deadlock in the Senate. Finally he decided to take his case to the country, as he had so often done in response to his ingrained "appeal habit." He had never been robust, and his friends urged him not to risk breaking himself down in a strenuous barnstorming campaign. But Wilson, having made up his mind, was unyielding. He had sent American boys into battle in a war to end wars; why should he not risk his life in a battle for a League to end wars?

Wilson's spectacular tour met with limited enthusiasm in the Middle West, the home of several million German-Americans. After him, like baying bloodhounds, trailed Senators Borah and Johnson, sometimes speaking in the same halls a day or so later, to the accompaniment of cries of "Impeach him, impeach him!" But on the Pacific Coast and in the Rocky Mountain area the enthusiasm for Wilson and the League was overwhelming. The high point—and the breaking point—of the trip came at Pueblo, Colorado, where Wilson, with tears streaming down his cheeks, pleaded for his beloved League of Nations.

That night Wilson's weary body rebelled. He was whisked back to Washington, where he suffered a stroke that paralyzed the left side of his body. For weeks he lay in bed, a desperately sick man. The Democrats, who had no first-rate leader in the Senate, were left rudderless. With the wisdom of hindsight, we may say that Wilson might better have stayed in Washington, providing the necessary leadership and compromising with the opposition, insofar as compromise was possible. A good deal of compromise had already gone into the treaty, and a little more might have saved it.

Senator Lodge, cold and decisive, was now in the driver's seat. His Fourteen Reservations, a sardonic parallel to Wilson's Fourteen Points, had been whipped into shape. Most of them now seem either irrelevant, inconsequential, or unnecessary; some of them merely reaffirmed principles and policies, including the Monroe Doctrine, already guaranteed by the treaty or by the Constitution.

But Wilson, who hated the sound of Lodge's name, would have no part of the Lodge reservations. They would, he insisted, emasculate the entire treaty. Yet the curious fact is that he had privately worked out his own set of reservations with the Democratic leader in the Senate, Gilbert M. Hitchcock, and these differed only in slight degree from those of Senator Lodge.

VII

As the hour approached for the crucial vote in the Senate, it appeared that public opinion had evidently veered considerably. Although confused by the angry debate, it still favored the treaty—but with some safeguarding reservations. A stubborn Wilson was unwilling to accept this disheartening fact, or perhaps he was not made aware of it. Mrs. Wilson, backed by the President's personal physician, Dr. Cary Grayson, kept vigil at his bedside to warn the few visitors that disagreeable news might shock the invalid into a relapse.

In this highly unfavorable atmosphere, Senator Hitchcock had two conferences with Wilson on the eve of the Senate ballot. He suggested compromise on a certain point, but Wilson shot back, "Let Lodge compromise!" Hitchcock conceded that the Senator would have to give ground but suggested that the White House might also hold out the olive branch. "Let Lodge hold out the olive branch," came the stern reply. On this inflexible note, and with Mrs. Wilson's anxiety mounting, the interview ended.

The Senate was ready for final action on November 19, 1919. At the critical moment Wilson sent a fateful letter to the Democratic minority in the Senate, urging them to vote down the treaty with the hated Lodge reservations so that a true ratification could be achieved. The Democrats, with more than the necessary one-third veto, heeded the voice of their crippled leader and rejected the treaty with reservations. The Republicans, with more than the necessary one-third veto, rejected the treaty without reservations.

The country was shocked by this exhibition of legislative paralysis. About four-fifths of the senators professed to favor the treaty in some form, yet they were unable to agree on anything. An aroused public opinion forced the Senate to reconsider, and Lodge secretly entered into negotiations with the Democrats in an effort to work out acceptable reservations. He was making promising progress when Senator Borah got wind of his maneuvers through an anonymous telephone call. The leading irreconcilables hastily summoned a council of war, hauled Lodge before them, and bluntly accused him of treachery. Deeply disturbed, the Massachusetts Senator said: "Well, I suppose I'll have to resign as majority leader."

"No, by God!" burst out Borah. "You won't have a chance to resign! On Monday, I'll move for the election of a new majority leader and give the reasons for my action." Faced with an upheaval within his party such as had insured Wilson's election in 1912, Lodge agreed to drop his backstage negotiations.

VIII

The second-chance vote in the Senate came on March 19, 1920. Wilson again directed his loyal Democratic following to reject the treaty, disfigured as it was by the Lodge reservations. But by this time there was no other form in which the pact could possibly be ratified. Twenty-one realistic Democrats turned their backs on Wilson and voted Yea; 23 loyal Democrats, mostly from the rock-ribbed South, joined with the irreconcilables to do the bidding of the White House. The treaty, though commanding a simple majority this time of 49 Yeas to 35 Nays, failed of the necessary two-thirds vote.

Wilson, struggling desperately against the Lodge reservation trap, had already called upon the nation, in a "solemn referendum," to give him a vote in favor of the League in the forthcoming Presidential election of 1920. His hope was that he could then get the treaty approved without reservations. But this course was plainly futile. Even if all the anti-League senators up for reelection in 1920 had been replaced by the pro-League senators, Wilson would still have lacked the necessary two-thirds majority for an unreserved treaty.

The American people were never given a chance to express their views directly on the League of Nations. All they could do was vote either for the voluble Democratic candidate, Cox, who stood for the League, or the stuffed-shirt Republican candidate, Harding, who wobbled all over the evasive Republican platform. If the electorate had been given an opportunity to express itself, a powerful majority probably would have favored the world organization, with at least some reservations. But wearied of Wilsonism, idealism, and self-denial, and confused by the wordy fight over the treaty, the voters rose up and swept Harding into the White House on a tidal wave of votes. The winner had been more anti-League than pro-League, and his prodigious plurality of 7,000,000 votes condemned the League to death in America.

IX

What caused this costly failure of American statesmanship? Wilson's physical collapse intensified his native stubbornness. A judicious compromise here and there no doubt would have secured Senate approval of the treaty, though of course with qualifications. Wilson believed that in any event the Allies would reject the Lodge reservations. The probabilities are that the Allies would have worked out some kind of acceptance, so dire was their need of America's economic support, but Wilson never gave them a chance to act.

Senator Lodge was also inflexible, but prior to the second rejection he was evidently trying to get the treaty through—on his own terms. As majority leader of the Republicans, his primary task was to avoid another fatal split in his party. Wilson's primary task was to get the pact approved. From a narrowly political point of view, the Republicans had little to gain by engineering ratification of a Democratic treaty.

The two-thirds rule in the Senate, often singled out as the culprit, is of little relevance. Wilson almost certainly would have pigeonholed the treaty, as he threatened, if it had passed with the Lodge reservations appended.

Wilson's insistence that the League be wedded to the treaty actually contributed to the final defeat of both. Either would have had a better chance if it had not been burdened by the enemies of the other. The United Nations, one should note, was set up in 1945 independently of any peace treaty.

Finally, the American public in 1919–20 was not yet ready for the onerous new world responsibilities that had suddenly been forced upon it. The isolationist tradition was still potent, and it was fortified by postwar disillusionment. If the sovereign people had cried out for the League with one voice, they almost certainly would have had their way. A treaty without reservations, or with a few reservations acceptable to Wilson, doubtless would have slipped through the Senate. But the American people were one war short of accepting that leadership in a world organization for peace which, as Wilson's vision perceived, had become a necessity for the safety and the welfare of mankind.

The blame for this failure of statesmanship cannot fall solely on the excessive partisanship of both parties, the shortsighted outlook of Lodge, or the rigidity of a sick and ill-informed President. Much of the responsibility must be placed at the door of a provincial population anxious to escape overseas responsibilities while basking in the sunshine of normalcy and prosperity.

THOMAS A. BAILEY (1902–1983) taught for nearly 50 years at Stanford University and was America's leading diplomatic historian. His major works include a two-volume exegesis titled *Woodrow Wilson's World War One Diplomacy* and the popular *A Diplomatic History of the American People* that went through ten editions.

William G. Carleton   → **NO**

A New Look at Woodrow Wilson

All high-placed statesmen crave historical immortality. Woodrow Wilson craved it more than most. Thus far the fates have not been kind to Wilson; there is a reluctance to admit him to as great a place in history as he will have.

Congress has just gotten around to planning a national memorial for Wilson, several years after it had done this for Theodore Roosevelt and Franklin D. Roosevelt. Wilson is gradually being accepted as one of the nation's five or six greatest Presidents. However, the heroic mold of the man on the large stage of world history is still generally unrecognized.

There is a uniquely carping, hypercritical approach to Wilson. Much more than other historical figures he is being judged by personality traits, many of them distorted or even fancied. Wilson is not being measured by the yardstick used for other famous characters of history. There is a double standard at work here.

What are the common errors and misrepresentations with respect to Wilson? In what ways is he being judged more rigorously? What are the reasons for this? Why will Wilson eventually achieve giant stature in world history?

☙❦❧

There are two criticisms of Wilson that go to the heart of his fame and place in history. One is an alleged inflexibility and intransigence, an inability to compromise. The other is that he had no real understanding of world politics, that he was a naïve idealist. Neither is true.

If Wilson were indeed as stubborn and adamant as he is often portrayed he would have been a bungler at his work, for the practice and art of politics consist in a feeling for the possible, a sense of timing, a capacity for give-and-take compromise. In reality, Wilson's leadership of his party and the legislative accomplishments of his first term were magnificent. His performance was brilliantly characterized by the very qualities he is said to have lacked: flexibility, accommodation, a sense of timing, and a willingness to compromise. In the struggles to win the Federal Reserve Act, the Clayton Anti-Trust Law, the Federal Trade Commission, and other major measures of his domestic program, Wilson repeatedly mediated between the agrarian liberals and the conservatives of his party, moving now a little to the left, now to the right, now back to the left. He learned by experience, cast aside pride of opinion, accepted and maneuvered for regulatory commissions after having warned of their danger during the campaign of 1912, and constantly acted as a catalyst of the opposing factions of his party and of shifting opinion.

The cautious way Wilson led the country to military preparedness and to war demonstrated resiliency and a sense of timing of a high order. At the Paris Conference Wilson impressed thoughtful observers with his skill as a negotiator; many European diplomats were surprised that an "amateur" could do so well. Here the criticism is not that Wilson was without compromise but that he compromised too much.

Actually, the charge that Wilson was incapable of compromise must stand or fall on his conduct during the fight in the Senate over the ratification of the League of Nations, particularly his refusal to give the word to the Democratic Senators from the South to vote for the Treaty with the Lodge Reservations, which, it is claimed, would have assured ratification. Wilson, say the critics, murdered his own brain child. It is Wilson, and not Lodge, who has now become the villain of this high tragedy.

Now, would a Wilsonian call to the Southerners to change their position have resulted in ratification? Can we really be sure? In order to give Southerners time to readjust to a new position, the call from the White House would have had to have been made several weeks before that final vote. During that time what would have prevented Lodge from hobbling the League with still more reservations? Would the mild reservationists, all Republicans, have prevented this? The record shows, I think, that in the final analysis the mild reservationists could always be bamboozled by Lodge in the name of party loyalty. As the fight on the League had progressed, the reservations had become more numerous and more crippling. Wilson, it seems, had come to feel that there simply was no appeasing Lodge.

During the Peace Conference, in response to the Senatorial Round Robin engineered by Lodge, Wilson had reopened the whole League question and obtained the inclusion of American "safeguards" he felt would satisfy Lodge. This had been done at great cost, for it had forced Wilson to abandon his position as a negotiator above the battles for national advantages and to become a suppliant for national concessions. This had resulted in his having to yield points in other parts of the Treaty to national-minded delegations from other countries. When Wilson returned from Paris with the completed Treaty, Lodge had "raised the ante," the Lodge Reservations requiring the consent of other signatory nations were attached to the Treaty, and these had multiplied and become more restrictive in nature as the months went by. Would not then a "final" yielding by Wilson have resulted in even stiffer reservations being added? Was not Lodge using the Reservations to effect not ratification but rejection, knowing that there was a point beyond which Wilson could not yield?

Wilson seems honestly to have believed that the Lodge Reservations emasculated the League. Those who read them for the first time will be surprised, I think, to discover how nationally self-centered they were. If taken seriously, they surely must have impaired the functioning of the League. However, Wilson was never opposed to clarifying or interpreting reservations which would not require the consent of the other signatories. Indeed, he himself wrote the Hitchcock Reservations.

Even had the League with the Lodge Reservations been ratified, how certain can we really be that this would have meant American entrance into the League? Under the Lodge Reservations, every signatory nation had to accept them before the United States could become a member. Would all the signatories have accepted every one of the fifteen Lodge Reservations? The United States had no monopoly on chauvinism, and would not other nations have interposed reservations of their own as a condition to their acceptance of the Lodge Reservations?

At Paris, Wilson had personally experienced great difficulty getting his own mild "reservations" incorporated into the Covenant. Now, at this late date, would Britain have accepted the Lodge Reservation on Irish self-determination? In all probability. Would Japan have accepted the Reservation on Shantung? This is more doubtful. Would the Latin American states have accepted the stronger Reservation on the Monroe Doctrine? This is also doubtful. Chile had already shown concern, and little Costa Rica had the temerity to ask for a definition of the Doctrine. Would the British Dominions have accepted the Reservation calling for one vote for the British Empire or six votes for the United States? Even Lord Grey, who earlier had predicted that the signatories would accept the Lodge Reservations, found that he could not guarantee acceptance by the Dominions, and Canada's President of the Privy Council and Acting Secretary for External Affairs, Newton W. Rowell, declared that if this Reservation were accepted by the other powers Canada would withdraw from the League.

By the spring of 1920, Wilson seems to have believed that making the League of Nations the issue in the campaign of 1920 would afford a better opportunity for American participation in an effective League than would further concessions to Lodge. To Wilson, converting the Presidential election into a solemn referendum on the League was a reality. For months, because of his illness, he had lived secluded in the White House, and the memories of his highly emotional reception in New York on his return from Paris and of the enthusiasm of the Western audiences during his last speaking trip burned vividly bright. He still believed that the American people, if given the chance, would vote for the League without emasculating reservations. Does this, then, make Wilson naïve? It is well to remember that in the spring of 1920 not even the most sanguine Republican envisaged the Republican sweep that would develop in the fall of that year.

If the strategy of Wilson in the spring of 1920 was of debatable wisdom, the motives of Lodge can no longer be open to doubt. After the landslide of 1920, which gave the Republicans the Presidency and an overwhelming majority in a Senate dominated by Lodge in foreign policy, the Treaty was never resurrected. The Lodge Reservations, representing months of gruelling legislative labor, were cavalierly jettisoned, and a separate peace was made with Germany.

What, then, becomes of the stock charge that Wilson was intolerant of opposition and incapable of bending? If the truth of this accusation must rest on Wilson's attitude during the Treaty fight, and I think it must, for he showed remarkable adaptability in other phases of his Presidency, then it must fall. The situation surrounding the Treaty fight was intricately tangled, and there is certainly as much evidence on the side of Wilson's forbearance as on the side of his obstinacy.

A far more serious charge against Wilson is that he had no realistic understanding of world politics, that he was an impractical idealist whose policies intensified rather than alleviated international problems. Now what American statesman of the period understood world politics better than Wilson—or indeed in any way as well as he? Elihu Root, with his arid legalism? Philander Knox, with his dollar diplomacy? Theodore Roosevelt or Henry Cabot Lodge? Roosevelt and Lodge had some feel for power politics, and they understood the traditional balance of power, at least until their emotions for a dictated Allied victory got the better of their judgment: but was either of them aware of the implications for world politics of the technological revolution in war and the disintegration of the old balance of power? And were not both of them blind to a new force in world politics just then rising to a place of importance—the anti-imperialist revolutions, which even before World War I were getting under way with the Mexican Revolution and the Chinese Revolution of Sun Yat-sen?

Wilson is charged with having no understanding of the balance of power, but who among world statesmen of the twentieth century better sated the classic doctrine of the traditional balance of power than Wilson in his famous Peace Without Victory speech? And was it not Theodore Roosevelt who derided him for stating it? With perfectly straight faces Wilson critics, and a good many historians, tell us that TR, who wanted to march to Berlin and saddle Germany with a harsh peace, and FDR, who sponsored unconditional surrender, "understood" the balance of power, but that Wilson, who fought to salvage a power balance by preserving Germany from partition, was a simple-simon in world politics—an illustration of the double standard at work in evaluating Wilson's place in history.

Wilson not only understood the old, but with amazing clarity he saw the new, elements in world politics. He recognized the emergence of the anti-imperialist revolutions and the importance of social politics in the international relations of the future. He recognized, too, the implications for future world politics of the technological revolution in war, of total war, and of the disintegration of the old balance of power—for World War I had decisively weakened the effective brakes on Japan in Asia, disrupted the Turkish Empire in the Middle East and the Austro-Hungarian Empire in Europe, and removed Russia as a make-weight for the foreseeable future. Wilson believed that a truncated Germany and an attempted French hegemony would only add to the chaos, but he saw too that merely preserving Germany as a power unit would not restore the old balance of power. To Wilson,

even in its prime the traditional balance of power had worked only indifferently and collective security would have been preferable, but in his mind the revolutionary changes in the world of 1919 made a collective-security system indispensable.

Just what is realism in world politics? Is it not the ability to use purposefully many factors, even theoretically contradictory ones, and to use them not singly and consecutively but interdependently and simultaneously, shifting the emphasis as conditions change? If so, was not Wilson a very great realist in world politics? He used the old balance-of-power factors, as evidenced by his fight to save Germany as a power unit and his sponsoring of a tripartite alliance of the United States, Britain, and France to guarantee France from any German aggression until such time as collective security would become effective. But he labored to introduce into international relations the new collective-security factors to supplement and gradually supersede in importance the older factors, now increasingly outmoded by historical developments. To label as doctrinaire idealist one who envisaged world politics in so broad and flexible a way is to pervert the meaning of words. . . .

⁂

Ranking the Presidents has become a popular game, and even Presidents like to play it, notably Truman and Kennedy. In my own evaluation, I place Wilson along with Jefferson and Lincoln as the nation's three greatest Presidents, which makes Wilson our greatest twentieth-century President. If rated solely on the basis of long-range impact on international relations, Wilson is the most influential of all our Presidents.

What are the achievements which entitle Wilson to so high a place? Let us consider the major ones, although of course some of these are more important than others.

. . . [B]etter than any responsible statesman of his day, Wilson understood and sympathized with the anti-imperialist revolutions and their aspirations for basic internal reforms. He withdrew American support for the Bankers' Consortium in China, and the United States under Wilson was the first of the great powers to recognize the Revolution of Sun Yat-sen. Early in his term he had to wrestle with the Mexican Revolution. He saw the need for social reform; avoided the general war with Mexico that many American investors, Catholics, and professional patriots wanted; and by refusing to recognize the counter-revolution of Huerta and cutting Huerta off from trade and arms while allowing the flow of arms to Carranza, Villa, and Zapata, he made possible the overthrow of the counter-revolution and the triumph of the Revolution. What merciless criticism was heaped on Wilson for insisting that Latin Americans should be positively encouraged to institute reforms and develop democratic practices. Yet today Americans applaud their government's denial of Alliance-for-Progress funds to Latin American countries which refuse to undertake fundamental economic and social reforms and flout democracy.

. . . [C]onfronted with the stupendous and completely novel challenge of having to mobilize not only America's military strength but also its civilian resources and energies in America's first total war, the Wilson Administration set up a huge network of administrative agencies, exemplifying the highest imagination and creativity in the art of practical administration. FDR, in his New Deal and in his World War II agencies, was to borrow heavily from the Wilson innovations.

. . . Wilson's Fourteen Points and his other peace aims constituted war propaganda of perhaps unparalleled brilliance. They thrilled the world. They gave high purpose to the peoples of the Allied countries and stirred their war efforts. Directed over the heads of the governments to the enemy peoples themselves, they produced unrest, helped bring about the revolutions that overthrew the Sultan, the Hapsburgs, and the Hohenzollerns, and hastened the end of the war.

. . . [T]he Treaty of Versailles, of which Wilson was the chief architect, was a better peace than it would have been (considering, among other things, the imperialist secret treaties of the Allies) because of Wilson's labors for a just peace. The League of Nations was founded, and this was to be the forerunner of the United Nations. To the League was assigned the work of general disarmament. The mandate system of the League, designed to prepare colonial peoples for self-government and national independence, was a revolutionary step away from the old imperialism. The aspirations of many peoples in Europe for national independence were fulfilled. (If the disruption of the Austro-Hungarian Empire helped destroy the old balance of power, it must be said that in this particular situation Wilson's doctrine of national autonomy only exploited an existing fact in the interest of Allied victory, and even had there been no Wilsonian self-determination the nationalities of this area were already so well developed that they could not have been denied independence after the defeat of the Hapsburgs. Wilson's self-determination was to be a far more *creative* force among the colonial peoples than among the Europeans.) The Treaty restrained the chauvinism of the Italians, though not as much as

Wilson would have liked. It prevented the truncating of Germany by preserving to her the Left Bank of the Rhine. The war-guilt clause and the enormous reparations saddled on Germany were mistakes, but Wilson succeeded in confining German responsibility to civilian damage and the expenses of Allied military pensions rather than the whole cost of the war; and had the United States ratified the Treaty and participated in post-war world affairs, as Wilson expected, the United States would have been in a position to join Britain in scaling down the actual reparations bill and in preventing any such adventure as the French seizure of the Ruhr in 1923, from which flowed Germany's disastrous inflation and the ugly forces of German nihilism. (There is poignancy in the broken Wilson's coming out of retirement momentarily in 1923 to denounce France for making "waste paper" of the Treaty of Versailles.) Finally, if Shantung was Wilson's Yalta, he paid the kind of price FDR paid and for precisely the same reason—the collapse of the balance of power in the immediate area involved.

. . . [T]he chief claim of Wilson to a superlative place in history—and it will not be denied him merely because he was turned down by the United States Senate—is that he, more than any other, formulated and articulated the ideology which was the polestar of the Western democracies in World War I, in World War II, and in the decades of Cold War against the Communists. Today, well past the middle of the twentieth century, the long-time program of America is still a Wilsonian program: international collective security, disarmament, the lowering of economic barriers between nations (as in America's support for the developing West European community today), anti-colonialism, self-determination of nations, and democratic social politics as an alternative to Communism. And this was the program critics of Wilson called "anachronistic," a mere "throw-back" to nineteenth-century liberalism!

America today is still grappling with the same world problems Wilson grappled with in 1917, 1918, and 1919, and the programs and policies designed to meet them are still largely Wilsonian. But events since Wilson's time have made his solutions more and more prophetic and urgent. The sweep of the anti-imperialist revolutions propels us to wider self-determination and social politics. The elimination of space, the increasing interdependence of the world, the further disintegration of the balance of power in World War II, and the nuclear revolution in war compel us to more effective collective security and to arms control supervised by an agency of the United Nations.

There will be more unwillingness to identify Wilson with social politics abroad than with the other policies with which he is more clearly identified. Historians like to quote George L. Record's letter to Wilson in which he told Wilson that there was no longer any glory in merely standing for political democracy, that political democracy had arrived, that the great issues of the future would revolve around economic and social democracy. But Wilson stood in no need of advice on this score. Earlier than any other responsible statesman, Wilson had seen the significance of the Chinese Revolution of Sun Yat-sen and of the Mexican Revolution, and he had officially encouraged both. Wilson believed that economic and social reform was implicit in the doctrine of self-determination, especially when applied to the colonial peoples. He recognized, too, that the Bolshevist Revolution had given economic and social reform a new urgency in all parts of the world. He was also well aware that those who most opposed his program for a world settlement were the conservative and imperialist elements in Western Europe and Japan, that socialist and labor groups were his most effective supporters. He pondered deeply how closely and openly he could work with labor and socialist parties in Europe without cutting off necessary support at home. (This—how to use social democracy and the democratic left to counter Communism abroad and still carry American opinion—was to be a central problem for every discerning American statesman after 1945.) Months before he had received Record's letter, Wilson himself had expressed almost the same views as Record. In a long conversation with Professor Stockton Axson at the White House, Wilson acknowledged that his best support was coming from labor people, that they were in touch with world movements and were international-minded, that government ownership of some basic resources and industries was coming, even in the United States, and that it was by a program of social democracy that Communism could be defeated.

In 1918 two gigantic figures—Wilson and Lenin—faced each other and articulated the contesting ideologies which would shake the world during the century.

Since then, the lesser leaders who have succeeded them have added little to the ideology of either side. We are now far enough into the century to see in what direction the world is headed, provided there is no third world war. It is not headed for Communist domination. It is not headed for an American hegemony. And it is not headed for a duality with half the world Communist and the other half capitalist. Instead, it is headed for a new pluralism. The emerging new national societies are adjusting their new industrialism to their own conditions and cultures; and their developing economies will be varying mixtures of privatism, collectivism, and welfarism. Even the Communist states differ from one another in conditions, cultures, stages of revolutionary development, and degrees of Marxist "orthodoxy" or "revisionism." And today, all national states, old and new, Communist and non-Communist, join the United Nations as a matter of course.

There will be "victory" for neither "side," but instead a world which has been historically affected by both. Lenin's international proletarian state failed to materialize, but the evolving economies of the underdeveloped peoples are being influenced by his collectivism. However, the facts that most of the emerging economies are mixed ones, that they are working themselves out within autonomous national frameworks, and that the multiplying national states are operating internationally through the United Nations all point to a world which will be closer to the vision of Wilson than to that of Lenin. For this reason Wilson is likely to become a world figure of heroic proportions, with an acknowledged impact on world history more direct and far-reaching than that of any other American.

William G. Carleton (1903–1982) was a professor emeritus at the University of Florida and author of the widely used textbook, *The Revolution in American Foreign Policy*.

EXPLORING THE ISSUE

Was Woodrow Wilson Responsible for the Failure of the United States to Join the League of Nations?

Critical Thinking and Reflection

1. Compare and contrast the roles of President Wilson and Senator Lodge in bringing about the defeat of the Treaty of Versailles in the Senate. Who should bear responsibility for this failure?
2. Given Bailey's interpretation, do you think Wilson would have compromised on the treaty with Senator Lodge had he not suffered a severe stroke? Discuss.
3. Critically analyze how Carleton defends Wilson from the charges of (1) inflexibility and (2) naïve optimism. Do you agree or disagree with these criticisms? Why?
4. Evaluate whether Wilson was a realist or an idealist.
5. Compare and contrast the interpretations of Bailey and Carleton regarding Wilson's approach to foreign policy.

Is There Common Ground?

Both Carleton and Bailey make strong cases for their points of view. Carleton blames the Republicans, in particular the chairman of the Senate Foreign Relations Committee, Henry Cabot Lodge, for stalling votes on the treaty by reading its provisions to an empty Senate for nearly two weeks. He also rejects the Freudian interpretation, which argues that Wilson was incapable of compromise.

Bailey, on the other hand, blames Wilson more than Lodge for killing the treaty and the opportunity for the United States to enter and influence the League of Nations. Had Wilson not been physically damaged by his stroke, he might have struck a deal with Republicans as he had done previously in passing his New Freedom legislative program. Perhaps Bailey best hits the mark when he argues that Wilson was ahead of his times, and the American people were not willing to overthrow their traditional isolationist views to join an international League of Nations. Carleton also agrees that Wilson was ahead of his time. Maybe it was impossible for the United States to have joined the League of Nations at this time.

Additional Resources

Lloyd E. Ambrosius, "Woodrow Wilson's Health and the Treaty Fight," *Wilsonianism: Woodrow Wilson and His Legacy in American Foreign Relations* (Palgrave Macmillan, 2002).

John M. Cooper, *Breaking the Heart of the World* (Cambridge University Press, 2001).

Arthur S. Link, "The Case for Woodrow Wilson," in *The Higher Realism of Woodrow Wilson* (Vanderbilt University Press, 1971).

Arthur S. Link, *Woodrow Wilson: Revolution, War, and Peace* (Johns Hopkins University Press, 1979).

John A. Thompson, *Woodrow Wilson* (Pearson Education, 2002).

Internet References . . .

The Treaty of Versailles and the League
of Nations

www.ushistory.org/us/45d.asp

U.S. Department of State

http://history.state.gove/milestones/1914-1920/WWI

Wilson—A Portrait: League of Nations

www.pbs.org/wgbh/amex/wilson/portrait/
wp_league.html

Wilson Embarks on Tour to Promote
League of Nations

www.history.com/this-day-in-history/wilson-embarks-
on-tour-to-promote-league-of-nations

Selected, Edited, and with Issue Framing Material by:
Kevin R. Magill and Tony L. Talbert, *Baylor University*

ISSUE

Is Media Propaganda Helpful in Supporting United States Democracy?

YES: Edward Bernays, from "Speak Up for Democracy," *Current History* (1940)

NO: Noam Chomsky, from "Democracy and the Media" in Pluto Press (1989)

Learning Outcomes

After reading this issue, you will be able to:

- Identify the positive and negative ways propaganda can play out in a democratic society.
- Analyze and historically contextualize the ways propaganda in the media has influenced American society specifically regarding political campaigns, foreign relations, public policy, and in the exchange of democratic ideas.
- Evaluate whether or not propaganda has served the interests of those in power or the larger interest of the American people.
- Deliberate how the media should function within democratic systems and assess whether or not there is room for propaganda within those systems.

ISSUE SUMMARY

YES: Edward Bernays believes that the media propaganda plays a vital role in developing the opinions, habits, tastes, and ideas within a democratic society. He suggests that this conscious and intelligent manipulation is vital because it helps to establish a basic framework by which citizens can understand the world, thereby avoiding chaos.

NO: Noam Chomsky rejects the idea that this type of propaganda is helpful, instead suggesting that it and other media mechanisms limit the exchange of democratic ideas. He argues that this propaganda has served to further the interests of those in power and business elites.

Issue framing with Lauren Bagwell, *University of Wisconsin-Madison*

Without question, the history of American Propaganda can be observed from the country's inception. It has ranged from framing ideas in particular ways to communicating messages that shape perceptions. Consider the history of propaganda in US history. The presentation of the Boston Massacre became a massive Revolutionary War propaganda piece that signaled to colonists

that they needed to revolt because the oppressive British Empire would never allow them to live free. Since that time, propaganda has been used to sway public opinion in the United States during wartime, in illegal spying and cold war tactics, in the war on drugs, in advertising, and in psychic warfare. Most often it has been used to develop consensus for controversial political action or as a way to change tastes and perceptions about ideas, goods, and people. It is perhaps as an important time as ever to consider propaganda in the era of so-called "fake news." Perhaps propaganda is a better description of the ideas that are being framed for public consumption.

Before evaluating whether propaganda is helpful to American democracy, it is important to center ourselves around a working definition of what propaganda is. Propaganda is applied psychology (Bernays, 1936) that uses symbols to evoke complex human emotions that in turn shape an individuals' attitudes and behaviors (Hobbs, 2017). In its simplest form, propaganda is an effective communication (Hobbs, 2017). At its core, it is a tool for communication that, when put in the hands of producers, synthesizes perspectives, later distributing those perspectives out to consumers on a mass scale. Hobbs (2017) writes:

> At its worst, propaganda leads to genocide. And in its best and highest use, propaganda can help shift public opinion and behavior to help create a 'more educated, healthier and progressive citizenry' (pg. 626).

The two articles selected for this issue offer two different positionalities that force readers to critically evaluate whether propaganda is helpful to American democracy. On one side of the table sits Edward Bernays. Referred to as "the father of public relations," Bernays believed propaganda was "the voice of the people in the democracy of today" (Bernays, 1936). Bernays argues that propaganda allowed ideas, namely minority ideas, to be communicated more quickly and effectively. On the other side of the spectrum sits Noam Chomsky. Sometimes referred to as the "father of modern linguistics," Chomsky is a scholar in the field of cognitive science. He argues that propaganda does not serve the voice of the people rather the voice of the elite, thus hindering the very nature of democracy.

The selected articles take into account both the producer and consumer of propaganda and the impact propaganda has on systems of democracy. In his piece (1989), Chomsky offers a conception of a propaganda model. In this model, he identifies the systems of power influencing a dominant media force entangled in the market system. The model suggests that aspects of mainstream media serve as elite institutions that filter the spread of ideas through the parameters of elite interests (Chomsky & Herman, 1988 cited in Bușu et al., 2014). Chomsky argues this is particularly problematic in a US context where citizens, though given the civil liberties to act as active citizens, typically situate themselves as consumers and observers but not as participants in their country's democracy (Chomsky, 1989). As a result, the average citizen is "unaware of their own stake in an issue or are immobilized by effective propaganda" (Bușu et al., 2014, pg. 87).

One way Chomsky notes the submissiveness of the American consumer is in reference to the Creel Commission. Established under the Woodrow Wilson Administration, the Creel Commission served as the Committee on Public Information. Noteworthy for their World War I propaganda campaign later known the Red Scare, Chomsky suggests that the commission best controlled the news by flooding news channels with endless cycles of facts or official information. Chomsky argues that the saturation of information flooding into news channels, combined with selective media coverage, indoctrinated a perceived truth into the American people. Chomsky writes:

> A prominent feature was the suppression of independent politics and free speech, on the principle that the state is entitled to prevent improper thought and its expression. Wilson's Creel Commission, dedicated to creating war fever among the generally pacifist population, had demonstrated the efficacy of organized propaganda with the cooperation of the loyal media and the intellectuals, who devoted themselves to such tasks as "historical engineering," the term devised by historian Frederic Paxson, one of the founders of the National Board for Historical Service established by U.S. historians to serve the state by "explaining the issues of the war that we might the better win it." The lesson was learned by those in a position to employ it. (Chomsky, 1989, pg. 47).

While the Chomsky suggests that Americans are unaware of the extent to which business elites and government entities use propaganda to influence daily decisions, opinions, and thought processes, the Bernays articles suggest otherwise. In contrast to Chomsky, Bernays argues that the influence of propaganda, when used altruistically, can contribute towards shared democratic visions. Bernays does not deny that propaganda can be misused; rather, he argues that misuse occurs when propaganda is exploited as a function of the state as in the case of many dictatorships. He argues too that propaganda in a democracy must be a function of the people. Bernays writes:

> So the program I propose falls into two fields. One would be cultivated by the leaders of every kind of group—social, educational, neighborhood, religious, athletic, and so on. The other would be cultivated by men and women of all sorts everywhere at all times (Bernays, 1940, pg. 22).

Bernays sees the United States as a collection made up of many groups each having their own group leaders or "molders of opinion." Propaganda as a function of the people involves each of these groups striving towards becoming more articulate in how they communicate principles of democracy to their constituents. The process, Bernays argues, is a combination of art, science, psychology, and sociology. It is up to the group leaders, the molders of opinion, to become experts in each field in order to be more efficient and effective advocates of democracy.

In both articles, Bernays and Chomsky offer commentary on the influence propaganda has on democratic systems. Both authors make a case that propaganda plays a critical role in developing societal norms, opinions, ideas, and framework for how individuals as citizens see and interpret the world around them. Chomsky argues that individuals are often unaware of the political and economic structures of power that use this as an organizational framework to propel the ideas of the business elites and limit minority perspectives. Bernays argues that propaganda can be used as a tool to fight for democracy when altruistically used by newspaper writers, radio commentators, and scenarists to whom Bernays refers to as "professional molders of public opinion in politics." Through engaging with these pieces of work, readers will develop a deeper understanding of the structures that influence propaganda in the media and decide for themselves whether or not this is helpful for American democracy.

YES ⬅

Edward L. Bernays

Speak Up for Democracy

A Program Outlined for Patriots . .
Group Members and Leaders . .
Believers in America.

MILLIONS of Americans are out of sympathy with American democracy. Native-born or foreign-born, Communists, Nazis, Fascists or fellow-travelers, these millions are more sympathetic with the institutions and policies of Soviet Russia, Nazi Germany or Fascist Italy than with those of the United States.

The depression, stripping men of assets and opportunities, weakened belief in democracy. Since then the military machines and dynamic propaganda of Communists, Fascists and Nazis have vanquished democracy in most of Europe and placed it squarely on the defensive in its last great stronghold, the United States.

I admit that democracy is on the defensive in the United States. I propose that it be defended. By constructing vast fighting forces, land, sea and air? That, of course—but that is only part of the proposal. In large degree, the strength of our fighting force will depend on the depth and breadth of our belief in our institutions. "Armies fight as the people think," a wise British general noted. To widen and deepen our belief in our institutions, I propose that all of us, our leaders as well as our rank and file, become propagandists for democracy.

"Speak up for democracy"—my message boils down to four words.

This program is not academic, not visionary. It is realistic, tangible. It applies proved methods of persuasion, of influencing, crystallizing and mobilizing public opinion. The mobilization of public opinion has been my profession and avocation for more than twenty-five years. My wife and I first called our joint work "counsel on public relations" eighteen years ago. In all modesty, may I say that my counsel has been sought and applied by many of America's greatest corporations, by highly placed individuals, by government. And so I ask for credence when I say that the program here suggested will work.

The billions of dollars being spent for national defense will be uselessly spent unless, throughout the country, there is a fundamental belief in and reliance upon democracy. Ignorance or rejection of the worth of democracy is a greater menace to this country than any "fifth column," than any foreign army or navy.

Now, how shall we go about revitalizing democracy—the whole of democracy for all the people? Men and women want to contribute something more personal to democracy than a few dollars or the use of their names on some organization's letterhead. And they can. The way to save democracy is to go out and save it. And the way to do that is for everyone to *mold public opinion for democracy to the limit of his own power.*

In the United States, there are thousands of professional molders of public opinion in politics, business and other fields—newspaper and magazine men, writers, scenarists, radio commentators, others. All can do their part in fighting for democracy. They do not need to be told how. They know. But in time of peril the United States does not entrust its defense to the professional soldier alone. Like the protection of the country militarily, its protection ideologically depends on the aggressive activity of all—and ideas are as valuable in defense as armaments.

The molding of public opinion for democracy must not come only from the top, from the Roosevelts and Willkies. Members of every group of society must assume responsibilities—and the value of democracy must be directly related to the individuals in that group.

"I like the American Way," an Eastern manufacturer said recently.

"Why?"

"Because my mail reaches me as it was sent—uncensored. No one taps my telephone. I can join any political party I wish. I can vote for what and whom I please. I can read, see and hear what I choose. I can express opinions openly, even when they are 'agin' government men and measures."

That statement dealt with abstractions—liberty, justice, rights—but they meant much to that American. They will mean as much to other Americans who think their meanings through. But there are people in this country who have thought no further than did many in Germany, when the Nazis were getting under way. They wanted to protect their property, as who doesn't? They gave money to a political leader named Hitler who excoriated democracy and promised them that their property would be secure. The rest they now know too well.

MANY here also fail to recognize the good fortune they enjoy under democracy, the misfortune that would come to them if democracy were to be displaced by Nazism, Fascism or Communism. Young college graduates, taxicab drivers, professional men—all sorts of people—go far astray.

A Harvard professor recently told me that, after a long lecture he had given to his class on democracy, one of his students said: "It's all hokum, but I believe it anyway." He really had no realization of what democracy meant to him.

Another college graduate I know, a young woman, feels that her country is a failure because it has not given her and the young man she wants to marry security for life. To her, all else is unimportant. She is interested only in a Utopian United States.

A taxicab driver, during a national political convention this year, took a good deal of his time and mine to belittle democratic processes. The convention delegates, he was sure, were interested solely in "women and the bottle," and so "a dictator would be a hell of a lot better." That taxicab driver should be taught how subjects are treated in dictator countries.

A professional man I know told me with chuckle-headed cheerfulness of a manufacturing concern in which he has an interest: "We aren't going to take war contracts. Why should we be stuck with them? While our competitors are loading up with war contracts on a cost-plus basis, we'll be doing a bang-up business in regular directions." It never occurred to him to identify himself with the government and national defense in this regard.

The cure for these misapprehensions in our democracy is, I believe, more democracy. In a dictatorship, propaganda is a function of the state. In a democracy it must be a function of the people. So the program I propose falls into two fields. One would be cultivated by the leaders of every kind of group—social, educational, neighborhood, religious, athletic, and so on. The other would be cultivated by men and women of all sorts everywhere at all times.

Many different kinds of groups function in the United States, and each has its group leaders, its molders of opinion. Each leader influences his constituents on matters of direct concern to his group. But he has influence extending beyond that particular subject. Realizing this, he should strive to become more articulate regarding democracy, more efficient as a molder of public opinion in its favor.

Molding public opinion is not a gift or an inspiration. Like other professions—law, engineering, architecture—it combines a science and an art. It applies established principles of psychology, sociology and other social sciences to the achievement of definite goals. It is up to our group leaders to study these principles and learn how they can be used to mold public opinion for democracy.

THE average group leader may be in a better position to do this than average group members. There are courses, at universities and elsewhere, in which the subject is taught. There are books on public opinion in libraries. To find them consult *A Reference Guide to Public Opinion*, issued by the Princeton University Press. Good books to start with are Walter Lippmann's *Public Opinion* and Peter Odegard's *The American Public Mind*. The author of this article has written *Propaganda* and *Crystallizing Public Opinion*.

To mold public opinion, the group leader must know what governs public actions; must understand the groups that make up society; must have a feeling for the value and effect of words and pictures. He must know the media through which facts and opinions are brought to the people in his community. When he does know, he can meet with effective counter-propaganda all attacks on democracy.

The great instruments—the press, the radio, the motion picture, the school, the lecture platform—that mold public opinion in his community are open to the group leader if he brings them the ideas and material their publics demand. He should make a study of their activities and needs. He should know what constituencies and ideas the newspapers in his city represent; what their policies are in news and editorial coverage; who the editors are; and on what basis they desire news referring to the activities for democracy which he may set in motion.

He should be acquainted, also, with the policies and personnel of the radio stations and press services in his territory. He should know the character and location of any public forum in his community. He should know who books the important speaking engagements in his town and why and when. He should know who in his community represents the leading newsreel companies.

WITH these facts before him he can plan his campaign for democracy in terms of the kind of material these media carry. If he finds leaders of other groups in his town who are of the same mind, together they can organize a joint executive committee to work for the common goal.

And every group member, as well as group leader, can do his part in selling democracy. If you believe in democracy, say so. If you understand its magnificent realities as they affect the individual's day to day life, stress them. Affirm the truth. Scotch the lie. All of us can be champions of democracy within our own sphere—to our friends and families, to the people we meet, to the butcher, baker, candlestick maker.

The most common accusations against democracy number less than a dozen. Each of us can have available strong and truthful answers to them, and help bury the accusations by incessant repetition of the answers.

Here is a list of common accusations against democracy in the United States:

1. Democratic processes are too slow, too inefficient.

   Answer: Democratic processes are planned to provide for full, free discussion, which takes time. Thus decisions can be reached between conflicting points of view, giving the greatest satisfaction to the greatest number. Normally, progress in our democracy comes the safe, lasting way, through evolutionary change. But we have often risen to an emergency—note the speed with which Congress enacted recovery legislation in 1933 and defense legislation in 1940. In such cases it has shown all the force and speed of the autocracies, without their abuse of power.

2. Freedom of speech is a meaningless freedom except for the man who acts as if it were license. Then it should be forbidden.

   Answer: Have *you* ever criticized this government, or specifically, Mr. Roosevelt? How would *you* like to be sent to a concentration camp for doing so? That is what would happen to *you* for criticizing the government in a dictatorship. The basic purpose of freedom of speech, and of the press, and of assembly, is to facilitate human communication, to enable the people, by free interchange, of ideas, to arrive at sound conclusions leading to intelligent action. As Lyman Bryson, distinguished American educator, puts it, "If every man can say what he pleases, we

have a fair chance of getting at the truth." If this freedom is meaningless, truth itself is meaningless. And so is rational action.

3. Security in a dictatorship is more important than liberty in a democracy.

   Answer: Liberty and security are not mutually exclusive—that is totalitarian propaganda. The greatest degree of economic security known on this earth was known in the Scandinavian democracies recently destroyed by Communism and Fascism. And they also enjoyed great liberty. In a dictatorship, on the other hand, there is no real security—not even security of life. Many of Hitler's good friends would testify to the fact had they not been murdered in the blood purge of 1934 or later.

4. Dictatorships are superior to democracy because they have eliminated unemployment.

   Answer: The alternative we face is not "no job under democracy" vs. "job under dictatorship." We Americans are striving constantly to combat unemployment, as our C.C.C., W.P.A. and other government projects indicate. Dictatorships, meanwhile, strive to create not the fact but the illusion that, under their systems, everyone has a job. In a dictatorship, everyone is actually or potentially part of a system of forced labor—tomorrow the expert accountant may be made to slaughter hogs; tomorrow the Montana cowboy may be forced to dig Bronx sewers. The right to strike is forfeit; the right to bargain is unknown. The activity in which, under dictatorship, labor shares is largely activity in preparation for war. In the U.S., labor is still free—to organize, to bargain collectively, to quit and take another job. Meanwhile, M. E. Tracy, former editor of CURRENT HISTORY, phrases it neatly: "Nazism, Communism and Fascism boast of the fact that they have no unemployment. Neither has a prison nor an army."

5. Most people are too ignorant and stupid to vote intelligently, as under democracy they should.

   Answer: Abraham Lincoln said, "No man is good enough to govern any other man without that other's consent." Those who accuse the majority of stupidity rarely class themselves among the majority. The real alternatives here are majority rule vs. dictator rule. In a democracy there is always opportunity under intelligent leadership for peaceful conversion of a venal, despotic or stupid majority opinion. Thomas Jefferson wrote: "I know of no safe depository of the ultimate powers of society but the people themselves; and if we think them not enlightened enough to exercise their control with a wholesome dis-cretion, the remedy is not to take it from them, but to inform their discretion by education." If a dictator has anti-social qualities—and also the 600,000 police supposedly in Hitler's Gestapo—what is to be done?

6. Gangsterism in this country shows that our democracy has rotted, and must be superseded by a stronger system like Fascism or Communism.

Answer: Here the gangsters are illegal. In dictator countries, the gangsters are legal. They are the government and the law. When the people of this country are sufficiently aroused, they invoke the law and gangsters are eliminated. In dictator nations only a bloody revolution can shake the gangsters from their hold.

7. Democracy has representative government, not democratic government. The men who govern act according to their constituents' desires. Their actions are not necessarily in the public interest. They are actions predicated on the self-interest of the individual legislator and of his group. How much better would be the decision reached by a strong man at the top!

Answer: This is presupposing that the strong man knows, and always acts on, the right answer. It is taking a much greater chance to place your trust in one man than in the self-interest of many men, representing the self-interest of many groups. Occasionally, beneficent despots arise. History quickly points out how very few they have ever been.

8. As science and invention continue, there will be less opportunity for the democratic state to function through its electorate. The best method for carrying on governmental activities will have been determined. And in a dictatorship the Fuehrer can quickly avail himself of all the find-ings of science and invention without having to convince the people of their validity.

Answer: How can we be sure that the dictator has the all-seeing wisdom to make only sound and scientific decisions? When he is wrong, his decisions carry the same force and weight as when he is right. The "scientific" blood theories of the Nazis have been disproved, and yet carry the weight of truth in Nazi Germany. Is it not better to let the people absorb truth and science more slowly than to let all suffer from someone's crackpot pseudo-scientific notions?

The refugees who have come to us from dictatorship countries give a picture that the individual who lives here can hardly comprehend. Whenever the house doorbell rang, they were in mortal fear that it might be the Gestapo or its equivalent. When they walked along the street and were eyed by a casual stranger, they were afraid of being picked up and never being heard from again. When the children did not come home exactly at the appointed hour, who knew but that they might have been appre-hended? No telephone conversation was safe. Every activ-ity was at the whim of an impersonal and arbitrary power.

Do we want that kind of life in these United States of America? You know we don't. Let's not have it. Let's speak up for *our* United States, *our* America, *our* democracy—now!

EDWARD BERNAYS (1891–1995) was an Austrian-American pioneer in the field of public relations and propaganda, referred to in his obituary as "the father of public rela-tions." He combined the ideas of Gustave Le Bon and Wilfred Trotter on crowd psychology with the psychoana-lytical ideas of his uncle, Sigmund Freud.

Noam Chomsky

→ **NO**

Democracy and the Media

Under the heading "Brazilian bishops support plan to democratize media," a church-based South American journal describes a proposal being debated in the constituent assembly that "would open up Brazil's powerful and highly concentrated media to citizen participation." "Brazil's Catholic bishops are among the principal advocates [of this] . . . legislative proposal to democratize the country's communications media," the report continues, noting that "Brazilian TV is in the hands of five big networks [while] . . . eight huge multinational corporations and various state enterprises account for the majority of all communications advertising." The proposal "envisions the creation of a National Communications Council made up of civilian and government representatives [that] . . . would develop a democratic communications policy and grant licenses to radio and television operations." "The Brazilian Conference of Catholic Bishops has repeatedly stressed the importance of the communications media and pushed for grassroots participation. It has chosen communications as the theme of its 1989 Lenten campaign," an annual "parish-level campaign of reflection about some social issue" initiated by the Bishops' Conference.

The questions raised by the Brazilian bishops are being seriously discussed in many parts of the world. Projects exploring them are under way in several Latin American countries and elsewhere. There has been discussion of a "New World Information Order" that would diversify media access and encourage alternatives to the global media system dominated by the Western industrial powers. A UNESCO inquiry into such possibilities elicited an extremely hostile reaction in the United States. The alleged concern was freedom of the press. Among the questions I would like to raise as we proceed are: just how serious is this concern, and what is its substantive content? Further questions that lie in the background have to do with a democratic communications policy: what it might be, whether it is a desideratum, and if so, whether it is attainable. And, more generally, just what kind of democratic order is it to which we aspire?

The concept of "democratizing the media" has no real meaning within the terms of political discourse in the United States. In fact, the phrase has a paradoxical or even vaguely subversive ring to it. Citizen participation would be considered an infringement on freedom of the press, a blow struck against the independence of the media that would distort the mission they have undertaken to inform the public without fear or favor. The reaction merits some thought. Underlying it are beliefs about how the media do function and how they should function within our democratic systems, and also certain implicit conceptions of the nature of democracy. Let us consider these topics in turn.

The standard image of media performance, as expressed by Judge Gurfein in a decision rejecting government efforts to bar publication of the *Pentagon Papers*, is that we have "a cantankerous press, an obstinate press, a ubiquitous press," and that these tribunes of the people "must be suffered by those in authority in order to preserve the even greater values of freedom of expression and the right of the people to know." Commenting on this decision, Anthony Lewis of the *New York Times* observes that the media were not always as independent, vigilant, and defiant of authority as they are today, but in the Vietnam and Watergate eras they learned to exercise "the power to root about in our national life; exposing what they deem right for exposure," without regard to external pressures or the demands of state or private power. This too is a commonly held belief.

There has been much debate over the media during this period, but it does not deal with the problem of "democratizing the media" and freeing them from the constraints of state and private power. Rather, the issue debated is whether the media have not exceeded proper bounds in escaping such constraints, even threatening the existence of democratic institutions in their contentious and irresponsible defiance of authority. A 1975 study on "governability of democracies" by the Trilateral Commission concluded that the media have become a "notable new source of national power," one aspect of an "excess of democracy" that contributes to "the reduction of governmental authority" at home and a consequent "decline in the influence of democracy abroad." This general "crisis of democracy," the commission held, resulted from the efforts of previously marginalized sectors of the population to organize and press their demands, thereby creating an overload that prevents the democratic process from functioning properly. In earlier times, "Truman had been able to govern the country with the cooperation of a relatively small number of Wall Street lawyers and bankers," so the American *rapporteur,* Samuel Huntington of Harvard University, reflected. In that period there was no crisis of democracy, but in the 1960s, the crisis developed and reached serious proportions. The study therefore urged more "moderation in democracy" to mitigate the excess of democracy and overcome the crisis.

Putting it in plain terms, the general public must be reduced to its traditional apathy and obedience, and driven from the arena of political debate and action, if democracy is to survive.

The Trilateral Commission study reflects the perceptions and values of liberal elites from the United States, Europe, and Japan, including the leading figures of the Carter administration. On the right, the perception is that democracy is threatened by the organizing efforts of those called the "special interests," a concept of contemporary political rhetoric that refers to workers, farmers, women, youth, the elderly, the handicapped, ethnic minorities, and so on—in short, the general population. In the U.S. presidential campaigns of the 1980s, the Democrats were accused of being the instrument of these special interests and thus undermining "the national interest," tacitly assumed to be represented by the one sector notably omitted from the list of special interests: corporations, financial institutions, and other business elites.

The charge that the Democrats represent the special interests has little merit. Rather, they represent other elements of the "national interest," and participated with few qualms in the right turn of the post-Vietnam era among elite groups, including the dismantling of limited state programs designed to protect the poor and deprived; the transfer of resources to the wealthy; the conversion of the state, even more than before, to a welfare state for the privileged; and the expansion of state power and the protected state sector of the economy through the military system—domestically, a device for compelling the public to subsidize high-technology industry and provide a state-guaranteed market for its waste production. A related element of the right turn was a more "activist" foreign policy to extend U.S. power through subversion, international terrorism, and aggression: the Reagan Doctrine, which the

media characterize as the vigorous defense of democracy worldwide, sometimes criticizing the Reaganites for their excesses in this noble cause. In general, the Democratic opposition offered qualified support to these programs of the Reagan administration, which, in fact, were largely an extrapolation of initiatives of the Carter years and, as polls clearly indicate, with few exceptions were strongly opposed by the general population.

Challenging journalists at the Democratic Convention in July 1988 on the constant reference to Michael Dukakis as "too liberal" to win, the media watch organization Fairness and Accuracy In Reporting (FAIR) cited a December 1987 *New York Times*/CBS poll showing overwhelming popular support for government guarantees of full employment, medical and day care, and a 3-to-1 margin in favor of reduction of military expenses among the 50 percent of the population who approve of a change. But the choice of a Reagan-style Democrat for vice president elicited only praise from the media for the pragmatism of the Democrats in resisting the left-wing extremists who called for policies supported by a large majority of the population. Popular attitudes, in fact, continued to move towards a kind of New Deal-style liberalism through the 1980s, while "liberal" became an unspeakable word in political rhetoric. Polls show that almost half the population believe that the U.S. Constitution—a sacred document—is the source of Marx's phrase "from each according to his ability, to each according to his need," so obviously right does the sentiment seem.

One should not be misled by Reagan's "landslide" electoral victories. Reagan won the votes of less than a third of the electorate; of those who voted, a clear majority hoped that his legislative programs would not be enacted, while half the population continues to believe that the government is run "by a few big interests looking out for themselves." Given a choice between the Reaganite program of damn-the-consequences Keynesian growth accompanied by jingoist flag-waving on the one hand, and the Democratic alternative of fiscal conservatism and "we approve of your goals but fear that the costs will be too high" on the other, those who took the trouble to vote preferred the former—not too surprisingly. Elite groups have the task of putting on a bold face and extolling the brilliant successes of our system: "a model democracy and a society that provides exceptionally well for the needs of its citizens," as Henry Kissinger and Cyrus Vance proclaim in outlining "Bipartisan Objectives for Foreign Policy" in the post-Reagan era. But apart from educated elites, much of the population appears to regard the government as an instrument of power beyond their influence and control;

and if their experience does not suffice, a look at some comparative statistics will show how magnificently the richest society in the world, with incomparable advantages, "provides for the needs of its citizens."

The Reagan phenomenon, in fact, may offer a foretaste of the directions in which capitalist democracy is heading, with the progressive elimination of labor unions, independent media, political associations, and, more generally, forms of popular organization that interfere with domination of the state by concentrated private power. Much of the outside world may have viewed Reagan as a "bizarre cowboy leader" who engaged in acts of "madness" in organizing a "band of cutthroats" to attack Nicaragua, among other exploits (in the words of Toronto *Globe and Mail* editorials), but U.S. public opinion seemed to regard him as hardly more than a symbol of national unity, something like the flag, or the Queen of England. The Queen opens Parliament by reading a political program, but no one asks whether she believes it or even understands it. Correspondingly, the public seemed unconcerned over the evidence, difficult to suppress, that President Reagan had only the vaguest conception of the policies enacted in his name, or the fact that when not properly programmed by his staff, he regularly came out with statements so outlandish as to be an embarrassment, if one were to take them seriously. The process of barring public interference with important matters takes a step forward when elections do not even enable the public to select among programs that originate elsewhere, but become merely a procedure for selecting a symbolic figure. It is therefore of some interest that the United States functioned virtually without a chief executive for eight years.

Returning to the media, which are charged with having fanned the ominous flames of "excess of democracy," the Trilateral Commission concluded that "broader interests of society and government" require that if journalists do not impose "standards of professionalism," "the alternative could well be regulation by the government" to the end of "restoring a balance between government and media." Reflecting similar concerns, the executive-director of Freedom House, Leonard Sussman, asked: "Must free institutions be overthrown because of the very freedom they sustain?" And John Roche, intellectual-in-residence during the Johnson administration, answered by calling for congressional investigation of "the workings of these private governments" which distorted the record so grossly in their "anti-Johnson mission," though he feared that Congress would be too "terrified of the media" to take on this urgent task.

Sussman and Roche were commenting on Peter Braestrup's two-volume study, sponsored by Freedom House, of media coverage of the Tet Offensive of 1968. This study was widely hailed as a landmark contribution, offering definitive proof of the irresponsibility of this "notable new source of national power." Roche described it as "one of the major pieces of investigative reporting and first-rate scholarship of the past quarter century," a "meticulous case-study of media incompetence, if not malevolence." This classic of modern scholarship was alleged to have demonstrated that in their incompetent and biased coverage reflecting the "adversary culture" of the sixties, the media in effect lost the war in Vietnam, thus harming the cause of democracy and freedom for which the United States fought in vain. The Freedom House study concluded that these failures reflect "the more volatile journalistic style—spurred by managerial exhortation or complaisance—that has become so popular since the late 1960s." The new journalism is accompanied by "an often mindless readiness to seek out conflict, to believe the worst of the government or of authority in general, and on that basis to divide up the actors on any issue into the 'good' and the 'bad'." The "bad" actors included the U.S. forces in Vietnam, the "military-industrial complex," the CIA and the U.S. government generally; and the "good," in the eyes of the media, were presumably the Communists, who, the study alleged, were consistently overpraised and protected. The study envisioned "a continuation of the current volatile styles, always with the dark possibility that, if the managers do not themselves take action, then outsiders—the courts, the Federal Communications Commission, or Congress—will seek to apply remedies of their own."

It is by now an established truth that "we tend to flagellate ourselves as Americans about various aspects of our own policies and actions we disapprove of" and that, as revealed by the Vietnam experience, "it is almost inescapable that such broad coverage will undermine support for the war effort," particularly "the often-gory pictorial reportage by television" (Landrum Bolling, at a conference he directed on the question of whether there is indeed "no way to effect some kind of balance between the advantages a totalitarian government enjoys because of its ability to control or black out unfavorable news in warfare and the disadvantages for the free society of allowing open coverage of all the wartime events"). The Watergate affair, in which investigative reporting "helped force a President from office" (Anthony Lewis), reinforced these dire images of impending destruction of democracy by the free-wheeling, independent, and adversarial media, as did the Iran-contra scandal. Ringing defenses of freedom of the press, such as those of Judge Gurfein and Anthony Lewis, are a response to attempts to control media excesses and impose upon them standards of responsibility.

Two kinds of questions arise in connection with these vigorous debates about the media and democracy: questions of fact and questions of value. The basic question of fact is whether the media have indeed adopted an adversarial stance, perhaps with excessive zeal; whether, in particular, they undermine the defense of freedom in wartime and threaten free institutions by "flagellating ourselves" and those in power. If so, we may then ask whether it would be proper to impose some external constraints to ensure that they keep to the bounds of responsibility, or whether we should adopt the principle expressed by Justice Holmes, in a classic dissent, that "the best test of truth is the power of the thought to get itself accepted in the competition of the market" through "free trade in ideas."

The question of fact is rarely argued; the case is assumed to have been proven. Some, however, have held that the factual premises are simply false. Beginning with the broadest claims, let us consider the functioning of the free market of ideas. In his study of the mobilization of popular opinion to promote state power, Benjamin Ginsberg maintains that

> western governments have used market mechanisms to regulate popular perspectives and sentiments. The "marketplace of ideas," built during the nineteenth and twentieth centuries, effectively disseminates the beliefs and ideas of the upper classes while subverting the ideological and cultural independence of the lower classes. Through the construction of this marketplace, western governments forged firm and enduring links between socioeconomic position and ideological power, permitting upper classes to use each to buttress the other … In the United States, in particular, the ability of the upper and upper-middle classes to dominate the marketplace of ideas has generally allowed these strata to shape the entire society's perception of political reality and the range of realistic political and social possibilities. While westerners usually equate the marketplace with freedom of opinion, the hidden hand of the market can be almost as potent an instrument of control as the iron fist of the state.

Ginsberg's conclusion has some initial plausibility, on assumptions about the functioning of a guided free market that are not particularly controversial. Those segments of the media that can reach a substantial audience are major corporations and are closely integrated with even larger conglomerates. Like other businesses, they sell a product to buyers. Their market is advertisers, and the "product" is audiences, with a bias towards more wealthy audiences, which improve advertising rates. Over a century ago, British Liberals observed that the market would promote those journals "enjoying the preference of the advertising public"; and today, Paul Johnson, noting the demise of a new journal of the left, blandly comments that it deserved its fate: "The market pronounced an accurate verdict at the start by declining to subscribe all the issue capital," and surely no right-thinking person could doubt that the market represents the public will.

In short, the major media—particularly, the elite media that set the agenda that others generally follow—are corporations "selling" privileged audiences to other businesses. It would hardly come as a surprise if the picture of the world they present were to reflect the perspectives and interests of the sellers, the buyers, and the product. Concentration of ownership of the media is high and increasing. Furthermore, those who occupy managerial positions in the media, or gain status within them as commentators, belong to the same privileged elites, and might be expected to share the perceptions, aspirations, and attitudes of their associates, reflecting their own class interests as well. Journalists entering the system are unlikely to make their way unless they conform to these ideological pressures, generally by internalizing the values; it is not easy to say one thing and believe another, and those who fail to conform will tend to be weeded out by familiar mechanisms.

The influence of advertisers is sometimes far more direct. "Projects unsuitable for corporate sponsorship tend to die on the vine," the London *Economist* observes, noting that "stations have learned to be sympathetic to the most delicate sympathies of corporations." The journal cites the case of public TV station WNET, which "lost its corporate underwriting from Gulf+Western as a result of a documentary called 'Hunger for Profit', about multinationals buying up huge tracts of land in the third world." These actions "had not been those of a friend," Gulf's chief executive wrote to the station, adding that the documentary was "virulently anti-business, if not anti-American." "Most people believe that WNET would not make the same mistake today," the *Economist* concludes. Nor would others. The warning need only be implicit.

Many other factors induce the media to conform to the requirements of the state-corporate nexus. To confront power is costly and difficult; high standards of evidence and argument are imposed, and critical analysis is naturally not welcomed by those who are in a position to react vigorously and to determine the array of rewards and punishments. Conformity to a "patriotic agenda," in contrast, imposes no such costs. Charges against official enemies barely require substantiation; they are, furthermore, protected from correction, which can be dismissed as apologetics for the criminals or as missing the forest for the trees. The system protects itself with indignation against a challenge to the right of deceit in the service of power, and the very idea of subjecting the ideological system to rational inquiry elicits incomprehension or outrage, though it is often masked in other terms. One who attributes the best intentions to the U.S. government, while perhaps deploring failure and ineptitude, requires no evidence for this stance, as when we ask why "success has continued to elude us" in the Middle East and Central America, why "a nation of such vast wealth, power and good intentions [cannot] accomplish its purposes more promptly and more effectively" (Landrum Bolling). Standards are radically different when we observe that "good intentions" are not properties of states, and that the United States, like every other state past and present, pursues policies that reflect the interests of those who control the state by virtue of their domestic power, truisms that are hardly expressible in the mainstream, surprising as this fact may be.

One needs no evidence to condemn the Soviet Union for aggression in Afghanistan and support for repression in Poland; it is quite a different matter when one turns to U.S. aggression in Indochina or its efforts to prevent a political settlement of the Arab-Israeli conflict over many years, readily documented, but unwelcome and therefore a non-fact. No argument is demanded for a condemnation of Iran or Libya for state-supported terrorism; discussion of the prominent—arguably dominant—role of the United States and its clients in organizing and conducting this plague of the modern era elicits only horror and contempt for this view point; supporting evidence, however compelling, is dismissed as irrelevant. As a matter of course, the media and intellectual journals either praise the U.S. government for dedicating itself to the struggle for democracy in Nicaragua or criticize it for the means it has employed to pursue this laudable objective, offering no evidence that this is indeed the goal of policy. A challenge to the underlying patriotic assumption is virtually unthinkable within the mainstream and, if permitted expression, would be dismissed as a variety of ideological fanaticism, an absurdity, even if backed by overwhelming evidence—not a difficult task in this case.

Case by case, we find that conformity is the easy way, and the path to privilege and prestige; dissidence carries personal costs that may be severe, even in a society that lacks such means of control as death squads, psychiatric prisons, or extermination camps. The very structure of the media is designed to induce conformity to established doctrine. In a three-minute stretch between commercials, or in seven hundred words, it is impossible to present unfamiliar thoughts or surprising conclusions with the argument and evidence required to afford them some credibility. Regurgitation of welcome pieties faces no such problem.

It is a natural expectation, on uncontroversial assumptions, that the major media and other ideological institutions will generally reflect the perspectives and interests of established power. That this expectation is fulfilled has been argued by a number of analysts. Edward Herman and I have published extensive documentation, separately and jointly, to support a conception of how the media function that differs sharply from the standard version. According to this "propaganda model"—which has prior plausibility for such reasons as those just briefly reviewed—the media serve the interests of state and corporate power, which are closely interlinked, framing their reporting and analysis in a manner supportive of established privilege and limiting debate and discussion accordingly. We have studied a wide range of examples, including those that provide the most severe test for a propaganda model, namely, the cases that critics of alleged anti-establishment excesses of the media offer as their strongest ground: the coverage of the Indochina wars, the Watergate affair, and others drawn from the period when the media are said to have overcome the conformism of the past and taken on a crusading role. To subject the model to a fair test, we have systematically selected examples that are as closely paired as history allows: crimes attributable to official enemies versus those for which the United States and its clients bear responsibility; good deeds, specifically elections conducted by official enemies versus those in U.S. client states. Other methods have also been pursued, yielding further confirmation.

There are, by now, thousands of pages of documentation supporting the conclusions of the propaganda model. By the standards of the social sciences, it is very well confirmed, and its predictions are often considerably surpassed. If there is a serious challenge to this conclusion, I am unaware of it. The nature of the arguments presented against it, on the rare occasions when the topic can even be addressed in the mainstream, suggest that the model is indeed robust. The highly regarded Freedom House study, which is held to have provided the conclusive demonstration of the adversarial character of the media and its threat to democracy, collapses upon analysis, and when innumerable errors and misrepresentations are corrected, amounts to little more than a complaint that the media were too pessimistic in their pursuit of a righteous cause; I know of no other studies that fare better.

There are, to be sure, other factors that influence the performance of social institutions as complex as the media, and one can find exceptions to the general pattern that the propaganda model predicts. Nevertheless, it has, I believe, been shown to provide a reasonably close first approximation, which captures essential properties of the media and the dominant intellectual culture more generally.

One prediction of the model is that it will be effectively excluded from discussion, for it questions a factual assumption that is most serviceable to the interests of established power: namely, that the media are adversarial and cantankerous, perhaps excessively so. However well-confirmed the model may be, then, it is inadmissible, and, the model predicts, should remain outside the spectrum of debate over the media. This conclusion too is empirically well-confirmed. Note that the model has a rather disconcerting feature. Plainly, it is either valid or invalid. If invalid, it may be dismissed; if valid, it *will* be dismissed. As in the case of eighteenth-century doctrine on seditious libel, truth is no defense; rather, it heightens the enormity of the crime of calling authority into disrepute.

If the conclusions drawn in the propaganda model are correct, then the criticisms of the media for their adversarial stance can only be understood as a demand that the media should not even reflect the range of debate over tactical questions among dominant elites, but should serve only those segments that happen to manage the state at a particular moment, and should do so with proper enthusiasm and optimism about the causes—noble by definition—in which state power is engaged. It would not have surprised George Orwell that this should be the import of the critique of the media by an organization that calls itself "Freedom House."

Journalists often meet a high standard of professionalism in their work, exhibiting courage, integrity, and enterprise, including many of those who report for media that adhere closely to the predictions of the propaganda model. There is no contradiction here. What is at issue is not the honesty of the opinions expressed or the integrity of those who seek the facts but rather the choice of topics and highlighting of issues, the range of opinion permitted expression, the unquestioned premises that guide reporting and commentary, and the general framework imposed

for the presentation of a certain view of the world. We need not, incidentally, tarry over such statements as the following, emblazoned on the cover of the *New Republic* during Israel's invasion of Lebanon: "Much of what you have read in the newspapers and newsmagazines about the war in Lebanon—and even more of what you have seen and heard on television—is simply not true." Such performances can be consigned to the dismal archives of apologetics for the atrocities of other favored states.

I will present examples to illustrate the workings of the propaganda model, but will assume the basic case to have been credibly established by the extensive material already in print. This work has elicited much outrage and falsification (some of which Herman and I review in *Manufacturing Consent*, some elsewhere), and also puzzlement and misunderstanding. But, to my knowledge, there is no serious effort to respond to these and other similar critiques. Rather, they are simply dismissed, in conformity to the predictions of the propaganda model. Typically, debate over media performance within the mainstream includes criticism of the adversarial stance of the media and response by their defenders, but no critique of the media for adhering to the predictions of the propaganda model, or recognition that this might be a conceivable position. In the case of the Indochina wars, for example, U.S. public television presented a retrospective series in 1985 followed by a denunciation produced by the right-wing media-monitoring organization Accuracy in Media and a discussion limited to critics of the alleged adversarial excesses of the series and its defenders. No one argued that the series conforms to the expectations of the propaganda model—as it does. The study of media coverage of conflicts in the Third World mentioned earlier follows a similar pattern, which is quite consistent, though the public regards the media as too conformist.

The media cheerfully publish condemnations of their "breathtaking lack of balance or even the appearance of fair-mindedness" and "the ills and dangers of today's wayward press."[29] But only when, as in this case, the critic is condemning the "media elite" for being "in thrall to liberal views of politics and human nature" and for the "evident difficulty most liberals have in using the word dictatorship to describe even the most flagrant dictatorships of the left"; surely one would never find Fidel Castro described as a dictator in the mainstream press, always so soft on Communism and given to self-flagellation. Such diatribes are not expected to meet even minimal standards of evidence; this one contains exactly one reference to what conceivably might be a fact, a vague allusion to alleged juggling of statistics by the *New York Times* "to obscure the decline of interest rates during Ronald

Reagan's first term," as though the matter had not been fully reported. Charges of this nature are often not unwelcome, first, because response is simple or superfluous; and second, because debate over this issue helps entrench the belief that the media are either independent and objective, with high standards of professional integrity and openness to all reasonable views, or, alternatively, that they are biased towards stylishly leftish flouting of authority. Either conclusion is quite acceptable to established power and privilege—even to the media elites themselves, who are not averse to the charge that they may have gone too far in pursuing their cantankerous and obstreperous ways in defiance of orthodoxy and power. The spectrum of discussion reflects what a propaganda model would predict: condemnation of "liberal bias" and defense against this charge, but no recognition of the possibility that "liberal bias" might simply be an expression of one variant of the narrow state-corporate ideology—as, demonstrably, it is—and a particularly useful variant, bearing the implicit message: thus far, and no further.

Returning to the proposals of the Brazilian bishops, one reason they would appear superfluous or wrongheaded if raised in our political context is that the media are assumed to be dedicated to service to the public good, if not too extreme in their independence of authority. They are thus performing their proper social role, as explained by Supreme Court Justice Powell in words quoted by Anthony Lewis in his defense of freedom of the press: "No individual can obtain for himself the information needed for the intelligent discharge of his political responsibilities … By enabling the public to assert meaningful control over the political process, the press performs a crucial function in effecting the societal purpose of the First Amendment."

An alternative view, which I believe is valid, is that the media indeed serve a "societal purpose," but quite a different one. It is the societal purpose served by state education as conceived by James Mill in the early days of the establishment of this system: to "train the minds of the people to a virtuous attachment to their government," and to the arrangements of the social, economic, and political order more generally. Far from contributing to a "crisis of democracy" of the sort feared by the liberal establishment, the media are vigilant guardians protecting privilege from the threat of public understanding and participation. If these conclusions are correct, the first objection to democratizing the media is based on factual and analytic error.

A second basis for objection is more substantial, and not without warrant: the call for democratizing the media could mask highly unwelcome efforts to limit intellectual

independence through popular pressures, a variant of concerns familiar in political theory. The problem is not easily dismissed, but it is not an inherent property of democratization of the media.

The basic issue seems to me to be a different one. Our political culture has a conception of democracy that differs from that of the Brazilian bishops. For them, democracy means that citizens should have the opportunity to inform themselves, to take part in inquiry and discussion and policy formation, and to advance their programs through political action. For us, democracy is more narrowly conceived: the citizen is a consumer, an observer but not a participant. The public has the right to ratify policies that originate elsewhere, but if these limits are exceeded, we have not democracy, but a "crisis of democracy," which must somehow be resolved.

This concept is based on doctrines laid down by the Founding Fathers. The Federalists, historian Joyce Appleby writes, expected "that the new American political institutions would continue to function within the old assumptions about a politically active elite and a deferential, compliant electorate," and "George Washington had hoped that his enormous prestige would bring that great, sober, commonsensical citizenry politicians are always addressing to see the dangers of self-created societies." Despite their electoral defeat, their conception prevailed, though in a different form as industrial capitalism took shape. It was expressed by John Jay, the president of the Continental Congress and the first chief justice of the U.S. Supreme Court, in what his biographer calls one of his favorite maxims: "The people who own the country ought to govern it." And they need not be too gentle in the mode of governance. Alluding to rising disaffection, Gouverneur Morris wrote in a dispatch to John Jay in 1783 that although "it is probable that much of Convulsion will ensue," there need be no real concern: "The People are well prepared" for the government to assume "that Power without which Government is but a Name . . . Wearied with the War, their Acquiescence may be depended on with absolute Certainty, and you and I, my friend, know by Experience that when a few Men of sense and spirit get together and declare that they are the Authority, such few as are of a different opinion may easily be convinced of their Mistake by that powerful Argument the Halter." By "the People," constitutional historian Richard Morris observes, "he meant a small nationalist elite, whom he was too cautious to name"—the white propertied males for whom the constitutional order was established. The "vast exodus of Loyalists and blacks" to Canada and elsewhere reflected in part their insight into these realities.

Elsewhere, Morris observes that in the post-revolutionary society, "what one had in effect was a political democracy manipulated by an elite," and in states where "egalitarian democracy" might appear to have prevailed (as in Virginia), in reality "dominance of the aristocracy was implicitly accepted." The same is true of the dominance of the rising business classes in later periods that are held to reflect the triumph of popular democracy.

John Jay's maxim is, in fact, the principle on which the Republic was founded and maintained, and in its very nature capitalist democracy cannot stray far from this pattern for reasons that are readily perceived.

At home, this principle requires that politics reduce, in effect, to interactions among groups of investors who compete for control of the state, in accordance with what Thomas Ferguson calls the "investment theory of politics," which, he argues plausibly, explains a large part of U.S. political history. For our dependencies, the same basic principle entails that democracy is achieved when the society is under the control of local oligarchies, business-based elements linked to U.S. investors, the military under our control, and professionals who can be trusted to follow orders and serve the interests of U.S. power and privilege. If there is any popular challenge to their rule, the United States is entitled to resort to violence to "restore democracy"—to adopt the term conventionally used in reference to the Reagan Doctrine in Nicaragua. The media contrast the "democrats" with the "Communists," the former being those who serve the interests of U.S. power, the latter those afflicted with the disease called "ultranationalism" in secret planning documents, which explain, forthrightly, that the threat to our interests is "nationalistic regimes" that respond to domestic pressures for improvement of living standards and social reform, with insufficient regard for the needs of U.S. investors.

The media are only following the rules of the game when they contrast the "fledgling democracies" of Central America, under military and business control, with "Communist Nicaragua." And we can appreciate why they suppressed the 1987 polls in El Salvador that revealed that a mere 10 percent of the population "believe that there is a process of democracy and freedom in the country at present." The benighted Salvadorans doubtless fail to comprehend our concept of democracy. And the same must be true of the editors of Honduras's leading journal *El Tiempo*. They see in their country a "democracy" that offers "unemployment and repression" in a caricature of the democratic process, and write that there can be no democracy in a country under "occupation of North American troops and contras," where "vital national interests are abandoned in order to serve the objectives of foreigners," while repression and illegal arrests continue, and the death squads of the military lurk ominously in the background.

In accordance with the prevailing conceptions in the U.S., there is no infringement on democracy if a few corporations control the information system: in fact, that is the essence of democracy. In the *Annals of the American Academy of Political and Social Science,* the leading figure of the public relations industry, Edward Bernays, explains that "the very essence of the democratic process" is "the freedom to persuade and suggest," what he calls "the engineering of consent." "A leader," he continues, "frequently cannot wait for the people to arrive at even general understanding … Democratic leaders must play their part in … engineering … consent to socially constructive goals and values," applying "scientific principles and tried practices to the task of getting people to support ideas and programs"; and although it remains unsaid, it is evident enough that those who control resources will be in a position to judge what is "socially constructive," to engineer consent through the media, and to implement policy through the mechanisms of the state. If the freedom to persuade happens to be concentrated in a few hands, we must recognize that such is the nature of a free society. The public relations industry expends vast resources "educating the American people about the economic facts of life" to ensure a favorable climate for business. Its task is to control "the public mind," which is "the only serious danger confronting the company," an AT&T executive observed eighty years ago.

Similar ideas are standard across the political spectrum. The dean of U.S. journalists, Walter Lippmann, described a "revolution" in "the practice of democracy" as "the manufacture of consent" has become "a self-conscious art and a regular organ of popular government." This is a natural development when "the common interests very largely elude public opinion entirely, and can be managed only by a specialized class whose personal interests reach beyond the locality." He was writing shortly after World War I, when the liberal intellectual community was much impressed with its success in serving as "the faithful and helpful interpreters of what seems to be one of the greatest enterprises ever undertaken by an American president" (*New Republic*). The enterprise was Woodrow Wilson's interpretation of his electoral mandate for "peace without victory" as the occasion for pursuing victory without peace, with the assistance of the liberal intellectuals, who later praised themselves for having "impose[d] their will upon a reluctant or indifferent majority," with the aid of propaganda fabrications about Hun atrocities and other such devices.

Fifteen years later, Harold Lasswell explained in the *Encyclopaedia of the Social Sciences* that we should not succumb to "democratic dogmatisms about men being the best judges of their own interests." They are not; the best judges are the elites, who must, therefore, be ensured the means to impose their will, for the common good. When social arrangements deny them the requisite force to compel obedience, it is necessary to turn to "a whole new technique of control, largely through propaganda" because of the "ignorance and superstition [of] ... the masses." In the same years, Reinhold Niebuhr argued that "rationality belongs to the cool observers," while "the proletarian" follows not reason but faith, based upon a crucial element of "necessary illusion." Without such illusion, the ordinary person will descend to "inertia." Then in his Marxist phase, Niebuhr urged that those he addressed—presumably, the cool observers—recognize "the stupidity of the average man" and provide the "emotionally potent oversimplifications" required to keep the proletarian on course to create a new society; the basic conceptions underwent little change as Niebuhr became "the official establishment theologian" (Richard Rovere), offering counsel to those who "face the responsibilities of power."

After World War II, as the ignorant public reverted to their slothful pacifism at a time when elites understood the need to mobilize for renewed global conflict, historian Thomas Bailey observed that "because the masses are notoriously short-sighted and generally cannot see danger until it is at their throats, our statesmen are forced to deceive them into an awareness of their own long-run interests. Deception of the people may in fact become increasingly necessary, unless we are willing to give our leaders in Washington a freer hand." Commenting on the same problem as a renewed crusade was being launched in 1981, Samuel Huntington made the point that "you may have to sell [intervention or other military action] in such a way as to create the misimpression that it is the Soviet Union that you are fighting. That is what the United States has done ever since the Truman Doctrine"—an acute observation, which explains one essential function of the Cold War.

At another point on the spectrum, the conservative contempt for democracy is succinctly articulated by Sir Lewis Namier, who writes that "there is no free will in the thinking and actions of the masses, any more than in the revolutions of planets, in the migrations of birds, and in the plunging of hordes of lemmings into the sea." Only disaster would ensue if the masses were permitted to enter the arena of decision-making in a meaningful way.

Some are admirably forthright in their defense of the doctrine: for example, the Dutch Minister of Defense writes that "whoever turns against manufacture of consent resists any form of effective authority." Any commissar would nod his head in appreciation and understanding.

At its root, the logic is that of the Grand Inquisitor, who bitterly assailed Christ for offering people freedom and thus condemning them to misery. The Church must correct the evil work of Christ by offering the miserable mass of humanity the gift they most desire and need: absolute submission. It must "vanquish freedom" so as "to make men happy" and provide the total "community of worship" that they avidly seek. In the modern secular age, this means worship of the state religion, which in the Western democracies incorporates the doctrine of submission to the masters of the system of public subsidy, private profit, called free enterprise. The people must be kept in ignorance, reduced to jingoist incantations, for their own good. And like the Grand Inquisitor, who employs the forces of miracle, mystery, and authority "to conquer and hold captive for ever the conscience of these impotent rebels for their happiness" and to deny them the freedom of choice they so fear and despise, so the "cool observers" must create the "necessary illusions" and "emotionally potent oversimplifications" that keep the ignorant and stupid masses disciplined and content.

Despite the frank acknowledgment of the need to deceive the public, it would be an error to suppose that practitioners of the art are typically engaged in *conscious* deceit; few reach the level of sophistication of the Grand Inquisitor or maintain such insights for long. On the contrary, as the intellectuals pursue their grim and demanding vocation, they readily adopt beliefs that serve institutional needs; those who do not will have to seek employment elsewhere. The chairman of the board may sincerely believe that his every waking moment is dedicated to serving human needs. Were he to act on these delusions instead of pursuing profit and market share, he would no longer be chairman of the board. It is probable that the most inhuman monsters, even the Himmlers and the Mengeles, convince themselves that they are engaged in noble and courageous acts. The psychology of leaders is a topic of little interest. The institutional factors that constrain their actions and beliefs are what merit attention.

Across a broad spectrum of articulate opinion, the fact that the voice of the people is heard in democratic societies is considered a problem to be overcome by ensuring that the public voice speaks the right words. The general conception is that leaders control us, not that we control them. If the population is out of control and propaganda doesn't work, then the state is forced underground, to clandestine operations and secret wars; the scale of covert operations is often a good measure of popular dissidence, as it was during the Reagan period. Among this group of self-styled "conservatives," the commitment to untrammeled executive power and the contempt for democracy reached unusual heights. Accordingly, so did the resort to propaganda campaigns targeting the media and the general population: for example, the establishment of the State Department Office of Latin American Public Diplomacy dedicated to such projects as Operation Truth, which one high government official described as "a huge psychological operation of the kind the military conducts to influence a population in denied or enemy territory." The terms express lucidly the attitude towards the errant public: enemy territory, which must be conquered and subdued.

In its dependencies, the United States must often turn to violence to "restore democracy." At home, more subtle means are required: the manufacture of consent, deceiving the stupid masses with "necessary illusions," covert operations that the media and Congress pretend not to see until it all becomes too obvious to be suppressed. We then shift to the phase of damage control to ensure that public attention is diverted to overzealous patriots or to the personality defects of leaders who have strayed from our noble commitments, but not to the institutional factors that determine the persistent and substantive content of these commitments. The task of the Free Press, in such circumstances, is to take the proceedings seriously and to describe them as a tribute to the soundness of our self-correcting institutions, which they carefully protect from public scrutiny.

More generally, the media and the educated classes must fulfill their "societal purpose," carrying out their necessary tasks in accord with the prevailing conception of democracy.

NOAM CHOMSKY is an institute professor in the Department of Linguistics and Philosophy at the Massachusetts Institute of Technology, Boston. A member of the American Academy of Science, he has published widely in both linguistics and current affairs. His books include At War with Asia, Towards a New Cold War, Fateful Triangle: The U.S., Israel and the Palestinians, Necessary Illusions, Hegemony or Survival, Deterring Democracy, Failed States: The Abuse of Power and the Assault on Democracy and Manufacturing Consent: The Political Economy of the Mass Media.

EXPLORING THE ISSUE

Is Media Propaganda Helpful in Supporting United States Democracy?

Critical Thinking and Reflection

1. How has the connotation of propaganda shifted over time? How has this impacted how citizens engage with mass media?
2. In a 1936 speech given at the University of Virginia, Bernays argues that propaganda is "an important tool of sound social evolution and change" that makes it possible for minority opinions and ideas to circulate and become effective more quickly. How might Chomsky respond to this statement?
3. In your opinion, would censoring the spread of propaganda violate freedom of the press? Why or why not?
4. In your opinion, does blaming propaganda in the media let the consumers of that media off the hook? Why or why not? What skills, knowledge, and competencies would an individual need to critically engage with propaganda?
5. How might propaganda in the media challenge American citizens to participate more fully in the democratic process of self-governance?

Is There Common Ground?

It would certainly be interesting to ask Bernays about how he feels about modern media and propaganda. He lived until 1995 and saw aspects of modern propaganda. Although Bernays and Chomsky approach the issue of propaganda from competing perspectives, both works allude to an invisible hand that deciphers and employs information mass-produced for the general public. Both Chomsky and Bernays acknowledge that the process of propaganda involves manipulating the news, inflating personality, and evoking specific emotions through symbols and images.

For Bernays, this type of communication is an effective method that in turn fosters an organized and functional democratic system. From this lens, propaganda is a tool used to consolidate and distribute the contributions of the past and present in an accessible way (Bernays, 1936). For Chomsky, this process hinders freedom of the press because the "freedom to persuade" is concentrated in the few hands of the elite rather the hands of the American people. Neither author denies the potential and power of propaganda as a tool to advance social change or influence cultural ways of thinking. Rather, Bernays and Chomsky diverge in how they interpret and analyze the invisible hands carrying that tool.

Additional Resources

Benkler, Y., Faris, R., & Roberts, H. (2018). *Network Propaganda: Manipulation, Disinformation, and Radicalization in American Politics*. Oxford University Press.

Bernays, E. (1936). Freedom of propaganda. *Vital Speeches of the Day, 2*(24), 744–746.

Bușu, O. V., Teodorescu, M., & Gîfu, D. (2014). Communicational positive propaganda in democracy. *International Letters of Social and Humanistic Sciences (ILSHS), 27*, 82–93.

Hobbs, R. (2017). Teaching and learning in a post-truth world. *Educational Leadership, 75*(3), 26–31.

Klanfer, J. (1939). Democracy and propaganda. *The Sociological Review, 31*(4), 422–448.

Lazarsfeld, P. F., & Merton, R. K. (1948). Mass communication, popular taste and organized social action. *Media Studies*, 18–30.

Orwell, George. 1984. London: Secker and Warburg, 1949. Print.

Internet References . . .

This American Life

https://www.thisamericanlife.org/575/poetry-of-propaganda

The Conversation

http://theconversation.com/how-woodrow-wilsons-propaganda-machine-changed-american-journalism-76270

Freedom House

https://freedomhouse.org/article/new-report-freedom-net-2017-manipulating-social-media-undermine-democracy

New York Public Library

https://www.nypl.org/events/exhibitions/overhere/more

Selected, Edited, and with Issue Framing Material by:
Kevin R. Magill and Tony L. Talbert, *Baylor University*

ISSUE

Were the First 100 Days of the New Deal Essentially Political Maneuvering?

YES: Gabriel Kolko, from "The New Deal Illusion," *CounterPunch* (2012)

NO: Franklin D. Roosevelt, from "On the Purposes and Foundations of the Recovery Program, July 24, 1933," Marist College (1933)

Learning Outcomes

After reading this issue, you will be able to:

- Describe how FDR's use of mass communications helped promote and gain public support for New Deal policies and the entry into World War II.
- Understands how the New Deal influenced public opinion (e.g., the public's belief in the responsibility of government to deliver public services).
- Compare and contrast the impact of media (radio, television, digital, and Internet technologies) on the nation during the 1930s and the 21st century.
- Discuss the significance and ideology of FDR and the New Deal (e.g., whether the New Deal was able to solve the problems of The Depression, who the New Deal helped the most and the least; how the New Deal changed the relationship between state and federal government).
- Evaluate the impact of New Deal Programs on the economy (relief, reform, and recovery) and Roosevelt's legacy on the American Presidency.

ISSUE SUMMARY

YES: Gabriel Kolko asserts that instead of implementing a successful progressive New Deal agenda President Franklin Delano Roosevelt and his administrative cabinet of advisors closely aligned with conservative "big business" interests that took advantage of the economic crises during America's 20th-century Great Depression to protect their financial and social power bases at the expense of the common person.

NO: To counter Gabriel Kolko's critical analysis of the FDR's New Deal motives, a primary document representing one of President Roosevelt's many "fireside chats" is offered as evidence that FDR's New Deal policies called upon all segments of the U.S. population to enter into a common commitment of sacrifice and service to address the economic and social crises of the day.

I never saw him—but I knew him. Can you have forgotten how, with his voice, he came into our house, the President of these United States, calling us friends. . .
—Carl Carmer, April 14, 1945
(quoted on Museum of Broadcast Communications website, Flashback: The 70th Anniversary of

FDR's Fireside Chats—linked from EDSITEment-reviewed Center for History and New Media)

The first two decades of the twentieth century saw the ebullient American spirit in full bloom as unbridled industrial expansion and technological innovations in manufacturing established the United States as the new global leader. The omnipotence of productivity became yet another example of American Exceptionalism that would be touted by political and business leaders. The 1928 election of Republican Herbert Hoover over the Democratic candidate Alfred E. Smith seemed to indicate the American voters comfort with the continuation of *laissez faire* capitalist economic policies as a counterbalance to the increasingly radicalized social reform movements that critiqued the greed and graft of America's economic systems.

And then it happened. The 1929 crash of the stock market set off a panic like no other seen before in American history. What began has a financial earthquake centered on New York's Wall Street resulted in trembling aftershocks that spread throughout the nation and across the globe. Unemployment was growing worldwide. In 1930, there were four million unemployed people in the United States. By 1932, that number had grown to nine million. If jobs were available, pay was reduced or came in the form of scrip to be used for barter to trade for goods and services. The industries of the Gilded Age that had fueled the American economy for over two decades were failing or had already collapsed. The great urban migration that had lured millions of persons from their agrarian lifestyles to the promise of a better life in the cities where manufacturing jobs were plentiful now found themselves without means of income, sustenance, and increasingly homeless. Across the nation millions of freight trains were filled not with manufactured or farm grown goods but people escaping debt and desolation. American citizens, migrants in their own homeland, wandered desperately in search of a way to feed, clothe, and house themselves and their families in what appeared to be both a literal and figurate Dust Bowl nation in what was once the world's economic leader.

Business and political leaders who had just a few years earlier bragged that good leadership consists of showing average people how to do the work of superior people were now themselves immobilized without answers to the crisis. Less than a year into his Presidency, Herbert Hoover would respond with some relief programs in an attempt to stave off the growing humanitarian crisis of unemployment, hunger, homelessness, and distress. Hoover's largely ineffective response to the nation's financial collapse and what promised to be a loss of confidence in the viability of the nation itself set off a series of economic, political, and social disruptions that would eventually lead to the wars, the revolutions, and the cultural shifts that would define the events of the remainder of the 20th century.

Into the economic maelstrom stepped Franklin Roosevelt with his stentorian voice and Groton accent (Stromberg, 2016). Throughout his governorship in New York, Roosevelt aggressively implemented relief measures that appeared to successfully bridge the wants of the business class and the needs of the working class. Comprehensive industrial welfare and unemployment remedies were enacted throughout the state. His critics from the political, economic, and social right and left labeled FDR as just another wealthy elitist offering false hope to a desperate nation of people seeking a savior. His supporters would retort that he was not a "traitor to his class" (as some businessmen claimed) or another wealthy narcissist seeking power (as some reformers claimed), he was instead a pragmatic and oft times distractible leader who professed a personal creed of organic collectivism that was needed during this time of crisis (Adelstein, 1991).

It is therefore no surprise that by 1932 the former U.S. Vice Presidential candidate and the current Governor of New York Franklin Delano Roosevelt would be the frontrunner for the Democrat Party ticket for the president of the United States. Presidential historians Thomas E. Cronin and William R. Hochman assert that

> *In the 1932 election, Roosevelt deftly campaigned both on Hoover's left and right. Where Hoover was cold, austere, remote and doctrinaire, Roosevelt was warm, personal, charming and uncommonly self-confident. Roosevelt may have lacked depth, but he had breadth. He liked politics, loved people and yearned to be in the center of things. He accepted the inevitability of change and seemed to have no fear of the future. He was confident of his own strength and ability to lead, to manage and to succeed. He was ready to use the power of government to deal with the crisis of the Great Depression.* (Cronin and Hochman, 1985)

FDR campaigned with confidence and presented an enthusiastic smile to cheering as well as critical crowds who assembled for his speeches at county fairs, convention centers, and coast-to-coast and in-between whistle-stop rallies. His speeches were topical and brief; they lifted people's spirits, especially when contrasted with the dour and impersonal Hoover message (Cronin and Hochman, 1985). Where Hoover offered excuses for economic failures, Roosevelt offered examples of how those failures could be remedied. Hoover's policy pronouncements seemed entangled in an ethic of Gilded Age greed and graft where Roosevelt's daring break with his own landed gentry constituency resonated with middle class business owners whose storefronts had been shuttered and the working class laborers long out of employment.

On Tuesday, November 8, 1932, the newly elected President Franklin D. Roosevelt and his colorful running mate Texas congressman and Speaker of the House of Representatives John Nance Garner could claim a landslide victory over the feckless campaign and presidency of Herbert H. Hoover. Celebration, however, was not what was called for on that winter day and the months ahead. Unemployment grew to over 25 percent of the nation's workforce, with more than twelve million Americans out of work. A new wave of bank failures hit in February 1933 one month prior to FDRs first presidential inauguration. Upon accepting the Democratic nomination, FDR had promised a "New Deal" to help America out of the Depression, though the meaning of that program was far from clear (Leuchtenburg, 1963; Leuchtenburg, 2009). By the time President Roosevelt delivered his historic inaugural address on March 4, 1933, the Great Depression had reached depths that seemed to dismantle not only the brick and mortar institutions of the United States but also the beliefs and confidence of the American people toward their systems of governance and finance. To the American public Roosevelts assertion that *we have nothing to fear but fear itself* was either a bold call to collective consciousness or a foolish platitude disconnected from the realities of rank and file Americans in distress.

It is against this backdrop of trembling American consciousness that we pose the inquiry, *Were the First 100 Days of the New Deal Essentially Political Maneuvering?* Perhaps an odd question given the nature of politics and politicians as both an art and science of maneuvering and manipulation. It would be quite easy to simply say, "Yes, of course FDR like all U.S. politicians engaged in political maneuvering. Isn't that, after all what all politicians do?" Setting aside this reasonable, though equally cynical, response this issue encourages the reader to delve deeply into the philosophical intent of the question. That being, epistemologically, ontologically, and axiologically was FDRs rhetoric and method grounded in a sincere and enlightened calling to rescue his nation and her people or was he simply securing his own fortunes and those of his elite peers by seizing the reins of power?

During his long Presidency, Franklin Delano Roosevelt so dominated the political culture that historians have called the period "the age of Roosevelt" (Leuchtenburg, 1982). Did the transformation of the presidency come about because of the crises Roosevelt confronted or because of his style and character? This is the juncture of the debate that Gabriel Kolko and vicariously Franklin Delano Roosevelt will confront in their essay and speech presented in the pages ahead. Both Kolko's and Roosevelt's words will be meticulously compared and contrasted as careful analysis of whether FDR's New Deal promises were sound and fury (Kolko) or substance and

fundamentals (Roosevelt) when addressing the economic and social foundations of the 1930s–40s United States and the world at-large.

Gabriel Kolko will assert that instead of implementing a successful progressive New Deal agenda President Franklin Delano Roosevelt and his administrative cabinet of advisors closely aligned with conservative "big business" interests that took advantage of the economic crises during America's 20th-century Great Depression to protect their financial and social power bases at the expense of the common person. Kolko's analysis is supported by numerous cited sources and examples that he skillfully uses to build his case that Roosevelt's New Deal was indeed political maneuvering more so than philosophical merit. An example of such cited evidence supporting Kolko's contention is represented in the work of Gary Dean Best's book *Pride, prejudice, and politics: Roosevelt versus recovery, 1933-1938*. Best contends that "Franklin Delano Roosevelt was, himself, the primary obstacle to American recovery from the Great Depression of 1933-38. [The depression continued] eight years of the Roosevelt administration, despite unprecedented intervention by the federal government in the nation's economic life" (Best, 1990). Like Best, Gabriel Kolko argues that FDRs lack of understanding about the economy coupled with his public posturing that put him at virtual war with the very groups she should have been encouraging (i.e., American business and financial communities) extended the economic crisis and further solidified Roosevelt's control over all branches of the government and segments of society. Simply put, Franklin Delano Roosevelt's New Deal transformed the way the public assesses the effectiveness of the U.S. Presidency.

Cronin and Hochman ask, "Did the transformation of the presidency come about because of the crises Roosevelt confronted or because of his style and character? The answer is both" (1985). The confluence of Cronin's, Hochman's, and Kolko's analysis emerges with the point that Roosevelts style was certainly distinctive from that of Hoover's but the substance of the policies responding to the economic crises were largely the same. Kolko (2012) notes, "In the end, Hoover and Roosevelt had much in common programmatically; both failed to reverse the depression, and many of the measures they adopted in the effort to do so were very similar. . . . one of Roosevelt's closest advisers, Rexford Tugwell, admitted that 'practically the whole New Deal was extrapolated from programs that Hoover started'". Grounded in the arguments of style over substance, sound over strategy, Kolko presents a case, with support from other cited historians, economists, and political scientists, that while there's no doubt FDRs first 100 days has become the standard that all other

U.S. presidents are judged the fundamental reality is that the New Deal was largely a brilliant façade of political maneuvering.

In sharp contrast to Kolko's case, we have Franklin Delano Roosevelt offering an important counterweight to the critical evaluations of his New Deal motivations and implementations. Drawing from one of Roosevelt's fireside chats, *On the Purposes and Foundations of the Recovery Program* (July 24, 1933), delivered just four months after his inauguration, President Roosevelt offers the American public his philosophical and operational interpretation of the first 100 days of his presidency. Primary documents are our best source for capturing both the letter and intent of the historical record. In this primary document and in several secondary supporting sources we better understand Roosevelt as most certainly a skilled politician as well as a strategic policy maker.

> *I think it will interest you if I set forth the fundamentals of this planning for national recovery; and this I am very certain will make it abundantly clear to you that all of the proposals and all of the legislation since the fourth day of March have not been just a collection of haphazard schemes but rather the orderly component parts of a connected and logical whole.* (Roosevelt, 1933)

With a reflective demeanor and against the backdrop of an uncharacteristically long silence from public radio addresses, President Roosevelt invites the nation to listen and perhaps better understand why he set into motion a flurry of reform and recovery efforts that had many accusing him of usurping Constitutional powers. Surrounded by a so-called "brain trust" of university professors and career policy strategist and aided by a largely supportive Democratic Congress, President Roosevelt seized the opportunity to take action with the immediate launching of his New Deal proposals. He wanted broad executive power "to wage a war against the emergency as great as the power that would be given me if we were in fact invaded by a foreign foe" (Roosevelt, 1933). Roosevelt's war against the depression was waged with the devices of the Wilson war years as many of the New Deal agencies resembled the executive agencies created by Wilson in the First World War (Cronin and Hochman, 1985). Within months of his swearing in ceremony FDR's progressive ideologies and initiatives were on full display in small towns and cities, in fields and factories across America. These included the Agricultural Adjustment Act, the National Industrial Recovery Act, the design and development of the Public Works Administration, the Tennessee Valley Authority, the Emergency Fleet Corporation and the U.S. Grain Corporation, and hundreds of other acronym laden agencies, entities, and initiatives that would not simply maneuver politics but manage policies that put America back on course.

Though Franklin D. Roosevelt's words are the primary source for the counter debate to Gabriel Kolko, secondary sources should be considered as supporting the "No" position in this dialogue. An example of this supporting secondary source evidence is offered by John Frendreis, Raymond Tatalovich, and Jon Schaff in their article *Predicting legislative output in the first one-hundred days, 1897-1995*. The authors apply a statistical modeling formula political assertion in constructing their arguments and more on a statistical modeling formula that supports their contention that the first 100 days of Franklin D. Roosevelt's administration reveals that his New Deal legislative agenda can be accurately characterized as a successful model for other U.S. presidents to consider (Frendreis, Tatalovich, and Schaff, 2001). Challenging Kolko's notion that the New Deal was largely political maneuvering, Frendreis, Tatalovich, and Schaff argue that the New Deal policies passed during FDR's first 100 days, though not perfect, have generally served as a benchmark of rating U.S. presidential effectiveness for the last 85 years. Further support of this position is Anthony J. Badger's assertion that while businessmen and business interests certainly played a role in the New Deal the policies passed in the first 100 days generally served to positively stabilize economic conditions for US citizens and their government" (Badger, 2008). Simply stated, Franklin Delano Roosevelt was a politician that employed political maneuvering coupled with proactive mobilization firmly grounded in a progressive ideological position. From November 8, 1932, until his death on April 12, 1945, Roosevelt's New Deal policies, expansive Executive Branch powers as a "war president," and virtuoso presidential performance not only bailed America out of the Great Depression but permanently redefined the presidency as a central leadership post for nation and world.

YES

Gabriel Kolko

The New Deal Illusion

What was the New Deal of the 1930s? There are so many myths surrounding it, and to a large extent the Democratic Party's credibility today is based on the assumption they were fundamental social innovators, progressive if you will, during the New Deal.

But the 1920s and 1930 was a very complex period and are best treated as one unified era because the administration of Herbert Hoover, the much-reviled president during the Great Depression that began in 1929 and lasted well into the 1930s, was also a part of the American "Progressive" tradition. As I have argued elsewhere, American "progressivism" was a part of a big business effort to attain protection from the unpredictability of too much competition. [See my book *The Triumph of Conservatism: A reinterpretation of American History, 1900-1916*, New York, 1962] In fact, the New Deal was many things, having numerous aspects: what was not made up on the spur of the moment was copied from earlier efforts. The Democrats did not have a real economic strategy when they came to power. Most of what they said about the economy during the election campaign was, naturally, simply designed to get votes. They certainly had no idea the day they came to office how to deal with the Depression. Hoover had more ideas than they did.

Most historians know this; Hoover was far from being a bloodless conservative. If he did not act decisively, his ostensible reason was usually that he needed more information. Politics aside, Hoover's alleged empiricism appealed to many Democrats, and both parties still retain a belief in the redeeming virtues, even the adequacy, of getting the facts first: on the assumptions reality or political exigencies can always wait for them. Sometimes they will, sometimes they will not.

Roosevelt was wholly dependent on his advisers. The only thing the Democrats were nominally committed to was balancing the budget; Hoover ran a deficit so the Democrats used it against him: it was strictly an election ploy. The Democrats—like the Republicans before and after, were

split, and some—Louis D. Brandeis and Felix Frankfurter were the most notable—wanted to follow Woodrow Wilson's more classic liberal "New Freedom" plan. Louis Johnson and those who were on Wilson's War Industries Board, wanted some form of centralized "planning."

By April 1933 Roosevelt had so much conflicting advice before him that he decided not to do anything for the time being, but changed his mind quickly when the Senate threatened to pass the Black Bill for a 30-hour work week, which big business immediately opposed. Roosevelt and most of his advisers opposed it also.

The Democratic Senate and House seemed ready to enact a more "radical" set of proposals. He authorized his Secretary of Labor, Francis Perkins, to present Congress an alternative to the Black Bill that would not arouse the ire of business, and he asked his leading adviser, Raymond Moley, to come up with a recovery plan based on business-government cooperation.

Though Herbert Hoover was clearly Roosevelt's intellectual superior, he was unlucky to have presided over an economic depression within eight months of taking office. The depression was the product of much larger forces in the world and the American economy rather than which party was in power. If the Democrats had been in the White House in 1929, there would have been an identical economic downturn. And in many regards Hoover's social thought was far more advanced than Franklin Roosevelt's, "progressive" in the sense that Theodore Roosevelt and Woodrow Wilson were. A Quaker, Hoover was an entirely self-made man, a very successful mining engineer-entrepreneur who made a fortune; he mastered Latin to the point that he made the still-standard translation of Georgius Agricola's *De re metallica* and knew Mandarin. Roosevelt was born into privilege, went to Harvard, where he was a "C" student and a cheerleader. He was an ardent stamp collector.

In 1920, Roosevelt said of Hoover, "There could not be a finer one." Wilson was alleged to want him to have the 1920 Democratic presidential nomination. Hoover didn't think the Democrats would win, and tied his star to the Republicans. But he was essentially an apolitical technocrat. There was always an empiricism about Hoover's actions and this often transcended politics. In 1947, President Harry Truman, Roosevelt's successor and a Democratic politician par excellence, appointed Hoover as chairman of a commission to reform the executive branch of government. He never sought glory but it came to him because of his substantial abilities. The Depression was more than a match for him, and it proved more than a match for Roosevelt. Basically, it was the Second World War that got the U.S. out of the Great Depression completely.

There was both ambiguity and ambivalence in Hoover's thinking, but there was in Roosevelt's also. Hoover regarded himself as part of the "progressive" continuum, and there were many things that he had in common with both the Democrats and Republicans who preceded him. Hoover tried to combat the ensuing Great Depression with public works projects such as major dams, volunteer efforts, new tariffs and raises in individual and corporate taxes. He created the Reconstruction Finance Corporation, mainly to give loans to weak banks. Roosevelt continued and expanded the RFC somewhat, also loaning the money to weak banks, railroads, and using it for work relief. Then the sums loaned dropped off in 1934 until World War Two, when the RFC began financing construction of munitions plants. Libertarians argued years later that Hoover's economics were statist, and that he belonged in the continuum of government and business collaboration that began around the turn of the century. I must agree with them.

Hoover's initiatives did not produce economic recovery, but served as the groundwork for various policies laid out in Franklin D. Roosevelt's "New Deal." As Secretary of Commerce under the preceding Republican presidents, he had been particularly active in creating trade associations in hundreds of industries, and these associations were to become the backbone of the National Recovery Administration, the first New Deal.

When the Democrats won in 1933 they favored business and government cooperation. Moley was joined by a group, including Hugh Johnson, who had served on Wilson's War Industries Board, Chamber of Commerce representatives, assorted trade association lawyers, bankers, and academics. Many people helped formulate the first phase of the New Deal. They were certainly not radicals nor did they want to be. The trade association movement was the heart of the first New Deal, but the Supreme Court outlawed the NRA in May 1935 as unconstitutional.

The NRA's trade association provisions actually consisted of nearly 600 association codes, and appears very complex because businesses are naturally divided by their different labor overhead, regional cost differences are often very great, and expenses vary. Whenever some firm has an advantage that produces profits they want to keep it and make money. That means that trade association codes, which deal with labor pay, output allowed, and the like, were often hotly contested by the various businesses in an industry—divided generally by region and size. The result was a mess of conflicts, but historians like Ellis Hawley, who have studied this period in great detail, concluded that big business was the major winner in the entire process of fixing the many codes. They were helped immensely because many key government officials were drawn themselves from business and industry, and Johnson, the head of the NRA, was sympathetic to business. Given the fact there were many codes there were many exceptions, but labor was generally very under-represented in the code authorities.

Roosevelt himself contributed little, perhaps nothing, to the formulation of the New Deal, most of which had existed in an early form in the trade associations. Trade associations wanted federal governmental protection from other members of the industry who competed too energetically—which classical economic theory declared was a good thing. Labor costs are equalized when labor is organized or child-labor outlawed; this became an issue when some codes, particularly in textiles, were formulated.

All this just shows what has been known for a long time: there is no difference between the parties and firms' use of federal regulations to make money. Labor unions can therefore emerge as many things, including as a form of intra-industry struggle. The coal, apparel, and textiles industries are good examples: Northern textiles were for limits on child labor, the Southern textile industry (which used children as cheap factory hands), against federal control of it.

Reform in the United States, beginning with the Interstate Commerce Commission of 1887 (which eventually regulated the trucking industry also), has embodied the principle that government sanctions are used to back private power in specific industries, meaning generally the biggest firms in the industries involved. The Democratic Administration under Roosevelt was explicitly for this principle, and the new Securities and Exchange Commission under Joseph P. Kennedy (the later President's father), a former speculator, made it explicit that the new SEC was intended to be the bankers' friend. And it was.

All the banking and financial legislation the Democrats passed proved very useful to at least some—generally the biggest—firms in the industry.

There were critics of whatever the Roosevelt Administration did: Some were ideological, some were regional—fearing that too much power would move to New York or Washington and damage their interests (Amadeo Giannini's Bank of America, which was then largely California-based), small business interests in the South, some coal mine operators, who detested high wage unions but were in fact often marginally economically whether or not they had unions. But the depression had shaken up many businessmen, financially and psychologically. They conceded change was needed, inevitable, or both. The Roosevelt Administration was ready to cooperate with them, and it did. Unions grew under the New Deal but largely because of the willingness of workers to strike and organize. Code rules sometimes helped them, especially in garments and highly competitive industries, but they were not the primary reason for their growth.

Roosevelt the Presidential candidate blasted the Republican incumbent for spending and taxing too much, increasing national debt, raising tariffs and blocking trade, as well as placing millions on the government dole. Roosevelt attacked Hoover for "reckless and extravagant" spending, of thinking "that we ought to center control of everything in Washington as rapidly as possible." Roosevelt's running mate, John Nance Garner, accused the Republicans of "leading the country down the path of socialism". Hoover believed the government should spend more money on dams and public works during business downturns, a kind of early Keynesism.

There was a complexity in Hoover and Roosevelt's responses to the Great Depression that makes very misleading their historical reputations that have survived in the common political rhetoric until now. Historians who have studied Hoover and Roosevelt in much greater detail, have come away with far better informed, nuanced, essentially critical judgments. The problem—among others—is that the general political community rarely reads their rather detailed academic monographs. But the persistence of the notion that somehow the Democrats are somehow better than Republicans is also related to the fact that the GOP more often falls under the sway of yahoos, making the Democrats seem less objectionable.

These simplifications have benefited the Democrats most, allowing them to portray themselves as somehow most able to meet the U.S.' social problems both then and thereafter. The interwar period was far more complex and does not lend itself to easy generalizations: it is a nuanced time and makes easy generalizations impossible.

Suffice it to say, unemployment went from 4.2 percent of the labor force in 1928 to 23.6 percent in 1932, the worst point in the Depression, fell back down to 16.0 percent in 1936 and shot back up to 19.0 in 1938. The Roosevelt Administration also introduced the Works Projects Administration (WPA), and while it employed some labor up to 30-hours a week, it could not teach these men and women skills until 1940 because some unions opposed doing so. Until the war had begun. WPA or not, unemployment remained very high. By 1939 the New Deal's social technology was exhausted and there was only a confused debate between Democrats about the virtues—or lack of them—of laissez faire and competition versus the panoply of ideas behind "planning" and control of competition. Only the Second World War, not the New Deal or Hoover's efforts, ended the depression. As the former NRA research director, Charles F. Roos, concluded, the ". . . NRA must, as a whole, be regarded as a sincere but ineffective effort to alleviate depression."

In the end, Hoover and Roosevelt had much in common programmatically; both failed to reverse the depression, and many of the measures they adopted in the effort to do so were very similar. There is certainly a continuity in the American "reform" tradition, such as it is, across the entire twentieth century. Both Hoover and Roosevelt were integral parts of it. Years later, one of Roosevelt's closest advisers, Rexford Tugwell, admitted that "practically the whole New Deal was extrapolated from programs that Hoover started." But Hoover had not started anything himself; he had only taken over efforts of a faction of the trade association movement to protect elements of specific industries—there were 100s—from poorer, smaller firms, generally but not always in the South—from the price-cutting and overproduction that some businessmen detested.

Americans are pragmatic and all-too-many dislike theoretical thinking. Sometimes they are simply unable, unwilling, or both, to generalize about their actions. Looking reality straight in the face can shatter myths that are politically useful. The "New Deal" is such a case, which the Democrats foster as if there is something uniquely pro-people about their party. But the so-called New Deal is an integral part of a movement in modern American history, one that largely reflected the business world's response to the complexities of the American economy after the late 1890s.

State intervention is used to resolve disputes or conflicting interests within specific industries that cannot be settled by competing firms by voluntary means. The problem is that these efforts to regulate the economy fail so often leaving the American economy devoid of an effective social technology to deal with crises. Wars—real and cold—have rescued it. But this intriguing enigma is a separate topic that would require too much time and space for me to deal with adequately here.

By 1936 the New Deal was at an analytic and programmatic impasse. It cobbled together new legislation that retained some of provisions of the old NRA—the Wagner Act on labor, explicitly allowing unions, but it could not legislate the end of unemployment. But while it had strong business opposition, the history of trade associations had revealed that there were also business elements that were pro-union because the equalization of labor costs proved vital to their interests. This was a major objective of many trade association codes. It can be debated whether businesses are pro-union but unions can be and are useful to the extent that they often eliminate labor cost differentials. Many of the so-called pro-labor provisions of the Wagner Act simply gave workers explicit rights they should have had earlier. Anyway, it sealed even more tightly the unions' bond with the Democratic Party and what are called liberals.

Anyone who looks at recent American history, the statements and policies of the Democrats and Republicans, will conclude that there is a much greater consensus between the parties than differences, and always has been. They frequently try to accentuate the differences, and sustaining political myths are often necessary to winning elections. The New Deal is one such myth that the Democrats gain from.

The New Deal illusion survives because it is very useful to today's Democratic Party. It needs myths, but if one knows the truth about it then we have the basis for understanding the essentially conservative nature of today's Democratic Party.

GABRIEL KOLKO (August 17, 1932–May 19, 2014) was an American-born Canadian historian and author. His research interests included American capitalism and political history, the Progressive Era, and US foreign policy in the 20th century. One of the best-known revisionist historians to write about the Cold War, he had also been credited as "an incisive critic of the Progressive Era and its relationship to the American empire." U.S. historian Paul Buhle summarized Kolko's career when he described him as "a major theorist of what came to be called Corporate Liberalism . . . [and] a very major historian of the Vietnam War and its assorted war crimes."

Franklin D. Roosevelt

➜ **NO**

On the Purposes and Foundations of the Recovery Program, July 24, 1933

Radio Address of the President from the White House—9:30pm.

After the adjournment of the historical special session of the Congress five weeks ago I purposely refrained from addressing you for two very good reasons.

First, I think that we all wanted the opportunity of a little quiet thought to examine and assimilate in a mental picture the crowding events of the hundred days which had been devoted to the starting of the wheels of the New Deal.

Secondly, I wanted a few weeks in which to set up the new administrative organization and to see the first fruits of our careful planning.

I think it will interest you if I set forth the fundamentals of this planning for national recovery; and this I am very certain will make it abundantly clear to you that all of the proposals and all of the legislation since the fourth day of March have not been just a collection of haphazard schemes but rather the orderly component parts of a connected and logical whole.

Long before Inauguration Day I became convinced that individual effort and local effort and even disjointed Federal effort had failed and of necessity would fail and, therefore, that a rounded leadership by the Federal Government had become a necessity both of theory and of fact. Such leadership, however, had its beginning in preserving and strengthening the credit of the United States Government, because without that no leadership was a possibility. For years the Government had not lived within its income. The immediate task was to bring our regular expenses within our revenues. That has been done.

It may seem inconsistent for a government to cut down its regular expenses and at the same time to borrow and to spend billions for an emergency. But it is not inconsistent because a large portion of the emergency money has been paid out in the form of sound loans which will be repaid to the Treasury over a period of years; and to cover the rest of the emergency money we have imposed taxes to pay the interest and the installments on that part of the debt.

So you will see that we have kept our credit good. We have built a granite foundation in a period of confusion. That foundation of the Federal credit stands there broad and sure. It is the base of the whole recovery plan.

Then came the part of the problem that concerned the credit of the individual citizens themselves. You and I know of the banking crisis and of the great danger to the savings of our people. On March sixth every national bank was closed. One month later 90 per cent of the deposits in the national banks had been made available to the depositors. Today only about 5 per cent of the deposits in national banks are still tied up. The condition relating to state banks, while not quite so good on a percentage basis, is shoving a steady reduction in the total of frozen deposits—a result much better than we had expected three months ago.

The problem of the credit of the individual was made more difficult because of another fact. The dollar was a different dollar from the one with which the average debt had been incurred. For this reason large numbers of people were actually losing possession of and title to their farms and homes. All of you know the financial steps which have been taken to correct this inequality. In addition the Home Loan Act, the Farm Loan Act and the Bankruptcy Act were passed.

It was a vital necessity to restore purchasing power by reducing the debt and interest charges upon our people, but while we were helping people to save their credit it was at the same time absolutely essential to do something about the physical needs of hundreds of thousands who were in dire straits at that very moment. Municipal and State aid were being stretched to the limit. We appropriated half a billion dollars to supplement their efforts and in addition, as you know, we have put 300,000 young men into practical and useful work in our forests and to

Franklin D. Roosevelt, "On the Purposes and Foundations of the Recovery Program," July 24, 1933.

prevent flood and soil erosion. The wages they earn are going in greater part to the support of the nearly one million people who constitute their families.

In this same classification we can properly place the great public works program running to a total of over Three Billion Dollars—to be used for highways and ships and flood prevention and inland navigation and thousands of self-sustaining state and municipal improvements. Two points should be made clear in the allotting and administration of these projects—first, we are using the utmost care to choose labor creating quick-acting, useful projects, avoiding the smell of the pork barrel; and secondly, we are hoping that at least half of the money will come back to the government from projects which will pay for themselves over a period of years.

Thus far I have spoken primarily of the foundation stones—the measures that were necessary to re-establish credit and to head people in the opposite direction by preventing distress and providing as much work as possible through governmental agencies. Now I come to the links which will build us a more lasting prosperity. I have said that we cannot attain that in a nation half boom and half broke. If all of our people have work and fair wages and fair profits, they can buy the products of their neighbors and business is good. But if you take away the wages and the profits of half of them, business is only half as good. It doesn't help much if the fortunate half is very prosperous—the best way is for everybody to be reasonably prosperous.

For many years the two great barriers to a normal prosperity have been low farm prices and the creeping paralysis of unemployment. These factors have cut the purchasing power of the country in half. I promised action. Congress did its part when it passed the farm and the industrial recovery acts. Today we are putting these two acts to work and they will work if people understand their plain objectives.

First, the Farm Act: It is based on the fact that the purchasing power of nearly half our population depends on adequate prices for farm products. We have been producing more of some crops than we consume or can sell in a depressed world market. The cure is not to produce so much. Without our help the farmers cannot get together and cut production, and the Farm Bill gives them a method of bringing their production down to a reasonable level and of obtaining reasonable prices for their crops. I have clearly stated that this method is in a sense experimental, but so far as we have gone we have reason to believe that it will produce good results.

It is obvious that if we can greatly increase the purchasing power of the tens of millions of our people who make a living from farming and the distribution of farm crops, we will greatly increase the consumption of those goods which are turned out by industry.

That brings me to the final step—bringing back industry along sound lines.

Last Autumn, on several occasions, I expressed my faith that we can make possible by democratic self-discipline in industry general increases in wages and shortening of hours sufficient to enable industry to pay its own workers enough to let those workers buy and use the things that their labor produces. This can be done only if we permit and encourage cooperative action in industry because it is obvious that without united action a few selfish men in each competitive group will pay starvation wages and insist on long hours of work. Others in that group must either follow suit or close up shop. We have seen the result of action of that kind in the continuing descent into the economic Hell of the past four years.

There is a clear way to reverse that process: If all employers in each competitive group agree to pay their workers the same wages—reasonable wages—and require the same hours—reasonable hours—then higher wages and shorter hours will hurt no employer. Moreover, such action is better for the employer than unemployment and low wages, because it makes more buyers for his product. That is the simple idea which is the very heart of the Industrial Recovery Act.

On the basis of this simple principle of everybody doing things together, we are starting out on this nationwide attack on unemployment. It will succeed if our people understand it—in the big industries, in the little shops, in the great cities and in the small villages. There is nothing complicated about it and there is nothing particularly new in the principle. It goes back to the basic idea of society and of the nation itself that people acting in a group can accomplish things which no individual acting alone could even hope to bring about.

Here is an example. In the Cotton Textile Code and in other agreements already signed, child labor has been abolished. That makes me personally happier than any other one thing with which I have been connected since I came to Washington. In the textile industry—an industry which came to me spontaneously and with a splendid cooperation as soon as the recovery act was signed—child labor was an old evil. But no employer acting alone was able to wipe it out. If one employer tried it, or if one state tried it, the costs of operation rose so high that it was impossible to compete with the employers or states which had failed to act. The moment the Recovery Act was passed, this monstrous thing which neither opinion nor law could reach through years of effort went out in a flash. As a British editorial put it, we did more under a Code in one day than they in England had been able to do under the common law in eighty-five years of effort. I use this incident, my friends, not to boast of what has already been done but to point the way to you for even greater cooperative efforts this Summer and Autumn.

We are not going through another Winter like the last. I doubt if ever any people so bravely and cheerfully endured a season half so bitter. We cannot ask America to continue to face such needless hardships. It is time for courageous action, and the Recovery Bill gives us the means to conquer unemployment with exactly the same weapon that we have used to strike down Child Labor.

The proposition is simply this:

If all employers will act together to shorten hours and raise wages we can put people back to work. No employer will suffer, because the relative level of competitive cost will advance by the same amount for all. But if any considerable group should lag or shirk, this great opportunity will pass us by and we will go into another desperate Winter. This must not happen.

We have sent out to all employers an agreement which is the result of weeks of consultation. This agreement checks against the voluntary codes of nearly all the large industries which have already been submitted. This blanket agreement carries the unanimous approval of the three boards which I have appointed to advise in this, boards representing the great leaders in labor, in industry and in social service. The agreement has already brought a flood of approval from every State, and from so wide a cross-section of the common calling of industry that I know it is fair for all. It is a plan—deliberate, reasonable and just—intended to put into effect at once the most important of the broad principles which are being established, industry by industry, through codes. Naturally, it takes a good deal of organizing and a great many hearings and many months, to get these codes perfected and signed, and we cannot wait for all of them to go through. The blanket agreements, however, which I am sending to every employer will start the wheels turning now, and not six months from now.

There are, of course, men, a few of them who might thwart this great common purpose by seeking selfish advantage. There are adequate penalties in the law, but I am now asking the cooperation that comes from opinion and from conscience. These are the only instruments we shall use in this great summer offensive against unemployment. But we shall use them to the limit to protect the willing from the laggard and to make the plan succeed.

In war, in the gloom of night attack, soldiers wear a bright badge on their shoulders to be sure that comrades do not fire on comrades. On that principle, those who cooperate in this program must know each other at a glance. That is why we have provided a badge of honor for this purpose, a simple design with a legend. "We do our part," and I ask that all those who join with me shall display that badge prominently. It is essential to our purpose.

Already all the great, basic industries have come forward willingly with proposed codes, and in these codes they accept the principles leading to mass reemployment. But, important as is this heartening demonstration, the richest field for results is among the small employers, those whose contribution will give new work for from one to ten people. These smaller employers are indeed a vital part of the backbone of the country, and the success of our plans lies largely in their hands.

Already the telegrams and letters are pouring into the White House—messages from employers who ask that their names be placed on this special Roll of Honor. They represent great corporations and companies, and partnerships and individuals. I ask that even before the dates set in the agreements which we have sent out, the employers of the country who have not already done so—the big fellows and the little fellows—shall at once write or telegraph to me personally at the White House, expressing their intention of going through with the plan. And it is my purpose to keep posted in the post office of every town, a Roll of Honor of all those who join with me.

I want to take this occasion to say to the twenty-four governors who are now in conference in San Francisco, that nothing thus far has helped in strengthening this great movement more than their resolutions adopted at the very outset of their meeting, giving this plan their instant and unanimous approval, and pledging to support it in their states.

To the men and women whose lives have been darkened by the fact or the fear of unemployment, I am justified in saying a word of encouragement because the codes and the agreements already approved, or about to be passed upon, prove that the plan does raise wages, and that it does put people back to work. You can look on every employer who adopts the plan as one who is doing his part, and those employers deserve well of everyone who works for a living. It will be clear to you, as it is to me, that while the shirking employer may undersell his competitor, the saving he thus makes is made at the expense of his country's welfare.

While we are making this great common effort there should be no discord and dispute. This is no time to cavil or to question the standard set by this universal agreement. It is time for patience and understanding and cooperation. The workers of this country have rights under this law which cannot be taken from them, and nobody will be permitted to whittle them away, but, on the other hand, no aggression is now necessary to attain those rights. The whole country will be united to get them for you. The principle that applies to the employers applies to the workers as well, and I ask you workers to cooperate in the same spirit.

When Andrew Jackson, "Old Hickory," died, someone asked, "Will he go to Heaven?" and the answer was, "He will if he wants to." If I am asked whether the American people will pull themselves out of this depression, I answer, "They will if they want to." The essence of the plan is a universal limitation of hours of work per week for any individual by common consent, and a universal payment of wages above a minimum, also by common consent. I cannot guarantee the success of this nationwide plan, but the people of this country can guarantee its success. I have no faith in "cure-alls" but I believe that we can greatly influence economic forces. I have no sympathy with the professional economists who insist that things must run their course and that human agencies can have no influence on economic ills. One reason is that I happen to know that professional economists have changed their definition of economic laws every five or ten years for a very long time, but I do have faith, and retain faith, in the strength of common purpose, and in the strength of unified action taken by the American people.

That is why I am describing to you the simple purposes and the solid foundations upon which our program of recovery is built. That is why I am asking the employers of the Nation to sign this common covenant with me—to sign it in the name of patriotism and humanity. That is why I am asking the workers to go along with us in a spirit of understanding and of helpfulness.

FRANKLIN D. ROOSEVELT, often referred to by his initials FDR, was an American statesman and political leader who served as the 32nd president of the United States from 1933 until his death in 1945. Roosevelt directed the federal government during most of the Great Depression, implementing his New Deal domestic agenda in response to the worst economic crisis in U.S. history. He realigned American politics by defining American liberalism throughout the middle third of the 20th century though World War II dominated his third and fourth terms. Roosevelt is widely considered to be one of the most important figures in American history, as well as among the most influential figures of the 20th century. Though he has been subject to substantial criticism, scholars often suggest he is one of the three greatest U.S. presidents.

EXPLORING THE ISSUE

Were the First 100 Days of the New Deal Essentially Political Maneuvering?

Critical Thinking and Reflection

1. How did FDR's fireside chats demonstrate his leadership? Explain how FDR combined the content of the New Deal with the power of his fireside chats to move the country forward in 1933.
2. Why did America as a whole accept FDR's vision for a new direction for America?
3. What are the most substantive critiques of FDR's style and substance outlined in this issue? What are the most substantive compliments of FDR's style and substance outlined in this issue?
4. How did FDR effectively or ineffectively use media technologies as compared to contemporary U.S. presidents?
5. What are other examples in U.S. history when the U.S. president or members of the U.S. Congress have "led the charge" to persuade the nation to follow a particular policy or viewpoint?

Is There Common Ground?

If Gabriel Kolko and President Franklin D. Roosevelt could carry on a conversation, it seems apparent that both would concur that his presidency revolutionized how we quantitatively and qualitative evaluate not only the first 100 days of an administration but the lasting impact of the entirety of one's presidency in the memories and matters of the American public. It is also likely that Kolko and Roosevelt would agree that President Herbert H. Hoover's legacy was both a political and philosophical casualty of Roosevelt's much superior acumen as a gifted politicians and policy strategist. Though, on the latter, Kolko and Roosevelt would differ on degrees.

Indeed, it would be quite intriguing to witness Kolko's and Roosevelt's debate on this matter of style and substance amidst the contemporary political environment of 24-hour news cycles and immediate information and misinformation moving about the globe at speeds unimaginable to the public some 30 years ago. One would believe that both Gabriel Kolko and FDR would find common ground in discussing the similarities and differences in how effective and ineffective media have been and are continuing to be applied by politicians, policy makers, pundits, and the public at-large. In particular, common ground might be found in analyzing the distinction in substance and style when comparing FDR's use of radio technologies to call for *esprit de corp* among all public and private sectors as compared to more contemporary U.S. Presidents' use of 21st-century digital technologies (e.g., Twitter) to sow division domestically and internationally.

Additional Resources

Badger, A.J. (2008). *FDR. The first hundred days*. New York: Hill and Wang.

Cronin, T., & Hochman, W. (1985). Franklin D. Roosevelt and The American Presidency. *Presidential Studies Quarterly, 15*(2), 277–286. Retrieved from http://www.jstor.org/stable/27550206

Kennedy, D. (2009). What the New Deal Did. *Political Science Quarterly, 124*(2), 251–268. Retrieved from http://www.jstor.org/stable/25655654

Leuchtenburg, W.E. (1963). *Franklin D. Roosevelt And The New Deal*, New York: Harper & Row.

Roosevelt, F.D. (1933). *First inaugural address* – March 4, 1933. Digital history. Retrieved from "http://www.digitalhistory.uh.edu/disp_textbook.cfm?smtID=3&psid=1240"psid=1240

References

Adelstein, R.P. (1991). The nation as an economic unit: Keynes, Roosevelt, and the managerial ideal. *Journal of American History, 78(1)*, 160–187

Badger, A.J. (2008). *FDR. The first hundred days*. New York: Hill and Wang.

Best, G.D. (1990). *Pride, prejudice, and politics: Roosevelt versus recovery, 1933-1938*. New York, NY: Praeger Publishers.

Cronin, T., & Hochman, W. (1985). Franklin D. Roosevelt and The American Presidency. *Presidential Studies Quarterly, 15*(2), 277–286. Retrieved from http://www.jstor.org/stable/27550206

Frendreis, J., Tatalovich, R., & Schaff, J. (2001). Predicting Legislative Output in the First One-Hundred Days, 1897-1995. *Political Research Quarterly, 54*(4), 853–870. https://doi.org/10.1177/10659 1290105400409History.com. The fireside chats (2010). Retrieved from https://www.history.com/topics/great-depression/fireside-chats

Kennedy, D. (2009). What the New Deal Did. *Political Science Quarterly, 124*(2), 251–268. Retrieved from http://www.jstor.org/stable/25655654

Kolko, G. (29 September 2012). "The New Deal Illusion". counterpunch.org. Retrieved 23 September 2013. Libertarians argued years later that Hoover's economics were statist, and that he belonged in the continuum of government and business collaboration that began around the turn of the century. I must agree with them.

Leuchtenburg, W.E. (1963). *Franklin D. Roosevelt and the New Deal*, New York: Harper & Row.

Leuchtenburg, W. (1982). The Legacy of FDR. *The Wilson Quarterly (1976-), 6*(2), 77–93. Retrieved from http://www.jstor.org/stable/40256266

Roosevelt, F.D. (1933) *On the Purposes and Foundations of the Recovery Program* - July 24, 1933. FDR Presidential Library & Museum. Retrieved from http://docs.fdrlibrary.marist.edu/042433.html%20%20

Roosevelt, F.D. (1933). *First inaugural address* – March 4, 1933. Digital history. Retrieved from "http://www.digitalhistory.uh.edu/disp_textbook.cfm?smtID=3&psid=1240"psid=1240

Stromberg, J.R. (2016). The new deal, part 1: Domestic policy. *Future of Freedom, 27*(11), 29–35.

Stromberg, J.R. (2016). The new deal, part 2: Foreign policy. *Future of Freedom, 27*(12), 27–35.

Internet References . . .

The American Presidency Project (University of California, Santa Barbara), Franklin D. Roosevelt Audio/Video page

http://www.presidency.ucsb.edu/medialist.php?presid=32

Franklin D. Roosevelt Presidential Library and Museum, Fireside Chats page (includes various transcriptions of chats, as well as audio files)

http://docs.fdrlibrary.marist.edu/firesi90.html

Gilder Lehrman Institute of American History - The Hundred Days and Beyond: What Did the New Deal Accomplish?

https://ap.gilderlehrman.org/essays/hundred-days-and-beyond-what-did-new-deal-accomplish

Miller Center (University of Virginia), Presidential Speeches holdings for Franklin D. Roosevelt (including all of FDR's fireside chats, most in audio format, all with transcripts)

http://millercenter.org/president/speeches#fdroosevelt and
http://millercenter.org/president/fdroosevelt

New Deal Network

http://newdeal.feri.org/

President Franklin D. Roosevelt and the New Deal (Library of Congress)

http://www.loc.gov/teachers/classroommaterials/presentationsandactivities/presentations/timeline/depwwii/newdeal/

ISSUE

Selected, Edited, and with Issue Framing Material by:
Kevin R. Magill and Tony L. Talbert, *Baylor University*

Was the World War II Era a Watershed for the Civil Rights Movement?

YES: James Nuechterlein, from "The Politics of Civil Rights: The FEPC, 1941–46," *Prologue: The Journal of the National Archives* (1978)

NO: Harvard Sitkoff, from "African American Militancy in the World War II South: Another Perspective," University Press of Mississippi (1997)

Learning Outcomes

After reading this issue, you will be able to:

- Explain what historians mean when they speak of a "watershed" event.
- Discuss the concept of the "long civil rights movement."
- Analyze the impact of World War II on the African American freedom struggle.
- Identify the key leaders and organizations that worked during the war to advance the cause of civil rights for black Americans.
- Describe the attitudes of African Americans toward the U.S. involvement in World War II.
- Understand the relationship between the U.S. federal government and civil rights initiatives during World War II.

ISSUE SUMMARY

YES: James Nuechterlein insists that the efforts to improve employment opportunities for African Americans during World War II, as exemplified by the establishment of the Fair Employment Practices Commission (1941–1946), marked the beginning of the modern civil rights movement in the United States and set the stage for broader civil rights successes in the 1950s and 1960s.

NO: Harvard Sitkoff challenges the "watershed" interpretation by pointing out that, after Pearl Harbor, militant African American protest against racial discrimination was limited by the constraints imposed on the nation at war, the dwindling resources for sustained confrontation, and the genuinely patriotic response by black Americans to dangers faced by the nation.

Historians have long sought to identify and write about specific moments in the past that produced a major shift in the political, economic, social, or diplomatic fortunes of a particular nation or group of people. As a result, extensive scholarship has been devoted to "revolutions," "turning points," and "sea changes," following which conditions were markedly different from what they had been previously. These "watershed" events that mark a change of course from the past can be positive or negative, depending upon one's point of view, and U.S. history is filled with them: the American Revolution, the Civil War, the Great War (World War I), the Great Depression, World War II, the Cold War, and 9/11.

For students of the modern American civil rights movement, there are several events that appear to serve the purpose of a watershed moment: the U.S. Supreme Court's landmark decision in the Brown case that overturned

Plessy v. Ferguson and set the stage for the dismantling of legally supported racial segregation; Rosa Parks' refusal to relinquish her seat on a Montgomery city bus in December 1955, which precipitated a year-long boycott and served as a springboard to Dr. Martin Luther King's rise to national prominence; the actions of four African American college students in Greensboro, North Carolina, who had grown weary of a contradictory Jim Crow system that allowed them to purchase products in a Woolworth's store but not sit down at the lunch counter for service in the rear of the same establishment. Each of these events altered the trajectory of African American activism in important ways and cleared the path for what many scholars characterize as the most successful social movement in American history.

Over the course of the past two decades, however, historians have begun to take a broader look at the African American freedom struggle and to identify significant precursors to the movement that many previously had placed within the chronological time frame of 1954–1968. For example, see Jacqueline Dowd Hall, "The Long Civil Rights Movement and the Political Uses of the Past," *Journal of American History* 91 (March 2005): 1233–1263, who argues for a much earlier starting point for the civil rights struggle and insists that the search for watershed events must be moved back farther in the twentieth century. In the hands of such scholars, the key historical moments came in the World War II, as the United States and its Allies combatted a fascist dictatorship firmly committed to an ideology of extermination; or during the Great Depression as Franklin Roosevelt's New Deal produced a much larger role for government to play in the lives of the American people; or as a consequence of the Wilson administration's effort to make the world safe for democracy while maintaining strict segregation of the races in his own nation. Still others claim that it is not unreasonable to push back the timeline of the civil rights movement to cover the intense antilynching efforts of Ida B. Wells-Barnett or to the Reconstruction period with its efforts to establish citizenship rights for African Americans who, while freed from the bonds of slavery at war's end, remained captive to Chief Justice Roger Taney's dictum in the *Dred Scott* case (1857) that peoples of African descent possessed no rights that whites were bound by law to respect.

The story of the United States' involvement in World War II involves much more than a delineation of military engagements in Europe and the Pacific. The war occurred on the heels of a devastating depression and helped to turn the economy around with nearly full production and employment. The war possessed significant social implications for many Americans, including women and ethnic and racial minorities, a subject that has received general scholarly attention from prominent historians Richard Polenberg, *War and Society: The United States, 1941–1945* (J. B. Lippincott, 1972); John Morton Blum, *V Was for Victory: Politics and American Culture during World War II* (Harcourt Brace Jovanovich, 1976); and Allan M. Winkler, *Home Front U.S.A.: America during World War II*, 2nd ed. (Harlan Davidson, 2000). The present issue examines the impact of World War II on efforts by black Americans to demonstrate their loyalty to the United States while at the same time insisting upon the same citizenship rights accorded white Americans. It builds upon the pioneering efforts of Richard Dalfiume, whose "The 'Forgotten Years' of the Negro Revolution," *Journal of American History* 55 (June 1968): 99–106, argued that scholars had overlooked World War II as a period in which African Americans aggressively combined patriotism and a challenge to Jim Crow. During these "forgotten years," Dalfiume argued, civil rights organizations such as the National Association for the Advancement of Colored People (NAACP) and A. Philip Randolph's March on Washington Movement (MOWM) applied pressure on the Roosevelt administration to eliminate discrimination in the military and in defense industry hiring practices. In doing so, mass militancy became a major strategy among blacks during the war and sowed the seeds for the civil rights revolution of the postwar period.

In the selections that follow, James Nuechterlein and Harvard Sitkoff debate the degree to which World War II deserves to be considered a watershed event in the history of the American civil rights movement. Nuechterlein subscribes to the interpretation introduced by Dalfiume and focuses upon the battle to combat employment discrimination in the nation's defense industries that led to the establishment of the Fair Employment Practices Commission (FEPC) via Franklin Roosevelt's Executive Order 8802 in 1941. According to Nuechterlein, FDR's decision was generated by A. Philip Randolph's threat to employ direct action strategies, including a march by 100,000 African Americans on the nation's capital. The debate over FEPC, he concludes, produced shifts in political power and strategy within the Democratic Party and provided models for the activism that would drive the modern civil rights movement of the 1950s and 1960s.

Harvard Sitkoff, who interestingly once had been a proponent of the conclusions reached by Dalfiume and Nuechterlein, now questions the validity of the "watershed" interpretation. He makes a clear distinction between the views expressed by African Americans before Pearl Harbor and the ideas they articulated after December 7, 1941, and concludes that black militancy declined sharply following the attack on the American fleet in Hawaii. Even African American Communists, he reports, softened their attacks on American racism during the war. According to Sitkoff, the types of black militancy that were evident prior to the Pearl Harbor attack were now inhibited by the constraints imposed by a nation at war, dwindling resources for sustained protest, and the patriotic response by blacks to the dangers faced by the United States.

YES

James Nuechterlein

The Politics of Civil Rights: The FEPC, 1941–46

It is now clear that the period of World War II marked the beginning of the modem civil rights movement in the United States. The most important event in that early development was the creation in 1941 by Franklin D. Roosevelt of the President's Committee on Fair Employment Practices. The history of the FEPC from its birth to its death in 1946 involved conflicts over political power and strategy within both major political parties but especially among the Democrats. The Roosevelt and Truman administrations were keenly sensitive to the party implications of the issue, while the congressional struggles over the FEPC, though involving the Republicans to some degree, essentially reflected shifts of strength and influence within the Democratic party. Those shifts heralded the later emergence of civil rights as the primary domestic political issue of postwar America. This essay builds on earlier studies of the FEPC by focusing in detail on the political aspects of the struggle, with particular reference to the conflicts within and between the parties in Congress. It attempts to illuminate, amplify, and specify a pattern of historical change in the politics of civil rights during this period that has frequently been asserted generally.

By 1940, blacks had become one of the most dependable voting blocs supporting the Democratic party. Politically and economically the appeal of the New Deal to the nation's "forgotten men" carried special significance for blacks, and although the Roosevelt administration avoided a frontal assault on discrimination before 1941, its legislative and administrative programs directed at the problems of the poor included, perforce, benefits for blacks. Responding to these programs, blacks in increasing numbers forsook their traditional Republican affiliation and became an important component of the Roosevelt coalition.

For blacks, economic progress was circumscribed by racial barriers, and returning prosperity highlighted their struggle. The preparedness program of 1940-41 brought the economic recovery that had always eluded the New Deal; unemployment dropped sharply under the demand of manpower for defense. Yet, for reasons beyond inadequate education and training, black reemployment continued to lag. Discrimination prevailed not only in corporations and in labor unions but also in the very government agencies charged with responsibility for managing manpower for the defense effort.

The government's apparent acquiescence in discrimination, evidenced also by continuing racial segregation in the armed forces, brought despair and bitterness to the black community. Protests from black organizations produced, at best, sporadic and inconclusive results. Government defense agencies regularly issued orders forbidding discrimination by defense contractors but the orders were just as regularly ignored.

Roosevelt, while not unsympathetic to black aspirations, had never placed civil rights high on his list of political priorities. Acutely aware that he had to depend on Southern Democratic congressmen to enact essential programs, he had remained cautiously noncommittal during the various struggles in the 1930s to pass federal antilynching legislation. By mid-1941, however, the pressures for action against job discrimination became more powerful, as substantial numbers of white liberals joined the newly militant black spokesmen in their protests.

The president put increasing pressure for action on William Knudsen and Sidney Hillman, co-chairmen of the Office of Production Management. Hillman, especially, continually urged government contractors not to discriminate, but the administration feared to use sanctions and urgings alone brought minimal results. Even government industrial training program administrators practiced discrimination, despite legal provisions to the contrary.

Where liberal protest and government suasion failed, organized pressure groups finally succeeded. The man most responsible for creating the FEPC was A. Philip Randolph, founder in 1925 of the Brotherhood of Sleeping Car Porters, American Federation of Labor, the most influential black body in organized labor. Having participated with other black leaders in several fruitless attempts to promote government action against discrimination in civilian and military affairs, Randolph decided late in 1940 that more direct action was required. To that end, in February 1941 he created the March on Washington Movement, an all-black organization dedicated to eliminating racial bias in war industries, labor unions, government agencies, and the armed forces.

Randolph established the movement's black only policy for three reasons: to prevent infiltration by white Communists, to stimulate black pride and self-confidence, and to attract the large numbers of lower-class blacks necessary for it to succeed. The MOWM planned a series of massive rallies in major cities to focus attention on the problems of blacks; should these fail to stimulate action, the organization threatened to stage a mass march on the nation's capital. To be credible, such a threat required evidence of broad and active support, and Randolph hoped for the kind of grassroots black enthusiasm that the middle-class, biracial National Association for the Advancement of Colored People and the Urban League had never enjoyed.

Throughout the first half of 1941, the MOWM organized rallies and put increased political pressure on the administration, setting July 1 as the date for its climactic march on Washington. Randolph may well have been unable to produce the massive march he predicted, but Roosevelt evidently decided that the threat could not be discounted. When new directives against discrimination from the Office of Production Management failed either to bring results or to appease black leaders, FDR assigned Fiorello LaGuardia, mayor of New York and director of civil defense, to negotiate with black spokesmen. At a White House conference held June 18, blacks pressed upon Roosevelt and other administration leaders their demands for a government agency to combat discrimination in employment.

In a meeting that LaGuardia termed "a fine example of democracy at work," the blacks won a clear, if not unqualified, victory. A week later, on June 25, Roosevelt issued Executive Order 8802 creating the President's Committee on Fair Employment Practices. For the first time since Reconstruction, an official government agency became responsible for safeguarding black rights. The

victory was especially notable since many liberals, convinced by mid-1941 that domestic concerns must be subordinated to crushing fascism abroad, had given only peripheral attention to black demands. Furthermore, Roosevelt knew that in creating the FEPC he risked losing the Southern congressional support so urgently needed in the areas of preparedness and foreign policy.

Yet the defense effort had given blacks new leverage with the administration. Production for defense demanded full use of manpower regardless of race; the nation quite literally could not afford to exclude blacks from jobs. Also, the ideological struggle against Hitler required closer correspondence between democratic dogma and social reality in terms of equality of races. The creation of the FEPC persuaded Randolph to "postpone" indefinitely the march on Washington, thereby saving the administration a major embarrassment at home and abroad. Political pressure was important as well: black leaders did not have to remind the president that the votes of their followers were an increasingly important factor in Democratic support.

Significantly, blacks had gained the victory on their own. They had bargained and won by operating as a pragmatic, determined pressure group. What they learned in 1941 they applied throughout the war years; as in World War I they supported the defense and war efforts, but contrary to the practice in 1917, they insisted that the demands of national unity must not preclude the expansion of black rights. They persisted in reminding the public of the implications for race relations of a war fought in the name of democratic ideals. Though they ultimately failed, and though the FEPC finally became another war casualty, they initiated a process that would, at another day, begin to give economic, political, and social substance to black equality.

Frustration marked the five-year history of the FEPC. Assigned the task of ending discrimination "in the employment of workers in defense industries or government because of race, creed, color, or national origin," it never received the power commensurate with that mandate. Throughout its career, the committee lacked the needed authority and adequate budget and personnel resources; these weaknesses, in turn, reflected inadequate political support from the Roosevelt administration and from Congress. Created only under duress, ignored by the general public and government officials alike, the FEPC struggled doggedly against prejudice among its enemies and indifference among those who claimed to be its friends.

The wording of the enforcement clause in Executive Order 8802 indicated the timidity of the administration's approach:

> The Committee shall receive and investigate complaints of this order and shall take appropriate steps to redress grievances which it finds to be valid. The Committee shall also recommend to the several departments and agencies of the government of the United States and to the President all measures which may be deemed by it necessary or proper to effectuate the provisions of this order.

To be effective, then, the FEPC needed full cooperation from the major government agencies involved in the defense effort. When corporations or labor unions refused to comply with nondiscrimination orders, the committee requested that the supervising agencies cancel or not renew any contracts with offenders. Some agencies complied with these requests; but most did not. In July 1942, for example, the United States Employment Service issued a directive to its field offices permitting them to discriminate in referring workers if employers insisted on it.

The absence of coercive power required the committee to rely mainly on publicity to fulfill its objectives. To this end, it conducted a series of public hearings in major employment centers during late 1941 and early 1942. The committee claimed, perhaps optimistically, that these hearings resulted in marked increases in the number of blacks employed in defense projects.

The hearings were of uncertain value politically. Predictably, they antagonized the FEPC's opponents while failing to satisfy its friends fully. The reaction in Birmingham, Alabama, was typical: blacks and some white liberals resented the committee's acceptance of social segregation; the city's commissioner of public safety, Eugene "Bull" Connor, on the other hand, warned Roosevelt that federal agencies were attempting "to destroy segregation and bring about amalgamation of the races." Only a quick countermand by the president, Connor said, could prevent "the annihilation of the Democratic Party" in the South.

The FEPC encountered continuing problems related to its own staff and also to its position within the executive branch. The original six-man committee reflected careful efforts by Roosevelt to achieve racial and ideological balance. Mark Ethridge, vice president and general manager of the Louisville *Courier-Journal,* became the first chairman, and the committee selected Lawrence W. Cramer, former governor of the Virgin Islands, as executive secretary. Ethridge, representing moderate Southern opinion, interpreted Executive Order 8802 in terms of the manpower needs of the war effort, not as a social document intended to put an end to racial segregation. Harassed from the outset by both Southern racists and Northern liberals, Ethridge resigned from the chairmanship early in 1942, although the president persuaded him to remain on the committee under the new chairman, Malcolm MacLean, president of the Hampton Institute. Under MacLean, the committee hoped to expand its scope and authority. It asked the president for broader enforcement power as well as a budget large enough to establish a dozen regional offices.

Though he at first appeared sympathetic, Roosevelt soon acted to weaken, rather than strengthen, the committee. Originally established in the Labor Division of the Office of Production Management and responsible only to the president, the FEPC was moved to the War Production Board after the OPM was abolished in January 1942, although it retained its independent status. Political pressure from Southern congressmen, heightened after the Birmingham hearings of June 1942, convinced many officials in the administration of the need for closer control of the agency's activities. Bowing to that pressure, the president, without consulting with committee members, transferred the FEPC to the War Manpower Commission on July 30, 1942, placing the agency under the supervision and control of Paul V. McNutt, WMC director.

The shift shocked committee members. Chairman MacLean loyally declared that he would obey orders, but warned, "All hell will break loose" among minority groups. Roosevelt responded characteristically by directing his secretary, Marvin McIntyre, to "get McLean [sic] and McNutt into the office together and have them talk over this whole thing;" he was sure that the dispute involved "a lot of smoke and very little fire."

The president was wrong. Over the next several months the FEPC and the WMC attempted without success to establish a mutually satisfactory working relationship. FEPC officials fought against being absorbed into the existing antidiscrimination agencies of the WMC, while McNutt, determined to keep the committee under close control, refused to approve a budget for the FEPC until it accepted his supervision. As negotiations dragged on, black protests over the transfer became increasingly bitter, despite White House assurances that the move would strengthen the committee. Walter White of the NAACP curtly wrote McNutt: "Abolition of the Committee altogether would be a more honest and honorable act in that blacks and other minorities would then be under no illusions" that the administration intended to fight discrimination in war industries or in the federal government.

With its precise status still undetermined, the FEPC nonetheless attempted to continue its work. After months of preparation, it scheduled public hearings for January 25 to 27, 1943, concerning claims of employment discrimination against blacks by Southern railroad unions and carriers. McNutt, disturbed by this further ruffling of Southern sensibilities, asked that the hearings be postponed; when the FEPC refused, he ordered them canceled himself early in January.

This blow to the committee's already shattered prestige evoked a storm of protest comparable to the one that had caused the agency to be formed originally. Liberals and minority groups saw the administration's retreat as a cave-in to increased pressure from Southern congressmen, emboldened by Democratic losses in the North after the 1942 elections. Their anger deepened when McNutt let it be known that the White House itself had ordered the hearings canceled. Convinced that the committee had lost the president's support, a number of staff members, headed by MacLean and Ethridge, handed in their resignations. While leaders of Randolph's March on Washington Movement again threatened to hold a massive demonstration in the nation's capital, Walter White, in a letter to Roosevelt, rehearsed the administration's failures: the FEPC had never enjoyed the direct access to the president that was originally envisioned; its staff and budget were not commensurate with the scope of its assignment; and it had never received adequate support from the White House when it was attacked by its enemies in and out of Congress.

Once again Roosevelt responded to the strongest political pressure of the moment. Early in February 1943, he directed McNutt to call a conference of minority group leaders to reconsider the committee's status. Nothing came of the conference, however, and for almost four months the administration conducted an intramural debate on the future of the FEPC. All agreed that the committee should be reconstructed and given autonomy, but some disagreed on what the proper scope of its activities should be.

By late May, Roosevelt had alternate drafts of a new executive order on his desk. Attorney General Francis Biddle argued that the committee needed authority to follow through on its findings of discrimination in war industries through the use of court injunctions requiring offending employers to stop discriminating and, where necessary, to reinstate improperly dismissed workers with back pay. Harold D. Smith, director of the budget, preferred to have the FEPC continue in its original pattern. He insisted that the problem of discrimination could be handled "by education, persuasion, and pressure [rather] than as a matter of law enforcement." He further argued that the draft from the Department of Justice would create serious work stoppages, strengthen the hand of "extremists" in minority groups, and arouse the ire of Southern congressmen. Although the newly appointed FEPC chairman, Monsignor Francis J. Haas, preferred Biddle's version, Roosevelt accepted the milder alternative. On May 27 he issued Executive Order 9346 creating a new FEPC on the basis of Smith's suggestions.

Though not as powerful as Biddle and others had hoped, the new FEPC was somewhat stronger than its predecessor. Restored to independent status within the Office of Production Management, the committee received a budget of almost a half million dollars, which enabled it to open twelve regional offices in major cities across the country. Still deprived of broad powers of enforcement, the FEPC could conduct hearings, make findings of fact, and take undefined "appropriate steps" to end discrimination.

During the next three years, the FEPC struggled, with mixed results, to fulfill its mandate. Considering its lack of legal, financial, and political resources, it established a commendable record. Over the period of its existence, the committee negotiated some five thousand cases and settled forty strikes set off by racial conflict. Increasing attacks from Congress provided one index of its impact on the problem of discrimination. Indeed, Southern congressional critics conducted a continuing, and eventually successful, war with the committee, one which plunged the Congress into turmoil and exacerbated existing differences within the Democratic party.

Until late in 1943, Congress took little official notice of the FEPC and its work, although Southern congressmen had, from the beginning, exerted private pressure on the administration to eliminate or cripple the agency. When the FEPC was revived and strengthened in mid-1943, however, its activities increasingly attracted congressional attention. . . .

Throughout 1944, the prospect of the national election conditioned congressional action on the FEPC. The Republicans, hoping to recapture the black vote and eager to exploit an issue that could divide the opposition, strongly endorsed the principle of a permanent FEPC. At the same time, distrust of the committee's New Deal character and eagerness to uphold their coalition with conservative Democrats dictated caution in taking legislative action. Roosevelt and the Democrats faced a similar dilemma: to act on the FEPC would lose needed Southern cooperation in Congress, but to ignore the FEPC might jeopardize the black vote in the upcoming election. . . .

Pressures of this kind prevented the Democrats from providing for a permanent FEPC in their legislative program for 1945. Congressmen from both parties continued the struggle, however, while Southerners renewed their efforts to destroy the agency altogether. Harry S. Truman's accession to the presidency following Roosevelt's death in April deepened the conflict, for Truman, unlike his predecessor, took a firm public stand in support of permanent FEPC legislation. . . .

With permanent legislation blocked, the FEPC's only hope for existence beyond June 30 lay in its being included in the new war agencies appropriations bill for fiscal year 1946. Again, Southerners on the Rules Committee intervened. . . .

As before, the Southerners were overwhelmingly preoccupied with the FEPC's effect on relations between the races. Race relations in the South, they argued, were steadily improving, and whatever prejudice that remained could not be legislated out of existence. Issues of this delicacy, they felt, should be left in local hands, since attempts by the federal government to legislate equality of any kind would only exacerbate existing tensions. [Mississippi Senator James] Eastland contended that discrimination was no worse in the South than in other areas of the country. [New Mexico Democrat Dennis] Chavez quickly agreed; it was precisely because the problem was a national one, he said, that it required national attention. Bested in that exchange, Eastland adopted a more ominous tone: "It appears to me that, for those who think, the bill would be the very last thing the Jews or other minority groups in the United States would want. If we can say that they may not be discriminated against, then we have the right to say that they may be discriminated against; and they are a minority group in this country."

For the South, the heart of the issue was white supremacy. "We do not attempt to hurt the colored man," said Allen Ellender of Louisiana, "but we simply make him realize that the white race is superior to the colored race in every respect." Given the innate disparity between the races, Southerners argued, total segregation would have to be maintained, and they were certain that the underlying goal of FEPC advocates was social equality. As in earlier debates, those supporting the bill emphasized equal economic opportunity, and generally denied being concerned with social equality. At one point, however, Joseph Guffey (D-Pa.) admitted under [Georgia Senator Richard] Russell's prodding that for businesses to maintain separate dining and toilet facilities was a violation of economic equality. Russell seized on this as proof "that this bill is designed to undertake to force social equality, miscegnation of the races, amalgamation of the races and eventually a mongrel American race."

The Southerners held the floor and dominated discussion throughout the three-week debate, but they allowed time for counter-arguments from supporters of the bill. Besides replying to specific criticisms, the Northerners attempted to construct a positive case for the FEPC. Chavez argued that since the war had imposed equality of sacrifice on minorities, peacetime should bring equality of employment. Referring to outbreaks of racial violence in Detroit and other urban centers during the war, he insisted that the FEPC, by limiting economic injustice, could prevent such incidents in the future. Examining the economic question in broader perspective, Senator [James] Mead saw discrimination as a threat to full employment and therefore as a drag on the entire economy. To most supporters of the FEPC, however, the moral question overshadowed economic considerations. H. Alexander Smith (R-N.J.) reminded the chamber that the nation had just fought a war against racist doctrines and that blacks and other minorities deserved equal employment opportunities as a matter of simple justice.

As the debate moved into its third week, Republicans on both sides of the issue demanded that cloture be invoked. Senator [Alben] Barkley, agreeing that the Senate should "either fish or cut bait," attempted to file the petition on February 4, but the Southerners continued to argue that the issue technically on the floor—amending the *Journal*—was not subject to cloture, and Senator [Kenneth] McKellar's rulings from the chair sustained their position.

The Southerners, however, having revived a useful weapon with which to sustain future filibusters, were now ready to proceed to a vote. Since they knew they would win a test on cloture, they renewed their offer to allow a vote provided that the FEPC's supporters would agree to withdraw legislation establishing the committee on a permanent basis. Persuaded that they could not break the filibuster and seeing no point in further debate, Senator Chavez and his allies accepted the Southerners' terms. Finally, on February 9, in a vote Russell termed "one of the most important which the Senate has taken in many years," the cloture attempt failed to gain the required two-thirds margin, 48 to 36. On that inglorious note, the last real hope for the FEPC disappeared, and on June 30, 1946, the agency closed its doors. Its final study reported wholesale revival of discriminatory practices against minorities.

The five-year struggle over the FEPC foreshadowed the emergence of civil rights as the primary domestic issue of American postwar politics. The emergence of that issue, in turn, heralded shifts in political power and strategy, especially within the Democratic party. The climactic 1946 debate in the Senate included a great deal of frank discussion on the political implications of civil rights legislation. Southerners frequently charged that Republicans and nonsouthern Democrats alike were interested less in black welfare than in black votes. To W. Lee O'Daniel of Texas, the FEPC was not an economic question at all: "It is purely and simply a trick to try to steal the votes of the northern blacks. It is a contest between northern Republicans and northern Democrats to steal the black votes." Throughout the dispute over the FEPC, Southerners regularly insisted, especially in the House, that on any secret congressional ballot, the FEPC would lose; much of its nominal support, they argued, simply represented political posturing.

For the Republican party, the FEPC and the race question in general raised perplexing problems. Aware at least rhetorically of their tradition as the party of Lincoln, Republicans in both houses gave official support to the agency and to racial equality. Yet they instinctively disliked extending federal control, which the FEPC seemed to require. They hesitated also to antagonize Southern Democrats with whom they had fashioned a powerful, though unofficial, political alliance against the New Deal. Finally, even wholehearted support of black rights could not guarantee electoral benefits. In 1944 the black vote was overwhelmingly Democratic, despite the Republicans' considerably stronger plank on civil rights. . . .

If the FEPC created problems for the Republicans, it produced a trauma among the Democrats. Senator [John] Overton spoke for the South in arguing that the party ought to be the white man's party. He and Eastland conducted a brief, revealing dialogue on the subject of the black vote:

> **Overton:** I believe the Negro [black] made a mistake when he yielded his friendship for the party which had stood by him through thick and thin in return for the aid which has been given to him during the last few years.

> **Eastland:** The Senator does not think the Democratic Party is friendly to the Negro, [black] does he?

> **Overton:** Certainly not the backbone of the Democratic Party.

The assumption that the South still constituted the backbone of the Democratic party ignored the political facts of the New Deal revolution. Chavez reversed Senator [Walter] George's argument that passage of the FEPC bill would wreck the party: "I say God pity the Democratic

Senators who now are chairmen of committees unless the Democratic party keeps itself liberal and votes to enact legislation such as . . . [FEPC]. . . . I know that unless we do so, the people will complain, as they will have a right to do, and the people will be resentful, as they will have a right to be, and the people will vote for a change." He pointed out that in recent years black votes had ensured the election of a number of Northern Democrats, including Guffey and Francis Myers of Pennsylvania and Scott Lucas of Illinois. [Senator Theodore] Bilbo conceded that blacks held the balance of power in many Northern states, even to the point of admitting that "the black vote controls the election of the President of the United States."

Gradually realizing that their importance within the party was declining, the Southerners felt frustrated, even persecuted. Eastland compared their situation to the suffering of the South during Reconstruction, and Senator Russell, in denying the South's indifference to minority aspirations, claimed that "if there is anyone in this body who is in a position to sympathize with any poor, maligned, and abused minority anywhere, it is one of those who bears the label of southern Democrat."

Southern Democrats saw the move for the FEPC as part of a continued ideological shift to the left within the party, a shift they felt less and less able to prevent. Time and again they identified the FEPC with the CIO, picturing the union as the sinister controlling power behind Northern party leadership. For all their hyperbole, the Southerners correctly discerned the long-range trend within their party on the issue of civil rights. Northern Democrats, increasingly willing to risk the loss of Southern support and lacking the Republicans' qualms about activist government, were moving slowly toward a commitment to black rights. By 1945 awakened black and liberal pressures, coinciding with FDR's personal sympathies, had led the president to more active, if still cautious, encouragement. From the outset of his presidency, his successor, Harry Truman, fought publicly though not always whole-heartedly, for black rights in employment and elsewhere. Democratic leaders in Congress, though remaining more sensitive to Southern pressures, nonetheless moved from total hostility to the FEPC to cautious, if notably unenthusiastic, support. By 1948, Northern liberals were willing to pay the price of a Dixiecrat revolt to include a strong civil rights plank in the party platform.

To be sure, fullscale conversion to the cause of black rights still lay considerably in the future for the Democrats. The death of the FEPC stemmed almost as much from its supporters' indifference as from its enemies' intransigence.

Analysis of the overall legislative history of the FEPC lends some credence to the accusations of perfidy made following the Senate filibuster. As Roy Wilkins of the NAACP charged, "neither the Democrats nor the Republicans wanted a real showdown on this legislation." Throughout the legislative history of the FEPC, its opponents displayed both shrewder parliamentary skill and greater political will than its supporters. Yet the pressures dictating the creation of the agency in 1941 continued to mount even after its death five years later. The struggle over the FEPC, both in the substance of debate and in the shape of the political dynamics surrounding the issue, foreshadowed later, more successful, struggles for the civil rights of black Americans.

JAMES NUECHTERLEIN is a Senior Fellow of the Institute on Religion and Public Life. He was formerly Professor of American Studies and Political Thought at Valparaiso University.

Harvard Sitkoff   → **NO**

African American Militancy in the World War II South: Another Perspective

It is now commonplace to emphasize the Second World War as a watershed in the African American freedom struggle, as a time of mass black militancy, and as the direct precursor to the civil rights protest movement of the late 1950s and 1960s. Even most textbooks today dramatize the wartime bitterness of African American protests against racial discrimination in the defense industry and the military, and highlight the phenomenal growth of the National Association for the Advancement of Colored People and the beginnings of the Congress of Racial Equality, which practiced direct-action civil disobedience to desegregate places of public accommodation. They quote the sardonic statement, supposedly popular during the war, of a black man, just drafted, who seethed: "Write on my tombstone—Here lies a black man, killed fighting a yellow man, for the protection of a white man." The individual military experience of a Jackie Robinson or a Medgar Evers is portrayed as representative of the turning point for African Americans as a whole; and virtually all devote the lion's share of space on blacks in the war to A. Philip Randolph's March-on-Washington Movement. Commonly described as the foremost manifestation of wartime mass black militancy, and singularly credited with forcing a reluctant President Franklin Roosevelt to issue Executive Order 8802 banning racial discrimination in defense and government employment, the MOWM is invariably pictured as the forerunner of the later Black Freedom Struggle's tactics and strategy. Most accounts also assert that the African American press during World War II was militantly demanding in a way it had never before been, and that the black masses, who actively, aggressively, even violently confronted Jim Crow, were yet far more militant. The war years, in sum, are depicted as a time when mass militancy became characteristic of the African American, when blacks belligerently assaulted the racial status quo, and when this watershed in black consciousness and behavior ignited the Negro Revolution that would later blaze.

Perhaps. Maybe. It is comforting to think that the destructiveness of mass warfare can have redeeming virtues; it is good to have forebears to admire and emulate. But if by a watershed in militancy we mean a crucial turning point in the aggressiveness of black actions, a far greater combativeness than previously exhibited, then the evidence to prove this argument conclusively has yet to appear; and major questions concerning this interpretation remain unanswered. This is especially so concerning the South, particularly the rural South, where most African Americans continued to live during World War II. Total war did, of course, generate major ruptures and upheavals in American life. Japan's sudden attack on the U.S. Pacific fleet at Pearl Harbor on December 7, 1941, evoked a widespread wave of patriotism and national purpose. Few Americans, black or white, dissented from the war spirit, intensified by media publicity and government-orchestrated campaigns to rally 'round the flag. Support for the war effort placed a premium on loyalty and unity. Even those who wished to protest had to tread carefully.

The angry demonstrations by African Americans against racial discrimination in the defense industry and in the armed services, the flurry of petitions and protests, so common in 1940 and 1941, diminished after the United States entered the war, and received decreasing attention as the war dragged on. In fact, the most militant editorials in the Negro press, the virulent threats by African American protest leaders and protest organizations, the indignant portents of black disloyalty or of tepid support by blacks for the Allied cause, almost without exception came *before* Pearl Harbor, before the United States entered the war. Pre-war actions are not instances of *wartime* militancy.

Indeed, soon after the attack on Pearl Harbor, Edgar G. Brown, director of the National Negro Council[,] telegraphed President Roosevelt that all African Americans pledge 100 percent loyalty to the United States. The National Urban League promised total support for the war effort. The Southern Negro Youth Congress raised money for defense bonds, sponsored an Army Welfare Committee to establish a USO Center for Negroes, and created its own Youth V for Victory Committee. W. E. B. Du Bois and A. Philip Randolph spoke at "Victory Through Unity" conferences. Father Divine donated a hotel to the Navy, and Paul Robeson travelled to training camps to entertain the troops. Dr. Charles Drew, whose research made blood transfusions possible, proclaimed that the priority of all Americans, "whether black or white, is to get on with the winning of the war" despite the scientifically unwarranted decision of the Red Cross to segregate the blood of black and white donors. Joe Louis promised the entire profits of his next two fights to the Army and Navy relief funds. Langston Hughes wrote plays for the War Writers Board and jingles for the Treasury Department. Josh White sang "Are You Ready?" promising to batter the Japanese "ratter till his head gets flatter," and Doc Clayton sounded a call for revenge in his "Pearl Harbor Blues." African Americans working in Hollywood formed a Victory Committee, headed by Hattie McDaniel. Richard Wright, who had earlier denounced American involvement in the war, immediately offered his literary services to the government for "the national democratic cause," and African Americans in the Communist Party hierarchy sought to aid the war effort by ordering that the attacks on racism in the script for the Broadway play based on Wright's *Native Son* be toned down.

The first issues of the Negro press after Pearl Harbor proclaimed in banner headlines "Mr. President, Count on Us," and "The Black Tenth is Ready." Major newspapers that had once excoriated Du Bois for penning his First World War "Close Ranks" editorial now repeated his very imagery to restate his plea that Negroes put aside their special grievances for the duration. The Norfolk *Journal and Guide* called upon African Americans to "close ranks and join with fervent patriotism in this battle for America." "The hour calls for a closing of ranks, for joining of hands, not for a widening of the racial gap" echoed the Chicago *Defender.* The California *Eagle* promised to shift its campaign from full citizenship rights to full citizenship duties. A study of twenty-four Negro newspapers in the first several months of the war found that only three harped on the grievances and complaints of African Americans; the other twenty-one stressed the necessity of racial cooperation to avenge Pearl Harbor and the common goal of both blacks and whites of defeating the United States' foreign enemies. Columnists who before the attack on Pearl Harbor had accentuated the similarities between Nazism and American racism, stressed their differences after Pearl Harbor; essayists who had trumpeted that the Black Yanks Are Not Coming changed their tune to the Need to Do Everything to Win the War. And the Negro Newspaper

Publishers Association, at its first meeting after the entry of the United States into the war, unanimously pledged its unequivocal loyalty to the nation and to the president. . . .

Instead of militant protest, the dominant theme of African American organizations and journals during the Second World War was that patriotic duty and battlefield bravery would lead to the Negro's advancement. The notion that blacks would gain from the war, not as a gift of white goodwill but because the nation needed the loyalty and manpower of African Americans, had been sounded in every one of America's previous armed conflicts, and it continued to reverberate throughout World War II. "War may be hell for some," columnist Joseph Bibb exulted, "but it bids fair to open up the portals of heaven for us." Whites will respond positively to the needs of African Americans if Negroes do their part as 100 percent loyal Americans declared Lester Granger. In order for African Americans to benefit later they must fight for the United States now, "segregation and Jim Crowism to the contrary notwithstanding," announced the New York *Age.* Full participation in the defense of the nation, claimed the Baltimore *Afro-American*, is the path to eventual equality. And the NAACP declared the slogan for its mid-1942 convention to be "Victory is Vital to Minorities."

In this vein, African Americans took up the call of the Pittsburgh *Courier* for a "Double V" campaign. Originating with a letter to the editor from James G. Thompson of Wichita, Kansas, who sought to join the army "to take his place on the fighting front for the principles which he so dearly loved," the *Courier* urged blacks to "fight for the right to fight" because wartime performance would determine postwar status. Opposing the war effort, or sitting on the sidelines, argued the *Courier*, would be the worst possible course for blacks to follow. Rather than calling for a massive attack on the Jim Crow system, the *Courier* added, African-Americans must join in the defense of their country. "The more we put in," argued columnist J. A. Rogers, "the more we have a right to claim." That notion was restated in hundreds of ways, as the *Courier* and the Negro press overall harped on the necessity of African Americans serving fully and faithfully so that they could prove their patriotism and later gain concessions. With cause, the Socialist Workers Party denounced the Double V as "a cover for unqualified support of the war." Yet even a fight for the right to fight could be misunderstood, and the space devoted to the Double V in the *Courier* declined by half between April and August 1942. By the end of 1942 the Double V campaign had been wholly superceded by less ambiguous, more positive, declarations of African American patriotism; and the *Courier* would go on to urge black soldiers to "insist on combat duty." "The most significant achievement of the Negro press during this crisis, in our estimation," bragged African American publishers in 1944, "lies in the fact that the Negro newspapers have brought home to the Negro people of America that this is their war and not merely 'a white man's war.'"

However much the great majority of African Americans desired the end of racial discrimination and segregation in American life, only a minority thought that their fight for rights should take precedence over defeating Germany and Japan, and far fewer flirted with militant protests that might be considered harmful to the war effort. Thus A. Philip Randolph's March-on-Washington Movement, generally depicted as the epitome of mass black militancy during the war, truly held center-stage in the Negro community only for a few months in 1941, before American entry into the war, and then gradually withered away. Shunned as "unpatriotic" by many of the mainstream Negro organizations and newspapers that had earlier supported it, Randolph's group labored in vain to rebut accusations of employing the "most dangerous demagoguery on record" and of "Marching Against the War Effort." Polls in the Negro press during 1942 revealed a steady diminution of black support for a March on Washington to demand a redress of grievances. When Randolph called for mass marches on city halls in 1942, no blacks marched. When he called for a week of non-violent civil disobedience and non-cooperation to protest Jim Crow school and transportation systems in 1943, a poll indicated that more than 70 percent of African Americans opposed the campaign, and no blacks engaged in such activities. And when he called upon the masses to come to his "We Are Americans, Too!" conference in Chicago in the summer of 1943, virtually no blacks other than members of his Sleeping Car Porters union attended. By then, as Randolph admitted, the March-on-Washington Movement was "without funds." Unable to pay the rent for an office or for the services of an executive secretary, the organization existed only on paper.

Asa Philip Randolph's brief shining moment had passed quickly. The March-on-Washington Movement ended with Randolph having never led a wartime mass march or a civil disobedience campaign. When he described the program of his organization in Rayford Logan's *What the Negro Wants* (1944), Randolph barely discussed mass militant protests. Instead, most of his essay was devoted to attacking American Communists, to explaining why racial change in the South must be gradual and piecemeal, and to advocating race relations committees that would take the necessary measures to prevent or stop race riots. Quite at odds with the image of the wartime Randolph in most current accounts, his wartime agenda for the

March-on-Washington Movement in fact differed little from that of the NAACP. Randolph, moreover, devoted the greatest amount of his time and energy during the war to criticizing discrimination within the American Federation of Labor and heading the National Council for a Permanent Fair Employment Practices Commission, a traditional legislative lobby which never advocated mobilizing the masses and which was controlled by an elite group of mainly white New York socialists and labor leaders. Penning the moribund March-on-Washington Movement's epitaph in 1945, Adam Clayton Powell, Jr., described it as an "organization with a name that it does not live up to, an announced program that it does not stick to, and a philosophy contrary to the mood of the times." Its former headquarters in Harlem had already been converted into a bookshop.

The Congress of Racial Equality suffered much the same fate as the March-on-Washington Movement during the war, but it did so in relative obscurity. The white media barely mentioned it, and the Negro press did so even less. A tiny interracial, primarily white, elite group of pacifist and socialist followers of A. J. Muste, CORE mainly engaged in efforts to counter discrimination in places of public accommodation and recreation in northern cities where those practices were already illegal. It did little to try to desegregate schools and housing, or to expand job opportunities for African Americans, or to influence civil rights legislation, and its wartime efforts proved negligible. Because its dozen or so local chapters took to heart the reconciliatory aspects of Gandhian non-violence, the vital importance of changing the consciousness of those engaged in racist practices, few of its Christian pacifist members went beyond negotiations to direct action in the streets. CORE's hopes of becoming a mass, broad-based movement lingered as only a dream during the war, and blacks at Howard University and in St. Louis who, independent of each other, thought they were inventing the sit-in in 1944, did not even know that CORE, too, sought to employ the tactics of the CIO's famous "sit-down" strikes to the fight against Jim Crow. Faced with public apathy, unstable chapters, and a budget of less than $100 a month for its national office, CORE did not even contemplate entering the upper South until 1947, when eight blacks and eight whites decided to test the compliance with the Supreme Court's 1946 ruling in the Irene Morgan case, declaring segregation in interstate carriers unconstitutional. Even then, CORE would not try to establish a chapter in the South for another decade.

The NAACP, on the other hand, saw its membership grow from 50,556 and 355 branches in 1940 to over half a million and more than a thousand branches in 1946.

Yet, it essentially remained middle-class in orientation and bureaucratic in structure, abhoring radical tactics and adhering to a legalistic approach that did not countenance collective action. This was especially so in the South, the site of three-quarters of the new wartime branches. None of the southern branches sanctioned confrontations, direct action, or extra-legal tactics. Ella Baker, who visited local chapters of the NAACP throughout the wartime South, first as an assistant field secretary of the Association and then as its national director of branches, never ceased hectoring the national office that most of those branches were little more than social clubs with no interest whatsoever in pursuing local protests. Thurgood Marshall also chafed at the reluctance of the southern branch officers to attack Jim Crow, and their tendency to devote themselves solely to teacher-salary equalization suits. Such suits "aroused little excitement, even in the Deep South," maintains George B. Tindall: "The tedious pace, the limited results, the manifest equity of the claim" muted white alarm. And that suited the NAACP's southern leadership of black academics, businessmen, and ministers just fine. The issue of inequitable salaries for Negro public school teachers would remain their top priority even in the immediate postwar years. The pursuit of traditional objectives by restrained tactics remained the hallmark of the Association in the South. As they had in the 1930s, the wartime southern branches lobbied and litigated against the poll tax, the white primary, and lynching, and requested a more equitable share of educational facilities and funds.

Continuity also characterized the work of the seven southern affiliates of the National Urban League. They held firm to their social work orientation and to their reliance on negotiations to expand employment, recreational, and housing opportunities for African Americans. Such matters as African American juvenile delinquency and family disorganization took precedence over the fight for equal rights. Their wariness toward demonstrations and protests reflected their fear of losing funding from the Community Chest and local philanthropies, their faith in being able to make progress by working in conventional channels, and their hostility toward the NAACP—which they viewed as a competitor for financial contributions. Confrontation and disruption, even harsh talk, did not fit the Urban League's pursuit of gradual and limited racial change. When Benjamin Bell, the newly appointed executive secretary of the Urban League in Memphis, angered white politicians and businessmen by denouncing Jim Crow, the national office quickly replaced him with someone more compliant.

Much as southern black leaders did not support direct action protests or forthright attacks on segregation during the war, the editorials of southern Negro newspapers rarely echoed the demands for racial equality of those in the North. Several African American newspapers in the South followed the wartime lead of the Savannah *Tribune* in discontinuing the practice of reprinting editorials from northern black newspapers. Most of the southern Negro press had never done so, and they continued, as did most southern black church and community leaders during the war, to stay on the sidelines of the civil rights struggle, to advocate upright behavior and individual economic advancement within the existing order, and to preach paternalism and "civility." Even when calling for "fair play" or an end to disfranchisement, they did so in a manner that posed no clear and present danger to white supremacy. Lest criticism be construed as unpatriotic, they accentuated African American loyalty and contributions to the war effort above all else. Surveying the Negro press in Mississippi during the war, Julius Thompson concluded: "Submission to the system was the watchword."

. . . African American Communists soft-pedaled their censure of racism in the United States during the war. Executing an about-face from the period of the Nazi-Soviet Pact, when they took the lead in exposing Jim Crow in the armed forces, the Communists opposed efforts by blacks to embarrass the military after Germany invaded the Soviet Union in June 1941. They even sought to prevent African American legal challenges against discrimination from coming before the courts. The party's wartime policy was to do nothing that might erode the unity necessary for prosecuting the war. Ben Davis vigorously denounced both the March-on-Washington Movement and the NAACP for placing the interests of blacks above the needs for "national unity, maximum war production, and the highest possible morale in the armed forces." Having opposed civil disobedience by blacks and mass protests against racism, and defended the military against its civil rights critics, Davis confessed after the war that he had "often lost sight of" the black liberation struggle. Communist leader and social scientist John Williamson later concurred. "Neglect of the problems of the Negro people," Williamson wrote, "and the cessation of organizing efforts in the South undoubtedly slowed the pace of the freedom movement which arose later.

As did most black Communists, Georgian Angelo Herndon and his *Negro Quarterly* followed Earl Browder's wartime policy of refraining from public censure of Jim Crow. Its articles and editorials downplayed racial militancy, emphasized the need for patriotic unity, dispelled the "dangerous fallacy" that this is "a white man's war," and subordinated all racial issues to victory over fascist aggression. Similarly, chapters of the National Negro Congress metamorphosed into Negro Labor Victory Committees;

Southern Negro Youth Congress cadre mainly worked within NAACP and CIO affiliates to promote victory abroad; and local party members in St. Louis hounded that city's March-on-Washington Movement and accused it of "disrupting the war effort" when it attempted to organize a demonstration to get more blacks jobs in defense plants. The response of the *Daily Worker* to the race riot in Detroit was to condemn the NAACP for making such a fuss and to urge everyone to get back to work quickly. . . .

With so many former allies in the fight for equal rights now counseling "go slow," most African American advocates of aggressive tactics to achieve fundamental racial change either trimmed their sails or foundered. Battling Hitler largely terminated the encouragement to black assertiveness that had been supplied in the 1930s by the Communists, militant labor union activists, supportive progressive government officials, and by the beliefs and sympathies spurred by the reform liberalism of the Great Depression-New Deal era. During the 1930s, at least ten cities had experienced NAACP-supported school boycotts protesting segregation. To demand employment, African Americans, with the support of major community leadership, had mounted sustained campaigns of picketing and boycotting retail establishments in at least thirty-five cities, including Atlanta, Baltimore, Durham, Houston, Memphis, New Orleans, and Richmond. In Charlotte, Greensboro, and Norfolk, as well as in Chicago, Philadelphia, and New York, blacks had sat-in at relief bureaus, conducted rent strikes, and led mass hunger marches. They had engaged in direct action protests against racial discrimination at restaurants, hotels, beaches, and theaters in both the South and North. In comparison, there was only one boycott against school segregation during the war, in Hillburn, New York, and not another one in the South until 1951; there were just a handful of direct action protests against Jim Crow in public accommodations, primarily by the largely white CORE in Chicago and Denver; and there were no sustained boycotts or mass demonstrations against job discrimination in World War II. As Meier and Rudwick state, in the only study to enumerate African American protest activities: the Depression—not the war—is the "watershed in Afro-American direct action." Militant black activism in the Thirties "achieved a salience in black protest that would not be equalled or surpassed until the late 1950s and 1960s." Indeed, they conclude, there "was less actual use of direct action tactics during World War II than in the 1930s"; the number of protest "demonstrations declined sharply during World War II compared to the 1930s"; and, overall, "the amount of direct action was minor compared to the Depression era."

These facts do not in the least suggest that African Americans wanted equal rights any less in 1944 than in 1937; or that blacks during the war complacently accepted second-class status. Discontent is ever-present among those who are discriminated against and oppressed. Indeed, as has been amply described, the war against Hitlerism intensified the civil rights consciousness of the New Deal years, raised the expectations of blacks considerably, and had a significant impact on American racial opinions, especially in heightening perceptions of the discrepancy between the democratic ideals of the United States and its undemocratic racial practices. But compared to the Depression decade, and far more to the 1960s, blacks in World War II faced greater resistance to change, in a milieu less hospitable to disruptive protests, with reduced internal wherewithal and external support. The constraints imposed by a nation at war, the dwindling resources for sustained confrontation, and the genuinely patriotic response of most African Americans to the dangers their nation faced all inhibited militant protest activity. . . .

Militant protest never entirely abated during the war, but it never assumed dominance in either black strategy or action. To the extent that it is now possible to gauge the amount and strength of the rupture, or the transformation, in civil rights protest activities, World War II does not appear to be a watershed. Change, of course, occurred. But in a limited manner. The status and protest cognition of southern blacks in 1945, their organizations, leadership, language, and strategies for reform were neither exactly the same nor fundamentally different than they had been in 1940. The goals considered a distant dream in the 1930s had not suddenly appeared attainable. The traditional tactics of African American protest groups had not suddenly become unacceptable, nor had new, more disruptive ones come into widespread use. Why? In part, because the nearly million young black men who might have been expected to be in the forefront of more militant forays against racist practices had been uprooted from their communities to serve in an armed forces which cramped organized protests. In part, because the optimism of African Americans for postwar progress, induced by the sudden prosperity of those who left mule and plow or domestic work for a job in a defense plant and by the din of democratic propaganda during the war, mitigated against a radical turn in practices. And, certainly in part, because wartime America proved an infertile ground for the seeds of protest planted in the 1930s. The needs of war came first. Period. The domestic unity, as well as manpower and production efficiency, required for victory took precedence over all else, for the Roosevelts, and for virtually every prominent African American, labor leader, white liberal, and progressive proponent of civil rights. And if that meant holding the color line, defusing conflicts, eschewing confrontation for compromise, well, the expected rewards for African Americans would come after the war. Furthermore, social, economic, and demographic alterations, no matter how vast or rapid, in and of themselves do not generate mass movements for social change by the aggrieved or oppressed. The resources for sustained mass confrontations with the Jim Crow system in the South were gestating but still embryonic, and the political climate that would facilitate rather than inhibit militant collective action had not yet emerged. The war had driven old Dixie downward, but not down and out.

The hopes of some, and dire warnings of others, "that a New Negro will return from the war," willing to fight and die rather than accept the traditional structure of white dominance in southern society, proved premature. Indeed, it appears that many of those southern African Americans most "modernized" by military service soon left the South in the greatest numbers to pursue their individual ambitions in northern cities, or re-enlisted in the armed forces, depleting the pool of potential southern black activists. The insurgent struggle for racial justice to come in the South would eventually draw sustenance from the many fundamental transformations in American life and world affairs catalyzed by the Second World War, but that mass movement would hardly be just an extension, a continuation, of previous civil rights reform efforts. Those militantly fighting for change in the 1960s would not look to the agenda and actions of World War II blacks and racial organizations as models to emulate.

Harvard Sitkoff is a professor of history at the University of New Hampshire and is the author of *A New Deal for Blacks: The Emergence of Civil Rights as a National Issue: The Depression Decade,* 30th anniversary edition (Oxford University Press, 1979, 2009); *The Struggle for Black Equality, 1954–1980* (Hill & Wang, 1981); and *King: Pilgrimage to the Mountaintop* (Hill & Wang, 2008).

EXPLORING THE ISSUE

Was the World War II Era a Watershed for the Civil Rights Movement?

Critical Thinking and Reflection

1. Discuss in detail the major complaints confronting African Americans in the World War II era.
2. Evaluate the success or failure of civil rights organizations in their efforts to improve the status of black Americans during the war.
3. Who was A. Philip Randolph, and how did he hope to advance the interests of African Americans during the war? How successful was he?
4. How did the battle over the creation of the Fair Employment Practices Commission (FEPC) impact leaders in both the Republican and Democratic parties and foreshadow the emergence of the postwar civil rights movement?
5. Based on your reading of the two selections in this issue, was World War II a watershed event in the African American freedom struggle?

Is There Common Ground?

Although the Roosevelt administration demonstrated considerable reluctance in positively addressing the concerns of African Americans during the war, FDR's decision to issue Executive Order 8802, in response to the threat by A. Philip Randolph to stage a march on the nation's capital, did pave the way for a federal commitment to eliminate employment discrimination in the nation's defense industries and to end segregation in the armed forces. Absent this level of black militancy, it is difficult to imagine Roosevelt acting on his own initiative to address these concerns within the African American community. With Roosevelt's death in 1945, it remained for Harry Truman, surprisingly but forthrightly, to carry these commitments to the end of the war and beyond.

Nuechterlein also is correct in pointing out that African Americans during the war, especially A. Philip Randolph, developed goals, tactics, and strategies of protest that typically are associated with Dr. Martin Luther King, Jr. in the 1950s and 1960s. Despite the tendency to attribute the development of nonviolent direct action techniques to Dr. King, this strategy was derivative of techniques pioneered by Randolph and the Congress of Racial Equality (CORE) in the 1940s. Similarly, it is important to keep in mind the prominent role played by the NAACP and its leaders, especially Walter White and Roy Wilkins, not only in lobbying the Roosevelt administration on civil rights issues but also for conducting a legal action strategy that resulted in numerous Supreme Court civil rights victories, during the 1940s, in the areas of housing, public education, and political enfranchisement.

Finally, the positive impact on the civil rights movement is evident in the lives of many African American veterans who returned from fighting fascism abroad and launched their own attacks to erase the limitations to full freedom in their local communities. Among the most well-known of these World War II veterans were Medgar and Charles Evers, Amzie Moore, Oliver Brown, Robert F. Williams, and Ralph Abernathy. In the lives of these individuals, we see a direct connection between World War II and the modern civil rights movement.

Additional Resources

Glenda Elizabeth Gilmore, *Defying Dixie: The Radical Roots of Civil Rights, 1919–1950* (W. W. Norton, 2008)

Darlene Clark Hine, *Black Victory: The Rise and Fall of the White Primary in Texas* (KTO Press, 1979)

August Meier and Elliott Rudwick, *CORE: A Study in the Civil Rights Movement, 1942–1968* (Oxford University Press, 1973)

Christopher S. Parker, *Fighting for Democracy: Black Veterans and the Struggle Against White Supremacy in the Postwar South* (Princeton University Press, 2009)

David Welky, *Marching across the Color Line: A. Philip Randolph and Civil Rights in the World War II Era* (Oxford University Press, 2014)

Internet References . . .

The African Americans: Many Rivers to Cross

www.pbs.org/wnet/african-americans-many-rivers-to-cross/history/what-was-black-americas-double-war/

The History Place: African Americans in World War II

www.historyplace.com/unitedstates/aframerwar/

Pictures of African Americans during World War II

www.archives.gov/research/african-americans/ww2-pictures/

Remembering Jim Crow

http://americanradioworks.publicradio.org/features/remembering/laws.html

World War II WWW Sites

http://besthistorysites.net/index.php/ww2

The Cold War and Beyond

UNIT

The Cold War and Beyond

World War II ended in 1945, but the peace that many had hoped for never came. In 1949, China came under totalitarian communist control, the Russians developed an atomic bomb, and communist subversion by high-level officials in the State and Treasury Departments of the U.S. government was uncovered. By 1950, a "Cold War" between the Western powers and the Soviets was in full swing, and American soldiers were fighting a hot war in Korea to "contain" "communist" expansion. These efforts scared many nations into cooperating with the new "Western" super power. In September 1962, the Soviets attempted to bring offensive missile sites onto the island of Cuba. By the end of the crisis, President Kennedy and Premier Nikita Khrushchev had developed a respect for one another, but not without bringing the world to the brink of nuclear war. Another hot spot was Southeast Asia, where President Lyndon B. Johnson (LBJ) escalated America's participation in the Vietnam War in 1965. President Nixon negotiated a peace in January 1973 to bring troops home, but 16 months later the South Vietnamese government surrendered to the communists.

From 1950 to 1974, most white American families were economically well off. Many white veterans had attended college under the G.I. bill (distribution of wealth based on race), moved to the suburbs, and began to work white-collar jobs. The nuclear family was frozen in a state described by one historian as "domestic containment." Ideally, dad went to work, mom stayed home, and the kids went to school. But fissures developed in the 1950s that affected African Americans who were segregated from the suburbs and from most white-collar jobs; women who questioned the role of stay-at-home mom; and children who felt alienated from the cultural values of their family. The first sign was the emergence of rock and roll and its white icon Elvis Presley. Was the music revolt the traditional acting out of children against their parents, or did it reflect a real change in values that would culminate in political protests and the establishment of a counterculture in the 1960s?

Over the course of the 1960s, the United States experienced challenges to traditional institutions and values from African Americans who successfully fought for civil and voting rights; students opposing the Vietnam War; young adults forming communes and engaging in "counterculture" values; and women's liberation, which extended well into the 1970s. Government, business, and others combated the counterculture and began to again limit democracy to privilege the powerful.

Lyndon Johnson waged his Great Society, although the War on Poverty had mixed results. The costs of the Great Society and the endless war in Vietnam created economic problems for LBJ's successors. Vietnam, like Korea, was an effort to maintain the U.S. position as unquestioned world power. In the 1970s, Presidents Nixon, Ford, and Carter were unable to manage an economy whose major problem was to balance the trade-off between low levels of unemployment and acceptable levels of inflation. New imperialist efforts and the manipulation of resources led to a more stable economic and political reality and eventually the fall of the Soviet Union, whose imperialism required the physical control of space and resources. The economy of the 1980s, however, exploded with new high-tech jobs and created a growing gap not only between the rich and the poor but also between the wealthy and the American middle class. "Reaganomics" and neoliberalism became assaults on the environment, and eventually the working and middle class, as the regulations and rights were removed in favour of economic policy supporting big business.

By the opening of the twenty-first century, in the wake of the collapse of the Soviet Union and the end of the Cold War, the United States had emerged as the only true superpower. At the same time, democratic political aspirations and a desire for market economies had spread throughout much of the developing world. Is the American Century over? What will nationalist and socialist political currents do to an already antidemocratic society? Can the United States continue with its anti-poor, anti-environment, continually imperialist approaches to the unique problems of the new century?

Selected, Edited, and with Issue Framing Material by:
Kevin R. Magill and Tony L. Talbert, *Baylor University*

ISSUE

Was President Truman Responsible for the Cold War?

YES: Walter LaFeber, from "America, Russia, and the Cold War, 1945–2000," McGraw-Hill (2002)

NO: John Lewis Gaddis, from "The Origins of the Cold War: 1945–1953," McGraw-Hill (1990)

Learning Outcomes

After reading this issue, you will be able to:

- List the major events leading to the Cold War from 1945 to 1950.
- Identify and give the significance of the following terms: "atomic diplomacy" and "containment."
- Assess President Truman's role as a "parochial nationalist."
- Evaluate Stalin's responsibility for the Cold War.
- Compare and contrast the orthodox and revisionist interpretations as to who caused the Cold War.

ISSUE SUMMARY

YES: Walter LaFeber argues that the Truman administration exaggerated the Soviet threat after World War II because the United States had expansionist political and economic global needs.

NO: John Lewis Gaddis argues that the power vacuum that existed in Europe at the end of World War II exaggerated and made almost inevitable a clash between the democratic, capitalist United States and the totalitarian, communist USSR and that Joseph Stalin, unwilling to accept any diplomatic compromises, was primarily responsible for the Cold War.

Less than a month before the war ended in Europe the most powerful man in the world, President Franklin Delano Roosevelt, died suddenly from a brain embolism. A nervous, impetuous, and inexperienced Vice President Harry S Truman became the president. Historians disagree whether Truman reversed Roosevelt's relationship with Soviet leader Joseph Stalin or whether the similarities in policy were negated by Truman's blunt negotiating style compared with FDR's suave, calm approach. But disagreements emerged over issues such as control over the atomic bomb, Germany, Poland, and the economic reconstruction of Europe.

The question of Germany was paramount. During the war it was agreed that Germany would be divided temporarily into zones of occupation with the United States, Great Britain, and the newly liberated France controlling the western half of Germany, whereas the Russians would take charge of the eastern half. Berlin, which was 90 miles inside of the Russian zone, would also be divided into zones of occupation. Arguments developed over boundaries, reparations, and transfers of industrial equipment and agricultural foodstuffs between zones. In May 1946, the Americans began treating the western zones as a separate economic unit because the Russians were transferring the food from their zone back to the Soviet Union. In September 1946, Secretary of State James Byrnes announced that the Americans would continue to occupy their half of Germany indefinitely with military troops. By 1948, a separate democratic West German government was established. The Russians protested by blocking ground access to the western zones of Berlin, but the Americans continued to supply the West Berliners with supplies through an airlift. After 10 months, because of the bad publicity, the Russians abandoned the Berlin blockade and created a separate, communist East German government.

Roosevelt and Winston Churchill had conceded Russian control over Eastern Europe during the World War II conferences. The question was how much control. Stalin was not going to allow anticommunist governments to be established in these countries. He had no understanding of how free elections were held. Consequently, when the Cold War intensified in 1947 and 1948, Russian-dominated communist governments were established in Hungary, Poland, and Czechoslovakia.

In February 1946, Stalin delivered a major speech declaring the incompatibility of the two systems of communism and capitalism. The next month, Churchill, now a retired politician, delivered his famous speech at a commencement ceremony at Westminster College in Fulton, Missouri, with the Truman administration's consent, in which he complained about the "iron curtain" that Russia was imposing on Eastern Europe. At the same time, George Kennan, a bright multi-linguist American diplomat who spent years in Germany and Russia and who would become the head of Truman's policy planning staff, wrote a series of telegrams and articles which set the tone for the specific policies the Truman administration would undertake. Kennan had coined the phrase "containment," a word that would be used to describe America's foreign policy from Truman to the first President Bush. Containment would assume various meanings and would be extended to other areas of the globe besides Europe in ways Kennan claims were a misuse of what his original intentions were. Nevertheless the Truman administration moved to stop further Russian expansionism.

In 1947, a series of steps were undertaken both to "contain" Russian expansionism and to rebuild the economies of Europe. On March 12, Truman took the advice of Senator Arthur Vandenberg to "scare the hell out of the American people." In an address before a Republican-controlled Congress, the President argued in somewhat inflated rhetoric that "it must be the policy of the United States to support free peoples who are resisting attempted subjugation by armed minorities or by outside pressures." In the same speech, in what became known as the "Truman Doctrine," the president requested and received $400 million in economic and military assistance to Greece and Turkey. Almost as an afterthought, American military personnel were sent to oversee the reconstruction effort,

a precedent that would later be used to send advisers to Vietnam.

In June 1947, Secretary of State George C. Marshall announced a plan to provide economic assistance to all European nations. This included the Soviet Union, which rejected the offer and formed its own economic recovery group. In April 1948, Congress approved the creation of the Economic Cooperation Administration, the agency that would administer the program. The Marshall Plan would be remembered as America's most successful foreign aid program, in which $17 billion was channeled to the Western European nations. By 1950, industrial production had increased 64 percent since the end of the war, whereas the communist parties declined in membership and influence.

When did the Cold War begin? Was it inevitable? Should one side or the other take most of the blame for the anxiety and occasional hysteria that this conflict created?

Revisionist historians of the Cold War are critical of American foreign policy. In his essay "Another Such Victory: President Truman, American Foreign Policy, and the Cold War," *Diplomatic History* (Spring, 1999), Arnold Offner takes issue with President Truman's recent biographers Robert H. Ferrell, *Harry S. Truman: A Life* (University of Missouri Press, 1994), Alonzo L. Hamby, *Man of the People: A Life of Harry S Truman* (Oxford, 1995), and especially David McCullough's *Truman* (Simon & Schuster, 1992), all of whom rank Truman among the near-great presidents. Offner describes Truman as a "parochial nationalist" whose outlook on foreign policy was ethnocentric and who made rash and quick decisions to cover his insecurities. Offner also accuses the Truman administration with practicing "atomic diplomacy" at the end of the war, when the United States was the sole possessor of the A-bomb, to make the Russians more manageable in Europe.

In his book *We Now Know: Rethinking Cold War History* (Oxford University Press, 1997), John Gaddis argues more strongly than he has in his previous works that Stalin was primarily responsible for the Cold War. Based upon newly discovered, partially opened Soviet archival materials, Gaddis describes Stalin, Khrushchev, and even Chairman Mao as prisoners of a peculiar world view: "Aging Ponce de Leons in search of an ideological fountain of youth."

Professor Gaddis accepts the fact that Truman was insecure. He also believes that throughout 1945 up to early 1946, the Truman administration was responding to the political and economic uncertainties of the post–World War II environment. Although the United States took the lead in creating the World Bank and the International Monetary Fund to supply money for rebuilding Europe's destroyed infrastructure, these institutions were woefully inadequate to the task. It was also unclear whether the United States was going to reenter a recession, as had occurred at the end of the World War I. Gaddis insists that the United States created its Western European empire by invitation through the implementation of the Truman Doctrine, the Marshall Plan, the rebuilding of West Germany, and the formation of NATO. On the other hand, Russia created its empire by force. Starting in Romania in 1945 and in Poland and Hungary in 1947 and ending with the takeover in Czechoslovakia in 1948, the Russians imposed totalitarian governments on its citizens.

Students who wish to study the Cold War in greater detail should consult *Containment: Documents on American Policy and Strategy, 1945–1950* edited by Thomas H. Etzold and John Lewis Gaddis (Columbia University Press, 1978). Another comprehensive work is Melvyn P. Leffler, *A Preponderance of Power: National Security, the Truman Administration, and the Cold War* (Stanford University Press, 1992). The two best readers to excerpt the various viewpoints on the Cold War are Thomas G. Paterson and Robert J. McMahon, eds., *The Origins of the Cold War*, 3rd ed. (D.C. Heath, 1991) and David Reynolds' edited series of essays *The Origins of the Cold War: International Perspectives* (Yale University Press, 1994).

Walter LaFeber's selection in this issue contains most of the arguments advanced by the revisionist critics of America's Cold War policies, Truman's diplomatic style was blunt and impetuous; and he tended to oversimplify complex issues into black and white alternatives. He believes that the Truman administration exaggerated the Russian threat to the balance of power in Europe. It is not clear whether this was a deliberate miscalculation or whether the Truman administration misperceived the motive behind the "iron curtain" that Russia drew around Eastern Europe. The author maintains that Stalin was more concerned with Russia's security needs than with world conquest.

John Gaddis's selection in the second reading is much less critical than LaFeber's of America's postwar policy. Gaddis believes that the United States and Russia would inevitably clash once the common enemy—Hitler—was defeated because the two countries had fundamentally different political and economic systems. He maintains that for nearly two years there was confusion and uncertainty in the United States' foreign policy in Europe. Truman, he says, did not reverse Roosevelt's policy. His manner was more blunt and, consequently, he showed less patience in dealing with Stalin. Gaddis acknowledges revisionist criticisms that the Americans misperceived Stalin's attempts to control Eastern Europe. The Soviet premier used expansionist rhetoric when he was primarily concerned with protecting Russia from another invasion. By early 1946, both sides were pursuing policies that would lead to an impasse. Still, Gaddis places most of the blame for the Cold War on Stalin, an authoritarian imperialist who "equated world revolution with the expanding influence of the Soviet state." In contrast, according to Gaddis, Truman was constrained by the democratic electoral system of checks and balances and a Republican-controlled Congress from 1946 to 1948, but Stalin had no such constraints. He purged all his real and potential revolutionary opponents in the 1930s and late 1940s and pursued foreign policy objectives as a romantic revolutionary. In summary, according to Gaddis, if Mikhail Gorbachev had been the Soviet leader in 1945, there might have been alternate paths to the Cold War, but with Stalin in charge, "there was going to be a cold war whatever the West did."

YES ⬋

Walter LaFeber

America, Russia, and the Cold War, 1945–2000

... Truman entered the White House [as a] highly insecure man. ("I felt like the moon, the stars, and all the planets had fallen on me," he told reporters.) And he held the world's most responsible job in a world that was changing radically. Truman tried to compensate for his insecurity in several ways. First, he was extremely jealous of his presidential powers and deeply suspicious of anyone who challenged those powers. Truman made decisions rapidly not only because that was his character but also because he determined "the buck stopped" at his desk. There would be no more sloppy administration or strong, freewheeling bureaucrats as in FDR's later years.

Second, and more dangerously, Truman was determined that these decisions would not be tagged as "appeasement." He would be as tough as the toughest. After only twenty-four hours in the White House, the new President confidently informed his secretary of state, "We must stand up to the Russians," and he implied "We had been too easy with them." In foreign-policy discussions during the next two weeks, Truman interrupted his advisers to assure them he would certainly be "tough."

His determination was reinforced when he listened most closely to such advisers as Harriman, Leahy, and Secretary of the Navy James Forrestal, who urged him to take a hard line. Warning of a "barbarian invasion of Europe," Harriman declared that postwar cooperation with the Soviets, especially economically, must depend on their agreement to open Poland and Eastern Europe. In a decisive meeting on April 23, Secretary of War Henry Stimson argued with Harriman. Stimson declared that peace must never be threatened by an issue such as Poland, for free elections there were impossible, Russia held total control, and Stalin was "not likely to yield . . . in substance." Stimson was not an amateur; he had been a respected Wall Street lawyer and distinguished public servant for forty years, including a term as Herbert Hoover's secretary of state.

But Truman dismissed Stimson's advice, accepted Harriman's, and later that day berated Soviet Foreign Minister Molotov "in words of one syllable" for breaking the Yalta agreement on Poland. Truman demanded that the Soviets agree to a "new" (not merely "reorganized") Polish government. An astonished Molotov replied, "I have never been talked to like that in my life." "Carry out your agreements," Truman supposedly retorted, "and you won't get talked to like that."

The next day Stalin rejected Truman's demand by observing that it was contrary to the Yalta agreement. The dictator noted that "Poland borders with the Soviet Union, what [sic] cannot be said of Great Britain and the United States." After all, Stalin continued, the Soviets do not "lay claim to interference" in Belgium and Greece where the Americans and British made decisions without consulting the Russians. . . .

Stimson had been correct. Truman's toughness had only stiffened Russian determination to control Poland.

An "iron fence" was falling around Eastern Europe, Churchill blurted out to Stalin in mid-1945. "All fairytales," the Soviet leader blandly replied. But it was partly true. The crises over Rumania and Poland only raised higher the fence around those two nations. In other areas, however, the Soviet approach varied. A Russian-sponsored election in Hungary produced a noncommunist government. In Bulgaria the Soviet-conducted elections satisfied British observers, if not Americans. Stalin agreed to an independent, noncommunist regime in Finland if the Finns would follow a foreign policy friendly to Russia. An "iron fence" by no means encircled all of Eastern Europe. There was still room to bargain if each side wished to avoid a confrontation over the remaining areas.

But the bargaining room was limited. Stalin's doctrine and his determination that Russia would not again be invaded from the west greatly narrowed his diplomatic options. So too did the tremendous devastation of the war. Rapid rebuilding under communism required security, required access to resources in Eastern and Central Europe, and continued tight control over the Russian people. The experience of war was indelible. Russians viewed almost everything in their lives through their "searing experience of World War II," as one psychologist has phrased it. The conflict had destroyed 1700 towns and 70,000 villages and left 25 million homeless. Twenty million died; 600,000 starved to death at the single siege of Leningrad. . . .

Some scholars have examined Stalin's acts of 1928–1945, pronounced them the work of a "paranoid," and concluded that the United States had no chance to avoid a cold war since it was dealing with a man who was mentally ill. That interpretation neatly avoids confronting the complex causes of the Cold War but is wholly insufficient to explain, those causes. However Stalin acted inside Russia, where he had total control, in his foreign policy during 1941–1946 he displayed a realism, a careful calculation of forces, and a diplomatic finesse that undercut any attempt to explain away his actions as paranoid. If he and other Soviets were suspicious of the West, they were realistic, not paranoid: the West had poured thousands of troops into Russia between 1917 and 1920, refused to cooperate with the Soviets during the 1930s, tried to turn Hitler against Stalin in 1938, reneged on promises about the second front, and in 1945 tried to penetrate areas Stalin deemed crucial to Soviet security.

American diplomats who frequently saw Stalin understood this background. In January 1945 Harriman told the State Department, "The overriding consideration in Soviet foreign policy is the preoccupation with 'security,' as Moscow sees it." The problem was that Americans did not see "security" the same way. They believed their security required an open world, including an open Eastern Europe. . . .

By mid-1945 Stalin's policies were brutally consistent, while Truman's were confused. The confusion became obvious when the United States, opposed to a sphere of interest in Europe, strengthened its own sphere in the Western Hemisphere. Unlike its policies elsewhere, however, the State Department did not use economic weapons. The economic relationship with Latin America and Canada could simply be assumed. . . .

But Latin America was not neglected politically. A young assistant secretary of state for Latin American affairs, Nelson Rockefeller, and Senator Arthur Vandenberg (Republican from Michigan) devised the political means to keep the Americas solidly within Washington's sphere. Their instrument was Article 51 of the U.N. Charter.

This provision was largely formulated by Rockefeller and Vandenberg at the San Francisco conference that founded the United Nations in the spring of 1945. The article allowed for collective self-defense through special regional organizations to be created outside the United Nations but within the principles of the charter. In this way, regional organizations would escape Russian vetoes

in the Security Council. The United States could control its own sphere without Soviet interference. . . .

The obvious confusion in that approach was pinpointed by Secretary of War Stimson when he condemned Americans who were "anxious to hang on to exaggerated views of the Monroe Doctrine [in the Western Hemisphere] and at the same time butt into every question that comes up in Central Europe." Almost alone, Stimson argued for an alternative policy. Through bilateral U.S.-U.S.S.R. negotiations (and not negotiations within the United Nations, where the Russians would be defensive and disagreeable because the Americans controlled a majority), Stimson hoped each side could agree that the other should have its own security spheres. But as he had lost the argument over Poland, so Stimson lost this argument. Truman was prepared to bargain very little. He might not get 100 percent, the President told advisers, but he would get 85 percent. Even in Rumania, where the Russians were particularly sensitive, the State Department secretly determined in August 1945, "It is our intention to attain a position of equality with the Russians." When, however, the Americans pressed, the Soviets only tightened their control of Rumania. . . .

Although Truman did not obtain his "85 percent" at Potsdam, en route home he received the news that a weapon of unimaginable power, the atomic bomb, had obliterated Hiroshima, Japan, on August 6. Eighty thousand had died. This was some 20,000 fewer than had been killed by a massive American fire bombing of Tokyo earlier in the year, but it was the newly opened secret of nature embodied in a single bomb that was overwhelming. Roosevelt had initiated the atomic project in 1941. He had decided at least by 1944 not to share information about the bomb with the Soviets, even though he knew Stalin had learned about the project. By the summer of 1945 this approach, and the growing Soviet-American confrontation in Eastern Europe, led Truman and Byrnes to discuss securing "further *quid pro quos*" in Rumania, Poland, and Asia from Stalin before the Russians could share the secret of atomic energy. . . .

Stimson, about to retire from the War Department, made one final attempt to stop an East-West confrontation. In a September 11 memorandum to Truman, Stimson prophesied "that it would not be possible to use our possession of the atomic bomb as a direct lever to produce the change" desired inside Eastern Europe. If Soviet-American negotiations continue with "this weapon rather ostentatiously on our hip, their suspicions and their distrust of our purposes and motives will increase." He again urged direct, bilateral talks with Stalin to formulate control of the bomb and to write a general peace settlement. Stimson's advice was especially notable because several months before he himself had hoped to use the bomb to pry the Soviets out of Eastern Europe. Now he had changed his mind.

Truman again turned Stimson's advice aside. A month later the President delivered a speech larded with references to America's monopoly of atomic power, then attacked Russia's grip on Eastern Europe. Molotov quickly replied that peace could not be reconciled with an armaments race advocated by "zealous partisans of the imperialist policy." In this connection, he added, "We should mention the discovery of . . . the atomic bomb."

With every utterance and every act, the wartime alliance further disintegrated. . . .

During early 1946 Stalin and Churchill issued their declarations of Cold War. In an election speech of February 9, the Soviet dictator announced that Marxist-Leninist dogma remained valid, for "the unevenness of development of the capitalist countries" could lead to "violent disturbance" and the consequent splitting of the "capitalist world into two hostile camps and war between them." War was inevitable as long as capitalism existed. The Soviet people must prepare themselves for a replay of the 1930s by developing basic industry instead of consumer goods and, in all, making enormous sacrifices demanded in "three more Five-Year Plans, I should think, if not more." There would be no peace, internally or externally. These words profoundly affected Washington. Supreme Court Justice William Douglas, one of the reigning American liberals, believed that Stalin's speech meant "The Declaration of World War III." *The New York Times* front-page story of the speech began by declaring that Stalin believed "the stage is set" for war.

Winston Churchill delivered his views at Fulton, Missouri, on March 5. The former prime minister exalted American power with the plea that his listeners recognize that "God has willed" the United States, not "some Communist or neo-Fascist state" to have atomic bombs. To utilize the "breathing space" provided by these weapons, Churchill asked for "a fraternal association of the English-speaking peoples" operating under the principles of the United Nations, but not inside that organization, to reorder the world. This unilateral policy must be undertaken because "from Stettin in the Baltic to Trieste in the Adriatic, an iron curtain has descended across the Continent" allowing "police government" to rule Eastern Europe. The Soviets, he emphasized, did not want war: "What they desire is the fruits of war and the indefinite expansion of their power and doctrines."

The "iron curtain" phrase made the speech famous. But, as Churchill himself observed, the "crux" of the message lay in the proposal that the Anglo-Americans, outside the United Nations and with the support of atomic weaponry (the title of the address was "The Sinews of Peace"), create "a unity in Europe from which no nation should be permanently outcast." The Soviets perceived this as a direct challenge to their power in Eastern Europe. Within a week Stalin attacked Churchill and his "friends" in America, whom he claimed resembled Hitler by holding a "racial theory" that those who spoke the English language "should rule over the remaining nations of the world." This, Stalin warned, is "a set-up for war, a call to war with the Soviet Union."

Within a short period after the Churchill speech, Stalin launched a series of policies which, in retrospect, marks the spring and summer of 1946 as a milestone in the Cold War. During these weeks the Soviets, after having worked for a loan during the previous fifteen months, finally concluded that Washington had no interest in loaning them $1 billion, or any other amount. They refused to become a member of the World Bank and the International Monetary Fund. These rejections ended the American hope to use the lure of the dollar to make the Soviets retreat in Eastern Europe and join the capitalist-controlled bank and IMF.

Actually there had never been reason to hope. Control of their border areas was worth more to the Russians than $1 billion, or even $10 billion. . . .

Truman's difficulties came into the open during the autumn of 1946, when he was attacked by liberals for being too militaristic and by conservatives for his economic policies.

The liberal attack was led by Henry Agard Wallace, a great secretary of agriculture during the early New Deal, Vice President from 1941–1945, maneuvered out of the vice-presidential nomination in 1944 so that Harry Truman could be FDR's running mate, and finally secretary of commerce in 1945. Here he devoted himself to the cause of what he liked to call the "Common Man," by extending increased loans to small businessmen and, above all, enlarging the economic pie by increasing foreign trade. Wallace soon discovered that Truman threatened to clog the trade channels to Russia, Eastern Europe, perhaps even China, with his militant attitude toward the Soviets.

At a political rally in New York on September 12, 1946, Wallace delivered a speech, cleared personally, and too rapidly, by Truman. The address focused on the necessity of a political understanding with Russia. This, Wallace declared, would require guaranteeing Soviet security in Eastern Europe. He hoped the capitalist and communist systems could compete "on a friendly basis" and "gradually become more alike." Wallace, however, added one proviso for his happy ending: in this competition "we must insist on an open door for trade throughout the world. . . . We cannot permit the door to be closed against our trade in Eastern Europe any more than we can in China." At that moment Byrnes and Vandenberg were in Paris, painfully and unsuccessfully trying to negotiate peace treaties with Molotov. They immediately demanded Wallace's resignation. On September 20, Truman complied. . . .

On March 12, 1947, President Truman finally issued his own declaration of Cold War. Dramatically presenting the Truman Doctrine to Congress, he asked Americans to join in a global commitment against communism. The nation responded. A quarter of a century later, Senator J. William Fulbright declared, "More by far than any other factor anti-communism of the Truman Doctrine has been the guiding spirit of American foreign policy since World War II.". . .

The Truman Doctrine was a milestone in American history for at least four reasons. First, it marked the point at which Truman used the American fear of communism both at home and abroad to convince Americans they must embark upon a Cold War foreign policy. This consensus would not break apart for a quarter of a century. Second, . . . Congress was giving the President great powers to wage this Cold War as he saw fit. Truman's personal popularity began spiraling upward after his speech. Third, for the first time in the postwar era, Americans massively intervened in another nation's civil war. Intervention was justified on the basis of anticommunism. In the future, Americans would intervene in similar wars for supposedly the same reason and with less happy results. . . .

Finally, and perhaps most important, Truman used the doctrine to justify a gigantic aid program to prevent a collapse of the European and American economies. Later such programs were expanded globally. The President's arguments about the need to fight communism now became confusing, for the Western economies would have been in grave difficulties whether or not communism existed. The complicated problems of reconstruction and U.S. dependence on world trade were not well understood by Americans, but they easily comprehended anticommunism. So Americans embarked upon the Cold War for the good reasons given in the Truman Doctrine, which they understood, and for real reasons, which they did not understand. . . .

The President's program evolved naturally into the Marshall Plan. Although the speech did not limit American effort, Secretary of State Marshall did by concentrating the administration's attention on Europe. Returning badly shaken from a Foreign Ministers conference in Moscow, the secretary of state insisted in a nationwide broadcast that Western Europe required immediate help. "The patient is sinking," he declared, "while the doctors deliberate." Personal conversations with Stalin had convinced Marshall that the Russians believed Europe would collapse. Assuming that the United States must lead in restoring Europe, Marshall appointed a policy-planning staff under the direction of George Kennan to draw up guidelines. . . .

Building on this premise, round-the-clock conferences in May 1947 began to fashion the main features of the Marshall Plan. The all important question became how to handle the Russians. Ostensibly, Marshall accepted Kennan's advice to "play it straight" by inviting the Soviet bloc. In reality the State Department made Russian participation improbable by demanding that economic records of each nation be open for scrutiny. For good measure Kennan also suggested that the Soviets' devastated economy, weakened by war and at that moment suffering from drought and famine, participate in the plan by shipping Soviet goods to Europe. Apparently no one in the State Department wanted the Soviets included. Russian participation would vastly multiply the costs of the program and eliminate any hope of its acceptance by a purse-watching Republican Congress, now increasingly convinced by Truman that communists had to be fought, not fed. . . .

The European request for a four-year program of $17 billion of American aid now had to run the gauntlet of a Republican Congress, which was dividing its attention between slashing the budget and attacking Truman, both in anticipation of the presidential election only a year away. In committee hearings in late 1947 and early 1948, the executive presented its case. Only large amounts of government money which could restore basic facilities, provide convertibility of local currency into dollars, and end the dollar shortage would stimulate private investors to rebuild Europe, administration witnesses argued. . . .

The Marshall Plan now appears to have signaled not the beginning but the end of an era. It marked the last phase in the administration's use of economic tactics as the primary means of tying together the Western world. The plan's approach . . . soon evolved into military alliances. Truman proved to be correct in saying that the Truman Doctrine and the Marshall Plan "are two halves of the same walnut." Americans willingly acquiesced as the military aspects of the doctrine developed into quite the larger part. . . .

The military and personal costs of the Truman Doctrine. . . . were higher than expected. And the cost became more apparent as Truman and J. Edgar Hoover (director of the Federal Bureau of Investigation) carried out the President's Security Loyalty program. Their search for subversives accelerated after Canadians uncovered a Soviet spy ring.

The House Un-American Activities Committee began to intimate that Truman was certainly correct in his assessment of communism's evil nature but lax in destroying it. In March 1948 the committee demanded the loyalty records gathered by the FBI. Truman handled the situation badly. Unable to exploit the committee's distorted view of the internal communist threat, he accused it of trying to cover up the bad record of the Republican Congress. He refused to surrender the records, ostensibly because they were in the exclusive domain of the executive, more probably because of his fear that if the Republicans saw the FBI reports, which accused some federal employees of disloyalty on the basis of hearsay, unproven allegations, and personal vendettas, November might be an unfortunate month for Truman's political aspirations. Unable to discredit the loyalty program he had set in motion, trapped by his own indiscriminating anticommunist rhetoric designed to "scare hell" out of the country, Truman stood paralyzed as the ground was carefully plowed around him for the weeds of McCarthyism. . . .

And then came the fall of Czechoslovakia. The Czechs had uneasily coexisted with Russia by trying not to offend the Soviets while keeping doors open to the West. This policy had started in late 1943, when Czech leaders signed a treaty with Stalin that, in the view of most observers, obligated Czechoslovakia to become a part of the Russian bloc. President Edvard Beneš and Foreign Minister Jan Masaryk, one of the foremost diplomatic figures in Europe, had nevertheless successfully resisted complete communist control. Nor had Stalin moved to consolidate his power in 1946 after the Czech Communist party emerged from the parliamentary elections with 38 percent of the vote, the largest total of any party. By late 1947 the lure of Western aid and internal political changes began to pull the Czech government away from the Soviets. At this point Stalin, who like Truman recalled the pivotal role of Czechoslovakia in 1938, decided to put the 1943 treaty into effect. Klement Gottwald, the Czech Communist party leader, demanded the elimination of independent parties. In mid-February 1948 Soviet armies camped on the border as Gottwald ordered the formation of a wholly new government. A Soviet mission of top officials flew to Prague to demand Beneš's surrender. The communists assumed full control on February 25. Two weeks later Masaryk either committed suicide, or, as Truman believed, was the victim of "foul play."

Truman correctly observed that the coup "sent a shock throughout the civilized world." He privately believed, "We are faced with exactly the same situation with which Britain and France were faced in 1938–9 with Hitler."

Two days before, on March 14, the Senate had endorsed the Marshall Plan by a vote of 69 to 17. As it went to the House for consideration, Truman, fearing the "grave events in Europe [which], were moving so swiftly," decided to appear before Congress.

In a speech remarkable for its repeated emphasis on the "increasing threat" to the very "survival of freedom," the President proclaimed the Marshall Plan "not enough." Europe must have "some measure of protection against internal and external aggression." He asked for Universal Training, the resumption of Selective Service (which he had allowed to lapse a year earlier), and speedy passage of the Marshall Plan. Within twelve days the House approved authorization of the plan's money. . . .

During the spring of 1948 a united administration, enjoying strong support on foreign policy from a Republican Congress, set off with exemplary single-mindedness to destroy the communist threat that loomed over Europe. Within two years this threat had been scotched. But the officials who created the policy had split, the Congress that ratified the policy had turned against the executive, the administration had fought off charges that it had been infiltrated by communists, and the United States found itself fighting a bloody war not in Europe but in Asia. These embarrassments did not suddenly emerge in 1950 but developed gradually from the policies of 1948–1949. . . .

The world in which NATO was to be born was undergoing rapid change. . . .

The Senate ratified the treaty 82 to 13. On the day he added his signature in mid-July 1949, Truman sent Congress a one-year Mutual Defense Assistance (MDA) bill providing for $1.5 billion for European military aid. This was the immediate financial price for the NATO commitment. A memorandum circulating through the executive outlined the purpose of MDA: "to build up our own military industry," to "create a common defense frontier in Western Europe" by having the Allies pool "their industrial and manpower resources, "and particularly, to subordinate "nationalistic tendencies." In the House, however, the bill encountered tough opposition from budget-cutting congressmen. On September 22 President Truman announced that Russia had exploded an atomic bomb. Within six days the NATO appropriations raced through the House and went to the President for approval.

Although publicly playing down the significance of the Russian bomb, the administration painfully realized that, in Vandenberg's words, "This is now a different world." Few American officials had expected the Soviet test this early. Because it was simultaneous with the fall of China, the American diplomatic attitude further stiffened. . . .

A grim President, pressed by domestic critics and the new Soviet bomb, demanded a wide-ranging reevaluation of American Cold War policies. In early 1950 the National Security Council began work on a highly secret document (declassified only a quarter of a century later, and then through an accident) that would soon be known as NSC-68. Truman examined the study in April, and it was ready for implementation when Korea burst into war.

NSC-68 proved to be the American blueprint for waging the Cold War. . . . It began with two assumptions that governed the rest of the document. First, the global balance of power had been "fundamentally altered" since the nineteenth century so that the Americans and Russians now dominated the world: "What is new, what makes the continuing crisis, is the polarization of power which inescapably confronts the slave society with the free." It was us against them. Second, "the Soviet Union, unlike previous, aspirants to hegemony, is animated by a new fanatic faith, antithetical to our own, and seeks to impose its absolute authority," initially in "the Soviet Union and second in the areas now under [its] control." Then the crucial sentence: "In the minds of the Soviet leaders, however, achievement of this design requires the dynamic extension of their authority and the ultimate elimination of any effective opposition to their authority. . . . To that end Soviet efforts are now directed toward the domination of the Eurasian land mass. . . .

In conclusion, therefore, NSC-68 recommended (1) against negotiations with Russia since conditions were not yet sufficient to force the Kremlin to "change its policies drastically"; (2) development of hydrogen bombs to offset possible Soviet possession of an effective atomic arsenal by 1954; (3) rapid building of conventional military forces to preserve American interests without having to wage atomic war; (4) a large increase in taxes to pay for this new, highly expensive military establishment; (5) mobilization of American society, including a government-created

"consensus" on the necessity of "sacrifice" and "unity" by Americans; (6) a strong alliance system directed by the United States; (7) and—as the topper—undermining the "Soviet totalitarian" from within by making "the Russian people our allies in this enterprise." How this was to be done was necessarily vague. But no matter. . . . Truman and Acheson were no longer satisfied with containment. They wanted Soviet withdrawal and an absolute victory.

But, as in early 1947 before Truman "scared hell" out of them, the American people were by no means prepared to pay such costs for victory. Republicans and many Democrats demanded lower taxes. Even Secretary of Defense Louis Johnson fought against NSC-68, arguing that Acheson's policies could bankrupt the country. The secretary of state finally brought the military around to accept the civilian call for larger defense budgets. The Soviet Union meanwhile appeared quiet and contained. The political circumstances threatened to destroy Acheson's hopes that NSC-68 could be used to build global "positions of strength." Only he, the President, and a few others seemed to have a clear idea of what had to be done. NSC-68 was a policy in search of an opportunity. That opportunity arrived on June 25, 1950, when, as Acheson and his aides later agreed, "Korea came along and saved us."

WALTER LAFEBER is the Andrew H. and James S. Tisch Distinguished University History Professor Emeritus and the Stephen H. Weiss Presidential Fellow in the department of history at Cornell University. He received his PhD from the University of Wisconsin-Madison in 1959, where he studied under William Appleman Williams. One of the nation's leading revisionist historians of United States foreign policy, LaFaber is also the author of *The New Empire: An Interpretation of American Expansion, 1860–1898* (Cornell University Press, 1963, 1998) and *Inevitable Revolutions: The United States in Central America*, 2nd ed. (W.W. Norton, 1993).

John Lewis Gaddis  **NO**

The Origins of the Cold War: 1945–1953

It is, of course, a truism that coalitions tend not to survive their enemies' defeat. Certainly during World War II most observers of the international scene had expected differences eventually to arise among the victors. The hope had been, though, that a sufficiently strong framework of common interests—whether the United Nations or some mutually acceptable agreement on spheres of influence—would develop that could keep these differences within reasonable limits. This did not happen. Although both sides sought security, although neither side wanted a new war, disagreements over how to achieve those goals proved too great to overcome. With a rapidity that dismayed policymakers in both Washington and Moscow, allies shortly before united against the Axis found themselves in a confrontation with each other that would determine the shape of the postwar era. Russian-American relations, once a problem of rarely more than peripheral concern for the two countries involved, now became an object of rapt attention and anxiety for the entire world.

I

It is no simple matter to explain how national leaders in the United States and the Soviet Union came to hold such dissimilar concepts of postwar security. There did exist, in the history of the two countries' encounters with one another, an ample basis for mutual distrust. But there were also strong motives for cooperation, not the least of which was that, had they been able to act in concert, Russians and Americans might have achieved something close to absolute security in an insecure world. Their failure to do so may be attributed, ultimately, to irreconcilable differences in four critical areas: perceptions of history, ideology, technology, and personality.

Clearly the divergent historical experiences of the two countries conditioned their respective views of how best to attain security. The Russians tended to think of security in terms of space—not a surprising attitude, considering the frequency with which their country had been

invaded, or the way in which they had used distance to defeat their adversaries. That such a concept might be outmoded in an age of atomic weapons and long-range bombers appears not to have occurred to Stalin; Hitler's defeat brought no alteration in his determination to control as much territory along the periphery of the Soviet Union as possible. "He regarded as sure only whatever he held in his fist," the Yugoslav Communist Milovan Djilas has written. "Everything beyond the control of his police was a potential enemy."

Americans, on the other hand, tended to see security in institutional terms: conditioned by their own atypical historical experience, they assumed that if representative governments could be established as widely as possible, together with a collective security organization capable of resolving differences between them, peace would be assured. That such governments might not always harbor peaceful intentions toward their neighbors, that the United Nations, in the absence of great power agreement, might lack the means of settling disputes, occurred to only a few informed observers. The general public, upon whose support foreign policy ultimately depended, tended to accept Cordell Hull's vision of a postwar world in which "there will no longer be need for spheres of influence, for alliances, for balance of power, or any of the special arrangements through which, in the unhappy past, the nations sought to safeguard their security or to promote their interests."

There was, of course, room for compromising these conflicting viewpoints. Neither the United States nor its British ally had been prepared wholly to abandon spheres of influence as a means of achieving their own postwar security; both accepted the premise that the USSR was entitled to have friendly countries along its borders. The great difficulty was that, unlike the expansion of American and British influence into Western Europe and the Mediterranean, the Soviet Union's gains took place without the approval of most of the governments and most of the people in the areas involved. The Anglo-Americans simply did not find it necessary, in the same measure as did the Russians, to ensure their own security by depriving people within their sphere of influence of the right to self-determination. Given Western convictions that only the diffusion of democratic institutions could guarantee peace, given Hitler's all-too-vivid precedent, Moscow's imposition of influence in Eastern Europe seemed ominous, whatever its motives. Stalin found himself able to implement his vision of security only by appearing to violate that of the West. The result was to create for the Soviet Union new sources of hostility and, ultimately, insecurity in the world.

Ideological differences constituted a second source of antagonism. Stalin had deliberately downplayed the Soviet commitment to communism during the war, even to the point of abolishing the Comintern in 1943. Some Americans concluded that the Russians had abandoned that ideology altogether, if on no other grounds than that a nation that fought Germans so effectively could not be all bad. The European communist movement remained very much the instrument of Soviet policy, however, and the Russians used it to facilitate their projection of influence into Eastern Europe. This development raised fears in the West that Soviet collaboration against the Axis had been nothing but a marriage of convenience and that, victory having been achieved, the Kremlin was now embarking upon a renewed crusade for world revolution.

This was, it now appears, a mistaken view. Stalin had always placed the security of the Soviet state above the interests of international communism; it had been the former, not the latter, that had motivated his expansion into Eastern Europe. Far from encouraging communists outside the Soviet Union to seize power, Stalin initially advised restraint, especially in his dealings with such movements in France, Italy, Greece, and China. But the Soviet leader's caution was not all that clear in the West. Faced with the sudden intrusion of Russian power into Europe, faced with a revival of anticapitalist rhetoric among communists throughout the world, faced with painful evidence from the recent past of what happened when dictators' rhetoric was not taken seriously, observers in both Western Europe and the United States jumped to the conclusion that Stalin, like Hitler, had insatiable ambitions, and would not stop until contained.

Technological differences created a third source of tension. The United States alone emerged from World War II with an industrial plant superior to what it had possessed before that conflict started; the Soviet Union, in turn, had come out of the war with its land ravaged, much of its industry destroyed, and some twenty million of its citizens dead. The resulting disparity of power caused some

Americans to exaggerate their ability to influence events in the rest of the world; it simultaneously produced in the Russians deep feelings of inferiority and vulnerability.

This problem manifested itself most obviously with regard to reconstruction. Stalin had hoped to repair war damage with the help of Lend-Lease and a postwar loan from the United States; his conviction that Americans would soon be facing a postwar depression led him to believe—drawing on clear Leninist principles—that Washington would have no choice but to provide such aid as a means of generating foreign markets for surplus products. His surprise was great when the United States passed up the economic benefits it would have derived from granting a loan in favor of the political concessions it hoped to obtain by withholding it. Nor would Washington allow the use of Lend-Lease for reconstruction; to compound the offense, the Truman administration also cut off, in 1946, the flow of reparations from the American zone in Germany. Whether more generous policies on these matters would have produced better relations with the Soviet Union is impossible to prove—certainly the Russians were never in such need of aid as to be willing to make major political concessions in order to get it. There is no doubt, though, that they bitterly resented their exclusion from these "fruits" of Western technology.

Another "fruit" of Western technology that impressed the Russians was, of course, the atomic bomb. Although Soviet leaders carefully avoided signs of concern about this new weapon, they did secretly accelerate their own bomb development project while simultaneously calling for the abolition of all such weapons of mass destruction. After much debate within the government, the United States, in the summer of 1946, proposed the Baruch Plan, which would have transferred control of all fissionable materials to the United Nations. In fact, however, neither the Russians nor the Americans had sufficient faith in the world organization to entrust their security completely to it. Washington at no point was willing to surrender its bombs until the control system had gone into effect, while Moscow was unwilling to accept the inspection provisions which would allow the plan to operate. Both sides had concluded by 1947 that they would find greater security in an arms race than in an unproven system of international control.

Finally, accidents of personality made it more difficult than it might otherwise have been to achieve a mutually agreeable settlement. The Russians perceived in the transition from Roosevelt to Truman an abrupt shift from an attitude of cooperation to one of confrontation. "The policy pursued by the US ruling circles after the death of Franklin D. Roosevelt," the official history of

Soviet foreign policy asserts, "amounted to renunciation of dependable and mutually beneficial cooperation with the Soviet Union, a cooperation that was so effective . . . in the period of joint struggle against the nazi aggressors." In fact, though, Roosevelt's policy had been firmer than Stalin realized; Truman's was not as uncompromising as his rhetoric suggested. What was different was style: where Roosevelt had sought to woo the Soviet leader by meeting his demands wherever possible, the new chief executive, like a good poker player, tried to deal from positions of rhetorical, if not actual, strength. His tough talk was designed to facilitate, not impede, negotiations—any appearance of weakness, he thought, would only encourage the Russians to ask for more.

What Truman failed to take into account was the possibility that Stalin might also be bluffing. Given the history of Western intervention to crush Bolshevism, given the Soviet Union's ruined economy and weakened population, and given the atomic bomb's unexpected confirmation of American technological superiority, it seems likely that the aging Soviet dictator was as frightened of the West as the West was of him. Truman's tough rhetoric, together with Hiroshima's example, may well have reinforced Stalin's conviction that if *he* showed any signs of weakness, all would be lost. Both leaders had learned too well the lesson of the 1930s: that appeasement never pays. Prospects for an amicable resolution of differences suffered accordingly.

There was nothing in this set of circumstances that made the Cold War inevitable—few things ever are inevitable in history. But a situation such as existed in Europe in 1945, with two great powers separated only by a power vacuum, seemed almost predestined to produce hostility, whether either side willed it or not. As a result, the United States, the Soviet Union, and much of the rest of the world as well would have to suffer through that prolonged period of insecurity that observers at the time, and historians since, have called the "Cold War."

II

The evolution of United States policy toward the Soviet Union between 1945 and 1947 can be seen as a three-stage process of relating national interests to national capabilities. From V-J Day through early 1946, there existed genuine confusion in Washington as to both Soviet intentions and appropriate methods for dealing with them. Coordination between power and policy was, as a result, minimal. By the spring of 1946, a consensus had developed favoring resistance to further Soviet expansion, but little had been done to determine what resources would be necessary to

accomplish that goal or to differentiate between areas of primary and secondary concern. It was not until 1947 that there began to emerge an approach to the Soviet Union that bore some reasonable relationship to American capabilities for projecting influence in the world.

There appeared to be no lack of power available to the United States for the purpose of ordering the postwar environment as it saw fit, but the task of transforming technological superiority into political influence proved frustratingly difficult. Secretary of State James F. Byrnes had hoped to trade reconstruction assistance and a commitment to the international control of atomic energy for Soviet concessions on such outstanding issues as implementation of the Yalta Declaration on Liberated Europe, peace treaties with former German satellites, and, ultimately, a final resolution of the German question itself. But the Russians maintained a posture of ostentatious unconcern about the atomic bomb, nor would they yield on significant issues to obtain reconstruction assistance. Congressional skepticism about Moscow's intentions ensured that any loan would carry a political price far beyond what the Russians would willingly pay, while public opinion pushed Truman into a decision to seek United Nations control of atomic energy before Byrnes had made any attempt to extract Soviet concessions in return. Economic and technological superiority thus won the United States surprisingly few practical benefits in its early postwar dealings with the USSR.

In Washington, moreover, there still existed a substantial number of officials who viewed Soviet hostility as the product of misunderstandings and who expected that, with restraint on both sides, a mutually satisfactory resolution of differences might still occur. It is significant that as late as November, 1945, a State Department representative could rebuke the Joint Chiefs of Staff for confidentially suggesting that the wartime alliance might not survive victory. "We must always bear in mind," a Department memorandum noted the following month, "that because of the differences between the economic and political systems [of the United States and the Soviet Union], the conduct of our relations requires more patience and diligence than with other countries." Despite his tough rhetoric, President Truman shared this view. Disagreements with the Russians were to be expected once the common bond of military necessity had been removed, he told his advisers; in time, they would disappear because "Stalin was a fine man who wanted to do the right thing."

But events made this position increasingly difficult to sustain. The Russians remained adamant in their determination to exclude Western influence from Eastern Europe and the Balkans, while a continued Soviet presence in Iran and Manchuria raised fears that Moscow might try to impose control over those territories as well. Russian interest in the eastern Mediterranean seemed to be growing, with demands for trusteeships over former Italian colonies, boundary rectifications at Turkey's expense, and a revision of the Montreux Convention governing passage through the Dardanelles. And in February, 1946, news of Soviet atomic espionage became public for the first time with the revelation that the Canadian government had arrested a group of Russian agents for trying to steal information about the bomb. That same month, Stalin in his first major postwar foreign policy speech stressed the incompatibility between communism and capitalism, implying that future wars were inevitable until the world economic system was restructured along Soviet lines.

It was at this point that there arrived at the State Department a dispatch from George F. Kennan, now *chargé d'affaires* at the American embassy in Moscow, which did much to clarify official thinking regarding Soviet behavior. Russian hostility toward the West, Kennan argued, stemmed chiefly from the internal necessities of the Stalinist regime: the Soviet dictator required a hostile outside world in order to justify his own autocratic rule. Marxism provided Soviet leaders with

> justification for their instinctive fear of the outside world, for the dictatorship without which they did not know how to rule, for cruelties they did not dare not to inflict, for sacrifices they felt bound to demand. . . . Today they cannot dispense with it. It is the fig leaf of their moral and intellectual respectability.

It followed that Stalin was, by nature, incapable of being reassured. "Nothing short of complete disarmament, delivery of our air and naval forces to Russia and resigning of the powers of government to American Communists would even dent this problem," Kennan noted in a subsequent dispatch, "and even then Moscow would smell a trap and would continue to harbor the most baleful misgivings." The solution, Kennan suggested, was to strengthen Western institutions in order to render them invulnerable to the Soviet challenge while simultaneously awaiting the eventual mellowing of the Soviet regime.

There was little in Kennan's analysis that he and other career Soviet experts had not been saying for some time. What was new was Washington's receptivity to the message, a condition brought about both by frustration over Soviet behavior and by growing public and Congressional resistance to further concessions. In contrast to its earlier optimism about relations with Moscow, the State Department now endorsed Kennan's analysis as "the most probable explanation of present Soviet policies and attitudes." The United States, it concluded, should demonstrate to the Kremlin, "in the first instance by diplomatic means and in the last analysis by military force if necessary that the present course of its foreign policy can only lead to disaster for the Soviet Union."

The spring and summer of 1946 did see a noticeable toughening of United States policy toward the Soviet Union. In early March, Truman lent public sanction to Winston Churchill's strongly anti-Soviet "iron curtain" speech by appearing on the platform with him at Fulton, Missouri. That same month, Secretary of State Byrnes insisted on placing the issue of Iran before the United Nations, even after the Russians had agreed to withdraw their troops from that country. The termination of German reparations shipments came in May; three months later, Byrnes publicly committed the United States to support German rehabilitation, with or without the Russians. In July, Truman endorsed the continued presence of American troops in southern Korea on the grounds that that country constituted "an ideological battleground upon which our whole success in Asia may depend." Soviet pressure on Turkey for bases produced a decision in August to maintain an American naval force indefinitely in the eastern Mediterranean. In September, White House aide Clark Clifford submitted a report to the president, prepared after consultation with top military and diplomatic advisers, arguing that "this government should be prepared . . . to resist vigorously and successfully any efforts of the U.S.S.R. to expand into areas vital to American security.". . .

Shortly thereafter a severe economic crisis, the product of remaining wartime dislocations and an unusually harsh winter, hit Western Europe. This development caused the British to announce their intention, in February, 1947, of terminating economic and military aid to Greece and Turkey, countries that had, up to that point, been regarded as within London's sphere of responsibility. It also raised the longer-range but even more frightening prospect that economic conditions in Western Europe generally might deteriorate to the point that communist parties there could seize power through coups or even free elections. Suddenly the whole European balance of power, which the United States had gone to war to restore, seemed once again in peril.

This situation, which appeared so to threaten European stability, was one the Russians had done little if anything to instigate; it was rather the product primarily of internal conditions within the countries involved. But there was little doubt of Moscow's ability to exploit the

European economic crisis if nothing was done to alleviate it. And action was taken, with such energy and dispatch that the fifteen weeks between late February and early June, 1947, have come to be regarded as a great moment in the history of American diplomacy, a rare instance in which "the government of the United States operat[ed] at its very finest, efficiently and effectively."

Such plaudits may be too generous. Certainly the language Truman used to justify aid to Greece and Turkey ("at the present moment in world history nearly every nation must choose between alternative ways of life. . . . I believe that it must be the policy of the United States to support free peoples who are resisting attempted subjugation by armed minorities or by outside pressures") represented a projection of rhetoric far beyond either the administration's intentions or capabilities. Whatever its usefulness in prying funds out of a parsimonious Congress, the sweeping language of the "Truman Doctrine" would cause problems later on as the president and his foreign policy advisers sought to clarify distinctions between vital and peripheral interests in the world. That such distinctions were important became apparent with the announcement in June, 1947, of the Marshall Plan, an ambitious initiative that reflected, far more than did the Truman Doctrine, the careful calibration of ends to means characteristic of the administration's policy during this period.

The European Recovery Program, to use its official title, proposed spending some $17 billion for economic assistance to the non-communist nations of Europe over the next four years. (Aid was offered to the Soviet Union and its East European satellites as well, but with the expectation, which proved to be correct, that Moscow would turn it down.) It was a plan directed, not against Soviet military attack, a contingency United States officials considered remote, but against the economic malaise that had sapped self-confidence among European allies, rendering them vulnerable to internal communist takeovers. It involved no direct military commitments; rather, its architects assumed, much as had advocates of the "arsenal of democracy" concept before World War II, that the United States could most efficiently help restore the balance of power in Europe by contributing its technology and raw materials, but not its manpower. . . .

III

Despite its limited character, the vigor of the American response to Soviet postwar probes apparently caught Stalin by surprise. His response was to try to strengthen further the security of his own regime, first by increasing safeguards against Western influences inside the Soviet Union;

second, by tightening control over Russia's East European satellites; and finally by working to ensure central direction of the international communist movement. By a perverse kind of logic, each of these moves backfired, as did a much earlier Soviet initiative whose existence only came to light at this point—the establishment, in the United States during the 1930s, of a major espionage network directed from Moscow. The result, in each of these cases, was to produce consequences that only made it more difficult for Stalin to obtain the kind of security he sought. . . .

Meanwhile, attempts to resolve the question of divided Germany had produced no results, despite protracted and tedious negotiations. In February, 1948, the three Western occupying powers, plus the Benelux countries, met in London and decided to move toward formation of an independent West German state. Stalin's response, after initial hesitation, was to impose a blockade on land access to Berlin, which the World War II settlement had left a hundred miles inside the Soviet zone. The Berlin crisis brought the United States and the Soviet Union as close to war as they would come during the early postwar years. Truman was determined that Western forces would stay in the beleaguered city, however untenable their military position there, and to reinforce this policy he ostentatiously transferred to British bases three squadrons of B-29 bombers. No atomic bombs accompanied these planes, nor were they even equipped to carry them. But this visible reminder of American nuclear superiority may well have deterred the Russians from interfering with air access to Berlin, and through this means the United States and its allies were able to keep their sectors of the city supplied for almost a year. Stalin finally agreed to lift the blockade in May, 1949, but not before repeating the dubious distinction he had achieved in the Russo-Finnish War a decade earlier: of appearing to be brutal and incompetent at the same time.

The Berlin blockade had two important consequences, both of which were detrimental from the Soviet point of view. It provided the impetus necessary to transform the Western Union into the North Atlantic Treaty Organization, a defensive alliance linking the United States, Canada, and ten Western European nations, established in April, 1949. Simultaneously, the blockade lessened prospects for a settlement of the German problem in collaboration with the Russians; the result was to accelerate implementation of the London program, a goal accomplished with the formation, in September, 1949, of the Federal Republic of Germany.

Stalin's efforts to tighten control over communists outside the Soviet Union also produced unintended consequences. In apparent reaction to the Marshall Plan, he authorized in September, 1947, the revival of a central directorate for the international communist movement, this time to be known as the Cominform. It is unlikely that Stalin had anything more in mind than to make international communism a more reliable instrument of Soviet foreign policy, but the effect in the West was to confirm lurking suspicions that his objective had always been world revolution. As Elbridge Durbrow, the American *chargé d'affaires* in Moscow, put it, the move was "patently a declaration of political and economic war against the U.S. and everything the U.S. stands for in world affairs."

Establishment of the Cominform substantially weakened the position of communist parties in Western Europe, whose success, up to that point, had been based largely on their ability to convince followers of their nationalist rather than internationalist credentials. Even worse, from the Soviet point of view, the effort to enforce ideological uniformity provoked an open split with Tito's Yugoslavia, heretofore the Kremlin's most reliable satellite. In Washington, the State Department's Policy Planning Staff immediately saw the importance of this development:

> For the first time in history we may now have within the international community a communist state. . . . independent of Moscow. . . . A new factor of fundamental and profound significance has been introduced into the world communist movement by the demonstration that the Kremlin can be successfully defied by one of its own minions.

Winning support from within the government and from Congress for a policy of actually aiding a communist regime took time, but by 1949 the United States was supporting Tito's position in the United Nations and providing economic assistance. After the outbreak of the Korean War, military aid would follow as well. Stalin's effort to impose monolithic unity had the ironic effect of producing the first visible crack in the monolith—an error of which the United States was quick to take advantage.

Yet another of Stalin's errors—this one made years earlier—came to light only at this point. There had long been rumors, and even some fragmentary evidence, of a Soviet espionage network operating within the United States, but Washington officials had not taken this information seriously nor had it been thoroughly investigated prior to the end of World War II. That situation changed, though, with the defection of Soviet code-clerk Igor Gouzenko in Ottawa shortly after V-J Day, together with the almost simultaneous confession of Elizabeth Bentley, an American who claimed to have been running spies for the Soviet KGB since 1940. These revelations suggested not only that Russians had been trying to steal atomic bomb secrets, but that an entire network of Soviet agents had been created during the 1930s for the purpose of infiltrating government agencies and conveying sensitive information to Moscow. The Truman administration responded by quietly removing suspected individuals from official positions and strengthening its security checks, but by 1948 the Congress had launched a series of sensational public hearings into the matter during which several highly-placed former officials—notably Harry Dexter White of the Treasury Department and Alger Hiss of the State Department—were accused of having committed espionage. White died before formal charges could be brought, but Hiss was convicted early in 1950 of having lied about his earlier communist connections; there quickly followed the arrests of British scientist Klaus Fuchs, who confessed to having transmitted atomic bomb information to the Russians while working on the wartime Manhattan Project, and of Julius and Ethel Rosenberg, who were eventually executed for the same crime in 1953. . . .

It might be argued that there was nothing unusual in all of this: espionage, after all, has a long and colorful history in relations between great powers. But there is, as yet, no evidence that the Americans or the British attempted to spy on the Russians in any substantial way during World War II; despite their success in breaking German and Japanese codes, they appear to have refrained from attempting a similar coup against the Russians, for fear of compromising the wartime alliance. The fact that Stalin felt no comparable inhibitions is revealing, both about his own mentality and about his expectations for cooperation after the war. It also causes one to wonder what the Russians gained from their elaborate espionage activities in Britain and the United States, as balanced against what they lost. For although Fuchs's treason may have accelerated the Soviet atomic bomb project by about a year, and although the Russians . . . may well have picked up sensitive inside information about the size of the American atomic stockpile, the cost to the Russians of their indulgence in espionage, once it became known in the West, was considerable. If Stalin ever hoped to win the trust of Western statesmen—and there is some reason to think he did—then this evidence of his own failure to reciprocate a wartime trust extended to him could only have defeated that purpose.

Through his own policies, therefore, Stalin brought about many of the things he most feared: an American commitment to defend Western Europe; a revived West German state, closely tied to his adversaries; the beginnings of fragmentation within the international communist movement; and a conviction on the part of Western leaders that, because the Soviet Union could not be trusted, negotiations with it on the resolution of outstanding differences could only be approached with the greatest caution and from positions of strength, if they were to take place at all. It was a sobering demonstration of the consequences that can follow from a chronic inability to anticipate the impact of one's own actions; it also provides evidence for the view that one of the West's major—if unappreciated—assets during the early Cold War was the persistent ineptitude of the Soviet dictator himself.

JOHN LEWIS GADDIS is the Robert A. Lovett Professor of History at Yale University in New Haven, Connecticut. He has also been distinguished professor of history at Ohio University, where he founded the Contemporary History Institute, and he has held visiting appointments at the United States Naval War College, the University of Helsinki, Princeton University, and Oxford University. He is the author of many books.

EXPLORING THE ISSUE

Was President Truman Responsible for the Cold War?

Critical Thinking and Reflection

1. Define "containment" as a policy. How did it originate? How did the Truman administration use it? Why was diplomat George F. Kennan critical of its long-term application?
2. Critically examine what Gaddis means by arguing that the United States created an "empire by invitation" in Europe after World War II. Also examine what LaFeber means when he argues that Truman was a "parochial nationalist." How did Truman's perception of the world affect the decisions he made during the years from 1945 to 1950?
3. Compare and contrast and critically evaluate the interpretation of the Cold War of Gaddis and LaFeber in regards to the following:
   a. The Munich analogy
   b. New strategic thinking (atomic diplomacy; containment)
   c. America's global interests
   d. Russia's global interests
   e. A combination of America's and Russia's military and economic power 1945–1950
   f. The lend-lease controversy
   g. Atomic diplomacy (threats or sincere arms control offers)
   h. Iran and Middle East issues
   i. Truman Doctrine
   j. Marshall Plan
   k. Korean War
   l. Truman's personality
   m. Stalin's personality
4. Do you think that if FDR had lived into 1948 that the Cold War could have been avoided? Was the Cold War the fault of Truman's "parochial nationalist" outlook?
5. Do you agree or disagree with Gaddis, who argues that the Cold War was inevitable because of Stalin's personality? Critically evaluate.

Is There Common Ground?

Both sides have hardened their positions in assessing blame for the Cold War. Revisionists believe that Americans did not recognize the legitimate concerns of the Soviet Union regarding its security. Understanding that Russia had suffered enormous casualties on the eastern front in World War II, the United States should have granted more concessions for Russian territorial control over Eastern Europe in order to prevent a third invasion from France or Germany through that weakened frontier. Meanwhile, after attempts to negotiate the Yalta agreements laid down by his predecessor FDR, President Truman recognized how difficult it would be to work with Stalin. There is a tendency among many Americans to lay blame for the Cold War at the feet of the Soviet Union whose leaders were captive to communist ideology. What is ignored is the degree to which the United States was equally driven by a competing ideology of democracy and free market capitalism. Consequently, both sides viewed each other as a threat.

Additional Resources

John Lewis Gaddis, *The Cold War: A New History* (The Penguin Press, 2005).

Melvyn P. Leffler and David S. Painter, eds., *Origins of the Cold War: An International History* (Routledge, 1994).

Ralph Levering et al., *Debating the Origins of the Cold War: American and Russian Perspectives* (Rowman and Littlefield, 2002).

Wilson D. Miscamble, C.S.C., *From Roosevelt to Truman: Potsdam, Hiroshima and the Cold War* (Cambridge, 2007).

Ellen Schrecker, ed., *Cold War Triumphalism* (The New Press, 2004).

Internet References . . .

Central Intelligence Agency (CIA) Electronic Reading Room

www.foia.cia.gov/

CWIHP: Cold War International History Project

http://legacy.wilsoncenter.org/coldwarfiles/index.html

Harry S Truman Library

http://www.trumanlibrary.org/library.htm

Selected, Edited, and with Issue Framing Material by:
Kevin R. Magill and Tony L. Talbert, *Baylor University*

ISSUE

Was Rock and Roll Responsible for Dismantling America's Traditional Family, Sexual, and Racial Customs in the 1950s and 1960s?

YES: Jody Pennington, from "Don't Knock the Rock: Race, Business, and Society in the Rise of Rock and Roll," Aarhus University Press (1992)

NO: Bruce Harrah-Conforth, from "Rock and Roll, Process, and Tradition," *Western Folklore* (1990)

Learning Outcomes

After reading this issue, you will be able to:

- Describe the origin of the term "rock and roll."
- Describe the roots of rock and roll music.
- Describe the revolutionary, evolutionary, and conservative aspects of 1950s' rock and roll music.
- Critically evaluate the controversy surrounding the effects of rock and roll music on society's values in the 1950s and 1960s.

ISSUE SUMMARY

YES: Jody Pennington believes that the emergence of rock and roll in the 1950s, along with new forms of consumerism, expressed "the inner conflict between conservative and rebellious forces for high school teenagers who wanted to rebel against their parents yet still grow up to be them."

NO: Bruce Harrah-Conforth argues that youth departure from lifestyles of previous generations left a lack of rites of passage into adulthood. As a result, America's youth sought community through the construction and manipulation of rock and roll allowing them to create their own rites of passage and mark the experiences of the generation. Rock and roll, therefore, was a new version of a time-honored experience through which American youth grappled with their place in the social world.

Issue framing with Ashleigh Maldonado, *Baylor University*

Most Americans assume that rock and roll has dominated American popular music since the 1950s, but this is not true. The phrase "rhythm and blues" was coined by the first white rock and roll Cleveland disc jockey Alan Freed who, when he went national, was pushed by a lawsuit in 1954 to abandon the name of his show from "The Moondog House" to "Rock 'n' Roll Party." An African American euphemism for sexual intercourse, "rock 'n' roll" had appeared as early as 1922 in a blues song and was constantly used by black singers into the early 1950s. It is not clear whether DJ Freed consciously made the name change to cultivate a broader audience, but that is precisely what happened. The phrase caught on, and Freed and station WINS secured a copyright for it.

Rock and roll was a fashion of rhythm and blues, black gospel, and country-western music. It combined black and white music, which explains why so many of the early rock singers came from the South and recorded their hit songs in New Orleans or Memphis. Between 1953 and 1955, the first true rockers—Fats Domino, Chuck Berry, and Little Richard—were African Americans. Fats Domino came from New Orleans, sang from his piano, and sold over 65 million records between 1949 and 1960, including "Ain't That a Shame," "I'm Walking," and "Blueberry Hill." Even more influential because of his electric guitar riffs, body and leg gyrations, and songs full of wit and clever wordplay, Chuck Berry's lifestyle (he did two stints in prison) and songs ("Maybellene," "Johnny B. Good," and "Roll Over Beethoven") influenced two generations of rockers, including sixties British rock bands the Beatles and the Rolling Stones. Another rocker, Little Richard, known as "the Georgia Peach," became famous as much for his flamboyant style of dress with his towering hair and multicolored clothes that reflected a teasing sexuality. He created a string of hits—"Tutti Frutti," "Long Tall Sally," and "Good Golly Miss Molly,"—which were recorded as cover records by white artists such as Pat Boone. Best known today for his Geico commercial, Little Richard scared the hell out of white middle-class American parents.

Even more threatening from these parents' perspective, however, was Elvis Presley, the "King of Rock and Roll," and the most influential pop icon in the history of the United States. But Elvis was not the inventor of rock and roll. His voice was average and his songs (written by others) were often mediocre, but his rugged good looks and his sexy gyrations on the stage threw young girls into spasms. Most importantly, he was white. More than 30 years after his death, Elvis still defines the age of rock and roll, and his music remains popular with sales of his recordings numbering over a billion.

Presley was the first star to take advantage of the new teenage consumer market. By the middle 1950s there were 16.5 million teenagers, half in high school and the other half in college or the work force, who possessed a lot of disposable income, available via allowances or part-time jobs. Suburban teenagers had their own rooms replete with radios and record players. "By the end of 1957," says Glenn Altschuler, "seventy-eight Elvis Presley items had grossed $55 million." Presley helped promote the products, making personal appearances in department stores.

There is little argument that a new generation of teenagers had emerged in the fifties. Historians can trace the adolescent generations back to the early twentieth century. The gap between parent and child always existed, but the new value system that set apart the two generations might have occurred earlier had the Great Depression and World War II not intervened. Television shows were geared to the very young and the parents. Radio had lost its nightly sitcoms to television and switched to news and music formats. Teenagers were tired of their parents' sentimental croon and swoon ballads, which did not address their feelings. New DJs emerged, who played the rock and roll songs for teenagers who sat in their rooms pretending to do their homework.

Between 1958 and 1963, rock and roll as a distinct form of music nearly disappeared. There were several reasons for this. First were the congressional investigations of 1959–61 into payoffs to DJs to push certain records on their shows. "Payola" ruined the careers of a number of rock DJs, including Alan Freed, who lost his two major jobs in New York, was hounded by the IRS for back taxes, and succumbed to alcoholism in 1965. But Dick Clark of American Bandstand fame was protected by the music establishment even though he became a multimillionaire with interests in a number of record companies whose songs he featured on his own show.

Second, "payola McCarthyism" receded in the early sixties as a result of rock and roll being fused into the mainstream of American popular music. Religious leaders appeared less worried about rock's perversion of the country's sexual moral values, southerners lost the fear of rock's racial mongrelization, and American parents no longer associated rock music with subversives, communists, and other radicals. How could they, when Elvis Presley cut his hair, was drafted into the Army, and sang ballads and religious songs that were often integrated into his two dozen forgettable movies? By the time Presley's manager finished reshaping the King's image, Elvis looked more like Pat Boone, the sanitized pop idol. At the same time, Dick Clark turned his Philadelphia-based show, American Bandstand, into an afternoon phenomenon that featured well-groomed teenagers dancing to the latest songs.

In 1963, serious rock was replaced by folk music. Greenwich Village, in the heart of downtown New York City, was its epicenter, Bob Dylan became its troubadour by writing new folk songs instead of retreading old ones, and the group Peter, Paul, and Mary popularized the music into commercial success. At the same time, folk music provided anthems for the civil rights and antiwar protest movements.

Meanwhile, a sixties rock revival came from two sources. First was the British invasion, symbolized by the arrival of the Beatles in 1963, followed by other groups, such as the Rolling Stones, who traced their roots to the early guitar riffs of Chuck Berry. Having come from working-class backgrounds in Liverpool, the Beatles grew up in an environment that challenged authority and poked fun at some of the hypocrisy of middle-class values. Their later songs influenced the protest movements in the United States.

A second source of revival for protest rock music came from the counterculture movement in San Francisco. Bands such as the Grateful Dead and Jefferson Airplane brought "underground" rock to the forefront. Soon, even the Beatles were imitating the San Francisco underground with their classic album, "Sgt. Pepper's Lonely Hearts Club Band," with a style that, according to one writer, combined "a peculiar blend of radical political rhetoric, of allusions to the drug culture, and of the excited sense of imminent, apocalyptic liberation."

Two events in 1969 symbolized the high and low points of sixties rock. In August, 500,000 people converged on a farm in upstate New York for a three-day rock festival. Woodstock became a legendary symbol. There was a scant political protest. Music was the common bond that united people sitting in the rain-filled mud, sharing food and drugs while drowning out the fears of participating in an endless war. In December, all the good will of Woodstock was destroyed at a free Rolling Stones concert in Altamont, California. Four people died, one of whom was clubbed, stabbed, and kicked to death by the Hell's Angles, hired as body guards for the Stones on the advice of the Grateful Dead.

Would the sixties "new left" and counterculture movements have taken place without the emergence of rock and roll in the 1950s? Did rock help to reshape America's values, or was it all one big commercial hustle?

The two best overviews of the early history of rock and roll are Glenn C. Altschuler, *All Shook Up: How Rock and Roll Changed America* (Oxford University Press, 2003) and James Miller, *Flowers in the Dustbin: The Rise of Rock and Roll, 1947–1977* (Simon & Schuster, 1999). Excellent overviews of the 1950s include Douglas T. Miller and Marion Nowak, *The Fifties: The Way We Really Were* (Doubleday, 1975); David Halberstam, *The Fifties* (Villard, 1993); and William L. O'Neill, *American High: The Years of Confidence, 1945–1960* (Simon & Schuster, 1986). For the decade of the 1960s, see William O'Neill's *Coming Apart: An Informal History of the 1960s* (Times Books, 1971); David Farber, *The Age of Great Dreams: America in the 1960s* (Hill & Wang, 1994); and Terry H. Anderson, *The Movement and the Sixties: Protest in America from Greensboro to Wounded Knee* (Oxford University Press, 1995). David Marcus examines the impact of the 1950s and 1960s upon present-day politics and pop culture in *Happy Days and Wonder Years: The Fifties and Sixties in Contemporary Cultural Politics* (Rutgers University Press, 2004).

In the first selection, Jody Pennington believes that the emergence of rock and roll in the 1950s along with new forms of consumerism expressed "the inner conflict between conservative and rebellious forces for high school teenagers who wanted to rebel against their parents yet still grow up to be them." According to one book reviewer, Pennington has written in 20 plus pages the best and most reliable synthesis . . . on the relationship of rock 'n' roll music to the body politic. He carefully covers every aspect of the popular music business in the fifties, analyzing the crucial role played by the 'indies' (the independent record companies), the impact of technology on market distribution (45s and LPs quickly replaced the old 78s), as well as the way radio and the record business had to compete against the suddenly ubiquitous television for control of the family entertainment medium.

In the second selection, Bruce Harrah-Conforth disagrees with Pennington's analysis. "In spite of . . . profound social changes and power" in a post-WWII and Cold War era he notes, "the lack of American rites of initiation into adulthood . . . saw many members of America's youth set about to use their new found power to produce their own circumstances in which a model of transitional ritual and social role playing could be enacted to their needs and desires." Rock and roll, rather than being the *cause* of disruption and disorder, was merely the tool by which America's youth developed community and established ritual in their otherwise chaotic, war-torn world.

YES

Jody Pennington

Don't Knock the Rock: Race, Business, and Society in the Rise of Rock and Roll

Forty Miles of Bad Road

From the beginning, rock 'n' roll was geared for movement, for dancing: it sounded best in a car, cruising down the highway or cutting down the boulevard. You could buy the record and play it at home above the din of parents yelling 'turn that crap down!' or 'you call that music?' But that was never the same as hearing it suddenly on the car radio (even if for the tenth time in the same day) when some cool disc jockey dropped the needle in the groove. The music was everywhere: blaring out of every apartment, a radio in every car, turned on all the time. In 1956, the year rock 'n' roll peaked, it was the perfect accompaniment for bombing around in a '49 Ford or a new '55 Chevy: raked and flamed, decked and lowered, chopped and channeled with fins and tails on a Saturday night; burning rubber zero to sixty to the first red light and then on to the next, looking for another chump with overhead cams, a 4.56 rear end to cut out.

Cars and kids came together in the 1950s, and rock 'n' roll was best man at the wedding. This was the latest generation of American Huck Finns running from routine and convention. Their rivers were the roads, highways, boulevards, avenues, and streets of America's big cities and small towns. Their rafts were their cars, and their Nigger Jim was the latest hit on the radio. The night was all beginning and without end.

Mobility meant escape: from the rigidity of home, from high school, from authority. Suburban mothers abhorred deviant behavior in their children and had little patience with wild rock 'n' rollers who threatened their own interests or the creeds and symbols they cherished. Dad wanted stability and order on the home front so he could go about his daily bread-winning tasks. Parents restrained their kids with 'restriction', a form of Levittown house arrest meant to quash any interest in music, dancing, motorcycles, souped-up cars, violence, and sex.

Rock 'n' roll reflected the interests and needs of its young public; it moved them. This raucous new music appeared in young people's lives at the crucial intersection of the dependency of puberty and the autonomy of the post-teen years. To millions at this age, sitting with the family around the tube watching Milton Berle or Sid Caesar was a drag. Instead they kept to themselves in their own rooms, listening to the hi-fi or radio, with posters of Little Richard, Elvis, and Buddy Holly on the wall; or they went to concerts or dated or hung out with friends at diners and juke joints. Whatever they did, they got away from parents; wherever they went, rock 'n' roll was there: reinforcing and enhancing the sensation of independence. Mom and Dad stayed home, secure in their own opinions, values, and standards of conduct. They knew bikers, greasers, and rock 'n' rollers who flouted them were ignorant or wicked.

The attitudes embodied by the music were rebellious and provocative. That in itself was nothing new. Jitterbuggers in the 1930s had had their music labeled 'syncopated savagery'. Now as parents, twenty years later, these former savages were shocked at how seriously their offspring took rock 'n' roll. Parents saw in rock 'n' roll a destructive force, not just a symptom of awkward adolescence. Partly because the kids of the postwar era had wealth like none before them, however, the generational conflict sharpened as never before. As Greil Marcus would later write: 'it's a sad fact that most of those over thirty cannot be a part of it [rock 'n' roll], and it cannot be a part of them.' Who, then, were these parents, these over-thirty enemies of rock 'n' roll?

Squaresville

Following their victory over fascist Germany and Japan, returning vets felt like national heroes. It was now time to earn a little money, have a family, and prosper. Commuting along the paved highways of the golden fifties in MG-TCs, ex-GIs basked perkily in the suburban afterglow of battlefield heroism. The world was theirs for the conquering: a promotion here, a new house there; a barbecue grill, 2.5 kids who would some day go to college, a wife at home enjoying—or enduring—what Betty Friedan would later call the feminine mystique. Heroes made good neighbors: conservative, a bit artificial, and stiff. Jumpy at the mention of Alger Hiss and Whittaker Chambers, communist spies and Congressional committees, good Americans wore loyalty oaths on their sleeves . . .

High school: educational institution and model of life. A world all its own, filled with pep rallies and glee clubs, dress codes and demerits, school papers and assembly programs, field trips and drill teams; a complex of hall passes and phi-deltas, cheerleaders and team spirit, Big-Man-on-Campus and jocks, clicks and outsiders; a realm where one dressed for success in letter jackets, chinos, and penny loafers. Students were groomed to compete in the toughest of schools: popularity. You were either neat or gross, peachy keen or spastic. Lose in this game and you were a creep, a turkey, a *nothing*.

In many small towns and city neighborhoods, school was the focus of students' social lives. They were whipped into enthusiastic abandon by the marching band and wooed by the majorettes at the Friday night football games in the fall under stadium lights or wowed by the cheerleaders at basketball games. There were hockey games, track meets, and the wrestling team, as well as a plethora of cultural activities, from car washes and banquets to brownie sells and parades. To cap it off there were the high school balls: Homecoming, the sock hops, and the Senior Prom, the culmination of four exciting, memorable years. Amidst all this there was still time for classes. Governed by the conservative norms and mores of the middle class, these were simulations of 'real life' designed to transfigure zitty-faced kids into government or company employees, replicas of what William H. Whyte's 1956 volume dubbed *The Organization Man*. Character was molded by disciplinary measures like restrictions and demerits, but the emphasis was always on the individual. American high schools in the 1950s churned out good citizens: members of the Key Club or the Beta Club, trained in the habits of good citizenship; good employees: members of VICA, prepared to enter the world of work, or DECCA, the future marketing leaders of America; and good wives: members of the Future Home-makers of America, a credit to their sex. Still bolstered by the legacy of McCarthyism, moreover, schools had little problem dishing out their version of the 'American Way'. More than any other age-group, teenagers felt under pressure to conform and to become achievers in a society preoccupied with belonging and success.

Off campus, teenagers were flooded with enticements to consume. If they turned on the television or the radio, flipped through a magazine, or went to the movies, they found themselves barraged with endless images of a stimulating world, one which appeared as the virtual antithesis of high school's drab halls, lockers, and desks. Hedonism beckoned, and teenagers from middle-class families responded with indulgence: girls filled their hope chests with the basics for a good marriage; boys filled the tanks of their cars. They bought radios, cameras, hoola-hoops, frisbees, pogo sticks, television sets, swim suits, clothes, i.d. bracelets, deo, 'greasy kid stuff'—anything that brought them pleasure.

Rock 'n' roll hit this world like a bomb. The ultimate safety valve, the ultimate escape for anyone destined for a nine-to-five office job, it was music for the moment (it barely lasted longer). For two or three minutes anybody could be a rebel: speed the car up, hang an arm out the window, cop an attitude, moon a cop, *anything*. The best tracks could obliterate time, creating a world you could vanish into, lose yourself in, and then return from with the help of the disc jockey's patter. Maybe the nine-to-five world could serve as a means to an end: consumption. But it couldn't give life a purpose.

Rock 'n' roll fit perfectly into the conflict between the new patterns of the consumer society and the traditional Puritan work ethic of abstinence and industriousness. For these well-to-do teenagers the day was divided between the two worlds: in the classroom teachers propagated the traditional values; in their free time teenagers lived a life of impulse shopping. Just as the stop-and-jerk pace of Chuck Berry's 'Sweet Little Sixteen' swings the young girl from pretty young wild thing to Daddy's little girl, so their lives oscillated between obedience and indulgence. Through the works of writers like Jerry Leiber and Mike Stoller (who wrote 'Hound Dog' and 'Jailhouse Rock' for Elvis Presley, and all the Coasters' hits); Felice and Boudleaux Bryant (who penned hits for the Everly Brothers); and especially rock 'n' roll poet laureate Chuck Berry, rock 'n' roll spoke to these teenagers: it dealt with their problems and frustrations, their dancing and dates, their likes, dislikes, and obsessions.

That'll Be the Day

As much medium as message, rock 'n' roll was one of the first strokes of cultural self-awareness to blossom in the 1950s. Maybe the lyrics were sometimes as trite or nonsensical as Tin Pan Alley's, maybe white kids had problems understanding the singing, but rock 'n' roll—with its solid backbeat and driving eighth-note rhythm—fit the pace and rhythm of a world which had grown modern during the war and which was now coming to grips with its modernity: coast-to-coast broadcasts, transatlantic jet flights, super highways, fast cars, transistors, the Bomb, roller derbies, instant coffee, Sputnik, desegregation, *Playboy*, the rat race, frisbees, and Sugar Ray Robinson. Let Mom and Pop Suburbia condemn the noise and the meaningless babble, let them fox-trot and cha-cha to Frank Sinatra and Rosemary Clooney: what a slow burn! For Junior, it was slow dancing with a rise in his Levis and a tale to take back to the guys: get much?

From the start rock 'n' roll had its prophets of doom: 'it'll never last' went the wisdom of schmaltz, and it seemed sound enough. This was, after all, *Leave it to Beaver-land:* fads came, fads went. In fact, rock 'n' roll never dominated the charts or musical tastes. As Charlie Gillet points out in *The Sound of the City,* even during its heyday 'from 1955 through 1959, just under half of the top ten hits . . . could be classified as rock 'n' roll'. During those years, according to Serge Denisoff, rock 'n' roll 'did not constitute all of popular music, and even in the heyday of Elvis Presley not all teenagers were into his music, as many rock histories seem to imply'. Nonetheless rock 'n' roll endured. It was exclusive and well-guarded, with a strong sense of awareness that the music was something special; it was almost elitist in its sense of being reserved for those hip enough to *dig it.* Rock 'n' roll was a fever, a craze; and a lot of kids in the 1950s were on the edge of a fighting mood: 'Your ass is grass! Get bent! You're cruisin' for a bruisin'! Don't give me any grief.' Rock 'n' roll caught the mood—'Blue Suede Shoes', 'That'll be the Day', 'Too Much Monkey Business', 'Hound Dog', 'Rip it Up'. Chuck Berry summed up the new generation's disdain for the older: 'Roll Over Beethoven.'

Rock 'n' roll alone did not induce the new teenage behavioral patterns in the 1950s. Prosperity, new forms of distribution, the portable radio, and television made their presence felt. Still, something in the music sparked fires where cinders glowed. Rock 'n' roll was the matrix inside which middle-class teenagers played out fantasies of rebellion within the context of family, home, and future career. With rock 'n' roll's distribution through radio, television, and film, these kids became the standard image of teenagers' lives and values for the entire social spectrum. With the appearance of Elvis, *they*—white, American, middle-class teenagers—could dream of performing the music as well. Elvis expressed the inner conflict between conservative and rebellious forces for high school teenagers who wanted to rebel against their parents yet still grow up to be them.

Graceland

If rock 'n' roll was the dominant music of white teenagers during the second half of the 1950s, then the key was the King: Elvis Presley. An outsider and a success, he summed up and incarnated the contradictions of the teenager's world. He was one of them: white and young. He had rejected the adult world and sneered his way to the pinnacle of stardom. Elvis not only got the Cadillac; Elvis was bigger and better than a Cadillac. In his music, in his stage act, in his voice, he demanded—and got—respect. As Peter Wicke puts it, he 'embodied the uncertain and consuming desire of American high school teenagers in the fifties, the desire somehow to escape the oppressive ordinariness which surrounded them without having to pay the bitter price of conformity. His quick success seemed to be the proof that, in principle, escape was possible'.

For parents and high school principals in an era when these words still meant something, Elvis Presley was sinful and wicked. He set a bad example. He was a hood, with his long sideburns, ducktail haircut, and curled upper lip. His blatant sexuality, aggressiveness, and bumping and grinding troubled adults. Inside the music industry, though, Elvis was King. From late April 1956, when 'Heartbreak Hotel' dethroned Nelson Riddle's 'Lisbon Antigua' and Les Baxter's 'The Poor People of Paris' at the top of the charts (remaining there for eight weeks), to his late March 1958 induction into the U.S. Army, Elvis ruled the hit parade. He had the number one single in no less than fifty-five out of one hundred and four weeks: 'I Want You, I Need You, I Love You'; 'Don't Be Cruel' and 'Hound Dog' (eleven weeks at number one); 'Love Me Tender' (five weeks); 'Too Much' (three weeks); 'All Shook Up' (nine weeks); 'Teddy Bear' and 'Jailhouse Rock' (seven weeks); and 'Don't' (five weeks).

Although his manager, 'Colonel' Tom Parker, and his record label, RCA, orchestrated his ascent to the top of the pop world, Elvis himself ultimately deserves credit. He had the charisma, the style, the personality, the voice, and (in contrast to Jerry Lee Lewis, who still hasn't lost his rough edges) he could adapt. Elvis had it all. As Greil Marcus would write: 'The version of the American dream that is Elvis's performance is blown up again and again, to contain more history, more people, more music, more hopes; the air gets thin but the bubble does not burst, nor will it ever. This is America when it has outstripped itself, in all of its extravagance.'. . .

The poverty and rural attitudes that were a part of life in the postwar South influenced the course of rock 'n' roll's development. Although the population of the Deep South had shifted during the twentieth century from ninety per cent rural to more than fifty per cent urban, transplanted bumpkins like the Presleys, who had themselves only recently moved to Memphis from Tupelo, Mississippi, stayed 'country'. They did so, moreover, in spite of an increase in their standard of living. (The

New Deal and World War Two had been important stimuli to economic growth in the South, but by the 1950s the region's average per capita income was still only half that of the national average). Like country truck driver Elvis, rock 'n' roll reflected this migration from the farm to the city. Elvis's first single had a blues number on the A-side and a country song on the flip side. Bill Haley had his roots in Texas and Oklahoma country swing in the tradition of Bob Wills. Jerry Lee (as well as Elvis and the other Sun label stars) had his roots in country swing and white gospel. The Everly Brothers had theirs in bluegrass and the country duet singing of Charlie and Ira Louvin and the Delmore Brothers.

Both the R&B and the country elements of rock 'n' roll have origins in the folk music traditions of the outsiders and outcasts of twentieth century America: on the one hand, the African-Americans who picked the cotton; on the other, the so-called 'white trash' who worked it through the cotton mills. The folk blues, typically in a first-person voice, express the experience of African-Americans living in the South during the first half of the twentieth century. The vocabulary is minimal and filled with images of traveling and country roads, field workers and prisoners. Although the dialect and diction are slightly different, the lyrics of country music deal with the realities of rural and city life in the South and the West, again in simple, straightforward language that incorporates the colloquialisms of these regions. Images of truck stops and sunsets, honky-tonks and fields, gamblers and drinkers, cheating and working tell the sentimental stories of taxing, emotional circumstances. The lyrics, sentiments, and, frequently, religious undertones common to both country blues and country and western reflected the inanity of segregation: Southerners of any race had more in common with each other than with anyone from other regions of the USA. Both forms feature expressive vocals: on the one hand, the sharp, nasal sound of country; on the other, the minor pentatonic sound of the blues. An original American sound was heard in the meeting of the two: first in minstrels and then in the songs of Stephen Foster, who was influenced not only by the minstrels but by the music of the African-American churches as well. Generations later, rock 'n' roll would emerge as a sort of electrified Stephen Foster in the unlikely form of Bill Haley.

Although both blues and country had long been commercialized when they merged in the guise of rock 'n' roll, Decca was taking a chance on Haley. And while the label enjoyed great success—at his first session with Decca, Haley recorded both 'Rock Around the Clock' and 'Shake, Rattle and Roll'— taking chances was not the norm for the majors. Their standard operating procedure had long been to chum out 'cover versions' of songs that had already been recorded by someone else. In the 1950s, however, the majors gave cover versions a new twist. Just as in the 1920s Paul Whiteman's orchestra had set out, in his words, to 'make a lady' of hot jazz, so thirty years later the industry recast R&B in an all-white form: performed by whites (such as Steve Lawrence, Andy Williams, Pat Boone, or the Fontane Sisters), recorded by whites, sold by whites, bought by whites, and profited from by whites. (Otherwise rejecting African-American music, the majors would at best record so-called 'black sepias' like Nat King Cole, who appealed to the white mainstream with sentimental, melodramatic crooning.)

As part of this tactic, the majors thus recorded white artists covering R&B tunes originally cut by African-American artists for the independent lablels or 'indies'. These white versions were arranged and perfomed to sound like banal pop music, with a unique beat but always in a simple 'sing-along' form that would be music to white ears. Working on assumptions derived from European classical music traditions, producers like Mitch Miller considered their cover versions to be an improvement on the originals, which they thought sounded like primitive jungle music: harsh, low-down, and dirty. Such assumptions were broadly shared by the white record-buying public. In mainstream America, Bill Haley was thought of as having introduced a new music, a new rhythm; hardly anyone bothered to mention that 'his sound came from the music of the black population, a people whose "great sense of rhythm" had always been admired, but who, white America insisted, otherwise had nothing non-physical to contribute'.

A Choice of Colors

Cultural interaction between African-Americans and the white majority was never strictly a matter of black *or* white. An irreducible component of Southern culture was the mutual influence of the races upon one another. At shows in towns like Macon, Georgia, white kids would sneak in (behind the backs of their parents and white authorities) and slip upstairs to see the African-American kids down on the floor. At first, the white kids would just sit and watch. In the end, however, they were bound to come down and dance. When some young white performers—like Jerry Lee Lewis, sneaking into the 'nigra' clubs in Ferriday, Louisiana, with his cousin Jimmy Lee Swaggart to hear artists like B.B. King—took the music at face value, they helped transform popular music and thereby American youth culture.

Sometimes these Southern rockers covered R&B hits, but more often they brought elements of R&B into their own tunes. Instead of adapting African-American styles to white tastes, they tried to imitate the originals as closely as they could, as when Elvis covered Big Mama Thornton's 'Hound Dog'. Perhaps the swing disappeared in these white attempts at R&B: simplified in rock 'n' roll to a more rigid, basic rhythm under the influence of Hank Williams and the hard-driving style of country pickers like Merle Travis, Joe Maphis, and James Burton. Still, rock 'n' roll was noisy and aggressive because these musicians had been singing and playing that way all along. The rock 'n' roll played by their native sons, rockabilly, frightened white Southerners most. Long in touch with African-American music, these musicians had sufficient spirit to sell records in the R&B, country, and pop markets. Since they were white, moreover, they could get away with it to such a degree that by 1956 even genuine R&B records started to gain acceptance in the mainstream pop market, much to the horror of many white Southerners.

It was no surprise, therefore, that 'the most extreme and bizarre expressions of antagonism towards rock 'n' roll tended to take place in the South. In April 1956, the *New York Times* reported several attempts by white Southern church groups to have rock 'n' roll suppressed. The whole movement towards rock 'n' roll, the church groups revealed, was part of a plot by the NAACP to corrupt white Southern youth'. A stepchild of R&B, the music was known dismissively in the South during those years as 'nigger music'. Rock 'n' roll was music played by and for *niggers* (African-American or white): Little Richard, Fats Domino, and Chuck Berry; Elvis Presley, Jerry Lee Lewis, Carl Perkins, and Buddy Holly. Renegade rednecks in the best Southern tradition, the white rock 'n' rollers were the very stuff of Southern nightmares. For although white Southerners deemed African-Americans rarely capable of attaining the same level of rectitude, white descent into blackness had to be averted. For decades Southern whites had drawn arms against an unseen enemy, evincing a distrust of both mulattoes (who *looked* white) and whites who behaved 'black'. Whites who, like the Southern rock 'n' rollers, strayed too close to African-Americans were known as 'white niggers': genetically white but 'black' in their behavior. The music they played, rock 'n' roll, which sounded like R&B, was the 'jungle music' of burr-heads, blue-skins, tar-pots, spies, jigaboos, darkies, and shines.

The white South's image of African-Americans in the 1950s was much as it had been since the turn of the century. Generations had grown up believing Booker T. Washington to have spoken for all African-Americans and spoken the truth: that they were content to 'cast down their buckets' where they were, chop cotton, lay rails, and work, work, work until Saturday night. By the 1950s, Booker T. was long dead, but in white minds Sambo continued to shuffle contentedly along, bucket in hand. Even while insisting that 'our Nigras are good Nigras', white Southerners had nonetheless devised dogmas and institutions that assured the greatest possible distance between the races. Known collectively as Jim Crow, these had consisted of both legal and extralegal means designed to keep African-Americans in their place and to compel them to behave 'properly' in the presence of whites. The legal measures—the poll tax, stiff residency requirements, literacy tests, and 'grandfather clauses'—kept African-Americans away from the polls and thus ensured the stability of a caste system which governed all aspects of African-American life. Extralegal steps helped guarantee the invisibility of most African-Americans and made those who were visible the Sambos whites needed to see: gullible children in grown-up bodies who slapped their knees, jumped, and turned, and whom whites could allow to run free within their own world without constant guidance after work on Saturday—as long as they showed up at work on Monday morning.

The white South's ability to sustain the system was, of course, challenged on a city bus in Montgomery, Alabama, on 1 December 1955, when Rosa Parks refused to yield her seat to a white man. Although it took years to secure its greatest gains (after Montgomery there was a lull), with Martin Luther King, Jr. more than rising to the occasion the civil rights movement was in the ascendant.

From the Station to the Train

By the time of the civil rights movement, another movement, primarily geographical and cultural rather than social and political, had long since begun: the exodus of millions of African-Americans from the countryside to the nation's cities. Prompted partly by the decline and subsequent mechanization of Southern agriculture, partly by the attraction of often military-spawned jobs, and partly by the dream of a better life beyond Jim Crow, this vast folk migration took hundreds of thousands to Northern industrial cities like New York, Chicago, and Detroit and, to a lesser degree, Southern cities like Memphis and New Orleans. Between 1860 and 1960 the African-American share of the total Southern population dwindled from almost fifty per cent to twenty-nine per cent.

Musical forms born and raised in the South—the blues, jazz, gospel, R&B, and soul—also traveled. On the road, gospel waited alongside the blues in bus depots; jazz and R&B rode together on trains. The movement to the cities helped turn the blue note electric, and African-American radio stations pumped it out. By the early 1950s, R&B stations dotted the urban landscape. Fans had only to turn their tuning knobs to hear the dance blues of singers like Amos Milburn, Roy Brown, Fats Domino, and Lloyd Price, and the 'hot' style of disc jockeys like Hamp Swain in Macon, Georgia, Zenas 'Big Daddy' Sears and 'Jockey Jack' Gibson in Atlanta, and 'Sugar Daddy' in Birmingham. Meanwhile, Alan Freed at WINS in New York set a precedent for white disc jockeys playing R&B; those who followed his lead included Al Benson in Chicago, Hunter Hancock in Los Angeles, and 'Poppa Stoppa' in New Orleans.

These and other artists and disc jockeys gave a voice to a nation of wanderers looking for home: a tricky concept, as James Brown once pointed out, for a people who had been told to move along for a century and a half. Newly-urbanized African-Americans faced a world very different from the one they had known before, but when it came to the question of color, they found themselves on familiar ground. Not surprisingly, when confronted by the racial prejudice of the North and West, they survived just as they and their predecessors had done in the South: by building up their community, families, clubs, and churches. Whether in the North or South, then, home was cut off from white society. White people may have heard R&B as it made its way across the air waves. What their ears didn't hear, what their eyes didn't see, what they wanted neither to hear nor to see, was the distinct *community* which it addressed, a largely self-contained world created by American apartheid: the chitlin' circuit. . . .

Gospel music spoke for and sustained a distinct community, retaining collective and communal features which expressed something of the suppression which so many in that community had experienced. It also helped to transform that community. It did so partly through its influence on rhythm and blues.

Boogie at Midnight

Cacophonous vocals shouted explicit lyrics; loud saxophones, pianos, and guitars honked, rolled, and wailed while drums banged out the heavy rhythm; delirious artists expressed emotions and ideas which exhilarated their audience. Until 1949, when Jerry Wexler gave it the more sophisticated name 'rhythm and blues' while writing for *Billboard,* the white music industry branded all this 'race music'. The lines between urban blues and R&B were tenuous (as are all popular musical categories), and the early R&B charts looked like a blues who's-who: John Lee Hooker's 'Boogie Chillen', Lonnie Johnson's 'Tomorrow Night', shouter Wynonie Harris's 'Good Rockin' Tonight',

as well as tunes by Howlin' Wolf, Charles Brown, Muddy Waters, Bull Moose Jackson, and Ivory Joe Hunter.

R&B was updated and mellowed as the influence of gospel smoothed over its rougher edges. Technology played a crucial part. Although different radio stations programmed specific genres, listeners were not so constrained; as a result gospel singles crossed over to the R&B charts: in 1950, for example, the Five Blind Boys' 'Our Father' was chasing Wynonie Harris's 'I Like My Baby's Pudding' up the charts. Quartet singing, long a crossover area for artists like the Mills Brothers and the Ink Spots, was the springboard for the 'bird groups' (the Ravens and the Orioles), who in turn inspired groups like the Clovers and the Dominoes. Founded in 1950 by Billy Ward, the Dominoes built their sound around the gospel-style vocals of Clyde McPhatter. Race restricted the success of songs like 'Do Something for Me' and 'Have Mercy Baby' to the R&B charts, until the appearance of rock 'n' roll enabled an R&B group, Frankie Lymon and the Teenagers, to hit the charts for sixteen weeks in 1956, peaking at number six, with 'Why Do Fools Fall in Love?' The original did better than the cover versions by the Diamonds and Gale Storm. The Platters, who had charted in 1955 with 'Only You' released three Top Ten pop and R&B hits in 1956. Many of the R&B acts that followed went on to become rock 'n' roll, rather than soul, stars. Imperial artist Fats Domino rode 'Blueberry Hill' and 'I'm in Love Again' into the Top Ten. Two other 'R&B' artists, Chuck Berry and Little Richard, hit the charts with 'Maybellene', 'School Days', and 'Sweet Little Sixteen'; and 'Tutti-Frutti', 'Long Tall Sally', and 'Rip it Up', respectively.

White listeners started to develop a better feeling for the music: they heard R&B differently. As it became familiar, it became acceptable on its own terms. In its initial cross over into white culture, R&B attracted a cult following among college and high school students. Its rhythm and forbidden thrills, though still contrasting sharply with the milquetoast sounds of Perry Como and company, had been made more palatable by gospel. White R&B fans could now accept the real thing, not covers.

Even though more and more people came to prefer R&B, the majors could not and did not start promoting the product; they seemed scarcely aware of the market. The indies—often using singers with regional appeal in a regional market—detected the trend more quickly. Largely through their efforts, some juke boxes began stocking R&B records, while white dance bands started to incorporate R&B hits in their sets. Whether through the efforts of the majors or the indies, singers and musicians like Chuck Berry, Bo Diddley, and Little Richard found themselves able to play African-American music *as* African-American music: no crooning sepia nonsense. Racial barriers were dissolving as sons of slaves and sons of Pilgrims broke sonic barriers to create the sound of rebellion and deliverance: rock 'n' roll.

Whatever their race, these artists were dependent upon the various media to get their music to the widest possible audience. The people who played rock 'n' roll could not have known they were making history, but they did know they were on to something new, something that broke with musical traditions. These early rock 'n' rollers were no navel-gazers: they were carnival sideshow entertainers with a product to sell and a get-rich-quick scheme: a number one record. The world of rock 'n' roll was not only a cultural and social expression but also a commercial network of musical commodities—singles and albums—which had to be recorded, distributed, and promoted.

Have You Heard the News?

The music industry has survived despite the appearance of successive new media that at one time or another seemed capable of subjugating it. Radio initially made the need to buy records appear obsolete—until swing music became so popular in the 1930s that a rush on records ensued. Later, television appeared to threaten the industry. Again, however, it endured (most recently by becoming a part of television through MTV). Recorded music has survived because of its unique ability to create an emotional bond between the listener and recorded sound. Everything else—the technology, the marketing, the profits—have resulted from that bond and its basic power.

During and after World War Two, the record industry, radio, and television all experienced changes that together radically altered the modes of musical production: new recording techniques and small-group recording budgets; new companies and a redefinition of the target audience; reductions in record prices; and a new affiliation with broadcast radio. The shift from 78 revolutions per minute to the $33^1/_3$ and 45 rpm speeds, a change in the sizes of records, the substitution of shellac by vinyl, and television's influence on radio station programming—each had an impact on the industry. Although its story cannot be reduced solely to technical innovations, rock 'n' roll did evolve out of and along with the technology of these media. What was new about rock 'n' roll was its relationship with the means of mass communication: record, radio, television, and film. American rock 'n' roll depended on the existence of these media and accepted them without compromise as a condition of artistic creativity.

This Year's Model

Notable technological improvements associated with the introduction of magnetic tape resulted in recording techniques which were not only inexpensive but which made both overdubbing (with remarkably improved microphones) and the correcting of mistakes possible. One pioneer was guitarist Les Paul, who by 1947 had started making 'sound-on-sound' recordings. Real multitrack recording was first used in 1954. Employing just two tracks, it was far from today's sixty-four track digital studios; the basic principle of studio music production—sound-on-sound—nevertheless remains unaltered. Multitrack technology was to influence both the sound and the structure of rock music, since a producer could now assemble the music from individually recorded parts in a final mix instead of reproducing a single take of a song: records no longer needed to be exact copies of live performances, rendering the large rooms previously employed for recording big band orchestras unnecessary. . . .

When the majors finally realized that rock 'n' roll was here to stay, they restructured their A&R departments and hired men who had a better feel for the sound and who understood the new standards. From this point on, the A&R men from the majors picked from the same flock of producers, song writers, arrangers, and session men as the indies.

The most conspicuous technological innovation triggered the 'Battle of the Speeds'. By 1948 CBS engineer Peter Goldmark had perfected the high fidelity long-playing record (LP), which reduced the playing speed from 78 to $33^1/_3$ rpm. With their low noise characteristics and extended duration, LPs transformed not only recording studios and the contents of records themselves, but also the industry's hierarchy, as Columbia first stole the lead on RCA only to see the latter respond with 45 rpm singles. The ascent of rock 'n' roll paralleled that of the 45 rpm single (along with the portable radio). Until the emergence of rock 'n' roll, and especially Elvis Presley, the 45 rpm single's role in popular music had been minimal. Aimed at the new teenage market and priced within reach of teenagers' pocket money, however, its popularity rose quickly.

Until rock 'n' roll appeared in the 1950s, radio programming had changed very little since the 1930s, when the friendly, conversational microphone styles of Al Jarvis at KFWB in Los Angeles, Martin Block at WNEW in New York, and Arthur Godfrey had first raised announcers to the status of 'personalities', who received as much attention from their listeners as the music they played. Jarvis pioneered the 'Make Believe Ballroom' format, which simulated the atmosphere of a ballroom through the use of real or contrived conversations with the performers and dancers. Block's use of this framework would engender *Your Hit Parade* and *Lucky Lager Dance Time*. Godfrey's irreverent style helped make the radio disc jockey someone not to be treated lightly; his early morning show attracted many listeners and thus numerous sponsors. Such sponsorship represented a commercialization of radio that would have profound consequences. When the American Tobacco Company started sponsoring *The Lucky Strike Hit Parade* nationwide, records began to be ranked according to their popularity. Air play became the most effective type of direct marketing. By the end of World War Two most singers, musicians, record companies, and sheet music publishers had become aware of the interaction between sales and air play. Record sales and taste trends increasingly engendered and reflected one another: each at once parasite on and host for the other; both having a symbiotic relationship with the charts (particularly *Billboard's*). A song could become a hit because a lot of people liked it and bought the record, and a lot of people liked a song and bought the record because it was a hit.

Since television during the 1950s rapidly took over the family entertainment role once held by radio, and since programs like *Monitor* (a weekend program of interviews, satire, and news features) proved failures, radio programming other than news broadcasts returned to the hands of station owners, who responded to the challenge of television by converting their stations to a 'Top-Forty' format in order to survive. Top-Forty programs shaped teenagers' perceptions of rock 'n' roll: music was ranked, and hits were important. Cheap, battery-driven portable radios made possible by transistor technology came on the market in 1954. Rock 'n' roll developed within a technological milieu increasingly beyond parental control. Teenagers' relative independence in deciding what they liked and what they wanted to listen to resulted in an age-specific audience, and rock 'n' roll developed on its audience's terms. . . . Between 1954 and 1959 the record industry increased its sales from $213,000,000 to $603,000,000. A large proportion of the increase in sales accrued to the indies, who made their break into the market by providing assorted kinds of rock 'n' roll. After the majors had dropped their 'race' and 'new jazz' artists during World War Two, the indies had moved into the 'race' market and begun recording rhythm and blues. In 1954 they extended their market to white kids as they developed distribution networks sufficient to give them as good a chance of having a hit with a new record as any of the majors; once they saw the possibilities of profit in rock 'n' roll, they recorded almost anybody singing almost anything and put all their energy and money into promoting

those records that seemed to stand a chance. The independents doubled their number of Top Ten hits between 1955 and 1956, then doubled them again by 1957. They succeeded in spotting and responding to the grassroots signs of rock 'n' roll's popularity partly because, unlike the majors, the indies often signed singers with regional or local appeal. . . . Although lacking the sales figures, budgets, and distribution facilities of the major music publishers, record companies, and radio networks, the indies nevertheless changed the direction of popular music and the structure of the record industry.

The indies had produced twice as many hits by the end of the decade as the majors, yet the struggle for survival never eased up. Few would survive the 1960s. Plagued by competition from bootleggers (who pirated copies of their hits) and always fighting to collect from their distributors, indie labels still had to pay 'consultancy fees' to disc jockeys, and the monthly overheads of staff and offices, on top of the costs of pressings. Sometimes their wisest move was to license a likely hit to larger companies like Mercury, ABC, or Dot (all of whom formed fruitful relationships with independent producers).

Through their influence over distribution networks, the majors effectively controlled most record stores, juke boxes, sheet music sales, and radio airplay. Slow to realize the closing of the American racial gap which accompanied and followed World War Two, the majors thus adopted a conservative strategy, deploying their sizeable resources to fight for the success of their established performers, mostly older artists from the dance band era still under five year contracts. The singers who operated under such contracts had to be musical chameleons and appeal to just about anyone (unlike rock 'n' roll madmen like Little Richard and Jerry Lee Lewis who were, by contrast, anything but malleable). The majors used their contract singers for the cover versions recorded, released, and promoted hot on the tail of R&B hits. The majors did renovate their commercial policy by releasing singles more quickly, while strengthening their promotion work by marketing from coast to coast. Confident in their market domination, however, they underestimated the ways in which a few radio disc jockeys who appreciated the power of rhythm and blues (such as Danny 'Cat Man' Stiles, Hal Jackson, and George 'Hound Dog' Lorenz) could penetrate the cracks of segregation and discrimination by playing it to anyone who would listen.

The majors slowly came to understand teenage record buyers, drop their traditional sales categories of popular music and rhythm and blues, and call anything that appealed to teenage record buyers 'rock 'n' roll'. When the majors finally acted, rock 'n' roll devolved into teenybopper music, designed for and chiefly bought by people between the ages of nine and twenty four, who determined what the record charts looked like by the manner in which they spent their own or their parents' money. When some seventeen-year-old Peggy Sue bought the latest hit single by the King, she cared little about the technology or money that had gone into its production and had little interest in knowing that she was dancing to a product made to be marketed and consumed for profit. She simply bought a record she *liked*. Her reasons for picking this particular record were, of course, influenced by many things—her age, gender, race, and social background as well as the forces of advertising and peer group pressure—which may have had little to do with the song itself. Later, as she grew older, the music would nevertheless bring back memories of those halcyon days and the experiences she and her friends had shared with a rock 'n' roll backdrop.

As the music industry itself matured, styles would change: from heavy to folk, from country to soft, from bubble gum to disco, from glitter to glam; all, however, were variations on the basic rock 'n' roll theme, products of industry attempts to sustain old or develop new markets, while kids tried to find a new sound that fit their world and their experiences. Musicians starting out as kids looking for new sounds came into the industry and developed new styles in the lacuna between the industry's creating and following trends. As a result, the various genres of rock music through the ages—and especially the records that came with them—had (and continue to have) one thing in common: what James Von Schilling has called the ability to 'capture in time a unique combination of music, performance, and artistry and then enable us to make this "timepiece" part of our personal experience'.

Afterword: Funeral Dirge American Pie

Legend has it that rock 'n' roll died. Estimates of the precise date differ, but most agree that at some point in the late 1950s rock 'n' roll passed away, only to be reborn as 'rock' in 1964 when the Beatles arrived in New York and Dylan went electric. . . .

Jody Pennington is an associate professor in the department of aesthetics and communication at the University of Aarhus in Denmark. He is the author of *Sex in American Film* (Praeger, 2007), and in 2008 served as president of the Denmark Association of American Studies.

Bruce Harrah-Conforth

Rock and Roll, Process, and Tradition

One of the most fascinating parts of being a folklorist is confronting the questions our discipline both evokes from the outside world and creates from its own interior dynamics. What is it that we do? What is the stuff we collect? And what do we do with it once we have it? I believe there would be general agreement among folklorists that at least one of our primary concerns is with tradition. Yet I have read and heard convincing arguments by leading psychologists calling tradition "The Dead Hope of Living People." How would we, as self-proclaimed celebrators of tradition, answer that assertion? Probably an equal number of folklorists would state that it is *process* that defines folklore, but to me this term appears to be no less anxiety-ridden than is tradition. Process has been used to describe everything from the sublime to the mystic; from the simple enumeration of performance traits to a super-organicism that seems to have folklore creating itself. How do we utilize these two ideas—tradition and process? How do we make them palatable to our discipline, unveiling of the workings of human culture, and usefully explanatory to the world-at-large? Further, how do we address the oft-heard belief that mass-media is graying our culture, destroying our folklore?

Paradoxically, I believe that the answers to these questions may be obtained by examining those items of cultural creation which are most often *not* understood in folkloric terms. No place is better to find out what folklore is, I believe, than where many people think it is not: contemporary mass-culture and in this case, rock and roll.

One of the elements that appears to make both process and tradition such elusive creatures is their context, for their roots begin long before the emergence of a recognizable focal point, such as a folk group, community, or specific cultural products. One can get a good idea of this notion of a continuum of process by examining the factors which contributed to the creation of the 1960s "hip" youth culture, or psychedelia.

The development of the 1960s counterculture had its roots in several historical factors: economics, technology, youth itself, politics, and culture. Perhaps first and foremost, however, was the change in numbers of America's young. Here the true seeds of the "process" of the 1960s hip community were, quite literally, born. In the first year after World War II, 1946, two and a quarter million couples were married, more than twice as many as in any previous year. Accompanying this nuptual increase was what has been called a "Procreation Ethic" (Jones, 1980).

The results of this new ethic were that in one year's time alone, 1945–46, the number of births jumped 19 percent. Between 1946 and 1947 the increase was 12 percent. During the years 1948 through 1953 more babies were born than in the previous thirty years. By the 1960s, therefore, there were more teenagers and young adults than ever before.

On the economic front, middle class white America, the group primarily responsible for the baby boom, was also flourishing as never before. The median income for white families (in constant dollars) nearly tripled between 1947 and 1968, and importantly, much of the attention of this new prosperity was directed toward, the new American youth.

This enormous new consumer audience, without ever being aware of it, was part of an historical process that was forever altering the face of American life, for as the marketplace shifted its focus to the attention of youth and their parents' dollars, the focus of American life also shifted to youth. And with that focus came power.

By holding the purse strings of the economy, America's youth were gaining the power to influence style, art, culture, politics, and all the elements of daily life hitherto mandated by their parents and other adults. A paradigm shift had begun toward a new youth-oriented culture. Assisting this new paradigm were the increasing numbers of America's college population. In 1950 only 13 percent of 18 to 24 year-olds were enrolled in college. By 1968 that figure had risen to 30.3 percent.

Although the paradigm was shifting to the young, all was not a bed of roses, for the baby boomers were also the first generation to live with the hauntingly pervasive anxiety that their lives might be instantaneously wiped out in a flash of white light: the only warning that a nuclear attack had occurred.

Though they had the world in the palm of their hands the young were also acutely aware that the Cold War could someday turn hot and not just snatch that world out of their palms, but turn their palms to cinder and ash. This existence of duality provided a foregrounding of the duality they eventually saw in the hypocrisy of America's attitude toward Civil Rights, sexual mores, the drive for capital, the Viet Nam war, and most of the sacred cows associated with what their parents would call "The Good Life."

In spite of these and other profound social changes and powers, however, the young in America were still denied the one thing they needed most: tradition and ritual, an initiation out of the naivete of youth and into the new role and status of socio-cultural power brokers.

Sometime during the nascent days of the hip youth movement someone suggested that, there is no such thing as the generation gap, there is but the absence of the rites of passage. This simple statement offers a means of understanding the youth revolution of the 1960s and begins to put its attendant socio-cultural underpinnings in perspective. The lack of American rites of initiation into adulthood contributed vastly to a situation which saw many members of America's youth set about to use their new-found power to produce their own circumstances in which a model of transitional ritual and social role-playing could be enacted to their needs and desires. This desire to reorder one's socio-cultural surroundings in a manner that is manipulable, understandable, and relevant to one's own life represents not only our deepest human traits, but lies at the heart of all folkloric process. The often elusive object of our folkloric studies lives within this realm of human action: more correctly a complex of action, manufactured by our own biochemical make-up and our culture-specific choices selected from the set of options offered to us by our biogenetics. This biogenetic base, described in the work of Eugene d'Aquili (1983, 1986), Charles Laughlin, Jr. (1975), and Victor Turner (1983), states in essence that, due to the very chemical workings of our brains, human beings have no choice but to construct [folklore] to explain their world in what often appears to be a capricious universe. Whenever this construction occurs, when this socio-cultural reordering is present, so too is folklore. How does this fit into a discussion of rock and roll and folk music? The answer lies in the simple fact that rock and roll, like all human products, has the capability of being used as a tool to both reorder and make sense out of that "capricious universe." And that, I will now address, is precisely what members of the 1960s hip community did.

Important to the reordering of our circumstances into folkloric modes is the creation of mutual identity, a sense of community. And important to the notion of community is a place in which its members feel safe to commune with one another and sense common bonds. The ceremonial behavior of ritual action accomplishes these ends. As sociologist Herbert Blumer has stated:

> . . . the paraphernalia of ritual possessed by every movement serves to foster feelings of common identity and sympathy. This paraphernalia consists of a set of sentimental symbols, such as slogans, songs, cheers, poems, hymns, expressive gestures, and uniforms. Every movement has some of these (Blumer, 1978).

The 60s hip community was no exception: it had slogans, "Turn On, Tune In, Drop Out," or "May the Baby Jesus Shut Your Mouth and Open Your Mind"; it clearly had songs; it had cheers, often obscure like the Digger's "Oooooooh, Aaaaaahhhh," or the mystic Buddhist chants supplied by Allen Ginsberg; it had poems written for it by Ginsberg, Michael McClure and others which appeared in *The Oracle*, the community paper; it had hymns like "Hare Krishna, Hare Krishna"; it had expressive gestures: the peace sign, the clenched fist; and it certainly had uniforms. And perhaps foremost, it had a church in which these elements were all unified: the church of rock and roll performance as manifested in the rock and roll venues, San Francisco's Fillmore Auditorium and Avalon Ballroom.

Within this area of rock and roll performance the hip community found a haven for the free expression and communal integration of their rituals of bonding. The patterns which were displayed in this expression linked the community with ritual design that is timeless, for the entirety of action surrounding the hip rock concert/ballroom scene corresponded to the traditional patterns of ritual.

To conceive of modern cultural performance as ritual may at first seem strange, but as Victor Turner had described, "Ritual is . . . a synchronization of many performance genres . . . All the senses of participants and performers may be engaged; they hear music and prayers, see visual symbols, taste consecrated foods, smell incense, and touch sacred persons and objects. They also have available the kinesthetic forms of dance and gesture" (Turner, 1982).

A better description of the ballroom performances could not be written. Turner's statement that "All the senses of participants and performers may be engaged" is particularly appropriate here, for not only were there bands to fill the ears, but light shows to fill the eyes, consecrated foods (Electric Acid Kool-Aid [LSD], and marijuana) to fill the taste, incense and marijuana to fill the nose, and dancing and caressing to fill the touch. Aesthetically, therefore, it is easy to see how the ballroom scene could replicate the trappings of ritual. Examining the concept and principles of rites of transition and intensification, helps explain how the ballroom concerts clearly functioned as rituals.

Arnold Van Gennep defined "rites de passage" as rituals marked by three phases: separation, limen, and aggregation. The first phase consists of certain symbolic behavior detaching the participants from either a "fixed point in the social structure or a set of cultural conditions." The second, or liminal phase, corresponds to an ambiguity of self. It is "a time and place lodged between all times and spaces defined and governed in any specific biocultural ecosystem by the rules of law, politics, and religion." The third phase consummates the ritual and returns the participants to a new state (Turner, 1967).

Advancing Van Gennep's theory, other scholars have noted that rites of passage rituals may serve as metaphors for community life. Yvonne Lockwood's work on the sauna as an expression of Finnish-American identity has shown that rites of passage may become the "manifestation and reassertion of . . . ethnic identity" (Lockwood, 1978). Robert S. McCarl has pointed out that formalistic interpretations of ritual as manifest transitional states may lose sight of their true esoteric function. Rather, he states that ritual should be viewed as a process that "explore[s] the boundaries of cultural experience . . . [through] . . . an intensification of meaning derived from the performance of everyday [expressive resources] in a ritual context" (McCarl, 1984). Also expanding Van Gennep's work, Elliot Chappie and Carleton Coon originated the concept of "rites of intensification": those group actions which "mobilize, focus, and intensify those elements within a culture's life course which must be routinely renewed so that orderly process and growth may be maintained" (Wallace, 1966). The ballroom/concert experience was constructed in such a way as to serve as a weekly "rite of intensification" into, reflecting, and renewing the ecstatic state of hippie life.

When one entered the Fillmore Auditorium or Avalon Ballroom it was tantamount to entering a church in that it was a "safe place," a "sanctuary" for the new community. Removed from the incursions of the parent society it was a domain specifically designed as a place apart from the usual trappings of "normal" existence. It was a place in which community members could "freak freely." The rooms were large and seatless caverns of Victorian architecture. They were dark and full of corners and balconies in which all sorts of behavior could, and often did, occur. They were also refitted with the accouterments of the counter culture so as to accommodate the light shows and other multi-media additions to the entirety of the performance/ritual. These rock and roll sanctuaries created a separation from the outside and provided a gradual immersion into the new space of the ballroom by a variety of means: giving attendees free gifts (sometimes a simple token like a piece of fruit, more often than not a souvenir post card replicating the psychedelic poster for that week's performance), the burning of incense, and the gradual immersion into the performance itself. The bands' performances were framed by the showing of fantasy movies or cartoons, or the appearance of wandering jugglers of acrobats.

The second or liminal stage was the bombardment of the senses by the intensity of the performance coupled with the freedom of the sanctuary. This complex allowed the participants to reach ecstatic states. The overwhelming sounds of the bands assaulted the ears; the light shows struck unfamiliar, remarkable images over the whole of the assemblage; the unbounded dance patterns permitted people to reach their peaks in groups or alone; and the assorted smells and sensations found within the sanctuary bombarded the rest of the senses. Add to this the fact that many of the participants in the ballroom scene were generally under the influence of some type of psychedelic drug, sufficient in itself to replicate the liminal state, and it is easy to see the power within these structured events.

The third phase, or aggregation, was accomplished by the framing of the end of the performance. Encores were a routine occurrence, and as such prepared the participants for the end of the event. The finale was usually followed by a return to the same kind of occurrences that preceded the event: showing of movies or cartoons, people circulating throughout the audience, or being given another gift upon leaving. These elements served to ease the participants back into their surrounding environs and to allow them to take a piece of the event with them: a tangible piece of evidence that they were, in fact, changed: they were members of a shared, unique experience.

The performance of rock and roll within this context of holistic ritual, however, serves as but one portion of a traditional event. Those critics who have failed to see rock and roll as anything but a mass-market commodity have extracted the item from the process, for within the realm of the folk community and its attendant rituals, even the standardized rock and roll product—the record album—may function as a portion of the folk process.

Although centered around the ballroom experience, these rituals, like those of traditional folk groups, extended into the home. While no rock and roll band could physically follow community members into their homes for the continuation of community ritual on a personalized basis, their recordings, as icons of the rites of passage, could.

The record album existed as an icon within the context of the hip counter culture. In line with Marshall Fishwick's description of icon, the record album was an amalgam of ". . . images and ideas converted into three dimensions. They [were] admired artifacts, external expressions of internal convictions. . ." (Fishwick, 1970).

Albums and their packaging were slices of the ritual life that surrounded the counter culture. A sampling of early hip albums uncovers a wealth of information about the culture that spawned them. The first Grateful Dead album had its cover designed by Alton "Mouse" Kelly, one of the best known psychedelic poster artists, and true to the genre, was an amalgam of psychedelic symbols: flowing, amorphous lettering, runic script, a colorful photo montage, and strange Indian deities all foregrounding a solar flare. The back cover is an equally disturbing design in which a photo of the group is reproduced in positive and negative mirror images with the negative image containing the only legible writing. The first Country Joe and the Fish album cover featured four full-color photos of a ballroom light show. Similar themes were explored on other album covers, but a highlight of album art/design was the poem written by high priest of LSD, Augustus Stanley Owsley III, for the back cover of Blue Cheer's debut album, *Vincebus Eruptum* (the name Blue Cheer, by the way, was also the name of a powerful form of LSD which was manufactured by Owsley):

> ON
> ONOFF
> ONOFF
> ONOFF
> ONOFF
> OMMMMMM
> The ground of BEING
> CHANGE
> The sound of TIME
> LIFE
> Seek the UNREVEALED
> LOVE
> Dance the WONDER yet concealed
> AID
> Subtle color of the MIND
> BLUE
> CHEER
>
> . . . .Owsley

The message of the poem is quite obscure, meaningful only to those who would also recognize the name of Owsley as the producer of extremely high-grade LSD. But that is precisely the point. Unlike previous record albums, which as products of a mass-market system were geared at reaching as many people as possible, the albums of the bands of the hip community, although also products of that same system, were aimed at a specific group that could understand and utilize the special information contained on their covers and in their songs.

When a community member put on one of these albums it served as a recreation of the community ritual played out in the ballroom churches. The album covers became true icons in the sense that one would study them, pass them around, and try to understand them. They might be prominently displayed during the album's playing. They served, in a sense, as proxy band members: pictures and symbols to replicate the actual experience of seeing the bands in person. Putting on an album also entailed many of the same rituals as attending a church/ballroom performance: the initial framing often signified a separation from the outer world. This often took place through the rolling of joints to be smoked while listening to the album, placing a rug or towel in front of the door to prevent the aroma of marijuana from seeping into the hall, moving the furniture so that dancing could take place, turning the lights off, or turning black lights on, lighting candles, and so on. In many ways, therefore, although the albums were mass-produced and standardized, they were traditionalized by the community, much like many other objects, to serve as bearers of subcultural identity. The continual, and in this case ritual, re-employment of these objects in a folkloric manner enabled them to become a part of the folklore "process." That they were, as items, singularly unfolkloric, does not matter. As a part of the action of living folklore they were employed, and served as much a folkloric function, as any hand-made artifact graced with the official sanction of "folkdom."

This note has addressed two points: that folklore is a combination of social and biogenetic forces, and that even mass-produced items can be traditionalized by communities in order that they may function as folk items. The performances of rock and roll within the hip community were such that the music was only a part of a larger, ritualistic event, purposely designed as a means of acting as a community rite. The setting, framing, and carrying out of performances at the rock and roll ballrooms closely paralleled that which is involved in the creation of traditional rites of passage and the creation of sanctuary, or church. Finally, the commercial products of these bands, while mass-produced and standardized, were employed by members of the community as iconic symbols for the larger experience of the counter culture and were utilized within their own homes as a form of church ritual by proxy. The hip rock and roll community, in true folkloric fashion, molded its resources, commercial or not, into a rich tapestry of folkloric process: the true nature of folklore as an articulation of culture and its resources.

Was this an isolated instance? Is rock and roll really fulfilling a folkloric need? Preliminary research I have done with punk, heavy metal, and speed metal bands indicates that the same reordering of society and culture is present in their respective communities. Is this a conscious articulation of a group's folk needs? To answer that I quote Mark Fisher, designer of the Rolling Stones current "Steel Wheels" tour. The design of the stage the Stones are using must reflect, in Mr. Fisher's own words, "a magic and tribal identity. . . . [it must] transform a football stadium into a temple for a night" (Brown, 1989).

Is tradition the "Dead Hope of Living People?" Quite the contrary; it is really a living hope, endowed by the past with the spark of life. Passed from one generation to another, it serves as a method for making the most of our life resources. What is process? An ongoing continuum of human biogenetics and cultural choice. How do we make these terms useful? By using them to demonstrate that contemporary society and culture is not shocking or alien, but merely a technologically new continuation of time-honored activities. Is our culture graying? Are we losing our folk traditions? Only if we are too blind to search for them in the newly emerging forms, vibrantly alive, all about us.

Indiana University
Bloomington, Indiana

References Cited

Blumer, Herbert. 1978. Elementary Collective Groupings. *Collective Behavior and Social Movements*, ed. Louis E. Genevie. Itasca: Peacock Publishers.

Brown, Patricia Leigh. 1989. For the Stones, A Stage Set Built of Steel and Magic. *New York Times* (October 5) n.p.

d'Aquili, Eugene. 1983. The Myth-Ritual Complex: A Biogenetic Structural Analysis. *Zygon* 18:247–268.

_____. 1986. Myth, Ritual and the Archetypal Hypothesis. *Zygon* 21:141–160.

Fishwick, Marshall. 1970. Entrance. In *Icons of Popular Culture*, ed. Marshall Fishwick and Ray B. Browne. Bowling Green: Bowling Green University Popular Press.

Jones, Landon Y. 1980. *Great Expectations: America and the Baby Boom Generation*. New York: Coward, McMann and Goohegan.

Laughlin, Charles, Jr. 1975. The Biopsychological Determinants of Religious Ritual Behavior. *Zygon* 10:32–58.

Lockwood, Yvonne. 1978. The Sauna: An Expression of Finnish-American Identity. *Studies in Folklore and Ethnicity*, ed. Larry Danielson. Los Angeles: California Folklore Society.

McCarl, Robert S. 1984. Performance in Fire Fighting Culture. *Journal of American Folklore* 97:395–422.

Turner, Victor. 1967. *The Forest of Symbols*. Ithaca: Cornell University Press.

_____. 1983. Body, Brain, Culture. *Zygon* 18:221–245.

Wallace, Anthony F. C. 1966. *Religion: An Anthropological View*. New York: Random House.

BRUCE HARRAH-CONFORTH was curator for the Rock and Roll Hall of Fame in Cleveland and, later, a professor in the American Studies Department at the University of Michigan in Ann Arbor, Michigan. He is the author of *African American Folksong and American Cultural Politics: The Lawrence Gellert Story* (2013).

EXPLORING THE ISSUE

Was Rock and Roll Responsible for Dismantling America's Traditional Family, Sexual, and Racial Customs in the 1950s and 1960s?

Critical Thinking and Reflection

1. Critically evaluate the controversy surrounding the effects of rock and roll music on society's values in the 1950s and 1960s.
2. Describe cover records. Explain how these records reflected the racial values of white Americans in the 1950s.
3. Compare and contrast the two major disc jockeys of rock and roll in the 1950s—Alan Freed and Dick Clark. Why was Freed driven to alcoholism and an early death while Clark sustained a successful career into the twenty-first century?
4. Explain why Elvis Presley was the key rock and roll figure of the 1950s? Could rock and roll have taken off and existed as the main form of popular music from the mid-1950s to the present without Elvis?
5. Discuss whether rock and roll influences the concerns and values of today's youth? Explain and compare with the concerns and values of the previous six decades of values.
6. In what ways, if any, did the youth use rock and roll to adhere to or perpetuate the norms and traditions of their parents?

Is There Common Ground?

Most historians agree on the basic facts surrounding the origins of rock and roll. They may disagree on details such as who were the first singers identified with rock and roll, but clearly by the mid-fifties a group of southern singers like Jerry Lee Lewis, Chuck Berry, and Elvis Presley fused rhythm and blues, country western and black gospel into a new form of music. The disagreement centers around the social impact of this music and whether local leaders and governmental authorities overreacted to rock and roll music by breaking up rock concerts and pressuring disc jockeys to stop playing rock music on the radio. Were the adolescents of the 1950s merely a younger generation in a traditional rebellion against the authority of their parents? Or was this generation in the process of breaking down the traditional norms of the family leading to the counterculture and political revolts of the 1960s?

Additional Resources

Matthew F. Delmont, *The Nicest Kids in Town: American Bandstand, Rock 'n' Roll, and the Struggle for Civil Rights in 1950s Philadelphia* (University of California Press, 2012).

Peter Guralnick, *Last Train to Memphis: The Rise of Elvis Presley* (Back Bay Books, 1994).

John A. Jackson, *Big Beat Heat: Alan Freed and the Early Years of Rock & Roll* (Schirmer Books, 1991).

John A. Jackson, *American Bandstand: Dick Clark and the Making of a Rock 'n' Roll Empire* (Oxford University Press, 1998).

Sean Wilenz, *Bob Dylan in America* (Doubleday, 2010).

Internet References . . .

Rock and Roll Museum—Cleveland

www.Cleveland.com/rockhall

Rock & Roll Music—YouTube

www.youtube.com/watch?v=IH8lrcvdID8

Rock and Roll Music—Listen Free at Last.fm

www.last.fm/tag/rock%20and%20roll

Selected, Edited, and with Issue Framing Material by:
Kevin R. Magill and Tony L. Talbert, *Baylor University*

ISSUE

Did President John F. Kennedy Cause the Cuban Missile Crisis?

YES: Thomas G. Paterson, from "When Fear Ruled: Rethinking the Cuban Missile Crisis," *New England Journal of History* (1995)

NO: Robert Weisbrot, from "Maximum Danger: Kennedy, the Missiles, and the Crisis of American Confidence," Ivan R. Dee, Publisher (2001)

Learning Outcomes

After reading this issue, you will be able to:

- Understand Premier Khrushchev's reasons for putting Soviet missiles in Cuba in the summer of 1962.
- Understand President Kennedy's response to the missiles placed in Cuba.
- Understand the traditional and revisionist interpretations of the Cuban missile crisis.
- Understand the impact of the newly declassified documents—such as minutes of the meetings and conferences between former American and Soviet officials—in changing our perceptions about decision making in the Oval Office.
- Understand the impact of the concepts of "crisis management" and "nation building" in the formation of our foreign/policy.

ISSUE SUMMARY

YES: Professor Thomas G. Paterson believes that President Kennedy, even though he moderated the American response and compromised in the end, helped precipitate the Cuban missile crisis by his support for both the failed Bay of Pigs invasion in April 1961 and the continued attempts by the CIA to assassinate Fidel Castro.

NO: Historian Robert Weisbrot argues that the new sources uncovered in the past 20 years portray Kennedy as a president who had not only absorbed the values of his time as an anti-Communist cold warrior but who nevertheless acted as a rational leader and was conciliatory toward the Soviet Union in resolving the Cuban missile crisis.

In 1959, the political situation in Cuba changed drastically when Fulgencio Batista y Zaldi'var was overthrown by a 34-year-old revolutionary named Fidel Castro, who led a guerilla band in the Sierra Maestra mountain range. Unlike his predecessors, Castro refused to be a lackey for American political and business interests. The new left-wing dictator seized control of American oil refineries and ordered a number of diplomats at the U.S. embassy in Havana to leave the country. President Dwight

D. Eisenhower was furious and responded shortly before he left office by imposing economic sanctions on the island and breaking diplomatic ties.

Eisenhower's successor, John F. Kennedy, supported an invasion of Cuba by a group of disaffected anti-Castro Cuban exiles that had been planned by the previous administration to foster the overthrow of Castro. The April 1961 Bay of Pigs invasion was a disaster as Castro's army routed the invaders, killing many and imprisoning others. The Kennedy administration responded by securing

Cuba's removal from the Organization of American States (OAS) in early 1962, imposed an economic embargo on the island, and carried out threatening military maneuvers in the Caribbean.

The isolation and possibility of a second invasion of this Caribbean communist client state probably influenced Soviet Premier Nikita Khrushchev to take a more proactive stance to defend Cuba. In the summer of 1962, he sent troops and conventional weapons to the island; by September 1962, missile launching pads had been installed. President Kennedy confronted criticism from Republicans, such as Senator Kenneth Keating of New York, who charged that the Russians were bringing not only troops but also nuclear weapons to Cuba. At first, Kennedy was concerned with the political implications of the charges for the 1962 congressional races, and on September 11, 1962, he assured reporters that the Cuban military buildup was primarily defensive in nature.

President Kennedy was probably caught off-guard with Khrushchev's bold actions in Cuba in the fall of 1962. Did Khrushchev want to compensate for the Russian "missile gap"? Did he want to trade Russia's withdrawal from Cuba with the American withdrawal from Berlin? Did Khrushchev wish to provide Cuba with military protection from another U.S. invasion? Forty years later, with much more evidence available from the Cuban and Russian participants in these events, Khrushchev's motives are still the subject of debate. President Kennedy, like most policymakers, had to make his decision to blockade Cuba on the basis of the best available information at the time.

The situation changed drastically on the morning of October 16, 1962, when National Security Council adviser McGeorge Bundy informed the president that photographs from U-2 reconnaissance flights over Cuba revealed that the Russians were building launching pads for 1,000-mile medium-range missiles as well as 2,200-mile intermediate-range missiles. The president kept the news quiet. He ordered more U-2 flights to take pictures and had Bundy assemble a select group of advisers who became known as the Executive Committee of the National Security Council (Ex-Comm). For six days and nights, the president favored a blockade, or what he called a "quarantine," of the island. On October 22, 1962, Kennedy revealed his plans for the quarantine over national television.

Mark J. White has succinctly summarized the resolution of the Cuban missile crisis in the introduction to his edited collection of documents entitled *The Kennedys and Cuba: The Declassified Documentary History* (Ivan R. Dee, 1999). "During the second week of the crisis," writes White, "from JFK's October 22 address to the achievement of a settlement six days later, Kennedy and Khrushchev initially fired off messages to each other, defending their own positions and assailing their adversary's. But a series of developments from October 26 to 28 suddenly brought the crisis to an end." Khrushchev offered to remove the missiles if the American president promised not to invade Cuba and removed the Jupiter missiles that the United States had installed along the Soviet border in Turkey. Kennedy publically promised not to invade Cuba and privately agreed to withdraw the missiles in Turkey, an arrangement that satisfied Khrushchev and brought an end to the most dangerous episode of the entire Cold War era.

Was President Kennedy responsible for the Cuban missile crisis? Professor Thomas Paterson, one of the best known revisionist diplomatic historians, has authored numerous books and articles critical of America's Cold War policies in Europe and Cuba, and is quite critical of what he sees as JFK's fumbling efforts to resolve the crisis via diplomacy. First he challenges the "Camelot image" of Kennedy as the hero who avoided nuclear war by negotiating a settlement with the Russians to take the missiles out of Cuba, thereby avoiding a military confrontation. In Paterson's view, Kennedy's reckless personal behavior was also carried out in his professional life. The president, according to Paterson, was looking for a way to manage the crisis. Rejecting the choices of Eisenhower, who wavered between threats of nuclear retaliation or doing nothing, Kennedy believed a third way, involving the use of "special forces" like the Green Berets, might alter the balance of power in the attempt to "nation build" third-world countries to favor the western way over the communist alternative. (The reader is not far off the mark if he perceives similar policies being pursued in Iraq and Afghanistan today.) Paterson admits that the Khrushchev–Castro decision to place missiles in Cuba "ranks as one of the most dangerous in the Cold War." Yet, he blames the policies of the Eisenhower–Kennedy administrations for this decision. As Paterson writes, "Had there been no exile expeditions at the Bay of Pigs, no destructive covert activities, no assassination plots, no military maneuvers and plans, and no economic and diplomatic steps to harass, isolate and destroy the Castro government, there would not have been a Cuban missile crisis." Was Kennedy's response a triumph of effective crisis management? Not in Paterson's view. "In the end," he says, "the two superpowers, frantic to avoid nuclear war and scared by the prospects of doomsday, stumbled toward a settlement."

In the NO selection, Professor Robert Weisbrot rejects both the earlier portraits of Kennedy partisans that JFK was an "effective crisis manager" and the assessments of critics who discern in the president's foreign policy "a dismal amalgam of anti-communist hysteria, reckless posturing, and a disturbing gleeful crisis orientation." Relying on new evidence made available over the past 20 years, such as the declassified Ex-Comm conversations and the transcripts of several conferences involving Soviet and American scholars and former officials (including Cuba's Castro), Weisbrot sees Kennedy not as a cold warrior but as a rational leader who defused the crisis. Concluding that Kennedy was neither the lone crisis hero as his chief speech writer Ted Sorenson portrayed him in *The Kennedy Legacy* (Macmillan, 1969) nor a macho anticommunist counterrevolutionary as many revisionists have insisted, Weisbrot credits a number of other participants for softening the crisis. Secretary of State Dean Rusk, for example, was not the "silent Buddha" as portrayed in the writings of earlier Kennedy admirers. It was Rusk who revealed that Kennedy's fall-back plan was to have U.N. Secretary General U. Thant propose a swap of missiles in Turkey and Cuba. It was Llewellyn Thompson, the former ambassador to the Soviet Union, and not Robert Kennedy who suggested accepting Khrushchev's tacit proposals and not the harsher terms of his public demands. Then there was Kennedy's National Security Adviser McGeorge Bundy who acknowledged: "The most important part of crisis management is not to have a crisis, because there's no telling what will happen once you're in one." Scott D. Sagan's, *Limits of Safety: Organizations, Accidents and Nuclear Weapons* (Princeton University, 1985), lists a number of potential disasters, which Professor Weisbrot recounts, that occurred during the Cuban missile crisis, some of which even President Kennedy was not aware. The real failure of crisis management occurred later, Weisbrot believes, when the Kennedy–Johnson team, full of exuberance over their success in Cuba, believed they could manage similar crises in Southeast Asia.

YES ⬅

Thomas G. Paterson

When Fear Ruled: Rethinking the Cuban Missile Crisis

Nikita Khrushchev cried and then rushed to the American Embassy in Moscow to sign the book of condolence. Fidel Castro remarked, again and again, "This is bad news," and then turned silent. In Bremen, Germany, a "sea of flowers" engulfed the U.S. consulate, and in Nice, France, construction crews stopped working. A Czech citizen asked: "Who will lead us now?" Europeans were left, said one of them, "Like children in the darkness."

"He glittered when he lived," wrote one of John F. Kennedy's admiring assistants and biographers, Arthur M. Schlesinger, Jr. "Everyone around him thought he had the Midas touch and could not lose." "It can be said of him," eulogized one editorial, "that he did not fear the weather, and did not trim his sails, but instead challenged the wind itself . . . to cause it to blow more softly and more kindly over the world and its people." "The man was magic," a congressman recalled, "He lit up a room. He walked in, and the air was lighter, the light was brighter."

In a time of wrenching turmoil at home and abroad, President John F. Kennedy, for people everywhere, represented hope, youthful energy, courage, determination, compassion, and innovative leadership. He envisioned a new order to pry America out of its doldrums, to get it moving again, as he so often put it. He had won popular approval from the American people and he had touched people abroad, becoming for many a legitimate hero. His wit, eloquent oratory, self-confident style, athleticism, and handsome looks captivated a generation seeking the light at the end of the tunnel. "Though I never met him, I knew him just the same," went the words of a song by the musical group, The Byrds. "He was a friend of mine."

Some thirty years after Kennedy's death, such words still resonate among Americans who feel the anguish of dashed hopes—their slain leader losing his chance to make a difference, taking with him the promise of a better future. Yet, now, we also have more perspective on the tumultuous decade of the sixties. We have had the terrible experience of Vietnam, many frightening Cold War confrontations, and the Watergate and Iron-Contra scandals to make us more skeptical of our leaders and more searching in our assessments. Most important, we now have what must undergird any careful account of the Kennedy era—declassified documents from the Kennedy Library in Boston, the Central Intelligence Agency, and East German and Soviet archives, among others. The massive documentary record, although incomplete, has generated scholarly studies that peel back the layers of once hidden stories, expose complexities, separate image from reality, and compel us to contend with a less satisfying past than the one we would prefer and have imagined. The positive images Kennedy's advisers so skillfully broadcast—the cosmetic cream of celebration that covered his blemishes—have not altogether disappeared but they have faded. We have more balance, more insight, more evidence. Our portrait of John F. Kennedy has become necessarily less flattering. Such is the nature of always evolving historical research and interpretation, although we can take no comfort from it.

We now have an unadorned Kennedy, a whole Kennedy, a very human Kennedy, whose character, judgment, and accomplishments have been called into question. The demythologizing of John F. Kennedy, for example, includes a reconsideration of the image of the family man. Although Kennedy genuinely loved his children, he was a brazen, reckless womanizer who named the women he wanted for sex and usually got them, including Hollywood starlets and Judith Campbell Exner, mistress to crime bosses as well as to the President. This is the stuff of sensationalism, of course, but these sexual indiscretions also endangered national security, his presidency, and his health. Kennedy, moreover, was gravely ill. Had the voting public known the extent of his ailments in 1960—especially his Addison's disease and severe back pain, for which he took injections of concoctions of amphetamines, steroids, calcium, and vitamins administered by a discredited doctor—had the public known, they may not have taken the risk of sending him to the White House. His reputation as a writer has also encountered the test of evidence. His book, *Profiles in Courage,* published in 1955, for which he took personal credit and won a Pulitzer Prize, was actually written for him by an aide and a university professor.

The 1960 presidential candidate who criticizing the Eisenhower Administration for permitting the Soviets to gain missile superiority—the famed charge of a "missile gap"—became the President who learned that the United States held overwhelming nuclear supremacy—yet he nonetheless tremendously expanded the American nuclear arsenal. CIA officers, believing that they were carrying out presidential instructions, tried to assassinate Cuba's Fidel Castro and send sabotage teams to destroy life and property on the island. For a President who said that Americans should "never fear to negotiate," Kennedy seemed more enamored with military than with diplomatic means: defense expenditures increased thirteen percent in the Kennedy years, counter-insurgency training and warfare accelerated, and U.S. intervention in Vietnam deepened.

Given the disparity between image and reality and the inevitable reinterpretation that new documentation and distance from events stimulate, it is not surprising that ambiguity now marks Kennedy scholarship. He appears as both confrontationist and conciliator, hawk and dove, decisive leader and hesitant improviser, hyperbolic politician and prudent diplomat, poor crisis preventer but good crisis manager, idealist and pragmatist, glorious hero and flawed man of dubious character. On the one hand he sponsored the Peace Corps, and on the other he attended personally to the equipment needs of the Green Berets. On the one hand he called for an appreciation of Third World nationalism, and on the other he intervened in Vietnam and Cuba to try to squash nationalist movements he found unacceptable. He said that the United States respected neutralism, yet he strove to persuade important neutrals such as India, Indonesia, and Egypt to shed their non-alignment for alliance with the United States in the Cold War.

Kennedy preached democracy, but sent military aid to oppressive Latin American regimes, and the Alliance for Progress did not meet its goals because it shored up elites, who took the money for their own purposes. He said he knew that the Sino-Soviet split compelled a new policy toward the People's Republic of China, but he spoke often about a monolithic Communism and rejected options to improve relations with the PRC. On the one hand he created the Arms Control and Disarmament Agency, and on the other expanded the number of American intercontinental ballistic missiles from some 60 to more than 420. On the one hand, seeing Eastern Europe as the "Achilles heel of the Soviet empire" and discarding John Foster

Dulles' provocative and failed policy of "liberation," he strove for improved relations with Soviet Russia's neighbors. But on the other he signed a trade bill that denied most-favored-nation treatment to Yugoslavia. On the one hand he called for a new Atlantic community, and on the other he refused to share decision-making power with increasingly disgruntled Western European allies.

Some analysts have argued that had Kennedy lived and won reelection in 1964, he would have withdrawn from Vietnam and transformed the Cold War from confrontation to peace and disarmament. Some Kennedy-watchers have emphasized that the President was evolving as a leader; that is, through education imposed by crises, Kennedy grew and began to temper his ardent Cold War anti-Communism, learning the limits of American power. "The heart of the Kennedy legend," the journalist James Reston has aptly noted, "is what might have been." We can never be sure about what Kennedy might have done, but we do know what he *did.* And that is were we must focus our attention—on the Kennedy *record.* Was it "stunningly successful," as one writer has claimed, or was it something quite less—high on image, but mixed if not low on results?

The centerpiece in the Kennedy record is his handling of the Cuban missile crisis. His role in this disturbing crisis—the closest the United States and the Soviet Union ever came to nuclear war—has especially undergone scrutiny in the last few years. Recent international conferences, featuring Kennedy-era decisionmakers, and the declassification of documents in Russia, Cuba, and the United States give us a new, more textured view of Kennedy and the missile crisis. It may be true, as Secretary of State Dean Rusk remembered, that "President Kennedy had ice water in his veins," but serious doubts have emerged about whether this event ranks as his "finest hour."

This dangerous moment in world history should not be championed as a supreme display of crisis management, calculated control, and statesmanship, but rather explored as a case of near misses that scared the crisis managers on both sides into a settlement because, in the words of National Security Affairs Adviser McGeorge Bundy, the crisis was "so near to spinning out of control."

New evidence also prompts us to investigate the Cuban missile crisis not as a simple good guys–bad guys drama foisted on the United States by an aggressive Soviet Union and crazed Castroite Cuba, but as a crisis for which Kennedy policies must bear some responsibility. This article plumbs the origins of the crisis, Kennedy's management of it, and the outcome, the "narrow squeak" that it was.

Those hair-trigger days of October 1962, stand out in the drama of the Cold War. Before that quaking month, the Soviets had boldly and recklessly placed medium-range missiles in Cuba—missiles that could carry nuclear warheads and destroy American cities. On October 14, an American U-2 spy-plane snapped photographs which revealed the construction of several missile sites. Determined to force the missiles from Cuba, Kennedy soon convened a council of wise men called the Executive Committee or ExComm. ExComm considered four policy options: "talk them out," "squeeze them out," "shoot them out," or "buy them out." Ultimately the committee advised the president to surround Cuba with a naval blockade as the best means to resolve the crisis. Kennedy went on television the evening of October 22 to explain the crisis and the U.S. response.

An international war of nerves soon began. More than sixty American ships went on patrol to enforce the blockade. The Strategic Air Command went on nuclear alert, moving upward to Defense Condition (DEFCON) 2 for the first time ever—the next level being deployment. B-52 bombers, packed with nuclear weapons, stood ready, while soldiers and equipment moved to the southeastern United States to prepare for an invasion of Cuba. Thousands of road maps of the island were distributed to anxious troops. Nail-biting days followed as Soviet ships steamed toward the U. S. armada. Grabbing a few hours of sleep on cots in their offices and expecting doomsday, Kennedy's advisers wondered if they would ever see their families again. And then, finally, with great relief, on October 28, Khrushchev appealed for restraint and the Americans and Soviets settled. In return for a Kennedy pledge not to invade Cuba and to withdraw U.S. Jupiter missiles from Turkey, Khrushchev promised to "dismantle," "crate, and return" his SS-4 missiles to the Soviet Union, and he fulfilled his pledge.

Kennedy's handling of the crisis, Arthur Schlesinger had effusively written, constituted a "combination of toughness and restraint, of will, nerve and wisdom, so brilliantly controlled, so matchlessly calibrated." "We've won a great victory," Kennedy himself told congressional leaders. In private, the President crowed to friends, "I cut his balls off."

"We have been had," growled Admiral George Anderson, in a quite different view. The no invasion pledge, complained Cuban exiles, "was another Bay of Pigs for us." "It's the greatest defeat in our history," snapped General Curtis LeMay. These statements about "victory" and "defeat" actually set the question too narrowly. A more revealing question is this: How did we get into the crisis in the first place?

Cuba and the United States had been snarling at one another ever since Fidel Castro came to power in early 1959 and vowed to reduce U.S. power on the island. While Cuba accelerated a bitterly anti-American revolution, the Eisenhower Administration imposed economic sanctions and initiated covert CIA actions. A defiant Castro moved Cuba steadily toward Communism and military alliance with the Soviet Union. Just before Kennedy's inauguration, President Eisenhower broke diplomatic relations with Cuba. Kennedy soon accelerated a multitrack program of covert, economic, diplomatic, and propagandistic elements designed to bring Castro down. Secretary of Defense Robert McNamara later remarked: "If I had been in Moscow or Havana at that time [of 1961–1962], I would have believed the Americans were preparing for an invasion."

Essential to understanding the frightening missile crisis of fall 1962, in fact, is the relationship between U.S. activities and Soviet/Cuban decisions. The time of events is critical, and there is no doubt that Castro saw Cuba's acceptance of the missiles as the formation of a military alliance with the Soviet Union, similar to membership in the Warsaw Pact. In May 1962, the Soviets and Cubans first discussed the idea of placing nuclear-tipped missiles on the island; in early July, during a trip by Raul Castro to Moscow, a draft agreement was initialed; in late August, during a trip by Che Guevara to Moscow, the final touches were put on the accord.

What was the United States doing during those critical months before August? By 1962, more than two hundred anti-Castro Cuban exile organizations operated in the United States. After the failed Bay of Pigs invasion of early 1961, Cuban exiles chafed at the bit in Florida, eager to avenge their losses. Many of them banded together under the leadership of Jose Miro Cardona, the former prime minister. Miro Cardona met with President Kennedy in Washington on April 10, 1962, and the Cuban exile left the meeting persuaded that Kennedy intended to use U. S. armed forces against Cuba. Indeed, after Miro Cardona returned to Miami, he and his Revolutionary Council began to identify recruits for a Cuban unit in the U.S. military.

If Havana worried about such maneuverings, it grew apprehensive too about the alliance between the exile groups and the CIA, whose commitment to the destruction of the Castro regime knew few bounds. Hit-and-run saboteurs burned cane fields and blew up oil depots and transportation facilities. In May, one group attacked a Cuban patrol boat off the northern coast of the island. The Revolutionary Student Directorate, another exile organization, used two boats to attack Cuba in August. Alpha 66 attacked Cuba on numerous occasions, as did other CIA saboteurs. CIA officers and "assets" were at the same time plotting to assassinate Fidel Castro.

Some of these activities came under the wing of Operation Mongoose, the covert effort engineered by Attorney

General Robert Kennedy to disrupt the Cuban economy and stir unrest on the island. As General Maxwell Taylor recalled, after the Bay of Pigs "a new urgency" was injected into "Kennedy's concern for counterinsurgency. . . ." Robert Kennedy told counterinsurgency specialist Colonel Edward Lansdale that the Bay of Pigs "insult needed to be redressed rather quickly."

Intensified economic coercion joined covert activities. The Kennedy Administration, in February 1962, banned most imports of Cuban products. Washington also pressed its NATO allies to support the "economic isolation" of Cuba. Soon Cuba was forced to pay higher freight costs, enlarge its foreign debt, and suffer factory shutdowns due to the lack of spare parts once [bought] in the United States. The effect on Cuba was not what Washington intended: more political centralization and repression, more state management, closer ties to the Soviet Union.

In early 1962, as well, Kennedy officials engineered the eviction of Cuba from the Organization of American States. The expulsion registered loudly in Havana, which interpreted it as "political preparation for an invasion."

At about the same time, the American military planning and activities, some public, some secret, demonstrated U.S. determination to cripple the Castro government. Mongoose director Lansdale noted in a top secret memorandum to the President that he designed his schemes to "help the people of Cuba overthrow the Communist regime from within Cuba. . . ." And if the revolt proved successful, the United States would have to sustain it. That is, he said, the United States would likely have to "respond promptly with military force. . . ." Indeed, "the basic plan requires complete and efficient support of the [U.S.] military." The chairman of the Joint Chiefs of Staff, General Taylor, explained in the spring of 1962 that "indigenous resources" would carry out the Operation Mongoose plan to overthrow the Cuban government, but, he added, the plan "recognizes that final success will require decisive U.S. military intervention." Because the scheme also required close cooperation with Cuban exiles, it is likely that Castro's spies picked up from the leaky Cuban community in Miami at least vague suggestions that the U. S. military was plotting action against Cuba. As CIA agents liked to joke, there were three ways to transmit information rapidly: telegraph, telephone, and tell-a-Cuban.

Actual American military maneuvers heightened Cuban fears. One well publicized U.S. exercise, staged during April—also in 1962—included 40,000 troops and an amphibious landing on a small island near Puerto Rico. Some aggressive American politicians, throughout 1962, were calling for the real thing: an invasion of Cuba. In the

summer of 1962, finally, the U. S. Army began a program to create Spanish-speaking units; the Cuban exiles who signed up had as their "primary" goal, as they put it, a "return to Cuba" to battle the Castro government.

By late spring/summer 1962, then, at the very time that Havana and Moscow were contemplating defensive measures that included medium-range missiles, Cuba felt besieged from several quarters. Havana was eager for protection. The Soviet Union had become its trading partner; and the Soviets, after the Bay of Pigs, had begun military shipments that ultimately included small arms, howitzers, armored personnel carriers, patrol boats, tanks, MIG jet fighters, and surface-to-air missiles. Yet all of this weaponry, it seemed, had not deterred the United States. And, given the failure of Kennedy's multitrack program to unseat the Cuban leader, "were we right or wrong to fear direct invasion" next, asked Fidel Castro. As he said in July l962, shortly after striking the missile-deployment agreement with the Soviets: "We must prepare ourselves for that direct invasion." He welcomed the Soviet missiles to deter the United States. And the Soviet Union grabbed at any opportunity to notch up its position in the nuclear arms race.

The Khrushchev-Castro decision to place missiles in Cuba ranks as one of the most dangerous in the Cold War. Yet had there been no exile expedition at the Bay of Pigs, no destructive covert activities, no assassination plots, no military maneuvers and plans, and no economic and diplomatic steps to harass, isolate and destroy the Castro government, there would not have been a Cuban missile crisis. "We'd carried out the Bay of Pigs operation, never intending to use American military force—but the Kremlin didn't know that," a pensive Robert McNamara recalled some twenty-five years after the event. "We were running covert operations against Castro" [and] "people in the Pentagon were even talking about a first strike [nuclear policy]. . . . So the Soviets may well have believed we were seeking Castro's overthrow *plus* a first strike capability." The former Defense Secretary concluded: "This may have led them to do what they did in Cuba."

To stress only the global dimension—Soviet-American competition, as is commonly done, is to slight the local or regional sources of the conflict. As somebody put it, we have looked too much at the international climate and too little at the local weather. To slight the local conditions is to miss the central point that Premier Nikita Khrushchev would never have had the opportunity to install dangerous missiles in the Caribbean if the United States had not been attempting to actively to overthrow the Cuban government.

If Kennedy's war against Cuba helped initiate the crisis, Kennedy must also bear responsibility for how the crisis unfolded so dangerously—how the crisis began to spin out of control. Kennedyites prided themselves on a calculated, well managed foreign policy; they believed that they could control events through the rational use of force and wise deciphering of the intentions and capabilities of friends and foes alike.

The sources for such confidence in "control" were many. First, the popularity of the concept of "control accounting" or "management control" in business and government, popularized by think tanks such as the RAND Corporation and personified in Secretary McNamara, who believed that numbers told much if not all and that almost everything could be reduced to fine-tuned plans and balances—including a "balance of terror."

Second, the Kennedy people admired a strong presidency. Critical of Dwight Eisenhower for weak leadership in the 1950s, the Kennedyites extolled a strong, activist executive who would generate policy, command the bureaucracy, and lead Congress—in short, a chief executive in firm control.

Third, at work were popular Clausewitzian notions of disciplined war—that "war in all its phases must be rationally guided by meaningful political purposes." Yet another source of the control mentality was the "can-do" style of the Kennedy team and its exaggerated sense of U.S. power and the American ability to right a world gone wrong, to remake other societies, to face down adversaries. The United States, McGeorge Bundy once remarked, "was the locomotive at the head of mankind, and the rest of the world [was] the caboose." Arthur Schlesinger captured the mood this way: "Euphoria reigned; we thought for a moment that the world was plastic and the future unlimited."

Last, Kennedy officials had a faddish fascination with anti-revolutionary, counter-insurgency doctrines, modernization theories, and covert methods, which suggested that the application of limited power could produce desired results; that violence could be managed; and that through nation-building, the United States could guide countries toward peace and prosperity, if not replicate itself abroad and win allies."

In the early 1960s, this faith in control did not go unchallenged within the administration. Schlesinger himself grew alarmed by the Administration's fervent embrace of counterinsurgency. As he wrote later, it became a "mode of warfarer . . . which nourished an American belief in the capacity and right to intervene in foreign lands, and which was both corrupting in method and futile in effect." Ambassador Adlai Stevenson remarked to a friend that "they've got the damndest bunch of boy commandos running around [here] . . . [that] you ever saw." Under Secretary of State George Ball never warmed to what he called the "high

priests, who talked a strange, sacerdotal language" with "a quaintly Madison Avenue ring." He criticized the nation-building ideas of Walt Rostow as a "most presumptuous undertaking," for Ball doubted that "American professors could make bricks without the straw of experience and with indifferent and infinitely various kinds of clay." This calls to mind Sam Rayburn's remark after Vice President Johnson came back from a White House meeting thoroughly excited about the brainpower of Kennedy's young assistants: "Well, Lyndon," Rayburn said, "they may be every bit as intelligent as you say, but I'd feel a whole lot better about them if just one of them had run for sheriff once."

As it turned out, the world was not malleable, events could not be predicted or controlled with pinpoint accuracy, and the rather heady people in the Kennedy entourage proved fallible. Recent studies of the Berlin crisis, for example, reveal just how difficult it is to control local leaders or commanders, be they General Lucius Clay in West Germany or Walter Ulbricht in East Germany. Clausewitz himself had warned about "uncertainty." The "general unreliability of all information," he wrote, "presents a special problem"—"all action takes place . . . in a kind of twilight, which, like fog or moonlight, often tends to make things seem grotesque and larger than they really are."

Still, the control mentality dominated the Kennedy Administration. Exploration of its place during the missile crisis helps scholars test the question of crisis management. What emerges from the mounds of documents is not so much an enviable exercise in crisis management, but rather a study in near misses, imperfect instructions, confusions, miscalculations, and exhaustion. These negative traits gained life because President Kennedy, at the start, ruled out negotiations with either the Soviet Union or Cuba. He decided to inform the Soviets of U.S. policy through a television address rather than through diplomatic channels. The stiff arming of diplomacy seriously raised the level of danger.

Some ExComm participants recommended that negotiations be tried first. In the beginning, McGeorge Bundy urged consideration not only of military plans but of a "political track" or diplomacy. But Kennedy showed little interest in negotiations. When McNamara mentioned that diplomacy might precede military action, for example, the President immediately switched the discussion to another question: How long would it take to get air strikes organized? Conspicuously absent from the first meeting of the crisis was a serious probing of Soviet and Cuban motivation or any reflection on how U.S. actions may have helped trigger the crisis. At the second ExComm meeting of October 16, Secretary of State Dean Rusk argued against the surprise air strike that General Taylor had bluntly advocated. Rusk recommended instead "a direct message to Castro." At the close of Rusk's remarks, Kennedy once again derailed such thoughts and returned to the military option, immediately asking: "Can we get a little idea about what the military thing *is?*

During the tense days that followed, former Ambassador to the Soviet Union Charles Bohlen advised that Moscow would have to retaliate against the United States if American bombs killed its technicians. A stern letter to Khrushchev should be "tested" first as a method to gain withdrawal of the missiles. Joined by former ambassador to the Soviet Union Llewellyn Thompson, Bohlen favored opening "talks" with Moscow—a "diplomatic approach." Bohlen told the President: "I don't see the urgency of military action." And a grim Ambassador to the United Nations, Adlai Stevenson, appealed to Kennedy: "The existence of nuclear missile bases anywhere is negotiable before we start anything." But, after helping to initiate the crisis, Kennedy bypassed diplomacy in favor of confrontation.

During the hair-trigger days after the October 22 speech, much went wrong, the level of danger constantly went up, and weary and irritable decisionmakers sensed that they were losing their grip. "A high risk of uncontrollable escalation" dogged the crisis. Robert Kennedy remembered that, on October 25, "we were on the edge of a precipice with no way off. . . . President Kennedy had initiated the course of events, but he no longer had control over them." So much unraveled, so much could not be reigned in. First, there was the possibility that what Robert Kennedy called a "crackpot" exile group would attempt to assassinate Castro or raid the island. Operation Mongoose sabotage teams were actually already inside Cuba; they had been dispatched there before the missile crisis and now they could not be reached by their CIA handlers. What if this "half-assed operation," the Attorney General worried, ignited trouble. One of these teams actually did blow up a Cuban factory on November 8. To cite another mishap: not until the 27th of October did the administration think to inform the Soviets that the quarantine line was an arc measured at 500 nautical miles around Cuba. What if a Soviet captain inadvertently piloted his ship into the blockade zone?

The legendary feud between McNamara and his admirals during the crisis revealed trouble. This exchange between the Defense Secretary and Admiral George Anderson could not have been reassuring at the time:

> McNamara: "When that ship reaches the line, how are you going to stop it?"
> Anderson: "We'll hail it."
> McNamara: "In what language—English or Russian?"
> Anderson: "How the hell should I know?"

> McNamara: "What will you do if they don't understand?"
> Anderson: "I suppose we'll use flags."
> McNamara: "Well, what if they don't stop?"
> Anderson: "We'll send a shot across the bow."
> McNamara: "Then what if that doesn't work?"
> Anderson: "Then we'll fire into the rudder."
> McNamara: "You are not going to fire a single shot at anything without my express permission, is that clear?". . .
> Anderson: "Don't worry, Mr. Secretary, we know what we are doing here."

The Soviet ships, fortunately, stopped and returned home.

The Navy's anti-submarine warfare activities also carried the potential of escalating the crisis. Soviet submarines prowled near the quarantine line, and, following the standing rules of engagement, Navy ships forced several of them to surface. In one case, a Navy commander exercised the high-risk option of dropping a depth charge on a Soviet submarine. As one specialist on crisis management has written, the President and McNamara "may not have fully understood the operational implications of their authorization of ASW [Anti-submarine warfare] operations."

Another opportunity for trouble occurred when the commander of the Strategic Air Command, General Thomas S. Power, issued DEFCON 2 alert instructions in the clear. Alerts serve to prepare American forces for war, but they also carry the danger of escalation, because movement to a high category might be read by an adversary as American planning for a first strike. Under such circumstances, the adversary might be tempted to launch a preemptive strike. The Soviets, feeling their way cautiously through the crisis, chose not to read it that way.

Two serious episodes in the air on October 27 also saw the breakdown of crisis management. In the morning, a U-2 was shot down over Cuba by a surface-to-air missile. Who did it? Did *Cubans,* after having fought Soviet soldiers to take over the SAM sites? Or did a Soviet general in Cuba, on his own, without Khrushchev's knowledge or authorization but perhaps with Castro's, order the shootdown? It seems that the senior Soviet officer, apparently following standing orders to shoot if an American invasion occurred—an invasion he apparently judged to be underway—made the decision during a time when "the psychological climate was . . . ripe for panic" and when "the United States was doing its best to flex its muscles in the region as visibly as possible." In any case, American decisionmakers assumed that Soviets manned the SAM batteries; thus, the shoot-down constituted a dangerous escalation.

General LeMay readied for a massive air strike. McNamara now thought "invasion had become almost inevitable." But President Kennedy hesitated to retaliate, surely scared, now increasingly timid about taking another step toward nuclear war. The President decided to seek an accommodation with Khrushchev. He bypassed ExComm and dispatched his brother to deliver an ultimatum—and a compromise—to Soviet Ambassador Anatoly Dobrynin: start pulling out the missiles within forty-eight hours or U.S. forces would remove them. After Dobrynin asked about a trade (a trade Khrushchev had requested)—the U. S. Jupiter missiles in Turkey for the Soviet missiles in Cuba—Robert Kennedy offered an important American concession: the Jupiters would be dismantled if the problem in Cuba were resolved. As the President said in an ExComm meeting, "we can't very well invade Cuba with all its toil . . . when we could have gotten them out by making a deal on the same missiles in Turkey."

The White House also learned on the 27th of October that an American U-2 plane overflew the northeastern part of the Soviet Union, probably because equipment malfunctioned. Soviet fighters scrambled to intercept it, and American jets from Alaska took flight to rescue the errant aircraft. Although the spy plane flew home without having unleashed a dog fight, Moscow might have read the incident as provocative—a prelude to a bombing attack. As in so many of these examples, decisionmakers in Washington lost control of the crisis to personnel at the operational level. That same afternoon, Cuban anti-aircraft batteries hit a low-flying U.S. reconnaissance aircraft. Castro savored more.

Another aspect of the control issue raises doubts about Kennedy's handling of the crisis. ExComm members represented considerable intellectual talent and experience, but a mythology of cool calculation has grown up around their role. ExComm actually debated alternatives under "intense strain," often in a "state of anxiety and emotional exhaustion." Some advisers suffered such stress that they seemed to become passive or unable to perform their responsibilities.

An assistant to Adlai Stevenson recalled that he had had to become an ExComm "back-up" for the ambassador because, "while he could speak clearly, his memory wasn't very clear . . ." Why? Vice Admiral Charles Wellborn explained that the "emotional state and nervous tension that was involved in [the missile crisis] had this effect." Stevenson, said Wellborn, was feeling "pretty frightened." So apparently was Dean Rusk. Robert Kennedy remembered that the Secretary of State "frequently could not attend our meetings," because "he had a virtually complete breakdown mentally and physically." Once, when Rusk's eyes swelled with tears, Dean Acheson barked at

him: "Pull yourself together, Dean, you're the only Secretary of State we have." We cannot determine how stress affected the advice ExComm gave Kennedy, or whether the President himself was speeding on his amphetamines, but at least we know that the crisis managers struggled against time, sleep, exhaustion, and themselves, and they did not always think clearheadedly at a time when the stakes were very high. Had Stevenson and Rusk, both of whom recommended diplomacy and compromise, been steadier, the option of negotiations at the start might have received a better hearing and the world might have been spared so grueling a confrontation. In any case, as McNamara has recalled, there was always the danger that "people may crack" and become "quivering, panicky, irrational people" if "you just keep piling it on."

As for the Soviets, they too sensed that the crisis was spinning out of control. Khrushchev's rambling letter of October 26 to Kennedy betrayed desperation, if not disarray, in the Kremlin. "You and I should not now pull on the ends of the rope in which you have tied a knot of war, because the harder you and I pull, the tighter the knot will become," the Soviet premier wrote. When the knot becomes too tight, Khrushchev observed, it will have to be cut, unleashing the "dread forces our two countries possess." Khrushchev also had to worry about his field commanders. Russian accounts indicate that Soviet forces in Cuba possessed short-range tactical nuclear missiles with warheads. Although the Soviet commander apparently did not have predelegated authority to fire the missiles, Kremlin decisionmakers had to worry about possible mishap, miscommunication or panic that might lead to a firing. These circumstances and the shootdown of the U-2 over Cuba meant that Khrushchev, too, was experiencing the failure of control and the possible ascendancy of accident.

Add to these worries his trouble with Fidel Castro, who demanded a bold Soviet response to U.S. actions and who might provoke an incident with the United States that could escalate the crisis. Castro was pressing the Soviets to use nuclear weapons to save Cuba should the United States attack. "Such adventurists," remarked a Soviet decisionmaker. Khrushchev sternly told his advisers: "You see how far things can go. We've got to get those missiles out of there before a real fire starts." He sensed that time was running out, that events were outpacing the wits of leaders. The United States might invade, and then what? Like Kennedy, to head off disaster, he appealed for a settlement— and the two men and nations compromised. Khrushchev did not consult Castro, but rather informed him, because "we did not have time." That Khrushchev was nervous and fearful about another dangerous twist in the crisis seems clear, because he took the unusual step of announcing the withdrawal of the missiles via Radio Moscow. He did not want to waste the precious time that would have been required to encode, transmit, decode, and translate a diplomatic message. "You see," McNamara has said, "from beginning to end, fear ruled." Khrushchev "shitted in his pants," crudely remarked one Soviet official."

A triumph of American and Kennedy prudence? A triumph of crisis management? Historians no longer think so. In the end, the two superpowers, frantic to avoid nuclear war and scared by the prospects of doomsday, stumbled toward a settlement. "We were in luck," remarked Ambassador John Kenneth Galbraith, "but success in a lottery is no argument for lotteries." If the crisis had lasted more than thirteen days, remembered a U.S. adviser, "the whole thing would have begun to unravel."

President Kennedy helped precipitate the missile crisis by harassing Cuba through his multi-track program. Then he reacted to the crisis by suspending diplomacy in favor of public confrontation. In the end, he frightened himself. In order to postpone doomsday, or at least to prevent a high-casualty invasion of Cuba, he moderated the American response and compromised. Khrushchev withdrew his mistake, while gaining what Ambassador Llewellyn Thompson thought was the "important thing" all along for the Soviet leader: being able to say, "I saved Cuba. I stopped an invasion."

After the missile crisis, Castro sought better relations with Washington, and he made gestures toward detente. He sent home thousands of Soviet military personnel. He publicly called for rapprochement. But, after Castro returned from a trip to the Soviet Union, where he patched up relations with Khrushchev and won promises of more foreign aid, Robert Kennedy asked the CIA to crank up another anti-Castro campaign. The National Security Council soon approved a new sabotage program, and the CIA devised new dirty tricks. The agency also revitalized its assassination option by making contact with a traitorous Cuban official, Rolando Cubela. Codenamed AM/LASH, he and the CIA plotted to kill Fidel Castro. On the very day that President Kennedy died, AM/LASH rendezvoused with CIA agents in Paris, where he received a ballpoint pen rigged with a poisonous hypodermic needle intended to produce Castro's instant death.

Months before, in June of 1963, President Kennedy had delivered an unusual speech at American University that seemed to mark a break with the past. He asked Americans to reexamine their hard-line, anti-Soviet attitudes and he appealed for negotiations with the Soviet Union. He also revealed his uneasiness with a strategic policy so dependent upon nuclear weapons. And the president urged the Soviets to join him in reducing nuclear-arms stockpiles.

This high-minded, conciliatory speech, coming just months before his assassination and at a time when he was preparing the country and the Senate for a limited test ban treaty, has persuaded some that Kennedy was shedding his Cold Warriorism. Yet, as the father of the containment doctrine and Kennedy's Ambassador to Yugoslavia, George F. Kennan, sadly remarked, "one speech is not enough." We can, for example, contrast the American University address with two speeches that Kennedy was prepared to deliver in Texas on November 22, 1963, had he not been killed. In the first, Kennedy boasted about his administration's high military buildup. The United States, he said, had to blunt the "ambitions of international Communism." As for Vietnam in particular, the United States "dare not weary of the task." Neither in this undelivered Dallas speech nor in another planned for Austin did Kennedy speak of negotiations. Indeed, the Cold War rhetoric that Kennedy had asked citizens to tone down just months earlier at American University had become revitalized in these two speeches.

Kennedy's foreign policy legacy, then, is mixed, his direction at the end of his life uncertain. Escalation in Vietnam, an arms race of massive proportion and fear, greater factionalism in the Atlantic alliance, and a globalism of overcommitment that ensured crises and weakened the American economy stand beside the Peace Corps and an end to the Berlin crisis. Kennedy surely had doubts about the cliches of the Cold War, but he never shed them. Despite the rhetoric of the bold, new thinking, Kennedy and his advisers never fundamentally reassessed American foreign policy assumptions. Instead, they endowed them with more vigor because they believed that they, unlike those before them, could control—could manage—events.

As historians digging into the documents, we have learned that the world was not plastic, that magic means not only enchantment but sleight of hand, and that President Kennedy did not have the Midas touch. We must reckon with a past colored more with subtle grays than with the extremes of blacks and whites. With such enlightenment comes much discomfort.

THOMAS G. PATERSON is a professor of history at the University of Connecticut in Storrs, CT. His articles have appeared in *Journal of American History and Diplomatic History* (where he has served upon the editorial boards) and *American Historical Review*. A past president of the Society for Historians of American Foreign Relations, he has authored, coauthored, or edited many books, including *Contesting Castro* (Oxford University Press, 1994) and *On Every Front*, 2nd ed. (W.W. Norton, 1993).

Robert Weisbrot

→ **NO**

Maximum Danger: Kennedy, the Missiles, and the Crisis of American Confidence

The Missile Crisis in Historical Perspective

In his history of nuclear policy, *Danger and Survival*, McGeorge Bundy acknowledged, "Forests have been felled to print the reflections and conclusion of participants, observers, and scholars" on the Cuban missile crisis. The first great wave of coverage occurred in the mid-1960s, as the nation savored a cold war triumph and saluted a martyred leader of untold promise. A second wave peaked in the 1970s, as critics dissected the episode not to extol President Kennedy's supreme feat but to expose his feet of clay. Beginning in the mid-1980s the deforestation again accelerated, as declassified sources and meetings by former officials from America, Russia, and Cuba provided a wealth of factual corrections to early, long unchallenged recollections. Yet this crisis, perhaps the most intensely scrutinized fortnight in American history, is just beginning to come into historical focus.

1. Early Histories: Kennedy's Matchless "Crisis Management"

Kennedy's admirers were first to the ramparts in the battle over the president's historical reputation. The president's speech writer and special counsel Theodore Sorensen, historian Arthur Schlesinger, Jr., columnists and presidential intimates Joseph Alsop and Charles Bartlett, NBC correspondent Elie Abel, and the president's brother and attorney general, Robert Kennedy (in his posthumously published memoir *Thirteen Days*), all depicted the Soviet placement of missiles in Cuba as a brazen, nuclear-tipped challenge that the president could not decline without compromising credibility and tempting still bolder provocations. Brimming with insiders' revelations of tense national security meetings, their narratives formed a paradigm of successful crisis management that, they suggested, future policymakers should study and emulate.

The early histories lauded President Kennedy for cool judgement "in steering a safe course between war and surrender." Although he had discounted diplomacy alone as inadequate to dislodge the missiles and, in any case, a poor answer to nuclear blackmail, Kennedy had rejected urgings to bomb the missile sites (possibly followed by an invasion of Cuba), which would likely have killed many Russians. According to Robert Kennedy, at least six of twelve top aides, both civilian and military, had pressed this doubtful "surgical" solution, prompting him to muse that had any of them been president, "the world would have been very likely plunged in a catastrophic war."

Kennedy drew further praise for conjuring a diplomatic miracle from an unpromising and increasingly volatile standoff. Elie Abel reported that Khrushchev's public demand that America remove its Jupiter missiles from Turkey was "a doubled sense of shock" to Kennedy, who "distinctly remembered having given instructions, long before" to remove the obsolete Jupiters. Now the president "reflected sadly on the built-in futilities of big government," for "not only were the missiles still in Turkey but they had just become pawns in a deadly chess game." Still, Sorensen observed, "The President had no intention of destroying the Alliance by backing down."

As the story was told: After much wrangling and confusion among Ex Comm members, Robert Kennedy offered "a thought of breathtaking simplicity and ingenuity: why not ignore the second Khrushchev message and reply to the first?" With his brother's approval, he informed the Soviet ambassador that while "there could be no quid pro quo or any arrangement made under this kind of threat or pressure. . . . President Kennedy had been anxious to remove those missiles" and still hoped to do so "within a short time after this crisis was over." The attorney general served this carrot on a stick, adding that either the Soviets must remove the missiles promptly or the Americans would do so. The next morning Khrushchev publicly acceded to these terms.

In the heady aftermath of the crisis, President Kennedy saluted the Soviet premier for his "statesmanlike" decision and privately cautioned aides that there should be "no boasting, no gloating, not even a claim of victory. We had won by enabling Khrushchev to avoid complete humiliation—we should not humiliate him now." Robert Kennedy recalled, "What guided all [the president's] deliberations was an effort not to disgrace Khrushchev," to leave the Soviets a path of graceful retreat.

For a nation emerging from a week of terror of the missile crisis, Henry Pachter wrote in the book *Collision Course*, the "style" and "art" of Kennedy's leadership had "restored America's confidence in her own power." Sorensen, haggard from two weeks of stress and fatigue, recalled pondering the president's achievement as he leafed through a copy of *Profiles in Courage* and read the introductory quotation from Burke's eulogy of Charles James Fox: "He may live long, he may do much. But here is the summit. He never can exceed what he does this day."

2. Revisionist Histories: Reckless Kennedy Machismo

Whether or not history moves in cycles, historians typically do, and by the 1970s the once-standard odes to President Kennedy had given way to hard-edged, often hostile studies. As portrayed by the new histories, the "brief shining moment" of Kennedy's Camelot was illumined by nothing more magical than the beacons of modern public relations. From his youth Kennedy had flaunted a reckless self-indulgence encouraged by the family's founding tyrant, Joseph P. Kennedy, who imparted to his male children his own ambition, opportunism, and a shameless *machismo* toward women. A succession of affairs unencumbered by emotional involvement; publication of an intelligent but amateurish senior thesis courtesy of family friends; embellishment of a war record marked by heroism but also by some unexplained lapses in leadership; and reception of a Pulitzer Prize for *Profiles in Courage*, written in significant part by his aide, Sorensen, all reflected a pursuit of expedience more than excellence.

Critics found that Kennedy's performance as president confirmed and extended rather than overcame this pattern of flamboyant mediocrity. They discerned in his conduct of foreign policy a dismal amalgam of anti-Communist hysteria, reckless posturing, and a disturbingly gleeful crisis orientation. The results were accordingly grim, ranging from the early disaster at the Bay of Pigs to the placement—or misplacement—of more than fifteen thousand U.S. military personnel in Vietnam by the time of Kennedy's death. Scarcely learning from his early mistakes, Kennedy ignored legitimate Cuban concerns for defense against American intervention and needlessly flirted with the apocalypse in order to force the removal of missiles that scarcely affected the world military balance. To judge from their skeptical recounting, this harrowing superpower confrontation might better be termed the "misled crisis," for it stemmed from Kennedy's perception of a threat to his personal and political prestige rather than (as Americans were misinformed) to the nation's security.

No crisis existed, then, until Kennedy himself created one by forgoing private diplomacy for a public ultimatum and blockade. Considering that the United States had already planned to remove its obsolete missiles from Turkey, Kennedy should have heeded Adlai Stevenson's advice to propose immediately a trade of bases, rather than rush into a confrontation whose outcome he could neither foresee nor fully control. Instead, "From the first, he sought unconditional surrender and he never deviated from that objective." "He took an unpardonable mortal risk without just cause," Richard J. Walton wrote. "He threatened the lives of millions for appearances' sake."

The prime historical mystery to the revisionists was why any American president would needlessly play Russian roulette in the nuclear age. Critics conceded that the president may have felt "substantial political pressures" over Cuba but blamed him for having largely created those pressures with shrill, alarmist speeches. "He had been too specific about what the United States would and would not tolerate in Cuba, and his statements reduced his options," Louise FitzSimons wrote. Garry Wills also saw Kennedy as a prisoner of his own superheated rhetoric about Khrushchev, Communists, and missiles, which aroused a false sense of crisis; "If he was chained to a necessity for acting, he forged the chains himself. . . . Having fooled the people in order to lead them, Kennedy was forced to serve the folly he had induced."

Revisionist writers detected a sad consistency in Kennedy's anti-Communist hyperbole, so that the missile crisis appeared to be a logical by-product of his style rather than simply a grisly aberration. During his bid for the presidency in 1960 Kennedy had stirred voters by charging his Republican opponent, Vice President Richard Nixon, with failing to "stand up to Castro" and to Khrushchev, or to prevent a potentially lethal "missile gap" with the Soviets (in fact Americans had a vast lead). Such ideological zeal remained evident in the Ex Comm, where, David Detzer claimed, Kennedy was "more Cold Warrior" than many, "worrying about America's reputation (and maybe his own) for toughness. . . ."

Scholars in the rising genre of psychohistory traced the nation's "perilous path" in the missile crisis to "the neuroticism of Kennedy's machismo." According to Nancy Gager Clinch, the president viewed the Cuban missiles "as a personal challenge to [his] courage and status," and "In the Kennedy lexicon of manliness, not being 'chicken' was a primary value." This interpretation radiated to other fields: Sidney Lens, in his study of the military-industrial complex, found in Kennedy's "willingness to gamble with the idea of nuclear war . . . a loss of touch with reality, almost a suicidal impulse."

The more judicious of the new historians, like Richard J. Walton, tempered their personal indictments by depicting the president as "an entirely conventional Cold Warrior." Still, in addition to "his fervent anti-communism, and his acceptance of the basic assumptions of American postwar foreign policy," "the *machismo* quality in Kennedy's character" pushed him to embark on "an anti-communist crusade much more dangerous than any policy Eisenhower ever permitted." Burdened by both personal flaws and political pressures, Kennedy failed during the missile crisis to keep American policy from exhibiting, in his own words, "a collective death-wish for the world."

Like traditional historians of the missile crisis, the revisionists identified a hero, but it was the Soviet premier, Nikita Khrushchev, who withdrew the missiles at risk to his prestige. "Had Khrushchev not done so, there might well have been no later historians to exalt Kennedy," for then Kennedy and his aides, so set on victory at any cost, "would burn the world to a cinder." In effect the new histories inverted the earlier images of Kennedy as a sentry for international order standing firm against a ruthless Soviet Union. To the revisionists, Kennedy's belligerence itself posed the chief threat of global annihilation, and only the belated prudence of his counterpart in the Kremlin salvaged the peace.

3. New Evidence, Old Myths

For more than two decades after the missile crisis, scholarship churned along these two interpretive poles, grinding ever finer a limited cache of primary sources. Denied access to most records of the Ex Comm meetings, historians continued to rely on memoirs by several of President Kennedy's aides. As for the Soviets, a commentator for *Izvestia* later lamented that their press "treated the episode with socialist surrealism," refusing even to concede Khrushchev's placement of nuclear weapons in Cuba. "The word 'missiles' never appeared in the newspapers, though later, in the Kennedy-Khrushchev letters, the phrase 'weapons the United States considers offensive' was used."

As late as 1982 a writer surveying the historical literature could reasonably assert, "There are no new facts about the Kennedys, only new attitudes." Seldom has an insight aged more rapidly or spectacularly. Beginning in the mid-to-late eighties the volcanic flow of information and inquiry in the era of *glasnost* enabled several conferences on the missile crisis in which Soviet and American scholars and former officials shared facts and feelings long guarded like vital national secrets. These exchanges, coinciding with the declassification of various Ex Comm conversations, overturned much of what both traditional and revisionist scholars had long believed, extending even to shared assumptions about the basic facts of the crisis.

The entire twenty-five-year debate over whether Kennedy was warranted in not pledging to withdraw the Turkish missiles was abruptly exposed as based on a faulty record of events. In 1987 former Secretary of State Dean Rusk revealed that Kennedy had secretly prepared a fallback plan to have UN Secretary General U Thant propose a mutual dismantling of missiles in Cuba and Turkey. This would have let the president appear to comply only with a UN request rather than a Soviet demand. Whether Kennedy would have resorted to this gambit is uncertain, but clearly he had been seeking ways to defuse the risk of war.

Kennedy's back-channel efforts to end the crisis went further still. At a conference in Moscow in 1989, the former Soviet ambassador to the United States, Anatoly Dobrynin, recalled an explicit American agreement to withdraw the missiles from Turkey, not simply a vague expression of hope that this might eventually occur. Robert Kennedy had asked him not to draw up any formal exchange of letters, saying it was important not to publicize the accord, for it could show the administration to be purveying a falsehood to the American public. Sorensen deepened the panelists' astonishment by confirming that Robert Kennedy's diaries, which formed the basis of the posthumously published book *Thirteen Days,* were indeed explicit on this part of the deal. But at the time it was still a secret even on the American side, except for the president and a few officials within the Ex Comm. Sorensen explained that in preparing *Thirteen Days* for publication, "I took it upon myself to edit that out of his diaries."

As a result of Sorensen's editing discretion, Kennedy's conciliatory policy on the Turkish missiles was distorted by histories of the crisis into a symbol of either his valiant resolve or his confrontational bent. Similarly historians had long emphasized the imminent danger of a U.S. attack on the Cuban missile sites, whether to highlight the president's grave choices or to further indict him for war-mongering. Yet McNamara insisted in 1987, "There was no way we were going to war on Monday or Tuesday [October 29 or 30]. No way!" McNamara had suggested in the Ex Comm an intermediate step of tightening the quarantine to include petroleum, oil, and lubricants, and felt "very certain" that the president would have preferred this step to authorizing an attack.

Some of the new evidence is considerably less flattering to President Kennedy's image as a peacemaker. Records of the first day of Ex Comm meetings, October 16, show both John and Robert Kennedy inclined, with most other participants, to a quick air strike. The president's vaunted containment of the risks of war also appears less reassuring than in the idealized portrayals of early histories and memoirs. The perennial boast that he only modestly opened a Pandora's box of nuclear dangers lost much of its luster as scholars inventoried what had nearly escaped. The president never learned that U.S. destroyers might have crippled a Soviet submarine with depth charges near the quarantine line, an episode that could have triggered a wider naval clash. Kennedy also did not know of a series of false nuclear alerts that, in combination with the Strategic Air Command's heightened combat readiness, DEFCON (Defense Condition) 2, posed risks of inadvertent escalation.

Still more alarming, on October 27 a U.S. reconnaissance pilot strayed into Soviet territory, a violation that Khrushchev indignantly likened to a preparation for a preemptive nuclear strike. "There's always some son of a bitch who doesn't get the word," the president said on learning of this provocation. Kennedy would have been still more displeased had he known that because of the heightened military alert, U.S. fighter planes scrambling to protect the lost pilot from Russian MiGs were armed not with conventional weapons but with nuclear missiles. Scott D. Sagan, whose resourceful study *The Limits of Safety* discloses various military miscues and malfunctions during the crisis that might have led to a wider conflict, concludes that while "President Kennedy may well have been prudent," he lacked "unchallenged final control over U.S. nuclear weapons."

Nor did the danger of unwanted escalation stem entirely from U.S. nuclear forces. According to Anatoli Gribkov, who headed operational planning for the Soviet armed forces in 1962, the Russians had placed in Cuba not only medium-range missiles but also twelve *Luna* tactical missiles with nuclear warheads designed for ground combat support. Had Kennedy ordered an invasion, the Soviet commander in Cuba, General Issa Pliyev, in the event he lost contact with Moscow, had authority to fire the *Lunas* at the American landing force. On hearing this

in 1992, a stunned McNamara exclaimed, "No one should believe that a U.S. force could have been attacked by tactical nuclear warheads without the U.S. responding with nuclear warheads. And where would it have ended? In utter disaster."

Even Ex Comm veterans who had long exalted the Kennedy administration's "rational crisis management" have renounced the very notion as romantic—and dangerous. President Kennedy's National Security Adviser, McGeorge Bundy, acknowledged, "The most important part of crisis management is not to have a crisis, because there's no telling what will happen once you're in one." McNamara agreed, "'Managing' crises is the wrong term; you don't 'manage' them because you *can't*. . . ." On the twenty-fifth anniversary of the missile crisis, Sorensen, Kennedy's loyal aide and biographer, termed the confrontation "unwise, unwarranted and unnecessary."

The new scholarship has further chipped at the Kennedys' larger-than-life image by crediting the much maligned foreign policy establishment with contributions hitherto unknown or attributed wholly to the president and his brother. Secretary of State Dean Rusk, belying later charges that he was ineffectual in the Ex Comm and nearing a breakdown, originated the contingency plan to have UN Secretary General U Thant request the withdrawal of missiles in both Turkey and Cuba. With the president's approval, Rusk prepared Andrew Cordier, the president of Columbia University and a former UN parliamentarian, to approach U Thant. Had Khrushchev not accepted an earlier American offer, Rusk's idea might have served as the basis for a settlement under UN auspices.

The administration's celebrated "acceptance" of Khrushchev's tacit proposals on October 26 rather than his sterner public demands the next day—a ploy once credited to Robert Kennedy alone—in fact had a complex patrimony, Llewellyn Thompson, the former ambassador to the Soviet Union, whom Robert Kennedy's memoir credits generously but generally for "uncannily accurate" advice that was "surpassed by none," may have first suggested the outlines of this strategy. Bundy, Assistant Secretary of State for Latin American Affairs Edwin Martin, and others also offered variations on this gambit in informal discussions. Robert Kennedy formally proposed the idea in an Ex Comm meeting and drafted a response with Sorensen. But the view that this was his exclusive brainchild—a view nurtured by his own seemingly definitive account— underscores that memoirs seldom reveal an author's limitations other than a selective memory.

The very machinery of government, long viewed as a cumbersome, bumbling foil to a dynamic chief executive, now appears to have been a responsive (if not fully respected) partner. Contrary to early accounts, the failure to remove American missiles from Turkey before the crisis did not stem from unwitting bureaucratic sabotage of a presidential directive. Rather, Kennedy himself had acquiesced in the delay to avoid embarrassing a Turkish government that had only recently hinged its prestige on accepting the missiles. The president may well have been dismayed by their continued presence, but he was in no way surprised by it in the Ex Comm meetings. Rusk dismissed reports of the president's alleged betrayal by a lazy State Department, saying, "He never expressed any irritation to me because he had been fully briefed by me on that situation."

These and other discoveries all augur a far richer, more precise understanding of Kennedy's role in the missile crisis. But they have yet to produce an interpretive framework to encompass them. Should historians conclude that the president was less militant than once thought because he sanctioned a trade of missile bases? Or more militant because he initially leaned toward bombing Cuba? Does he now appear more adept at crisis management, given his elaborate fallback plans for a possible settlement through the UN? Or simply lucky to survive his own ignorance of swaggering American officers, false nuclear alerts, and nuclear-equipped Soviet forces in Cuba? Was the president more dependent on the Ex Comm in light of contributions by unsung heroes such as Llewellyn Thompson? Or did he treat the Ex Comm as having limited relevance, as in his concealment from most members of the private deal on the Turkish missiles? On these and other issues, the additions to our knowledge have been individually striking but cumulatively chaotic.

A way to make sense of these seemingly disparate and even conflicting pieces of evidence is to view President Kennedy as a moderate leader in a militant age. His vision at all times extended beyond the Ex Comm's deliberations, encompassing the formidable national consensus that the Soviet base in Cuba should be challenged militarily. Honing his policies on the grindstone of political necessity, Kennedy ordered a blockade of the island and considered still bolder action because he knew that Soviet leaders and the American public alike would otherwise view him as fatally irresolute. Yet within his circumscribed political setting, he proved more willing than most Americans, both in and outside his circle of advisers, to limit bellicose displays and to offer the Russians timely, if covert, concessions.

Despite a growing awareness of Kennedy's political constraints, the revisionist image of a man driven by both insecurity and arrogance to rash policies has proven extraordinarily resilient. Thomas G. Peterson, who incisively recounts the covert war against Castro waged by two administrations, judges Kennedy's brand of cold war leadership more dangerous than Eisenhower's. "Driven by a desire for power," Paterson writes, "Kennedy personalized issues, converting them into tests of will." Far from simply continuing "his predecessor's anti-Castro policies," Kennedy "significantly increased the pressures against the upstart island" out of an obsession with Castro. "He thus helped generate major crises, including the October 1962 missile crisis. Kennedy inherited the Cuban problem—and he made it worse."

In *The Dark Side of Camelot* (1997) the award-winning journalist Seymour Hersh cranks up to full strength the assault on Kennedy's character that had stamped revisionist writings of the 1970s. Contrasting Khrushchev's "common sense and dread of nuclear war" with Kennedy's "fanaticism" during the missile crisis, Hersh concludes: "For the first time in his presidency, Kennedy publicly brought his personal recklessness, and his belief that the normal rules of conduct did not apply to him, to his foreign policy. . . . The Kennedy brothers brought the world to the edge of war in their attempts to turn the dispute into a political asset."

Textbooks too have incorporated into their "objective" look at American history the notion that Kennedy's belligerence is the key to understanding his foreign policy. In a leading work, *Promises to Keep: The United States Since World War II* (1999), Paul Boyer finds that "Kennedy's approach to Cold War leadership differed markedly from Eisenhower's. Shaped by an intensely competitive family and a hard-driving father whom he both admired and feared, he eagerly sought to prove his toughness to the Soviet adversary."

The focus on Kennedy's supposed confrontational bent to explain his policies reaches its fullest—and most problematic—development in the aptly titled study by Thomas C. Reeves, *A Question of Character*. Reeves's Kennedy was "deficient in integrity, compassion, and temperance," defects that clearly influenced his Cuban policy, from the decision [in 1961] to ignore the moral and legal objections to an invasion, and through the creation of Operation Mongoose." During the missile crisis too, "Kennedy at times seemed unduly militant, and his aggressive and competitive instincts led him to grant the [diplomatic] initiative to the Soviets at critical points where more skilled diplomacy might have avoided it." Reeves dismisses claims that the president sought never to "challenge the other side needlessly," with the comment, "Neither, of course, were the Kennedys prepared to accept anything short of victory." Faced with the mounting evidence of Kennedy's prudence, Reeves allows that the president's "personal agony over the conflict, his several efforts to avoid bloodshed, and his willingness to make a trade of Turkish for Cuban missiles, revealed a deeper concern for the nation and the world than many who knew him well might have suspected." But little else leavens Reeves's generally dour portrait of a president whose personal failings compounded the risks of war. Like other revisionist scholars, Reeves dutifully ingests the new scholarship on the missile crisis but cannot easily digest it.

The hazards of treating presidential character as the Rosetta stone to make sense of policies in the missile crisis should by now give pause to even the most confirmed of Kennedy's admirers or detractors. The emergence of contributions by Rusk, Thompson, Bundy, Martin, and other establishment figures has made it more difficult to portray the Kennedys as lonely titans striding across the political stage with ideas and policies uniquely their own. And, granted that Kennedy was "the key decisionmaker," he nonetheless acted within tightly defined parameters that had little to do with the character of the chief executive.

The amplified record of decision-making has also recast or removed issues that long galvanized and framed debates over Kennedy's character. Interpretations of the president's supposedly tough policy on the Jupiter missiles now appear to have rested on accounts that, by embellishment and concealment alike, exaggerated his brinkmanship. The puncturing of those distortions should deflate as well the images of Kennedy as either a surpassingly valiant leader or a Neanderthal cold warrior.

Traditional historians, it is now clear, both sanitized and romanticized the historical record in portraying President Kennedy as an ideal fusion of hawkish resolve and dovish reserve, who forced out the Cuban missiles without making needless concessions or taking heedless risks. In fact Kennedy resolved the crisis not simply through toughness and diplomatic legerdemain but by pledging to remove the missiles from Turkey, a deal he publicly spurned and his partisans long proudly but wrongly denied. And while Kennedy's defenders lauded his rejection of calls for air strikes and invasion, they overlooked the provocation of his actual policies, including the plots against Castro, the push for ever greater American nuclear superiority, and, of course, the blockade of Cuba.

The historical record is even more resistant to revisionist portraits of a president whose psychological deformities impelled him to risk peace for the sake of personal glory or catharsis. These accounts were from the first suspect, whether in drawing tortured connections between Kennedy's womanizing and his foreign policy or deriding him for sharing the beliefs of his own generation rather than a later one. They simply collapse under the weight of evidence that, during the gravest crisis of the cold war, Kennedy repeatedly proved more prudent than many aides, both civilian and military. As he told his brother Robert on October 26, "If anybody is around to write after this, they are going to understand that we made every effort to find peace and every effort to give our adversary room to move. I am not going to push the Russians an inch beyond what is necessary."

Ernest May and Philip Zelikow, editors of an invaluable annotated record of the Ex Comm sessions, marvel that "[Kennedy] seems more alive to the possibilities and consequences of each new development than anyone else." On October 27, with pressure mounting for decisive action, the president "is the only one in the room who is determined not to go to war over obsolete missiles in Turkey." May and Zelikow acknowledge Kennedy's partial responsibility for this superpower clash but deem it "fortunate" that "[he] was the president charged with managing the crisis."

The most telling dismissal of revisionist rhetoric comes from Kennedy's adversaries themselves. Shortly after the crisis ended, Khrushchev admitted to an American journalist, "Kennedy did just what I would have done if I had been in the White House instead of the Kremlin." In his memoirs the former Soviet leader lamented Kennedy's death as "a great loss," for "he was gifted with the ability to resolve international conflicts by negotiation, as the whole world learned during the so-called Cuban crisis. Regardless of his youth he was a real statesman." As for those "clever people" who "will tell you that Kennedy was to blame for the tensions which might have resulted in war," Khrushchev said, "You have to keep in mind the era in which we live." Castro, for his part, believed Kennedy "acted as he did partly to save Khrushchev, out of fear that any successor would be tougher."

The misrepresentations of Kennedy's leadership go deeper than the debates over whether he was heroic or merely reckless, idealistic or expedient, poised or impulsive. Scholars have so focused on Kennedy's style, aura, temperament, and character as to slight, if not obscure, the crucial framework of national values that he necessarily accommodated and largely shared. The missile crisis, as much as anything, is the story of how Kennedy faithfully reflected a remarkable consensus in political institutions and public opinion regarding America's role as Free World champion in the nuclear age.

Contrary to the impression left by Kennedy's partisans, the Executive Committee he formed to advise him during the missile crisis was never a sealed laboratory for reinventing American policy. Nor was it, as the revisionists later had it, a forum for venting personal demons at public expense. Rather, like any leader in a democracy, Kennedy self-consciously labored under constraints imposed by public opinion, the Congress, the military, the CIA, and a host of civilian constituencies. To argue that he could or should have disdained these pressures is to imply a preference for philosopher kings over accountable presidents. Whatever the appeal of such arguments, they leave little room for either the ideal or the reality of American democracy.

Americans in the early sixties overwhelmingly regarded the prospect of missiles in Cuba as intolerably threatening and judged leaders by their firmness against Soviet encroachments. Whoever occupied the Oval Office would therefore have faced intense pressures to demand removal of the missiles, direct low-level military action against Cuba, and avoid apparent concessions to the Russians. Buffeted by partisan sniping, public opinion, and the force of inherited policies, President Kennedy pursued all of these options. Throughout he sought to minimize confrontation with the Soviet Union to a degree consistent with his political survival.

Accounting for the full political weight of entrenched national attitudes can help resolve the central paradox of Kennedy's policies during the missile crisis, which reflected elements of both recklessness and restraint. Considered against the background of his times, Kennedy appears a rational leader, conciliatory and even empathetic towards his counterpart in the Kremlin. Yet he also represented a political culture marked by fear and bluster, qualities stoked by an uncontrolled arms race and Manichean visions of the East-West divide. To ask which was the "real" Kennedy is to speak of a chimera: a leader somehow extricable from his era.

Kennedy embodied the anti–Soviet, anti-Communist values—and obsessions–of his day, though with more skepticism and caution than most contemporaries. His relative detachment from cold war dogmas was not enough to avoid a crisis caused by mutual misjudgments. Still, it allowed for a crucial modicum of flexibility and restraint that helped keep this crisis from spiraling toward war.

It may be tempting to conclude that Kennedy's avoidance of a wider conflict warrants cynicism rather than celebration, as the bare minimum one should expect of any sane leader in the nuclear age. Yet the obstacles to military restraint between states are no less daunting simply because the dangers are so great. Whatever Kennedy's missteps, he proved—together with Soviet Premier Khrushchev—that leaders can resist the lures of unchecked escalation even while mired in a climate of mutual suspicion, fear, and hostility. This achievement may yet gain new luster as nuclear weapons spread to other nations steeped in their own bitter rivalries, a development auguring two, three, many missile crises to come.

ROBERT WEISBROT is a professor of history at Colby College in Waterville, Maine, where he is also on the advisory committee for the African American Studies Program. He is the author of *From the Founding of the Southern Christian Leadership Conference to the Assassination of Malcolm X* (1957–65) (Chelsea House, 1994).

EXPLORING THE ISSUE

Did President John F. Kennedy Cause the Cuban Missile Crisis?

Critical Thinking and Reflection

1. Critically analyze the disparity between the image of President Kennedy's foreign policy versus the reality.
2. Critically analyze the strengths and weaknesses of the new sources about the Cuban missile crisis—such as declassified government memos, transcriptions of the Ex-Comm meetings, and transcriptions of several conferences held in Moscow and Havana where participants and their children recalled the roles they played during the crisis.
3. Compare and contrast the traditional view, the revisionist view, and the post-revisionist view of the roles of Kennedy and Khrushchev in resolving the Cuban missile crisis.
4. Compare and contrast and critically evaluate the interpretations of Paterson and Weisbrot as to the causes and solutions of the Cuban missile crisis.

Is There Common Ground?

All writers agree on the timing of the events. Khrushchev started the crisis in the summer of 1962 when Russian ships brought offensive Intercontinental Ballistic Missiles (IBMs) to the island. Kennedy responded in a nontraditional way in the beginning by announcing over radio and television that the United States was establishing a "quarantine" or "blockade" around the island. After several attempts at back door diplomacy with Robert Kennedy, the Attorney General and the President's brother, pledging not to invade Cuba and privately to withdraw obsolete missiles in Turkey and Italy within the next six months, Khrushchev's negotiator agreed to take the missiles out of Cuba immediately.

The basic question asked is which national leader was most responsible for bringing the post–World War II superpowers to the brink of nuclear war. Both Kennedy and Khrushchev wanted to work out a compromise. Both were pressured by hard liners on their respective advising committees. Suppose the Russian ships crossed the blockade line and refused to turn back? Did the Russian commander have the right to start a war without checking with Khrushchev? If the United States had invaded Cuba, how much damage would American ships have suffered? If troop losses mounted because the CIA underestimated the number of Russian soldiers and ICBMs on the island, would the war have escalated to a full-scale nuclear one?

Two random incidents occurred, which might have led to war had more belligerent leaders other than the two Ks been in power. First, on October 27 a U-2 was shot down over Cuba by a surface-to-air missile. Who did it? Cubans?

Russians? Kennedy decided to bypass his own committee and have his brother go behind the scenes to negotiate with Khrushchev's aide. Meanwhile, Khrushchev ignored a U-2 flight whose pilot accidentally overflew the northeastern portion of the Soviet Union and was rescued by American planes without incident.

Managing a crisis such as the showdown in Cuba demonstrates that there is a lot of luck to keep events from spinning out of control. The reader need only study America's crisis over the Pearl Harbor attack, the escalation of the Vietnam War, and the 9/11 attacks, which led to the war on terror to realize the value of peacefully resolving the Cuban missile crisis.

Additional Resources

Michael Dobbs, *One Minute to Midnight: Kennedy, Khrushchev, and Castro on the Brink of Nuclear War* (Alfred A. Knopf, 2008).

Aleksandr Fursenko and Timothy Naftali, *"One Hell of a Gamble": Khrushchev, Castro, and Kennedy, 1958–1964* (W.W. Norton, 1997).

Ernest R. May and Philip D. Zelikow, eds., *The Kennedy Tapes: Inside the White House During the Cuban Missile Crisis* (Harvard University Press, 1997).

James A. Nathan, ed., *The Cuban Missile Crisis Revisited* (St. Martin's Press, 1997).

Sheldon M. Stern, *The Cuban Missile Crisis in American Memory: Myths Versus Reality* (Stanford University Press, 2012).

Internet References . . .

Cold War: Cuban Missile Crisis

www.loc.gov/exhibits/archives/colc.html

Cuban Missile Crisis

www.history.com/topics/cold-war/cuban-missile-crisis

Cuban Missile Crisis

www.jfklibrary.org/JFK/JFK-in-History/Cuban-Missile-Crisis.aspx

The Cuban Missile Crisis, 1962: The 40th Anniversary

www2.gwu.edu/~nsarchiv/nsa/cuba_mis_cri/moment.htm

The Cuban Missile Crisis, October 1962

https://history.state.gov/milestones/1961-1968/cuban-missile-crisis

Selected, Edited, and with Issue Framing Material by:
Kevin R. Magill and Tony L. Talbert, *Baylor University*

ISSUE

Did Southern White Christians Actively Support Efforts to Maintain Racial Segregation?

YES: Carolyn Renée Dupont, from "A Strange and Serious Christian Heresy: Massive Resistance and the Religious Defense of Segregation," New York University Press (2013)

NO: David L. Chappell, from "Broken Churches, Broken Race: White Southern Religious Leadership and the Decline of White Supremacy," University of North Carolina Press (2004)

Learning Outcomes

After reading this issue, you will be able to:

- Understand the role religion played both in support of and in opposition to the desegregation movement.
- Evaluate the ways in which white southerners employed theological arguments to support racial segregation.
- Discuss the response of southern white ministers and laity to the goals of the civil rights movement.
- Assess the connection between religion and politics in reaction to desegregation campaigns in the South.
- Analyze the apparent contradiction between adherence to Christian principles and attitudes toward racial equality among many white southerners.

ISSUE SUMMARY

YES: Carolyn Renée Dupont argues that in the post-*Brown* years of the 1950s and 1960s most white Mississippians, including Christian ministers and laypersons, zealously drew upon biblical texts, religious tracts, and sermons to craft a folk theology supporting massive resistance to racial segregation.

NO: David L. Chappell concludes that white southern religious leaders from the mainline Protestant denominations, preferring peace and social order, failed to provide sufficient support to enable segregationist politicians to mount a united front in defending the doctrine of white supremacy.

On May 17, 1954, the U.S. Supreme Court announced the results of its deliberation in the case of *Brown v. Board of Education of Topeka et al*. In a unanimous decision engineered by new Chief Justice Earl Warren, the Court paved the way for the collapse of a legally supported racial segregation system that had dominated black-white relations in the United States since the *Plessy v. Ferguson* case of 1896.

The *Brown* ruling represented a significant victory for the National Association for the Advancement of Colored People (NAACP), the nation's leading civil rights organization, which had spearheaded a legal action campaign for four decades that had produced constitutional victories in the areas of housing, transportation, and voting, as well as education, in an effort to restore enforcement of the Fourteenth and Fifteenth Amendments in matters regarding race. Most African Americans saw the *Brown* decision as a vital step in finally eliminating separate and unequal facilities throughout the country and realizing the democratic promise of life in the United States. In contrast, the Warren Court's decision sent shock waves through the white South, and even as local school board representatives publicly announced that they would comply with the Court's ruling, back-channel efforts were quickly underway to block biracial schools. Unintentionally aided by the Supreme Court's refusal to establish a definite time frame by which desegregation of public schools should take place, many white southerners interpreted the Court's dictum to act "with all deliberate speed" to mean "never." Following the lead of a group of over one hundred southern congressmen who signed "The Southern Manifesto" that charged the Warren Court with abuse of power and pledged resistance to the enforcement of *Brown*, southern politicians at the local and state level, business leaders who formed White Citizens' Councils, and members of a reinvigorated Ku Klux Klan all joined to resist implementation of the *Brown* decision, claiming that they were only protecting traditional regional mores from the intrusive arm of the federal government.

In the face of this program of "massive resistance," many African Americans came to the conclusion that the NAACP's legal strategy was insufficient to guarantee genuine change in the realm of civil rights. The time seemed to be ripe for a new approach and a broader focus beyond public school desegregation. In 1955, the arrest of Rosa Parks and the subsequent bus boycott in Montgomery, Alabama, appeared to offer a powerful new weapon in the form of nonviolent direct action. Although most closely associated with the leadership approach of Dr. Martin Luther King, Jr., who rose to national prominence from his leadership role in the Montgomery campaign, direct action had long been an instrument for change in the black community. Black residents had employed this strategy in several American cities in the first decade of the twentieth century to oppose segregated seating on municipal streetcars; labor leader A. Philip Randolph had threatened the Roosevelt administration with direct action protests in 1941 in an effort to end racially discriminatory hiring practices in the nation's defense industries and segregation in the armed services; and the Congress of Racial Equality, organized in 1942, had conducted numerous nonviolent challenges to Jim Crow in the 1940s and 1950s. Beginning in 1960, African American college students, joined by their peers at all-white colleges and universities, sparked wide national attention to direct action and passive resistance through sit-in demonstrations that succeeded in desegregating lunch counters and restaurants in over 200 southern communities. For his own part, Martin Luther King depended on nonviolent direct action to carry the day in his campaign to desegregate downtown facilities in Birmingham, Alabama, to lobby for federal action leading to the Civil Rights Act of 1964, and to stimulate broad support for political empowerment though voter registration drives in Selma, Alabama, and passage of the Voting Rights Act in 1965.

The literature on the civil rights movement is extensive. August Meier, Elliott Rudwick, and Francis L. Broderick, eds., *Black Protest Thought in the Twentieth Century*, 2nd ed. (Bobbs-Merrill, 1971) present a collection of documents that places the activities of the 1950s and 1960s in a larger framework. The reflections of many of the participants of the movement are included in Howell Raines, *My Soul Is Rested: The Story of the Civil Rights Movement in the Deep South* (G. P. Putnam, 1977). August Meier's contemporary assessment, "On the Role of Martin Luther King," *Crisis* (1965), in many ways remains the most insightful analysis of King's leadership. More detailed studies include David J. Garrow's Pulitzer Prize winning *Bearing the Cross: Martin Luther King, Jr., and the Southern Christian Leadership Conference* (William Morrow, 1986); and Harvard Sitkoff, *King: Pilgrimage to the Mountaintop* (Hill and Wang, 2008). Taylor Branch's award-winning trilogy *America in the King Years* (Simon & Schuster, 1988, 1998, 2006) is a wonderful read. For an understanding of the major civil rights organizations in the 1960s, see August Meier and Elliott Rudwick, *CORE: A Study in the Civil Rights Movement, 1942–1968* (Oxford University Press, 1973), Clayborne Carson, *In Struggle: SNCC and the Black Awakening of the 1960s* (Harvard University Press, 1981), Adam Fairclough, *To Redeem the Soul of America: The Southern Christian Leadership Conference and Martin Luther King, Jr.* (University of Georgia Press, 1987), and Patricia Sullivan, *Lift Every Voice: The NAACP and the Making of the Civil Rights Movement* (New Press, 2009). Finally, the texture of the civil rights movement is captured brilliantly in Henry Hampton's documentary series *Eyes on the Prize*.

The issue under consideration examines the role of religion in the modern civil rights movement. On the one hand, there is little doubt that religion, especially in the form of the Christian church, played an indisputable role in the efforts of African Americans to win full equality through their freedom struggle. As Aldon Morris has insisted in *The Origins of the Civil Rights Movement: Black Communities Organizing for Change* (Free Press, 1984), "The black church functioned as the institutional center of the modern civil rights movement. Churches provided the movement with an organized mass base; a leadership of clergymen largely economically independent of the larger white society and skilled in the art of managing people and resources; an institutionalized financial base through which protest was financed; and meeting places where the masses planned tactics and strategies and collectively committed themselves to the struggle." Martin Luther King, Jr.'s leadership reinforces the importance of this connection between religion and social struggle and is evident in virtually all of his sermons, speeches, and writings. For King, the strategy of nonviolent direct action was as much a way of life as his Christian witness. See, for example, James Melvin Washington, ed., *Testament of Hope: The Essential Writings of Martin Luther King, Jr.* (Harper & Row, 1986) and Clayborne Carson, ed., *The Autobiography of Martin Luther King, Jr.* (Warner Books, 1998). It should be remembered, however, that King was not alone in this regard. Most early CORE members came to the cause of civil rights through their commitment to Christian pacifism; many of the early members of the Student Nonviolent Coordinating Committee (SNCC), such as John Lewis, James Bevel, Sandra Cason, and Dorothy Burlage, were drawn to the movement by their religious associations; and all of the members of the Southern Christian Leadership Conference, like King, couched their civil rights commitments within the tenets of their faith.

But what about the vast majority of white southerners for whom religious (especially Christian) faith and practice was a central part of their everyday lives? For some, there is no doubt that their understanding of the Gospels and the teachings of Jesus led them to support efforts by their African American brothers and sisters to gain full citizenship rights, though such sympathies could incur the wrath of their friends and neighbors, leading to physical harassment and social ostracism. Along this interpretational line, historian Paul Harvey, in *Freedom's Coming: Religious Culture and the Shaping of the South from the Civil War through the Civil Rights Era* (University of North Carolina Press, 2007), describes a "folk theology of segregation" that originated in the postbellum South and explains how black and white religious folk challenged the theologically grounded racism held by most white southerners and ultimately helped to end Jim Crow. For others, religion became a bulwark to thwart attempts to bring down the walls of racial segregation. Charles Marsh, in his *God's Long Summer: Stories of Faith and Civil Rights* (Princeton University Press, 1997) reveals how white leaders as different as Douglas Hudgins, the pastor of First Baptist Church of Jackson, Mississippi, and Sam Bowers, the Imperial Wizard of the White Knights of the Ku Klux Klan, subscribed to a theology that reinforced a commitment to segregation and racial purity.

The essays that follow evaluate how white southerners related to assaults on the Jim Crow system through the prism of their religious faith and practices. Focusing on the state of Mississippi, Carolyn Renée Dupont asserts that segregationists called upon religion to defend the racial status quo by weaving together biblical literalism, political conservatism, and racial segregation. Ordinary pastors and laypersons produced religious tracts and sermon reprints that portrayed segregation as a universal natural law of God, and secular organizations, such as the White Citizens' Councils, recruited clergy to their ranks to help promote a religious defense of segregation.

In contrast, David Chappell notes that while most white southerners held deeply racist beliefs, the ministers of the dominant Protestant denominations (Baptists, Methodists, and Presbyterians) condemned racial prejudice as unbiblical and wrong, and the major organizations representing Southern Presbyterians and Southern Baptists even called for compliance with the *Brown* decision. For most white southern religious authorities, Chappell says, maintaining peace and social order were more important than defying desegregation and prevented them from aligning their interests with segregationist politicians who fomented anti-civil rights efforts in the 1950s and 1960s.

YES ↵

Carolyn Renée Dupont

A Strange and Serious Christian Heresy: Massive Resistance and the Religious Defense of Segregation

"During the past two years there has been a deluge of materials spread over the face of the South in which various Biblical proofs are given for divine sanction of racial segregation . . . not only the ignorant woolhat-hill folk [are] accepting the exegesis of the hate mongers but the more refined as well. . . . The pamphlets, articles, and tracts [are] written by preachers and religious educators well known in the circle of the target audience." Thus observed Will Campbell, the progressive Mississippi Baptist expatriate, in 1957. The writer Lillian Smith confirmed that "[t]here is a great deal of this kind of talk going around these days, quoting chapter and verse, etc." Other religious leaders described how "many segregationists cloak their activities with quotations from the scriptures . . . [and] claims [are] made by certain ministers that the Bible endorse[s] segregation." Indeed, southern Christians seemed so zealous to cite biblical proofs for segregation that Campbell concluded "some of the racial hate being peddled in the name of Jesus Christ" constituted "a strange and serious Christian heresy."

The biblical case for racial segregation enjoyed a renaissance after the *Brown* decision because religion itself seemed a threat to southern apartheid. Religious assaults on segregation included the major denominations' support for *Brown*, the faith-based activism of many black leaders, and the growing conviction in some circles that the Christian faith mandated racial equality. While black activists and their sympathizers wished that white religion would offer a more vigorous call to racial justice, white southerners regarded as dangerous even the limited support religion had conferred on the quest for black equality.

The faith-based indictment of the southern social system, left unchallenged and allowed to grow, could prove disastrous for the project of massive resistance. If Mississippians heeded the voices of their coreligionists outside the Deep South, their energy for the fight against integration might flag. If they heard about the sinfulness of segregation in their churches and religious literature, they might come to doubt the rightness of Mississippi's path of defiance. Surely, they would lack the conviction to resist the Supreme Court, to suffer the closing of public schools, and to visit punishment on their fellows who violated the bonds of white solidarity. Only at great peril could massive resisters forego a religious defense, for the moral challenge to segregation could cost their campaign what it needed most—the enthusiastic and unwavering support of ordinary Mississippians. Because religion now jeopardized segregation, segregationists called on religion to defend it.

The religious case for segregation took a variety of guises and appeared in many places in the form of an influential and pervasive phenomenon Paul Harvey has described as "segregationist folk theology." Though it drew on biblical texts describing the curse of Ham, the tower of Babel, and the example of Israel as a racially exclusive people, segregationist folk theology functioned as an orthodoxy that wove together biblical literalism, political conservatism, and racial segregation, elevating all three to equally revered status. Tugging at any single strand constituted a heretical unraveling of the entire fabric. Those who articulated these ideas took as natural and God-ordained the social world they saw around them, but except for the essential assumption that heaven smiled on the racial hierarchy, the arguments they marshaled displayed little consistency.

Given the thorough blending of its secular and religious aspects, this belief system cropped up in venues outside pulpits, Sunday school classes, radio sermons, and religious literature. Indeed, segregationist folk theology found expression nearly everywhere—in secular newspapers and organizations, at the state's universities and schools, at county rallies, and in legislative chambers. Though it lay dormant much of the time, when segregation seemed imperiled, it erupted with fury through the normally placid surface of life-as-usual. . . .

Segregationist Folk Theology

. . . The multifaceted nature of this religious defense—its reliance on a variety of extra-biblical evidence and claims—displayed the strength, rather than the weakness, of these arguments in the minds of those who espoused them. These expositors believed they had identified a principle so pervasive in its practice and application that it extended beyond the Bible. In a world defined by a God-ordained principle so significant and sacrosanct as they imagined, hierarchies of all sorts revealed themselves throughout the created order.

Layfolk and ministers without powerful denominational connections articulated this theology far more often than religious elites or pastors of large and prominent congregations. The leaders of the Mississippi Baptist Convention, the editors of the *Baptist Record*, and the pastor of Mississippi's largest Baptist church never gave voice to it as such. Neither did the bishop of Mississippi's two white Methodist conferences and the pastors of large Methodist congregations. At the same time, however, Mississippi's most influential Presbyterian leader, Dr. G. T. Gillespie, provides an important exception to this generalization. President of the Mississippi Synod of the Southern Presbyterian Church, Gillespie authored "A Christian View of Segregation," perhaps the best-known and most representative example of the folk theology of segregation. Gillespie and a few others notwithstanding, the folk theology of segregation came far more often from Mississippi's ordinary pastors and from its eager laymen.

Of extant sermons or tracts advertised as "biblical defenses of segregation," few hewed so exclusively to biblical sources as a 1953 sermon preached by Reverend J. C. Wasson, a Methodist minister in the small Delta town of Itta Bena. Wasson offered classic segregationist readings of two texts often employed for this purpose: Genesis 9:18–27, which details the story of Noah's curse on his grandson, "Cursed be Canaan; a slave of slaves shall he be to his brothers," and Deuteronomy 7:1–6, in which God tells the children of Israel, "You shall not make marriages with [surrounding tribes], giving your daughters to their sons or taking their daughters for your sons." In elucidating the Genesis account, Wasson explained that Noah pronounced the curse because Canaan's father, Ham, having found Noah drunk and naked in his tent, had informed his brothers and so "had on this occasion treated his father with contempt or reprehensible levity." Wasson continued: "The word, Ham, means hot and it signifies burnt or

black. Ham's descendants moved southward into Africa, a hot country, without any doubt this was the beginning of the niger [*sic*] race." Wasson preferred the spelling "niger" because, "the words negro and nigger are not in the Bible. In Acts 13:1 is the only place in the Bible where the black race is designated by its proper name: 'And Simeon that was called Niger,' niger the I is a long I, pronounced Ni-ger, the word means black." The Deuteronomy text prescribed "death" as "the penalty for violating the law of segregation," from which Wasson inferred, "No intelligent Bible student can deny that God is the author of segregation." Wasson then proceeded to identify the law of Moses as a command to "be segregated to keep their race pure" and to elucidate other Old Testament stories—the division of Israel into two kingdoms and the Babylonian captivity—as punishment for the sin of miscegenation.

Another Methodist, the prominent attorney John Creighton Satterfield, elaborated the biblical foundations of segregation at a forum at Millsaps College in 1958. While acknowledging that both segregationists and integrationists could find biblical support for their views, Satterfield proceeded to dismember integrationists' favorite passages. Explicating a passage from the apostle Paul's sermon at Mars Hill in Acts 17:26, "God has made of one blood all nations of men for to dwell on all the face of the earth," the Methodist layman argued that integrationists who used this verse "imply that there are no differences in men and read into Paul's statement something that he probably did not have in mind." Furthermore, Satterfield maintained, those who favored racial mixing stopped reading the verse too soon. "Paul went on to say 'and hath appointed the bounds of their habitation.'" That last phrase, Satterfield claimed, "justifies the segregation of the races." Satterfield proceeded next to Galatians 3:26–28, another reference favored by religious enemies of segregation: "In Christ Jesus, you are sons of God through faith—there is neither Jew nor Greek, there is neither slave nor free, there is neither male nor female, for you are all one in Christ Jesus." Stripping this verse of its racially egalitarian implications, Satterfield observed: "I am sure neither you nor I believe it is necessary to abolish the differences between male and female in order to live a Christian life." He went on to explain that the "South's system of segregation is not based on 'race prejudice' but on 'race preference.'"

Most biblical defenses of segregation, however, did not stick so closely to biblical texts, and many actually mixed scriptural arguments with other types of evidence. William W. Miller's sermon, "The Bible and Segregation," presented on radio station WTOK in early March, 1956, followed this model. Even though Miller, pastor of the Bible Baptist Church in Meridian, declared that "THE BIBLE DOES CLEARLY AND INDISPUTABLY TEACH SEGREGATION OF THE RACES [emphasis in the original]," only a fraction of his sermon enumerated the classic segregationist texts. He devoted the far greater bulk of his message to assailing the theological credentials of those who advanced a Christian mandate for black equality and elucidating the communist-inspired origins of the movement for racial justice and, especially, of the NAACP. Miller concluded his address with an admonition to the "dear Negro friends and brethren" who might have been in his listening audience: "renounce, the devil inspired, Communist supported and directed NAACP as the slithering serpent that it is. . . . Don't imagine that in following the NAACP segregation line you are walking in the Christian faith. Don't think for a moment that you can pray to God and get His blessing upon a course of action which is antithetical to the Christian faith."

The Hattiesburg Baptist layman, D. B. Red, authored two tracts in the pattern of Miller's sermon. Red's "A Corrupt Tree Bringeth Forth Evil Fruit" took its title from Matthew 7:17, advertising on its cover its purpose as "A plea for RACIAL SEGREGATION Based on Scripture, History and World Conditions." The first half of the tract traced the history of Israel as a people commanded to remain distinct from those around them. Moses, Ezra, Nehemiah, and Hosea had all admonished the Israelites not to intermarry with neighboring tribes. In this rendering, as in Wasson's, the children of Israel failed to obey, sought integration, and reaped dire consequences. Red then turned from biblical texts to world politics, history, and geology. He cited turmoil in Africa and India as a result of integration, explained the role of communism in instigating the movement for racial equality, offered the example of Reconstruction as a moment when the South almost lost its way in the face of forced integration, and finally, detailed the beauty of the created order: "Was it not wise to separate the various minerals instead of pouring them all together?" Mississippi's Senator James O. Eastland endorsed the tract for its "masterful job in marshalling both biblical and secular arguments." Red's other self-published tract, "Race Mixing A Religious Fraud," used much of the same material as an attempt to answer religious "race mixers" who advocated integration. Red admonished in his closing paragraphs: "Is your denomination helping to push us down the Devil's highway of racial integration? If so, remember who is paying the bills and whose civilization is going down the drain. . . . The best way to be heard is to speak through the ballot box and collection plate."

Mississippians contributed to and drank from the stream of tracts and sermon reprints with similar themes, content, and format that circulated throughout the South. While probably the most famous and well-traveled biblical defense of segregation came from the Mississippi Presbyterian divine, Dr. G. T. Gillespie, his polemic also leaned heavily on secular as well as religious arguments, though its Citizens' Council promoters circulated it under the title "A Christian View on Segregation." The piece began by describing white southerners' abhorrence of racial intermarriage as part of their elevated culture and depicted segregation as a universal law of nature that resulted in improvements wherever it was applied: "The phenomenal development of the race horse, the draft horse, the beef and dairy breeds of cattle furnish impressive evidence that segregation promotes development and progress . . . whereas the intermingling of breeding stock results invariably in the production of 'scrubs' or mongrel types, and the downgrading of the whole herd." When Gillespie turned to the Bible for evidence, he cited many of the same passages and examples as those developed by Wasson and Red, and then finished with a quick tour of American history, calling on statements by Thomas Jefferson, Abraham Lincoln, and Booker T. Washington to argue that segregation "represents the best thinking of representative American leadership." Though the treatise ostensibly qualified itself by asserting that "the Bible contains no clear mandate for or against segregation," Gillespie nonetheless clearly intended to identify segregation as in keeping with the will and plan of God: "[the Bible] does furnish considerable data from which valid inferences may be drawn in support of the general principle of segregation as an important feature of the Divine purpose and Providence throughout the ages."

The fine distinctions of hermeneutics and exegesis that drew fire from Gillespie's theological critics outside the state (and that still invite the musings of scholars) failed to concern the white southern layfolk who served as the pamphlet's primary audience. Gillespie and his promoters likely did not hope to convert integrationists. Rather, they primarily wanted to assure southern segregationists that the Bible did not condemn the practice. Erle Johnston, publicist for Ross Barnett's successful gubernatorial campaign and later director of the state's Sovereignty Commission, understood the goals of Gillespie's sermon and explained that it gave "those segregationists who needed some kind of Biblical inspiration to feel comfortable . . . what they wanted." The address suited the purposes of the racial hierarchy so well that it became one of Governor Barnett's "favorite moral sources" when he cited "pastors and ministers of various faiths [who] supported his position." Indeed, the Brandon, Mississippi, editor who claimed that "Dr. G. T. Gillespie . . . can convince anyone that segregation is neither immoral nor un-Christian and is God's will," demonstrated that legions of Mississippians understood the intent of Gillespie's message.

Such pamphlets, tracts, and sermons represented the formal articulation of the biblical case for segregation, but white Mississippians more often expressed their belief in the divine nature of the racial hierarchy in less structured and formal settings. Segregationist folk theology announced itself in the ordinary operations of life; it wove itself into workday exchanges, peppered private ruminations, and bubbled up in conversation. Charging a grand jury in Scott County, Circuit Judge O. H. Barnett explained: "Segregation is right, it is Christian, and it ought to be taught in the homes and preached from every pulpit in the state and nation." A Presbyterian confided to his diary that "the pure white race and the pure black have been bred naturally and by Divine Providence over a long, long period of time." Similarly, a state highway patrolman demanded that a civil rights worker use his Bible to "[l]ook it up where it says about mongrelizin' of black and white degeneratin' the races." When the activist asked for the exact reference, the patrolman replied, "I don't know, but it's in there.". . .

"God Separated the Races": The Citizens' Councils and the Religious Defense of Segregation

Immediately after the *Brown* decision and in direct response to the threat it posed, leading citizens from the Mississippi Delta organized grass-roots support for segregation. As the South's most avid promoters of the case for segregation, the Citizens' Councils flourished, and the religious argument figured importantly in their program. The organization attracted 25,000 members among the state's middle and upper-middle classes within months after its birth in July 1954. In two years, it grew to 85,000 members in sixty-five chapters in Mississippi alone. In its wild nascent success, the movement spread quickly to other states, reaching a national membership of 250,000 by the end of 1956. By 1960, the Citizens' Councils promoted the gospel of racial purity through annual rallies, a regional paper with a circulation of 40,000, weekly television programs broadcast by twelve stations, and radio shows aired on more than fifty stations. The organization's success owed, in part, to its disavowal of violence, its pledge to maintain segregation by legal methods, its polished and sophisticated use of public media, and a somewhat socially elevated constituency that included senators, lawyers, and prominent businessmen.

In their capacity as self-appointed defenders of "racial integrity and states' rights," the Citizens' Councils recognized that ignoring religious arguments would leave potentially dangerous streams of thought unguarded. Understanding both religion's danger and its possibilities, the group's original mastermind, Robert Patterson, exhorted laymen to "straighten these churches out" and secure their cooperation in the fight against integration. The Mississippi Gulf Coast chapter purposefully solicited "all clergymen occupying pulpits in this community," appealing "for their continued support of racial segregation in our churches." As fellow Christians, the councilors explained, "we . . . feel ourselves entitled to the honest support of our own pastors in this frightening situation." Reverend J. L. Pipkin of Blue Mountain urged the organization to pursue the religious argument more aggressively: "I believe this may be the Christians['] greatest challenge, to get up and tell the truth against these great odds." Indeed, conspicuously Christian councilors, frightened for the future of segregation, militantly advanced an understanding of their faith and segregation as mutually linked.

While the Citizens' Councils deployed an army of Christian spokesmen, they regarded ministers as a prize catch. One chapter proudly boasted "the accession to its ranks of five very fine men of God from the local clergy." Clergyman occupied prominent places in the organization, as did laymen with very public religious commitments. Local pastors commonly offered the invocation at rallies, and prominent ministers served as keynote speakers. Presbyterian ministers who performed these tasks included Dr. G. T. Gillespie, the . . . Reverend [John Reed] Miller of First Presbyterian Church in Jackson, and Reverend William Arnett Gamble, stated clerk of the Central Mississippi Presbytery, who served on the board of the Jackson Citizens' Council. Among Baptists, Dr. David M. Nelson spoke for Council events and wrote literature for the organization; Baptist Reverend Charles C. Jones of Mendenhall, along with the laymen Louis Hollis of First Baptist Church, Jackson, and D. B. Red of Hattiesburg, also occupied a variety of posts in the organization. Methodist pastors who served the organization included Reverend B. K. Hardin of Jackson's Boling Street Methodist Church, and Delmar Dennis, who spoke at rallies and other events. By showcasing this phalanx, the Councils sought to create the impression that they had unanimous support among Mississippi's religious leaders. In 1957 the group claimed that "only two ministers in the state are not with us," an assertion that smacked of hyperbole.

Ministerial participation afforded the Councils a symbolic religious imprimatur and an aura of respectability, but the organization understood that religious *thought* constituted the real battleground for Mississippians' hearts and minds. Thus, to its arsenal of printed segregationist polemics, the Councils added a subset designed specifically for its Bible-reading audience. These Christian defenses of segregation offer prime examples of segregationist folk theology and its multi-faceted foundations. In addition to Dr. Gillespie and his "A Christian View on Segregation," Mississippi College president Dr. Nelson endowed the Citizens' Councils with considerable prestige. Though his pamphlet on "Conflicting Views on Segregation" seemed to suggest a concern with open-mindedness and fair play, the piece aimed primarily to contravene the moral case for integration as a well-intentioned but naïve and unsophisticated perversion of God's divine plan. The text ostensibly reproduced Nelson's correspondence with "Tom," a pseudonymous Mississippi College alumnus. Nelson repeatedly challenged Tom's understanding of segregation as a "moral question" and repudiated his conviction that Christian faith required that "there should be no racial differences." Nelson argued that, in striking down legal segregation, the Supreme Court had attempted "to do what the good Lord in His infinite wisdom did not do. He made the people into races, with racial characteristics, with inherent likes and dislikes, similarities and dissimilarities, and it would be as fallacious for mere man to try to improve upon the work of the Lord as it proved to be in his attempt to build a tower to heaven." When Tom countered that "The promotion of the Missionary Work in the Baptist Church and the teaching [of Christianity] at Mississippi College . . . seemed to be out of line with our practice of excluding Negroes from our colleges and churches," Nelson replied, "Again we demur and call for the chapter and the verse of the Bible. The whole tenor of the Scriptures is against mixed marriages and the pollution of the blood of distinct and separate races."

The Citizens' Councils did not confine their religious defense of segregation to the tract publications and sermon collections that they advertised for sale in their weekly paper. Nearly every issue of the organization's paper, *The Citizens' Council* and its refurbished successor after mid-1961, *The Citizen*, contained an article, op-ed piece, cartoon, letter to the editor, or news item calculated to establish, elucidate, and defend the orthodoxy that God himself had established segregation to spare whites from contamination by blacks and that any attempt "to destroy these God-given distinctions . . . opposes God's plan." A multipart "Manual for Southerners," aimed at school-aged children and printed over several issues in 1957, developed the case for God's blessing on segregation, as indicated by the subheadings "God separated the

Races," "God Doesn't Want Races to Mix," and "Segregation is Christian." Many issues of *The Citizen* included segregationist sermon reprints among its articles. The authors of these included spokesmen from Mississippi's religious communions—the Presbyterian pastor Al Freundt, the Baptist deacon Louis Hollis, and the Methodist Sunday school teacher Dr. Medford Evans. Mississippians, however, represented only part of the team of southern religious spokesmen who made similar arguments in the organization's journal. The paper pulled in the commentary of religious leaders from across the South, including Dr. Bob Jones, Sr., president and founder of Bob Jones University in Greenville, South Carolina, North Carolina Episcopal minister James Dees, and the Texas Episcopalian rector Robert T. Ingram.

Though the Citizens' Councils advanced several different and even contradictory religious arguments for segregation, the organization probably made its most effective faith-based case by tying religious advocacy for racial equality to liberal theology. A corollary line of reasoning maintained that only the proponents of segregation remained loyal to biblical truth and the old-time Gospel of salvation. Council literature repeatedly advanced the trope of liberal ministers as effeminate, deluded, and educated beyond their own capacities to understand or communicate. Such ministers, they argued, were not harmless, over-zealous, do-gooders, but apostates and heretics who flirted dangerously with socialism, if not outright communism, in emphasizing equality and social engagement. The abstruse theology of racial justice preached by such ministers bore little resemblance to the easily understood evangelical Gospel that issued from southern pulpits. Thus, the Council argument made a short leap from advocacy for racial justice to the kind of religious liberalism Mississippians had decried for decades, and the religious defense of segregation remained intimately tied to a defense of conservative, evangelical Christianity. Commitment to segregation became part and parcel of Mississippians' own cherished faith, and they could fear for their own souls if they accepted the argument for racial equality.

Thus, in the religious and racial worlds of white Mississippians, churches and ministers who advocated racial equality dangerously perverted both the Bible and the divine plan, and they constituted an evil worthy of the Christian's most vigorous opposition. As if to confirm the dangerous status of denominations that had endorsed racial equality, the Citizens' Councils included the Episcopal Church and the Methodist Church on a list of organizations under the jarring heading "Here is the enemy." Other Citizens' Council material decried apostasy in the

Catholic Church, the Lutheran Church, and the American Baptist Convention. Almost the entire May 1958 issue of *The Citizens' Council* explored the pernicious "doctrine" of integration in American religious communities. Under the heading "Southern Churches Urge Mixing," the issue featured articles condemning Southern Baptist and Presbyterian literature and documenting the rise of communist influence within the churches. Dr. Nelson closed the issue with a defense of the place of race in the divine plan: "races are different, radically different, and man is not responsible for this difference, but God [is] . . . [to] attempt to merge them in the crucible of miscegenation . . . is the height of blasphemy."

Will Campbell understood the genius of tying the religious defense of segregation to the conservative faith of Mississippians. When he wanted to draft a short series of publications aimed at "Mississippi Cockle Burrs and Georgia Crackers" as a riposte to the Citizens' Council argument, he planned to approach Mississippians with the same kind of chapter and verse method they favored. Though he did "not believe in the Biblical method of proof text," he "want[ed] to encounter them . . . using their own language, own Biblical methods." Wrote Campbell, "If they want to believe a big fish swallowed Jonah, I won't argue with them." Yet he also knew that even "good fundamentalism [c]ould as successfully deny the racist biblical claims" as more modernist or historical critical methods. Such a tract series as Campbell envisioned might have been Mississippi's only prayer for changing its resistant trajectory, for Mississippians who wanted to keep the faith that had been delivered unto them could find no resonance with the idea that God would champion the cause of black equality. . . .

CAROLYN RENÉE DUPONT received her PhD from the University of Kentucky in 2003 and is an associate professor of history at Eastern Kentucky University.

David L. Chappell   ➡ **NO**

Broken Churches, Broken Race: White Southern Religious Leadership and the Decline of White Supremacy

The standard image of the white South in the civil rights struggle is a mob—united in anger against nine black students at Little Rock in 1957 or against James Meredith at the University of Mississippi in 1962. With amazing discipline, southern politicians projected a more organized image of unanimity. . . . But the black minority in the region saw through what turned out to be a veneer of defiance and solidarity. Probably the most important reason they saw through it was that the religious leadership of the white South showed none of the militancy and discipline of the political leadership. . . .

There was a split in the white southern church that never became formalized, though it was conspicuous to those involved in it at the time. The split was over how to deal with the racial crisis of the mid-twentieth century. It was not as neat as the North-South split of the mid-nineteenth century, which is probably why it never became formalized. . . .

Interested observers like Martin Luther King and James Lawson sensed the disarray when they looked at white southern Christians: there was no way these people could measure up to the image of unity and defiance their politicians had created. King and others saw where the weak points were, and they drove in wedges. Scholars, blinded by the abiding racism of most of the white southern clergy, miss this crucial point. The historically significant thing about white religion in the 1950s–60s is not its failure to join the civil rights movement. The significant thing, given that the church was probably as racist as the rest of the white South, is that it failed in any meaningful way to join the anti-civil rights movement. . . .

The historically significant failure of white southern churches was their inability to live up to the militant image that southern politicians had shown. The churches failed to elevate their whiteness—the institutions and customs

that oppressed black folk—above their other concerns. That is what they needed to do to defend those institutions and customs effectively. Members of the churches were a pretty good cross-section of the white South. They loved feeling superior to black folk and they loved segregation; every election and opinion poll makes that clear. But the civil rights militants perceived something that opinion polls and, so far, historians have not examined deeply enough to grasp: that white churches were unwilling to make sacrifices to preserve segregation. They loved other things—peace, social order—more. They could not make defense of segregation the unifying principle of their culture.

Some prominent white southern religious leaders *tried* to achieve unity on the question of segregation—and were for a time confident that they could get it. But they were on the other side. Before the Supreme Court's desegregation decision of 1954, the southern Presbyterians, known as the Presbyterian Church in the United States (PCUS), and, shortly after the decision, the Southern Baptist Convention (SBC) overwhelmingly passed resolutions supporting desegregation and calling on all to comply with it peacefully. People—even historians—are surprised to hear this. The pro-integration resolutions were reiterated later. Both southern denominations elected presidents who were viewed as strong opponents of segregation. Both desegregated their southern seminaries well ahead of most public schools. (By 1958 all SBC seminaries accepted black applicants.) Of course, there was dissent and conflict within the white southern denominations. They were not as unified for compliance with desegregation as their senators were for defiance. Still, it is striking how, initially, the South's religious assemblies sharply opposed the position taken by its elected politicians.

This is not to suggest that the assemblies supported the civil rights movement. They were in their own eyes expressing cautious respect for the duly constituted authority of the Supreme Court. To them, and to us, that may have been a moderate, even conservative, gesture. But the South's political spokesmen believed, at any rate they consistently said, that the high court had abrogated the Constitution and tried to impose a dangerous and insulting revolution on southern society. The battle over forced desegregation in the 1950s began with the white South's religious bodies lined up on one side and its politicians on the other. . . .

Degrees of Segregationism

In opposition to the denominational resolutions, there were occasional fiery statements from southern white clergymen, such as the Rev. Carey Daniel, whose First Baptist Church of West Dallas became a platform for paranoid extremism. Daniel, also executive vice president of the Dallas Citizens' Council, said that Christians had a duty to disobey the Supreme Court, for the Court, in ordering desegregation, had unaccountably contradicted its long established tradition of approving segregation laws. . . .

Another militant segregationist, the Rev. Leon Burns of Columbia, Tennessee, was less interested in the Bible, which he did not get around to until the end of his speech, than he was in sex:

> The average Negro who wants integration is not interested in equal educational and economic advantages with the White race, and when these things are dangled before him by the NAACP he is unmoved, but when they whisper in his ear that someday he will be able to live with a White woman he is very interested. In a survey made among several thousand Negroes a few years ago, it was found that the secret desire of almost every Negro man questioned was to be able to sleep with a White woman. Several flatly stated that they would risk death in the electric chair to do it.

There are other examples of this sort of militant and dishonest rhetoric from clergymen, but they are rare.

Only a few preachers appear in segregationist periodicals and in the widely circulated segregationist pamphlets. Conversely, most secular segregationists avoided discussion of religious themes. Of the small number of southern white ministers who identified themselves with the segregationist cause, most were much less decisive, much less defiant, than Daniel or Burns. . . .

The lack of commitment among white southerners who nominally favored segregation was what made clergymen's statements so important. The most widely published and often-cited segregationist preacher was the Rev. G. T. Gillespie of Jackson, Mississippi. He was known for a single speech in 1954—his only known segregationist statement, much reprinted but apparently never developed. (He died in 1958.) Gillespie said, "While the Bible contains *no clear mandate* for or against segregation as between the white and negro races, it does furnish *considerable data* from which valid *inferences may* be drawn in support of the *general principle* of segregation as *an* important feature of the Divine purpose and Providence throughout the ages" (emphasis added). The most obvious inference to draw from Gillespie's hesitant language was that even committed segregationists were unwilling to claim biblical sanction. Most of them saw no point in trying to be dishonest about that. Gillespie could never articulate a fighting faith for his parishioners. He was hedging segregationists' bets, not exhorting them with a vigorous call to arms.

The most decisive statement Gillespie made was: "Concerning matters of this kind, which in the inscrutable wisdom of God have been left for mankind to work out in the light of reason and experience without the full light of revelation, we dare not be dogmatic." Similarly, in a segregationist collection of essays, the Rev. Edward B. Guerry, an Episcopal priest in Charleston, South Carolina, wrote: "We should endeavor to respect the sincere convictions of those who disagree with us. No one can assume for himself an attitude of infallibility on a matter so complex as this racial question."

Other than careful, respectable, and nearly unassailable arguments like Gillespie's (if they can be called arguments), segregationist publications rarely gave space to clergymen or to religious appeals. Segregationist preachers who deviated from the careful, not very helpful pattern of Gillespie and Guerry tended to be even less useful to the cause. They showed little interest in disciplined strategy or unity behind a party line.

For segregationist leaders who were trying to maintain their authority and respectability, if it was not dangerous to indulge zealots like Carey Daniel and Leon Burns, it was probably not worth the trouble. The Rev. T. Robert Ingram of Houston, a "born-again" Episcopalian, herded Guerry and four other "born-again" southern Episcopalians into a little volume of essays that poured cold water on religious agitation for civil rights in 1960.

But Ingram had a far more ambitious agenda than most segregationists. He seems to have been more interested in the publicity surrounding segregationism than in segregation itself. In August 1960 he laid out his scheme in a letter to Thomas Waring, editor of the influential segregationist newspaper, the *Charleston News and Courier:*

> Briefly, my plan is this: I am in the process of organizing a propaganda drive to explain how the system of law in the United States and all Christian countries . . . is rooted and grounded in the Ten Commandments. Further, to show that each of the Commandments is under attack by an organized movement of liberals and socialists, the spearhead of which is for the abolishment of capital punishment. . . . I am persuaded that my propaganda drive will tie all the loose ends together for Christian people and throw the liberals into [a] position of attacking not [s]imply a series of isolated issues but the whole law of God.

This is the kind of grandiosity that sensible propagandists like Waring eschewed. For all his racism and fear of federal encroachment, Waring was a practical man who knew the importance of concentrating one's fire.

Most segregationist clergymen felt more compelled to act like Waring than like Ingram. The urge to appear moderate and reasonable while proving their segregationism, however, made them unreliable. The Rev. James Dees—an Episcopal priest from South Carolina who would break away from his denomination in 1963 and start his own, the Anglican Orthodox Church—made flexible as well as rigid statements on segregation. In 1955 Dees published a pamphlet, circulated widely in the South, renouncing all gradualism and defeatism and vowing to oppose integration to the bitter end. Yet at the end, Dees admitted:

> There are certain areas where I think that segregation is not practicable [or] sensible. I am glad to note that at the professional level, the races are coming together for what I believe is for good. I observe that the State Medical Society has voted to admit negro doctors. It has long been a practice for ministerial associations to be inter-racial. I think that it behooves the seminaries of our Church to receive negro students, since it would not be practicable to try to provide a separate seminary for the mere handful of negro seminary students that we have.

Most segregationists thought that concessions like these only legitimated the principle of integration.

It is surprising how little southern white clergymen contributed to the record of the segregationist cause, considering how important religion was in the white South in the period. One reason may be that the Bible, which had so much slavery in it, offered so little objective support for postemancipation racism. There was no biblical equivalent of legal segregation or disfranchisement. There were separate nations and tribes in the Bible, but these were not defined the way race was in the modern South: by laws based on biological concepts. The nations and tribes in the Bible were defined by linguistic and cultural divisions. But the two "races" in the modern South both spoke English and practiced evangelical Protestantism.

For whatever reason, the few prominent religious figures associated with segregationism rarely emphasized the Bible, and when they did mention it they betrayed a complete lack of confidence in its usefulness. Generally they aimed to show only that Scripture was ambivalent on equality and brotherhood on this earth, not that it offered any positive warrant for segregation. Dr. Medford Evans ("an active Methodist layman" and former Sunday school teacher), writing in the Citizens' Council organ in January 1963, outlined St. Paul's insistence on certain earthly social distinctions. He thought that these distinctions might be loosely analogous to race, but he was careful to hedge the analogy: "Whether these injunctions of St. Paul are literally binding on Christians today or not, they certainly prove that St. Paul's statement that we are all one in Christ cannot be used to require indiscriminate integration" on earth. Evans cannot have expected such anticlimactic residues of his exegesis to be very useful in rallying apathetic white southerners. Yet his was typical of would-be religious leaders' statements.

A few lay segregationists and occasional clergymen invoked Acts 17:26, where God created the "nations of men" and determined "the bounds of their habitation." But this was selective quotation of a verse that worked better for integrationists: that verse also said (as Fannie Lou Hamer emphasized) that God "made of one blood all the nations of men." It was not a verse that segregationists could rely on or articulate forcefully. Evans avoided it altogether. Gillespie conceded the main point, emphasized not only in Acts but also elsewhere in the Bible: "Paul affirms the unity of the race"—meaning the human race—"based upon a common origin, concerning which there can be no difference of opinion among those who accept the authority of the Bible." He did not mention that popular scientific arguments for racism required a rejection of biblical monogenesis.

Gillespie's position, like that of most literate ministers who supported segregation, was hesitant and inconclusive as to its biblical bona fides. There were references in the Old Testament that he found useful, especially the curse laid on Noah's son Ham after the Flood (Genesis 9:18-29). The point is not that the curse on Ham was universally understood, by anybody literate in biblical studies, to have nothing to do with racial distinctions. Rather, the point is that Gillespie himself could not do much with it. The story of Ham showed that Providence must have been "responsible for the distinct racial characteristics, which seem to have become fixed in prehistoric times, and which are chiefly responsible for the segregation of racial groups across the centuries and in our time." This was not enough to fuel propaganda. In a sense it was not even relevant, since no one was fighting "racial characteristics." Gillespie needed a justification for man-made legal barriers—barriers that applied even to those who had no distinct racial characteristics, who passed for white. Gillespie was on slightly firmer ground in drawing analogies to Old Testament restrictions on intermarriage and cross-breeding of crops. But his qualifications show that he was on the defensive and not entirely confident even there: the permissibility of modern racial laws was "a possible though not necessary inference" from the ancient Hebrew restrictions.

At any rate, when he got to the New Testament, Gillespie nullified what little support he had shaken out of the Old: "There is no question but that the emphasis placed by Our Lord upon the love of God for the whole world (John 3:16 and other passages) was intended in part at least as a rebuke to the bigotry and intolerance of the Jewish leaders, and to counteract the attitude of contempt and indifference which the Jewish people as a whole manifested toward the other peoples of the world." The best Gillespie could do was to argue, with many qualifications, that the New Testament did not *prohibit* segregation and did not positively *require* integration. So, too, Gillespie's colleague at Bellhaven College, Morton Smith, concluded, "We would have to say first of all that the Bible does not condemn segregation. On the other hand it does not necessarily condemn integration. This being the case this whole matter falls into the realm of Christian liberty. Where the Bible is not clearcut . . . the individual must decide . . . on the basis of his own conscience."

On the fringes of the segregation movement, a few clergymen made more out of the curse on Ham, attempting to claim that God created and intended to maintain racial distinctions. But literate ministers either avoided biblical references or, in the manner of Gillespie, qualified them into uselessness. Again, Carey Daniel was exceptional. The *way* Daniel used the Bible seems to make it clear why he was exceptional. Not content with the curse on Ham or God's setting the "bounds of habitation"

of nations, Daniel constructed an obsessive reading of Scripture, entitled "God the Original Segregationist." This took racial segregation to be the central idea of God's plan. Its section titles included "Moses the Segregationist," "Jesus the Segregationist," "Paul the Segregationist," "Nimrod the Original Desegregationist." Christians could be deeply committed to segregation and still not stomach such a distortion of God's sense of priorities. Whatever comfort they might draw from such a reading in private, most were too embarrassed to be associated with anything of the kind in public.

It must be stressed that in public was where it mattered. It is not in dispute that white southerners held deeply racist views (though one might wonder at the strength of a commitment that required such contortions as Daniel's). The question is whether they could organize themselves effectively—publicly—to defend a way of life built on those views.

The Rev. W. A. Criswell, the most celebrated and popular segregationist minister, in a famous address to the South Carolina legislature (again reprinted much but apparently not developed later), mentioned the Bible only once, in passing—not in his actual discussion of segregation, but in the warm-up jokes he told to ingratiate himself with the audience. . . . Criswell made a ringing if somewhat incoherent defense of segregation, drawing on common notions of social traditions, animal breeding, and so forth, but like most segregationist clergymen he contributed little that drew on his expertise. It certainly helped the segregationist cause that men of the cloth lent their authority to commonsensical, pragmatic, traditionalist, or scientific justifications of segregation. But these justifications were not ones that men of the cloth were specially qualified to provide, or were very good at providing.

The question remains whether a significant number of local ministers, especially in the unaffiliated Baptist congregations and independent sects, might have preached segregation more wholeheartedly (and dishonestly) or, when the Word failed them, might have contributed to segregationist militancy by winks and blinks and nods. The printed evidence reveals two things: segregationist organizations and leaders felt a strong need to add religious authority to their cause (else they would not have pulled the tentative ruminations of Gillespie, Evans, and others into their propaganda at all), and they could not find anything more decisive than what these writers offered (else they would naturally have printed it in their periodicals and pamphlets).

On occasion Criswell—and other preachers—may have indulged in some hocus-pocus to show that the Bible sanctioned segregation. Virtually every historian who has touched on the matter assumes that this went on, though no one has produced much evidence. In his published speech on the matter, at any rate, Criswell did not stoop to claim that the Bible sanctioned segregation. Interestingly, it only took him until 1968 to repudiate segregationism altogether, at which time he made a point of admitting that his earlier position had never been justified biblically. Nor did the Rev. Albert Freundt, a prominent segregationist Presbyterian in Mississippi, bother with the Bible in the article he published for the Citizens' Council.

Segregation's biblical sanction was a matter of deep concern that should not be underestimated. The South was the Bible Belt: inerrantist and literalist views ran high. The question of the biblical provenance of their taboos and traditions was, for many white southerners, a subject of great soul-searching. It was not simply propaganda. The soul-searching required honest and literate segregationists to drop any pretensions of conservative views on biblical interpretation: they would have to become radically unbiblical in their derivation of moral support for, let alone commands to maintain, their political institution. It is necessary to read carefully the anguished writings of the moderate segregationists, and would-be segregationists, on the matter.

During the historic struggle in Little Rock in 1957, some of the city's fringe churches had hitherto obscure preachers (Wesley Frank Pruden, for example) making cases for segregation. But two days before the crisis erupted at Central High, the Rev. Dale Cowling, a prominent local minister strongly connected with and supported by the SBC, preached at Second Baptist Church of Little Rock (the church of Congressman Brooks Hays, who later became president of the SBC). Cowling said: "Those who base their extreme opposition to integration upon their interpretation of the Scripture . . . are sincere beyond question. They are simply greatly mistaken in their efforts to prove that God has marked the Negro race and relegated it to the role of servant." Cowling dismissed the segregationist interpretation of Noah's curse on Ham: "A serious study of this section of scripture and History" would reveal that the imputation of Negro descent to Ham's line "is only the conjecture of man. We might as well reason that the Negro is the descendant of any other Old Testament character." Cowling also confined the strictures against intermarriage in Leviticus to the Old Testament dispensation: "Since the coming of the Savior, the clear insistence of the Word of God is that 'in Christ there is neither bond nor free, Greek [n]or Hebrew.'"

The white pastor of First Baptist Church in Poplarville, Mississippi, the Rev. Clyde Gordon, who dissociated himself from "northern agitators" and did not think "immediate" integration was practical, still condemned race prejudice as unbiblical and wrong. "There are some false impressions and conceptions that we need to fight bitterly today. Some of our writers try to take the Bible and prove by it that God is color conscious and, in such an attempt, reveal a staggering ignorance of God and His word." One example sufficed: "Some say that Noah placed a curse on Ham and he became black. That is not truth. It is not so stated in the Bible. . . . The Negro race, along with every one of us, had its beginning back there in Eden." The Negro "is a human being made in the image of God." Gordon did not want to attack segregation; he simply wanted its defenders not to blaspheme themselves.

Such statements infuriated the segregationists but put them on the defensive. Though it is probably impossible to make a complete tally of biblical references, it seems that antisegregationists and moderates refer to Bible stories like the curse on Ham more often than prominent segregationists do. Segregationists' enemies used the curse on Ham story as a foil. It was an opportunity to ridicule the segregationists, to expose their ignorance and failures of reason. Segregationists, in turn, were sensitive to the way people like Carey Daniel exposed their weaknesses, perhaps made segregationist ideology appear weaker than it was. . . .

The Wages of Neutrality

. . . A major variation on the theme of opposition to political preaching is a startling anticlericalism among segregationists. In Chattanooga, a segregationist denounced the PCUS's pro-integration position: "The sad part of this is that just as the rulings of the Supreme Court and their violations of the Constitution have made so many people lose respect for and confidence in the Courts—so the leaders in our churches are forcing many members to lose respect for and confidence in our churches and its leaders." A month after the *Brown* decision, one of the major segregationist leaders of South Carolina, Congressman William Jennings Bryan Dorn, complained to supporters about widespread southern white acquiescence in the decision. He was "alarmed over the tendency exhibited by many of our church leaders, particularly their influence with youth." Another leader of the South Carolina segregationists, state senator Marion Gressette, told the American Legion and other groups during the election campaign of 1956 that his opposition came from two sources: "a few NAACP Mbrs and Church leaders." . . .

Perhaps the ultimate anticlerical statement came from a fan of Strom Thurmond's in 1955: "By now it should be evident to the pro-segregation forces that their real opponent in the fight to provide for the preservation of the white race in America is the so-called christian religion. . . . It should also be evident that segregation in the U.S. is a lost cause unless the prosegregration forces organize across state lines, po[o]l their knowledge and resources, and launch a frontal assault on organized religion by telling all men the truth about themselves and the so-called christian religion." This fan wanted Thurmond to organize all leaders of the southern states to expose falsehood, suggesting that he "notify the heads of the various religious organizations sponsoring integration that they will be exposed as [frauds] and their religion as a myth, just so much modern witchcraft." . . .

The higher segregationists looked in their churches, the worse it got. They blamed preachers more than laymen or laywomen, big-city preachers more than rural and small-town ones, bishops or regional and denominational board members more than preachers. Universities and colleges were, of course, the worst of all. The segregationists spent a lot of time bemoaning the takeover of southern seminaries by integrationists. . . .

In some cases, divinity faculty were indeed disproportionately outspoken in favor of civil rights. In June 1952, when the trustees of the University of the South (Sewanee) rejected a directive of October 1951 from the Synod of Sewanee Province (fifteen southern dioceses) to admit black students, eight of the ten members of the theology faculty protested. The eight maintained that the trustees' position was "untenable in the light of Christian ethics and of the teaching of the Anglican Communion." . . .

Some followed the logic of anticlericalism so far as to dissociate themselves from religion altogether. Roy Harris, the Georgia power broker and sometime officeholder, was one of the most gifted propagandists in the South. When the Methodist hierarchy dared to send his church a new minister who had signed a statement against closing the schools to prevent integration, Harris

boasted, "I ain't been to church since." In June 1954 an Atlanta racist attacked the head of the PCUS, Wade Boggs, who had made forthright statements against segregation. Referring to Boggs's "burning desire to establish a mixed race," the Atlanta racist said, "I *was* a member of your denomination, but left Druid Hills [Presbyterian Church] and the faith along with others when Dr. [Donald] Miller ranted and raved to have the races mixed." He compared clergymen like Boggs with "those Senator Eastland speaks of as 'racial politicians in judicial robes,'" that is, Supreme Court justices, who made "desperate" efforts to force racial mixing by law. "THANK GOD THERE IS NO LAW WHICH REQUIRES CHURCH ATTENDANCE." The best-selling segregationist author Carleton Putnam addressed the southern white clergy with even sterner language: "You watch the federal government take forcibly from the South while you sit with your hands folded in prayer. I'm tired of the sort of combined ignorance and stupidity you have shown. I'm tired of your timid conformity with the popular drift. And finally, I'm tired of your milk and water suggestions that we pass the buck to God while you support a policy which forces the white children of the South against the wishes of their parents into associations they understand better than you do," This sort of rhetoric further divided prominent segregationist spokesmen from the white South's religious authorities, making unity ever more difficult.

DAVID L. CHAPPELL earned his PhD in history from the University of Rochester and is the Rothbaum Professor of Modern American History at the University of Oklahoma. His other books include *Inside Agitators: White Southerners in the Civil Rights Movement* (Johns Hopkins, 1994), which earned the Gustavus Myers Award for Outstanding Book on Human Rights in North America, and *Waking from the Dream: The Struggle for Civil Rights in the Shadow of Martin Luther King, Jr.* (Random House, 2014).

EXPLORING THE ISSUE

Did Southern White Christians Actively Support Efforts to Maintain Racial Segregation?

Critical Thinking and Reflection

1. How did some white southerners employ biblical evidence to support racial segregation in the 1950s and 1960s?
2. Explain the concept of "segregationist folk theology" as it is discussed in Carolyn Dupont's essay.
3. To what extent did religion play a supportive role in the civil rights movement?
4. What distinction does David Chappell make between the racial views of denominational organizations, leading ministers, and segregationist politicians in the South during the civil rights era?
5. Compare and contrast the arguments of Dupont and Chappell in assessing the influence of religion among white southerners with respect to the goals of the civil rights movement.

Is There Common Ground?

Neither Carolyn Dupont nor David Chappell would dispute the fact that religion played a significant role in the civil rights movement of the 1950s and 1960s, but one must be aware of the complexity involved in fully addressing that role. First of all, while this movement for social justice for African Americans possessed a moral and ethical component, it was also primarily a social and political movement. Second, people of various religious backgrounds and affiliations participated in some phase of the movement, but they did not represent a majority of the American people, including those Americans who shared their religious associations. Third, many people from these same religious affiliations actively opposed the goals of the civil rights movement or took a moderate stance that questioned the speed with which racial change seemed to be occurring. The best example of this separation of religious views on civil rights can be seen in Martin Luther King, Jr.'s "Letter from Birmingham Jail," written in 1963 during the Birmingham, Alabama, campaign. Here King is answering an open letter from eight Birmingham religious leaders, both Christian and Jewish, who expressed concern that King and his followers were asking for too much change too fast. King's irritation with white "moderates" is evident as he insists that a century since emancipation is enough time to have waited for the nation to make good on its promise of equality. Similarly, it is worth pointing out that not all African Americans were comfortable from a religious perspective in taking on the goals of the civil rights campaigns. For them, both ministers and laity, fighting for particular civil rights amounted to political action which fell outside the more essential cause of individual salvation.

The same differences can be found among white southerners. Some carried their religious views directly into the movement; some employed religious arguments to challenge the goals of desegregation; some condemned non-southerners who insisted that their religious faith demanded that they come south to join the struggle; many rejected the linkage between religion and civil rights. As both Dupont and Chappell recognize, the vast majority of white southerners in the 1950s and 1960s were reluctant to turn their backs on what seemed to be the traditional folkways of segregation. Even when the national, regional, or state institutions of particular denominations, such as the Southern Baptist Convention, articulated a position favorable to desegregation, religious followers often failed to follow.

Additional Resources

Joel Alvis, *Religion and Race: Southern Presbyterians, 1946–1983* (University of Alabama Press, 1994)

James F. Findlay, Jr., *Church People in the Struggle: The National Council of Churches and the Black Freedom Movement, 1950–1970* (Oxford University Press, 1993)

Davis W. Houck and David E. Dixon, eds., *Rhetoric, Religion, and the Civil Rights Movement: 1954–1965* (Baylor University Press, 2006)

Charles Marsh, *The Beloved Community: How Faith Shapes Social Justice from the Civil Rights Movement to Today* (Basic Books, 2006)

Mark Newman, *Getting Right with God: Southern Baptists and Race* (University of Alabama Press, 2001)

Internet References . . .

Southern Christian Leadership Conference

nationalsclc.org

The Martin Luther King, Jr. Center

www.thekingcenter.org

The Role of Religion in the Civil Rights Movements

https://www.americanprogress.org/issues/civil-liberties/news/2004/06/09/861/the-role-of-religion-in-the-civil-rights-movements/

Selected, Edited, and with Issue Framing Material by:
Kevin R. Magill and Tony L. Talbert, *Baylor University*

ISSUE

Did the Nixon–Kissinger "Peace with Honor" Strategy Fulfill the Conservative Commitment to Containment of Communism?

YES: Richard Nixon, from "Peace with Honor" and "14 Addresses to the Nation on Vietnam," Richard Nixon (1973)

NO: Jeffrey Kimball, from "Debunking Nixon's Myths of Vietnam," *The New England Journal of History* (2000)

Learning Outcomes

After reading this issue, you will be able to:

- Analyze the United States' policy of containment, tracing the significant events leading to the United States' involvement in Vietnam.
- Explain President Nixon's "Vietnamization" policy during the war.
- Discuss the impact of Nixon's speeches on the conservative lobby's support of his presidency during the Vietnam War.
- Describe Nixon's strategic change in Vietnam and the "decent-interval" theory.
- Evaluate the "Nixon Doctrine" and determine if Nixon's "Peace with Honor" strategy fulfilled his commitment to containment.

ISSUE SUMMARY

YES: Richard Nixon believed his policy of Vietnamization and the Paris Peace Accords of 1973 would bring lasting peace in Vietnam, ultimately fulfilling his promise of containment and satisfying his "Peace with Honor" strategy.

NO: Jeffrey Kimball suggests the Nixon–Kissinger "Peace with Honor" promise remained unfulfilled at the conclusion of the Vietnam war due to misrepresentations of the truth used to salvage the reputations of the president and his conservative staff.

Issue framing with Nathan Scholten

Through the execution of policies including the Marshall Plan, the Truman Doctrine, and containment, the United States communicated its stance against communism to the world following the conclusion of WWII. Believing the Soviet Union to be an expansionist-driven country, desiring authority and influence outside of its legally defined territories, the United States' containment policy aimed to deter recently formed governments, primarily in Asia and Africa, from falling victim to the communist agenda. Any communist country, in the eyes of the United States, aligned with the empire and ideals of the Soviet Union. With the creation and practice of containment through foreign policy decisions abandoning the isolationist, noninterventionist ideologies of the pre-WWII era, the United States established a clear distinction between the ideals of democracy in the West, and communism in the East.

Prior to the conflict in Vietnam, Korea presented the United States with an initial opportunity to implement its policy of containment. With the conclusion of WWII, Korea was divided at the 38th parallel. North Korea, overseen by the Soviet Union, instituted a communist regime, while South Korea, overseen by the United States, instituted a democratic regime. The growing tension and division between the north and south led to North Korea's invasion of its southern neighbor in June of 1950. With the backing of the United Nations, the United States entered an active conflict with North Korea. After three years of fighting, the Korean War ended where it began: a communist North and a democratic South, divided once again at the 38th parallel.

Clearly, Korea delivered little success for the United States and its use of containment. Nevertheless, the threat of communist influence in Asia resurfaced in Vietnam, once again prompting American involvement. For much of the 19th century, and into the years prior to the start of WWII, Vietnam was a colony of France. However, in 1940, Japan invaded the region, holding brief control of Vietnam and other surrounding territories until its surrender in August of 1945. Although the British and Dutch granted independence to previously held colonies in the Indochina region following the end of WWII, France attempted to regain control of Vietnam after Japan's surrender. Vietnam, however, desired independence, and with the leadership of Ho Chi Minh, ignited a revolution against France. The First Indochina War lasted eight years, culminating in France's devastating loss in the battle of Dien Bien Phu in May of 1954. In accordance with the Geneva conference of 1955, Vietnam was divided at the 17th parallel, establishing a communist North controlled by Ho Chi Minh, and a democratic South controlled by Ngo Diem.

France's departure from Vietnam, and the communist rule of Ho Chi Minh in the North, concerned the United States, prompting military and financial support for Diem's regime. Perceiving another opportunity for the Soviet Union to expand its communist influence with an invasion of South Vietnam, the United States again implemented its policy of containment. Coined the "domino theory" by Dwight Eisenhower in 1954, the United States characterized Vietnam as the first domino, and if allowed to fall to communism, would begin a chain reaction of countries within the region. Even with the support of the United States, the people of South Vietnam were dissatisfied with Diem's rule and its abrasiveness toward the largely populated Buddhist citizenry. Fearing an unstable South Vietnam under Diem's control, the United States launched a coup in 1963, leading to Diem's capture and unintended murder. Shortly after, another American-supported government was established, placing Nguyen Van Thieu and Nguyen Cao Ky in power.

Following the assassination of John F. Kennedy, newly appointed president Lyndon B. Johnson strengthened military involvement in Vietnam due to the murky circumstances surrounding the Gulf of Tonkin incidents of 1964. Claiming two separate torpedo attacks on the USS Maddox by the North Vietnamese (evidence later proved no second attack occurred), Johnson communicated the urgency of increased U.S. involvement in Vietnam. Consequently, Congress passed the Gulf of Tonkin Resolution, granting the president "all necessary action" to protect U.S. forces in Indochina. With his newly acquired power, Johnson executed mass-bombing raids throughout North Vietnam, while raising the total number of United States ground forces in Vietnam to 550,000 by 1968. Unfortunately, the North Vietnamese remained unphased, launching the Tet Offensive that same year and defeating American hopes for a swift end to the war.

Amid the rising anti-war sentiment in the United States, coupled with the uncertain effectiveness of the growing military involvement in Vietnam, Johnson declined reelection for his second term. His successor, Richard Nixon, vowed to end the conflict in Vietnam once and for all. At the time of Nixon's inauguration in 1969, the United States involvement in the region tallied over four years. Understanding the complexity of ending the war while ensuring an American victory, Nixon adopted "Vietnamization." Under his plan, Nixon would strengthen South Vietnam, incrementally restoring military responsibility to the South Vietnamese, while simultaneously reducing the presence of United States troops, effectively de-Americanizing the war. However, Nixon's backed invasion of Cambodia in 1970, combined with strategic bombings along the Vietnam-Cambodia border, revived anti-war protests resulting in the death of four students at Kent State in Ohio. By 1973, following the Christmas (1972) bombings of Cambodian and North Vietnamese cities, the Paris Peace Accords declared a cease-fire between North and South Vietnam. Unfortunately, the cease-fire lasted two years, and Nixon's resignation surrounding the Watergate scandal passed responsibility onto previous vice president, Gerald Ford. Congress, not swayed by Ford's pleas for military aid to the South Vietnamese, refused involvement. In the Spring of 1975, with the collapse of South Vietnam's government, North Vietnam seized Saigon. Estimates detail 1.2 million Vietnamese and 55,000 Americans soldiers died in combat, with financial costs for the United States reaching $150 billion.

The YES selections consist of "Nixon's 14 Addresses to the Nation of Vietnam" and Nixon's "Peace with Honor" radio broadcast on January 23, 1973. In these documents, the president details his plan for Vietnamization and strict adherence to the conservative, anti-communist ideology. Utilizing the supposed effectiveness and reach of his many speeches to the American public, Nixon believed his strategies throughout the war and the eventual treaty agreement through the Paris Peace Accords provided a stable, lasting peace for Vietnam, satisfied the goals of American allies in the region, and honored the lives of those who served in the conflict. Nixon further suggests Vietnamization, and the ensuing Nixon–Kissinger "Peace with Honor' strategy utilizing conventional bombing strategies throughout North Vietnam and Cambodia, aligned with the conservative agenda and reduced American casualties. Moreover, Nixon argues this approach was instrumental in garnering continued support from "The Great Silent Majority" and contributed to victory in both the conflict in Vietnam and in his reelection efforts in 1972.

In the NO selection, "Debunking Nixon's Myths of Vietnam," Jeffrey Kimball questions Nixon's claims of fulfilling the "Peace with Honor" strategy and successfully ending the war in Vietnam. Rather than acknowledging the flaws of Vietnamization and containment, Kimball argues Nixon and his staff blamed South Vietnam's fall after the Paris Peace Accords on Congress' refusal to provide necessary aid to the Saigon regime. Furthermore, Kimball highlights Nixon's revised plans in 1971 as a clear rejection of "Peace with Honor." Although ensuring the success and freedom of South Vietnam after the war was a requirement for Nixon during the initial stages of his presidency, he was forced to change his policy. No longer guaranteeing the freedom of South Vietnam, Nixon's adapted strategy now focused on affording South Vietnam a surviving chance at the conclusion of the war. Nixon's adjusted decent-interval, or "stop-gap" option (1971), combining intensified bombings in North Vietnam with a rapidly strengthened South Vietnamese government, hoped to produce a significant length of time between the withdrawal of American forces and the fall of Saigon. Thus, this plan ensured Nixon could argue an acceptable solution was reached in Paris, saving his credibility and the "Peace with Honor" doctrine. Kimball concludes by discussing the subsequent official, historical narratives surrounding Nixon and the end of war, which he feels ignore the true nature of the peace agreement and prove the "Peace with Honor" strategy was not achieved.

Richard Nixon

"Peace With Honor" Broadcast
January 23, 1973

Good evening:

I have asked for this radio and television time tonight for the purpose of announcing that we today have concluded an agreement to end the war and bring peace with honor in Vietnam and in Southeast Asia.

The following statement is being issued at this moment in Washington and Hanoi:

> At 12:30 Paris time today, January 23, 1973, the Agreement on Ending the War and Restoring Peace in Vietnam was initialed by Dr. Henry Kissinger on behalf of the United States, and Special Adviser Le Duc Tho on behalf of the Democratic Republic of Vietnam.

The agreement will be formally signed by the parties participating in the Paris Conference on Vietnam on January 27, 1973, at the International Conference Center in Paris.

The cease-fire will take effect at 2400 Greenwich Mean Time, January 27, 1973. The United States and the Democratic Republic of Vietnam express the hope that this agreement will insure stable peace in Vietnam and contribute to the preservation of lasting peace in Indochina and Southeast Asia.

That concludes the formal statement. Throughout the years of negotiations, we have insisted on peace with honor. In my addresses to the Nation from this room of January 25 and May 8 [1972], I set forth the goals that we considered essential for peace with honor.

In the settlement that has now been agreed to, all the conditions that I laid down then have been met:

A cease-fire, internationally supervised, will begin at 7 p.m., this Saturday, January 27, Washington time.

Within 60 days from this Saturday, all Americans held prisoners of war throughout Indochina will be released. There will be the fullest possible accounting for all of those who are missing in action.

During the same 60-day period, all American forces will be withdrawn from South Vietnam.

The people of South Vietnam have been guaranteed the right to determine their own future, without outside interference.

By joint agreement, the full text of the agreement and the protocol to carry it out will be issued tomorrow.

Throughout these negotiations we have been in the closest consultation with President Thieu and other representatives of the Republic of Vietnam. This settlement meets the goals and has the full support of President Thieu and the Government of the Republic of Vietnam, as well as that of our other allies who are affected.

The United States will continue to recognize the Government of the Republic of Vietnam as the sole legitimate government of South Vietnam.

We shall continue to aid South Vietnam within the terms of the agreement, and we shall support efforts by the people of South Vietnam to settle their problems peacefully among themselves.

We must recognize that ending the war is only the first step toward building the peace. All parties must now see to it that this is a peace that lasts, and also a peace that heals—and a peace that not only ends the war in Southeast Asia but contributes to the prospects of peace in the whole world.

This will mean that the terms of the agreement must be scrupulously adhered to. We shall do everything the agreement requires of us, and we shall expect the other parties to do everything it requires of them. We shall also expect other interested nations to help insure that the agreement is carried out and peace is maintained.

As this long and very difficult war ends, I would like to address a few special words to each of those who have been parties in the conflict.

First, to the people and Government of South Vietnam: By your courage, by your sacrifice, you have won the precious right to determine your own future, and you have developed the strength to defend that right. We look forward to working with you in the future—friends in peace as we have been allies in war.

To the leaders of North Vietnam: As we have ended the war through negotiations, let us now build a peace of reconciliation. For our part, we are prepared to make a major effort to help achieve that goal. But just as reciprocity was needed to end the war, so too will it be needed to build and strengthen the peace.

To the other major powers that have been involved even indirectly: Now is the time for mutual restraint so that the peace we have achieved can last.

And finally, to all of you who are listening, the American people: Your steadfastness in supporting our insistence on peace with honor has made peace with honor possible. I know that you would not have wanted that peace jeopardized. With our secret negotiations at the sensitive stage they were in during this recent period, for me to have discussed publicly our efforts to secure peace would not only have violated our understanding with North Vietnam, it would have seriously harmed and possibly destroyed the chances for peace. Therefore, I know that you now can understand why, during these past several weeks, I have not made any public statements about those efforts.

The important thing was not to talk about peace, but to get peace—and to get the right kind of peace. This we have done.

Now that we have achieved an honorable agreement, let us be proud that America did not settle for a peace that would have betrayed our allies, that would have abandoned our prisoners of war, or that would have ended the war for us but would have continued the war for the 50 million people of Indochina. Let us be proud of the 2½ million young Americans who served in Vietnam, who served with honor and distinction in one of the most selfless enterprises in the history of nations. And let us be proud of those who sacrificed, who gave their lives so that the people of South Vietnam might live in freedom and so that the world might live in peace.

In particular, I would like to say a word to some of the bravest people I have ever met—the wives, the children, the families of our prisoners of war and the missing in action. When others called on us to settle on any terms, you had the courage to stand for the right kind of peace so that those who died and those who suffered would not have died and suffered in vain, and so that where this generation knew war, the next generation would know peace. Nothing means more to me at this moment than the fact that your long vigil is coming to an end.

Just yesterday, a great American, who once occupied this office, died. In his life, President Johnson endured the vilification of those who sought to portray him as a man of war. But there was nothing he cared about more deeply than achieving a lasting peace in the world.

I remember the last time I talked with him. It was just the day after New Year's. He spoke then of his concern with bringing peace, with making it the right kind of peace, and I was grateful that he once again expressed his support for my efforts to gain such a peace. No one would have welcomed this peace more than he.

And I know he would join me in asking—for those who died and for those who live—let us consecrate this moment by resolving together to make the peace we have achieved a peace that will last.

Thank you and good evening.

President Richard Nixon's 14 Addresses to the Nation on Vietnam

Achieving "Peace With Honor"—1969 to 1973.

Introduction

The most pressing problem facing Richard Nixon when he assumed the presidency on January 20, 1969, was the war in Vietnam. When he took office, nearly 36,000 Americans had been killed in Vietnam. During the 1968 campaign, Nixon promised to end the war in Vietnam, secure the return of American POWs, and create a framework for a generation of peace.

According to the Gallup Poll, it had been more than three years since President Johnson's handling of the war had received majority support, and he had lost the support of even a plurality in December 1966, 2½ years earlier, and never regained it.

Conversely, from 1969 to 1972, the Gallup Poll asked on 20 separate occasions "Do you approve or disapprove of the way President Nixon is handling the situation in Vietnam?" Eighteen of the 20 times, more Americans said they approved than disapproved.

Nixon's 14 speeches, and the countless other times he articulated his strategy in press conferences, interviews, and speeches around the country, won him the consistent support of the American people—the people he called "the great silent majority"—and were a key component to his historic landslide re-election in 1972.

May 14, 1969

In his first address to the nation on Vietnam, the President spoke of the steps his new administration was already taking to "bring lasting peace to Vietnam" and spelled out his comprehensive peace plan.

In his opening lines he made clear the principle that would guide his policy and his strategy:

> Since I took office four months ago, nothing has taken so much of my time and energy as the search for a way to bring peace to Vietnam. I know

that some believe that I should have ended the war immediately after the inauguration by simply ordering our forces home. This would have been the easy thing to do. It might have been a popular thing to do. But I would have betrayed my solemn responsibility as President of the United States if I had done so . . . . We want to end [this war] so that the younger brothers of our soldiers in Vietnam will not have to fight in the future in another Vietnam someplace else in the world.

A Gallup Poll taken soon after the speech revealed that more than twice as many people approved of the new President's handling of the situation in Vietnam than disapproved.

November 3, 1969

In President Nixon's second prime-time address to the nation on Vietnam, he made clear that the United States would not abandon its South Vietnamese allies. While said the U.S. would continue to fight the North Vietnamese Communists, he also explained his commitment to reducing American's military presence in Vietnam, including cutting American combat forces in Vietnam by 20 percent by December 15, 1969.

The most memorable part of the speech was his call for the support of the American people for his policy in Vietnam: *"Tonight, to you—the great silent majority of my fellow Americans—I ask for your support."*

The response from the American people was overwhelmingly positive. Within hours, more than 50,000 telegrams and 30,000 letters had flooded the White House mail room, the vast majority supporting the President. President Nixon would later write, "Very few speeches actually influence the course of history. The November 3 speech was one of them."

December 15, 1969

Nixon, Richard M. 14 Addresses to the Nation on Vietnam.

Six weeks after his "Silent Majority" address of November 3, 1969, President Nixon took to the airwaves again to report on the progress toward peace in Vietnam. The President did not attempt to sugarcoat the situation:

> I must report to you tonight with regret that there has been no progress whatever on the negotiating front since November 3. The enemy still insists on a unilateral, precipitate withdrawal of American forces and on a political settlement which would mean the imposition of a Communist government on the people of South Vietnam against their will, and defeat and humiliation for the United States. This we cannot and will not accept.

Nevertheless, the President announced further reductions to America's presence in Vietnam. By April 15, 1970, the number of American troops would be cut by 115,500 from the nearly 550,000 that were in Vietnam when the President took office on January 20, 1969.

April 20, 1970

In his fourth "Address to the Nation" on Vietnam, President Nixon announced his decision to withdraw another 150,000 Americans from Vietnam based on the progress that was achieved in training and equipping the South Vietnamese military to assume responsibility of its own defense. He also confirmed that his earlier goal of reducing American troops in Vietnam by 115,500 had been accomplished on schedule. The President reported that American combat deaths in the first three months of 1970 had dropped to the lowest first quarter level in five years. Near the end of his speech, he expressed his ongoing concern for American prisoners of war and praised the *"dedication, the bravery, the sacrifice of hundreds of thousands of young men who have served in Vietnam."*

But it wasn't all good news. The President spoke of his regret that "no progress has taken place on the negotiating front" and repeated his commitment to the right of people of South Vietnam to determine their own political future. And foreshadowing what would be his next speech on Vietnam just 10 days later, the President also discussed the ongoing use of sanctuaries in Cambodia by the North Vietnamese, to attack American forces.

April 30, 1970

In what would be one of the most controversial actions of his presidency, President Nixon announced that he was launching joint American-South Vietnamese military action to *"clean out major enemy sanctuaries on the Cambodian-Vietnam border"* that were being used as *"bases for attacks on both Cambodia and American and South Vietnamese forces in South Vietnam." Using a map to explain the action he had ordered, the President pledged that "Once enemy forces are driven out of these sanctuaries and once their military supplies are destroyed, we will withdraw."*

Acknowledging that his decision would be hotly debated, President Nixon asserted that his decision went beyond political differences because *"the lives of American men are involved. The opportunity for 150,000 American to come home in the next 12 months is involved. The future of 18 million people in South Vietnam and 7 million people in Cambodia is involved. The possibility of winning a just peace in Vietnam and in the Pacific is at stake."*

June 3, 1970

One month after announcing the Cambodian actions, President Nixon addressed the nation to report on its results. Calling it "the most successful operation of this long and very difficult war," the President declared that he was keeping his pledge to withdraw American forces from Cambodia once the objectives of the actions were achieved.

While film of captured enemy material appeared on the nation's television screens, the President announced, *"In the month of May, in Cambodia alone, we captured a total amount of enemy arms, equipment, ammunition, and food nearly equal to what we captured in all of Vietnam in all of last year."*

The President also said that as a result of the success of the Cambodian operation, the next 50,000 Americans would be brought home from Vietnam by October 15.

October 7, 1970

In one of his shortest addresses on Vietnam, the President explained the five elements of his new proposal, which had already been agreed to by South Vietnam, Laos, and Cambodia.

- First, a cease-fire-in-place throughout Indochina (North and South Vietnam, Laos, and Cambodia).
- Second, convening an Indochina Peace Conference.
- Third, negotiating a set timetable for the complete withdrawal of American troops as part of an overall settlement.
- Fourth, agreement to reach a fair political settlement in South Vietnam that respects the right of the people of South Vietnam to self-determination.
- Fifth, the immediate release of all prisoners of war held by both sides.

The President concluded his speech by calling on the leaders of North Vietnam to agree to this initiative for peace. They would not.

April 7, 1971

President Nixon made just one televised address to the nation on Vietnam in 1971, although he discussed his efforts to end the war on more than 100 other occasions in press conferences, speeches around the country, interviews, on radio, and other venues.

In this speech, the President announced that by May 1, more than 265,000 American troops will have been brought home from Vietnam—cutting almost in half the number there when he took office on January 20, 1969. He also announced that from May 1 to December 1, 1971, another 100,000 would be withdrawn.

Citing the drawdown of American forces, and the increasing ability of the South Vietnamese military to defend its country, the President said, *"I can assure you tonight with confidence that American involvement in this war is coming to an end."*

January 25, 1972

Two weeks after approving the withdrawal of an additional 70,000 American troops from Vietnam, President Nixon made his ninth primetime address to the nation about the war. The President revealed for the first time that the United States had been pursuing secret talks with North Vietnam. He explained that over the previous 2½ years his National Security Advisor, Henry Kissinger, had held 12 meetings in Paris with senior officials of the North Vietnamese government, working to bring the war to an end.

The President outlined the elements of the numerous proposals the United States had made during these negotiations, only to see them repeatedly rejected by North Vietnam.

"We are ready to negotiate peace immediately . . . . We want to end the war not only for America but for all the people of Indochina. The plan I have proposed tonight can accomplish that goal." It would take another year before the North Vietnamese would finally agree to a negotiated peace.

April 26, 1972

On March 30, 1972, the North Vietnamese launched a full-scale invasion of the South, crossing the neutral territory of the Demilitarized Zone with as many as 120,000 troops. *"What we are witnessing here,"* the President said, *"what is being brutally inflicted upon the people of South Vietnam, is a clear case of naked and unprovoked aggression across an international border."*

Citing the performance of the South Vietnamese army's success in resisting the attack without the involvement of any American ground troops, the President announced the withdrawal of 20,000 more Americans within the coming two months—a reduction of nearly 500,000 from when he took office in January 1969.

He closed his speech with a call for national unity: *"My fellow Americans, let us therefore unite as a nation in a firm and wise policy of real peace—not the peace of surrender,*

but peace with honor—not just peace in our time, but peace for generations to come."

May 8, 1972

Fewer than two weeks later, President Nixon was again given television and radio time to speak to the American people. This time the message was much more sobering. During the prior two weeks, the North Vietnamese had launched three new attacks against the South, and, in the President's words, *"the risk that a Communist government may be imposed on the 17 million people of South Vietnam has increased, and the Communist offensive has now reached the point that it gravely threatens the lives of 60,000 American troops who are still in Vietnam."*

The President described the hard choices he now faced: to either undertake the "immediate withdrawal of all American forces, continued attempts at negotiation, or decisive military action to end the war."

He chose the third option, but offered an olive branch. If the North would agree to return all American POWs and would agree to a ceasefire in all of Indochina, the United States would complete a total withdrawal of American troops within four months.

The President's announcement re-energized swaths of protestors—and protests—around the country. But as they had done over the previous 3½ years, a majority of the American people continued to support the President.

November 2, 1972

Five days before the 1972 election, the President gave a wide-ranging speech to the nation from the Library in the White House, laying out his vision for the next four years should he be re-elected. Early in his talk he reviewed the record of his Vietnam policy and reported that *"we have reached substantial agreement on most of the terms of a settlement"* with North Vietnam.

Five days later, the President won an historic victory, carrying 49 of the 50 states (96.7 percent of the total electoral votes) and winning nearly 61 percent of the popular vote. It was quite a contrast to just four years earlier, when then-President Johnson refused to run for reelection and then-candidate Nixon won just 43.4 percent of the popular vote (and just 56 percent of the electoral votes) in one of the closest presidential elections in history.

January 23, 1973

"I have asked for this radio and television time tonight for the purpose of announcing that today we have concluded an agreement to end the war and bring peace with honor in Vietnam and in Southeast Asia." With those words, President Nixon announced to the nation that four years and three days after he first took the oath as president, the war in Vietnam was over.

During the course of the previous four years, the Gallup Poll asked on 20 separate occasions, "Do you approve or disapprove of the way President Nixon is handling the situation in Vietnam?" Eighteen of the 20 times, more Americans said they approved than disapproved.

Following the President's 13th speech, the Gallup Poll asked the question one last time. Fully 75 percent of those polled approved of the President's policy; just 18 percent disapproved.

March 29, 1973

Two months after announcing the peace agreement, President Nixon addressed the nation for the last time about Vietnam:

For the first time in 12 years, no American military forces are in Vietnam. All of our American POWs are on their way home. The 17 million people of South Vietnam have the right to choose their own government without outside interference . . . . We can be proud tonight of the fact that we have achieved our goal of obtaining an agreement which provides peace with honor in Vietnam.

After paying tribute to *"every one of the 2½ million Americans who served honorably in our Nation's longest war,"* he thanked the American people for their support of his policy:

Tonight I want to express the appreciation of the Nation to others who helped make this day possible. I refer to you, the great majority of Americans listening to me tonight, who, despite an unprecedented barrage of criticism from a small but vocal minority, stood firm for peace with honor. I know it was not easy for you to do so . . . . Because you stood firm—stood firm for doing what was right—[Air Force Lt.] Colonel [George G.] McKnight was able to say for his fellow POWs when he returned home

a few days ago, "Thank you for bringing us home on our feet instead of on our knees."

President Nixon achieved the goals he established at the beginning of his presidency—and he did so, in no small part, through these speeches—speeches that earned him the consistent support of the American people to win peace with honor, bring the POWs home, and establish the framework for a generation of peace.

RICHARD M. NIXON was elected as the 37th president of the United States and held office from 1969 to 1973. After serving in the navy for four years (1942–1946), Nixon was elected to the U.S. House of Representatives in 1946. In 1950, Nixon successfully ran for the United States Senate and won the nomination for the vice presidency under Dwight D. Eisenhower in 1952, serving two terms. Losing the presidential election of 1960, Nixon spent eight years (1960–1968) practicing law in New York City and studying the intricacies of foreign policy and affairs, eventually winning the presidential election of 1968 by defeating Democratic Candidate, Hubert H. Humphrey. After a landslide victory over Democratic candidate George McGovern in the 1972 presidential election, Nixon became the first president to resign from office in 1974 amidst the Watergate scandal stemming from illegal activities during his campaign efforts in 1972. While president, Nixon instituted a number of significant domestic and foreign legislation and policies, from the creation of the Environmental Protection Agency (EPA), the Occupational Safety and Health Administration (OSHA), and the revenue-sharing "New Federalism" program, to Vietnamization and the reestablishment of direct relations with the People's Republic of China in 1970–1971.

Jeffrey Kimball

Debunking Nixon's Myths of Vietnam

". . . an account or belief that is demonstrably untrue, in whole or substantial part."

— Thomas A. Bailey

"The time has come to debunk these myths."

— Richard Nixon

Richard Nixon will long be remembered in history textbooks and encyclopedias for having been the first American president to resign his office. It seems almost as likely that he will also be remembered as a president who was uncommonly effective in the arena of foreign policy, because at the turn of the twenty-first century, Nixon's own embattled appraisal of the diplomatic history of his administration—reinforced by Henry A. Kissinger's nuanced variation—occupies a commanding position on the historiographic and public-opinion battlefields. The basic building blocks comprising this intellectual framework are Nixon's claims about his leadership regarding rapprochement with the People's Republic of China, detente with the Soviet Union, and "peace with honor" in Vietnam. Rapprochement and detente are the most celebrated of his policies; his management of the U.S.-Vietnam War is the most controversial and complex.

For many academics, policymakers, journalists, and others among the citizenry, the Nixon-Kissinger paradigm defines in whole or large part their conventional wisdom about the achievements of Nixon-administration foreign policy between the years 1969 and 1974. I venture that it constitutes the canonical perspective of Nixon's diplomatic record. His claim of having opened China has, in particular, achieved the status of historiographic orthodoxy *and* folk legend, which Nixon, a student and practitioner of legend-making, defined as "an artful intertwining of fact and myth, designed to beguile, to impress, to inspire, or sometimes simply to attract attention."

Nixon was ever mindful of Winston Churchill's dictum that history would only treat him well if he wrote his own history. In speeches, interviews, memoirs, and essays during and after his presidency, he portrayed himself as a discerning presidential leader who—possessing a unified conception of global politics—challenged the bureaucracy's narrow-minded, ossified thinking and the public's naive idealism. Maintaining that he had developed a strategy for restoring relations with the PRC even before his election as president, he claimed credit for having initiated rapprochement, and he contended that his motives were noble as well as sensible: bringing China back into the family of nations, reopening trade, ending the U.S.-Vietnam War, and creating an environment for regional peace and stability. Characterizing' his steps toward detente with the Soviet Union as both realistic and imaginative, he claimed successes in advancing nuclear arms control, broadening trade, promoting European stability, and terminating the U.S.-Vietnam War. He lauded the prudent practicality of his Nixon Doctrine, the promising initiatives of his Mideast policies, the righteous realism of linkage diplomacy, and the clever effectiveness of triangular diplomacy in bringing an honorable conclusion to the U.S.-Vietnam War on January 27, J973, through the Paris Agreement on Ending the War and Restoring Peace in Vietnam. Citing his self-styled masterful handling of this intractable conflict—which, he claimed, he had inherited from his Democratic predecessors—he maintained that he had snatched victory from the jaws of defeat, brought American soldiers home, rescued POWs, given the Saigon regime the ability to endure and survive protected the rising capitalist tigers of the Pacific Rim from communism, and preserved American credibility. These putative accomplishments—but especially his claims that he brought an end to the U.S.-Vietnam War, reestablished relations with China, and reduced tensions with the Soviet Union—constituted the key pillars of what Nixon called his "structure of peace."

Kissinger's version of this history was a nuanced variation of Nixon's. As had Nixon, he put a positive spin on the major benchmarks of their joint foreign policy, but he gave himself more credit for having made crucial contributions to the creation of a new international order. He, too, singled out administration opponents for his severest criticism, but he grudgingly acknowledged the dark side of

Jeffrey Kimball, "Debunking Nixon's Myths of Vietnam," New England Journal of History, vol 56, 2–3, Winter/Spring 2000, pp. 31–46.

Nixon's psyche as well as his excessive partisanship, and he noted that these inherent flaws of Nixon's personality had detrimental consequences for his policies and presidency. Kissinger, however, portrayed himself as having been a restraining influence on Nixon and his hardline advisers in the White House.

Nixon, Kissinger, former aides, and some journalists and historians amended the script of this historical drama in the months and years after his resignation from the presidency. They cast the Watergate scandal as the main culprit in causing the breakdown of his administration's foreign policies, particularly regarding South Vietnam, which was ultimately lost, they claimed, because Congress, emboldened by Watergate and in Nixon's absence, failed to provide adequate support to the Saigon regime. Obversely, they portrayed his foreign policy achievements as having redeemed his historical reputation from the embarrassment of Watergate. Appreciated for policies that were seen by many as bold, imaginative, and realistically constructive, Nixon emerged from the ruins of resignation with the prestige of a statesman and peacemaker.

The weakest link in the chain of historical claims that Nixon and his aides and supporters forged in constructing their legend of foreign policy was and is their treatment of the U.S.-Vietnam War. Nevertheless, key elements of their version of history enjoy wide acceptance, in part because they parallel hawkish and pro-war tenets concerning the conflict. For example: North Vietnam (the Democratic Republic of Vietnam; DRV) and South Vietnam (the Republic of Vietnam; RVN) were two separate nations; the military aggression of the Communist North against the potentially democratic South caused the war; it was a just and necessary war; the danger of a regional and global domino effect was real; the key strategic errors were made by liberal Democratic policymakers; the war was militarily winnable; Congress, the press, and the antiwar movement caused U.S. defeat in Vietnam. Even less partisan and more detached historians have not been immune from some of Nixon's claims; for example, that his policies in Vietnam, such as Vietnamization, were guided by a farsighted principle for a new direction in American foreign policy vis-a-vis the third world—the Nixon Doctrine.

Believing that his administration had to seize the moment before antiwar intellectuals and the liberal press preempted the public-relations battlefield, Nixon had begun as early as December 1972 to remold the history of the war. On the nineteenth, the day after the "Christmas bombings" of Hanoi had commenced, he instructed his chief of staff H. R. Haldeman to assemble a spin-control group that would assure him "for all time the coveted title[s] of Peacemaker" and "peace *bringer*." The strategy that emerged at the time of the signing of the Paris Agreement in late January 1973 was to build on the emerging "revisionist school" of history, which defended the morality and purpose of the war, "take advantage of the current crest" of public emotion about the return of the POWs, and launch an "all out effort" to "get a lot of people out selling our line" with a few "key points to emphasize."

At another propitious moment twelve years later, Nixon concisely recapitulated his historical "line" on the U.S.-Vietnam War in a small polemical book entitled *No More Vietnams*. Nineteen-eighty-five, its year of publication, marked the tenth anniversary of the fall of Saigon and the first year of President Ronald Reagan's second term. It was also the year in which the movie *Rambo: First Blood, Part-Two* was released—one of several eighties' motion pictures about the war that appealed to those who wanted to believe that Americans could triumph against their old and new enemies around the globe from Vietnam to Iran to Central America. The U.S.-Vietnam War stood as a symbol of victory betrayed, especially to many military veterans of the conflict, but also to those among the larger public who were dismayed about defeat in Vietnam and cynical about politicians after Watergate. How better for Nixon to advance his personal rehabilitation than to reprise his history of the U.S.-Vietnam War in a politically-correct light for the eighties, thereby ingratiating himself with the resurgent new Right and the diplomatically militant administration of President Reagan, who had often proclaimed the war to have been a betrayed noble cause? Although he stressed the triumph of his own policies, Nixon dedicated *No More Vietnams* to "those who served," comparing their competence and bravery to the pernicious naivete and irresponsibility of antiwar demonstrators. As he had previously, Nixon defended his record in Vietnam, arguing once more that his victory had been overturned by the faithlessness of Congress. Now rejecting detente, Nixon issued a call to arms against an expansionist Soviet Union, world Communism, and a revolutionary Third World in the book's last chapter, which was entitled "Third World War."

Because of the U.S.-Vietnam War, the post-World War II cold war consensus on foreign policy had been shattered; yet, by the 1980's the U.S.-Vietnam War had replaced World War II as the most resonant source of historical lessons for citizens and decisionmakers engaged in debate about the best foreign policy course to take in the present and future. Drawing on their interpretation of the history of the U.S.-Vietnam War, noninterventionist opponents of the Reagan administration argued that America's past intervention in Vietnam had been a failed, tragic mistake; therefore, there should be "no more Vietnams."

From the point of view of interventionists like Nixon and Reagan, the U.S.-Vietnam War had been a necessary war that could have been a military and political success had proper strategies been pursued and the war's opponents not undermined the will of the nation to persist. Military intervention in the third world remained in their opinion a viable and necessary option as long as it was properly executed; therefore, there should be more Vietnams—but no more failed Vietnams of the sort allegedly caused by weak-willed liberal politicians, the press, and the antiwar movement.

Nixon intended the title of his little book to be ironic. In an "author's note," he declared that "both during and after the war, as President and private citizen, I found that television and newspaper coverage of the U.S.-Vietnam War described a different war from the one I knew, and that the resulting misimpressions formed in the public's mind were continuing to haunt our foreign policy." He wrote the book, he said, in order to debunk these misimpressions, or myths, as he more often referred to them, thereby correcting the historical record and contributing to the avoidance of more *failed* Vietnams—while encouraging more *successful* Vietnams.

In the course of debunking myths, Nixon created and perpetuated myths through lack of candor about his own management of the war and by misrepresenting accounts that did not correspond with his. An example was his assertion that among the hundreds of "books, thousands of newspaper and magazine articles, and scores of motion pictures and documentaries" about the war, the "great majority" have concluded that "the United States lost the war militarily." It would not have bolstered Nixon's historical image, of course, to have admitted that the war had been lost militarily, since this would have suggested that he had been forced to accept the Paris Agreement, implying in turn that he had settled for something less than victory. Thus, in *No More Vietnams* and elsewhere, he claimed to have won the war militarily by late 1972. In contrast to Nixon, my own sampling of the mountain of books, articles, and movies about the war to which he referred leads me to conclude that the overwhelming majority of authors, producers, directors, and editors have not claimed that the U.S. had been militarily defeated but instead that the U.S. had simply failed to win militarily, with the result that the U.S. government's longstanding policy goals had gone down to defeat.

Several volumes would be required to confute all of Nixon's own myths of the U.S.-Vietnam War, but perhaps it will suffice here to look at two representative issues that illustrate why core elements of Nixon's history of his handling of the war are demonstrably untrue, if not in whole part, at least in substantial part: What was Nixon's plan for the prosecution of the war, and why did it fail?

Straddling the political center of his electoral constituency during the presidential campaign of 1968, Mr. Nixon alternately implied and denied that he had a secret plan to achieve "peace with honor" in Vietnam. As president in 1969, however, he and his assistant for national security affairs, Henry Kissinger, privately assured select groups that they did have a plan and that it would bear fruit before the year was out—but they were secretive in revealing all of its components. Many years later, Nixon explained that before his inauguration he had reviewed strategic options and during "the first months" of his administration had "put together a five-point strategy to . . . end the war and win the peace":

— Vietnamization (the accelerated equipping and training of South Vietnamese armed forces);

— De-Americanization (the gradual withdrawal of U.S. troops and reductions in draft calls);

— Pacification (counter-guerrilla measures);

— Linkage and triangular diplomacy (using rapprochement and detente to lever Beijing and Moscow into pressuring Hanoi);

— Negotiations with Hanoi coupled with "irresistible military pressure" (incursions into Cambodia and Laos and intensified, expanded bombing against North Vietnam, its army in the South, the Southern Vietcong, and the Ho Chi Minh trail).

Nixon's postwar description of his strategy was only superficially accurate. His careful wording obscured complex and dark realities about the details and underlying assumptions of his plan, its contingent, improvised, and evolving nature, and the goals of his strategy.

Regarding his plan's details and assumptions, Nixon neglected to report that his "madman theory" undergirded the conjoined components of negotiations and military pressure. Guided by this theory, he aimed to force concessions from Hanoi not only by damaging their military and logistical capabilities through stepped-up bombing but also by threatening them with the possibility of more drastic escalations, such as invading North Vietnam, mining Northern ports, bombing Hanoi, Haiphong, and Red River dikes, and using nuclear weapons. Threats of this sort were intended to indicate to Hanoi that he was willing to destroy North Vietnam even at the risk of Chinese and Soviet intervention. They were "irrational" in the sense of exceeding the accepted or predictable norms of "rational" statecraft in the circumstances of the time. Because of his past reputation as a zealous anticommunist and his present campaign of bombing in the rest of Indochina, Nixon theorized that the North Vietnamese would soon come to believe that he was indeed a risk-taker who was capable of escalating the war against the DRV out of vengeful anger or unpredictable impulsiveness.

In the anti-detente political climate of the eighties, Nixon was willing to report in *No More Vietnams* that he had also tried to use the carrots of rapprochement and detente to seduce Beijing and Moscow into using sticks of persuasion against Hanoi; that is, that he had attempted to entice them into reducing their shipments of war materiel to North Vietnam, thereby forcing Hanoi to make concessions in its negotiations with Washington. What he did not report or at least make clear in his discussion of triangular diplomacy was that he had additionally sought to play a "China card" against the Soviets by communicating to Moscow that Washington was prepared to improve relations with Beijing in order to facilitate the containment of the Soviet Union. In addition, he incorporated his mad-threat strategy into his dealings with the Soviets, repeatedly hinting to them that dire military measures in Indochina would result from Hanoi's continued "intransigence," with unfortunate consequences for U.S.-USSR relations. Denoting his tilt toward the PRC, he did not, however, employ this approach in his talks with Beijing. Nixon's strategy—developed in private sessions with Kissinger, who also assisted in its tactical implementation—was not only to link other issues to the settlement of the Vietnam War but to link linkage itself to threats designed to induce anxiety in the Soviets and North Vietnamese.

Nixon initiated these strategies of threat, linkage, and triangulation in a series of steps during the first half of 1969. In February, for example, he informed Ambassador Anatolii Dobrynin that the U.S. would link progress in detente to progress in settling the war in Vietnam, and, establishing his credentials as a mad bomber, he escalated bombing raids in South Vietnam and Laos. In March he launched a massive B-52 bombing campaign against Vietnamese Communist forces in Cambodia. At least as early as July 12, Kissinger, on behalf of his boss, cautioned Moscow through Dobrynin that if it failed in persuading Hanoi to negotiate in a way that pleased Washington, Nixon would dramatically expand U.S. bombing against North Vietnam. A few days later, Nixon warned Hanoi in a personal letter that "if by November 1, no major progress was made toward a solution, we will be compelled . . . to take measures of greatest consequence." He subsequently disseminated this threat through other diplomatic channels. By September Kissinger's National Security Council staff and the Joint Chiefs of Staff were finalizing plans to carry out the threat in operation Duck Hook. In

mid-October, however, Nixon retreated, abandoning Duck Hook in the face of opposition from Secretary of State William Rogers and Secretary of Defense Melvin Laird, NSC staff criticism of the operation's potential efficacy, North Vietnamese defiance, Soviet noncooperation, and his own anxiety about ongoing antiwar demonstrations and latent negative public reaction.

Duck Hook's cancellation spelled the failure of Nixon's original plan to "end the war and win the peace," and it also exposed the contingent, improvised, and evolving nature of his strategy. In postwar memoirs and histories, Nixon emphasized themes of personal control and farsighted consistency: he described himself as having been on top of things and his plan as having successfully unfolded from beginning to end. The reality was that in the beginning—that is, in 1969—all parts of the plan had not been fully in place, and they had also been unusually subject to the vicissitudes of circumstances and events, which neither Nixon nor Kissinger had adequately anticipated. Secretary Laird, for example, doggedly advocated accelerated de-Americanization, leading Nixon, against Kissinger's opposition, to carry out more rapid troop withdrawals than originally envisioned, which had the effect of eroding his military leverage on the ground in Vietnam. Moreover, the DRV and the USSR proved more impervious to mad threats and linkage diplomacy than Nixon and Kissinger had hoped.

For his part, Nixon was less resistant to home-front pressures than he allowed in his postwar accounts, in which he attempted to portray defeats as victories. He described his televised address to the nation on November 3, 1969, for example, as the most significant and effective of his presidency, because it was well-received by a majority of the public, serving to blunt the impact of the antiwar demonstrations of October and November. What he failed to mention, however, was that the speech was originally intended as his announcement of the commencement of Duck Hook but became instead an attempt to energize the Silent Majority. It was also an acknowledgment that the war was now perceived as "his war."

The November 3 address marked the transition from his original plan to a revised plan. Forced to rearrange strategic priorities, he had decided to place more emphasis than before on Vietnamization and pacification (and to be more aggressive in attacking his opponents on the home front). In addition, he revamped his approach to the Soviets: he would continue to use the lure of detente to induce their assistance with Hanoi, but he would now redouble his efforts to bring about rapprochement with Beijing in order not only to foster its cooperation vis-a-vis Hanoi but also to play the China card against Moscow. (Nixon was encouraged in this direction by the border clashes between Soviet and Chinese forces in 1969 and by the coincidence of Beijing's own diplomatic initiatives to break out of its diplomatic isolation in order to play an "American card" against the Soviets.) As before, Nixon intended to buttress his strategy with forceful threats and military measures: continued bombing in Indochina, threats of expanded bombing against North Vietnam, and, if the opportunity presented itself, decisive ground operations.

Nixon's decision to invade Cambodia in April 1970 was the result of a dynamic process that had begun with his search in the fall of 1969 for a more effective blueprint for victory. It was animated not only by the administration's desire to make a "big play" in 1970 but also by the March 18 military coup against Prince Norodom Sihanouk (which Nixon endorsed), the internecine turmoil that had preceded it, and the administration's concerns about the threat that Communist Vietnamese forces on South Vietnam's Cambodian flank posed to Vietnamization and pacification. The invasion—or incursion, as Nixon called it—produced mixed and tragic consequences. Although it did temporarily disrupt Communist Vietnamese troop deployments and logistics, the operation fell far short of the decisive results for which Nixon had hoped; it brought about a military alliance of convenience between Khmer, Vietnamese, and Chinese Communists; and it helped plunge Cambodia into an abyss of civil war. On the home front, Nixon was unnerved by widespread demonstrations against the incursion, by the killing and wounding of students at Kent State University at the hands of Ohio National Guard troops, and by the intensification of congressional opposition to his direction of the war. The strategic results were that he would not be able to send U.S. troops into Laos or again into Cambodia, he would feel more than before the need to carry out large-scale troop withdrawals from South Vietnam, and his hope of bringing the war to a favorable conclusion by the end of 1970 or the beginning of 1971 had been shattered.

Frustrated by his diminished options, and growing more concerned about citizen impatience with the war and the war's potential impact on his chances for reelection in 1972, Nixon considered yet another revised plan during the fall of 1970. He would placate Americans by rapidly withdrawing all remaining U.S. ground forces except those considered "residual"; he would compensate for that step and also apply pressure on Hanoi by canceling negotiations, issuing an ultimatum, and massively bombing, mining, and blockading North Vietnam. Kissinger successfully argued against this "bug out" strategy, maintaining that a pullout by the end of 1971 would leave them incapable of dealing with setbacks in South Vietnam when the 1972 presidential election took place; it would be better, therefore, to continue with negotiations and extend the timing of troop withdrawals until the end of 1972, "so that we won't have to deliver finally until after the elections."

Implicit in this approach was their acceptance of a stopgap option that Nixon subsequently claimed he had steadfastly rejected; namely, the "decent-interval" solution. The term referred to a scenario in which a somewhat weakened enemy and strengthened Saigon regime would ensure that there would be a sufficiently lengthy period of time between the withdrawal of American forces and the ultimate collapse of the Saigon government, whose preservation had long been the fundamental goal of U.S. policy. For Nixon, such a solution would lend credence to his claim that he had negotiated a satisfactory agreement, thus, in turn, salvaging U.S. credibility and Nixon's honor. Nixon had not abandoned hope of achieving his fundamental goal, but he had come to realize that he might fail.

Nixon's policy goal in South Vietnam was the same as that of Presidents Eisenhower, Kennedy, and Johnson before him. Since the late 1950s, the U.S.-Vietnam War had been a struggle over the political status of South Vietnam. The U.S. was committed to the preservation of a non-Communist, pro-capitalist government in an independent state of South Vietnam. Communist and allied Vietnamese nationalists were committed to the expulsion of U.S. forces and the reunification of North and South, preferably, for the Communists, in the form of a "socialist" nation under a Communist government. Thus, in the secret negotiations held in Paris between the delegations led by Kissinger and Le Due Tho, which began fitfully in August 1969, Kissinger sought to win agreement primarily on two main issues: the mutual withdrawal from South Vietnam of American and North Vietnamese forces and the continuance of the Saigon regime of Nguyen Van Thieu. Tho sought to win agreement on the unconditional, unilateral withdrawal of U.S. troops and the removal of Thieu from power although, as events proved, this was not quite as important to them as unilateral American withdrawal. There were several other ancillary issues, but these four were fundamental.

Nixon and Kissinger began to abandon the mutual withdrawal formula in principle in September 1970, thereby shifting from a victory strategy—in the sense of ensuring Thieu's survival—to a strategy that allowed for the possibility of a decent-interval solution. Hanoi abandoned its demand for Thieu's removal by the U.S. in October 1972 but received de jure recognition of the Provisional Revolutionary Government (PRG; the government arm of the Southern National Liberation Front) in the territories it controlled.

My interpretation of documentary and secondary evidence leads me to conclude that the two sides agreed to a compromise in which each accepted less than its maximum terms because each had come by mid-1972 to realize that the war was indeed militarily stalemated and that its chances of achieving an acceptable settlement would be better in October, just before Nixon's reelection, than they would be afterward. Moreover, the costs of the war—that is, the monetary, human, political, and international toll—had become unacceptably palpable. Hence, both sides now deemed a compromise solution to be necessary and, therefore, realistic.

Nixon and Kissinger later argued that their triangular policies vis-a-vis Beijing and Moscow had caused Hanoi to accept a diplomatic solution that favored Saigon and Washington. It appears that the PRC and USSR did exert pressure on the DRV in the form of diplomatic advice or admonition, but at the same time, there is no evidence that it was decisive. Instead, it seems that North Vietnam. acted mostly in response to its assessment of the balance of forces on the ground and in the air in South Vietnam, which would favor them after a U.S. withdrawal, and also to its assessment of the American political scene, which limited Nixon's options and exerted pressure on him to compromise. Neither Chinese nor Soviet pressure was the primary contributing cause of Hanoi's decision to negotiate and sign the Paris agreement. Nor is there any compelling evidence that Linebacker I and II, Nixon's two massive bombing campaigns in 1972, forced Hanoi to come to an agreement. Instead, it seems that the military and political consequences of the North Vietnamese Spring Offensive of 1972, which were not favorable to Saigon, were more, significant in bringing about a settlement.

Who won and who lost the war—the U.S. or the DRV? The proof of the pudding is that in the compromise Paris settlement, the U.S., on balance, conceded the most: it withdrew its ground, air, and naval forces; although Thieu remained in power, the PRG was recognized as a legitimate political entity; despite Nixon's Enhance Plus program of military aid for Thieu, his long-term prospects of survival were not good. Thus, the situation in Vietnam had basically returned to the conditions established in the 1954 Geneva Accords, but with significant improvements for Communist forces: the North Vietnamese Army remained in the South; the PRG and its military arm, the Vietcong, possessed de facto and de jure control of significant portions of Southern territory; the U.S. could not reintroduce troops in the future and not likely re-intervene with air power; and the international community accepted the legitimacy of Vietnam's reunification. It was a cease-fire agreement that might have been achieved in any one of the years before its actual signing in January 1973.

Nixon's argument that the war was won in the Paris Agreement but subsequently lost as the result of Congress's failure to deliver sufficient amounts of aid to Saigon ignored the true terms of the settlement, as well as the demonstrable fact that he and Kissinger had been forced to accept the military realities of the war in 1972 and had yielded to political pressure from congressional liberals and conservatives to get out of Vietnam. What he succeeded in doing, however, was to win, or at least score successes, in the battle for the verdict of history. Through myth-laden accounts of his foreign policies in general and his war policies in particular, as well as his emphasis on Congress's betrayal of the cause, he convinced many that he had forced the other side to accept a peace agreement that favored Saigon. In effect, he and Kissinger succeeded in creating a decent interval—not for Thieu, not for "those who served," not for those on both sides who lost their lives, limbs, or loved ones, and not for the American citizenry or the Indochinese, but for their own reputations. Their's was a message, moreover, that not only helped redeem their prestige but made the war a political football, ill-preparing Americans to understand the meaning and lessons of the war they had just fought.

JEFFREY P. KIMBALL is a Professor Emeritus of History at Miami University (Ohio, USA). He received his PhD from Louisiana State University. He has been the author of books, journal articles, and book chapters on foreign relations, war, alternatives to war, war termination, popular culture, and historiography from the late eighteenth century to the Vietnam and Afghanistan wars. His books include *To Reason Why: The Debate About the Causes of American Involvement in the Vietnam War* (1990), *Nixon's Vietnam War* (1998), which was a History Book Club selection, received the Robert Ferrell Book Prize and was nominated for a Pulitzer Prize; and *The Vietnam War Files: Uncovering the Secret History of Nixon-Era Strategy* (2004), which won the Arthur Link/Warren Kuehl Prize. His latest book, with coauthor William Burr, is *Nixon's Nuclear Specter: The Secret Alert of 1969, Madman Diplomacy, and the Vietnam War* (2015).

EXPLORING THE ISSUE

Did the Nixon–Kissinger "Peace with Honor" Strategy Fulfill the Conservative Commitment to Containment of Communism?

Critical Thinking and Reflection

1. What were the United States' previous foreign policy practices/doctrines of isolationism and containment (in Vietnam prior to Nixon's involvement and elsewhere) and how did they impact Nixon's perspective and decisions regarding the war in Vietnam?
2. How did Nixon's policies change during the Vietnam war? Could Congress have saved Vietnam in 1973 and 1975? Did Nixon and Kissinger really expect Vietnam to fall after a decent interval? Explain.
3. How did the circumstances in Vietnam and growing anti-war sentiment in the United States alter the conservative stance regarding the war? (Trace the specific events leading to this altered conservative perspective)
4. Was Nixon's "Peace with Honor" strategy fulfilled? Do you believe Nixon's strategies succeeded in bringing a true peace to Vietnam? Why or why not?
5. In what ways can the foreign policies decisions made during the Vietnam War provide insight and direction for President Trump in creating policy in Yemen, Venezuela, and Syria?

Is There Common Ground?

Both Kimball and the two artifacts from Richard Nixon highlight the initial strategy of Vietnamization and containment of communism in Vietnam. As all three documents iterate, Vietnamization incrementally restored military responsibility to the South Vietnamese, reduced the involvement of American troops, and hoped to ensure an American victory and the perpetual freedom of South Vietnam. Furthermore, the three selections explicitly discuss the controversy surrounding the invasion or "incursion" of Cambodia by the United States along the border between Cambodia and South Vietnam in 1970. While Kimball and Nixon concur regarding the invasion's adherence to Nixon's policy of containment and its success in appeasing the conservative base within the United States before the 1972 presidential election, unlike Nixon, Kimball is unable to ignore the invasion's effect on increased Chinese–Khmer–Vietnam relations and Cambodia's eventual dissent into Civil War. As the artifacts detail, Nixon's concern after the invasion focused exclusively on the home front, as his efforts to satisfy conservatives allowed the president to overlook the Kent State protest and the growing opposition in Congress.

After 1971, Kimball and Nixon agree the United States' strategy for victory and freedom in Vietnam changed and now focused on providing South Vietnam a chance of survival after the departure of the United States' military. Even with the continued growth in anti-war sentiment and protests within the United States, the documents argue many supporters of the president simply overlooked his change in rhetoric and strategy, offering continued praise for the president's commitment to containment. With the institution of Operation Linebacker I and II in the summer of 1972, Nixon showed an intensified aspiration for reelection in trying to appease the "Great Silent Majority." Although the documents differ in their analysis regarding the success of these operations in Vietnam, Nixon's efforts in garnering electorate support in the United States proved successful, as the incumbent carried 49 out of the 50 states and 61 percent of the popular vote. Ultimately, it was the Paris Peace Accords that sealed the moral and supposed "Peace with Honor" victory for Nixon. While Kimball challenges the message of a complete and lasting victory in Vietnam as observed in the official, historical knowledge surrounding the war, he concedes the agreement was well supported on the home front, as observed by a Gallup poll taken in 1973 where 75 percent of respondents approved of the President's policy for peace.

Additional Resources

George C. Herring, "The 'Vietnam Syndrome' and American Foreign Policy," *The Virginia Quarterly Review*, Volume 57, Issue 4, Fall 1981, Pages 594–612.

James H. Willbanks, *Abandoning Vietnam: How America Left and South Vietnam Lost the War* (University Press of Kansas, 2004).

Ken Hughes, "Fatal Politics: Nixon's Political Timetable for Withdrawing from Vietnam," *Diplomatic History*, Volume 34, Issue 3, June 2010, Pages 497–506.

Richard Reeves, *Alone in the White House* (Simon and Schuster, 2001).

Internet References . . .

The American Experience: Vietnam Online

www.pbs.org/wgbh/amex/vietnam

Foreign Affairs: Vietnam

https://www.foreignaffairs.com/search?qs=Vietnam

Vietnam Center and Archive

http://vietnam.ttu.edu/

White House Tapes: The Presidential Recordings Program

http://millercenter.org/academic/presidential recordings/

Selected, Edited, and with Issue Framing Material by:
Kevin R. Magill and Tony L. Talbert, *Baylor University*

ISSUE

Has the Women's Movement of the 1970s Failed to Liberate American Women?

YES: F. Carolyn Graglia, from "Domestic Tranquility: A Brief against Feminism," Spence Publishing (1998)

NO: Jo Freeman, from "The Revolution for Women in Law and Public Policy," McGraw-Hill Education (1995)

<table>
<tr><td>

Learning Outcomes

After reading this issue, you will be able to:

- Identify and explain the significance of the "cult of womanhood" and its major components.
- Summarize the conservative critique of the women's liberation movement.
- Understand the political implications of the women's movement.
- Identify specific changes in the law and public policy pertaining to the status of women in the United States that were products of the women's movement of the 1960s and 1970s.
- Assess the positive and negative consequences of the women's movement of the 1970s.

</td></tr>
</table>

ISSUE SUMMARY

YES: Writer and lecturer F. Carolyn Graglia argues that women should stay at home and practice the values of "true motherhood" because contemporary feminists have discredited marriage, devalued traditional home-making, and encouraged sexual promiscuity.

NO: Jo Freeman claims that the feminist movement produced a revolution in law and public policy in the 1960s and 1970s that completed a drive to remove discriminatory laws regarding opportunities for women in the United States.

In 1961, President John F. Kennedy established the Commission on the Status of Women to examine "the prejudice and outmoded customs that act as barriers to the full realization of women's basic rights." Two years later, Betty Friedan, a closet leftist from suburban Rockland County, New York, wrote about the growing malaise of the suburban housewife in her best-seller *The Feminist Mystique* (W. W. Norton, 1963).

The roots of Friedan's "feminine mystique" go back much earlier than the post–World War II "baby boom" generation of suburban America. Historians of American women have traced the origins of the modern family to the early nineteenth century. As the nation became more

stable politically, the roles of men, women, and children became segmented in ways that still exist today. Dad went to work, the kids went to school, and mom stayed home. Women's magazines, gift books, and religious literature of the period ascribed to these women a role that Barbara Welter has characterized as the "Cult of True Womanhood," in which the ideal woman upheld four virtues—piety, purity, submissiveness, and domesticity. See Welter's essay in *American Quarterly* (Summer 1996), as well as Barbara Berg's earlier work *The Remembered Gate: Origins of American Feminism: The Woman & the City, 1800–1860* (Oxford University Press, 1978).

In nineteenth-century America, most middle-class white women stayed home. Those who entered the workforce as teachers or became reformers were usually extending the values of the Cult of True Womanhood to the outside world. This was true of the women reformers in the Second Great Awakening and the peace, temperance, and abolitionist movements before the Civil War. The first real challenge to the traditional value system occurred when a handful of women showed up at Seneca Falls, New York, in 1848 to sign the Women's Declaration of Rights.

At the beginning of the twentieth century, a number of middle-class women from elite colleges in the Northeast were in the vanguard of a number of progressive reform movements—temperance, antiprostitution, child labor, and settlement houses. Working in tandem with the daughters of first-generation immigrants employed in the garment industry, the early feminists realized that laws affecting women could be passed only if women had the right to vote. After an intense struggle, the Nineteenth Amendment was ratified on August 26, 1920. The "suffragettes" overcame the arguments of male and female antisuffragists who associated women voters with divorce, promiscuity, and neglect of children and husbands with the ratification of the Nineteenth Amendment. Once the women's movement obtained the vote, however, there was no agreement on future goals. The movement stalled between the two world wars for a variety of reasons: women pursued their own individual freedom in a consumer-oriented society in the 1920s; and the Great Depression of the 1930s placed the economic survival of the nation at the forefront. But World War II had long-range effects on women. Minorities—African Americans and Hispanics, in particular—worked at high wages for over three years in factory jobs traditionally reserved for white males; so did married white females, often in their thirties.

World War II brought about major changes for working women. Six million women entered the labor force for the first time, many of whom were married. "The proportion of women in the labor force," writes Lois Banner, "increased from 25 percent in 1940 to 36 percent in 1945. This increase was greater than that of the previous four decades combined." Many women moved into high-paying, traditionally male jobs as police officers, firefighters, and precision toolmakers. Steel and auto companies that converted over to wartime production made sure that lighter tools were made for women to use on the assembly lines. The federal government also erected federal childcare facilities.

When the war ended in 1945, many of these women lost their nontraditional jobs. The federal day-care program was eliminated, and the government told women to go home, even though a 1944 study by the Women's Bureau concluded that 80 percent of working women wanted to continue in their jobs after the war. Most history texts emphasize that women did return home, moved to the suburbs, and created a baby boom generation, which reversed the downward size of families in the years from 1946 to 1964. What is lost in this description is the fact that after 1947 the number of working women again began to rise, reaching 31 percent in 1951. The consciousness of the changing role of women during World War II would reappear during the 1960s. When Friedan wrote *The Feminine Mystique* in 1963, both working-class and middle-class college-educated women experienced discrimination in the marketplace. When women worked, they were expected to become teachers, nurses, secretaries, and airline stewardesses—the lowest-paying jobs in the workforce. In the turbulent 1960s, this situation was no longer accepted, and by 1973, at the height of the Women's Liberation Movement, women comprised 42 percent of the American workforce. By the beginning of the twenty-first century, middle-class women had made substantial gains in the professions compared with 1960. They represented 43 percent of law school classes as opposed to 2 percent in 1960; 35 percent of students in MBA programs as compared to 4 percent in 1960; 38 percent of all physicians and dentists in contrast to 6 and 1 percent, respectively, in those categories in 1960; and 39 percent in doctoral programs today, up from 11 percent in 1960. Working-class women, on the other hand, have been much less successful in breaking into traditional blue-collar jobs such as truck driving and construction.

One of the consequences of the resurgence of conservatism in the Reagan Era of the 1980s was a blistering criticism of the feminist movement in the United States. Pundit Rush Limbaugh spoke frequently about "feminazis" who were undermining the traditional structures of American society, most particularly the family, and his characterizations were echoed by social critics such as Phyllis Schlafly, Camille Paglia, and others who decried what they viewed as the dangerous excesses of the "radical feminists." The late Elizabeth Fox-Genovese contended that contemporary feminists have not spoken to the concerns of married women, especially women from poor to lower-middle-class families who must work in order to help support the family. Fox-Genovese's *Feminism Is Not the Story of My Life: How Today's Feminist Elite Have Lost Touch with the Real Concerns of Women* (Doubleday, 1996) is peppered with interviews of whites, African Americans, and Hispanic Americans of different classes and gives a more complex picture of the problems women face today. Moderate feminists, such as Cathy Young, author of *Cease Fire! Why Women Must Join Forces to Achieve True*

Equality (Free Press, 1999), challenged the conservatives' arguments that dismissed the real discrimination women had faced in the job market in the 1950s and which seemed to attempt to restore a view of female sexuality as essentially submissive. Historian and feminist Sara M. Evans responded to much of the contemporary criticism of the women's movement by describing a resurgence of feminism in the 1980s and 1990s. Born in large part out of the concern over judicial limitations to abortion rights and highly publicized cases of sexual harassment in the workplace, women's rights advocates rallied to protest against the illusion of equality in the United States that had come to replace acts of more overt discrimination. According to Evans, these conditions resulted in increased membership in the National Organization of Women (NOW) and the National Abortion Rights Action League (NARAL) and mobilized younger women who had taken their improved opportunities in American society for granted. The end result was the emergence of Third Wave feminists who have broken down class, racial, and sexual orientation barriers to achieve a new sense of solidarity and who have joined with women's rights advocates in other countries to globalize their protest. See *Tidal Wave: How Women Changed America at Century's End* (Free Press, 2004).

In the first selection in this issue, F. Carolyn Graglia's critique of contemporary feminism is a throwback to attitudes toward women of the late nineteenth and early twentieth century which applauded the "Cult of True Womanhood" and opposed the women social workers and suffragists who appeared to be intruding upon the man's world. Graglia argues that contemporary feminism ignores women's primary role in raising children and preserving the moral character of the family. She blames "second-wave" feminists, along with the Great Society's social programs, for promoting a sexual revolution that has destroyed the American family by fostering a high divorce rate and sexually transmitted diseases.

In the second selection, Jo Freeman enumerates legislative initiatives championed by activists for women's rights in the 1960s and 1970s—from the Equal Pay Act of 1963 to prohibitions against sex discrimination in employment in 1964 to changes in restrictive abortion laws—and characterizes them as a truly revolutionary shift in American law and public policy. Most notable, according to Freeman, was the introduction of a focus in favor of equality of opportunity and individual choice for women as opposed to an earlier reformist mentality of protective legislation.

YES

F. Carolyn Graglia

Domestic Tranquility

Introduction

Since the late 1960s, feminists have very successfully waged war against the traditional family, in which husbands are the principal breadwinners and wives are primarily homemakers. This war's immediate purpose has been to undermine the homemaker's position within both her family and society in order to drive her into the work force. Its long-term goal is to create a society in which women behave as much like men as possible, devoting as much time and energy to the pursuit of a career as men do, so that women will eventually hold equal political and economic power with men. . . .

Feminists have used a variety of methods to achieve their goal. They have promoted a sexual revolution that encouraged women to mimic male sexual promiscuity. They have supported the enactment of no-fault divorce laws that have undermined housewives' social and economic security. And they obtained the application of affirmative action requirements to women as a class, gaining educational and job preferences for women and undermining the ability of men who are victimized by this discrimination to function as family breadwinners.

A crucial weapon in feminism's arsenal has been the status degradation of the housewife's role. From the journalistic attacks of Betty Friedan and Gloria Steinem to Jessie Bernard's sociological writings, all branches of feminism are united in the conviction that a woman can find identity and fulfillment only in a career. The housewife, feminists agree, was properly characterized by Simone de Beauvoir and Betty Friedan as a "parasite," a being something less than human, living her life without using her adult capabilities or intelligence, and lacking any real purpose in devoting herself to children, husband, and home.

Operating on the twin assumptions that equality means sameness (that is, men and women cannot be equals unless they do the same things) and that most differences between the sexes are culturally imposed, contemporary feminism has undertaken its own cultural impositions. Revealing their totalitarian belief that they

know best how others should live and their totalitarian willingness to force others to conform to their dogma, feminists have sought to modify our social institutions in order to create an androgynous society in which male and female roles are as identical as possible. The results of the feminist juggernaut now engulf us. By almost all indicia of well-being, the institution of the American family has become significantly less healthy than it was thirty years ago.

Certainly, feminism is not alone responsible for our families' sufferings. As Charles Murray details in *Losing Ground*, President Lyndon Johnson's Great Society programs, for example, have often hurt families, particularly black families, and these programs were supported by a large constituency beyond the women's movement. What distinguishes the women's movement, however, is the fact that, despite the pro-family motives it sometimes ascribes to itself, it has actively sought the traditional family's destruction. In its avowed aims and the programs it promotes, the movement has adopted Kate Millett's goal, set forth in her *Sexual Politics*, in which she endorses Friedrich Engels's conclusion that "the family, as that term is presently understood, must go"; "a kind fate," she remarks, in "view of the institution's history." This goal has never changed: feminists view traditional nuclear families as inconsistent with feminism's commitment to women's independence and sexual freedom.

Emerging as a revitalized movement in the 1960s, feminism reflected women's social discontent, which had arisen in response to the decline of the male breadwinner ethic and to the perception—heralded in Philip Wylie's 1940s castigation of the evil "mom"—that Western society does not value highly the roles of wife and mother. Women's dissatisfactions, nevertheless, have often been aggravated rather than alleviated by the feminist reaction. To mitigate their discontent, feminists argued, women should pattern their lives after men's, engaging in casual sexual intercourse on the same terms as sexually predatory males and making the same career commitments as men. In pursuit of these objectives, feminists have fought unceasingly for the ready availability of legal abortion and consistently derogated both motherhood and the worth of full-time homemakers. Feminism's sexual teachings have been less consistent, ranging from its early and enthusiastic embrace of the sexual revolution to a significant backlash against female sexual promiscuity, which has led some feminists to urge women to abandon heterosexual sexual intercourse altogether.

Contemporary feminism has been remarkably successful in bringing about the institutionalization in our society of the two beliefs underlying its offensive: denial of the social worth of traditional homemakers and rejection of traditional sexual morality. The consequences have been pernicious and enduring. General societal assent to these beliefs has profoundly distorted men's perceptions of their relationships with and obligations to women, women's perceptions of their own needs, and the way in which women make decisions about their lives.

Traditional Homemaking Devalued

The first prong of contemporary feminism's offensive has been to convince society that a woman's full-time commitment to cultivating her marriage and rearing her children is an unworthy endeavor. Women, assert feminists, should treat marriage and children as relatively independent appendages to their life of full-time involvement in the workplace. To live what feminists assure her is the only life worthy of respect, a woman must devote the vast bulk of her time and energy to market production, at the expense of marriage and children. Children, she is told, are better cared for by surrogates, and marriage, as these feminists perceive it, neither deserves nor requires much attention; indeed, the very idea of a woman's "cultivating" her marriage seems ludicrous. Thus, spurred on by the women's movement, many women have sought to become male clones.

But some feminists have appeared to modify the feminist message; voices—supposedly of moderation—have argued that women really are different from men. In this they are surely right: there are fundamental differences between the average man and woman, and it is appropriate to take account of these differences when making decisions both in our individual lives and with respect to social issues. Yet the new feminist voices have not conceded that acknowledged differences between the sexes are grounds for reexamining women's flight from home into workplace. Instead, these new voices have argued only that these differences require modification of the terms under which women undertake to reconstruct their lives in accordance with the blueprint designed by so-called early radicals. The edifice erected by radical feminism is to remain intact, subject only to some redecorating. The foundation of this edifice is still the destruction of the traditional family. Feminism has acquiesced in women's desire to bear children (an activity some of the early radicals discouraged). But it continues steadfast in its assumption that, after some period of maternity leave, daily care of those children is properly the domain of institutions and paid employees. The yearnings manifested in women's palpable desire for children should largely be sated, the new voices tell us, by the act of serving as a birth canal and then spending so-called quality time with the child before and after a full day's work.

Any mother, in this view, may happily consign to surrogates most of the remaining aspects of her role, assured that doing so will impose no hardship or loss on either mother or child. To those women whose natures make them less suited to striving in the workplace than concentrating on husband, children, and home, this feminist diktat denies the happiness and contentment they could have found within the domestic arena. In the world formed by contemporary feminism, these women will have status and respect only if they force themselves to take up roles in the workplace they suspect are not most deserving of their attention. Relegated to the periphery of their lives are the home and personal relationships with husband and children that they sense merit their central concern.

Inherent in the feminist argument is an extraordinary contradiction. Feminists deny, on the one hand, that the dimension of female sexuality which engenders women's yearning for children can also make it appropriate and satisfying for a woman to devote herself to domestic endeavors and provide her children's full-time care. On the other hand, they plead the fact of sexual difference to justify campaigns to modify workplaces in order to correct the effects of male influence and alleged biases. Only after such modifications, claim feminists, can women's nurturing attributes and other female qualities be adequately expressed in and truly influence the workplace. Manifestations of these female qualities, feminists argue, should and can occur in the workplace once it has been modified to blunt the substantial impact of male aggression and competitiveness and take account of women's special requirements.

Having launched its movement claiming the right of women—a right allegedly denied them previously—to enter the workplace on an *equal* basis with men, feminism then escalated its demands by arguing that female differences require numerous changes in the workplace. Women, in this view, are insufficiently feminine to find satisfaction in rearing their own children, but too feminine to compete on an equal basis with men. Thus, having taken women out of their homes and settled them in the workplace, feminists have sought to reconstruct workplaces to create "feminist playpens" that are conducive to female qualities of sensitivity, caring, and empathy. Through this exercise in self-contradiction, contemporary feminism has endeavored to remove the woman from her home and role of providing daily care to her children—the quintessential place and activity for most effectively expressing her feminine, nurturing attributes.

The qualities that are the most likely to make women good mothers are thus redeployed away from their children and into workplaces that must be restructured to accommodate them. The irony is twofold. Children—the ones who could benefit most from the attentions of those mothers who do possess these womanly qualities—are deprived of those attentions and left only with the hope of finding adequate replacement for their loss. Moreover, the occupations in which these qualities are now to find expression either do not require them for optimal job performance (often they are not conducive to professional success) or were long ago recognized as women's occupations—as in the field of nursing, for example—in which nurturing abilities do enhance job performance.

Traditional Sexual Morality Traduced

The second prong of contemporary feminism's offensive has been to encourage women to ape male sexual patterns and engage in promiscuous sexual intercourse as freely as men. Initially, feminists were among the most dedicated supporters of the sexual revolution, viewing female participation in casual sexual activity as an unmistakable declaration of female equality with males. The women in our society who acted upon the teachings of feminist sexual revolutionaries have suffered greatly. They are victims of the highest abortion rate in the Western world. More than one in five Americans are now infected with a viral sexually transmitted disease which at best can be controlled but not cured and is often chronic. Sexually transmitted diseases, both viral and bacterial, disproportionately affect women because, showing fewer symptoms, they often go untreated for a longer time. These diseases also lead to pelvic infections that cause infertility in 100,000 to 150,000 women each year.

The sexual revolution feminists have promoted rests on an assumption that an act of sexual intercourse involves nothing but a pleasurable physical sensation, possessing no symbolic meaning and no moral dimension. This is an understanding of sexuality that bears more than a slight resemblance to sex as depicted in pornography: physical sexual acts without emotional involvement. In addition to the physical harm caused by increased sexual promiscuity, the denial that sexual intercourse has symbolic importance within a framework of moral accountability corrupts the nature of the sex act. Such denial necessarily makes sexual intercourse a trivial event, compromising the act's ability to fulfill its most important function after procreation. This function is to bridge the gap between males and females who often seem separated by so many differences, both biological and emotional, that they feel scarcely capable of understanding or communicating with each other.

Because of the urgency of sexual desire, especially in the male, it is through sexual contact that men and women can most easily come together. Defining the nature of sexual intercourse in terms informed by its procreative potentialities makes the act a spiritually meaningful event of overwhelming importance. A sexual encounter so defined is imbued with the significance conferred by its connection with a promise of immortality through procreation, whether that connection is a present possibility, a remembrance of children already borne, or simply an acknowledgment of the reality and truth of the promise. Such a sex act can serve as the physical meeting ground on which, by accepting and affirming each other through their bodies' physical unity, men and women can begin to construct an enduring emotional unity. The sexual encounter cannot perform its function when it is viewed as a trivial event of moral indifference with no purpose or meaning other than producing a physical sensation through the friction of bodily parts.

The feminist sexual perspective deprives the sex act of the spiritual meaningfulness that can make it the binding force upon which man and woman can construct a lasting marital relationship. The morally indifferent sexuality championed by the sexual revolution substitutes the sex without emotions that characterizes pornography for the sex of a committed, loving relationship that satisfies women's longing for romance and connection. But this is not the only damage to relationships between men and women that follows from feminism's determination to promote an androgynous society by convincing men and women that they are virtually fungible. Sexual equivalency, feminists believe, requires that women not only engage in casual sexual intercourse as freely as men, but also that women mimic male behavior by becoming equally assertive in initiating sexual encounters and in their activity throughout the encounter. With this sexual prescription, feminists mock the essence of conjugal sexuality that is at the foundation of traditional marriage.

Marriage as a Woman's Career Discredited

Even academic feminists who are considered "moderates" endorse doctrines most inimical to the homemaker. Thus, Professor Elizabeth Fox-Genovese, regarded as a moderate in Women's Studies, tells us that marriage can no longer be a viable career for women. But if marriage cannot be a woman's career, then despite feminist avowals of favoring choice in this matter, homemaking cannot be a woman's goal, and surrogate child-rearing must be her child's destiny. Contrary to feminist claims, society's barriers are not strung tightly to inhibit women's career choices. Because of feminism's very successful efforts, society encourages women to pursue careers, while stigmatizing and preventing their devotion to child-rearing and domesticity.

It was precisely upon the conclusion that marriage cannot be a viable career for women that *Time* magazine rested its Fall 1990 special issue on "Women: The Road Ahead," a survey of contemporary women's lives. While noting that the "cozy, limited roles of the past are still clearly remembered, sometimes fondly," during the past thirty years "all that was orthodox has become negotiable." One thing negotiated away has been the economic security of the homemaker, and *Time* advised young women that "the job of full-time homemaker may be the riskiest profession to choose" because "the advent of no-fault and equitable-distribution divorce laws" reflect, in the words of one judge, the fact that "[s]ociety no longer believes that a husband should support his wife."

No-fault divorce laws did not, however, result from an edict of the gods or some force of nature, but from sustained political efforts, particularly by the feminist movement. As a cornerstone of their drive to make women exchange home for workplace, and thereby secure their independence from men, the availability of no-fault divorce (like the availability of abortion) was sacrosanct to the movement. *Time* shed crocodile tears for displaced homemakers, for it made clear that women must canter down the road ahead with the spur of no-fault divorce urging them into the workplace. Of all *Time's* recommendations for ameliorating women's lot, divorce reform—the most crying need in our country today—was not among them. Whatever hardships may be endured by women who would resist a divorce, *Time's* allegiance, like that of most feminists, is clearly to the divorce-seekers who, it was pleased to note, will not be hindered in their pursuit of

self-realization by the barriers to divorce that their own mothers had faced.

These barriers to divorce which had impeded their own parents, however, had usually benefited these young women by helping to preserve their parents' marriage. A five-year study of children in divorcing families disclosed that "the overwhelming majority preferred the unhappy marriage to the divorce," and many of them, "despite the unhappiness of their parents, were in fact relatively happy and considered their situation neither better nor worse than that of other families around them." A follow-up study after ten years demonstrated that children experienced the trauma of their parents' divorce as more serious and long-lasting than any researchers had anticipated. *Time* so readily acquiesced in the disadvantaging of homemakers and the disruption of children's lives because the feminist ideological parameters within which it operates have excluded marriage as a *proper* career choice. Removing the obstacles to making it a *viable* choice would, therefore, be an undesirable subversion of feminist goals.

That *Time* would have women trot forward on life's journey constrained by the blinders of feminist ideology is evident from its failure to question any feminist notion, no matter how silly, or to explore solutions incompatible with the ideology's script. One of the silliest notions *Time* left unexamined was that young women want "good careers, good marriages and two or three kids, and they don't want the children to be raised by strangers." The supposed realism of this expectation lay in the new woman's attitude that "I don't want to work 70 hours a week, but I want to be vice president, and *you* have to change." But even if thirty hours were cut from that seventy-hour workweek, the new woman would still be working the normal full-time week, her children would still be raised by surrogates, and the norm would continue to be the feminist version of child-rearing that *Time* itself described unflatteringly as "less a preoccupation than an improvisation."

The illusion that a woman can achieve career success without sacrificing the daily personal care of her children—and except among the very wealthy, most of her leisure as well—went unquestioned by *Time*. It did note, however, the dissatisfaction expressed by Eastern European and Russian women who had experienced, as a matter of government policy, the same liberation from home and children that our feminists have undertaken to bestow upon Western women. In what *Time* described as "a curious reversal of Western feminism's emphasis on careers for women," the new female leaders of Eastern Europe would like "to reverse the communist diktat that all women have to work." Women have "dreamed," said the Polish

Minister of Culture and Arts, "of reaching the point where we have the choice to stay home" that communism had taken away. But blinded by its feminist bias, *Time* could only find it "curious" that women would choose to stay at home; apparently beyond the pale of respectability was any argument that it would serve Western women's interest to retain the choice that contemporary feminism—filling in the West the role of communism in the East—has sought to deny them.

Nor was its feminist bias shaken by the attitudes of Japanese women, most of whom, *Time* noted, reject "equality" with men, choosing to cease work after the birth of a first child and later resuming a part-time career or pursuing hobbies or community work. The picture painted was that of the 1950s American suburban housewife reviled by Betty Friedan, except that the American has enjoyed a higher standard of living (particularly a much larger home) than has the Japanese. In Japan, *Time* observed, being "a housewife is nothing to be ashamed of." Dishonoring the housewife's role was a goal, it might have added, that Japanese feminists can, in time, accomplish if they emulate their American counterparts.

Japanese wives have broad responsibilities, commented *Time,* because most husbands leave their salaries and children entirely in wives' hands; freed from drudgery by modern appliances, housewives can "pursue their interests in a carefree manner, while men have to worry about supporting their wives and children." Typically, a Japanese wife controls household finances, giving her husband a cash allowance, the size of which, apparently, dissatisfies one-half of the men. Acknowledging that Japanese wives take the leadership in most homes, one husband observed that "[t]hings go best when the husband is swimming in the palm of his wife's hand." A home is well-managed, said one wife, "if you make your men feel that they're in control when they are in front of others, while in reality you're in control." It seems like a good arrangement to me.

Instead of inquiring whether a similar carefree existence might appeal to some American women, *Time* looked forward to the day when marriage would no longer be a career for Japanese women, as their men took over household and child-rearing chores, enabling wives to join husbands in the workplace. It was noted, however, that a major impediment to this goal, which would have to be corrected, was the fact that Japanese day-care centers usually run for only eight hours a day. Thus, *Time* made clear that its overriding concern was simply promoting the presence of women in the work force. This presence is seen as a good *per se,* without any *pro forma* talk about the economic necessity of a second income and without any question raised as to whether it is in children's interest to spend any amount of time—much less in excess of eight hours a day—in communal care. . . .

The Awakened Brünnhilde

. . . Those who would defend anti-feminist traditionalism today are like heretics fighting a regnant Inquisition. To become a homemaker, a woman may need the courage of a heretic. This is one reason that the defense of traditional women is often grounded in religious teachings, for the heretic's courage usually rests on faith. The source of courage I offer is the conviction, based on my own experience, that contemporary feminism's stereotypical caricature of the housewife did not reflect reality when Friedan popularized it, does not reflect reality today, and need not govern reality.

Feminists claimed a woman can find identity and fulfillment only in a career; they are wrong. They claimed a woman can, in that popular expression, "have it all"; they are wrong—she can have only some. The experience of being a mother at home is a different experience from being a full-time market producer who is also a mother. A woman can have one or the other experience, but not both at the same time. Combining a career with motherhood requires a woman to compromise by diminishing her commitment and exertions with respect to one role or the other, or usually, to both. Rarely, if ever, can a woman adequately perform in a full-time career if she diminishes her commitment to it sufficiently to replicate the experience of being a mother at home.

Women were *never* told they could *not* choose to make the compromises required to combine these roles; within the memory of all living today there were always some women who did so choose. But by successfully degrading the housewife's role, contemporary feminism undertook to force this choice upon all women. I declined to make the compromises necessary to combine a career with motherhood because I did not want to become like Andrea Dworkin's spiritual virgin. I did not want to keep my being intact, as Dworkin puts it, so that I could continue to pursue career success. Such pursuit would have required me to hold too much of myself aloof from husband and children: the invisible "wedge-shaped core of darkness" that Virginia Woolf described as being oneself would have to be too large, and not enough of me would have been left over for them.

I feared that if I cultivated that "wedge-shaped core of darkness" within myself enough to maintain a successful career, I would be consumed by that career, and that thus desiccated, too little of me would remain to flesh out my roles as wife and mother. Giving most of myself to the market seemed less appropriate and attractive than reserving myself for my family. Reinforcing this decision was my experience that when a woman lives too much in her mind, she finds it increasingly difficult to live through her body. Her nurturing ties to her children become attenuated; her physical relationship with her husband becomes hollow and perfunctory. Certainly in my case, Dr. James C. Neely spoke the truth in *Gender: The Myth of Equality:* "With too much emphasis on intellect, a woman becomes 'too into her head' to function in a sexual, motherly way, destroying by the process of thought the process of feeling her sexuality."

Virginia Woolf never compromised her market achievements with motherhood; nor did the Brontë sisters, Jane Austen, or George Eliot. Nor did Helen Frankenthaler who, at the time she was acknowledged to be the most prominent living female artist, said in an interview: "We all make different compromises. And, no, I don't regret not having children. Given my painting, children could have suffered. A mother must make her children come first: young children are helpless. Well, paintings are objects but they're also helpless." I agree with her; that is precisely how I felt about the briefs I wrote for clients. Those briefs were, to me, like helpless children; in writing them, I first learned the meaning of complete devotion. I stopped writing them because I believed they would have been masters too jealous of my husband and my children.

Society never rebuked these women for refusing to compromise their literary and artistic achievements. Neither should it rebuke other kinds of women for refusing to compromise their own artistry of motherhood and domesticity. Some women may agree that the reality I depict rings truer to them than the feminist depiction. This conviction may help them find the courage of a heretic. Some others, both men and women, may see enough truth in the reality I depict that they will come to regret society's acquiescence in the status degradation of the housewife. They may then accept the currently unfashionable notion that society should respect and support women who adopt the anti-feminist perspective.

It is in society's interest to begin to pull apart the double-bind web spun by feminism and so order itself as not to inhibit any woman who *could* be an awakened Brünnhilde. Delighted and contented women will certainly do less harm—and probably more good—to society than frenzied and despairing ones. This is not to suggest that society should interfere with a woman's decision to follow the feminist script and adopt any form of spiritual virginity that suits her. But neither should society continue to validate destruction of the women's pact by the contemporary feminists who sought to make us all follow their script. We should now begin to dismantle our regime that discourages and disadvantages the traditional woman who rejects feminist spiritual virginity and seeks instead the very different delight and contentment that she believes best suits her.

F. Carolyn Graglia is a trained lawyer, writer, and lecturer whose articles and books challenge the viewpoint of the modern women's movement.

Jo Freeman

The Revolution for Women in Law and Public Policy

A revolution in public policy toward women happened in the 1960s and 1970s. Beginning with passage of the equal pay act in 1963 and the prohibition against sex discrimination in employment in 1964, Congress added numerous laws to the books that altered the thrust of public policy toward women from one of protection to one of equal opportunity. While implementation is incomplete, and equal opportunity by itself will not eradicate women's secondary position in society, the importance of this fundamental change should not be underestimated.

Parallel to this development the Supreme Court fundamentally altered its interpretation of women's position in society. Until 1971, the judicial approach to women was that their rights and responsibilities, opportunities and obligations, were essentially determined by their position in the family—the role of wife and mother. Women were viewed first and foremost as members of a dependent class whose individual rights were subservient to their class position. From this perspective virtually all laws that classified by sex were constitutional. Today most such laws have been found unconstitutional. The remaining laws and practices that treat the sexes differently are subject to more searching scrutiny than in the past, and the Court is particularly disapproving of rationalizations for them that encourage dependency. . . .

Family Law

Under the English common law a woman lost her legal identity upon marriage; it *merged* into that of her husband under the feudal doctrine of *coverture*. The result was succinctly stated by Justice Black in 1966 as resting "on the old common-law fiction that the husband and wife are one . . . [and] that . . . one is the husband.". . .

In 1979 Louisiana became the last state to give both spouses the legal right to manage the community property. The case that led to its revocation is a good example of how little protection joint ownership really gave to a wife. Louisiana's "head and master" law permitted a husband the unilateral right to dispose of jointly owned community property without his wife's knowledge or consent. In 1974 Joan Feenstra had her husband incarcerated for molesting their minor daughter. To pay the attorney who represented him in this action, he executed a mortgage on their home. Louisiana law did not require the husband to get his wife's permission to do this or even to inform her of his action, although the house had been paid for solely out of her earnings. After the charges were dropped, a legal separation obtained, and the husband left the state, the attorney foreclosed on the mortgage, and Joan Feenstra challenged the constitutionality of the statute in federal court. During legal proceedings Louisiana changed the law to permit equal control, but only prospectively. However, the Supreme Court declared that the original statute had been unconstitutional and invalidated the mortgage. . . .

The Turning Point: Reed and Frontiero

It was not until 1971 that the Court demonstrated displeasure at a State's "drawing a sharp line between the sexes," when it unanimously held unconstitutional an Idaho statute giving preference to males in the appointment of administrators of estates. In *Reed v. Reed* the Court found the "administrative convenience" explanation of the preference for males to have no rational basis. Although unexpected, this development was not unforeseeable. During the previous few years the Court had been adding a bit of bite to the rational basis test by looking more closely at state rationalizations as they applied to *some* statuses or *some* interests that did not trigger strict scrutiny. In the previous two years the emerging women's movement had become publicly prominent, and the Equal Rights Amendment had been battling its way through Congress. Despite the Court's assertion that "the Constitution does not require legislatures to reflect sociological insight, or shifting social standards," the Court itself often does just that. A still stronger position was taken seventeen months later, when Air Force Lieutenant Sharon Frontiero challenged a statute that provided dependency allowances for males in the uniformed services without proof of actual economic dependency but permitted them for females only if they could show they paid one-half of their husband's living costs. Eight members of the Court found the statute unconstitutional, but they split as to the reason. Four applied strict scrutiny, using language very different from that of previous cases.

> There can be no doubt that our Nation has had a long and unfortunate history of sex discrimination. Traditionally, such discrimination was rationalized by an attitude of "romantic paternalism" which, in practical effect, put women not on a pedestal, but in a cage. . . .
>
> Moreover, since sex, like race and national origin, is an immutable characteristic determined solely by the accident of birth, the imposition of special disabilities upon the members of a particular sex because of their sex would seem to violate "the basic concept of our system that legal burdens should bear some relationship to individual responsibility. . . ." *Weber v. Aetna Casualty Surety Co.*, 406 U.S. 164, 175 (1972). And what differentiates sex from such nonsuspect statuses as intelligence or physical disability, and aligns it with the recognized suspect criteria, is that the sex characteristic frequently bears no relation to ability to perform or contribute to society. As a result, statutory distinctions between the sexes often have the effect of indiviously relegating the entire class of females to inferior legal status without regard to the actual capabilities of its individual members.

Three justices found the statute unconstitutional on the authority of *Reed*—that administrative convenience was not a rational basis—while deliberately avoiding the characterization of sex as a suspect classification. They gave as the compelling reason for such avoidance the fact that

> the Equal Rights Amendment, which if adopted will resolve the substance of this precise question, has been approved by the Congress and submitted for ratification by the States. If this Amendment is duly adopted, it will represent the will of the people accomplished in the manner prescribed by the Constitution. By acting prematurely and unnecessarily, . . . the Court has

assumed a decisional responsibility at the very time when state legislatures, functioning within the traditional democratic process, are debating the proposed Amendment. It seems . . . that this reaching out to pre-empt by judicial action a major political decision which is currently in process of resolution does not reflect appropriate respect for duly prescribed legislative processes.

Intermediate Scrutiny

In cases after *Reed* and *Frontiero* the Court applied a "strict rational basis" standard with greater and greater scrutiny, until in 1976 a new standard, subsequently referred to as one of "intermediate scrutiny," was articulated. On the surface, *Craig v. Boren* did not appear to be a potentially momentous case. It concerned an Oklahoma law that prohibited the selling of "3.2" beer to men under twenty-one but allowed its sale to women over eighteen. The state's rationale for this law was that more than ten times as many males as females between eighteen and twenty-one were arrested for drunk driving. The Court found the law unconstitutional, holding that "classifications by gender must serve important governmental objectives and must be substantially related to achievement of those objectives." It was not satisfied that "sex represents a legitimate, accurate proxy for the regulation of drinking and driving." . . .

New Protections

The Constitution protects individuals only from action by the state, not from action by private parties. Thus private parties can discriminate on any basis they choose unless the state says otherwise. Many statutes have been passed prohibiting discrimination; sometimes those statutes are challenged as themselves violative of a Constitutional provision. The Supreme Court has heard three cases brought by private associations challenging restrictions on their membership policies as interfering with their First Amendment right of free association, California, Minnesota, and New York City all passed ordinances prohibiting sex (and some other) discriminations by some types of clubs often thought of as private. Their rationale was that many of these clubs were in fact arenas for the conduct of business or the exchange of information important to people's careers, and that therefore discrimination was "invidious." The Court has unanimously upheld all of these statutes, ruling that any "slight infringement on . . . members' rights of expressive association . . . is justified because it serves the State's compelling interest in eliminating discrimination against women." . . .

Abortion

The movement to change restrictive abortion laws began independently of and earlier than the women's liberation movement, but when that movement emerged it quickly captured the abortion issue as its own, energizing and publicizing it along the way. It was the impetus of the feminist movement that led to *Roe v. Wade*, the 1973 Supreme Court decision that eliminated most state abortion laws, after only a few years of public debate and state action on abortion. In some ways the Court was ahead of its time, because public debate had not yet created a consensus. The Court's sweeping removal of a century of legal restriction sparked massive efforts to reduce and reverse its effects. The legal and political controversy has become so polarized that it borders on civil war. It has also tainted many issues that are not obviously related to abortion, with the result that some legislation that might have passed or passed sooner has been stymied. The state battles over ratification of the ERA were infected by opponents' claims that restrictions on abortion would be precluded by it as a denial of equal rights on account of sex. The Court decisions and legislative initiatives that followed *Roe v. Wade* can only be understood within a political context. Rather than reflect changes in legal doctrine that often follow social change, as exemplified by the reinterpretation of the Equal Protection Clause, new decisions and laws are best seen as the victories and defeats of an ongoing political struggle. . . .

In 1967 Colorado became the first state to adopt a law permitting therapeutic abortions if the life or mental health of the mother was threatened, if pregnancy occurred from rape or incest, or if the fetus was deformed. That same year several referral services were set up by nonphysicians to direct women to safer illegal abortions. The public debate over abortion laws became more vociferous, and in the next couple years another ten states adopted therapeutic exceptions. Four states—Alaska, Hawaii, New York, and Washington—went further and repealed virtually all restrictions on abortion. Both of these developments were boosted by the women's movement and the injection into the medical debate of the idea that reproductive freedom was a woman's right. Cases began to reach the lower courts in the late 1960s. Initially these just chipped away at the legal restrictions. Then, in 1969 and 1970, the California Supreme Court and several federal district courts declared their states' laws unconstitutional. In 1971 the Supreme Court granted certiorari to two cases from Texas and Georgia; seven justices heard oral argument in 1971, but the Court asked for a rehearing in 1972 with a full Court. Its decision was announced on January 22, 1973.

Justice Blackmun, writing the majority opinion in *Roe v. Wade* and *Doe v. Bolton*, did not stick to legal analysis. Recognizing the "sensitive and emotional nature of the abortion controversy," he surveyed medical, religious, moral, and historical material before concluding that "this right of privacy, whether it be founded in the Fourteenth Amendment's concept of personal liberty . . . or, . . . in the Ninth Amendment's reservation of rights to the people, is broad enough to encompass a woman's decision whether or not to terminate her pregnancy." While asserting "that the word 'person,'" as used in the Fourteenth Amendment, "does not include the unborn," the Court did recognize that "a State may properly assert important interests in safeguarding health, in maintaining medical standards and in protecting potential life.". . .

Antiabortion forces organized and tested *Roe*'s limits by passing laws and bringing test cases. One group of laws restricted the use of public funds for abortions. Called the "Hyde Amendments" for their most outspoken sponsor, Cong. Henry Hyde (R. Ill.), these attachments to annual appropriations bills deny any federal money authorized by these bills to be used for abortions. Included are restrictions on abortions for military personnel, Peace Corps volunteers, Indians served by federal health programs, health benefits for federal employees, and foreign assistance programs for which abortion is a family planning method. These laws exempt abortions to save the life of the mother; some of them also exempt pregnancies from rape or incest. All of these laws have stimulated acrimonious conflict.

The most controversial have been the restrictions on federal funds for Medicaid recipients—poor people. Several states responded to *Roe* by refusing to pay for Medicaid abortions. In 1977 the Court held that the States did not have to fund abortions for Medicaid-eligible women and could choose to fund only "medically necessary" abortions without violating the Equal Protection clause. The first Hyde Amendment passed Congress in 1976; it reached the Supreme Court in 1980. The Court held that the federal government had no constitutional or statutory obligation to fund abortions even when they were medically necessary. As a result of the Hyde Amendments, the number of federally funded abortions went from 294,600 in 1977 to 165 in 1990. States still have the option of paying for the procedure with state money. In 1990 thirteen states spent sixty-five million dollars for 162,418 abortions. The District of Columbia used to be one of the biggest state funders of abortions, but because much of its budget comes from the federal government, it is subject to Congressional control. Since 1988 Congress has amended the annual appropriations bills to forbid the District to use locally raised funds for abortions.

The other set of cases have tested the extent to which states can regulate the performance of abortion. The success of state restrictions has varied with the composition of the Court, which changed significantly during the Reagan and Bush administrations. Initially the Court affirmed *Roe* and applied strict scrutiny to state regulations. It upheld requirements that a doctor inform a woman about abortion and obtain written consent, but only if the requirements did not interfere with the physician-patient relationship. It found spousal consent statutes unconstitutional but parental notification requirements acceptable if a minor could present her request to a judge when a parent would not agree. Reporting requirements about abortions to the State were constitutional, but mandatory hospitalization and twenty-four-hour waiting periods were not. Advertising could not be restricted, and fetal protection statutes could only apply to viable fetuses.

By 1989 enough conservatives had been added to the Court for the balance of opinions to shift. On July 3, 1989, the Court upheld Missouri's prohibition of abortions on public lands or by public employees and its requirement that viability tests be done on women more than twenty weeks pregnant, by five to four. While it did not overrule *Roe*, the multiple opinions in *Webster* gave the states much more room for regulation than they had had before. Several states quickly passed laws prohibiting or strictly regulating abortion in anticipation that this Court would overrule *Roe* when given the opportunity to do so. The Court agreed to hear only one of the three cases appealed to it and on June 29, 1992, declined to overrule *Roe*, again by five to four. Three of the Reagan appointees, O'Connor, Kennedy, and Souter, wrote the joint opinion in which they opted to follow the judicially conservative tradition of sticking to precedent. "The Constitution serves human values, and while the effect of reliance on *Roe* cannot be exactly measured, neither can the certain cost of overruling *Roe* for people who have ordered their thinking and living around that case be dismissed." However, this decision did away with the trimester framework and dropped strict scrutiny as the standard by which regulations must be judged. Instead it held that the state's interest in protecting human life extends throughout pregnancy; it may regulate at any stage provided that the regulation does not impose an "undue burden" on a woman's right to obtain an abortion. . . .

Legislative Gains

The legislative changes in public policy have been as vast as the judicial changes, but they began earlier. . . .

Although the ERA was not ratified, the two-year battle had some very beneficial side effects. It created a climate in Congress that there was a serious constituent interest in women's rights and established liaisons between feminist organizations and Congressional staff. With this impetus the 92nd Congress, which sent the ERA to the states, passed a bumper crop of women's rights legislation in 1971–72. In addition to the ERA there were laws that (1) expanded the coverage of Title VII and the enforcement powers of the EEOC; (2) prohibited sex discrimination in all federally aided education programs (Title IX); (3) added sex discrimination to the jurisdiction of the U.S. Commission on Civil Rights; (4) prohibited sex discrimination in state programs funded by federal revenue sharing; (5) provided free day care for children of poor families and a sliding fee scale for higher income families (which was vetoed by President Nixon); (6) provided for a child care tax deduction for some parents; (7) added prohibitions against sex discrimination to a plethora of federally funded programs, including health training, Appalachian redevelopment, and water pollution.

Subsequent Congresses have also been active. New laws included the Equal Credit Opportunity Act; the Women's Educational Equity Act, which provides grants to design programs and activities to eliminate stereotyping and achieve educational equity; creation of the National Center for the Control and Prevention of Rape; an amendment to the Foreign Assistance Act requiring particular attention be given to programs, projects, and activities that tend to integrate women into the national economies of foreign countries; prohibitions of discrimination in the sale, rental, or financing of housing; an amendment to Title VII to include pregnancy in employment disability insurance coverage; admission of women to the military academies; and the addition of still more antidiscrimination provisions to federally funded programs such as small business loans.

The States have also been active arenas. Laws have been passed in most states prohibiting sex discrimination in employment, housing, and credit and in some states prohibiting discrimination in insurance, education, and public accommodations. Most states now have no-fault divorce provisions; all but four have equal custody and support laws (two others have equal custody but provide support for only the wife). The changes have been partially a result of pressure from feminist and other public interest groups and partially in response to changes in federal legislation and Supreme Court decisions. Many states have followed the lead of the Federal government in conducting studies to identify gender-based distinctions in their laws and recommend changes. Most of these studies were in response to efforts to adopt a state ERA or ratify the federal amendment.

The Family—Again

Toward the end of the 1980s both the federal and state governments turned their attention toward the family, which had undergone profound changes in the previous two decades. Although family law was traditionally a state prerogative, it had never been completely off limits to the federal government. . . .

In 1990 Congress finally got serious about providing child care to working parents. For decades child care had a negative connotation as something resorted to by poor women who *had* to work. The federal government subsidized some child care during World War II when it wanted women in the factories so the men could go to war, but those funds were eliminated after the war. In 1971 President Nixon vetoed a two-billion-dollar child care bill because of its "family-weakening implications." Presidents Ford and Carter also expressed disapproval of bills in Congress during their Presidencies, though in 1976 some funds were made available to the States that could be used for day care. Finally, in 1988, after four decades of increasing labor force participation by mothers of young children, Congress proposed a major child care bill. It quickly became embroiled in turf battles between committees and conflicts over church and state (e.g., should federal money be used for church-sponsored day care). These were resolved by 1990, and Congress passed a five-year program of tax credits and state grants that President Bush signed into law on November 5, 1990.

The President was not as enthusiastic about signing a bill to mandate unpaid leave for employees on the birth or adoption of a child or illness of a family member. His concern about increasing the costs to business outweighed his commitment to "family values," even though the United States was the only major industrialized country that did not provide such benefits. President Bush vetoed bills passed by Congress in 1990 and 1992 after eight years of wrangling; and said he would support only voluntary leave. However, once a new administration was elected, Congress rushed to pass H.R. 1, the Family and Medical Leave Act, which President Clinton signed on February 5, 1993.

"Family values" also delayed government intervention into family violence. Traditionally, how a family conducted its internal affairs has been considered a private matter. Despite growing evidence of child and spousal abuse, it was many years before legislatures overcame opposition to mandate action where there was abuse of children, and even more before services were created for spouses—virtually always wives. By 1984, when Congress passed the Family Violence Prevention and Services Act, thirty-two states had domestic violence programs, usually funding for emergency shelters and other programs run by nonprofit organizations. Today virtually all states have such programs, though funding is inadequate. . . .

The Challenges Ahead

The contemporary feminist movement finished the drive to remove discriminatory laws begun after Suffrage. It also altered public perceptions and public policy on the role of women to one that favors equality of opportunity and individual choice. This is reflected in the addition of "sex" to the pantheon of laws that prohibit discrimination in private conduct and in the Court decisions that recognize women's right to equal protection and due process. These changes, which largely occurred during the decade of the 1970s, are nothing less than a revolution in public policy. As late as 1963, the President's Commission on the Status of Women cautioned that "[e]xperience is needed in determining what constitutes *unjustified* discrimination in the treatment of women workers."

As is true of any revolution, the changes that were made created new problems in their wake. Once equal opportunity became a possibility, the fact that it by itself would not lead to equality became clearer. Essentially this policy means that women who are like men should be treated equally with men. It accepts as standard the traditional male life-style, and that standard in turn assumes that one's primary responsibility should and can be one's job, because one has a spouse (or spouse surrogate) whose primary responsibility is the maintenance of house and family obligations. Women whose personal life-style and resources permit them to fit these assumptions could, in the absence of sex discrimination, succeed equally with men.

Most women cannot, however, because our traditional conception of the family, and women's role within the family, make this impossible. Women still bear the primary responsibility for home and child care whether or not they are married and regardless of what their spouse does. The typical woman has more tasks to perform in a typical day than a typical man and thus has less time. Couples who equalize family responsibilities, or singles who take them all on, pay a price for deviancy. And women who spend the greater part of their lives as dependent spouses often find their "career" ended by death or divorce with little to show for it.

What is necessary is a total social reorganization that abolishes institutionalized sex role differences and the concept of adult dependency. It needs to recognize the individual as the principal economic unit, regardless of what combinations individuals do or do not choose to live in, and to provide the necessary services for individuals to support themselves and help support their children. In pursuit of these goals, programs and policies need to make participation by everyone in the labor force to the full extent of their abilities both a right and an obligation. They should also encourage and facilitate the equal assumption of family responsibilities without regard to gender, as well as develop ways to reduce conflict between the conduct of one's professional and private lives. While transition policies are necessary to mitigate the consequences of adult dependency, the goal should be abolition of the sexual division of labor. They should not be ones that permanently transfer dependency from "bread-winners" (male earners) to society in general, nor should they be ones that encourage dependency for a major portion of one's life by extolling its benefits and minimizing its costs. Instead, transitional policies should be ones that educate women to the reality that they are ultimately responsible for their own economic well-being, but are entitled to the opportunities to achieve it.

This too is not enough. Even while the revolution was in process, the feminist movement was generating new public policies to address problems not solved by the mere removal of discriminatory laws and practices. The pervasiveness of violence, the degradation of pornography, and the lack of affordable, available child care are burdens particularly borne by women that equal opportunity programs do not address. As women moved into positions of power, feminist inquiry disclosed new or hidden discriminations, such as the "glass ceiling" and inadequate research into women's health needs. As the family became open to public inspection, a host of problems that more heavily affected women, such as incest, sexual abuse, and domestic violence, became apparent. As science created new ways of reproducing, it compelled reconsideration of the concept of motherhood. And as people diversified their ways of living together, the nature of the family was questioned.

Not all of the new problems can be mitigated by changes in law and public policy. But many can be. As the consequences of the legal revolution ripple throughout society, one task will be to identify where the law can be a useful tool for more social change and to devise appropriate policies to achieve it.

Jo Freeman earned a PhD in political science from the University of Chicago in 1973 and a J.D. degree in 1982 from the New York University School of Law. She is the author of 11 books on the topics of feminism, social movements, and political parties, including *The Politics of Women's Liberation* (1975), *A Room at a Time: How Women Entered Party Politics* (2000), and *We Will Be Heard: Women's Struggles for Political Power in the United States* (2008).

EXPLORING THE ISSUE

Has the Women's Movement of the 1970s Failed to Liberate American Women?

Critical Thinking and Reflection

1. Discuss the role that women should fulfill in American society in the twenty-first century, according to Graglia. Critically analyze her views of contemporary feminism.
2. List and describe the characteristics of the nineteenth-century "Cult of True Womanhood." Compare the similarities and differences of Graglia's views of what women's roles should be today with the nineteenth-century ideal of womanhood.
3. According to Jo Freeman, in what ways did the women's movement influence changes in laws and public policies concerning the status of women in American society?
4. Compare the analyses of Graglia and Freeman on the impact of the women's movement on American society. Where do they agree, and where do they disagree?

Is There Common Ground?

Both women on the left and women on the right of the political spectrum would deny there is common ground between the two movements. Upon closer inspection, however, an interesting study would be to see how many conservative women active in business and politics took advantage of the Equal Rights Amendment in 1972 and the Higher Education Act (especially Title IX), which opened the doors of collegiate athletics and higher educational opportunities in traditional male fields such as law, medicine, and scientific research. One should also study the number of conservative women politicians, such as Michelle Bachman and Sarah Palin, who have benefited from the expanding political role of women in the past three decades. How much do Bachman, Palin, and other conservative women politicians embody both the liberated woman and the traditional mother?

One of the chief criticisms of the feminist movement of the 1970s stemmed from the fact that the vast majority of its participants were white, middle-class women focused on advancing their own personal goals. Since that time, the women's movement has expanded globally to incorporate women of all classes, races, and ethnicities, including many from developing nations in Africa, Asia, and Latin America. Additionally, in the United States, many women who had never viewed themselves as "feminists" have become more keenly attuned to the debates over women's roles in the public sphere and the workplace, as well as the impact of challenges pertaining to personal decision making tied into the highly charged debate over abortion rights.

Additional Resources

William H. Chafe, *The Paradox of Change: American Women in the Twentieth Century* (Oxford University Press, 1991)

Johnetta B. Cole and Beverly Gray-Sheftall, *Gender Talk: The Struggle for Women's Equality in African American Communities* (Ballantine, 2003)

Sara M. Evans, *Personal Politics: The Roots of Women's Liberation in the Civil Rights Movement and the New Left* (Alfred A. Knopf, 1979)

Estelle B. Freedman, *No Turning Back: The History of Feminism and the Future of Women* (Ballantine, 2001)

Ruth Rosen, *The World Split Open: How the Modern Women's Movement Changed America* (Viking, 2000)

Internet References . . .

Documents from the Women's Liberation Movement

http://library.duke.edu/rubenstein/scriptorium/wlm/

National Women's Liberation

http://www.womensliberation.org/

The 1960–70s American Feminist Movement

https://tavaana.org/en/content/1960s-70s-american-feminist-movement-breaking-down-barriers-women

Phyllis Schlafly Still Championing the Anti-Feminist Fight

http://www.npr.org/templates/story/story.php?storyId=134981902

Teach Women's History Project

www.feminist.org/research/teachersguide/teach1.html

Selected, Edited, and with Issue Framing Material by:
Kevin R. Magill and Tony L. Talbert, *Baylor University*

ISSUE

Do Economic Policies Associated with Reagan, Thatcher, and Friedman Promote Freedom in a Liberal Democracy?

YES: Milton Friedman, from "Capitalism and Freedom," *New Individualist Review* (1981)

NO: Daniel Stedman Jones, from "The American Roots of Neoliberalism," History News Network (2013)

Learning Outcomes
After reading this issue, you will be able to:
• Contextualize the historical development of Western liberal democratic thought as it related to capitalism and freedom.
• Understand the intersection of Western liberal democracy and capitalist market principles.
• Consider opposing arguments related to how liberal democracy ought to be framed and pursued.

ISSUE SUMMARY

YES: Milton Friedman argues that liberalism, in its quest to combat authoritarian elements, has naturally aligned with markets, individualism, and freedom. He further claims that the so-called economic freedom (meaning privatization) is a way of maintaining the personal liberties of people against the government and tries to give historical examples attempting to illustrate this point.

NO: Daniel Stedman Jones critiques and tracks how privatization has come to be understood as neoliberalism, the economic ideology that has come to permeate all American political life. Jones argues that in understanding the history of neoliberal thought can help us better make sense of the complexity of the present economic situation.

Issue framing with Victoria Davis, *Baylor University*

Looking at economics and politics together places one in what seems to be a complicated space between freedom and equality—two seemingly conflicting values. In the United States, the question is certainly posed so that these values seem in conflict: Can we be free and maintain inequality? Can we be equal and also be free? It seems that in order to ensure equality, individuals need to relieve some of their freedom and in order to ensure freedom individuals must be okay with some level of inequality. This tension between freedom and equality exists at the intersection of politics and economics within a society that has so completely tied itself to capitalism. At the core of most political-economic debates is the extent to which the state should influence our social existence and whether such influence by the state pushes us in the direction of protecting equality or protecting freedom, considering that most believe protecting both at similar levels is impossible. Perhaps the framing and naming of "equality" and "freedom" demands our attention.

Given the question at hand regarding the economic policies of Reagan, Thatcher, and Freidman, we might first consider what liberal democracy has come to mean. We might look to Lindblom (1977) to contextualize our analysis. Lindblom reminds us that "the history of democracy is largely an account of the pursuit of liberty" and points to historical events such as the American and French Revolutions as reflecting the ways in which liberal democracy came to be primarily attached to notions of freedom rather than the principle of rule by the people (p. 162). Concerning equality as a goal of democracy, Lindblom points to the ways in which the egalitarian ideas of democracy taken up by Marx and the socialist became positioned in opposition to more historically established libertarian notions of democracy (p. 163). Therefore, Lindblom notes:

> If in its actual historical origins polyarchy is an institution for introducing that amount and those forms of popular control that serve liberty, then it is not at all surprising that men who create polyarchies will also preserve market systems. For much of the fuller development of personal liberty that men have sought is freedom to engage in trade and to establish enterprises to pursue the gains of trade, freedom also to move about, to keep one's earnings and assets, and to be secure against arbitrary exactions" (pp. 163–164)

So, if modern Western democratic thought is primarily about preserving liberty, then perhaps the economic policies as presented by Friedman (1981) do indeed promote freedom in a liberal democracy. However, Jones (2013) in his outline of the American roots of neoliberalism brings us back to an important underlying question— what is meant by liberal democracy and what do we want it to mean as our political system evolves?

Lindblom's (1977) consideration of the why existing polyarchies are market oriented helps to unpack Friedman's (1981) argument for the necessity of economic freedom as a precursor to political freedom. However, Lindblom is offering an analysis of how we have historically arrived at the present intersection of liberal democracy and the market system and not an argument for or against the marriage between democracy and market principles. It makes sense that Friedman sees democracy rooted primarily in maintaining equality as being conflated with welfare and an over reliance on the state rather than on private arrangements considering that he is writing at the end of the Cold War and from the position of favoring the free market system (pp. 1–2). Additionally, understanding Friedman requires we consider how he primarily positions liberalism as a means to combat elements of authoritarianism. Therefore, it follows

for Friedman that ensuring the freedom of the markets ensures freedom in general. It is important to note too that Friedman uses historical analysis as his primary support to argue in favor of free markets as the ultimate protection of liberty. This relates to Lindblom, whose historical analysis suggests Western liberal democracy has primarily emphasized notions of liberty and therefore the protection of private over public interests. Further, Lindblom notes that the protection of private property is at the foundation of the development of our country as our constitution notes in the words of "life, liberty, and the pursuit of happiness" a more or less direct reference to Lockean principles of private property.

Mark Fischer (2009) claims it is almost impossible for us to see ourselves as existing outside of a neoliberal capitalist logic. Jones (2013) helps us to look past a blind acceptance of neoliberal capitalist logic by outlining the historical development of this ideology. What we gain from reading Jones is a more nuanced and complicated understanding of the production of neoliberal ideology. As Jones shows us, there is a history behind how neoliberalism came to be seen "as being as American as apple pie." The historical development of think tanks in both the United States and Western Europe served as a type of "economic imperialism" that gave neoliberal ideology and discourse a means to infiltrate all aspects of social life. The core thoughts being pushed out of these institutions was and still is meant to produce and disperse "a reformation of liberalism that would recover the classical liberal focus on individual liberty." Jones' concise outline of the history of American neoliberal ideology serves not only as a means to understanding present economic policies in both the United States and parts of Europe, but also as a cautionary tale. Jones is asking us to problematize the interwar thinking of intellectuals like Friedman and to not blindly accept economic freedom as a natural precursor to political freedom. Lindblom (1977) reminds us that focusing on freedom and equality often causes us to overlook the point of democracy as a form of polyarchy. Perhaps moving forward, we might more closely consider how neoliberal ideology came to permeate all levels of American and Western European social thought and choose to see the market and democracy as independent from one another.

Deciding how we want to define liberal democracy moving forward may seem daunting and overwhelming. It may also seem unrealistic to think we can pursue a couple of readings related to the topic and walk away with a strong sense of where we might land in the political-economic debates of our time. Perhaps, rather than starting from the larger more theoretical debate on the meaning of liberal democracy, we should consider how the present emphasis on liberal democracy as dependent on market principles materializes in our everyday existence and ask ourselves if this is working for us both as individuals and as a part of a larger social collective. It seems both Friedman (1981) and Jones (2013) would argue that much is at stake in how we choose to conceptualize democracy and no matter the angle or side from which you approach the topic, one must always look for underlying assumptions and consider how our political-economic ideology materializes.

YES ⤶   Milton Friedman

Capitalism and Freedom

IN DISCUSSING the principles of a free society it is desirable to have a convenient label and this has become extremely difficult. In the late 18th and early 19th centuries, an intellectual movement developed that went under the name of Liberalism. This development, which was a reaction against the authoritarian elements in the prior society, emphasized freedom as the ultimate goal and the individual as the ultimate entity in the society. It supported *laissez faire* at home as a means of reducing the role of the state in economic affairs and thereby avoiding interfering with the individual; it supported free trade abroad as a means of linking the nations of the world together peacefully and democratically. In political matters, it supported the development of representative government and of parliamentary institutions, reduction in the arbitrary power of the state, and protection of the civil freedoms of individuals.

Beginning in the late 19th century, the intellectual ideas associated with the term liberalism came to have a very different emphasis, particularly in the economic area. Whereas 19th century liberalism emphasized freedom, 20th century liberalism tended to emphasize welfare. I would say welfare instead of freedom though the 20th century liberal would no doubt say welfare in addition to freedom. The 20th century liberal puts his reliance primarily upon the state rather than on private voluntary arrangements.

The difference between the two doctrines is most striking in the economic sphere, less extreme in the political sphere. The 20th century liberal, like the 19th century liberal, puts emphasis on parliamentary institutions, representative government, civil rights, and so on. And yet even here there is an important difference. Faced with the choice between having the state intervene or not, the 20th century liberal is likely to resolve any doubt in favor of intervention; the 19th century liberal, in the other direction. When the question arises at what level of government something should be done, the 20th century liberal is likely to resolve any doubt in favor of the more centralized level—the state instead of the city, the federal government instead of the state, a world organization instead of a federal government. The 19th century liberal is likely to resolve any doubt in the other direction and to emphasize a decentralization of power.

This use of the term liberalism in these two quite different senses renders it difficult to have a convenient label for the principles I shall be talking about. I shall resolve these difficulties by using the word liberalism in its original sense. Liberalism of what I have called the 20th century variety has by now become orthodox and indeed reactionary. Consequently, the views I shall present might equally be entitled, under current conditions, the "new liberalism," a more attractive designation than "nineteenth century liberalism."

It is widely believed that economic arrangements are one thing and political arrangements another, that any kind of economic arrangement can be associated with any kind of political arrangement. This is the idea that underlies such a term as "democratic socialism." The essential thesis, I believe, of a new liberal is that this idea is invalid, that "democratic socialism" is a contradiction in terms, that there is an intimate connection between economic arrangements and political arrangements, and that only certain combinations are possible.

It is important to emphasize that economic arrangements play a dual role in the promotion of a free society. On the one hand, "freedom" in economic arrangements is itself a component of freedom broadly understood, so "economic freedom" is an end in itself to a believer in freedom. In the second place, economic freedom is also an indispensable means toward the achievement of political freedom.

The first of these roles of economic freedom needs special emphasis. The citizen of Great Britain who after World War II was not permitted, by law, to spend his vacation in the United States because of exchange control was being deprived of an essential freedom no less than the citizen of the United States who was denied the opportunity to spend his vacation in Russia on the grounds of his political views. The one was ostensibly an economic limitation on freedom and the other a political limitation, yet there is no essential difference between the two.

The citizen of the United States who is compelled by law to devote something like 10% of his income to the purchase of a particular kind of retirement contract, administered by the government, is being deprived of a corresponding part of his own personal freedom. How strongly this particular deprivation may be felt, and its closeness to the deprivation of religious freedom, which all would regard as "civil" or "political" rather than "economic," was dramatized by the recent episode involving a group of Ohio or Pennsylvania farmers of a particular religious sect. On grounds of principle, this group regarded compulsory federal old age programs as an infringement on their own personal individual freedom and refused to pay taxes or accept benefits. As a result, some of their livestock were sold at auction in order to satisfy claims for social security levies. A citizen of the United States who under the laws of various states is not free to follow the occupation of his own choosing unless he can get a license for it, is likewise being deprived of an essential part of his freedom. So economic freedom, in and of itself, is an extremely important part of total freedom.

The reason it is important to emphasize this point is because intellectuals in particular have a strong bias against regarding this aspect of freedom as important. They tend to express contempt for what they regard as material aspects of life and to regard their own pursuit of allegedly higher values as on a different plane of significance and as deserving special attention. But for the ordinary citizen of the country, for the great masses of the people, the direct importance of economic freedom is in many cases of at least comparable importance to the indirect importance of economic freedom as a means of political freedom.

VIEWED AS a means to the end of political freedom, economic arrangements are essential because of the effect which they have on the concentration or the deconcentration of power. A major thesis of the new liberal is that the kind of economic organization that provides economic freedom directly, namely, organization of economic activities through a largely free market and private enterprise, in short through competitive capitalism, is also a necessary though not a sufficient condition for political freedom. The central reason why this is true is because such a form of economic organization separates economic power from political power and in this way enables the one to be an offset to the other. Historical evidence speaks with a single voice on the relation between political and economic

freedom. I cannot think of a single example at any time or any place where there was a large measure of political freedom without there also being something comparable to a private enterprise market form of economic organization for the bulk of economic activity.

Because we live in a largely free society, we tend to forget how limited is the span of time and the part of the globe for which there has ever been anything like political freedom. The 19th century and the early 20th century in the Western world stand out as striking exceptions from the general trend of historical development. It is clear that freedom in this instance came along with the free market and the development of capitalist institutions.

History suggests only that economic freedom is a necessary condition for political freedom. Clearly it is not a sufficient condition. Fascist Italy or Fascist Spain, Germany at various times in the last 70 years, Japan before World Wars I and II, Czarist Russia in the decades before World War I are all societies that cannot conceivably be described as politically free yet in which private enterprise was the dominant form of economic organization. So it is possible to have economic arrangements that are fundamentally capitalist and yet political arrangements that are not free.

Yet, even in those cases, the citizenry had a good deal more freedom than citizens of a modern totalitarian state like Russia or Nazi Germany in which economic totalitarianism is combined with political totalitarianism. Even in Russia under the Czars it was possible for some citizens under some circumstances to change their jobs without getting permission from political authority because the existence of private property and of capitalism provided some kind of offset to the centralized power of the state.

The relation between political and economic freedom is complex and by no means unilateral. In the early 19th century, Bentham and the Philosophical Radicals were inclined to regard political freedom as a means to economic freedom. Their view was that the masses were being hampered by the restrictions that were being imposed upon them, that if political reform gave the bulk of the people the vote, they would do what was good for them, which was to vote for *laissez faire*. In retrospect, it is hard to say that they were wrong. There was a large measure of political reform that was accompanied by economic reform in the direction of a great deal of *laissez faire*. And an enormous increase in the well-being of the masses followed this change in economic arrangements.

Later in the 19th century, when there began to be a movement away from freer economic arrangements and *laissez faire* toward a greater measure of collectivism and centralization, the view developed, as expressed for example by Lord Acton and in the 20th century by Henry Simons and Friedrich Hayek, that the relation was more nearly the opposite—that economic freedom was the means to political freedom.

In the period since World War II, I think we have seen still a different interconnection between political and economic freedom. In the post-war period, the fears that economic intervention would destroy political freedom seemed to be on the way to being realized. Various countries, and again Britain is perhaps the outstanding example because it has been so much a leader in the realm of ideas and social arrangements, did extend very greatly the area of state intervention into economic affairs and this did threaten political freedom. But the result was rather surprising. Instead of political freedom giving way, what happened in many cases was that economic intervention was discarded. The striking example in British post-war development was the Control-of-Engagements Order issued by the Labor Government. In trying to carry out their economic plans, the Labor Government found it necessary to do something which several years before it had said it would never do, namely, to exercise control over the jobs which people could take. Thanks to widespread popular objection, the legislation was never enforced at all extensively. After being on the books for one year, it was repealed. It seems clear that it was repealed precisely because it quite directly threatened a cherished political freedom. And from that day to this, there has been a trend toward a reduction in the extent of political intervention in economic affairs.

The dismantling of controls dates from the repeal of the Control-of-Engagements Order; it would have occurred even if the Labor Government had stayed in power. This may, of course, turn out to be a purely temporary interlude, a minor halt in the march of affairs toward a greater degree of intervention into economic affairs. Perhaps only innate optimism leads me to believe that it is more than that. Whether this be so or not, it illustrates again in striking fashion the close connection between economic arrangements and political arrangements. Not only in Britain but in other countries of the world as well, the post-war period has seen the same tendency for economic arrangements to interfere with political freedom and for the economic intervention frequently to give way.

Historical evidence that the development of freedom and of capitalist and market institutions have coincided in time can never by itself be persuasive. Why should there be a connection? What are the logical links between economic and political freedom? In discussing these questions, I shall first consider the market as a direct component of freedom and then the indirect relation between market

arrangements and political freedom. In the process, I shall in effect outline the ideal economic arrangements of the new liberal.

THE NEW LIBERAL takes freedom of the individual as his ultimate goal in judging social arrangements. Freedom as a value in this sense has to do with the interrelations among people; it has no meaning whatsoever to a Robinson Crusoe on an isolated island (without his man Friday). Robinson Crusoe on his island is subject to "constraint," he has limited "power," he has only a limited number of alternatives, but there is no problem of freedom in the sense that is relevant to the present discussion. Similarly, in a society, freedom has nothing to say about what an individual does with his freedom; it isn't an all-embracing ethic by any manner of means. Indeed, a major aim of the believer in freedom is to leave the ethical problem for the individual to wrestle with. The "really" important ethical problems are those that face an individual in a free society—what an individual should do with his freedom. There are thus two sets of values that a liberal will emphasize—the values relevant to relations among people which is the context in which he assigns first priority to freedom; and the values that are relevant to the individual in the exercise of his freedom, which is the realm of individual ethics and philosophy.

Fundamentally there are only two ways in which the activities of a large number of people can be co-ordinated: by central direction, which is the technique of the army and of the totalitarian state and involves some people telling other people what to do; or by voluntary co-operation, which is the technique of the market place and of arrangements involving voluntary exchange. The possibility of voluntary co-operation in its turn rests fundamentally on the proposition that both parties to an exchange can benefit from it. If it is voluntary and reasonably well informed, the exchange will not take place unless both parties do benefit from it.

The simplest way to see the principle at work is to go back to the economist's favorite abstraction of Robinson Crusoe, only to have a number of Robinson Crusoe households on different islands, each of which is initially self-sufficient. Let the households come into contact with one another. The possibility of trade now emerges. What is it that gives them an incentive to trade? The answer clearly is that if each household concentrates on a small range of activities, producing things for itself indirectly, by trade, rather than doing everything for itself, everybody can be better off. This possibility arises for two reasons: one is that an individual can achieve a higher degree of competence in an activity if he specializes in it rather than engaging in many activities; the other, closely associated but not identical, is that people are different and each can specialize in those activities for which he has special capacities. Even if everyone were identical in all his capacities and abilities, there would still be a gain from division of labor which would make a larger total return possible because each individual could concentrate on a particular activity. But in addition, diversity among people becomes a source of strength because each individual can concentrate on doing those things that he can do best. So the incentive for the households to engage in trade and to specialize is the possibility of a greater total output.

The protection to Household A is that it need not enter into an exchange with Household B unless both parties benefit. If exchange is voluntary, it will take place if, and only if, both parties do benefit. Each individual always has the alternative of going back to producing for himself what he did before so he can never be worse off; he can only be better off.

OF COURSE, specialization of function and division of labor would not go far if the ultimate productive unit were the household. In a modern society, we have gone much farther. We have introduced enterprises which are intermediaries between individuals in their capacities as suppliers of services and as purchasers of goods. And similarly, specialization of function and division of labor could not go very far if we had to continue to rely on the barter of product for product. In consequence, money has been introduced as a means of facilitating exchange and of enabling the act of purchase and of sale to be separated into two parts.

The introduction of enterprises and the introduction of money raise most of the really difficult problems for economics as a science. But from the point of view of the principles of social organization, they do not fundamentally alter the essential character of economic arrangements. In a modern complex society using enterprises and money it is no less true than in the simple idealized world that co-ordination through the markets is a system of voluntary co-operation in which all parties to the bargain gain.

So long as effective freedom of exchange is maintained, the essential feature of the market is that it enables people to co-operate voluntarily in complex tasks without any individual being in a position to interfere with any other. Many of the difficult technical problems that arise in applying our principles to actual economic arrangements are concerned with assuring effective freedom to enter or not to enter into exchanges. But so long as people are effectively free to enter into an exchange and are reasonably well informed the essential feature of the market remains that of our ideal example. It provides

for co-operation without coercion; it prevents one person from interfering with another. The employer is protected from being interfered with or coerced by his employees by the existence of other employees whom he can hire. The employee is protected from being coerced by his employer by the existence of other employers for whom he can work; the customer by the existence of other sellers, and so on.

Of course, it is partly this feature of the market that leads many people to be opposed to it. What most people really object to when they object to a free market is that it is so hard for them to shape it to their own will. The market gives people what the people want instead of what other people think they ought to want. At the bottom of many criticisms of the market economy is really lack of belief in freedom itself.

The essence of political freedom is the absence of coercion of one man by his fellow men. The fundamental danger to political freedom is the concentration of power. The existence of a large measure of power in the hands of a relatively few individuals enables them to use it to coerce their fellow man. Preservation of freedom requires either the elimination of power where that is possible, or its dispersal where it cannot be eliminated. It essentially requires a system of checks and balances, like that explicitly incorporated in our Constitution. One way to think of a market system is as part of a broader system of checks and balances, as a system under which economic power can be a check to political power instead of an addition to it.

If I may speculate in an area in which I have little competence, there seems to be a really essential difference between political power and economic power that is at the heart of the use of a market mechanism to preserve freedom. With respect to political power, there is something like a law of conservation of energy or power. The notion that what one man gains another man loses has more applicability in the realm of politics than in the realm of economic arrangements. One can have many different small governments, but it is hard to think of having many different small centers of political power in any single government. It is hard for there to be more than one really outstanding leader, one person on whom the energies and enthusiasms and so on of his countrymen are centered. If the central government gains power, it is likely to do so at the expense of local governments. While I do not know how to formulate the statement precisely, there seems to be something like a fixed total of political power to be distributed.

There is no such fixed total, no law of conservation of power, with respect to economic power. You cannot very well have two presidents in a country, although you may have two separate countries, but it is perfectly possible to have a large number of additional millionaires. You can have an additional millionaire without there being any fewer millionaires anywhere else. If somebody discovers a way to make resources more productive than they were before, he will simply add to the grand total of economic wealth. Economic power can thus be more readily dispersed than political power. There can be a larger number of independent foci of power. Further, if economic power is kept in separate hands from political power, it can serve as a check and an offset to political power.

This is a very abstract argument and I think I can illustrate its force for our purpose best by turning to some examples. I would like to discuss first a hypothetical example that helps to bring out the principles involved and then an actual example from recent experience that also illustrates the way in which the market works to preserve political freedom.

I think that most of us will agree that an essential element of political freedom is the freedom to advocate and to try to promote radical changes in the organization of society. It is a manifestation of political freedom in our capitalist society that people are free to advocate, and to try to persuade others to favor socialism or communism. I want to contemplate for a moment the reverse problem. It would be a sign of political freedom in a socialist society that people in that society should be free to advocate, and try to persuade others to favor capitalism. I want to ask the hypothetical question: how could a socialist society preserve the freedom to advocate capitalism? I shall assume that the leading people and the public at large seriously wish to do so and ask how they could set up the institutional arrangements that would make this possible.

THE FIRST problem is that the advocates of capitalism must be able to earn a living. Since in a socialist society all persons get their incomes from the state as employees or dependents of employees of the state, this already creates quite a problem. It is one thing to permit private individuals to advocate radical change. It is another thing to permit governmental employees to do so. Our whole post-war experience with un-American activities committees and the McCarthy investigations and so on shows how difficult a problem it is to carry over this notion to governmental employees. The first thing that would be necessary would therefore be essentially a self-denying ordinance on the part of the government that would not discharge from public employment individuals who advocate subversive doctrines—since of course, in a socialist state the doctrine that capitalism should be restored would be a subversive doctrine. Let us suppose this hurdle, which is the least of the hurdles, is surmounted.

Next, in order to be able to advocate anything effectively it is necessary to be able to raise some money to finance meetings, propaganda, publications, writings and so on. In a socialist society, there might still be men of great wealth. There is no reason why a socialist society shouldn't have a wide and unequal distribution of income and of wealth. It is clear, however, that most, if not all of the people, of great wealth or income would be the leading figures in the government, directly or indirectly—high level civil servants or favored authors, actors, and the like. Perhaps it doesn't strain the bounds of credulity greatly to suppose that the government would countenance and tolerate the advocacy of capitalism by minor civil servants. It's almost incredible that it could tolerate the financing of subversive activity by leading civil servants. It is, therefore, hard to believe that these wealthy or high income individuals could be a source of finance. The only other recourse would be to try to get small sums from a large number of people. But this evades the issue. In order to get a lot of people to contribute you first have to persuade them. How do you get started persuading?

Note that in a capitalistic society radical movements have never been financed by small amounts from many people. They have been financed by a small number of wealthy people being willing to foot the bill. To take an example that is quite old but very striking, who financed Karl Marx? It was Engels, and where did Engels get his money? He was an independent business man of wealth. (In the modern day it's the Anita McCormick Blaines and Frederick Vanderbilt Fields, the Corliss Lamonts and so on who have been the source of finance of the radical movement.) This is the important source of the strength of freedom in a capitalist society. It means that anybody who has a "crazy" idea that he wants to propagate and promote has only to persuade a small number out of a very large number of potential backers in order to be able to get an opportunity to try out his crazy notions in the market place of ideas.

Moreover, the situation is even more extreme. Suppose somebody has an idea that he thinks will appeal to a large number of people. He doesn't even have to persuade somebody that he is right. He just has to persuade some capitalist in the society—in this particular case say a publisher or a magazine editor—that there's a chance that a lot of people will be willing to pay to read about his idea. A publisher, for example, will have an incentive to publish a book, with whose ideas he doesn't agree in the slightest, if there is a substantial chance that the book will sell enough copies to make money.

By contrast, let's go back to the hypothetical socialist society. How does the proponent of capitalism in such a society raise money to propagate his ideas? He can't get it from the wealthy individuals in the society. It is hard to believe that it is feasible for him to raise the necessary amount by getting small sums from a large number of people. Perhaps one can conceive of the socialist society being sufficiently aware of this problem and sufficiently anxious to preserve freedom to set up a governmental fund for the financing of subversive activities. It is a little difficult to conceive of this being done, but even if it were done it would not meet the problem. How would it be decided who should be supported from the fund? If subversive activity is made a profitable enterprise, it is clear that there will be an ample supply of people willing to take money for this purpose. If money is to be got for the asking, there will be plenty of asking. There must be some way of rationing. How could it be rationed?

Even if this problem were solved, the socialist society would still have difficulties in preserving freedom. The advocate of capitalism must not only have money, he must also be able to buy paper, print his material, distribute it, hold meetings, and the like. And, in the socialist society, in each instance this would involve dealing with an instrumentality of the government. The seller of paper in a capitalist society doesn't care or indeed know whether the paper he's selling is going to be used to print the *Wall Street Journal* or the *Worker*.

In the circumstances envisaged in the socialist society, the man who wants to print the paper to promote capitalism has to persuade a government mill to sell him the paper, a government printing press to print it, a government post office to distribute it among the people, a government agency to rent him a hall in which to talk and so on. Maybe there is some way in which one could make arrangements under a socialist society to preserve freedom and to make this possible. I certainly cannot say that it is utterly impossible. What is clear is that there are very real difficulties in preserving dissent and that, so far as I know, none of the people who have been in favor of socialism and also in favor of freedom have really faced up to this issue or made even a respectable start at developing the institutional arrangements that would permit freedom under socialism. By contrast, it is clear how a free market capitalist society fosters freedom.

A striking example, which may be found in the January 26, 1959, issue of *Time*, has to do with the "Black List Fade-Out." Says the *Time* story, "The Oscar" awarding ritual is Hollywood's biggest pitch for dignity but two years ago dignity suffered. When one Robert Rich was announced as top writer for *The Brave One*, he never stepped forward.

Robert Rich was a pseudonym masking one of about 150 actors blacklisted by the industry since 1947 as suspected Communists or fellow travelers. The case was particularly embarrassing to the Motion Picture Academy because it had barred any Communist or 5th Amendment pleader from Oscar competition.

"Last week both the Communist rule and the mystery of Rich's identity were suddenly revealed. Rich turned out to be Dalton (*Johnny Got His Gun*) Trumbo, one of the original Hollywood Ten writers who refused to testify at the 1947 hearing on Communism in the movie industry. Said producer Frank King who had stoutly insisted that Robert Rich was a young guy in Spain with a beard, 'We have an obligation to our stockholders to buy the best script we can. Trumbo brought us *The Brave One* and we bought it . . .' In effect it was the formal end of the Hollywood black list. For barred writers, the informal end came long ago. At least fifteen per cent of current Hollywood films are reportedly written by black list members. Said producer King, 'There are more ghosts in Hollywood than in Forest Lawn. Every company in town has used the work of black listed people; we're just the first to confirm what everybody knows'."

One may believe, as I do, that Communism would destroy all of our freedoms, and one may be opposed to it as firmly and as strongly as possible and yet at the same time also believe that in a free society it is intolerable for a man to be prevented from earning his living because he believes in or is trying to promote Communism. His freedom includes his freedom to promote Communism. The Hollywood black-list is a thoroughly unfree act that destroys freedom. It didn't work, however, precisely because the market made it costly for people to preserve the black list. The commercial emphasis, the fact that people who are running enterprises have an incentive to make as much money as they can, protected the freedom of the individuals who were black listed by providing them with an alternative form of employment, and by giving people an incentive to employ them.

If Hollywood and the movie industry had been government enterprises or if in England it had been a question of employment by the BBC it is difficult to believe that the Hollywood Ten or their equivalent would have found employment.

The essential feature of the market which is brought out by these examples, and one could multiply them many fold, is essentially that it separates the economic activities of the individual from his political ideas or activities and in this way provides individuals with an effective support for personal freedom. The person who buys bread doesn't know whether the wheat from which it was made was grown by a pleader of the 5th Amendment or a McCarthyite, by a person whose skin is black or whose skin is white. The market is an impersonal mechanism that separates economic activities of individuals from their personal characteristics. It enables people to co-operate in the economic realm regardless of any differences of opinion or views or attitudes they may have in other areas. You and I may buy Mennen drug products even though we may think "Soapy" Williams was a terrible governor of the state of Michigan. This is the fundamental way in which a free-market capitalist organization of economic activity promotes personal freedom and political freedom.

MILTON FRIEDMAN was a senior research fellow at the Hoover Institution, Stanford University, and the Paul Snowden Distinguished Service Professor Emeritus of Economics at the University of Chicago. In 1976, he was awarded the Nobel Prize in economics. He has written a number of books, including two with his wife, Rose D. Friedman—the bestselling Free to Choose and Two Lucky People: Memoirs, the latter published by the University of Chicago Press.

Daniel Stedman Jones   ➡ **NO**

The American Roots of Neoliberalism

3-18-13

Daniel Stedman Jones is a barrister in London. He was educated at the University of Oxford and at the University of Pennsylvania, where he earned a PhD in history. He has worked as a policy adviser for the New Opportunities Fund and as a researcher for Demos.

The word "neoliberalism"—the ideology of free markets, deregulation and limited government—is easily lost in translation from the European to the American context. In part this is a reflection of the different meanings of liberalism in Europe and the United States. But it also highlights a gap in historical understanding, which is only just beginning to be filled.

In Europe (and much of the wider world), neoliberalism is often seen as an American model of unrestrained market capitalism that has wrought havoc both on the developing world through the structural adjustment policies of the "Washington Consensus" and, most recently, by causing the financial crisis that brought the world economy to its knees in 2008. In the United States, by contrast, mention of the word often raises a quizzical glance, an assumption that it has something to do with Bill Clinton's New Democrats who claimed to reform liberalism in the late 1980s and 1990s or prompts a conversation about the rights or wrongs of the worldview of Paul Wolfowitz, the archetypal neo-*conservative*. Free markets are anyway viewed in the United States by advocates as being as American as apple pie and little attention is paid to the trans-Atlantic influences that have led to a distinctively neoliberal conception of free enterprise taking hold among American policymakers.

These misconceptions are unhelpful because they obscure important elements of recent transatlantic history. It is of course true that American historians, since Alan Brinkley's famous 1994 essay, "The Problem of American Conservatism," have opened up in all sorts of fruitful directions the study of the rightward turn taken in the United States since the 1960s. But it remains a strange feature of the debate, perhaps another hangover of oft-noted American exceptionalism, that the history of the set of ideas that much of the rest of the world most associates with the American model of capitalism, neoliberalism, is only imperfectly understood in the United States itself. In my book, *Masters of the Universe: Hayek, Friedman and the Birth of Neoliberal Politics*, recently published by Princeton University Press, I trace the history of neoliberalism, which I argue obtained a distinctively American inflection in the postwar period.

Neoliberalism first emerged in the interwar period, primarily in Austria, Germany, France and the United Kingdom, among thinkers and economists, who saw a need to reform liberalism. Writers like Friedrich Hayek, Ludwig von Mises, Walter Eucken, Wilhelm Röpke, Raymond Aron and Jacques Rueff thought that the "nightwatchman state" of laissez faire, exemplified by nineteenth century Britain, had proved inadequate for the problems of the early twentieth century. They saw a threat to individual freedom in the defeat of liberal politics by the totalitarianism of fascism and communism. Neoliberals also saw the activist and interventionist liberalism of Franklin Roosevelt's New Deal, along with that of the British Liberal governments of Herbert Henry Asquith and David Lloyd George, as a perversion of liberalism.

These primarily European neoliberals (though there were some Americans like Chicago economist Henry Simons) sought a reformulation of liberalism that would recover the classical liberal focus on individual liberty. *Neoliberalism was therefore an attempt to find a new middle way between what the neoliberals saw as failed laissez faire on the one hand and a new form of liberalism dominated by economic planning on the other that would form the basis of a counterattack against totalitarian impulses of left and right. Famously, Hayek became the chief proponent of this early neoliberal movement in his book *The Road to Serfdom* (1944). The defining features of the movement were a focus on anti-trust and fostering the conditions for a competitive economy and a concomitant acceptance of the need for a social safety net.

In the 1940s Hayek also developed an intellectual strategy for political influence, which he outlined in a seminal article entitled "The Intellectuals and Socialism" (1949). The central idea was that the neoliberals needed to learn from the success of the liberal left in Britain and the United States in the early twentieth century. Like the Fabian Society in Britain and the Brookings Institution in the United States the task was to influence intellectual opinion, which would force a change in the public debate over the long term. For Hayek, intellectuals encompassed all educated opinion from journalists, scientists and civil servants to experts in particular fields. The best way to attain political success would be to establish thinktanks to promote the neoliberal agenda. To this end, Hayek had already founded the Mont Pelerin Society (MPS), whose first meeting was held in Switzerland in 1947.

In retrospect, the first meeting of the MPS can be seen as a turning point in the history of neoliberalism. The meeting was attended by a number of young American scholars, Milton Friedman, George Stigler and James Buchanan, all of whom would profoundly influence the development of neoliberal ideas in the postwar period and shift the centre of gravity of the movement from Europe to the United States.

American neoliberalism took on a more radical character than its European precursors as Hayek's intellectual strategy came to fruition. In the 1950s and 1960s, both Hayek, who had moved the University of Chicago in 1950, and Friedman, who was already based there, became the leading hubs of a trans-Atlantic network of thinktanks and business-funded foundations such as the American Enterprise Institute (founded in 1943), the Foundation for Economic Education (1946), the William Volker Fund (1932, run by Harold Luhnow after 1944), the Earhart Foundation (1929) and the Institute for Humane Studies (1961). These organisations and others were joined by a second wave in the 1970s with the establishment of the Heritage Foundation (1973), the Cato Institute (1977), the Manhattan Institute (1980) and the Charles Koch Foundation (1980).

Friedman and Stigler became the leaders of the "Chicago School" of economics and Buchanan and his colleague Gordon Tullock established the "Virginia School" of political economy. Both "schools" sought to introduce market-based analysis to new areas. Friedman reformulated macroeconomics around a revival of the quantity theory of money. Stigler critiqued the dominant approaches to economic regulation whereby the regulated too often captures the regulator. Buchanan and Tullock applied the model of the individual pursuing his rational self-interest in the market to the realms of politics and government. Another Chicago economist and fellow Nobel prizewinner Gary Becker applied Chicago market-based theories to crime, the family, health and education. The process became known as economics imperialism.

At the same time as this expansion of market ideas was taking place the original emphases of neoliberal thought were changing. A crucial project, the Free Market Study, was undertaken in the 1950s at Chicago, led by Aaron Director, Friedman's brother-in-law. This study began to reformulate key neoliberal assumptions. The problem of monopoly was no longer seen as one of market failure but as one of government failure. In other words, government intervention, by favouring particular players, distorted the effective operations of the market. Large corporations had built into them self-correcting mechanisms and incentive structures that replicated the conditions of competition. Instead of market failures, the real problem of monopoly was now revealed to be, in the Chicago view, the distorting role played by labor unions. Lastly, Milton Friedman, in his famous book *Capitalism and Freedom* (1962) and his weekly *Newsweek* columns substituted the supposedly more efficient market mechanism for the welfare state in a range of social policy spheres.

This moment when neoliberalism becomes a distinctively American idea incubated in interwar Europe but refined in Chicago also marks its political breakthrough in both the United States and in Britain. To be sure for such an advance to occur required the perceived failings of liberalism in general and of neo-Keynesian demand management in particular, a policy approach that was proving powerless in the face of the novel problem of the 1970s: 'stagflation'. But there is no doubt that the change in neoliberalism from its early European origins to those in postwar America represented a radical clarification that sharpened the political message and made it more easily digestible. Key tenets of the Chicago world-view would become the centrepieces of the new political settlement after 1975.

At first, politicians of the left introduced neoliberal policies, such as Friedman's monetarism and Stigler's deregulation. For example, Carter appointed Paul Volcker to the Fed and introduced legislation to deregulate airlines, transport and finance. The Labour Government of James Callaghan in Britain introduced similar changes. But afterwards a more wholesale philosophy of free markets took hold under Reagan and Thatcher. The radical nature of American neoliberalism was made clear in the 'trickle-down' economics supported by Reagan's leading economic advisers and influences, Arthur Laffer, Martin Feldstein and Milton Friedman. Clinton, Larry Summers and Robert Rubin left this radical free market ideology substantially un-tampered with. Certainly, in welfare reform, the pursuit of 'flexible labour markets' and the repeal of Glass-Steagall, it was possible to see the entrenchment of key neoliberal policy prescriptions.

The legacies of American neoliberalism—guileless faith in markets and overweening hatred of government and public expenditure—still dominate the Republican Party today in the perpetual crises over debt ceilings, fiscal cliffs and sequesters. But they also influence the agendas of President Obama and his Treasury team too. After a brief Keynesian resurgence in early 2009, the dominant economic agenda is once again an awkward mix of Hayekian deficit reduction and sub-Friedmanite monetary stimulus. Only by examining this complicated and layered history of neoliberalism and its political breakthrough can some sense be made of the economic predicament that we find ourselves in today.

DANIEL STEDMAN JONES is a barrister in London. He was educated at the University of Oxford and at the University of Pennsylvania, where he earned a PhD in history. He has worked as a policy adviser for the New Opportunities Fund and as a researcher for Demos.

EXPLORING THE ISSUE

Do Economic Policies Associated with Reagan, Thatcher, and Friedman Promote Freedom in a Liberal Democracy?

Critical Thinking and Reflection

1. Create a diagram in which you write and describe the ways in which market principles help to promote freedom in a liberal democracy and the ways in which market principles work against the principles of a liberal democracy.
2. What examples from your personal lived experience show the intersection of market principles and democracy? Do you see any of these examples as beneficial/detrimental to you or others?
3. What is your definition of democracy? How has it been reaffirmed or challenged by these readings? Do you find yourself more aligned with Freidman or Jones?
4. Lindblom (1977) considers whether or not it is possible to conceive of a democracy more focused on collective interest than the protection of individual interests (p. 165). Do you think this is possible? Explain.

Is There Common Ground?

Coming from complex opinions concerning the intersection of the market and democracy, both Friedman (1981) and Jones (2013) highlight the importance of taking seriously the ways in which we define and conceptualize neoliberal economic policies. Friedman does this by using history as a warning for how to approach democracy in an effort to avoid authoritarian rule. Jones uses the historical development of neoliberal economic thought to help us better appreciate how it came to be the dominate ideology in American sociopolitical life.

In both articles, a focus on the intersection of market principles with democracy leaves us wondering what is actually meant by liberal democracy and whether it ought to place such a heavy emphasis on individual liberty. For Freidman, it is inconceivable to think that individual liberty can exist without complete economic freedom. For Jones, the historical development of modern neoliberal

thought might cause us some pause for using this ideology to guide our future political motivations.

Additional Resources

Foner, E. (1998). *The story of American freedom*. New York, NY: Norton

Lindblom, Charles, E. (1977). Market and democracy. *Politics and markets: The world's political-economic systems*. (161–169). New York, NY: Basic Books, Inc.

Macpherson, C. B. (1992). *The real world of democracy*. Toronto, ON: House of Anansi Press, Inc.

Sabine, G. H. (1952). The two democratic traditions. *The Philosophical Review, 61*(4), 451–474.

Fisher, M. (2009). *Capitalist realism: Is there no alternative?* John Hunt Publishing.

Internet References . . .

The Collective Works of Milton Friedman

https://miltonfriedman.hoover.org/collections;jsessio
nid=04821C5C37D8FEACD929D84CF2FB0576

Commanding Heights: On Freedom and
Free Markets

https://www.pbs.org/wgbh/commandingheights/
shared/minitext/int_miltonfriedman.html

Naomi Klein: how power profits from
disaster

https://www.theguardian.com/us-news/2017/jul/06/
naomi-klein-how-power-profits-from-disaster

Theory: The Shock Doctrine

https://beautifultrouble.org/theory/the-
shock-doctrine/

Selected, Edited, and with Issue Framing Material by:
Kevin R. Magill and Tony L. Talbert, *Baylor University*

ISSUE

Is the American Century Over?

YES: Andrew Bacevich, from "Farewell, the American Century," *The Nation* (2009)

NO: Joseph S. Nye Jr., from "The American Century Will Continue But It Won't Look the Same," *Politico* (2015)

Learning Outcomes

After reading this issue, you will be able to:

- Understand the impetus and context for Henry R. Luce's "The American Century."
- Identify the multiple dates, ideas, and events associated with the American Century.
- Identify the key tenets of Luce's argument for the American Century.
- Understand the arguments for the end of the American Century.
- Understand the arguments for the continuation of the American Century.

ISSUE SUMMARY

YES: Andrew Bacevich argues that the American Century is over. He believes we need to see ourselves as we are now by casting aside the problematic mythology of the American Century.

NO: Joseph S. Nye believes the American Century will continue; however, he suggests that if the United States would like to maintain its leadership role, it must recognize that the role will look very different from what it was in the 20th century.

Issue framing with Justin Kruger, *University of Texas at Austin*

Henry Luce wrote of the American Century:

> America cannot be responsible for the good behavior of the entire world. But America is responsible, to herself as well as to history, for the world-environment in which she lives. Nothing can so vitally affect America's environment as America's own influence upon it, and therefore if America's environment is unfavorable to the growth of American life, then America has nobody to blame so deeply as she must blame herself.

Henry R Luce famously argued that the 20th century was the American Century. Appearing in *Life* magazine on February 17, 1941, it provided an international vision for the United States as the force that would lead and ultimately transform the world by and through its leadership. In 1941, the United States was unquestionably on the rise in the traditional sense. She was an economic, political and cultural powerhouse in an increasingly interconnected world. These factors and more have led many to agree that the 20th century was indeed dominated by the United States. However, we now enter an era where the geopolitical landscape looks very differently. What will the future of the United States and indeed the World hold?

In the United States, greed and profit currently drive domestic and foreign policy. Domestically, the nation is dealing with some of the biggest wealth disparities in human history. Citizens are working harder than ever for less pay. Some individuals loose their life savings when forced to pay for healthcare because systems developed for the public good have been privatized. This is the case across sectors, government and industry where profit comes before people. Though citizens have been sufficiently propagandized to ignore or misinterpret the causes of this inhumane system, they are aware of it and are rejecting the status quo as evidenced in recent elections. However, rather than developing solidarity, citizens have once again been convinced to align with power rather than take it for the people. In foreign affairs, the United States continues its hegemony, largely because she is able to manipulate economic systems and maintain the largest and most capable military force in human history. Her air force occupies strategic places throughout the globe to enforce US values and influence. However, does her waning economic power necessarily mean the nation will relinquish her grasp on world values, culture, and dominance? Unquestionably, something will change, but will her spheres of influence or will it be something else? Will the United States relinquish her military might or yield her position as economic hegemon? The question our authors discuss is will US domination continue—differently than the previous century, or is her influence a myth?

Joseph S. Nye believes the American Century will continue, but that it will look differently than it has in the past. Andrew Bacevich believes the myth needs to go away. Nye begins his piece by noting that many people believe the United States has already, or will soon be, overtaken by China as the world's pre-eminent super power. He suggests, in brief, that the idea of the United States as a super power juggernaut is inconsistent with reality. Nye argues that the United States has curated a "feel-good notion of itself," playing fast and loose with facts, allowing America to over-extend its role in world affairs and for people to maintain an inflated sense of self. Nye argues that the American Century is a completely arbitrary concept. He believes that Henry Luce, publisher of Life magazine, released his article, "The American Century" in 1941 as a form of propaganda in an attempt to stir support for an American return to international leadership. At the time, he notes that isolationist ideas defined American foreign policy even as war raged in Europe.

Therefore, it may be prudent to ask what exactly does the American Century mean and how do we define it? For Nye, the idea of an American Century itself is debatable. He questions, is being the namesake for the control of a century about economic power? If so, is total GDP or per capita income the best measure? Is it military strength? Which data points offer a good measure of geopolitical power? What about a start date? When did the supposed American century begin? Is it 1914 as suggested by Michael Lind? Or 1991 with the fall of the Soviet Union?

Nye points to 1947 as a proposed date for the start of the American Century. He claims power should be the central idea upon which we consider the American Century. Power, as he defines it, it is about the ability to get what is wanted through coercion, payment, and/or attraction. Therefore, power in this sense is less about having omnipotent power, but rather is about having the resources to achieve one's aims. In this way, Nye believes the United States excels citing a series of events such as investing in the Marshall Plan in 1948, creating NATO in 1949, and aiding a UN coalition in Korea in 1950. The ability to set these events in motion demonstrates U.S. power. However, even within these examples, Nye also highlights U.S. shortcomings in world leadership. He mentions the Soviet ability to move nukes, the Korean War stalemate, Castro taking hold in Cuba, and the Soviet Union quashing revolts in the Eastern European countries of Hungary and Czechoslovakia.

It is from this perspective that Nye claims the United States will still continue to be a central player in foreign affairs but that she will be unable to control of world affairs as it has previously. Nye believes that the growing interconnectedness and complexity of the 21st century will demand such a coalition. For Nye, the American Century will continue, "at least a number of decades more, it will simply look very different than it did when Henry Luce first articulated it." He claims that cooperation with other nations will be central to building alliances and strengthening networks that will allow the United States to maintain its position as the central actor in world politics.

Bacevich believes that the concept of the American Century has not aged well. He begins by arguing what he understands to be the folly in Luce's appeal for America to "accept wholeheartedly our duty and our opportunity as the most powerful and vital nation in the world . . . to exert upon the world the full impact of our influence, for such purposes as we see fit and by such means as we see fit." While, he claims, the concept served a purpose in 1941, the call for American leadership has led to what he calls the myth of the American Century. Bacevich describes the myth, which he suggests the American people mostly accepted that the United States is leading the righteous fight against evil. He argues that the creation and continued acceptance of the idea of an American Century is dangerous because it is based on half-truths, misunderstandings and faulty assumptions. For Bacevich, the American Century has no place in our collective memory because it misarticulates our present and blinds us to what needs to be done in the future.

Bacevich gives examples of how the American Century myth functions. His central argument is that the so-called American Century is historical sugar-coating. It tends to over extend the power and virtue of the United States and downplays or leaves out the significant contribution of other countries. He equates the dominant narrative of the U.S. claiming victory for World War II to being "the equivalent of Toyota claiming credit for inventing the automobile," yet U.S. citizens commonly maximize the U.S. role in the conflict while minimizing the role of other nations—the USSR, for example. Bacevich argues that believing the American Century promotes American bombast, which has proved problematic in many ways. When we look to many of the military interventions following World War II political missteps such as those in Cuba, the use of nuclear bombs in Japan, or of the destabilization and fighting in the Middle East, there seems to be support for Bacevich's thesis because of little to no acknowledgment of many of these ill-advised efforts. Acknowledging that there is no way to know if past events might have turned out differently, Bacevich nonetheless believes that in order to move beyond the American Century, the United States needs to publicly apologize "without any expectations for reciprocity" as a show that the country is moving beyond its illusions pronounced in Luce's "American Century." Is the American Century a reality, is it merely a form of propaganda or is it something that was and will be?

YES ↵

Andrew J. Bacevich

Farewell, the American Century

In order to solve our problems Americans must begin to see ourselves as we really are.

In a recent column, the *Washington Post's* Richard Cohen wrote, "What Henry Luce called 'the American Century' is over." Cohen is right. All that remains is to drive a stake through the heart of Luce's pernicious creation, lest it come back to life. This promises to take some doing.

When the *Time-Life* publisher coined his famous phrase, his intent was to prod his fellow citizens into action. Appearing in the February 7, 1941, issue of *Life*, his essay "The American Century" hit the newsstands at a moment when the world was in the throes of a vast crisis. A war in Europe had gone disastrously awry. A second, almost equally dangerous conflict was unfolding in the Far East. Aggressors were on the march.

With the fate of democracy hanging in the balance, Americans diddled. Luce urged them to get off the dime. More than that, he summoned them to "accept whole-heartedly our duty and our opportunity as the most powerful and vital nation in the world.... to exert upon the world the full impact of our influence, for such purposes as we see fit and by such means as we see fit."

Read today, Luce's essay, with its strange mix of chauvinism, religiosity and bombast ("We must now undertake to be the Good Samaritan to the entire world"), does not stand up well. Yet the phrase "American Century" stuck and has enjoyed a remarkable run. It stands in relation to the contemporary era much as "Victorian Age" does to the nineteenth century. In one pithy phrase, it captures (or at least seems to capture) the essence of some defining truth: America as alpha and omega, source of salvation and sustenance, vanguard of history, guiding spirit and inspiration for all humankind.

In its classic formulation, the central theme of the American Century has been one of righteousness overcoming evil. The United States (above all the US military) made that triumph possible. When, having been given a final nudge on December 7, 1941, Americans finally

accepted their duty to lead, they saved the world from successive diabolical totalitarianisms. In doing so, the US not only preserved the possibility of human freedom but modeled what freedom ought to look like.

Thank You, Comrades

So goes the preferred narrative of the American Century, as recounted by its celebrants.

The problems with this account are twofold. First, it claims for the United States' excessive credit. Second, it excludes, ignores or trivializes matters at odds with the triumphal story line.

The net effect is to perpetuate an array of illusions that, whatever their value in prior decades, have long since outlived their usefulness. In short, the persistence of this self-congratulatory account deprives Americans of self-awareness, hindering our efforts to navigate the treacherous waters in which the country finds itself at present. Bluntly, we are perpetuating a mythic version of the past that never even approximated reality and today has become downright malignant. Although Richard Cohen may be right in declaring the American Century over, the American people—and especially the American political class—still remain in its thrall.

Constructing a past usable to the present requires a willingness to include much that the American Century leaves out.

For example, to the extent that the demolition of totalitarianism deserves to be seen as a prominent theme of contemporary history (and it does), the primary credit for that achievement surely belongs to the Soviet Union. When it came to defeating the Third Reich, the Soviets bore by far the preponderant burden, sustaining 65 percent of all Allied deaths in World War II.

By comparison, the United States suffered 2 percent of those losses, for which any American whose father or grandfather served in and survived that war should be saying: Thank you, Comrade Stalin.

For the United States to claim credit for destroying the Wehrmacht is the equivalent of Toyota claiming credit for inventing the automobile. We entered the game late and then shrewdly scooped up more than our fair share of the winnings. The true "Greatest Generation" is the one that willingly expended millions of their fellow Russians while killing millions of German soldiers.

Hard on the heels of World War II came the cold war, during which erstwhile allies became rivals. Once again, after a decades-long struggle, the United States came out on top.

Yet in determining that outcome, the brilliance of American statesmen was far less important than the ineptitude of those who presided over the Kremlin. Ham-handed Soviet leaders so mismanaged their empire that it eventually imploded, permanently discrediting Marxism-Leninism as a plausible alternative to liberal democratic capitalism. The Soviet dragon managed to slay itself. So thank you, Comrades Malenkov, Khrushchev, Brezhnev, Andropov, Chernenko and Gorbachev.

Screwing the Pooch

What flag-wavers tend to leave out of their account of the American Century is not only the contributions of others, but the various missteps perpetrated by the United States—missteps, it should be noted, that spawned many of the problems bedeviling us today.

The instances of folly and criminality bearing the label "made-in-Washington" may not rank up there with the Armenian genocide, the Bolshevik Revolution, the appeasement of Adolf Hitler or the Holocaust, but they sure don't qualify as small change. To give them their due is necessarily to render the standard account of the American Century untenable.

Here are several examples, each one familiar, even if its implications for the problems we face today are studiously ignored:

Cuba. In 1898, the United States went to war with Spain for the proclaimed purpose of liberating the so-called Pearl of the Antilles. When that brief war ended, Washington reneged on its promise. If there actually has been an American Century, it begins here, with the US government breaking a solemn commitment, while baldly insisting otherwise. By converting Cuba into a protectorate, the United States set in motion a long train of events leading eventually to the rise of Fidel Castro, the Bay of Pigs, Operation Mongoose, the Cuban Missile Crisis and even today's Guantánamo Bay prison camp. The

line connecting these various developments may not be a straight one, given the many twists and turns along the way, but the dots do connect.

The Bomb. Nuclear weapons imperil our existence. Used on a large scale, they could destroy civilization itself. Even now, the prospect of a lesser power like North Korea or Iran acquiring nukes sends jitters around the world. American presidents—Barack Obama is only the latest in a long line—declare the abolition of these weapons to be an imperative. What they are less inclined to acknowledge is the role the United States played in afflicting humankind with this scourge.

The United States invented the bomb. The United States—alone among members of the nuclear club—actually employed it as a weapon of war. The US led the way in defining nuclear-strike capacity as the benchmark of power in the postwar world, leaving other powers like the Soviet Union, Great Britain, France and China scrambling to catch up. Today, the US still maintains an enormous nuclear arsenal at the ready and adamantly refuses to commit itself to a no-first-use policy, even as it professes its horror at the prospect of some other nation doing as the United States itself has done.

Iran. Extending his hand to Tehran, President Obama has invited those who govern the Islamic republic to "unclench their fists." Yet to a considerable degree, those clenched fists are of our own making. For most Americans, the discovery of Iran dates from the time of the notorious hostage crisis of 1979-1981 when Iranian students occupied the US embassy in Tehran, detained several dozen US diplomats and military officers and subjected the administration of Jimmy Carter to a 444-day lesson in abject humiliation.

For most Iranians, the story of US-Iranian relations begins somewhat earlier. It starts in 1953, when CIA agents collaborated with their British counterparts to overthrow the democratically elected government of Mohammed Mossadegh and return the Shah of Iran to his throne. The plot succeeded. The Shah regained power. The Americans got oil, along with a lucrative market for exporting arms. The people of Iran pretty much got screwed. Freedom and democracy did not prosper. The antagonism that expressed itself in November 1979 with the takeover of the US embassy in Tehran was not entirely without cause.

Afghanistan. President Obama has wasted little time in making the Afghanistan War his own. Like his predecessor he vows to defeat the Taliban. Also like his predecessor he has yet to confront the role played by the United States in creating the Taliban in the first place. Washington once took pride in the success it enjoyed funneling arms and assistance to fundamentalist Afghans waging *jihad* against foreign occupiers. During the administrations of Jimmy Carter and Ronald Reagan, this was considered to represent the very acme of clever statecraft. US support for the Afghan mujahedeen caused the Soviets fits. Yet it also fed a cancer that, in time, exacted a most grievous toll on Americans themselves—and has US forces today bogged down in a seemingly endless war.

Act of Contrition

Had the United States acted otherwise, would Cuba have evolved into a stable and prosperous democracy, a beacon of hope for the rest of Latin America? Would the world have avoided the blight of nuclear weapons? Would Iran today be an ally of the United States, a beacon of liberalism in the Islamic world, rather than a charter member of the "axis of evil?" Would Afghanistan be a quiet, pastoral land at peace with its neighbors? No one, of course, can say what might have been. All we know for sure is that policies concocted in Washington by reputedly savvy statesmen now look exceedingly ill-advised.

What are we to make of these blunders? The temptation may be to avert our gaze, thereby preserving the reassuring tale of the American Century. We should avoid that temptation and take the opposite course, acknowledging openly, freely and unabashedly where we have gone wrong. We should carve such acknowledgments into the face of a new monument smack in the middle of the Mall in Washington: we blew it. We screwed the pooch. We caught a case of the stupids. We got it ass-backwards.

Only through the exercise of candor might we avoid replicating such mistakes.

Indeed, we ought to apologize. When it comes to avoiding the repetition of sin, nothing works like abject contrition. We should, therefore, tell the people of Cuba that we are sorry for having made such a hash of US-Cuban relations for so long. President Obama should speak on our behalf in asking the people of Hiroshima and Nagasaki for forgiveness. He should express our deep collective regret to Iranians and Afghans for what past US interventionism has wrought.

The United States should do these things without any expectations of reciprocity. Regardless of what US officials may say or do, Castro won't fess up to having made his own share of mistakes. The Japanese won't liken Hiroshima to Pearl Harbor and call it a wash. Iran's mullahs and Afghanistan's *jihadists* won't be offering to a chastened Washington to let bygones be bygones.

No, we apologize to them, but for our own good—to free ourselves from the accumulated conceits of the American Century and to acknowledge that the United States participated fully in the barbarism, folly and tragedy that defines our time. For those sins, we must hold ourselves accountable.

To solve our problems requires that we see ourselves as we really are. And that requires shedding, once and for all, the illusions embodied in the American Century.

What better epitomizes the follies and failures of US foreign policy than the endless war in Afghanistan, a country on the other side of the world with illusory strategic importance? The United States has squandered over $1 trillion on the war. Over 2,000 US soldiers have lost their lives, with 20,000 wounded. The war goes on with no plan for victory.

The current chair of the Joint Chiefs of Staff, Joseph Dunford, admitted that the war is a "stalemate." Yet, when Donald Trump tweeted that he was going to begin pulling troops out of Afghanistan, the foreign-policy establishment howled in disapproval. Richard Haass, a vicar of that establishment, rushed to defend the current course in a recent op-ed.

ANDREW J. BACEVICH JR. is an American historian specializing in international relations, security studies, American foreign policy, and American diplomatic and military history. He is a Professor Emeritus of International Relations and History at the Boston University Frederick S. Pardee School of Global Studies.

Joseph S. Nye Jr.  **NO**

The American Century Will Continue but It Won't Look the Same

America's global leadership won't dissipate as quickly as its loudest Cassandras have warned.

You'd be forgiven for thinking that the American century was already over. Most people around the world think it is—including most Americans. In recent years, polls showed that in 15 of 22 countries surveyed, most respondents said China either will replace or has replaced the United States as the world's leading power. A Pew poll in 2014 found only 28 percent of Americans thought their country "stands above all others." For the first time in nearly 40 years a majority of the American public said the United States plays a less important and powerful role as a world leader than it did a decade ago.

But a closer look at our country's recent past—and our future—makes clear that the nation was never quite as powerful as its biggest boosters have claimed, nor, though, will its global leadership dissipate in the years ahead as quickly as its loudest Cassandras have warned.

The very idea of "the American century" has always been somewhat arbitrary. The term was coined early in 1941 by Henry Luce, the famed publisher of Time magazine, as a political slogan in the domestic battle to reverse the isolationism of the period and press the United States to enter World War II. At the time, we were the world's largest power, but we did not act like one. The 19th century was often seen as "the British century," and Luce's idea of the "American century" was meant to capture the nation's attention to its power and global leadership—and set up a clear contrast with Britain's weakening state.

There has always been something odd about our fascination with centuries. How does such a time measurement apply to the life cycle of a country? Political entities are social constructs without clear life spans. Rome started its rise to power in the pre-Christian era and reached its apogee in 117 AD, but the Western Roman empire did not

collapse until some 3½ centuries later, and the Eastern Roman empire persisted until 1453.

Despite such problems, some analysts and historians have tried to discern century-long patterns in the life cycles of dominant countries. It's always been hard to predict what's right around the corner. For example, after Britain lost its North American colonies in the 18th century, the statesman Horace Walpole lamented that Britain was now reduced to the status of a miserable little island like Sardinia. He uttered this erroneous judgment on the eve of Britain's "second century," ushered in by the Industrial Revolution.

How should we measure the American century? If one defines it as the period since the U.S. became the country with the largest economy, it roughly coincides with the 20th century, reaching its peak in mid-century, and it is likely to end in the next decade or so when analysts expect China to pass the U.S. as the world's largest economy. But that's not necessarily a good measurement of geopolitical success. Power—the ability to affect others to get what you want—has three aspects: coercion, payment and attraction. Economic might is just part of the geopolitical equation. Even when China passes the U.S. in total economic size, which measured at exchange rates some economists think may occur in the late 2020s, we will not automatically be witnessing the end of the American century. Even in economic power China will still lag in per capita income, a better measure of the sophistication of an economy.

Michael Lind believes the American century began in 1914 with our entry into World War I, and he argues that it ended in 2014 because America's foreign policy is in a state of collapse, America's economy doesn't work well and American democracy is broken. It is more accurate, however, to date the American century with the end of

World War II. After the war, when Britain was too weak to support Greece and Turkey in 1947, the U.S. stepped up and took its place—investing in the Marshall Plan in 1948, creating NATO in 1949 and leading a United Nations coalition that fought in Korea in 1950.

Some might say that 1991 is a third potential mark for the beginning of the American century—the date when, following the collapse of the Soviet Union, the United States became the world's only country able to project military power on a global scale. The American Navy was equal in size to the next 17 navies; American forces had air superiority; the United States took the lead in space and the dawn of cyberspace; and the American military budget represented nearly half the globe's total defense spending. In such circumstances, it became very difficult for other states to balance American power. But that is too short a perspective.

There has always been a lot of fiction mixed with the facts of the "American century." To borrow a comedian's line, "Hegemony ain't what it used to be, but then it never was." The United States had a terrific run after World War II, but we never built a truly global order. The American world order has never represented more than half the globe; our system didn't include large countries like China, India, Indonesia and the Soviet bloc. The peak of America's share of world power resources was from 1945—when the U.S. had nearly half the world economy—to 1970, when the U.S. share of world product returned to its pre-war level of a quarter of the world product. Yet even during this period of peak influence, the U.S. often failed to get what it wanted: Witness Soviet acquisition of nuclear weapons; communist takeover of China and half of Vietnam; stalemate in the Korean War; Soviet suppression of the revolts in Hungary and Czechoslovakia; Castro's control of Cuba; and so forth.

So if we define "the American century" as the period since World War II when the United States—without full control—became the central actor in the global balance of power, will those same geopolitical circumstances still be true in 2041? My guess is yes. The U.S. is the only major developed country that will hold its place (third) in the demographic ranking of countries, rather than shrinking in population or being overtaken by other countries. Its dependence on imported energy has decreased; it remains in the forefront in development of key technologies (bio, nano, information) that are central to this century's economic growth; American universities dominate in the area of higher education; and our culture remains open and entrepreneurial. It's going to take years—decades even—for other countries to wrest leadership on those issues from the United States.

On the key new transnational issues—financial stability, climate change, pandemics, terrorism and cyber strife—American leadership will be important, but success in the years ahead cannot be one-sided. Achieving our goals in the 21st century will require the cooperation of other nations, both friendly and not. In this sense, power becomes a positive-sum game. If the American century is to continue, it will not be enough to think in terms of American power *over* others. One must also think in terms of power to accomplish joint goals—goals that will involve sharing power *with* others such as China, Europe, Japan, India, Brazil and so forth. On many transnational issues, empowering others can help the U.S. to accomplish its own goals. In this world, networks and connectedness become an important source of our power. The United States is involved in more alliances and networks than any other country.

Contrary to those who proclaim this the "Chinese century," we have not entered a "post-American world." Yet the continuation of our American century will not look like our strengths of the 20th century. Our share of the world economy will be less than it was in the middle of the past century, and the complexity represented by the rise of other countries—as well as the increased role of nonstate actors—will make it more difficult for anyone to wield influence and organize action. We should stop using clichés about "uni-polarity" and "multi-polarity." We will have to live with both situations at the same time. And we should stop talking and worrying about "decline," a fear that mixes many different trends and leads to mistaken policy conclusions.

Instead, we must focus on what we can do well: With slightly less relative power in the midst of a much more complex world, the United States will need to make smart strategic choices both at home and abroad if we wish to maintain our leadership. The American century will continue for at least a number of decades or more; it will simply look very different than it did when Henry Luce first articulated it.

JOSEPH SAMUEL NYE JR. is an American political scientist. He is the co-founder, along with Robert Keohane, of the international relations theory of neoliberalism, developed in their 1977 book Power and Interdependence. Together with Keohane, he developed the concepts of asymmetrical and complex interdependence.

EXPLORING THE ISSUE

Is the American Century Over?

Critical Thinking and Reflection

1. What is meant by Nye's assertion that American power should become a positive sum game?
2. How is the American Century dreamed of by Luce different from the one Nye suggests for the future?
3. Why does Bacevich argue it is necessary for the United States to acknowledge and apologize for its mistakes on the world stage?
4. What does Bacevich consider to be the weaknesses of the American Century ideology?
5. How is the notion of power constituted and discussed in the arguments of Luce, Bacevich, and Nye?

Is There Common Ground?

Drawing on different perspective of Luce's "The American Century," Bacevich and Nye argue similarly that the United States is important on the world stage and must adapt in order to maintain international standing in the 21st century. Both Authors recognize that Luce's arguments for "The American Century" were a by-product of frustration with U.S. isolationist foreign policy in the early 20th century. Further, both recognize that ideas promoted in "The American Century" as constituted by Henry R. Luce are no longer applicable as a contemporary foreign policy because it is too exclusionary.

While arguing different aspects of the American Century ideal, both authors note that the 1941 call for the United States to assume its place as the purveyor of world guardianship and to intervene as necessary is both overly nationalistic. It is also out of touch with more contemporary notions of modern leadership. The authors believe that moving forward requires that the United States shed both its past behaviors and notions of world grandeur for a more inclusive approach of shared leadership. For Bacevich, this means that the United States come to terms with its own grandiose ideals of superiority touted by Luce and own up to past mistakes while, Nye argues that the U.S. must alter course and lead through alliances with other countries.

Additional Resources

Acharya, A. (2018). *The end of American world order*. John Wiley & Sons.

Bacevich, A. J. (Ed.). (2012). *The Short American Century*. Harvard University Press.

Cummings, B. (1999). Still the American Century. *Review of International Studies*, 25, 271-299.

Evans, H., Buckland, G., & Baker, K. (1998). *The American Century*. Random House.

LaFeber, W., & Woloch, N. (2015). *The American Century: A History of the United States Since the 1890s*. Routledge.

McCoy, A. W. (2017). *In the Shadows of the American Century: The Rise and Decline of US Global Power*. Haymarket Books.

Meltzer, A. H. (2008). End of the 'American Century.' *World Economics*, 9(4), 1-11.

Nye Jr, J. S. (2015). *Is the American century over?*. John Wiley & Sons.

Painter, D. S. (2012). Oil and the American century. *The Journal of American History*, 99(1), 24-39.

Walker, W. O. (2018). *The Rise and Decline of the American Century*. Cornell University Press.

Internet References . . .

The End of the American Century.

Stengel, R. (2017, January 26). *The Atlantic*, Retrieved from https://www.theatlantic.com/politics/
archive/2017/01/end-of-the-american-century/514526/

The End of the American Century

Michael, T. (2011, February 16). The End of the
American Century. *Reason*, Retrieved from
https://reason.com/2011/02/16/the-end-of-
the-american-centur

Thanks to no-drama Obama, American
leadership is gone.

Cohen, R. (2016, December 26). *The Washington* Post,
Retrieved from https://www.washingtonpost.com/
opinions/thanks-to-no-drama-obama-american-lead-
ership-is-gone/2016/12/26/672481e8-cb9c-11e6-a747-
d03044780a02_story.html?noredirect=on&utm_
term=.fb093d6b4b4f